Population Theory and

SELECTED REA

Population Theory and Policy

SELECTED READINGS

EDITED BY

JOSEPH J. SPENGLER
Duke University

and

OTIS DUDLEY DUNCAN
University of Chicago

THE FREE PRESS, GLENCOE, ILLINOIS

Contents

INTRODUCTION

This volume is one of two companion collections of papers and other selections that have to do with demographic analysis, population theory, and population policy. The points of view of the two volumes differ somewhat, however. In the companion volume, *Demographic Analysis: Selected Readings,* are assembled readings which present varied demographic information, exemplify the work of the research demographer when he is dealing with delimited concrete problems and, in a number of instances, illustrate various points of methodological interest. In the present volume the results of demographic analysis are taken more or less for granted. Herein are readings which treat primarily of the implications of demographic phenomena for social structure and for socio-economic change and welfare, or which are concerned with development and applications of "population theory" and with policy aspects of population movements. In neither volume is major emphasis placed upon techniques of analysis, since several excellent treatises on methods of population research have already been published or are about to appear.

The editors have not attempted to write a textbook dealing with theory and policy, but have supplied brief introductions to the several chapters. These provide a framework for the selected readings and, in some instances, cover important points which have not received sufficient attention in those readings.

This volume may be used by itself as a relatively self-contained basis for a course in population theory and policy, or in combination with the companion volume in a one or two semester course emphasizing demographic analysis as well as population theory and policy, or as a source book of outside readings in conjunction with one of the standard texts on population problems or methods of demographic research. The large number of reading selections and the diversity of the sources from which they are drawn permit the instructor a good deal of latitude in adapting the material to his own course outline. Since no single volume can cover the entire field exhaustively, supplementary bibliographies have been included. These may be useful to instructors who wish to develop a given topic more intensively, to students working on individual projects or reports, and generally to the reader who wishes to gain an overview of current research on population. The bibliography is limited largely to recent (post-World War II) literature in periodicals and symposia; it is assumed that book-length monographs and treatises are better known and more accessible than fugitive journal literature.

We want to express our thanks to the authors who generously gave permission to reprint their papers, and to absolve them of responsibility for any erroneous impression of their work that may be conveyed by our remarks in chapter introductions. We also gratefully acknowledge the permissions to republish these selections granted by the original publishers and copyright holders.

JOSEPH J. SPENGLER
OTIS DUDLEY DUNCAN

February, 1956

Population Theory and Policy

SELECTED READINGS

CHAPTER 1

DEVELOPMENT OF POPULATION THEORY

The three selections comprising this chapter review the evolution of population theory from its primitive beginnings in pre-Christian times to its present state of development. This summary suggests that the progress of population theory—here understood to embrace principally men's views concerning the causes and the consequences of population movement and change—closely paralleled the evolution of economic and sociological theory. In ancient times already one encounters conjectures concerning causes and effects of population changes, but the conjectures do not become transformed into explanatory principles until after the Renaissance, and these principles in turn do not begin to be combined into an organized body of scientific knowledge centered about population until late in the eighteenth century. Moreover, until this century one finds in the literature on population, as in the literature of social science generally, much emphasis upon political and ethical objectives and little emphasis upon the operation of what may loosely be called cause and effect.

Demographic science assumed definite form considerably later than did economics (which took modern shape in the eighteenth century), or than did anthropology, political science, and sociology, all of which broke off from history, moral science and economics and achieved autonomy in the nineteenth century. Even today, in fact, men differ respecting the scope of demographic science, since population study has contact points with anthropology, biology, ecology, economics, sociology, and other sciences and concerns itself with aspects of problems that customarily are dealt with by these sciences. The papers included in this volume and its companion, however, provide a conspectus of the subject matter with which population study is primarily concerned and also suggest in what manner it overlaps various of the social and life sciences.

While population theory may not properly be said to include the statistical and mathematical tools utilized by students of population, the advancement of population study has been facilitated by the development of these tools and by the gradual accumulation of quantitative and related information in the analysis of which these and other tools may be employed. Vital statistics began to be utilized in the late seventeenth century, more than a hundred years before the undertaking of careful censuses and the improvement and spread of the practice of recording births, deaths, and marriages with care: births were compared with deaths, marriages, and population; deaths were contrasted with population; birth and death rates began to be approximated; and the principles of life-table construction were anticipated and applied. About 1800, age-specific fertility rates were constructed, and somewhat later, ratios of both births and young children to females of reproductive age were computed. Life-table construction was improved, and standardized birth and death rates were made use of. Net reproduction rates were not calculated, however, until near the close of the nineteenth century, and gross reproduction rates and replacement ratios came into use somewhat later. The shortcomings, for purposes of population forecasting, of net reproduction and replacement rates, together with static life tables, were not emphasized until after the 1930's when earlier forecasts began to prove wide of the mark. The analytical fruitfulness of the stable and other mathematical population models only gradually came to be perceived in the present century, largely as a result of Lotka's work (see Chapter 3). The improvements effected in these various tools are significantly attributable to improvements in population theory, to increasing concern with population problems, and to a resulting augmentation and diversification of the quantitative information assembled in censuses, registry systems, and so on.

Inasmuch as the role of population theory is examined in Chapter 2 and the development of the theory of population growth as such is treated in Chapter 3, it will here suffice merely to indicate several of the factors responsible for the progress of population study. Improvements in the tools of quantitative analysis have already been noted, together with advances in the social and the life sciences. Inasmuch as the concepts of equilibrium, disequilibrium, stabilizing forces, destabilizing conditions, etc., have come to play an important role in population study, the development of these concepts by the seventeenth-century founders of mechanical science and their gradual transplantation to social and life sciences must be considered important. The introduction into population study of the related concept of a system of interdependent parts, represented in economics by the price system, in sociology by the "social system," and in demography by various population models, must also be considered significant. Recognition, already in the eighteenth century, that population growth was conditioned by the availability of subsistence—later, of the means of existence, and then of income—contributed importantly to formulation of some population problems. So also did the population student's finding, 150–200 years ago, that the average level of consumption required by man might rise or fall and the economist's conclusion that, under specifiable conditions, the output of goods and services could not keep pace with an unrestricted growth of population. It is noted in Chapter 3 that already in the early nineteenth century economists realized that the theory of population is but a part of a larger, all-inclusive theory of socio-economic growth. Recognition that natural increase might vary from one segment of a population to another, when coupled with the proposition that men varied in hereditary capacities, gave rise in the last half of the nineteenth century to emphasis upon qualitative aspects of population growth. Observation of the behavior of international migrants led to the formulation, in the late nineteenth century, of "laws" of migration, while the decline in fertility drew attention to the economic importance of variations in a population's age composition. With the gradual suppression, especially after 1860, of laissez-faire individualism by a social philosophy favorable to collectivistic intervention in socio-economic affairs, questions of demographic policy ranging from concern with population optima and depopulation to interest in fertility-affecting distributivist schemes (e.g., family wage) drew attention and gave new direction to scientific inquiry.

HISTORY OF POPULATION THEORIES*

By the Population Division, United Nations

A. INTRODUCTION. Questions of population have occupied the attention of statesmen and philosophers since ancient times, but it is only recently that scholars have attempted to investigate systematically the factors of population growth or decline and the specific ways in which population changes may influence social institutions and human welfare. The early writers in this field were concerned primarily with questions of public policy relevant to population; the policies which they recommended or attempted to justify were predicated, of course, on certain assumptions as to the causes and consequences of population changes, but the assumptions were not always explicitly stated and there was generally little effort to test them by factual investigations. It is hardly surprising that this is so, since few of the statistical records that are necessary for such investigations were in existence more than two centuries ago, and the pertinent methods of analysis were only crudely developed before that time.[1] Consequently, the thought of early writers on these subjects was influenced more than that of modern scholars by their preconceptions and relatively superficial observations. Their works do not contain many useful ideas that cannot be found better developed in more recent literature on population theory. Nevertheless, some of the early writings are briefly reviewed in this chapter, in order to show how much of modern thought concerning the causes and consequences of population changes has been inherited from the past, and how much men's thinking on this subject has been influenced, in all ages, by the conditions of the times.

The publication of Malthus' Essay at the end of the eighteenth century brought the question of population for the first time into a prominent position in the literature on economics and related subjects. The works on population theory published since that time are far more numerous and weightier than the earlier writings in the field, and more relevant to the problems of the present day. An effort has therefore been made in the present summary to indicate their contents in greater detail. Even with reference to the writings of the nineteenth and twentieth centuries, however, the summary is inevitably highly selective and compressed. In selecting the material to be included, the aim has been not only to indicate the trends in the development of modern thought on population questions, but also to present an epitome of the theories of certain representative writers.

* Reprinted from *The Determinants and Consequences of Population Trends* (New York: United Nations, 1953), Chapter III, by permission of the publisher.

B. Ancient and Medieval Writings on Population. Germs of certain ideas which have figured prominently in recent theoretical works on population can be found in very ancient writings. The thesis that excessive growth of population may reduce output per worker, depress the level of living of the masses, and engender strife is of great antiquity. It appears in the works of Confucius and his school, as well as in the works of other schools of ancient Chinese philosophers. In fact, these writers had the concept of optimum numbers, so far as the population engaged in agriculture is concerned. They postulated an ideal proportion between land and population, any major deviation from which would create poverty. They held the government primarily responsible for maintaining such a proportion by moving people from over-populated to under-populated areas, though they noted that governmental action was reinforced at times by spontaneous migration.

These ancient Chinese writers also paid some attention to another topic which has occupied much space in subsequent literature on population theory—namely, the checks to population growth. They observed that mortality increases when the food supply is insufficient; that premature marriage makes for high infant mortality rates; that war checks population growth; and that costly marriage ceremonies reduce the marriage rate. They did not attempt to show how the variations of mortality, fertility, and nuptiality, as well as migration, might affect the balance between population and resources.[2]

Plato and Aristotle[3] considered the question of optimum size of population in their discussions of the ideal conditions of a city-state in which man's potentialities could be fully developed and his "highest good" realized. Their treatment of this question was by no means limited to its economic aspects. The "good life" could be attained, they believed, only if the population was large enough to be economically self-sufficient and capable of defending itself, but not too large for constitutional government. Self-sufficiency required the possession of enough territory to supply the needs of the people and to make possible a moderate level of living.[4] However, neither Plato nor Aristotle inquired explicitly into the relation between population density and *per capita* output or the connexion between the size of the population and the opportunities for division of labour. Plato specified 5,040 as the number of citizens "most likely to be useful to all cities," because it has "fifty-nine divisors" and "will furnish numbers for war and peace, and for all contracts and dealings, including taxes and divisions of the land."[5] Aristotle was less specific with regard to the optimum number, but he held that unless the size of the population was appropriately limited, poverty would be the result, for land and property could not be increased as rapidly as population would grow; civil discord would ensue, and it would be impossible for the government to function effectively.[6]

The views of Plato and Aristotle regarding the means of controlling the size of population are noteworthy. Plato proposed to restrict births, if necessary, by restraining the reproduction of those "in whom generation is afflu-ent"; if a higher birth rate were required, he would achieve it by means of re-wards, stigmas, advice and rebuke to the young men from their elders. Should the population grow too large in spite of these precautions, it could be reduced by colonization, and immigration could be used if absolutely necessary to replenish a population greatly diminished by wars or epidemics.[7] Aristotle mentioned child-exposure and abortion as suitable means of preventing an excessive number of children, and in this connexion paid some attention to eugenics.[8]

The Romans, like the Chinese, viewed population questions in the per-spective of a great empire rather than a small city-state. They were less con-scious than the Greeks of possible limits to population growth and more alert to its advantages for military and related purposes. Perhaps partly because of this difference in outlook, Roman writers paid less attention than the Greeks to population theory, but were much concerned with the practical problem of stimulating population increase. Their attitude was indicated by their dis-approval of celibacy, their writings in defence of marriage and procreation, and by their legislation aimed at raising the marriage and birth rates.[9] Cicero, touching upon this subject, rejected Plato's communism in wives and chil-dren and held that the State's population must be kept up by monogamous marriage.[10] He listed various checks to population growth—floods, epidemics, famines, wild animals, war, revolution—but did not attempt to state a general theory of the determinants of population increase or decrease.[11]

Medieval Christian writers considered questions of population almost en-tirely from a moral and ethical standpoint. Since they were concerned more with the next world than with the present, they did not stress material values. Their doctrines were mainly populationist, but they placed less emphasis than earlier Hebrew and other religious writers on maxims adjuring men to multi-ply and people the earth.[12] On the one hand, they condemned abortion, in-fanticide, child-exposure, divorce, and polygamy; on the other hand, they glorified virginity and continence, considered celibacy superior to marriage though suited only to certain persons, and frowned on second marriage.[13] Unlike the Greeks and Romans, early medieval authors did not attach great importance to population growth as a source of strength for the State, but in time, with the reappearance of Aristotle's influence, this point was again em-phasized.[14] Some medieval defenders of ecclesiastical celibacy resorted to economic arguments of a vaguely proto-Malthusian character, noting the ex-tent to which the population of the world had grown, attributing observed poverty and want to this cause, and citing pestilence, famine, war, etc., as na-ture's means of pruning excess population.[15] The prevailing tendency, how-ever, was to favour population increase, as it had been in earlier times. The high rates of mortality which were found throughout the world, and the con-stant threat of sudden depopulation through famines, epidemics and wars predisposed ancient and medieval writers alike to favour maintenance of a high birth rate.[16]

Arguments in favour of population increase predominated in the writings of European authors on population during the early modern, as well as the medieval, period. The discovery of the New World, the increase of commerce between Europe and Asia, the rise of national states, and the Protestant Reformation[17] brought some revision of the terms of discussion of population questions, but until the latter part of the eighteenth century there was no widespread change of attitude with regard to the desirability of a large and increasing population.[18]

Two writers of the period now under consideration require special mention. One is Ibn Khaldun, a fourteenth-century Muslim author, who expounded in detail a theory of cyclical variations of population and their relation to economic, political, and social-psychological conditions. Khaldun held that a densely settled population was conducive to high *per capita* income, since it permitted a greater division of labour, a greater variety of occupations, more military and political security, and more effective use of resources than could be achieved by a sparse population. Population growth was affected by what men believed the future held in store; favourable expectations made for fertility and growth while unfavourable expectations made for decline. Good economic conditions and political order stimulated population growth by increasing natality and checking mortality. The populations of states tended to undergo cyclical change. With the establishment of domination, came political order, population growth, division of labour, and rising income; in their wake came luxury, rising taxes and other changes which in several generations produced political decay, economic decline, and depopulation.[19] Khaldun's writings, though perceptive, apparently had little influence in the East and remained unknown in the West until the nineteenth century. The other writer worthy of special note is Botero, an Italian of the sixteenth century, who set forth ably some of the arguments later developed by Malthus. Botero held that man's generative powers operate with undiminished vigour irrespective of his numbers, whereas man's capacity to produce subsistence is subject to limits. The limitation of subsistence limits population through war, strife and various secondary checks to which the struggle for a limited subsistence gives rise. Presumably, Botero believed that the limits of subsistence had been reached, and that a further increase in population could not in general augment the flow of the means of support, since he declared that the population and the supply of food had remained constant for three thousand years or longer.[20]

C. MERCANTILIST AND RELATED THEORIES. The mercantilist and cameralist schools of political economy, which flourished in Europe during much of the seventeenth and eighteenth centuries, emphasized the economic, political and military advantages of a large and growing population,[21] and favoured various measures to stimulate population growth. These measures included the imposition of disabilities on celibates; the employment of penalties, favours, and monetary rewards to encourage marriage and production of large families; the removal of disabilities on illegitimate children; checks to emigration and stimuli to immigration; and improvements in medicine and public health. Writers in these traditions were concerned primarily with the ways and means of increasing the wealth and power of the state, and in particular its supplies of precious metals. Their aim was not to raise *per capita* income but to increase either the aggregate national income or the excess of national income over the wage-cost of production, which excess was viewed as a source of tax revenues for the state. Population growth would augment national income and at the same time depress the hourly wage rate, giving the workers an incentive to work longer hours and widening the margin between national income and wage costs. The benefit to the state would be especially great if the additional labour supply were used to develop manufactures, for manufactured goods could be exchanged abroad for gold and silver. Many writers thought that manufacturing yielded increasing returns, presumably because of the greater possibilities of division of labour in a larger population; some held that agriculture was subject to diminishing returns and that there were limits to its expansion.[22] It was generally recognized that a large labour supply was useful only if it could be employed, and certain writers stated the thesis that population was determined by the amount of employment that could be made available.

The mercantilists paid special attention to the relation between population and foreign trade. Cantillon suggested that, if the agriculture of a country could not be expanded in proportion to the population, or if such an expansion would involve diminishing returns, additional agricultural products could be obtained abroad in exchange for manufactured goods.[23] Steuart put it that "work" should be exported and "matter" imported so long as satisfactory terms of trade could be obtained; otherwise, population would have to be contained within the limits of home-produced subsistence.[24] Several writers remarked that the size of a country's population was determined by the amount of subsistence that could be produced at home or obtained abroad. Few mercantilist or cameralist writers attempted a systematic explanation of population changes, but they did discuss a variety of checks to population growth: plagues, wars, accidents, uncongenial climate, infecundity due to urbanization and other causes, vice, abortion, deferment of marriage, celibacy, monopoly, luxurious living, emigration, etc. In England, before the mid-seventeenth century, emigration to colonies was approved on the ground that it relieved population pressure at home; during the century that followed it was sometimes condemned on the ground that it reduced the size of the domestic population. This latter view was usually rejected, however, on the ground that colonies were complementary to the mother country and that emigrants to colonies brought into being supplies and markets which operated in time to increase the population capacity of the mother country.[25] Franklin developed the argument that the American population was complementary to the British, and hence its expansion would augment the population of Britain.[26]

The period in which mercantilism flourished saw the beginning of scientific analysis and measurement of population trends.[27] The first of the writers to discern an underlying order in vital statistics was Graunt, who observed "the numerical regularity of deaths and births, of the ratios of the sexes at death and birth, and of the proportions of deaths from certain causes to all deaths in successive years and in different areas; in general terms, the uniformity and predictability of many important biological phenomena in the mass."[28] Petty, more speculative than Graunt, stressed the advantages of a large population on fiscal, administrative, and economic grounds. He noted that, should the population double every 360 years, there would in 2,000 years be one person for every two acres of habitable land, and, in consequence, "wars and great slaughter."[29]

Süssmilch, author of the first complete treatise on population, was influenced by the work of both Graunt and Petty.[30] Birth and death rates were regular, he observed, and numbers normally increased, although urban mortality sometimes exceeded urban natality. Süssmilch thought that population normally tended to double every century, but that the period required for doubling would lengthen as population grew. Fixing the population capacity of the world at 4,000 to 5,000 million and the present world population around 1,000 million, he inferred that population could grow without causing difficulties for at least two centuries and probably much longer if the rate of increase fell and agriculture were greatly improved. Population growth, he said, was restrained by celibacy and deferred marriage and, above all, by pestilence, war, earthquakes, floods and starvation. Because he expected only advantages from population growth, and because he set no store by a rising standard of living, Süssmilch favoured measures which would accelerate growth.[31]

D. The Theories of Malthus and His Immediate Predecessors. During the last half of the eighteenth century, more and more writers on economic and social questions rejected mercantilist doctrine and, with it, the long-established idea that population growth was advantageous and should be actively encouraged by the State.[32] Particularly in England, France, and Italy, there was increasing emphasis on the dependence of population upon subsistence and increasing appreciation of the complex manner in which checks on population growth operated. Certain writers, including Cantillon and his followers, developed the thesis that population growth was dependent upon the scale of living and upon how much of the subsistence produced was available for the support of the people. In Cantillon's view the amount of subsistence produced would depend upon the uses to which proprietors put their land; while the number of people a given amount of subsistence could support would depend upon how poorly people were "content to live."[33] Few writers asserted that population was *determined* by the means of subsistence; most tended to say that, since the standard of living varied, numbers were merely *affected* by the means of subsistence. Among the checks to further growth of population mentioned were dangerous occupations, poor sanitary conditions, contraceptive practices, divorce, urbanization and hindrances to production. It was noted that with the advance of civilization, physical checks gave way somewhat to psychological checks and that the operation of checks became more complex.

The opponents of mercantilist doctrine tended, as a rule, to minimize the possible achievements of the state in augmenting subsistence and improving the lot of the people, and to favour a policy of *laissez-faire*. In this connexion, it was pointed out that, if population adjusted itself to the food supply or to the demand for labour, legislation designed to influence natural increase or migration could have little effect. Some authors, especially in England and France, opposed arrangements for poor relief on the ground that they might undermine frugality, make for labour immobility and misuse of resources, and thus increase the pressure of numbers on subsistence. These arguments were turned against such advocates of social reform as Godwin and Condorcet, in an effort to show that any benefits from reform would be cancelled by a consequent increase of population.[34]

It was in this period of reaction against mercantilist doctrine that Malthus wrote the first edition of his essay on the "principle of population."[35] The first edition was essentially a polemic directed primarily against Condorcet's conjectures regarding the perfectibility of man, against Godwin's system of equality and his allegation that the vices of mankind originated in human institutions, and against Wallace's contention that overpopulation would develop only in the distant future. Malthus asserted "the absolute impossibility from the fixed laws of our nature, that the pressure of want can ever be completely removed from the lower classes of society"; and that schemes for social reform such as Condorcet and Godwin had proposed would only increase the number of the poor by removing existing barriers to marriage and multiplication.

Malthus' argument rested upon the supposition that man's capacity to increase his means of subsistence was much less than his capacity to multiply; he asserted that man could increase his subsistence only in arithmetical progression, whereas his numbers tended to increase in geometrical progression. The history of mankind demonstrated, he said, that population always tended toward the limit set by subsistence and was contained within that limit by the operation of positive and preventive checks. The checks (e.g., want, famine, pestilence, premature mortality) were all resolvable into terms of "misery" and "vice," he declared, though he did describe as a check deferment of marriage "from a foresight of the difficulties attending a family." It followed, he believed, that existing institutional and psychological barriers to marriage and population growth should not be relaxed, since such relaxation would make matters even worse; but it did not follow that salutary population pressure should be eliminated were that possible.[36]

In the second and later editions of his *Essay*, Malthus examined at greater length what he regarded as the principal cause of mass poverty, namely, population pressure and the diversion of too large an amount of productive resources to population growth. While still maintaining that "population is necessarily limited by the means of subsistence" and "population invariably increases where the means of subsistence increase, unless prevented by some very powerful and obvious checks," he introduced a new check, "moral restraint," or the deferment of marriage by prospective spouses until they were in a position to support a family.

In opposition to the assertion that an indefinite increase of population could be supported, since in agriculture returns were at least in proportion to the labour bestowed upon the land, Malthus suggested the law of diminishing returns in agriculture.[37] He argued that fertile land was limited in amount and not capable of continuous and sufficient improvement.[38] Therefore, the practice of "moral restraint," together with frugal conduct, appeared as the only practicable and morally satisfactory alternative to unrestrained population growth. Since this practice was most likely to prevail in a society founded upon individual responsibility, Malthus advocated the abolition of poor laws and other arrangements which freed the individual of responsibility for the results of his behaviour.[39]

Malthus anticipated no significant change in the structure and the class composition of society, but asserted that "the principal and most permanent cause of poverty has little or no *direct* relation to forms of government, or the unequal division of property." Poverty had its origin in the pressure of population upon subsistence, and were this truth to become generally known, prudence might increase. In fact, with the progress of society and civilization and under the impact of man's desire to better his condition, the "prudential check to marriage" had increased in Europe, and the "evils resulting from the principle of population" had diminished. Britain's population, "in the course of some centuries, might double or treble" and yet every man in the kingdom be much better fed and clothed than he is at present.[40]

Malthus' contribution to the development of population theory was far greater than his writings reveal. His essay aroused a storm of controversy which long outlived Malthus himself and which made both his followers and his opponents conscious of the need for adequate information about population trends and for painstaking investigation of their relations with social and economic conditions. Thus Malthus was indirectly responsible for a large measure of the progress which has been made since his time, in developing population censuses and vital statistics, improving the techniques of demographic analysis, and formulating better grounded population theories.

E. WRITINGS OF THE NINETEENTH CENTURY "CLASSICAL SCHOOL" OF ECONOMISTS. The development of population theory from the early part of the nineteenth century up to about 1870 was largely dominated by two distinct schools of thought: first, the "classical school" of political economy in England and its counterparts on the European continent and in America, and second, the writers in the socialist and Marxian traditions.

The theorists of the "classical school"[41] were concerned with the causes and consequences of population changes in their efforts to discover the "laws" governing the levels and trends of production, wages, interest, rents and profits. From their theories flowed arguments, far more sophisticated than Malthus' ratios, to support the thesis that population growth tended to depress wages and create poverty.

One such argument was derived from the "laws" of diminishing or increasing returns in various branches of economic activity, which had been advanced by earlier writers, such as Serra, Adam Smith, and his contemporaries,[42] as well as by certain mercantilist writers. It was generally believed that the cost of production of agricultural commodities tended to rise as a result of increases in population and consequent increases in demand and output, while the cost of producing manufactured goods tended to fall. Decreasing costs (i.e., "increasing returns") in manufacturing presumably occurred because of the possibilities of increasing division of labour and continuing technical improvements. Increasing costs in agriculture[43] were expected, at least in the long run, since it was thought that (a) land was nearly fixed in quantity and quality, and an increase in the volume of production, with given techniques, involved the use of poorer lands or a less efficient combination of labour and capital with lands already in use; and (b) within agriculture there was little opportunity for the extension of division of labour and the application of invention.[44] It followed that, as population increased and more labour was employed in agriculture and manufactures, the increase in agricultural output would be less than proportional.[45] Thus, depending on the relative strength of the opposing tendencies in manufacturing and in agriculture, population growth would be accompanied either by an increase or by a decrease in output *per capita.*

Economists of this period varied in the emphasis placed on diminishing returns in agriculture; also some did not agree that manufacturing was characterized by increasing returns. Mill held that the tendency of returns in agriculture to fall as population increased could not be indefinitely offset by capital accumulation or by extension of division of labour and the introduction of technological improvements in non-agricultural industries. Since manufacturing was dependent upon the land for raw materials, "the general law of production from the land, the law of diminishing return, must in the last resort be applicable to manufacturing as well as to agricultural history." Without improvements in techniques, therefore, "the average condition of the people" must deteriorate if population continued to increase. "After a degree of density has been attained, sufficient to allow the principal benefits of combination of labour, all further increase tends in itself to mischief, so far as regards the average condition of the people; but the progress of improvement has a counteracting operation, and allows of increased numbers without any deterioration, and even consistently with a higher average of comfort." However, Mill apparently doubted whether improvements in the techniques of production would be made rapidly enough to offset the depressing effect of undue population growth on *per capita* income.[46]

Certain writers noted that the operation of the laws of returns in any particular country engaged in international trade might differ from that which would be expected in a closed economy or in the world as a whole. A nation might avoid diminishing returns in agriculture by exchanging manufactured products for agricultural commodities; and it might maintain satisfactory terms of trade by sending emigrants and capital to other parts of the world.[47] This view was criticized by those who believed the amount of accessible land to be limited and continuous, large-scale emigration to be impractical.[48]

Classical economists of this period also developed theories of distribution of the product among the factors of production, which were relevant to population theory. That the level of wages depended largely on the ratio of population to capital was a commonly held view, the inference being that wages would rise if capital increased more rapidly than population.[49] The rate of population increase was regarded as a function of the level of wages and the standard of living of the workers, since in the long run, wages must cover the cost of production of labour. Thus, while an increase in capital and hence in wage levels stimulated population growth, population increase would be greater if the standard of living remained relatively low, or rose only temporarily, than if it rose permanently. Workers could therefore improve their position by insisting on higher standards of living and thus keeping the rate of increase in their numbers below the rate of capital formation.[50]

The relationships of population growth to wages and capital formation were incorporated into the classical theory of the "stationary state," a theory designed to explain how the forces making for economic growth became equilibrated.[51] According to this theory, continuing increases in capital and labour would eventually reduce the rate of returns on capital to a level where the stock of capital was constant, while the level of wages would reach a point exactly commensurate with the standard of living. The growth of both capital and population would then cease, and the stationary state would be at hand. This equilibrium would be compatible either with a relatively small population and high wages or a larger population and lower wages. It could be modified by new changes in the stock of capital, by changes in population due to a rise or fall of living standards, by improvements in the methods of production, or by extension of the known and accessible stock of land.

A different theory of wages, to the effect that the remuneration of workers depended largely on the value of their services, was expounded by von Thünen, Longfield, Senior, Say, and most of the orthodox theorists following Say.[52] Von Thünen attributed the low wages of workers to their low marginal

productivity and to their exposure to exploitation by employers, both conditions which were largely traceable to the rapidity (about 1 per cent per year,
he said) with which population increased. The remedy consisted in reducing
the ratio of workers to capital and to the entrepreneurial and bureaucratic
classes. Other German economists observed that the level of wages was affected both by the productivity and the standard of life of the workers, and
that with an increase in the number of workers, there was often a diminution
in the welfare of the working population.[53]

The French liberal economists of this period, including Say, Destutt de
Tracy, Courcelle-Seneuil, Liesse, and others, called attention to the importance of the distribution of income as a factor affecting population growth.
They contended, in general, that the size of a country's population varies inversely with the *per capita* consumption, which in turn varies directly with
the degree of inequality of incomes.[54] A similar view was put forward by von
Storch, founder of the Germano-Russian school of economics.[55]

The relation of the size and growth of population to unemployment was
also given some consideration during this period. The Venetian economist
Ortes had stated earlier that, as a rule, the demand for labour was not sufficient to afford employment for more than half the population,[56] and a similar
view was held by certain nineteenth-century French economists.[57] To refute
the argument that an increase of population and labour supply would increase
unemployment, Say developed his "law of markets," that an increment in
supply tends to generate its own demand.[58]

Various views regarding the need for controlling population growth were
held during this period. Mill believed that population growth must be effectively controlled, since there were limits in the extent to which the flow of
goods and services in any particular country could be increased and since
international trade and emigration could afford little relief from population
pressure should numbers continue to grow. According to Mill, the supply of
food actually and potentially available from exporting countries was quite
limited, for their accessible territory was restricted, their population was
growing, and their productive efforts were subject to diminishing returns and
capital shortage.[59] Mill believed that in the most populous countries a desirable density had been achieved, and he hoped that the people of these
countries would be content to keep their numbers constant, lest by necessity
they be compelled to do so. Regarding man's capacity to control numbers,
Mill was more optimistic than Malthus; he observed that checks always operated to contain population growth within the limits set by man's resources
and his productive efforts. In primitive societies the increase was checked
largely by misery and premature mortality; in more advanced societies by
man's "fear of want" and his indisposition to give "existence to beings born
only to misery and premature death." Circumstances, such as peasant ownership, the independence of women, national education, and progress in civilization, restricted population growth. Most effective were changes such as an

increase in the scale of comfort, sufficiently great and lasting to produce a permanent alteration of a people's habits. Mill declared it quite possible that socialism would prove the most suitable form of society to deal with the population problem.[60]

In America, where the works of Smith, Say, and later Mill were popular, Malthus's inferences had been anticipated in part by Franklin and Madison. Perhaps the most outstanding of the American disciples of Malthus was Tucker, who discovered that the rate of natural increase was falling and predicted that it would continue to fall; who indicated that the terms of trade would turn against manufacturing countries where population continued to increase; and who supposed that increasing population pressure might depress the wages of free labour to the point where it would displace slave labour. Several defenders of the slave economy contended that this type of economy was relatively immune to such population pressure as tended to develop in free-labour economies. In general the American writers distinguished between old countries, where population pressure was manifesting itself, and new countries like America, where it would develop eventually should the rate of increase not gradually fall to an insignificant level as some anticipated it might.[61]

Although Say did not emphasize the need for moral restraint as did Malthus, presumably because he believed increments in population to be desirable as long as they could produce enough to live comfortably,[62] certain other French writers[63] supported Malthus more vigorously. Garnier, after formulating Malthus' main findings and their implications for man's welfare, proceeded to refute various criticisms which had been directed against Malthus' *Essay* and to question the adequacy of the various palliatives which had been proposed for the relief of poverty attributable, in Garnier's opinion, to population pressure. Garnier was, however, more optimistic than Malthus, since he believed men could escape poverty through the practice of prudence, through capital formation, through the regulation of family size, and through work and effort.[64] De Molinari, proceeding upon the hypothesis that population has a supply price and that man seeks pleasure and avoids pain, believed that credit and related institutions could be established which would assure something like the appropriate number of births.[65]

Reactions to Malthus elsewhere on the European continent were various. Roscher, in Germany, gave qualified support to Malthus, stressing the need for a "morally rational check on the sexual impulse" and noting that with the advance of civilization and technology, people became more free of Malthusian poverty and became more concerned with the future and with wants other than "subsistence."[66] In the Netherlands, Malthus had a supporter in Mees,[67] and in Geneva, Sismondi, though believing that the food supply would prove adequate, asserted that the prevailing distribution of property checked production and undermined prudence. He recommended that workers regulate their numbers and that institutional arrangements conducive to such regulation (e.g., peasant ownership) be promoted. Perhaps his most important contribution consisted in the observation that industrial capitalism had undermined the institutional and psychological checks to population growth which the precapitalist system provided, and as yet no suitable substitutes had appeared.[68] Rossi, although advocating moral restraint and thrift, believed that with advances in civilization changes in man's wants and productive capacity would establish a satisfactory equilibrium between numbers and resources.[69] Francesco Ferrara, somewhat influenced by Carey's views on rent and cost, supported Malthus's position in part although he placed a more optimistic interpretation upon the working of the principle of population and upon the population prospect.[70] Messedaglia criticized Malthus' progressions on the ground that they were not independent of one another as Malthus implied, since man was both a producer and a being disposed to increase in response to improvements in the opportunity to produce. The progression of population, being dependent on that of subsistence, was also necessarily arithmetical, but was double the progression of subsistence.[71]

Certain early nineteenth-century authors fundamentally disagreed both with Malthus and with the writers in the tradition of the "classical school," so far as population questions were concerned. Apart from the socialists and Marxists, whose views will be taken up in a later section of this chapter, there were some writers who contended either that an increase in population density made for an increase in productivity, or that, irrespective of the rate of population growth, there was a tendency for productivity to increase, thus insuring a steady rise in *per capita* income. Such writers have either denied the law of diminishing returns altogether, or admitting its existence at least in agriculture, have asserted that its action was more than counterbalanced by a law of increasing return outside agriculture, by technical progress, or by a combination of increasing non-agricultural returns and technical progress.[72] As a rule, the argument of Malthus's early critics rested upon the supposition that division of labour increased as population became more dense,[73] though some were content to note that technical progress would be more than sufficient to counterbalance population growth, or to infer from past trends that output per head would continue to increase.[74]

One of those subscribing to the idea that with population increase there was further division of labour was Everett, who contended in addition that population did not tend to grow so rapidly as Malthus supposed and, further, that any nation could import raw produce. Everett declared "that an increase of population on a given territory necessarily and naturally produced a division of labour, and a consequent increase of skill in its application." The natural result, he said, was an extension of manufacturing and trade, with a rise in wages due to the increasing productivity of labour.[75]

Carey stressed what he called "the power of association," which grew as population grew and thereby made possible greater diversity of employments, greater development of the human faculties, and increasing *per cap-*

ita output.[76] In Carey's opinion, this tendency was not checked, as some of Malthus's other critics asserted,[77] by diminishing returns in agriculture, since, contrary to Ricardo's assumption, cultivation proceeded from inferior to superior soils,[78] with the result that *per capita* output in agriculture tended to increase as population grew and settlement spread.[79] Carey believed that population growth would long continue to be conducive to increasing output *per capita*, though he admitted the existence of limits to production.[80] He did not anticipate population pressure, for he supposed that man would so develop mentally, morally, and physiologically that a suitable balance would be established between natality and mortality, on the one hand, and the resources at man's disposal, on the other.[81]

Rogers was one of the writers who did not specifically argue that population growth was a source of abundance, as did Everett and Carey, but noted that, historically, *per capita* output had tended to increase, in part because of technical progress and the fact that the better lands were sometimes the last to be brought under cultivation.[82]

Late nineteenth century opponents of Malthus seem to have placed more importance upon technical progress as such and less emphasis upon increasing specialization and division of labour than did the earlier writers. For example, Leroy-Beaulieu stated that technical progress, together with capital accumulation and the development of international division of labour, would continue to increase output per man.[83] In the view of Oppenheimer, the continuing improvement in the welfare of the masses indicated that any tendency to diminishing returns in agriculture was more than compensated for by an improved facility in manufacturing, and that an increasing productivity of labour was associated with an increasing population.[84] Much later, Wagemann stated that in the long run the law of diminishing returns was more than counterbalanced by technical progress. A condition of over-population might be replaced by one of under-population due to improved methods of social organization and production, capital formation, and other adjustments to the initial condition of over-population. But in time this condition of under-population would be again replaced by one of over-population to which further adjustments must be made. Thus Wagemann viewed demographic history as a sequence of alternating under- and over-population, with population growth both responding to and helping to generate economic change.[85]

The writers who drew conclusions contrary to those of Malthus from arguments relating to the "preventive checks" to population growth can be divided into three main groups. One group maintained that preventive checks would become more and more effective in slowing down population growth, though they offered little rationale to support this belief. Representatives of this group during the early part of the nineteenth century include Hazlitt, who supposed that moral restraint would prove adequate; Hamilton, who held the opinion that the rate of increase would fall as civilization advanced;

Moreton, who inferred that the failure of the "higher orders" to replace themselves and the consequent opportunity for ascent in social scale generated a tendency for a lower rate of reproduction to spread through the ranks of society; Weyland, who thought that population would cease to grow when a sufficiently high proportion of the people had located in cities, where birth rates tended to be below death rates; and many French, American, and other writers who presumed that the standard of living would continue to rise and check undue population growth.[86]

The second group of writers, not content to say that preventive checks would probably come more and more into play, attempted to demonstrate that such checks were the inevitable result of social and economic progress, and the guarantee of continuing progress. In the early part of the nineteenth century, such critics of Malthus as Senior,[87] Rickards,[88] and Alison[89] argued that as the real income of workers rose, they tended to adjust their standards of life accordingly, and that the higher standards, once attained, would not willingly be relinquished. As they became more self-respecting, workers would protect their position the more zealously by postponing marriage and limiting their families, as well as in other ways.[90] Later, as the practice of contraception became more general, anti-Malthusian writers placed increasing emphasis on arguments in this vein.[91]

The third group of anti-Malthusian writers dealing with preventive checks emphasized the reduction of natural fecundity which, they believed, would necessarily occur in the course of economic development, as a result of social selection and changes in the milieu. Many writers believed that man's fecundity would decline in response to increases in mental exertion and inbreeding and to modifications of diet,[92] and Spencer attempted to infer a self-adjusting biological principle of population growth. Spencer supposed that there existed an antagonism between the power to maintain life and the power to propagate; he considered that fertility varied inversely, while the power to maintain life varied directly, with the development of the nervous system. Where the power to maintain life was low, survival of the population required high fertility, and this in turn made the struggle for existence severe. The high fertility under such conditions tended, Spencer reasoned, to produce population pressure; and this pressure was conducive to improvements in the methods of production; intensified the need for skill, intelligence, self-control, and education; and made difficult the survival of the mentally sluggish. In consequence, man's nervous centres became enlarged, with the result that his power to maintain life increased while his power to reproduce diminished. The evolutionary tendency initially set in motion by excess fertility would tend to persist until both fertility and mortality had declined to a low level where they would balance one another.[93]

F. SOCIALIST AND MARXIST WRITINGS. Socialist and Marxist writers since the early part of the nineteenth century have, for the most part, either denied the existence of a population problem or maintained that it would be solved through reorganization of society. They have generally attributed human misery, not to excessive population growth, but to the maldistribution of income and other supposed defects in the existing social order. They have held that under the new form of society which they advocate adequate preventive checks on population growth would operate, and that the productive forces of the people would increase more rapidly than their numbers.[94]

Among the pre-Marxian socialists of the nineteenth century, such views were not so consistently and fully developed as they were later by Marx and his followers.

Pre-Marxian socialists, concerned in one way or another with matters of population, included the English Ricardian socialists and various socialist groups in France, Germany and Italy. Considerable differences in thought on matters of population are evident from the writings of these various groups. English Ricardian socialists in general tended to reject Malthus's views. Thompson believed that population growth could be controlled in his envisioned co-operative society. Gray criticized Malthus's ratios and implied that numbers would be brought under control. Gray indicated that, since labour produced all wealth, production would keep pace with population as long as raw materials were available; hence there would be no population problem for centuries. Hodgskin, after initially accepting Malthus's views, in part rejected them, since he believed that population growth was desirable insofar as it generated a division of labour and stimulated invention.[95]

Most early French socialists opposed Malthus's views, but for different reasons than the English Ricardian socialists. Malthus's views were opposed because of their ascetic implications, their denial of the bounty of nature, their opposition to social reform and reorganization, and also because of their denial that maldistribution was a major source of misery.[96] Fourier, while believing that France was over-populated and that the world's population capacity probably did not exceed 5,000 millions, advocated emigration and control of conception for the time being instead of moral restraint as recommended by Malthus. However, Fourier and certain of his followers believed that, with the establishment of the "societary state," physiological, dietary, and other changes would bring numbers under effective control. Malthus's solution was rejected by the Saint Simonians for the reason, among others, that it denied happiness to the worker. Louis Blanc and Pierre Leroux were critical of Malthus's views and asserted that imprudence itself was the product of misery. If misery were removed through reorganization of society, numbers would be brought under control with the more productive system which would be introduced. Proudhon, too, argued that under a system of social organization that insured justice, the population problem would disappear, since numbers would increase no more than was desirable in view of the new arrangements for production.[97] Ferdinand Lassalle believed that the reason why average wages of workers did not rise above the level necessary to provide subsistence and to permit the maintenance of the population, was the exploitation of workers by consolidated capital. He indicated, however, that with an increase in the wage bill the population tended to increase. His solution for this dilemma was the organization of workers' productive associations.[98] Rodbertus too believed that workers normally received only a subsistence wage, but held that population increases tended to intensify the exploitation of workers. He denied that productivity tended to fall in agriculture and declared that, as a result of the devolpment of chemistry and mechanics, "the increase in productiveness is incalculable." The solution for depressed wages and rapid population growth was to be found initially in reform and eventually in social reorganization.[99]

Achilla Loria and others developed the thesis that population pressure is characteristic only of certain stages of economic development.[100] According to Loria, an excess of population in his day—by which he meant an excess with respect to capital rather than to food—had its origin in the prevailing capitalistic wage system which operated, on the one hand, to restrict production, capital formation, and the productive employment of capital and, on the other hand, to compel the masses to work for miserable wages, thereby undermining their continence and exciting them to excessive procreation. Given sufficient capital formation and the productive use of capital, wage-depressing unemployment would be removed, wages would rise, and the living conditions and aspirations of the workers would improve, with the result that they would procreate less without resorting to contraceptive practices. Population growth itself, being the primary cause of economic evolution and of the historical succession of social forms, would directly and indirectly bring into being a form of organization free of excess population and attendant evils. This growth had long ago eliminated free land and caused the more productive system of forced association of labour, which was typical of capitalism, to replace the previous system of isolated labour. It would eventually cause the capitalistic system in turn to give place to a system of freely associated labour, since only under this latter system could agricultural workers produce enough to maintain themselves under conditions of high population density.[101]

Nitti also attributed the level of the birth rate to economic factors. Birth rates were high where poor economic conditions restricted the pleasures of the "popular classes." Each improvement in their economic condition operated to bring about a lowering of the birth rate.[102] Nitti did not consider the solution of the population problem as inevitable, but believed that it would gradually be realized by establishing a strong social organization with opportunity for the development of individuality. According to Nitti: "In every society where individuality will be strongly developed, but where progress of socialisation will not extinguish individual activity; in every society where wealth will be largely sub-divided and where the social cause of inequality will be eliminated by an elevated form of co-operation, the birth-rate will tend to become equal with the means of subsistence, and the regular variations of demographic evolution will not have, as in the past, an element of fear and terror."[103]

Marx's characterization of the population problem differed considerably from that of earlier socialist writers concerned with the Malthusian question.[104] He held that there could be no universal law of population, and that the source of existing "overpopulation" was not to be found in man's supposed biological proclivities but in the prevailing capitalist mode of production. This "over-population" arose from the fact that, because of capital accumulation, "variable capital," the source of demand for labour, increased less rapidly than did the labouring population.[105] The capitalistic mode of production thus created its own "relative surplus-population" or army of unemployed, independently of the actual rate of population increase. This Marx took to be the "law of population" under capitalism, and he held that every mode of production had its peculiar laws of population. Surplus population was not only a necessary consequence of capitalistic accumulation, but also a necessary condition to the existence and continuation of the capitalistic form of economic organization, for that mode of production required "the readily exploitable manpower."[106] Only when this reserve was sufficiently great could the pretensions of the employed workers be held in check and the rates of surplus value and profit be maintained.[107]

Marx identified three forms of "relative surplus population," or unemployment: "the floating, the latent, the stagnant." The *floating* category was recruited in large part from those displaced by machinery. The *latent* category was made up of that part of the agricultural population which was on the verge of migrating to the cities, and the *stagnant* form comprised workers with highly irregular employment. Natural increase alone could not supply enough recruits for the industrial reserve army, partly because death and morbidity rates were high and because youthful workers were preferred in many employments.[108] Therefore, according to Marx, it was essential to the capitalist system that capital of the sort that displaced labour be accumulated in sufficient volume to generate unemployment.[109] Surplus population could be created also through expropriation of land and the movement of dispossessed peasants out of agriculture.[110]

Marx's explanation implied that relative over-population of the sort associated with the capitalist mode of production would disappear when capitalism was superseded by a collective mode of production. He had little to say explicitly about the manner in which population would grow thereafter. His analysis of reproductive behaviour under capitalism suggested, however, that the increase of income, the reduction of inequalities in income distribution, and the improvements in the living conditions of the masses, which he expected to result from the reorganization of society, would bring about a decline of the death rate. The birth rate also would presumably decline because of the rise in living standards and the ending of the exploitation of children.[111]

Marx apparently placed no value upon moral restraint as a remedy to over-population. He stated, but did not elaborate, that a decline in the rate of population growth[112] might accentuate the tendency toward under-consumption and reduced profits, and thus expedite the breakdown of capitalism.[113]

The followers of Marx were not always in agreement in their views regarding the population problem, although in general they supported Marx. Bebel pointed, on the one hand, to the possibility of greatly augmenting the food supply, and on the other, to the presumption that, with improved economic conditions, human fertility would fall. He held that population was likely to increase more slowly in a socialistic society than in a bourgeois society, mainly because of the superior position of women under socialism.[114] Kautsky, unlike most socialists, initially attached considerable importance to the population question, suggesting among other things the possibility of both Marxian relative over-population and Malthusian absolute over-population.[115] Following Marx more closely in his later writings, he explained over-population as a result of the "variable constituent" of capital increasing less rapidly than both total capital and the labouring population. There might ensue an excess of population relative to variable capital and a deficiency of numbers relative to the means of life, with the result that wages would be depressed and profits would rise. This situation would disappear upon the collectivization of the economy.[116] He believed that under socialism conditions more conducive both to the appropriate regulation of numbers and to the increase of production would develop.[117]

Lenin, like Marx, rejected the Malthusian principle of population. He denied, also, that the law of diminishing returns applied under conditions of technological progress and changing methods of production, and maintained that it was applicable only where techniques remained unchanged.[118] By way of evidence, he pointed to the decline, or negligible increase, in the agricultural population of advanced countries, which had occurred simultaneously with the expansion of agricultural production.[119]

Although certain socialist writers in the 1920's and 1930's showed Malthusian leanings, the emphasis of contemporary socialist writings has been strongly anti-Malthusian.[120] The later writers have continued to assert that relative over-population, though characteristic of the capitalist mode of production, is avoided under socialism; and they have given much attention to the problem of converting rural population into the kind of manpower needed for a modern economy.[121] They have also given considerable attention to the actual and prospective trends of natural increase, noting that in capitalistic countries, particularly mature ones, relative over-population and other conditions were slowing down population growth and might eventually bring about depopulation. In socialist countries, on the contrary, they have held that a healthy growth of population was assured, since the philosophy of family limitation was there disapproved, [122] and socialism did not necessitate family limitation as did capitalism.[123]

Stalin has looked with favour upon population growth, but in view of the teaching of dialectical and historical materialism, has said that the growth of population was not an important determinant of the character of the social system. Population growth facilitates or retards the development of society, but it does not determine its development. For example, population growth does not, in itself, explain why the primitive communal system has given way to the slave system, the slave system to the feudal system, and the feudal system to the bourgeois system, instead of to other forms of social and economic organization. Stalin has also pointed out that, were social development determined by the growth of population, "a higher density of population would be bound to give rise to a correspondingly higher type of social system." He has noted, however, that types of social systems are not correlated with the degree of population density. The chief force determining the character of the social system has not been population growth but "the *method of procuring the means of life* necessary for human existence, the *mode of production of material values* . . . which are indispensable for the life and development of society."[124]

While present day Russian writers are opposed to concern with matters of over-population because they believe that such a problem is non-existent under socialism, the subject has not been completely ignored by certain post-revolutionary writers.[125] The possibility has been noted of at least temporary relative over-population under socialism until the achievement of a desirable level of productivity and development. Lubny-Gertsyk stated that a condition of over-population existed when the actual population exceeded the number that could attain a desirable level of productivity and development with the existing resources and technical conditions. Over-population might exist because natural resources were insufficient, because consumers' needs could not be satisfied, or because for various reasons production had fallen relative to population. Of the alternative remedies, a decrease in numbers or an increase in productivity, the latter was preferable. If, however, this was not easily accomplished, a regulation of fertility was indicated.[126] While over-population, defined in terms of unused time,[127] has existed in various parts of the U.S.S.R., it has generally been believed that in the long run Malthusian fears were unwarranted.[128]

G. RECENT DEVELOPMENT OF NON-SOCIALIST THEORIES RELEVANT TO POPULATION. During the period since about 1870, non-socialist writings on population have generally departed much more from Malthus' views than did those during the earlier part of the nineteenth century, with the result that the cleavage between socialist and non-socialist doctrine on this subject is no longer as distinct as it formerly was. The developments in non-socialist, like those in socialist theories, have been affected by several important changes in circumstances. First, statistical information relevant to population has been greatly extended and the methods of analysing demographic statistics have been much improved. Second, after about 1870 the birth rate and the rate of natural increase began to decline in certain of the economically most advanced countries. Third, significant improvements continued to be made in both manufacturing and the extractive industries, with the result that living conditions improved. Fourth, writers devoted to the developing science of sociology and the study of social evolution have taken an increasing part in the study of population questions. Meanwhile, new emphases have been introduced in economics. The marginalist school of economics, though not greatly concerned with population problems,[129] developed explanations of the principles governing production and the shares of labour and capital in the total product, which had evident bearings upon population theory.[130]

In England, Germany, Holland, the United States, and, to a lesser degree, in France and elsewhere a significant number of writers in the late nineteenth century and in the twentieth continued to emphasize that, unless population growth slowed down, the economic condition of the people would be adversely affected.[131] In England, perhaps more than elsewhere, the supposed benefits of emigration were stressed,[132] while in the United States and France the alleged disadvantages of immigration were expounded.

(1) *Development of Theory Concerning the "Laws of Returns."* While earlier nineteenth-century writers had commonly believed that manufactures were subject to constant or increasing returns and that the augmentation of production in the extractive industries involved increasing difficulties and rising costs in spite of technical progress, it came to be accepted before the close of the century that, other things being equal, average output per worker would fall in non-extractive as well as in extractive industries after the ratio of workers to the resources with which they work passed a certain point.[133] It was recognized, however, that other things were not equal, and that the effects of population growth upon wages and *per capita* income depended upon accompanying changes in social organization, technological skill and productive wealth. The latter factors might change as a result of population growth, or for independent reasons, in such a way as to counter-balance the tendency toward diminishing returns.[134]

Out of consideration of these ideas came the modern notion of a dynamic variable optimum population advanced by Cannan and other writers.[135] Cannan defined optimum as a population that was moving in the right direction with respect to the increase of output *per capita*. "The right movement is that which will give the largest returns to industry in the long run, the interests of the people of all the generations being taken into account." Cannan envisioned a "point of maximum return to all industries taken together," that is, a population, given which the productivity of labour would be at a maximum.[136] He indicated that the optimum magnitude changed as circumstances changed, usually faster than the actual population; generally, it tended to increase.[137]

Sidgwick, a late nineteenth-century economist, considered that the density of population in Great Britain had reached such a point that, without an adequate volume of foreign trade at satisfactory terms of exchange, no known improvements in the industrial arts could prevent further increases of population from depressing output per worker. He apparently anticipated no other change that would cause an increase in population density in Britain to augment average output.[138] Marshall, on the other hand, held that an increase of labour and capital generally led to improved organization and efficiency, thus offsetting the tendency toward diminishing returns which was inherent in "the part which nature plays in production." This proposition he called the "law of increasing return." He declared that an increase of population "accompanied by an equal increase in the material sources of enjoyment and aids to production" was likely to result in an economic benefit to the people, provided adequate supplies of raw materials could be obtained without too great difficulty and overcrowding did not impair health and opportunities for recreation. He believed that the growth of population in England and other "civilized countries" was, on the whole, advantageous. Should circumstances change, however, for instance, should foreign supplies be cut off, this growth might have disadvantageous effect.[139] But elsewhere in the world Marshall believed that the population situation was less favourable; only if numbers were effectively regulated could the "iron" law of wages be escaped and the comforts of western Europe be spread throughout the world.[140]

The fear that food imports might cease to be available to European countries was shared by Crookes and Giffen. From statistical evidence they inferred that the volume of food exports of export countries with a continuing growth of population would decline and, consequently, that the importing countries would be more dependent upon domestic production, that emigration to the new world would diminish, and that the condition of European workers would be adversely affected.[141] In Germany, which has become more dependent upon grain imports as industrialization proceeded,[142] Adolf Wagner and others were apprehensive lest the population become too dependent upon foreign food supplies and thereby purchase numbers at the expense of security. Brentano and others challenged this view and the protectionist policies based on it. Brentano denied that diminishing returns and other circumstances would make it impossible for Germany's suppliers to provide agricultural commodities on terms satisfactory to Germany.[143]

Following World War I, Keynes pointed to the supposedly unfavourable trend in the terms of trade as evidence of over-population.[144] In his view, with Europe already dependent upon the agriculture of the new world and with agriculture there already subject to diminishing returns, the position of the population of Europe was precarious and the terms on which agricultural imports were to be had would turn increasingly against her.[145] The issue was discussed occasionally in the 1920's and 1930's[146] and received more attention after World War II as a result of the difficulties encountered by countries greatly dependent upon foreign trade.[147]

Some writers also expected that exhaustion or deterioration of natural resources would make it difficult for European industry to continue expanding more rapidly than population would grow. Jevons predicted that, with the exhaustion of Britain's richer veins of coal, the cost of extracting coal would steadily rise and check Britain's industrial progress. If changes in other countries did not bring Britain to "a stationary condition," it "must come when our mines have reached a certain depth."[148] While Jevons' view received relatively little favourable attention in France,[149] it did command interest in England and eventually elsewhere.[150]

A number of writers took exception to the so-called law of increasing returns as formulated by Marshall and others, on the ground that it minimized the problems of realizing the potential increase in efficiency and output that growth of capital and labour supply might seem to make possible.[151] Wicksell pointed out that the validity of Marshall's "law" depended on the assumption, which he considered unacceptable, "that the raw materials required are to be found in practically unlimited quantities at an unchanged, or almost unchanged, price." Although increasing returns might well prevail for a time, Wicksell thought that diminishing returns would prevail in the long run.[152] Wolfe pointed out that natural resources always set a limit to production, though the limit was in all cases at least somewhat elastic and in some cases might be far in the future. Continuing population growth would therefore eventually bring the law of diminishing returns into operation, so that changed economic, social and political policies would be necessary to ensure continued progress in the material well-being of the people.[153]

Budge held that the limitations to human progress were to be found in nature rather than in man's institutions, and that population was tending to increase beyond the means of subsistence. He denied that diminishing returns in agriculture would be offset indefinitely by improvements in agricultural technique or counterbalanced by increasing returns in manufactures and transportation, or that population increases caused *per capita* product to rise.[154] Wolf drew attention to the various limitations to which technical progress itself is subject, thereby in effect denying the way of escape which many sought from the Malthusian problem.[155] Mombert, while admitting the operation of diminishing returns in agriculture and the limitations on technical progress, described by Wolf, believed that there existed many ways by which these tendencies could be counterbalanced; thus, he anticipated improving living conditions rather than increasing population pressure for some time to come.[156]

In recent literature less emphasis has been devoted to "laws of returns"[157] as such than to the sum total of the factors which affect the trends of aggregate income and *per capita* income, population being considered one of the more important of these factors.[158]

(2) *Development of Theories Concerning the Determinants of Population Growth.* Writers in the eighteenth and the early nineteenth centuries generally thought that the increase of the food supply regulated the growth

of population.[159] In more recent literature the idea has been developed that certain requirements other than food, which cannot readily be replaced by substitutes, may become population-limiting factors.[160] More and more the growth of population has been treated as a function of increasing income; thus the pertinence of Malthusian theory regarding the increase of "subsistence" and its relation to population growth has diminished.[161] There has, moreover, been an increasing recognition of the complexity of the factors affecting the rate of population growth. Bagehot, for example, stated that "the causes which determine the increases of mankind are little less than all the causes, outward and inward, which determine human action."[162] Pareto held a similar view, although he emphasized the importance of the economic factor in the slowing down of population growth in Europe.[163]

The reasons for the declining birth rates and natural increase rates in various European countries were a subject of considerable conjecture among writers of the late nineteenth and early twentieth centuries. A number of writers believed that similar development could be expected to occur elsewhere. Certain writers sought to demonstrate that a decline in the birth rate was inevitable in view of the natural processes of social change and the limits of economic expansion. Benini held that, when the earth had been peopled, natality and mortality would be brought into balance by the natural development of new customs relating to age at marriage and other factors.[164] Clark believed that in advanced countries the progress toward ever higher standards of living and wages was self-perpetuating, and that it could be stopped only by "perversion of the system" through monopoly, war, bad government, or class struggle.[165] Pigou drew the conclusion that almost certainly population growth would not be allowed to absorb all the fruits of economic development.[166] However, some writers, like Pierson,[167] were not so sure that the birth rate would decline with advancing civilization and the Malthusian problem would be solved in this way.

Certain French theorists, while noting that economic changes affected population growth by diminishing the value of children as assets, stressed changes in the underlying pattern of values which were associated only indirectly with economic development. Most of all they stressed "arrivisme" and social capillarity, the tendency for modern civilization to value the development of the individual more than that of the group, and hence a more rationalistic attitude toward procreation.[168] Not only did these tendencies remove the threat of undue population growth; in France they had brought the birth rate below the death rate and they would have this effect elsewhere as civilization developed. Some of the exponents of this theory advocated state intervention for the purpose of stimulating population growth.[169]

Brentano argued that advances in income produced various cultural effects which in turn made for family limitation.[170] This interpretation was compatible with the theory of civilization developed by Patten, who wrote: "As civilization is the principle antagonistic to the law of diminishing returns, so productive power is the principle antagonistic to the law of increasing population. . . . Every stage in the advancing civilization, accompanied by an increase in the number of industrial qualities, will open up new sources of pleasure and create new social forces through which the strength of the primitive appetites and passions will be reduced."[171]

The influence of biological factors on fertility has been emphasized by some writers. For example, Hankins observed that in highly civilized societies the energies of the people tend to be diverted from reproduction to the demands of mental and physical activities. Group differences in fertility reflected in some degree differences in the pressure of these demands, and Hankins therefore attributed the decline in natality partly to an increase in these pressures.[172]

Gini assembled statistical data which he interpreted as indicating that the rate of reproduction of a population tended to describe a parabola reflecting, not variation in the amount of subsistence or in the environment, but changes in the quality of the "germinal cells." According to his theory, a population cycle is initiated as a result of crossbreeding between groups that have become appropriately differentiated. Fecundity increases and the rate of growth rises for a time because fecundity is somewhat hereditary and each generation is largely the product of the relatively more fecund components of the preceding generation. In time, however, the forces making for an increase in fecundity are more than counterbalanced by the forces of "physical exhaustion"—principally a deterioration in the germinal cells which is accentuated by the movement of a relatively large fraction of the population into social classes which have characteristically low fecundity. In consequence, the rise in the rate of natural increase gives place to a decline which may continue to the zero level or below unless the population is reinvigorated through further crossbreeding (for example, with immigrants). [173] Gini's thesis has been criticized on the logical ground that it is impossible "to attribute any specific part of [an individual's] neuro-muscular patterns or other characteristics to inherent qualities of the germ plasm and others to cultural or other environmental factors."[174]

In general, the majority of writers toward the end of the nineteenth century and early in the twentieth were more optimistic than the earlier nineteenth-century writers in their estimates of man's ability to control his numbers. Their optimism had its origin in the spread of contraceptive practices and the decline of birth rates in economically advanced countries,[175] and was reinforced by the thesis that the birth rate tends to decline with the advance of civilization.[176] This view has been considerably modified in the more recent literature. Many writers now hold that the decline of the birth rate in Europe and in certain countries populated by European stock overseas was associated with industrialization, urbanization, and accompanying changes in modes of living and attitudes of the various classes within these societies. Many agree in general with earlier writers that population growth will eventually be brought under control. They emphasize that as some of the changes characteristic of countries experiencing declines in the birth rate are spread to areas where the birth rate is still high, it is to be expected that birth and death rates will decline, thus resulting in less rapid population increase and less pressure upon resources.[177]

(3) *Logistic and Related "Laws" of Population Growth.* Attempts to formulate mathematical "laws" of population growth have been encouraged by the increasing availability of statistics relating to population trends, as well as by the development of mathematical techniques for analysing such data. One of the first attempts at such a statement of population growth was that advanced by Quetelet in 1835. He asserted that "the resistance or the sum of the obstacles opposed to the unlimited growth of population, increases in proportion *to the square of the velocity with which the population tends to increase.*" Accordingly, in the absence of a change in "social state," a population tends to grow more and more slowly.[178] At Quetelet's request Verhulst submitted this principle to examination. In 1838 Verhulst suggested that a symmetrical theoretical curve which he named the "logistic" was suitable to describe the course of population growth. A few years later he made use of it to estimate the population of Belgium, to which he assigned maxima of 6.6–9.4 millions. Initially he supposed that the obstacles increase *"exactly in the same proportion* as the superabundant population" but he replaced this supposition with the hypothesis that that obstacles *"increase in proportion to the ratio of the superabundant population to the total population."*[179]

For a long time the logistic curve was little used, in part because census data were lacking.[180] As a result Verhulst's work was generally forgotten until after 1920, when the logistic curve was independently rediscovered by Pearl and Reed.[181]

Certain assumptions underlie the theory of growth implicit in the simple logistic curve of population growth.[182] First, the physical environment or the area which the population under analysis utilizes for its support is constant. Second, the population N increases from a lower asymptotic limit of zero toward an upper asymptotic limit K, which represents the maximum population that can exist in the stipulated environment under the given cultural conditions and methods of production. Third, the proportional rate of population growth R steadily declines,[183] because of the damping effect produced by the increase of population density.[184] The absolute increase per year or other time period generates a symmetrical bell-shaped curve which rises to a peak at the point where $N = K/2$—that is, where the actual population is one-half the maximum—and then moves downward toward zero. Thus, the population follows an S-shaped curve as it moves from a very low value toward the maximum K.[185]

The logistic "law," and the modified logarithmic equation employed by Pearl and Reed to express it, commanded much attention in the 1920's,[186] and fairly distinctive types of criticism of the logistic were developed. First, it was noted that the logistic was not always the type of curve that best described the past population growth of a given country or region. Second, even where a logistic described the past growth more precisely than other curves, it did not follow that the population would continue to follow the curve.[187] Third, it had not been established that, because of the inherent nature of the growth process, a population must pursue the path of a logistic even when there were strong grounds for supposing that an S-shaped curve would be traced.[188] Fourth, and most important, it was asserted that the logistic law did not effectively take account of the changes in culture which permit a population to exploit its resources more effectively and to alter its relations with other populations, nor did it anticipate changes in aspirations, in tastes, and hence in reproductive behaviour. Yet, the magnitude of K, the trend of R, and the progress of population in general was largely dependent upon such changes.[189] Accordingly, until such changes could be foreseen, and their relation to population growth determined, population forecasting by means of the logistic curve would be attended with considerable hazard. Critics of the logistic "law" therefore looked upon it primarily as an empirical formula which sometimes described the past course of population growth and might well represent the future tendency under certain conditions.[190]

The influence of immigration upon the domestic rate of natural increase as interpreted by certain nineteenth-century students of population has not been found to be incompatible with logistic theory. For example, Walker concluded, as Franklin had already said in the eighteenth century, that net immigration into the United States had not augmented the population of the United States but had reduced natural increase in the native population by an amount equal to the net immigration.[191] Logistic theory implies that Walker's thesis is essentially valid, at least in countries with relatively large populations, so long as immigration produces no cultural change;[192] however, given such change, immigration may increase or decrease a country's population in the long run.

Several theorists have tried to formulate a general law of population development which would not be based upon oversimplified hypotheses and predominantly biological analogies, and which would take account of various influences, particularly those within the economic sphere. In the opinion of these writers, hypotheses such as Verhulst's about the rate of growth, or Delevsky's about acceleration,[193] are not adequate.[194] They have argued that what is needed is a dynamic scheme of analysis of population growth.

An attempt at such a scheme was made by Amoroso[195] when he introduced the concept of "demographic elasticity" to represent the relation "between the logarithmic derivative of the population, considered as a function of time, and the corresponding logarithmic derivative of an index of economic activity."[196] This concept, in turn, was used by Vinci to obtain a "so-called generalized logistic curve." According to Vinci's formulation, (a) "demographic elasticity, consistently with an unknown function of time, becomes smaller and smaller as the population in its absolute value becomes greater and greater"; and (b) the "relative increase of real incomes is a function, also unknown, of time and of the relative magnitude of population."[197] Vianelli, on the basis of Vinci's scheme, undertook to discover, not the secular trend of population growth as Pearl had attempted, but the manner in which economic and demographic evolution, as represented by suitable indices, had mutually influenced one another in Italy and the United States. He found that demographic elasticity and the response of output to population growth varied in time and by country. He concluded, therefore, that demographic evolution was not a natural biological phenomenon, and that, given knowledge of the future behaviour of the functions which he employed, rational forecasts of population trends were possible.[198]

A summary of the thinking of Amoroso, Vinci, and Vianelli can perhaps be presented in the following simplified terms: Let it be assumed that the population of a community increases in a small proportion, x, and its net income in a small proportion, y. Further, let it be assumed that the increment of income is composed of two parts, one of which (y_1) is due to population growth and the other (y_2) to other factors such as the advance of technology and discovery of new resources. Then the demographic elasticity, e, is represented by the ratio x/y and the elasticity of productivity of population, E, by the ratio y_1/x. If the demographic elasticity, e, is 0.5 per cent and the elasticity of productivity, E, is zero, and if the independent increase of income, y_2, is 2 per cent per annum, the population increases at the rate of 1 per cent per annum. But if E rises to, say 0.5 per cent, the rate of population growth becomes approximately 1.33 per cent per annum; that is, the contribution of population growth to the increase of income raises the rate of population growth by about one-third.

Should the values of e and E change, as population grows, these changes would be reflected in the rate of increase of population, as well as of income. The elasticity of productivity of population, E, may rise or fall, depending, inter alia, on the size of the population, the resources available and the techniques of production.[199] The demographic elasticity, e, depends on the trends of mortality, fertility, and migration, which respond differently to changes of income under various conditions; and these responses may change as the population increases. Also, the increment to income which comes from sources other than population changes, y_2, may be indirectly influenced by the growth of population. For example, the rate of population increase may affect the development of technology and the rate of capital formation. Thus, on the basis of present information, it is not possible to construct precise formulations of the relationships among these variables.

(4) *Population "Types" and "Stages" of Demographic Evolution.* If population always grew logistically or in accordance with any standard pattern of development, it would be possible always to describe precisely what point of demographic evolution any given population had attained. Certain demog-

raphers who have rejected the logistic "law" have sought other means of making such a description. They have assumed that populations tend to evolve through certain stages, having characteristic tendencies of growth, and have subsequently classified given populations according to their position in this sequence of stages.

Blacker has identified five stages in demographic growth: (1) *the high stationary,* marked by high natality and mortality; (2) *the early expanding,* with high natality and high but declining mortality; (3) *the late expanding,* with declining natality but with mortality declining more rapidly; (4) *the low stationary,* with low natality balanced by equally low mortality; and (5) *the declining,* with low mortality, lower natality, and an excess of deaths over births.[200]

Thompson and others have reduced Blacker's stages or types to three: (1) that in which neither mortality nor natality is under reasonably secure control and where the potential growth is large despite a possible current low rate of increase; (2) that in which, while both natality and mortality are declining, natality decreases at first less rapidly and then more rapidly than mortality, and the population grows until it finally reaches the third stage; (3) that in which natality and mortality are low and under secure control, and the population is stationary or in a state of incipient decline.[201]

It has been suggested that another stage of growth or type of population should be added to those included in Blacker's and Thompson's classifications; namely, one in which natality, while relatively low and stable, remains above mortality and permits a significant rate of increase,[202] or one in which natality periodically rises above a low-level mortality, yielding alternately a stationary and a growing population.[203]

Another such classification has been presented by Landry, who has identified three "demographic régimes" based in large part upon the observations of Cantillon on the relation between production and consumers' preferences in determining population growth.[204] The three régimes are as follows: (1) A *primitive régime* exists during the period when population growth is controlled by the means of subsistence; a maximum population is reached when mortality, rising as the increase of population lowers the conditions of living, fluctuates around the level of fertility. The maximum population may rise or fall with changes in the conditions of production. (2) An *intermediate demographic régime* continues for the period in which the interests of individuals and of societies in the maintenance of a standard of living affects the growth of population by influencing marriage. Economic production tends to determine the size of population, but only indirectly and in relation to certain standards of living. (3) A *modern epoch,* introduced by the "demographic revolution," is characterized by general decline in fertility. Population changes no longer conform to any "population law" and economic influences no longer determine the trend of population. This period is characterized by "limited procreation" as contrasted with "unlimited procreation." Under the first two demographic régimes, technological advances are the prime source of increase of population. In the modern society technology progresses at an accelerated rate but ceases to have the same direct relationship with population changes.

REFERENCES

1. On the careless use of statistics by early writers, see H. Delbrück, *Numbers in history* (1913); H. Delbrück, *Geschichte der Kriegskunst in Rahmen der politische Geschichte* (1908), Vol. I, pp. 20–24.

2. C. Huan-Chang, *The economic principles of Confucius and his school* (1911), Vol. I, pp. 180, 186–187, 249–250, 297–309, 322–323, 328–330, 338–339, 345–346, 355–356, 361–362; L. Chi-Chao, *History of Chinese political thought during the early Tain period* (1930), pp. 65–66, 128–129, 187–188; M. P.-H. Lee, *The economic history of China with special reference to agriculture* (1921), pp. 144–146, 155–156, 159, 201, 229, 292, 416–417, 419, 436–437; M. Weber, *Gesammelte Aufsätze zur Religionssoziologie* (1920), pp. 276–536. That little attention was paid to the manner in which numbers are adjusted to resources is implied, for example, by the treatment of population and migration in N. L. Swann (Trans.), *Food and money in ancient China* (1950), pp. 61, 126–127, 302, and K. A. Wittfogel and F. Chia-Sheng, *History of Chinese society: Liao, 907–1125* (1949), pp. 41–112.

3. The theories of Plato and Aristotle were treated by J. Moreau in "Les théories démographiques dans l'antiquité grecque," *Population*, 4 (1949). Other ancient Greek writers had little to say about questions of population. Xenophon described certain population policies of the Lacedaemonians and Persians in his *Constitution of the Lacedaemonians* (ca. 370 B.C.), and in his *The Oeconomicus* (ca. 370 B.C.). For a brief account see A. A. Trever, *A history of Greek economic thought* (1916), Chapter 4; also H. Michell, *The economics of ancient Greece* (1940), paras. 40, 224, 352. Herodotus in his *History* (ca. 440 B.C.; 1921 edit.), Bk. I, paras. 58, 66, 136; Bk. II, paras. 44, 60, 87, 103–104; Bk. III, paras. 65, 108–109, 159; Bk. IV, paras. 13, 147, 150, occasionally referred to population growth and migration, but did not discuss the causes and consequences of these phenomena. Thucydides in *History* (ca. 145 B.C.; 1919 edit.), Bk. I, paras. 1–3, made passing references to migrations caused by population pressure. See also F. Bilabel, *Die ionische Kolonisation* (1920), pp. 2–5.

4. Plato, *Laws* (ca. 340 B.C.; 1926 edit.), Bk. V, para. 737; Aristotle, *Politica* (ca. 354 B.C.; 1932 edit.), Bk. I, para. 1; Bk. VII, para. 4. These two authors did not share the opposition of the Greek primitivists to the concentration of population in cities. A. O. Lovejoy and others (eds.), *A documentary history of primitivism and related ideas* (1935).

5. Plato, *Laws* (ca. 340 B.C.; 1926 edit.), Bk. V, paras. 737–738. See also Plato, *Republic* (ca. 370–380 B.C.; 1930 edit.), Bk. II, para. 372; Bk. IV, para. 423; Bk. V, paras. 459–461. A state with 5,040 citizens would have a total population of about 60,000 and, given the various amounts of territory assigned to ideal city-states, a population density of 75 to 300 per square mile. C. B. Welles, "The economic background of Plato's communism," *Journal of Economic History*, VIII (1948). In Plato's time the density of population in Attica was about 200 per square mile, and did not permit a comfortable level of living. G. Glotz, "La cité grecque," in *L'evolution de l'humanité* (1928), pp. 29–31.

6. Aristotle, *Politica* (ca. 354 B.C.; 1932 edit.), Bk. VII, paras. 4–5; Bk. II, paras. 6–9. In the latter place Aristotle declared that failure to limit population was "a never-failing cause of poverty," and that poverty was "the parent of revolution and crime." However, in his criticism of Plato's proposed community of women and property, he did not include the later Malthusian argument that such arrangements would stimulate excessive population growth. *Ibid.*, Bk. II, paras. 1–5; von Bortkiewicz did not consider Aristotle a forerunner of Malthus; see L. von Bortkiewicz, "War Aristoteles Malthusianer?" *Zeitschrift für die gesamte Staatswissenschaft*, 62 (1906). But see M. Moissides, "Le Malthusianisme dans l'antiquité grecque," *Janus*, 36 (1932), and N. E. Himes, *Medical history of contraception* (1936), Chapter 4.

7. Plato, *Laws* (ca. 340 B.C.; 1926 edit.), Bk. V, paras. 739–741, and on colonization

Bk. IV, paras. 707–709; Bk. V, para. 736; Bk. VI, para. 754. Colonization was a traditional Greek remedy for over-population. See H. Michell, *The economics of ancient Greece* (1940), pp. 217–224; Isocrates, *Panegyricus* (ca. 80 B.C.; 1928 edit.), paras. 34–36.

8. See Aristotle, *Politica* (ca. 354 B.C.; 1932 edit.), Bk. VII, para. 16, where exposure of deformed children is advocated. Aristotle mentioned homosexuality as a means of population control used by the Cretans; *ibid.*, Bk. II, para. 10. For his views on colonization, see *ibid.*, Bk. II, para. 11; Bk. VI, para. 5.

9. C. E. Stangeland, *Pre-Malthusian doctrines of population* (1904), Chapter 1; R. Gonnard, *Histoire des doctrines de la population* (1923), Chapters 2–3; J. Ferlet, *L'abaissement de la natalité à Rome et la dépopulation des campagnes, les réformes d'Auguste* (1902), Chapters 1–4; T. Frank, *An economic survey of Ancient Rome* (1933), Vol. I, pp. 40–42; Vol. III, pp. 313–322; Vol. V, p. 130; V. G. Simkovitch, *Toward the understanding of Jesus* (1937), pp. 128 ff.; E. Ciccotti, "Considerazioni sulle leggi matrimoniali di Augusto," *Congrès International de la Population* (1938); C. N. Cochrane, *Christianity and classical culture* (1944), pp. 198–201, 219–220. For examples of references to Roman population laws in the works of contemporary writers, see Suetonius, *Octavius Augustus* (ca. A.D. 123; 1914 edit.), pp. 123–287; Tacitus, *Annals* (ca. A.D. 104–109; 1931 edit.), Bk. III, paras. 25–28; and *ibid.*, Bk. XV, para. 19; Plutarch, *De amore prolis* (ca. A.D. 100; 1939 edit.), pp. 331–497. See also citations in A. O. Lovejoy and others (eds.), *A documentary history of primitivism and related ideas* (1935), pp. 408–411.

10. Cicero, *De re publica* (ca. 44 B.C.; 1928 edit.), Bk. IV, para. 5.

11. Cicero, *De officis* (ca. 44 B.C.; 1913 edit.), Bk. II, para. 5. The list of checks is from a non-extant work, "The destruction of human life" by Dicaerchus, a pupil of Aristotle and a primitivist. Diodorus Siculus in his *Library of history* (ca. 60 B.C.; 1933 edit.), Bk. I, para. 80, attributed the large population of Egypt to the ease and cheapness of rearing children there. Pliny's works contain almost nothing about population, although they did imply that immigration might check population and that cities grew through immigration. Pliny, *Historia naturalis* (ca. A.D. 75; 1942 edit.), Bk. IV, paras. 21 and 24.

12. With the exception of certain Brahmins and Buddhists the spokesmen for the Oriental religions appear to have favoured fertility and multiplication. See C. E. Stangeland, *Pre-Malthusian doctrines of population* (1904), Chapter 2. For the earlier Hebrew view see *Genesis*, Chapter i, verse 28; Chapter ix, verse 1; Chapter xiii, verse 6; *Leviticus*, Chapter xxvi, verse 9; *Deuteronomy*, Chapter xiv, verse 28; Chapter xvii, verse 6. Apparently, upon Palestine's becoming fully peopled, it was the preservation of the race rather than its increase that was emphasized. See N. E. Himes, *Medical history of contraception* (1936), pp. 69 ff.

13. See, among the ante-Nicene writers: St. Paul, *I Corinthians* (ca. A.D. 60), Chapter vii, verse 1–40; St. Paul, *I Timothy* (ca. A.D. 66), Chapter v, verses 3, 11–14; Ignatius, "Epistle to the Philadelphians" (ca. A.D. 80), in *The Fathers of the Church*, L. Schopp, ed. dir. (1947); Origen, "Commentaries on Matthew" (ca. A.D. 246–248), in *Ante-Nicene Christian Library*, A. Menzies, ed. (1903); Cyprian, "Of the discipline and advantages of chastity" and "On works and alms" (ca. A.D. 240), in *Ante-Nicene Christian Library*, A. Roberts and J. Donaldson, eds. (1880); Clement of Alexandria, "The miscellanies: on marriage" (ca. A.D. 170), *ibid.* (1869). See among the post-Nicene writers: Athemasius, "Letter 48" (ca. A.D. 354), in *A Select Library of the Nicene and Post-Nicene Fathers of the Christian Church*, P. Schaff, ed. (1892); Chrysostom, "Homilies on the gospel of St. John" (ca. A.D. 390), *ibid.* (1890); Cyril, "Lecture 12" (ca. A.D. 340), *ibid.* (1894); Basil, "Letter to a fallen virgin" (ca. A.D. 350), in *Nicene and Post-Nicene Fathers of the Christian Church*, P. Schaff, ed. (1895); Ambrose, "Concerning virgins" (ca. A.D. 377), in *A Select Library of Nicene and Post-Nicene Fathers of the Christian Church*, P. Schaff, ed. (1896); Nazianzen, "On the death of his father" (ca. A.D. 374), *ibid.* (1894); St. Augustine, "City of God" (ca. A.D. 413–426) and "Good of marriage" (ca. A.D. 400), *ibid.* (1887); Gregory the Great, "Book of pastoral rule: on the life of the pastor" (ca. A.D. 580), *ibid.* (1895); Tertullian, "Against Marcion" (ca. A.D. 200), in *Ante-Nicene Christian Library*, A. Roberts and J. Donaldson, eds. (1868); Tertullian, "To his wife" (ca. A.D. 200), *ibid.* (1869); Tertullian, "On monogamy" (ca. A.D. 200), *ibid.* (1870); Irenaeus, "Against heresies" (ca. A.D. 182–188), *ibid.* (1868). See also C. E. Stangeland, *Pre-Malthusian doctrines of population* (1904), pp. 55–82; R. P. Riquet, "Christianisme et population," *Population*, 4 (1949). Some of these views are reflected in the instructions for the clergy incorporated in the

medieval handbooks of penance. J. T. McNeil and H. M. Gamer, *Medieval handbooks of penance* (1938), see for example p. 294; also J. C. Russell, *British medieval population* (1948), pp. 159–164. The social arrangements in effect often made for the postponement of marriage, the ideal in medieval England being, according to Russell, "that a living must precede marriage." *Ibid.*, p. 164.

14. R. Gonnard, *Histoire des doctrines économiques* (1930), p. 41; P. Mombert, *Geschichte der Nationalökonomie* (1927), p. 81; Thomas Aquinas, "De regemine principum" (ca. A.D. 1260), in *On the governance of rulers* (1939); Thomas Aquinas, "Summa theologica" (ca. A.D. 1265–1272), in *The Summa theologica of St. Thomas d'Aquinas* (1935), Question 186, Art. 4, Sec. 3.

15. Theophilus, "Theophilus to Antolychus" (ca. A.D. 170), in *Ante-Nicene Christian Library*, A. Roberts and J. Donaldson, eds. (1867), Bk. II, para. 32; Bk. III, para. 6; Methodius, "The banquet of the ten virgins; or concerning chastity" (ca. A.D. 270), *ibid.* (1869); Jerome, "Letter 22" (ca. A.D. 384), in *Nicene and Post-Nicene Fathers of the Christian Church*, P. Schaff, ed. (1893); Dionysius Exiguus, "Libri de creatione hominis" (ca. A.D. 520), in *Patrologiae cursus completus*, J.-P. Migne, ed. (1848); Tertullian, "De anima" (ca. A.D. 200), in *Ante-Nicene Christian Library*, A. Roberts and J. Donaldson, eds. (1870); Eusebius, "Oration in praise of Constantine" (ca. A.D. 300), in *Nicene and Post-Nicene Fathers of the Christian Church* P. Schaff, ed. (1890). Raoul des Presles argued in a like manner in the fourteenth century; see V. L. J. Brants, *L'économie politique au moyen-âge* (1895), pp. 238–240.

16. With regard to the bearing of mortality experience on both custom and collective policy concerning marriage and child-bearing, see R. Korherr, "Die Bevölkerungspolitik der alten Kulturvölker," in *Démographie historique*, Congrès international de la population, Paris, 1937. Tome II (1938).

17. Luther and other leaders of the Reformation condemned celibacy, but otherwise their teachings on matters relevant to population did not greatly differ from the medieval Christian doctrines.

18. An exception should be noted in the case of England, where most writers until near the middle of the seventeenth century believed the country to be overpopulated and in need of colonies to draw off the excess. For summaries of the many works relevant to population during the fifteenth and sixteenth centuries, too numerous to list here, see K. E. Knorr, *British colonial theories* (1944), pp. 41–47, 68–81; C. E. Stangeland, *Pre-Malthusian doctrines of population* (1904), Chapter 3; also R. Gonnard, *Histoire des doctrines de la population* (1923), pp. 89–129; J. J. Spengler, *French predecessors of Malthus* (1942), Chapter 1; G. L. Beer, *The origins of the British colonial system* (1908), Chapters 1–2.

19. Representative selections from Khaldun's "Prolegomena" are available in C. Issawi, *An Arab philosophy of history* (1950), Chapter 5, which is based on the Quatremère and Beirut-Cairo editions. A French translation by W. M. de Slane, *Notices et extraits de la bibliothèque imperiale et autres bibliothèques*, Vols. 19–21, appeared in 1862–68. See also N. A. Quadir, "The economic ideas of Ibn Khaldun," *Indian Journal of Economics*, 22 (1942).

20. G. Botero, *Delle cause della grandezza delle città* (1558), pp. 220–224, 376–381.

21. The views of individual writers in these schools are summarized in dictionaries and encyclopedias of political economy. Mercantilist and cameralist views on population are summarized in C. E. Stangeland, *Pre-Malthusian doctrines of population* (1904), Chapters 4–6, and parts of 7–9; R. Gonnard, *Histoire des doctrines de la population* (1923), Part 2; P. Reynaud, *La théorie de la population en Italie du xvie au xviiie siècle* (1904), Part I; E. S. Furniss, *The position of the laborer in a system of nationalism* (1920), pp. 5, 31, 59, 62; A. W. Small, *The Cameralists: the pioneers of German social policy* (1909); J. Viner, *Studies in the theory of international trade* (1937), Chapters 1–2; E. A. J. Johnson, *Predecessors of Adam Smith: the growth of British economic thought* (1937), especially Part 2; E. F. Heckscher, *Merkantilismen* (1931), Vol. 2, pp. 139–145; J. J. Spengler, *French predecessors of Malthus* (1942), Chapters 2–3, 9; C. W. Cole, *French mercantilist doctrines before Colbert* (1931), especially Chapters 1 and 4; C. W. Cole, *Colbert and a century of French mercantilism* (1939), Vol. I, pp. 19–26, 45; C. W. Cole, *French mercantilism (1683–1700)* (1943), pp. 3–6, 229–272, 284–286; M. Beer, *Early British economics* (1938), pp. 41, 62, 78, 183–184; E. Silberner, "La guerre dans la pensée économ-

ique du xvie au xviiie siècle," in *Etudes sur l'histoire des théories économiques* (1939); M. T. Wermel, *The evolution of the classical wage theory* (1939).

22. Such was the view of A. Serra, as stated in his "Breve trattato delle cause che possono far abbondare li regni d'oro e d'argento dove non sono miniere con applicazione al Regno di Napoli" (1631) in *Economisti del cinque e seicento*, A. Graziani, ed. (1913 edit.).

23. R. Cantillon, *Essai sur la nature du commerce en général* (1755; 1952 edit.), Chapters 15–16.

24. J. Steuart, *An enquiry into the principles of political economy* (1767), Bk. 2, Chapters 24–25. See also Johnson, *Predecessors of Adam Smith, op. cit.* (1937), Chapters 11–12, 15.

25. See K. E. Knorr, *British colonial theories* (1944), pp. 41–48, 68–81.

26. See J. J. Spengler, "Malthusianism in late eighteenth century America," *American Economic Review*, XXV (1935).

27. For a concise summary of the views of British writers on fecundity and factors affecting fertility, see R. R. Kuczynski, "British demographers' opinions on fertility, 1660 to 1760," in *Political Arithmetic*, L. Hogben, ed. (1938).

28. W. F. Willcox in his introduction to J. Graunt's *Natural and political observations made upon the Bills of Mortality* (1662; 1939 edit.), p. xii of introductory chapter.

29. Here Petty was under the influence of M. Hale's *Primitive origination of mankind* (1677), Section II, Chapter 9. Hale, observing that population increased geometrically and could double in as few as 35 years, and that the available means of subsistence could not long sustain such a rate of growth, concluded that the growth of population was restrained by war, famine, floods, pestilence, and earthquakes. Petty's main writings are included in C. H. Hull, *The economic writings of Sir William Petty* (1899), especially Vol. II, pp. 537–548. For Halley's life table, which was much more complete than Graunt's skeleton table, see E. Halley's "An estimate of the degree of the mortality of mankind," *Philosophical Transactions*, 17 (1693). On these writers and their relation to the originators of actuarial science see J. Bonar, *Theories of population from Raleigh to Arthur Young* (1931), Chapters 3–5, 7.

30. Süssmilch was influenced also by others who had noted that population grew in geometric progression, among them Nichols, Scheucher, Wideburg, Euler, Whiston, Hume, Wallace, Gregory King, and Charles Davenant. Süssmilch knew W. Derham's *Physico-theology* (1723), p. 208, in which it was asserted that Divine Providence had established a balance in the world of living creatures to which man's numbers were made to conform, sometimes apparently through plagues and war. See J. Bonar, *Theories of population from Raleigh to Arthur Young* (1931), Chapter 5. Süssmilch's contemporary, Gottfried Achenwall, and his predecessor, Herman Conring, have sometimes been honoured as the founders of statistics, though their works bear no resemblance to modern statistical studies. Conring, who stressed the military value of large populations, discussed the checks to population operating in Spain; he included emigration and celibacy among the checks. See H. Conring, "Examen rerum publicarum potiorum totius orbis" (1677) in *Herman Conring's Staatenkunde*, R. Zehrfeld, ed. (1926 edit.).

31. J. P. Süssmilch, *Die Göttliche Ordnung in den Veränderungen des menschlichen Geschlechte aus der Geburt, dem Tode und der Fortpflanzung desselben erwiesen* (1775), Vol. I, pp. 17 ff.

32. For summaries of late eighteenth century writings on population see C. E. Stangeland, *Pre-Malthusian doctrines of population* (1904), pp. 224–356; R. Gonnard, *Histoire des doctrines de la population* (1923), pp. 160–258; J. J. Spengler, *French predecessors of Malthus* (1942), especially Chapters 4–9; P. Reynaud, *La théorie de la population en Italie du xvie au xviiie siècle* (1904), Part 2; J. Bonar, *Theories of population from Raleigh to Arthur Young* (1931), Chapters 6–8; M. T. Wermel, *The evolution of the classical wage theory* (1939), Chapters 2–6; K. E. Knorr, *British colonial theories* (1944), pp. 219–228. See also P. Vincent, "French demography in the eighteenth century," *Population Studies*, 1 (1947). A number of writers touched upon factors affecting the location of cities, but these views are not considered here. For example, see R. Maunier, "Théories sur la fonction des villes," *Revue d'économie politique*, 24 (1910).

33. See R. Cantillon, *Essai sur la nature du commerce en general* (1755; 1952 edit.), Part I, Chapter 15. The full implication of this theory and its development have been

treated by A. Landry in "Une théorie négligée. De l'influence de la direction de la demande sur la productivité du travail, les salaires et la population," *Revue d'économie politique,* 24 (1910). Landry examined the Physiocratic argument, usually denied by the contemporaries of Physiocrats, that, under certain conditions, an increase in food consumption per head or in grain exports could stimulate domestic prosperity and population growth. See A. Landry, "Les idés de Quesnay sur la population," *Revue d'histoire des doctrines économiques et sociales,* II (1909). Condillac pointed out that the population of a country would not exceed that number which it could nourish. The population would be less if *per capita* consumption increased; it would decrease further if land were used for production which did not increase consumption. E. B. de Condillac, *Le commerce et le gouvernement* (1776), p. 252. Ferguson argued, "men will crowd where the situation is tempting, and in a few generations will people every country to the measure of its subsistence"; but he added that, other conditions being given, numbers would vary inversely with the "standard" according to which men wished to live, and that this standard tended to rise with civilization. A. Ferguson, *An essay on the history of civil society* (1767), pp. 216–218; G. Chalmers, *An estimate of the strength of Great Britain during the present and four preceding reigns* (1794), pp. 1–2. For other works during this period concerned with the balance of population and subsistence and its consequences for population growth, see P. Reynaud, *La théorie de la population en Italie du xvie au xviiie siècle* (1904), pp. 109, 131; J. J. Spengler, *French predecessors of Malthus* (1942), pp. 230–241; C. E. Stangeland, *Pre-Malthusian doctrines of population* (1904), pp. 227, 237–238, 266, 275 ff., 347; A. Smith, *An enquiry into the nature and causes of the wealth of nations* (1776; 1937 edit.), Book I, Chapter 8.

34. See R. Wallace, *Various prospects of mankind, nature, and providence* (1761), p. 114. Godwin denied that such could be the final outcome, while Condorcet considered the possibility only to indicate that man could cope with it. W. Godwin, *Political justice* (1793), Bk. 8, Chapter 7. On Condorcet see J. J. Spengler, *French predecessors of Malthus* (1942), pp. 259–263, Chapters 7–8; C. E. Stangeland, *Pre-Malthusian doctrines of population* (1904), pp. 228, 273, 283, 344. See also G. T. Griffith, *Population problems of the age of Malthus* (1925), Chapter VI.

35. T. R. Malthus, *An essay on the principle of population* (1798). See also G. T. Griffith, *Population problems of the age of Malthus* (1925), Chapter IV. On the condition giving rise to Malthus's *Essay,* see F. S. Nitti and M. C. Buer, "The historical setting of the Malthusian controversy," in *London essays in economics in honour of Edwin Cannan,* T. E. Gregory and H. Dalton, eds. (1927).

36. T. R. Malthus, *An essay on the principle of population* (1798), Chapters 2, 4, 7. In Chapters 18–19 population pressure was described as part of the scheme of life, as compatible with Providential design, and as essential to man's development.

37. T. R. Malthus, *Observations on the effects of the Corn Laws, and of a rise or fall in the price of corn on the agriculture and general wealth of the country* (1814), pp. 40–41. Better formulations were expressed by West and Ricardo. See E. Cannan, *A history of the theories of production and distribution in English political economy* (1903), especially pp. 147–182. The law had been suggested earlier but had not been incorporated into the body of population theory. See M. Byé, *Les lois des rendements non proportionnels: Leur évolution et leurs formes modernes* (1928), Chapter 4. Turgot had formulated the law but had not explicitly used it in his treatment of population.

38. T. R. Malthus, *An essay on the principle of population; or a view of its past and present effects on human happiness, with an inquiry into our prospects respecting the removal or mitigation of the evils which it occasions* (1803), pp. 7 and 473.

39. He advocated public works in times of cyclical unemployment, in part because the unemployed were not responsible for the occurrence of such unemployment.

40. See T. R. Malthus, *An essay on the principle of population; or a view of its past and present effects on human happiness, with an inquiry into our prospects respecting the removal or mitigation of the evils which it occasions* (1803), Bk. 3, Chapter 14; Bk. 4, Chapters 4, 13–14. The checks are treated in Bks. 1–2; past expedients for coping with population pressure and poverty are appraised in Bk. 3, while the role of moral restraint and man's future prospects are discussed in Bk. 4. For a summary of Malthus' views as set forth in the various editions of Malthus, *An essay on the principle of population* (1803); and T. R. Malthus, *Principles of political economy considered with a view to their prac-*

tical application (1836), see J. J. Spengler, "Malthus's total population theory: a restatement and reappraisal," *Canadian Journal of Economics and Political Science,* 11 (1945). Malthus's sources are indicated. See also J. Bonar, *Malthus and his work* (1924), especially Bk. I, Chapter III, pp. 319 ff. The critical literature is discussed below.

41. See E. Cannan, *A review of economic theory* (1929), especially Chapters 1 and 4; C. Gide and C. Rist, *Histoire des doctrines économiques* (1947), Vol. I, Bk. I, Chapters 2–3; Bk. II, Chapter 1. Adam Smith, Jeremy Bentham, James Mill, David Ricardo, T. R. Malthus and others contributed to the formation of the classical system.

42. A. Smith, *An enquiry into the nature and causes of the wealth of nations* (1776; 1937 edit.), Bk. I, Chapter 11; T. R. Malthus, *The nature and progress of rent* (1815), p. 45; E. West, *Essay on the application of capital to land, with observations shewing the impolicy of any great restriction of the importation of corn, and that the bounty of 1688 did not lower the price of it* (1815), p. 7; A. Serra, "Breve trattato delle cause che possono far abbondare li regni d'oro e d'argento dove non sono miniere con applicazione al Regno di Napoli" (1613) in *Economisti del cinque e seicento,* A. Graziani, ed. (1913 edit.).

43. Some writers denied this, suggesting that agriculture too was subject to increasing returns. H. C. Carey, *Principles of social science* (1858), Vol. I, p. 267; A. D. H. Kaplan, *Henry Charles Carey: A study in American economic thought* (1931), Chapters 2–3. While Carey believed agriculture and manufacturing to be subject to increasing returns only within limits, he did not suggest that these would soon be attained.

44. Ricardo observed that mineral production too was subject to increasing cost, but this point was not immediately stressed by writers on population, since minerals did not bulk as large in living budgets as agricultural produce did. D. Ricardo, *Principles of political economy and taxation* (1821), Chapters 2–3.

45. For example, see N. W. Senior, "An outline of the science of political economy," in *Encyclopaedia Metropolitana* (1850); M. Bowley, *Nassau Senior and classical economics* (1937), pp. 122–126; J. E. Cairnes, *Some leading principles of political economy newly expounded* (1874), pp. 130–135; S. Bailey, *A critical dissertation on the nature, measures, and causes of value* (1825), pp. 125 ff.; J. S. Mill, *Principles of political economy* (1848; 1936 edit.), Bk. IV, Chapter 2; J. R. McCulloch, *Principles of political economy* (1864), Part III, Chapter 6; E. Cannan, *A History of the theories of production and distribution in English political economy* (1903), Chapter 5. See also J.-B. Say, *Traité d'économie politique* (1826), Bk. I, Chapter 8; J.-G. Courcelle-Seneuil, *Traité d'économie politique* (1857; 1891 edit.), Bk. I, Chapter 7.

46. J. S. Mill, *Principles of political economy* (1848; 1936 edit.), Bk. I, Chapters 10–13.

47. See H. Fawcett, *Manual of political economy* (1863), pp. 159–160, 249–250. Fawcett, though a disciple of Mill, put the advent of world over-population in the remote future, since Australia alone could "maintain in comfort a population of 100,000,000." Presumably, so long as unoccupied fertile land existed, emigrants could move there and provide the mother country with "cheap food." *Ibid.,* p. 160; H. F. von Storch, *Cours d'économie politique* (1823), Vol. III, pp. 318–322.

48. J. S. Mill, *Principles of political economy* (1848; 1936 edit.), Bk. I, Chapter 13. Say stressed, as had Malthus, the risks involved in a nation's becoming dependent in part upon foreign produce. J.-B. Say, *Traité d'économie politique* (1826), Bk. II, Chapter 11. Presumably Cairnes did not take much stock in the trade and emigration arguments, though he failed to treat them specifically. J. E. Cairnes, *The character and logical method of political economy* (1875), pp. 149–181, 207–313; see also J. Garnier, *Du principe de population* (1857; 1885 edit.), pp. 71–75, 149–156.

49. See E. Cannan, *A history of the theories of production and distribution in English political economy* (1903), Chapter 17; H. F. von Storch, *Cours d'économie politique* (1823), Vol. I, pp. 309–321.

50. F. W. Taussig, *Wages and capital* (1896), p. 224; M. Bowley, *Nassau Senior and classical economics* (1937), Chapters 3 and 5.

51. J. A. Schumpeter, *Epochen der Methoden- und Dogmengeschichte* (1914), pp. 53 ff.; W. J. Baumol, *Economic dynamics, an introduction* (1951), Chapter 2; L. Robbins, "On a certain ambiguity in the conception of stationary equilibrium," *Economic Journal,* XL (1930).

52. M. Bowley, *Nassau Senior and classical economics* (1937), pp. 75–81, 179–200. One of the best of the early statements of a marginal productivity theory of wages is M.

Longfield's *Lectures on political economy* (1834), Lecture X. See J. H. von Thünen, *Der isolierte Staat* (1850; 1921 edit.), Bk. II, Part I, pp. 43–51, 140–148, 185–193, 206–212; Part II, pp. 140–145.

53. R. von Mohl, *Geschichte und Literatur der Staatswissenschaften* (1856), pp. 462–517; H. K. E. von Mangoldt, "Bevölkerung," in *Deutsches Staatswörterbuch* (1857); L. Elster, "Bevölkerungswesen," in *Handwörterbuch der Staatswissenschaften* (1909).

54. Such a proposition had been stated in a different form by Cantillon. Ortes had reasoned similarly. J.-G. Courcelle-Seneuil stated this view in his *Traité d'économie politique* (1857), but later rejected it. *Ibid.*, (1891, 3rd edit.), p. 151. See A. Liesse, *Leçons d'économie politique* (1892), pp. 44–52, 70–74; also M. Block's criticism in *Les progrès de la science économique* (1890), Vol. I, pp. 540–541.

55. H. F. von Storch, *Cours d'économie politique* (1823), Vol. 3, Part II, Bk. ii, Chapter 2. The Italian, Scialoja, reasoned that population varied inversely with the number and intensity of man's wants and directly with the means of existence available. A. Scialoja, *I principi della economia sociale* (1846), pp. 153–160.

56. G. M. Ortes, *Riflessioni sulla popolazione delle nazioni per rapporto all'economia nazionale* (1790), Chapter 7. See also P. Reynaud, *La théorie de la population en Italie du xvie au xviiie siècle* (1904), Part 2, Chapter 1; A. Marsigli, *Il problema demografico nelle dottrine politiche ed economiche Italiani* (1934), Chapter 5.

57. See for example A. L. C. Destutt de Tracy, *Traité d'économie politique* (1823), pp. 185–197, 226.

58. J.-G. Courcelle-Seneuil, *Traité d'économie politique* (1857; 1891 edit.), Bk. I, Chapter 7.

59. J. S. Mill, *Principles of political economy* (1848, 1936 edit.), Bk. I, Chapter 13.

60. *Ibid.*, Bk. I, Chapters 10 and 13; Bk. II, Chapters 6 and 11; Bk. III, Chapters 2–3, 6–7; also J. S. Mill, "Chapters in socialism," *Fortnightly Review*, XXV (1879). On Mill's connexion with the early birth control movement see N. E. Himes, "John Stuart Mill's attitude toward Neo-Malthusianism," *Economic Journal*, Economic History Series, No. 4 (1929), and N. E. Himes, *Medical history of contraception* (1936). Mill's views concerning the influence of peasant ownership were inspired by Sismondi. See also H. Fawcett, *Manual of political economy* (1863), Bk. II, Chapters 4, 6, 8. J. N. Keynes, in *The scope and method of political economy* (1890, 1904 edit.), Chapter 9, Section 2, found in the permanent rise of wages after the Black Death an illustration of Mill's theory that large improvements are most likely to have permanent effects.

61. J. Dorfman, *The economic mind in American civilization* (1946), pp. 178–195, 365; G. J. Cady, "The early American reaction to the theory of Malthus," *Journal of Political Economy*, XXXIX (1931); J. J. Spengler, "Population doctrines in the United States," *Journal of Political Economy*, XLI (1933); J. J. Spengler, "Population theory in the ante-bellum South," *Journal of Southern History*, II (1936); J. J. Spengler, "Evolutionism in American economics 1800–1850," in *Evolutionary thought in America*, S. Parsons, ed. (1950).

62. J.-B. Say, *Cours complet d'économie politique* (1840), Part 6; J.-B. Say, *Traité d'économie politique* (1826), Bk. II; M. Bowley, *Nassau Senior and classical economics* (1937), pp. 74–81.

63. The views of French writers on population have been summarized by R. Gonnard, *Histoire des doctrines de la population* (1923), Part III; C. Gide and C. Rist, *Histoire des doctrines économiques* (1947), Vol. I, Bk. I, Chapter 2; J. Kretschmann, *Storia delle dottrine economiche* (1949), Chapter 31. See also J. J. Spengler, "French population theory since 1800," *Journal of Political Economy*, XLIV (1936) and J. J. Spengler, *France faces depopulation* (1938). French as well as Italian, German and English views are summarized in F. S. Nitti, *La popolazione e il sistema sociale* (1894).

64. J. Garnier, *Du principe de population* (1857; 1885 edit.), Chapters 1, 4–11. G. de Molinari, *La viriculture* (1897), pp. 118–119, 228–230; De Molinari's introduction to Garnier's *Du principe de population* (1857; 1885 edit.).

65. G. de Molinari, *Cours d'économie politique* (1855), Leçon 8–10; G. de Molinari, *La viriculture* (1897), pp. 118–119, 228–230; De Molinari's introduction to J. Garnier's *Du principe de population* (1857; 1885 edit.).

66. W. Roscher, "Grundlagen der Nationalökonomie," in *System der Volkswirtschaft* (1880); see also G. Rumelin, *Reden und Aufätze* (1881), pp. 305–332.

67. A. Mees, *Overzicht van enige Hoofdstukken der Staathuishoudekunde* (1866), pp. 26 ff.

68. J. C. L. S. de Sismondi, *Les nouveaux principes d'économie politique ou de la richesse dans ses rapports avec la population* (1819; 1827 edit.), Vol. II, Bk. 7. See also A. Amonn, *Simonde de Sismondi als Nationalökonom* (1949), Bk. II, pp. 324–378.

69. P. Rossi, *Cours d'économie politique* (1840), Bk. I, pp. 200–256. His contemporary, Romagnosi, was a critic of Malthus. On the Italian theories see A. Marsigli, *Il problema demografico nelle dottrine politiche ed economiche Italiani* (1934); J. Kretschmann, *Storia della dottrine economiche* (1949), especially Chapter 24; and E. Cossa, *Il principio di popolazione de Tomaso Roberto Malthus* (1895).

70. F. Ferrara, *Œuvres économiques choisies* (1938), pp. 28–29, 146–147; R. D. Volta, "Francisco Ferrara et son œuvre économique," *Revue d'économie politique*, XVI (1902); F. Virgilii, "Il problema della popolazione negli scritti di F. Ferrara," *Giornale degli Economisti e Rivista di Statistica*, XI (1895).

71. A. Messedaglia, *Della teoria della popolazione, principalmente sotto l'asoetto del metodo* (1858). For appraisals of Messedaglia's treatment of Malthus's two progressions, see R. Benini, *Principi di demografia* (1901), pp. 229–233; V. Pareto, *Cours d'économie politique* (1896), Vol. I, para. 192. See also F. Virgilii, "Il problema della popolazione negli scritti di F. Ferrara," *op. cit.*, for treatment of the amendments to Malthus's progressions suggested by Messedaglia, Pareto, Quetelet, and others.

72. Some writers stressed rather the argument that returns in agriculture long tended to be constant. For example, see A. Alison, *The principles of population and their connection with human happiness* (1840), Bk. I, pp. 35–36, 55, 62, 217–220. Alison admitted that there were limits to food production, but he expected that population growth would cease before these limits were reached. *Ibid.*, pp. 42–46, 84–85. See also P. A. Kropotkin's *The conquest of bread* (1907), especially Chapter 17; P. A. Kropotkin, *Fields, factories and workshops* (1899), especially Chapters 3–5.

73. For summaries of such arguments, see K. Smith, *The Malthusian controversy* (1951), pp. 58, 118–119, 147, 191, 229; G. J. Cady, "The early American reaction to the theory of Malthus," *Journal of Political Economy*, XXXIX (1931); J. J. Spengler, "Population doctrines in the United States," *Journal of Political Economy*, XLI (1933); M. Bowley, *Nassau Senior and classical economics* (1937), pp. 123–126; R. von Mohl, *Geschichte und Literatur der Staatswissenschaften* (1856), pp. 462–467, 490–517. H. George reasoned in *Progress and poverty* (1879), Bk. 2, Chapter 4, that the economies arising out of increasing division of labour would in the long run more than compensate for the resort to poorer soils which accompanied population growth; and that so long as this was the case, but presumably not longer, population would grow.

74. Critics of Malthus who subscribed to the "theory of increasing misery" had to build their argument on the premise that prevailing institutional conditions were making for increasing inequality. For one of the earliest critiques of Malthus's *Essay*, see C. Hall's *The effects of civilization on the people in European states* (1805), in which the growth of inequality was stressed. Hall said that since 0.5–0.7 acre would support a person, overpopulation would not develop in England for more than a century. By contrast Godwin indicated that 2.75 acres were required per person. See K. Smith, *The Malthusian controversy* (1951), pp. 54, 129. On the sources and the development of the doctrine of increasing misery see R. Michels, *La teoria di C. Marx sulla miseria crecente e le sue origini* (1922).

75. A. H. Everett, *New ideas on population* (1823), Chapters 4–5, and especially pp. 28, 38–42, 111, 120–121. See also J. J. Spengler, "Alexander Hill Everett, early American opponent of Malthus," *New England Quarterly*, IX (1936).

76. Carey's doctrine of association resembles somewhat Spencer's doctrine of increasing heterogeneity. Spencer indicated that population growth made for increasing specialization and skill. "In all ways increase of population by its actions and reactions develops a social organism which becomes more heterogeneous as it grows larger." H. Spencer, *Principles of sociology* (1896), Vol. III, Part VIII, Chapters 2–3. Spencer subscribed in essence to Mill's doctrine of the "stationary state." H. Spencer, *First principles* (1898), Part II, Chapter 22.

77. M. Bowley, *Nassau Senior and classical economics* (1937), pp. 123–126.

78. Certain earlier writers, as Chalmers, attributed increases in agricultural yields to

improvements in agricultural techniques. Later writers, including Mill and Hearn, argued that Ricardo's assumption of progression from superior to inferior soils did not necessarily hold for new countries. J. S. Mill, *Principles of political economy* (1848; 1936 edit.), Bk. I, Chapter 12, Section 2; W. E. Hearn, *Plutology* (1863), pp. 13–14; T. Chalmers, *On political economy, in connexion with the moral state and moral prospects of society* (1832), Section 2, pp. 10–14.

79. H. C. Carey, *Principles of social science* (1858), Vol. I, Chapters VII–X; A. D. H. Kaplan, *Henry Charles Carey, op. cit.*, Chapters 3–4.

80. H. C. Carey, *Principles of social science* (1859), Vol. III, Chapter XLVI, Section 1. Bastiat and his disciples, some of whom were influenced by Carey, were less optimistic concerning the possibility of increasing output; but they supposed that man's growth would be brought under voluntary control. The French writers were not hostile to Malthus as was Carey. See J. J. Spengler, "French population theory since 1800," *Journal of Political Economy*, XLIV (1936).

81. H. C. Carey, *Principles of social science* (1859), Vol. III, Chapters XLVI–XLIX. Carey employed Spencer's physiological theory.

82. J. E. T. Rogers, *A Manual of political economy* (1869), pp. 14, 69, 154–159.

83. P. Leroy-Beaulieu, *Traité théorique et pratique d'économie politique* (1900), Bk. I, pp. 740–776; Bk. III, p. 314. Not even agriculture was an exception to the law of falling price or falling labour input per unit of output.

84. F. Oppenheimer, *Das Bevölkerungsgesetz des T. R. Malthus unter der neuen Nationalökonomie* (1900), Chapters 2 and 4. Oppenheimer's views have been severely criticized. J. Wolf, "Une nouvelle loi de la population," *Revue d'Economie Politique*, XVI (1902); H. Dietzel, "Der Streit um Malthus' Lehre," in *Festgaben für Adolph Wagner zur Siebenzigsten Wiederkehr seines Geburtstages* (1905).

85. E. F. Wagemann, *Menschenzahl und Völkerschicksal, eine Lehre von den optimalen Dimensionen gesellschaftlicher Gebilde* (1948), pp. 30 ff., 48–98, 135 ff., 210 ff., 269 ff., 308 ff. He suggested also that the earth could support in comfort 30,000 million inhabitants, given sufficient improvement. *Ibid.*, p. 229.

86. W. Hazlitt, *A reply to the essay on population by the Rev. T. R. Malthus* (1807), Letter 4; R. Hamilton, *The progress of society* (1830), Chapter 18; A. H. Moreton, *Civilization, or a brief analysis of the natural laws that regulate the numbers and condition of mankind* (1836), Chapter 9; J. Weyland, *Principles of population and production as they are affected by the progress of society, with a view to moral and political consequences* (1816), Bk. 1, Chapters 2, 7; Bk. 3, Chapter 11; J. J. Spengler, "Population doctrines in the United States," *Journal of Political Economy*, XLI (1933); J. J. Spengler, "French population theory since 1800," *Journal of Political Economy*, XLIV (1936); K. Smith, *The Malthusian controversy* (1951), especially Bk. 4.

87. N. W. Senior, *Two lectures on population, delivered before the University of Oxford in Easter term, 1828, to which is added, a correspondence between the author and the Rev. T. R. Malthus* (1829), pp. 27, 34–35; also M. Bowley, *Nassau Senior and classical economics* (1937), Chapter 3.

88. G. K. Rickards, *Population and capital* (1854), p. 251.

89. A. Alison, *The principles of population and their connection with human happiness* (1840), p. 105.

90. M. T. Sadler, in *The law of population: a treatise, in six books; in disproof of the super-fecundity of human beings, and developing the real principle of their increase* (1830), Bk. IV, went so far as to propose as a law that the prolificness of men varied inversely with population density.

91. Even in the early part of the nineteenth century, some writers, including Francis Place and Robert Owen, indicated that more than moral restraint was required. See N. E. Himes, *Medical history of contraception* (1936), Chapter 11.

92. For example, on diet see T. Doubleday, *The true law of population, shown to be connected with the food of the people* (1841); G. Purves (Simon Gray), *Gray versus Malthus* (1818), Bk. 2. On mental exertion see T. Jarrold, *Dissertations on man, philosophical, physiological, and political; in answer to Mr. Malthus's "Essay on the Principle of Population"* (1806), pp. 245–274, 306–313. On diet and inbreeding, see W. E. Hickson, "Laws of population," *Westminster and Foreign Quarterly Review*, LII (1850). Recently protein

deficiency has been described as favourable to fertility by J. de Castro in *The geography of hunger* (1952), pp. 70–72.

93. See H. Spencer, *The principles of biology* (1867), Bk. II, pp. 406–410, 479–508. Spencer's theory, first announced in 1852, was adopted by Henry Carey and other American writers, as well as by a number of continental writers.

94. For general accounts of socialism and the theory of population, see L. Dumas, *Le socialisme et le principe de population* (1908); H. Sonolet, *Principe de population et socialisme* (1907); H. Soetbeer, *Die Stellung der Sozialisten zur Malthusischen Bevölkerungslehre* (1886); M. T. Martello, *L'economia politica antimalthusiana e il socialismo* (1894); P. Mombert, *Geschichte der Nationalökonomie* (1927), pp. 410–416; P. Mombert, *Bevölkerungslehre* (1929), pp. 214–235; E. Lowenthal, "The Ricardian socialists," *Studies in history, economics and public law*, XLVI (1911). For later representative statements that collectivism made for imprudence in matters of population, see A. Naquet, *Socialisme collectiviste, et socialisme liberal* (1890), Chapter IV; A. T. Hadley, *Economics* (1896), pp. 45–51; S. Budge, *Das Malthusische Bevölkerungsgesetz und die theoretische Nationalökonomie der letzten Jahrzehnte* (1912), p. 218. Lloyd early questioned this thesis on the ground that since the gain from restricting family size is largely diffused to others, the individual under capitalism has little incentive to restrict family size. See W. F. Lloyd, *Two lectures on the checks to population* (1833), p. 22.

95. See E. Lowenthal, "The Ricardian Socialists," *Studies in history, economics and public law* (Faculty of Political Science of Columbia University, ed.), XLVI (1911); K. Smith, *The Malthusian Controversy* (1951), Bk. II, Chapter IV; Bk. IV, Chapter III.

96. R. Gonnard, *Histoire des doctrines de la population* (1923), pp. 317 ff.

97. For detailed reference to the works of Fourier, the Saint-Simonians, Blanc, Leroux, and Proudhon, see L. Dumas, *Le socialisme et le principe de population* (1908); F. S. Nitti, *La popolazione e il sistema sociale* (1894), Bk. I; J. J. Spengler, "French population theory since 1800," *Journal of Political Economy*, XLIV (1936), pp. 747–753. See also H. Bergues, "La population vue par les utopistes," *Population*, VI (1951).

98. See F. Lassalle, *Kapital und Arbeit* (1864), Chapter 4, pp. 237–239.

99. See K. Rodbertus, "Zweiter Brief," in *Beleuchtung der sozialen Frage* (1899), pp. 5 ff., 35 ff., 71–74, 78–80; E. C. K. Gonner, *The social philosophy of Rodbertus* (1899), especially the introduction, Part II, Chapters 2–3, 5. On Lassalle and Rodbertus, see W. H. Dawson, *German socialism and Ferdinand Lassalle* (1888), especially Chapters 3, 6, 12–13.

100. In a sense, this was Schäffle's opinion also, but he believed that enforced birth-limitation and relative labour scarcity would so modify economic organization as to remove the existing pressure of numbers upon subsistence. See A. E. F. Schäffle, *Bau und Leben des sozialen Körpers* (1878), Zweiter Band; also K. Marlo, *Untersuchungen über die Organisation der Arbeit, oder System der Weltökonomie* (1885), Bk. I, pp. 238–239; Bk. II, Chapter 12.

101. A. Loria, *La legge di poplazione ed il sistema sociale* (1882). A. Loria, *Analisi della proprietà capitalista* (1889).

102. F. S. Nitti, *La popolazione e il sistema sociale* (1894), p. 162. This book is dedicated to Loria. Nitti emphasized the importance of social capillarity, as defined by Dumont, and of "civilisation" which made for "human individuality" (i.e., "an increase of functions, either in number or in density") and was antagonistic to "individualism" (i.e., "egotistical sentiment"). *Idem.*, pp. 86–88, 126–140, 149–170, 182. Spencer's theory, too, received his qualified approval. *Ibid.*, pp. 66–71, 175–178, 182–184.

103. *Ibid.*, p. 191.

104. For accounts see P. M. Sweezy, *The theory of capitalist development. Principles of Marxian political economy* (1942), pp. 86–92, 222–226; S. M. Levin, "Marx versus Malthus," *Papers of the Michigan Academy of Science, Arts and Letters*, XXII (1936); J. Robinson, *An essay on Marxism economics* (1949); and J. Robinson, "Marx on unemployment," *Economic Journal*, LI (1941); M. Dobb, *Political economy and capitalism* (1937), pp. 85–89, 98–103, 124, 207; M. Dobb, *Studies in the development of capitalism* (1947), especially Chapters 6–8; N. I. Bukarin and others, *Marxism and modern thought* (1938), pp. 193–195, 216–217.

105. K. Marx, *Das Kapital. Kritik der politischen Oekonomie* (1867); (1903 edit.), Erster Band, p. 594.

106. *Ibid.*, pp. 596–597. See also K. Marx, *Letters to Dr. Kugelmann* (1934), p. 111; F. Engels, *Dialectics of nature* (1940), pp. 208–209, 235.

107. K. Marx, *Das Kapital, op. cit.*, Erster Band, pp. 598, 602–604; *ibid.* (1894; 1904 edit.), Dritter Band, p. 217.

108. *Ibid.*, Erster Band, pp. 606–608. Marx indicated that when the industrial reserve army was large and wages were kept down natural increase was greater. Birth rates, death rates, and the size of families, he held, varied in inverse proportion to the level of wages and the amount of means of subsistence at the disposal of various groups of workers. *Ibid.* (1867; 1903 edit.), Erster Band, pp. 608, 476–477; *ibid.* (1894; 1904 edit.), Dritter Band, pp. 198–199.

109. Crises and depressions also increased the number unemployed. For Marx's explanation of the manner in which capital accumulation generated unemployment, see *ibid.* (1867; 1903 edit.), Erster Band, pp. 372, 577–585, 594–596, 603, 610–611; *ibid.* (1894; 1904 edit.), Dritter Band, pp. 202–204. He recognized that at times the needs for accumulating capital were such that the demand for labour rose more rapidly than its supply, with the result that wages advanced. *Ibid.* (1867; 1903 edit.), Erster Band, pp. 577, 584–585. For Marx's views on emigration and urbanization, see *ibid.* (1867; 1903 edit.), Erster Band, pp. 470, 536–539. For his comment on the difficulties attending the formation of an industrial reserve army in colonies and newly settled lands, see *ibid.* (1867; 1903 edit.), Erster Band, pp. 729–739; also H. O. Pappe, "Wakefield and Marx," *Economic History Review*, IV (1951).

110. K. Marx, *Das Kapital, op. cit.* (1867; 1903 edit.), Erster Band, pp. 682–714.

111. *Ibid.*, pp. 606–608, 621–624, 629. Elsewhere Marx indicated that, in the capitalistic society, a temporary excess of "surplus capital" over the working population would raise wages and thus reduce mortality and raise the marriage rate, so that the working population would increase. The relative over-population would be augmented also by the technological unemployment due to this capital surplus. *Ibid.* (1894; 1904 edit.), Dritter Band, pp. 198–199.

112. *Ibid.* (1867; 1903 edit.), Erster Band, pp. 584–585. Engels pointed out to Bebel in a letter (March, 1875) that Marx had refuted the Malthusian basis for Lassalle's iron law of wages. See K. Marx and F. Engels, *Correspondence, 1846–1895* (1934), p. 335.

113. P. M. Sweezy, *The theory of capitalist development, op. cit.*, pp. 222–226. Dobb pointed out, however, that a high correlation did not exist between the volume of employment and the rate of population growth in various countries.

114. See A. Bebel, *Die Frau und der Sozialismus* (1894), pp. 441–463.

115. See K. Kautsky, *Der Einfluss der Volksvermehrung auf den Fortschritt der Gesellschaft* (1880), especially Chapter 5 on the control of population growth. See also M. Schippel, *Das moderne Elend und die moderne Ubervölkerung* (1883), p. 242, and conclusion.

116. See K. Kautsky, *The economic doctrines of Karl Marx* (1925), Part III, Chapter 5.

117. See K. Kautsky, *Vermehrung und Entwicklung in Natur und Gesellschaft* (1920), especially Chapter 16.

118. V. I. Lenin, *Theory of the agrarian question* (1938 trans.), pp. 52–54, 314–321; V. I. Lenin, *Marx-Engels Marxism* (1935 trans.), p. 23.

119. V. I. Lenin, *Theory of the agrarian question* (1938 trans.), pp. 58–63. On the movement of migrants, imperialism, and the state of development of economies, see Lenin's *Imperializm* (1917), Chapter 8. Lenin used Marx's conception of "capitalist overpopulation" and the industrial reserve army, and made reply to those who misinterpreted Marx's views on population and related matters. See *Marx-Engels Marxism, op. cit.*, pp. 19–20, 24.

120. B. Smulevich, *Burzhuaznye teorii narodonaseleniya v svete marksistskoleninskoy kritiki* (1936), Smulevich severely criticized Malthusian, racist, organic, Sombartian, fascist, and Nazi population theories; appraised bourgeois analyses of the decline in natality in capitalist countries; and attempted to account for this decline. See also A. Sauvy, "Doctrine soviétique en matière de population," *Rivista Italiana di Demografia e Statistica*, II (1948).

121. For example, see S. Trubnikov, "Gosudarstvennye trudovye reservy SSSR," *Planovoye khozyaystvo*, No. 11 (1940); M. Sonin, *Voprosy balansa rabochei sily* (1949); P. Mastikov, "Po vuprosa sa dvizhenieto na selskoto rabotno naselenie b Bulgariia," *Narodostopanski Arkhiv*, Tom 4, Nr. 2 (1949). See also E. Granovsky, "Sotsialisticheskaya i kapi-

talisticheskaya industrializatsiya," *Mirovoye Khozyaystvo i Mirovaya Politika*, No. 9 (1947). M. I. Latsis in his *Agrarnoye perenaseleniye i perspektivy borby s nim* (1929), noting that "agrarian over-population" was a result of existing but modifiable conditions, indicated that it could be eliminated but only through efforts spread over some years. See also A. Leontiev, *Political economy* (1935), pp. 122–125, 210–211; R. P. Dutt, *The problem of India* (1943), Part II. Dutt attributed the agricultural over-population of India to what he called "de-industrialization."

122. For Lenin's views on neomalthusianism and the working class, see V. I. Lenin, *Sochineniya* (1930), Vol. 16, pp. 497–499.

123. For example, see S. Y. Sulkevich, *Territoriya i naseleniye SSSR* (1940), pp. 8–9; D. Bosin and L. Dubrowitzki, "Perviye Itogi Vsesoyuznoi Perepisi Naseleniya 1939 g," *Planovoye Khozyaistvo*, No. 6 (1939), p. 23; Besher attributed the decline of fertility in workers' families in capitalist countries to the recruitment of women for industry, and Smulevich to the hard conditions under which women worked. R. Besher, *Problemy naseleniya v narodnokhozyaystvennom planirovanii* (1937), p. 10; B. Smulevich, *Materinstvo pri kapitalizme i sotsializme* (1935), Chapter I. In an earlier study Smulevich observed that the entry of women into industry, assisted by the practice of contraception, was reducing fertility in capitalistic countries, and that even in socialist countries, in the transitional stage before socialistic organization could counteract individualism, motives resembling those characteristics of capitalist countries operated to produce family limitation. In time, however, under socialism these motives would disappear and the population would be under pressure to conform to the pattern of fertility established in the socialist society. Under socialism, therefore, population growth of desirable proportions would take place. But under capitalism the circumstances making for the limitation of numbers would gain in strength and perhaps finally make for depopulation. It was to be expected, therefore, that the demographic futures of capitalist and socialist countries would differ. See B. Smulevich, *Zabolevayemost i smertnost naseleniya gorodov i mestechek BSSR* (1928), especially Chapter 3. Smulevich stated that the rate of population increase depended upon the type of social organization, each type having its own law of population. Under capitalism natality tended to fall below mortality, and capitalist policies could not greatly modify this tendency. Under capitalism the wealthy restricted their families because they did not wish to subdivide their property holdings unduly; the petty bourgeois did so because they wanted to educate their children and prevent their becoming proletarians. The proletarians were less fertile than they had been formerly when they married early and did not seek to limit family size; for now, with child-labour and compulsory education laws, children could not begin to earn at so early an age, and more women were entering arduous employment outside the home. Under capitalism mortality was higher among the poor than existing medical knowledge warranted.

124. See J. V. Stalin, *Voprosy leninizma* (1934), pp. 535–563.

125. Peshchanskiy, for example, suggested that the observed decline in fertility might be considered as a positive achievement of the October revolution. V. Peshchanskiy, "Osnovnye pokazateli yestestvennogo dvizheniya naseleniya Evropeyskoy chasti RSFSR v 1927 godu," *Statisticheskoye obozreniye*, 11 (1928).

126. L. I. Lubny-Gertsyk, *Chto takoye perenaseleniye* (1923), pp. 46, 16, 98, 100.

127. L. E. Mints, *Agrarnoye perenaseleniye i rynok truda v SSSR* (1929).

128. See, for example, A. L. Prasolov, "Kratkiy obzor geografii pochv vsey sushi," *Mirovoe khoziaistro i mirovaia politika*, 6 (1945).

129. For example, Jevons said that the doctrine of population, though valid and important, "forms no part of the direct problem of economy" which had to do with maximizing the return from a given stock of productive agents. W. S. Jevons, *The theory of political economy* (1871), pp. 254–255. See also the treatment of population by M. Pantaleoni in his *Principii di economia pura* (1889), especially Chapter 1.

130. See P. H. Douglas, "Elasticity of supply as a determinant of distribution," in *Economic essays contributed in honour of John Bates Clark*, J. H. Hollander, ed. (1929); also P. H. Douglas, *The theory of wages* (1934), Part I. See also H. J. Davenport, *The economics of enterprise* (1913), pp. 180–181, 425–426.

131. Representative of the views of the British economists are those of A. Marshall, *Principles of economics* (1898), especially the preface and Bk. IV, Chapter 4; Bk. VI, Chapter 2; W. Cunningham, "On the statement of the Malthusian principle," *Macmillan's*

Magazine, XLIX (1883); B. Price, *Chapters on political economy* (1878), pp. 185, 191–196; T. H. Huxley, *Methods and results* (1896), p. 315; G. D. Campbell, *The unseen foundations of society* (1893), pp. 452–503; W. Smart, *Studies in economics* (1895), p. 38; J. A. Hobson, *Problems of poverty: an enquiry into the industrial condition of the poor* (1896), p. 133; J. Bonar, "The centenary of Malthus," *Economic Journal*, VIII (1898); J. S. Nicholson, *Principles of political economy* (1893), pp. 187 ff. On the American and French writers, see J. J. Spengler, "Population doctrines in the United States," *Journal of Political Economy*, XLI (1933); J. J. Spengler, "Population theory in the ante-bellum South," *Journal of Southern History*, II (1936); J. J. Spengler, "French population theory since 1800," *Journal of Political Economy*, XLIV (1936). On the German writers see L. Elster, "Bevölkerungswesen," in *Handwörterbuch der Staatswissenschaften* (1909). On the Dutch writers see N. G. Pierson, *Leerboek der Staathuishondkunde* (1902), Vol. II, Part 3; A. M. de Jong, *Inleiding tot het Bevolkingsvraagstuk* (1946), especially Chapter 6. On the Italian writers see A. Marsigli, *Il problema demografico nelle dottrine politiche ed economiche Italiani* (1934); and E. Cossa, *Introduzione allo studio dell'economia politica* (1892). Cossa subscribed to the substance of Malthus's doctrine. The Dutch, Italian, and other schools of economists are discussed in T. Palgrave's *Dictionary of political economy* (1915), Vol. I, especially pp. 656–660; Vol. II, pp. 460–470.

132. See W. A. Carrothers, *Emigration from the British Isles* (1929), Chapter 3, 13–15; C. Erickson, "The encouragement of emigration by British trade unions, 1850–1900," *Population Studies*, III (1949); H. Fawcett, *Manual of political economy* (1863), pp. 249 ff.; Hobson, *Problems of poverty, op. cit.* p. 133; W. Farr, *Vital statistics* (1885), pp. 59–62; J. G. Godard, *Poverty: its genesis and exodus* (1892), p. 141.

133. G. J. Stigler, *Production and distribution theories* (1941), pp. 49 ff., 258, 265 ff., 358. Among the first to stress the universal character of the law of diminishing incremental returns under static conditions were J. R. Commons, in *The distribution of wealth* (1893), Chapters 3–4, and the Australian economist, W. E. Hearn, in *Plutology* (1863), pp. 117–119. Hearn pointed out that "in the absence of any increase of skill or improved machinery," diminishing returns must characterize manufacturing as well as agriculture, fishing, and other activities based upon the exploitation of "natural agents"; and that output per worker had not fallen with the growth of population only because of increases in the knowledge and skill of workers and in the equipment put at their disposal. Hearn was not apprehensive concerning the population prospect, however, even though he noted man's great capacity for natural increase and the limits to which augmentation of production was subject. He thought that growth of population, if accompanied by complex industrial reorganization, makes for "more complete control over nature" and for economies of the sort associated with extension of the division of labour. He believed that the effectiveness of the prudential check to population growth increased as a community advanced in civilization and wealth, though never enough, apparently, to stop population growth and remove the pressure of numbers upon wealth. *Ibid.*, pp. 389–395.

134. Some writers paid little attention to the laws of returns. See G. Cassel, *Theoretische Sozialökonomie* (1918), Bk. I, Kap. III, para. 13; Bk. II, Kap. VI, para. 24; Bk. II, Kap. VIII, para. 35; F. von Wieser, "Theorie des gesellschaftlichen Wirtschaft," in *Grundriss der Sozialökonomik*, S. P. Albrecht, E. Altmann, Th. Beckerath, and G. Brauer, eds. (1924); J. B. Clark, *Essentials of economic theory* (1907), Chapter 23. The opinions expressed in these works were formed around the turn of the century. G. Cassel, in *Theoretische Sozialökonomie* (1918), p. 306, agreed with Marshall that the "iron law of wages" held in most of the world. Von Wieser noted that the "law of population always exerts the most oppressive influence on the lowest strata of the workers." F. von Wieser, "Theorie des gesellschaftlichen Wirtschaft," *op. cit.*, p. 370. Pierson supported Malthus' views and emphasized the limits to production in N. G. Pierson, *Leerboek der Staathuishondkunde* (1902), Vol. II, Part III, Chapter 3. Clark stated that population growth tended to depress average output. J. B. Clark, *Essentials of economic theory* (1907), p. 317.

135. See E. Cannan, *Elementary political economy* (1888), Part 1, para. 7; E. Cannan, *A history of the theories of production and distribution in English political economy from 1776–1848* (1894), Chapter 5; E. Cannan, *Wealth* (1928), Chapter 4. Historical accounts of the development of the optimum concept are given in S. S. Cohn, *Die Theorie des Bevölkerungsoptimums: Ein Beitrag zur dogmengeschichtlichen und dogmenkritischen*

Behandlung des Bevölkerungsproblems (1934), Part 3, Kap. 2; and G. Fua, *La conception économique de l'optimum du peuplement; population et bien-etre* (1940), Part I, div. 2. For shorter accounts see A. B. Wolfe, "The population problem since the World War: a survey of literature and research," *Journal of Political Economy*, XXXVI (1928); L. Robbins, "The optimum theory of population," in *London Essays in Economics: in honour of Edwin Cannan*, T. E. G. Gregory and H. Dalton, eds. (1927); P. Mombert, *Bevölkerungslehre* (1929); P. Mombert, "L'optimum de population," *Revue économique internationale*, 27 (1935); A. M. de Jong, *Inleiding tot het Bevolkingsvraagstuk* (1946), Chapter 6. On the more recent history of the optimum see M. Gottlieb, "The theory of optimum population for a closed economy," *Journal of Political Economy*, 53 (1945); M. Gottlieb, "Optimum population, foreign trade and world economy," *Population Studies*, III (1949). See also I. Ferenczi, *The synthetic optimum of population: an outline of an international demographic policy* (1938); F. C. Wright, *Population and peace: a survey of international opinion on claims for relief from population pressure* (1939). For further discussion of optimum population, see *The determinants and consequences of population trends* (New York: United Nations, 1953), Chapter XIII, Section G. 1.

136. See E. Cannan, *Wealth* (1928), Chapter 3. Wicksell, like Cannan, located the optimum at the point where the gains from division of labour, co-operation, industrial organization, etc., just balanced the productivity-decreasing effect of the diminution in land and natural resources *per capita* occasioned by population growth. This point was not fixed, but shifted with the introduction of new inventions and technical knowledge. For Wicksell's views see S. S. Cohn, *Die Theorie des Bevölkerungsoptimums, op. cit.*, pp. 81–83.

137. Cannan was not apprehensive concerning over-population since upon analysis of trends he expected the English rate of growth to descend to a trifling level by 1950 and to zero by the close of the century. E. Cannan, "The probability of a cessation of the growth of population in England and Wales during the next century," *Economic Journal*, V (1895).

138. H. Sidgwick, *Principles of political economy* (1887), Chapter 6, paras. 3–5. L. Robbins in "The optimum theory of population," *op. cit.*, noted that "with a little judicious editing" a strong case "could be made out for the claim of Sidgwick to be the real parent" of the modern optimum theory. See H. Sidgwick, *The methods of ethics* (1890), p. 413; H. Sidgwick, *The elements of politics* (1897), pp. 317–318.

139. See A. Marshall, *Elements of economics of industry* (1899), Bk. IV, Chapter 13; A. Marshall, *Principles of economics* (1898), Bk. IV, Chapter 13. In the same chapter, however, Marshall said that perhaps output per head would rise faster in advanced countries if population grew less rapidly. See also J. Wolf, "Ein neuer Gegner des Malthus" (1901); J. Wolf, *Nationalökonomie als exakte Wissenschaft* (1908), pp. 13, 191, 197. In his 1901 paper Wolf observed that within limits, increases in population density increased *per capita* output. In his 1908 work he regularly employed the term "optimum," indicating there was an optimum for each industry, and one for the whole population where labour input per unit of output was at a minimum. Also see S. S. Cohn, *Die Theorie des Bevölkerungsoptimums, op. cit.*, pp. 89–92.

140. A. Marshall, *Principles of economics* (1898), pp. 180 and 531.

141. See J. S. Davis, "The spectre of the dearth of food: history's answer to Sir William Crookes," in *Facts and factors in economic history* (1932); R. Giffen, *Economic enquiries and studies* (1904), Vol. I, pp. 382 ff.; Vol. II, pp. 14–27, 35–38, 46, 230, 340–344.

142. List, critic of Malthus, advocate of German industrialization, and proponent of temporary protectionism for under-industrialized countries, had implied that Germany's population would be larger and of better quality, given industrialization. See F. List, *Das Nationale System der Politischen Oekonomie* (1841), pp. 573–586.

143. A. Wagner, *Agrar und Industriestaat* (1902), pp. 23–38, 143, 152–160; L. Brentano, *Die Schrecken des überwiegenden Industriestaats* (1902), pp. 5–52. H. Dietzel, in *Weltwirtschaft und Volkswirtschaft* (1900), pp. 112–120, estimated that the world wheat supply would be adequate. On the controversy and the relevant literature see G. Haberler, "Der internationale Handel. Theorie der weltwirtschaftlichen Zusammenhänge sowie Darstellung und Analyse der Aussenhandelspolitik," in *Enziklopädie der Rechts- und Staatswissenschaft*, E. Kohlrausch, H. Peters, and A. Spiethoff, eds. (1933). See also Pierson's account of the inability of foreign trade to supply a growing and adequate volume of

raw produce. N. G. Pierson, *Leerboek der Staathuishondkunde* (1902), Vol. II, pp. 152–156.

144. Keynes's argument was criticized by Beveridge, who sought to show that Keynes had misinterpreted the data. For a later comment by W. Beveridge, see his "Mr. Keynes' evidence for over-population," *Economica*, IV (1924). Concerning the difficulties attendant upon using the terms of trade as an index of population maladjustment, see W. W. Rostow, "The terms of trade in theory and practice," *Economic History Review*, III (1950); W. W. Rostow, "The historical analysis of the terms of trade," *Economic History Review*, IV (1951). See also C. Clark, *The conditions of economic progress* (1940), Chapter 14. Recently Clark predicted that, in part because of the growth of population, the terms of trade would turn increasingly in favour of exporters of food and raw materials. C. Clark, "The future of the terms of trade," UNESCO, *International Social Science Bulletin*, III (1951).

145. J. M. Keynes, *The economic consequences of the peace* (1920), Chapter 2. Keynes' inferences, together with a number of studies that purported to show the rate of natural increase to remain high, led to "the rediscovery of the geometrical ratio" and fear of eventual over-population. See A. B. Wolfe, "The population problem since the World War," *op. cit.*

146. See P. Mombert, in *Bevölkerungslehre* (1929), pp. 373–419.

147. It was suggested in an Australian study that "the advantage of protection is in the maintenance of a larger population than could have been expected at the same standard of living without the protective tariff. It is not an advantage to every part of the population, nor has it produced the maximum of income per head." See J. B. Brigden and others, *The Australian tariff* (1929), p. 140. Haberler pointed out that, if protection results in a net increase in population, it is at the expense of a diminution of social product per head. G. Haberler, "Der internationale Handel," *op. cit.* Clark stated, however, that industrial protectionism was restricting Australia's population capacity by preventing agricultural expansion. C. Clark, "Australian over-industrialisation," *Manchester Guardian Weekly* (1952).

148. See W. S. Jevons, *The coal question: an inquiry concerning the progress of the nation, and the probable exhaustion of our coal-mines* (1865), Chapter 10. Already in the early 1860's Jevons, concerned with the growth of the demand for coal, thought he detected the approach of the British population toward a stationary condition. Babbage, as early as 1832, indicated that the world's coal mines might ultimately be exhausted. C. Babbage, *On the economy of machinery and manufacturers* (1832), p. 317.

149. Kerrilis stated that by the time the coal supplies of the world had been exhausted, men would be using the energy of the sun. L. Kerrilis, "Les ressources houillères du globe," *Journal des économistes*, 3ᵉ serie, XLIII (1876). Leroy-Beaulieu suggested, following Berthelot, that man would probably develop synthetic food and learn to harness the energy of the sun and of the interior of the earth. P. Leroy-Beaulieu, *Traité théorique et pratique d'économie politique* (1900), Vol. I, pp. 767–778; Vol. II, pp. 40–42, 283, 546; Vol. IV, pp. 537–540. Leroy-Beaulieu's optimism was shared by Jevons, who said solar energy would take the place of coal. See H. S. Jevons, *The British coal trade* (1915), p. 798. Charles Gide noted that manufacturing, while exempt from the working of the "law of decreasing returns," was subject to limits, but he did not include among them the decline in the coal supply to which he drew attention. He doubted whether synthetic food would ever be available for the support of a dense population. See C. Gide, *Principes d'économie politique* (1889).

150. R. Giffen, *Economic enquiries and studies* (1904), Vol. 2, p. 276, described metals as "presenting as much, or even more, difficulty than food." For subsequent developments see A. B. Wolfe, "The population problem since the World War," *op. cit.* For later treatments of the mineral exhaustion problem, see F. G. Tryon and L. Mann, "Mineral resources for future populations," in *Population problems in the United States and Canada*, L. I. Dublin, ed. (1926), Chapter 8; and President's Research Committee on Social Trends, *Recent social trends in the United States* (1933), Bk. I, Chapter 2.

151. On the manner in which some of these laws of returns were formulated, see G. J. Stigler, *Production and distribution theories* (1941), pp. 48 ff., 350. An increase in average returns occasioned by fuller use of large, relatively indivisible, factors is of much less import for population theory than for cost theory and so is ignored here. But see E. H. Cham-

berlin, "Proportionality, divisibility and economies of scale," *Quarterly Journal of Economics*, LXII (1948).

152. See K. Wicksell, *Föreläsningar i nationalekonomi* (1928), Bk. I, p. 112. Wicksell wrote extensively on the mechanics of population growth and was one of the formulators of the concept of optimum population. See K. Kock, "Nymalthusianismens genombrott i Sverige," in *Studier i ekonomi och historia. Tillägnade Eli F. Heckscher* (1945), pp. 73–88.

153. A. B. Wolfe, *Readings in social problems* (1916), p. 1. Wolfe emphasized the value of the optimum population theory in focusing attention upon the problem of achieving a satisfactory adjustment of numbers to resources. A. B. Wolfe, "The population problem since the World War," *op. cit.;* A. B. Wolfe, "The optimum size of population," in *Population problems in the United States and Canada*, L. I. Dublin, ed. (1926); A. B. Wolfe, "The theory of optimum population," *Annals of the American Academy of Political and Social Science*, 188 (1936); A. B. Wolfe, "The rationalisation of production and of reproduction," in *Economics, sociology of the modern world*, N. E. Himes, ed. (1935).

154. S. Budge, *Das Malthus'sche Bevölkerungsgesetz und die theoretische Nationalökonomie der letzten Jahrzehnte* (1912), especially Chapter 2. Budge attributed the decline in the birth rate to the fact that men wanted to maintain or elevate their standard of living; consequently, a falling death rate entailed a falling birth rate, since if more children survived the standard of living could be preserved only if fewer were born. He believed that socialism might weaken the tendency to restrict family size and that populations which did not regulate their numbers might over-run those which did. See *ibid.*, pp. 156, 184–185, 217–220.

155. Wolf identified four factors limiting economic progress and accordingly formulated four "laws of retardation of progress." One of these "laws" was that "every technical improvement . . . bars the way to further progress" by reducing the number and the range of possibilities still open in a field until finally all possibilities have been exhausted and technical development has ceased. J. Wolf, *Die Volkswirtschaft der Gegenwart und Zukunft* (1912), pp. 335 ff.; J. Wolf, *Nahrungsspielraum und Menschenzahl* (1917), pp. 19–27.

156. P. Mombert, *Bevölkerungslehre* (1929), pp. 356–372. Mombert indicated that a country might attempt to expand its capacity to support a population at a given level by augmenting domestic production for domestic consumption, or by exchanging products that embodied much labour for raw materials in foreign markets. He indicated, however, that the countries whence these raw materials came would in time require most of them for domestic use, and that consequently, both the terms of trade and the rate of capital formation in countries short of raw materials would be affected adversely. *Ibid.*, pp. 373–406. Some of the issues discussed in the text at this point are reviewed by S. S. Cohn in *Die Theorie des Bevölkerungsoptimums, op. cit.*, Part 3.

157. For representative recent accounts of the operation of "laws of returns" see A. A. Young, "Increasing returns and economic progress," *Economic Journal*, XXXVIII (1928); A. B. Wolfe, "Arten und Erscheinungsformen von Kosten und Ertragen," *Weltwirtschaftliches Archiv*, 40 (1934); G. T. Jones, *Increasing return* (1933), Parts 3–6; S. Kuznets, *Secular movements in production and prices* (1930), especially Chapter 4; A. F. Burns, *Production trends in the United States since 1870* (1934), especially Chapters 3–4, 6; G. J. Stigler, "The division of labour is limited by the extent of the market," *Journal of Political Economy*, LIX (1951).

158. S. Kuznets (ed.), *Problems in the study of economic growth* (1949), Parts 3–4; S. Kuznets, *Economic growth* (1952).

159. Chalmers, under the influence of Smith and perhaps Cantillon, declared that "the market cannot permanently be over-laden with corn" since, every increase of food being "followed up by an increase of population," a temporary surplus of corn "creates a market for itself" by stimulating population growth. "It is not so with any other manufactured goods, save in as far as they may work an increase of food." See T. Chalmers. *On political economy, in connexion with the moral state and moral prospects of society* (1832), pp. 56–57. A. Smith, *An enquiry into the nature and causes of the wealth of nations* (1776; 1937 edit.), Bk. I, Chapter 11, Parts 1 and 3. Malthus, as S. Budge did in *Das Malthus'sche Bevölkerungsgesetz und die theoretische Nationalökonomie der letzten Jahrzehnte* (1912), pp. 27 ff., conceived of the standard of living in elastic terms.

160. On the development of consumption theory see C. C. Zimmerman, *Consumption and standards of living* (1936), especially Chapter 3.

161. However, the diminishing pertinence of Malthus's notions was only slowly recognized. For example, Virgilii, who justified Malthus's use of the two progressions as a first approximation, supposed, following Berthelot, that the development of synthetic food would solve the population problem thereby ignoring the fact that the standard of living included many scarce elements besides food. Virgilii denied that technical progress in agriculture alone would make sufficient food available. See F. Virgilii, *Il problema della popolazione* (1924), pp. 177, 513, 547, 551, 577; F. S. Nitti, *La popolazione e il sistema sociale* (1894), pp. 109–123.

162. See F. Morgan (ed.), *The works of Walter Bagehot* (1889), Vol. IV, pp. 570–574; Vol. V, pp. 332–338. Bagehot rejected Mill's thesis that a great change in income is most likely to elevate living standards, saying that the response of a people to changes, large or small, depends on what today are called values and aspirations.

163. See V. Pareto, *Manuel d'économie politique* (1909), translated from the Italian, especially Chapter 7; also J. J. Spengler, "Pareto on population," *Quarterly Journal of Economics*, LIX (1945). In fact, a number of writers, both critics and supporters, indicated that, since societies are made up of different classes, the impact of any given changes upon population growth may vary by class.

164. R. Benini, *Principi di demografia* (1901), p. 286.

165. J. B. Clark, *Essentials of economic theory* (1907), Chapter 19.

166. A. C. Pigou, *The economics of welfare* (1932), Part I, Chapter 9.

167. N. G. Pierson, *Leerboek der Staathuishondkunde* (1902), Vol. 2, pp. 172–188. He implied that moral restraint was inadequate, and pointed to the high fertility of the working classes as evidence that birth rates did not necessarily decline as civilization advanced.

168. Concerning the rationalization of procreation, see M. Monheim, *Rationalisierung der Menschenvermehrung* (1928), especially part B; also H. Rost, "Der Wille zum Kinde bei den Kulturvölkern der Erde," *Allgemeines Statistisches Archiv*, 30 (1941).

169. See A. Dumont, *Dépopulation et civilisation. Etude démographique* (1890), Chapter 9; P. Leroy-Beaulieu, *La question de la population* (1913), Bk. 5, Chapter 11. For summaries see R. Gonnard, *Histoire des doctrines de la population* (1923), Part III especially 341–350; J. J. Spengler, *France faces depopulation* (1938), especially Chapter 7. On the development of state intervention, see D. V. Glass, *Population policies and movements in Europe* (1940), especially pp. 86–99. For the application of a kind of social-capillarity approach to the study of differential fertility, see R. A. Fisher, *The social selection of human fertility* (1932); R. A. Fisher, *The genetical theory of natural selection* (1930), Chapters 8–12.

170. For the development of this argument early in the twentieth century, see L. Brentano, *Konkrete Grundbedingungen der Volkswirtschaft* (1924), Chapters 2–3; L. Brentano, "Die Malthussche Lehre und die Bevölkerungsbewegung der letzten Dezennien," *Abhandlungen der Historischen Klasse der Königlich Bayerischen Akademie der Wissenschaften*, 24 (1909). See also Beatrice and Sidney Webb, *Industrial democracy* (1902), p. 636. That fertility had declined in spite of, and not because of, increases in income was inferred by many students who emphasized the relatively autonomous role of tastes and values. For an early study of this kind, see K. A. Wieth-Knudsen, *Natalité et progrès* (1908), Chapter 3 and 8. See J. Meerdink, *De achteruitgang der geboorten* (1937), pp. 123–146, for development of the argument that the decline in natality was attributable immediately to changes in human mentality.

171. S. N. Patten, *Essays in economic theory* (1895; 1924 edit.), pp. 199–201.

172. See F. H. Hankins, "Does advancing civilization involve a decline in natural fertility?" *Publications of the American Sociological Society*, XXIV (1930). For an analogous sociological explanation, see J. J. Spengler, *France faces depopulation* (1938), pp. 280–288. For an account of the hereditary aspect of fertility as affected by social selection, see W. Wagner-Manslau, "Human fertility," *Eugenics Review*, XXIV (1932).

173. See C. Gini, "The cyclical rise and fall of population," in *Population* (1930), and the extensive bibliography included. See also C. Gini, *Le basi scientifiche della politica della popolazione* (1931); C. Gini, *Saggi di demografia* (1934), pp. 281 ff.; C. Gini, "Real and apparent exceptions to the uniformity of a lower natural increase of the upper classes,"

Rural Sociology, I (1936); C. Gini, "Les facteurs de la décroissance de la natalité à l'époque contemporaine," in *Actas, memórias communicaçoes do congresso nacional de ciencias da população* (1940). See also D. Camavitto, *La decadenza delle popolazione messicane al tempo della Conquista* (1935), pp. 304–310; G. D. Snell, "Hybrids and history. The role of race and ethnic crossing in individual and national achievement," *Quarterly Review of Biology*, XXVI (1951); G. L. Vida, "La teoria della circolazione delle aristocrazie del Pareto e la teoria del ricambio sociale del Gini. Studio comparativo," *Genus*, II (1936).

174. See G. A. Lundberg, "The biology of population cycles," *Social Forces,* IX (1931).

175. See N. E. Himes, *Medical history of contraception* (1936), Part 6; A. Newsholme and T. H. C. Stevenson, "The decline of human fertility in the United Kingdom and other countries as shown by corrected birth-rates," *Journal of the Royal Statistical Society,* LXIX (1906); A. Newsholme, *The declining birth-rate* (1911), pp. 33 ff., Chapter 7; A. Grotjahn, *Geburtenrückgang und Geburten-regelung im Lichte der individuellen und der sozialen Hygiene* (1914), pp. 21–31; S. Budge, *Das Malthus'sche Bevölkerungsgesetz und die theoretische Nationalökonomie der letzten Jahrzehnte* (1912). A. Landry, *Traité de démographie* (1945), p. 566. However, Virgilii attributed the decline in Australian natality to moral restraint rather than to contraception. See F. Vergilii, *Il problema della popolazione* (1924), p. 468. On the impact of contraception on natality, see M. Monheim, *Rationalisierung der Menschenvermehrung* (1928), pp. 42–48. See also A. B. Wolfe, "The population problem since the World War," *op. cit.*

176. Perhaps the most vigorous exponent of this view was Leroy-Beaulieu. See his *La question de la population* (1913), Bk. III, Chapter 1. Landry believed that the changes which had taken place could be summarized much as follows: Eighteenth-century writers had considered two population types: (a) the type conceived of by Townsend, in which it was assumed that man was governed by sex and hunger, that his standard of life was fixed, and that his numbers were *determined* by subsistence and kept adjusted thereto by variations in mortality; (b) the type conceived of by Cantillon, in which it was assumed that the standard of life was variable, and that numbers were *conditioned* by subsistence and adjusted thereto by variations in nuptiality. The late nineteenth-century writers, such as Dumont and Mombert, had pointed to a third type of population in which natality and growth were governed largely by psychological and sociological circumstances. Where this type was found—in advanced countries—it was possible to stimulate natality by governmental action. See A. Landry, *La révolution démographique. Etudes et essais sur les problèmes de la population* (1934), pp. 169–192.

177. See F. W. Notestein (ed.), *Demographic studies of selected areas of rapid growth* (1944); K. Davis, *The population of India and Pakistan* (1951), Chapter 23, especially pp. 229 ff.

178. See A. Quetelet, *Sur l'homme et le développement de ses facultés* (1835), Bk. I, pp. 277–278. On Quetelet's other contributions to population statistics see F. H. Hankins, *Adolphe Quetelet as statistician* (1908), Chapters 3–5.

179. P. F. Verhulst, "Notice sur la loi que la population suit dans son accroissement," in *Correspondance mathématique et physique publiée par A. Quetelet* (1838); P. F. Verhulst, "Recherches mathématiques sur la loi de'accroissement de la population," in *Nouveaux mémoires de l'Académie royale des sciences et belles-lettres de Bruxelles*, XVIII (1845); P. F. Verhulst, "Deuxième mémoire sur la loi d'accroissement de la population," in *Nouveaux mémoires de l'Académie royale des sciences et belles-lettres de Bruxelles*, XX (1847). See also J. R. Miner, "Pierre-François Verhulst, the discoverer of the logistic curve," *Human Biology*, V (1933), pp. 684–685; G. U. Yule, "The growth of population and the factors which control it," *Journal of the Royal Statistical Society*, LXXXVIII (1925).

180. J. R. Miner, "Pierre-François Verhulst, the discoverer of the logistic curve," *op. cit.*, p. 674, found but one modern reference to Verhulst's work, that of L.-G. du Pasquier, "Esquisse d'une nouvelle théorie de la population," *Vierteljahrsschrift der Naturforschenden Gesellschaft in Zürich*, 63 (1918).

181. See R. Pearl and L. J. Reed, "On the rate of growth of the population of the United States since 1790 and its mathematical representation," *Proceedings of the National Academy of Sciences*, 6 (1920). Following the rediscovery of the logistic, it was discussed at great length. For example, see R. Pearl, *Medical biometry and statistics*

(1940), especially Chapter 18; R. Pearl, *The biology of population growth* (1925), pp. 4, 17, 119, 125–130, 157; A. J. Lotka, *Elements of physical biology* (1925), pp. 66–76; A. J. Lotka, *Théorie analytique des associations biologiques* (1939), pp. 48–62; W. C. Allee, O. Park, A. E. Emerson, T. Park, and K. P. Schmidt, *Principles of animal ecology* (1949); H. T. Davis, *The analysis of economic time series* (1941), pp. 524–529; E. C. Rhodes, "Population mathematics," *Journal of the Royal Statistical Society*, Series A, CIII (1940); D. G. Kendall, "Stochastic processes and population growth," *Journal of the Royal Statistical Society*, Series B, XI (1949); P.-E. Corblau, "La fonction logistique et la description des phénomènes de développement économiques et sociaux," *Bulletin de l'Institut de recherches économiques et sociales*, 13 (1947); L. Dor, "Analyse des phénomènes logistiques à l'aide de la courbe normale intégrale," *Bulletin de l'Institut de recherches économiques et sociales*, XIV (1948); A. Afzalipour, *Contribution à l'étude de la théorie mathématique de la démographie* (1936), Chapter VII; R. G. Glenday, *The economic consequences of progress* (1934), especially Part II.

182. On the asymmetrical generalized logistic, see R. Pearl, *Medical biometry and statistics* (1940), p. 460; S. Vianelli, "A general dynamic demographic scheme and its application to Italy and the United States," *Econometrica*, 4 (1936). pp. 271 ff.; S. Vianelli, "Evoluzione economica e demografica negli schemi delle curve logistiche," *Rivista Italiana di Scienze Economiche*, VII (1935), pp. 407 ff. See also H. S. Will, "On a general solution for the parameters of any function with application to the theory of organic growth," *Annals of Mathematical Statistics*, 7 (1936); H. Hotelling, "Differential equations subject to error, and population estimates," *Journal of the American Statistical Association*, New Series, XXII (1927); V. A. Kostitzin, *Biologie mathématique* (1937), Chapter IV; A. J. Lotka, *Elements of physical biology* (1925), Chapters 7–10.

183. Let b represent the biotic potential, or maximum rate of increase per time period of which a population is capable in the absence of that environmental resistance to population growth which increases as N approaches the maximum K. A. J. Lotka, in *Théorie analytique des associations biologiques* (1939), p. 12, put the value of b at .03–.04; P. Vincent and L. Henry in "Rythme maximum d'accroissement d'une population stable," *Population*, 2 (1947), pp. 668 ff., put the value of b at nearly .045 today and about .03 in Malthus's time. Let $(K - N)/K$ represent the fraction of the maximum population that remains to be brought into being before the population becomes stationary. The absolute increment per time period is $bN (K - N)/K$. The value of R is $b(K - N)/K$; it declines as N increases. See G. F. Gause, *The struggle for existence* (1934), Chapter 3, for an outline account.

184. While Volterra noted that the damping effect could be traced to a steady decline, as population grows, in the ratio of births to matings between males and females, the damping effect is usually attributed to the diminution in the ratio of physical resources to population as N grows. The decline in this ratio is accompanied, in animal populations, by an increase in mortality and a decrease in natality, and in human populations, by a decrease in natality and sometimes by an increase in mortality. V. Volterra, "Population growth, equilibria, and extinction under specified breeding conditions: a development and extension of the theory of the logistic curve," *Human Biology*, X (1938), pp. 1–4; W. C. Allee and others, *Principles of animal ecology* (1949), pp. 346 ff.; A. J. Lotka, *Théorie analytique des associations biologiques* (1939), pp. 48–63.

185. Concerning the conditions under which the logistic is superior to other growth curves, see C. P. Winsor, "A comparison of certain symmetrical growth curves," *Journal of the Washington Academy of Science*, XIII (1932); C. P. Winsor, "The Gompertz curve as a growth curve," *Proceedings of the National Academy of Science*, XVIII (1932).

186. Concerning the early reactions to this "law," see A. B. Wolfe, "The population problem since the World War," *op. cit.* The favourable reaction was prompted in part by the fact that, though social scientists were postulating declining rates of growth, no mode of increase which seemed appropriate for the more distant future had been discovered by writers who had fitted curves to past population growth. This problem, moreover, had not received attention in the nineteenth and early twentieth century works on vital statistics. For example, see W. Farr, *Vital statistics* (1885); A. Newsholme, *The elements of vital statistics* (1899); R. Mayo-Smith, *Statistics and sociology* (1895); G. C. Whipple, *Vital statistics* (1919).

187. It has been shown that the probable error of a future population estimate derived

from a logistic increases continuously with time. See H. Hotelling, "Differential equations subject to error, and population estimates," *Journal of the American Statistical Association,* New Series, XXII (1927), p. 311; H. Schultz, "The standard error of a forecast from a curve," *Journal of the American Statistical Association,* New Series, XXV (1930).

188. Such a basis was not provided by the physiological theories of fertility change developed by Pell, Rutgers, Brownlee, Carli, Gini, Stieve and others, some of which continued the Spencer tradition. A. B. Wolfe, "The population problem since the World War," *op. cit.* It was essential to show that, as population density increased, fertility and/or mortality had to respond in such a way as to yield the appropriate slackening of the rate of increase. Pearl attempted to show that as the density of the relevant populations increased, egg production per hen, fertility of the fruit fly, and the human birth rate fell in an appropriate manner. R. Pearl, *The biology of population growth* (1925), Chaper 6. It is generally accepted, however, that even though a rationale can be established for expecting a non-human population to grow in a certain predetermined manner, not even the empirical descriptions of growth of such populations are applicable to human populations. See V. Volterra and U. d'Ancona, *Les associations biologiques au point de vue mathématique* (1935); also N. Rashevsky, *Advances and applications of mathematical biology* (1940); N. Rashevsky, *Mathematical theory of human relations: an approach to a mathematical biology of social phenomena* (1947). See also R. Pearl, *The natural history of population* (1939), Chapter I.

189. Adherents to the logistic theory, when confronted by the possibilities of major cultural changes, looked upon the results as new logistic cycles of growth. For example, see A. B. Wolfe, "Is there a biological law of human population growth?" *Quarterly Journal of Economics,* XLII (1927); S. Vianelli, "A general dynamic demographic scheme and its application to Italy and the United States," *Econometrica,* 4 (1936); H. Hart, "Technological acceleration and the atomic bomb," *American Sociological Review,* II (1946).

190. On these matters see A. B. Wolfe, "Is there a biological law of human population growth?" *Quarterly Journal of Economics,* XLII (1927), pp. 557 ff.; G. H. Knibbs, "The growth of human populations and the laws of their increase," *Metron,* V (1925); L. Dor, "Analyse des phénomènes logistiques à l'aide de la courbe normale intégrale," *Bulletin de l'Institut de recherches économiques et sociales,* XIV (1948), pp. 327 ff.; E. B. Wilson and R. R. Puffer, "Least squares and population growth," *Proceedings of the American Academy of Arts and Sciences,* LXVIII (1933); A. J. Lotka, *Elements of physical biology* (1925), p. 67; L. T. Hogben, *Genetic principles in medicine and social science* (1931), Chapter 7; P. H. Douglas, *The theory of wages* (1934), especially Chapter 13; M. C. MacLean and A. W. Turner, "The logistic curve applied to Canada's population," *Canadian Journal of Economics and Political Science,* 3 (1937).

191. F. A. Walker, *Discussions in economics and statistics* (1899), Vol. II, pp. 43, 121, 206, 419–425, 441; B. Franklin, *Observations concerning the increase of mankind, peopling of countries, etc.* (1755; 1918 edit.), pp. 8–10; A. H. Smyth, *The writings of Benjamin Franklin* (1907), Vol. III, pp. 43–44, 63–73.

192. Pearl concluded that "the sole effect of the *net* immigration has been somewhat to steepen the general upward slope of the United States logistic curve, without either altering its fundamental shape or putting irregular waves in its course." R. Pearl, *The biology of population growth* (1925), p. 13.

193. Delevsky indicated that the rate of growth might sometimes increase and that a population might describe a sinusoidal curve. J. Delevsky, "Une formulation mathématique de la loi de la population," *Metron,* VII (1928).

194. See S. Vianelli, "A general dynamic demographic scheme and its application to Italy and the United States," *Econometrica,* 4 (1936), p. 270.

195. L. Amoroso, "L'equazione differenziale del movimento della popolazione," *Rivista Italiana di statistica,* 1 (1929).

196. See S. Vianelli, "A general dynamic demographic scheme and its application to Italy and the United States," *Econometrica,* 4 (1936), p. 270.

197. F. Vinci, "La logica della curva logistica," *Rivista Italiana di statistica,* I (1929), pp. 386–392; F. Vinci, "Ancora sulla curva logistica," *Rivista Italiana di statistica,* II (1930), pp. 105–106; and F. Vinci, *Manuale di statistica* (1934), Vol. II.

198. See S. Vianelli, "A general dynamic demographic scheme and its application to Italy and the United States," *Econometrica,* 4 (1936), and S. Vianelli, "Evoluzione eco-

nomica e demografica negli schemi delle curve logistiche," *Rivista Italiana di Scienze Economiche*, VII (1935). Demographic elasticity apparently was influenced by variation in the rate of saving, since this variation produced changes in the rate of growth of consumption. Vianelli's scheme has since been applied with some modification by Figueroa, who has considered a variety of social and economic factors. E. de Figueroa, "Un modelo dinámico general de desarrollo demográfico y sus aplicaciones," *Revista Internacional de Sociologia*, V (1947).

199. Changes in the rate of population growth entail changes in the age distribution of the population, which affect the ratio of the number of workers to the total population, and thus influence the trend of E.

200. See C. P. Blacker, "Stages in population growth," *Eugenics Review*, 39 (1947).

201. W. S. Thompson, "Population," *American Journal of Sociology*, XXXIV (1929); W. S. Thompson, *Plenty of people* (1948), Chapter 6; and W. S. Thompson, *Population and peace in the Pacific* (1946), especially Chapter 2. For a different approach in terms of diverse assumptions, see United Nations, "The past and future growth of world populations: a long range view," *Population Bulletin*, 1 (1951).

202. See J. S. Davis, "Population and resources, " *Journal of the American Statistical Association*, XLV (1950), pp. 346 ff.

203. See the "future" type of growth pattern described by Cowgill and distinguished from the "primitive" type in which mortality periodically falls below a high-level natality, and the "modern" type in which natality, though moving downward with mortality towards equilibrium at a low level, long exceeds mortality and permits considerable population growth. D. O. Cowgill, "The theory of population growth cycles," *American Journal of Sociology*, LV (1949).

204. A. Landry, *Traité de démographie* (1945), Chapter IX; R. Cantillon, *Essai sur la nature du commerce en général* (1755; 1952 edit.), Part I, Chapter XV.

THE POPULATION PROBLEM SINCE THE WORLD WAR: A SURVEY OF LITERATURE AND RESEARCH*

By A. B. Wolfe

The decade since the close of the World War has been a period of remarkable recrudescence of interest in population problems, much activity in population research, and some striking changes in population policy. It seems therefore an opportune moment to survey the main currents of post-war population literature and research, and, following such a survey, to make certain suggestions concerning the direction research should take now.

The survey which follows is limited to problems of the quantity of population. The literature of the problem of quality is omitted. To include it would make the presentation unduly long. For the same reason the great mass of American immigration literature is ignored, though some reference is made to the literature of migration in its international political aspect.

Even for the literature of the problem in its quantitative aspects, the well-informed reader will note many omissions. An effort has been made to include all the more important contributions in English, but doubtless not a few have been overlooked. In no case has this been intentional—at least further than was absolutely necessary to keep the presentation within manageable compass. Naturally the bulk of the references are to contributions by English and American writers, though others have not been altogether neglected. Two objects have been kept in mind: first, to distinguish the main trends or types of post-war contributions, and secondly, to give a sufficient number of citations to guide the student who may wish to make a serious survey, on his own account, of the recent literature.

Pre-war and Post-war Interest in Population Problems. For decades prior to the World War the problem of population had been slumbering in innocuous desuetude. Indeed, the popular impression was that a population problem in an economic or Malthusian sense no longer existed. There was, however, plenty of literature on other aspects of population. Sociologists and biologists competed in viewing with alarm differential fertility and the declining birth-rate. The "science" of eugenics was becoming popularized by enthusiasts far beyond a point justified by its thin foundation in scientifically established fact. To many, in America and England, the problem of quality was the only aspect of population worthy of much attention. In Germany and France, for twenty years preceding the war, the literature of population con-

* Excerpt from a paper of the same title which appeared in *The Journal of Political Economy*, 36 (October and December 1928); pp. 529–542 and 677–685 excerpted. Reprinted by permission of the University of Chicago Press.

sisted preponderantly of statistical analyses and disquisitions on the evils of
the decline in the birth-rate. While there was a monotonous sameness in it,
the German literature was on a higher scientific plane, on the average, than
the French. In France men like Lucien March did beautiful work in vital
statistics, but thanks to French nationalism and fear of Germany, a library of
pre-war French population books consists mainly of propagandism for large
families. In the United States the propagandist element was a little less pronounced, but it was sharpened by the racial contacts and prejudices engendered by immigration. The lamentations were over the decline in the birth-
rate of the native American stocks—a point of view or sentiment traceable at
least as far back as Francis A. Walker's famous articles on the effects of immigration on the size of the American family.[1] Professor Ross coined the
phrase "race suicide," and with characteristic energy Theodore Roosevelt
quickly made it a popular moral catchword. The declining birth-rate was supposed to have disproved the Malthusian doctrine once for all. Few persons
took the trouble to examine rates of natural increase or the significance of the
unprecedented absolute increases in population.

In this country the immigration problem naturally claimed much attention, from both economic and political points of view, but hardly at all as a
matter having even remote relation to any Malthusian fear of redundancy in
numbers. Organized labor favored restriction because of the belief that immigration made for low wages and unemployment, but any suggestion that immigration would tend to produce overpopulation would have been laughed
at. Discussion of neo-Malthusian ideas was taboo; the phrase "birth control"
had not been invented. Only here and there a sociologist and a few economists, whose opinions had negligible influence on the flow of public sentiment, gave thought to the probability of impending overpopulation, and
clung steadfastly, though passively, to the Malthusian doctrine. Not till 1912
does population appear as the subject of a presidential address before the
American Economic Association. In that year Professor Fetter addressed the
Association on the topic "Population or Prosperity."[2] This address can still be
read with profit, for Fetter was a far deeper student of population, and especially of the Malthusian doctrine, than most economic theorists. He pointed
out the humanitarian character of Malthus' ideas, the significance of the disappearance of the American frontier, the extravagance of current estimates
of future population capacity, the need of conserving natural resources, and
the altered conditions which made a change in our traditional immigration
policy desirable.[3] The slightness of interest in the population problem on the
part of American economists is perhaps indicated by the fact that on only
two or three other occasions in forty years has population been the subject of
a presidential address before the Association. Prior to 1910 there were few, if
any, college or university courses devoted specifically to population.[4]

Before the war, in the opening years of the present century, the westward
movement of population in this country was still in progress, though at greatly

diminished tempo. The people had gradually come to realize that the old frontier and free land were things of the past. Still, there was the boom in the Prairie Provinces of Canada, and our own western ranches were being rapidly and somewhat prematurely cut into farms. Also, thanks to the influence of interests which need not be analyzed, the program of irrigation and the Federal Reclamation Service was developed, with little thought and less investigation of the needs of the country or the economic feasibility of many of the reclamation projects. The voice of the booster was still blatant in the land. No discordant notes were sounded. Urbanization was proceeding apace, and the popular ranking of towns and cities was according to size and rapidity of growth, with scant regard for character or culture. Always afflicted with it to a distressing degree, the American people exhibited an exaggerated case of chronic megalomania. Some one has yet to write this chapter in folk psychopathology. In the mind of the American business man, especially the real estate agents—they had not yet become "realtors"—population increase was synonymous with progress. Unfortunately this confusion is still by no means uncommon. Even the conservation movement, sponsored by Charles R. Van Hise, Gifford Pinchot, and President Roosevelt, did little to bring to the people at large or to the captains of competitive business any real sense of responsibility for the accelerated rate of exploitation and waste of fixed natural inheritances of basic resources, as the later history of the oil and coal industries has abundantly shown.

To the European peoples the war revealed in high light the basically vital significance of raw materials and agricultural resources. There was nothing in the war, however, to bring directly to Americans at large such a realization. Nevertheless, by a sort of vicarious process our attention was gradually drawn to the problem of world-resources, especially foodstuffs, in relation to population and survival. Practical interest in the population problem was stimulated by the strain to which our productive resources were put to supply the allies with raw materials and to get foodstuffs to France and England. Academic interest in population was revivified in part through the current belief, fostered by quotations from Bernhardi and other German imperialists, that at least one of the German war motives was desire to secure additional territory for the rapidly expanding German population.[5] The unprecedented losses of life as the war wore on and famine stretched its lethal touch across the continent provided a tragic background for this interest. How would these losses be repaired? What would be their effect on family relations and sex mores?[6] Would the average lot of the surviving peoples ultimately be better or worse than that of pre-war populations? Above all—and this was the focus of American questioning—would post-war poverty produce a surge of European emigration, headed like a tidal wave for our shores, and destined, unless we raised adequate barriers in time, to swamp us in a flood of unneeded and unwanted numbers? As things turned out, we did raise the barriers, in the nick of time, and thereby shoved the migration problem out onto the stage of international politics, where it now promises to play no inconsiderable rôle.

In seeking the significant causes for post-war recrudescence of interest in the population problem we must not overlook the American birth-control movement, embodied in the vigorous and courageous propaganda of the American Birth Control League and the Voluntary Parenthood League, and popularly personified in Margaret Sanger. It was in the nature of sheer co-incidence that this movement should come so prominently and insistently on the stage in war time, though it is quite likely that the quickening of moral questioning which came out of war stimulation opened the way for a more ready hearing for the propaganda than it otherwise could have secured. The stupid attempts of city officials and Catholic prelates to prevent meetings for the discussion of birth control had the usual effect of advertising the propaganda and quickening interest among people who otherwise would have been apathetically indifferent. While danger of overpopulation is only one of the arguments advanced by the advocates of birth control, the idea of population pressure was nevertheless given public presentation in places and on occasions where formerly it would not have been mentioned, or, if mentioned, would have been regarded merely as a curious academic vagary.

One other specific impulse to the renewed interest may be mentioned. That was the emphasis which John M. Keynes gave to the population problem in *The Economic Consequences of the Peace* (1920). Discussing "Europe before the War," Keynes selected for emphasis what he regarded as the three or four greatest factors of instability: "The instability of an excessive population dependent for its livelihood on a complicated and artificial organization, the psychological instability of the laboring and capitalist classes, and the instability of Europe's claim, coupled with the completeness of her dependence, on the food supplies of the New World."[7] So prominent a place given to the Malthusian specter in the prologue of a book of this kind, so widely read at so psychological a moment, could not fail to bring home to thousands of readers the fact that the population problem is far more than an academic pastime.[8]

To whatever causes the post-war renewal of interest in the problem of population may be attributed, the new interest soon manifested itself in a phenomenal output of books and articles, especially in England and the United States, and to only slightly less extent in Germany. Closely related to the statistical and other analyses of population itself is the literature of natural resources, land utilization, problems of colonization, including tropical resources and health problems, and a certain amount of the literature of human geography. These are all fields into which, among others, the serious student of population must make rather extensive excursions, and in which the expansion of knowledge by research is a condition to general progress in population research. In all these fields there has been remarkable activity since the war. A bibliography of the scientific monographs and papers issued since 1914 and likely to be of importance in the study of this or that aspect of the population problem—the problem of numbers, resources, and standard of living—would fill a volume. In this brief survey of post-war population literature we cannot ignore these collateral fields, but we can do no more than mention some of the outstanding sources and contributions.

A striking feature of the post-war period has been the number of books dealing with population problems in the by and large, and intended for the general reader. The only American textbook on conventional lines thus far to appear is E. B. Reuter's *Population Problems* (1923). Outstanding among these general treatments of the subject are E. M. East's *Mankind at the Crossroads* (1923), a book which appeared at the right psychological moment and was widely read, and E. A. Ross's *Standing Room Only?* (1927), in the United States; and in England Harold Cox's *The Population Problem* (1923), Harold Wright's *Population* (1923), J. Swinburne's *Population and Social Problems* (1924), Carr-Saunders' smaller book, *Population* (1925), and P. S. Florence's *Overpopulation* (1926). There was thus an outburst of books, and also of journal articles, about five years after the close of the war. Carr-Saunders' first and larger book, *The Population Problem: A Study in Human Evolution* (1922), can hardly be classed as popular, though it has been widely cited. It devotes about half its space to the problem of quantity, and attempts, through extensive anthropological evidence, to sustain the thesis that human societies have always pursued an optimum population policy. Of the popular and general discussions of population, Cox's book is perhaps the most cogent in thought and the most readable in style. Written simply, without parade of scholarship, and unburdened with an unnecessary load of statistics, it goes directly to the heart of the problem. No one can read it without being impressed. East's book is excellent in parts, and contains a valuable popular presentation of potential agricultural resources, but is marred, in the eugenics sections (which so many writers appear to deem indispensable), by an uncritical attitude toward the unproved assumption of organically inherited racial superiorities and inferiorities.

It cannot be said, perhaps, that much of this new popular, or quasi-popular, literature has attempted any very deep analysis of fundamental economic and psychological forces, or that it has added much that is wholly new to population theory. The aggregate effect, however, is that of new contribution. Whatever the shortcomings of the type of literature under consideration, it has done more, especially in England and America, to promote and extend awareness and understanding of the reality of the population problem than had been done for decades preceding the war. Students of population in its quantitative economic aspects may now without apology claim to be dealing with an actual, present problem, one of tremendous import to the national welfare and world-civilization of the immediate future, a problem which no reasonably well-informed and open-minded person can any longer regard as a mere academic exercise, an obsession of astigmatic reformers, or a set of unfounded pessimistic and fanciful forebodings of disaster in a future so distant that no practical-minded person need care anything about it.

Curiously, the French, who before the war were so prolific of popular and propagandistic publications on population, have since the war published comparatively little.[9] The post-war German literature has been copious but dull. Much of it still reflects pre-war nationalism, as does the French, and a somewhat irrational solicitude over the failure of the German birth-rate to stem its downward course. Both French and German students, taken generally, have failed to break new ground or to make use of the newer methods of statistical analysis now so prevalent in England and America. In Germany *Bevölkerungsbewegung* and *Bevölkerungspolitik*, in all their traditional systemization and exhausting statistical content, still claim the central attention.[10]

The Rediscovery of the Geometrical Ratio. From the standpoint of educating the public on a problem of such basic importance as that of population in relation to natural resources perhaps the most significant achievement of the post-war literature in England and America is its virtual rediscovery of the geometrical ratio, or at least its new and pointed emphasis on the meaning of geometrical rates of increase as revealed by statistics of population growth during the nineteenth century. While militarists and realtors were congratulating themselves on the phenomenal growth of population, and French patriots were bemoaning France's stationary population and trying to think up expedients to induce a reluctant populace to have larger families *pour la patrie,* and while the self-appointed National Council of Public Morals, in England, was instituting a Birth-Rate Commission, composed largely of the higher clergy, to inquire into the causes of the declining birth-rate and report remedies for it,[11] certain persons on both sides of the Atlantic were making a thoughtful examination of rates of natural increase and of absolute increases, and rereading Malthus.

In his Columbia doctoral dissertation, *Population, a Study in Malthusianism,*[12] Warren S. Thompson, now director of the Scripps Institute for Research in Population Problems, Miami University, made an extended analysis of the relative increase of population and food production in the leading countries. He concluded that "the vital question to us is whether the United States can keep up its rate of increase indefinitely and still offer the good conditions of life which it does at present." This conclusion, conservatively enough expressed, was presently stated more decidedly and positively by Harold Cox, editor of the *Edinburgh Review.*[13] Cox brought out distinctly the impossible numbers which would result from continuation, even for a century or two, of present rates of natural increase; for instance, that England in the short space of 360 years would have two and a third *billion* people—a third more than the entire world's present population. He also emphasized, as the older literature never did, the magnitude of absolute increases. To be told that the annual rate of natural increase in England and Wales before the war was 11 per thousand is not necessarily impressive; but when this is shown to mean an absolute increase of over three and a half million people in a decade, for whom, if they are not to starve, English industry must find employment and subsistence, the facts of increase begin to take on rather more vivid significance.

If we digress a moment and, following Cox's lead, consider the magnitude of American population growth, we find that the 16,000,000 increase, 1900 to 1910, was only about a million short of our total population in 1840. It was twice as large as the absolute increase of 1850–60, although the percentage increase then was 36 as against 21 in 1900–10. The percentage increase in 1910–20 was only 14.9, but in that decade we added 13,788,000, a number nearly equal to the combined populations in 1920 of the two empire states, New York and California, or to the total population of all the South Atlantic states. The excess of births over deaths in the Birth Registration Area in 1925 (when our birth-rate was 21.4), was 848,000.[14] If the same rate held for the whole country, we added in 1925, by natural increase alone, considerably over a million people. How many persons, one may wonder, realize that even an arithmetical increase of ten million people means the addition, each decade, of a population equal to the 1920 population of metropolitan and upstate New York? It is clear that to calculate increase as a rate per thousand is a poor way to bring out the magnitude of current population growth.

Some very striking calculations on the significance of present rates of increase have been made by Sir George H. Knibbs, statistician for the Commonwealth of Australia. His monumental *Mathematical Theory of Population* appeared in 1917 in nearly 500 folio pages.[15] While much of it is probably due to the author's mathematical curiosity and is of no immediate applicability, and while most of it is beyond the comprehension of the non-mathematical reader, matter of signal interest and import is presented. Knibbs calculates, for instance, for each of twenty-six different countries, the number of years it takes population to double at the rates of increase current in the quinquennium 1906–11. The period of doubling varies from 436 years for France to 23.6 years for Canada, that for the United States being (on the rate for 1900–1910) 38.4 years. The weighted average for the twenty-six countries is 60.1 years.[16] At this rate, Knibbs shows, the world's population would mount to the following numbers:[17] at the end of 50 years, 2,796,000,000; at the end of 100 years, 4,598,000,000; at the end of 150 years, 7,562,000,000; at the end of 200 years, 12,437,000,000. For the period 1804–1914, Knibbs puts the world's average rate of increase at 0.864 per cent per annum, and for the twenty-six countries for which accurate statistics are available, 1.159 per cent per annum for the period 1906–11. At a rate of 1 per cent per year, the progeny of a single pair would in 10,000 years require the physical mass of 1,340,000,000,000,000,000,000 ($1,340 \times 10^{18}$) earths to compose their bodies. To the myopic vision of the average man, 10,000 years are an unthinkably, and therefore a negligibly, long period; to the geologist they are but a fleeting moment, and to the anthropologist only a minute fraction of the time during which man has been on the earth or of the time during which he will probably be able to remain on it. Since statements of what may happen in 10,000 or even 1,000 years may fail to register in the mind of the average reader, it is better to draw attention to a shorter period. Knibbs calculates that at the rate of 0.864 per cent per year the world's population would reach 7,400,-000,000 in 160 years, and the same figure in 120 years if the rate of 1906–11, 1.159 per cent, were to continue.[18] Even a phlegmatic imagination should be able to envisage so short a time.

The earth's population limit can be estimated, of course, only on certain assumptions as to standard of living, area of potentially productive land, improvement in agricultural technique, and the degree to which the people of the world can bring themselves to co-operate in order to use the earth's material resources to the best technical advantage. Knibbs notes estimates, involving various but reasonable assumptions, ranging from three to thirteen billions. While he thinks it doubtful whether the five billion limit will ever be attained, he concedes that science may enable the seven billion limit to be reached.[19] The dean of German geographers, Albrecht Penck, puts the limit at eight billions, which limit, he thinks, the present rate of increase would reach in 300 years. Whatever limit, within reason, be taken, it is evident that continuation of present rates of increase would bring us to it in a very short time.[20]

Other writers who have presented similar lines of analysis are E. M. East,[21] J. Swinburne,[22] W. S. Rossiter,[23] W. B. Pitkin,[24] and E. A. Ross.[25] Many writers point out the fact that the rate of population growth since the middle of the eighteenth century is, so far as we know, entirely unprecedented. Assuredly, so far as absolute human numbers are concerned, the world has never before witnessed anything even remotely comparable. It is shown by Knibbs that in view of the hundreds of thousands of years of man's previous sojourn on the earth, past rates of increase must have been extremely low.[26]

What are the causes of this extraordinary and astounding explosion of growth? No one seriously questions Malthus' assumption of the constancy of the sex instinct. The causes of the rapid modern growth are of course fundamentally economic: the opening up of great virgin areas of fertile alluvial plains, like the Mississippi Valley, previously practically unoccupied, revolution in transportation facilities, and the phenomenal increase in capacity to produce wealth, due to modern invention, machinery, and organization. But science in another direction has made the high rates possible. We know from tables of birth-rates and death-rates that a country may have a high rate of natural increase either with a high death-rate and a high birth-rate or a low death-rate and a low birth-rate. When the death-rate is low and the birth-rate is high, the rate of natural increase is correspondingly elevated.[27] Medical science has brought about a very great reduction in the death-rate in the

Western world, with a corresponding increase in the average length of life. The literature of this aspect of the population problem, in the medical and statistical journals, is very extensive, but since it is not essentially a post-war literature, we need not attempt to review it. Most general writers on population, however, have failed to give the decline in the death-rate more than passing notice and inadequate emphasis. This defect has been ably remedied by Professor Ross in his recent book, *Standing Room Only*.[28] In analyzing at length the significance of the declining death-rate, Ross makes a distinct and valuable contribution to population literature.

"Laws" of Population Increase. At a constant geometrical rate, such as Malthus assumed, population would accrue like a sum at compound interest. Whether population actually does grow at such a uniform rate over an indefinite period of time, or whether the rate of increase is itself subject to change, possibly in accordance with some regularity or law, is a question which Malthus did not consider. Paradoxical as it may seem, Malthus was not primarily interested in a law of growth. He was interested in the results of growth rather than in its precise mode. He saw, or thought he saw, that whatever the rate, and whether the rate be constant or variable, population tends to increase faster than subsistence, and thereby produce some inconvenient results. He took the simple assumption of a constant geometrical rate, for which he had some statistical evidence, rather than a varying rate. Like Malthus, practically all of the economists of the nineteenth century were interested in the results of population increase rather than its mode. With few exceptions they did not take the trouble to inquire whether the rate is constant or not.

The first exception, so far as the present writer has noted, was Edward Cannan, who in 1895 pointed out reasons for expecting the English rate of growth gradually to decline and finally become zero.[29] Another economist who noted the declining rate of increase was Pareto.[30] A mathematician or statistician would be more likely to raise the question than an economist, and we find, before the middle of the nineteenth century, the Belgian mathematician, P. F. Verhulst[31] and the Belgian statistician, Quetelet,[32] taking up the problem of the "law" or mode of increase, indicating thus early recognition of the fact that the rate is not necessarily constant. In 1891 H. S. Pritchett found that the actual mode of growth of the population of the United States up to 1890 was described fairly well by a third-order parabola. The trouble was that such a curve projected into the future leads to impossibly high numbers.[33] Finally, in 1920, Raymond Pearl and L. J. Reed evolved a modified logarithmic formula,[34] their so-called "logistic," much like that worked out in 1838–45 by Verhulst, whose formula, however, had not yet come to their attention.

The work of Pearl and Reed is so widely known and so frequently quoted that we need not make extended comment on it. Suffice it to say that the Pearl-Reed growth curve is S-shaped, concave before a point of inflexion, thereafter convex, and gradually approaching (but never reaching), at a continuously retarded rate, an upper limit or asymptote which for the United

States is put at 197,274,000. The theory assumes, or reveals, a "growth cycle," in the early stages of which population increases by accelerated rates, in the later stages by decreasing rates. Practically no one now supposes, or assumes, that population increases at a uniform geometrical rate up to the saturation limit and then abruptly stops. This change in conception has been brought about by two influences: first, census data indicate diminishing rates of increase; secondly, biological research has shown that the rate of growth of an individual organism is logarithmic, not constant, and this has been carried over to be applied analogically to the study of the increase of human populations.

Not for decades has a contribution to the theory of population commanded the attention which Pearl's logistic formula has received. This is partly due to Pearl's prominence as a biometrician, partly to the new interest of biologists in human population problems, and partly, perhaps, to the fact that the logistic formula or "law" of growth seems to some to free us from the old Malthusian fear of overpopulation. The statistician, whether in the natural or the social sciences, easily falls into a frame of mind in which he tacitly regards an empirical formula as a sort of law, governing phenomena. According to this more or less unconscious attitude there is some mystical virtue in Pearl's logistic equation and its constants, by which the population of the United States is fated in all probability not to exceed 197,274,000. Another cause for the popularity of the formula is that such a mode of approach is in line with present scientific fashion, that is, the extraordinary post-war development of mathematical statistics and the attempt to apply statistical methods to all sorts of problems, not always with adequate attention to the question whether they are amenable to valid methods of statistical analysis. Since one of the chief values of a growth formula is the ability it is supposed to give us to predict future growth, it makes a strong appeal to the many statisticians who today are concerning themselves with time series and the forecasting of business and economic movements. Even the attempts made from time to time by mathematical statisticians who are not satisfied with Pearl's formula to develop others is evidence of the appeal which mathematical methods have made.

Adverse criticisms of the Pearl-Reed formula have come from two sources: first, from those mathematicians and statisticians who see defect or error in Pearl's mathematics of curve-fitting,[35] and secondly from economists who object to all attempts to reduce to a mathematical formula a phenomenon so deeply influenced by human motivation and changing social environment as is the growth of population.[36]

On the other hand, the Pearl-Reed formula has been accepted by some statisticians, notably Yule,[37] and has been made use of, without much critical examination, by a number of writers on population. The biologists not unnaturally look with favor upon Pearl's mode of approach, since it seems to be a method that makes it possible for the biometric laboratory to contribute something really scientific to the theory of population growth, which it is apparently thought the social sciences have scarcely done.

While not questioning that vital phenomena are in the last analysis just as mechanistic as others, most economists and sociologists will be slow to think that the "law" of population growth is so simple, or that we can soon secure enough data on the influences which affect growth to justify committing ourselves to a mathematical formula, or to admission that "biological" factors override the social and economic. For two reasons—entirely apart from the mathematical questions involved—social scientists will be indisposed to think the biometric method of approach adequate. The first is the analogical procedure which such an approach involves. Pearl's conclusions are based almost entirely on analogical reasoning from the behavior of fruit flies in a bottle to that of human beings in a complex social environment. This is altogether too far a cry. The other reason is the entirely empirical nature of the Pearl-Reed or any other formula so far suggested. Without denying that all knowledge is derived through processes involving analogy and empirical induction, we may nevertheless make a distinction between relations the mechanism of which we know, and relations or correlations the mechanism of which we do not know. A mathematical formula of population growth, even if it fits the census data of growth exactly, belongs to the latter, or empirical, category. Pearl has recognized the purely empirical character of his "law" and has attempted to support it by evidence which will transform it into a "rational" law, that is, show the causative steps, or the mechanism, by which population must be expected to grow in accordance with the formula. His evidence is very slender, again partly analogical, and unconvincing. It needs rational explanation as much as the formula itself. Briefly, it is that human fertility is inversely correlated with density; but as to the causes or mode of such a correlation, if it exists, Pearl tells us nothing.[38]

There is a similarity between certain aspects of Pearl's biological approach and the physiological theories of fertility such as were propounded by Doubleday and Spencer in the mid-nineteenth century. In both types of theory a causal association is asserted, but no information is forthcoming with regard to its step-by-step nature. Recently C. E. Pell has tried to revive the physiological type of theory, but he shows little understanding of the exacting requirements of scientific method, and his attempt is a weak one. He formulates what he calls the "principle of the vital optimum"—"animal fertility in response to the direct action of the environment will be directly proportional to the nervous charge until the optimum point for fertility is reached; it will thenceforward bear an inverse proportion to the nervous charge."[39] Such a formula, even if it could be substantiated, is too general to mean much. Much the same idea as that advanced by Pell was presented a decade earlier by Dr. J. Rutgers, the well-known Dutch protagonist of birth control.[40] He called it the "physiological optimum." For every species there are environmental extremes, maxima and minima of tolerance—heat, cold, light, food, electrical tension, and so on. There is also an optimum point in the intensity of these environmental factors, individually and collectively, at which the individual will have the best health and the most energy. Accordingly Rutgers desires neither too low nor too high a material standard of living. "All ethics is a kind of higher hygiene."

Another writer, not a biologist, but a leading English public health official, Dr. John Brownlee, thinks there is some hidden biological or physiological law by which the human birth-rate rises and falls in cycles of long duration, probably two or three centuries.[41] Again the evidence is exceedingly slight. An Italian writer, F. Carli, has set forth a hypothesis similar to that advanced by Thomas Doubleday in 1843. "Beyond certain limits," thinks Carli, "an increase of wealth goes against the interests of the species and checks fertility."[42] C. Gini, at present the most prolific Italian writer on population, is quite certain that there are fundamental biological or physiological influences connected with the declining birth-rate and differential fertility.[43] Pearl's findings with regard to frequency of sexual intercourse in different economic classes may possibly, though not necessarily, be interpreted from a physiological point of view. If further research should substantiate Pearl's results as to differential sexual activity, the question would remain whether the differences were due to physiological causes or were volitional. In any case the differences which he finds are too small, and the frequencies in all classes too high, to serve as explanation of the differential birth-rate.[44]

So far as the present writer's reading goes, Dr. H. Stieve, of the University of Halle, comes the nearest to showing, both through reference to the results of experimentation on certain lower vertebrates (mice and fowls) and through certain anatomical observations on human individuals, physiological, or rather pathological, causes of sterility or of weakened reproductive powers. It has long been known that certain poisons, e.g., lead, may produce sterility, and recent research has connected reproductive power with the vitamin content of diet. Animal and plant breeders also know that overfeeding, under certain conditions, is detrimental to fertility, but the mechanism of the relation is ill understood. To these influences Stieve adds lack of exercise, too high external temperature, and sudden change of environment—"all the many influences which by way of the nervous system impair health and through their effect on the activity of the sex glands affect fertility." When he comes to the influence of modern culture, especially city life, on the activity of the sex glands, however, Stieve adds little to what has been brought forward in the past—the strain and stress of modern life, the idleness and overfeeding of the well-to-do classes, especially the women, and the undernourishment and bad housing of the masses.[45] To suspect a relation here and to demonstrate it are two different things. And it is by no means beyond question that modern conditions of living, even in industrial cities, are more detrimental to health and reproductive power than were the conditions in Europe in the 1870's, say, when the birth-rate was at a high point. To demonstrate an influence of culture on physiology it is necessary to find correlative changes in both. And this, thus far, the advocates of the physiological theory have failed to do.[46] Moreover, were the physiological theory demonstrated to be true, it would still be impossible to say how much of the decline in the birth-rate is pathological and how much volitional.

REFERENCES

1. "The Great Count of 1890," *Forum*, XI (June, 1891), 406–18; "Immigration and Degradation," *Forum* XI (August, 1891), 634–44.

2. *American Economic Review Supplement*, III (March, 1913), 5–19.

3. Fetter's interest in population went back to his student days at Jena, where he wrote his "Versuch einer Bevölkerungslehre," 1894. See also his "The Essay of Malthus: A Centennial Review," *Yale Review* VII (1898–99), 143–67.

4. Probably the first such courses in this country were offered at the University of Chicago by the late J. A. Field, at the University of Wisconsin by E. A. Ross, and at Oberlin College by the present writer.

5. Cf. Committee on Public Information, *Conquest and Kultur: Aims of the Germans in Their Own Words* (Washington, 1918); Jules Courmont, "La guerre et la repopulation," *Le Musee Social, Memoires et Documents* (January, 1918), pp. 11–13; Harold Cox, *The Problem of Population* (1923), pp. 80–82; G. Lowes Dickinson, *The Choice before Us* (1917), pp. 116–19. See also the more recent quotations in E. A. Ross, *Standing Room Only?* (1927), pp. 168–70.

6. Cf. for example, J. A. Field, "Economic Problems after the War," *American Economic Review Supplement* (March, 1917), pp. 233–37; A. B. Wolfe, "Economic Conditions and the Birth-Rate after the War," *Journal of Political Economy* (June, 1917), pp. 521–41; S. Šećerov, *Economic Phenomena before and after War* (London, 1919).

7. *Op. cit.*, p. 25. Cf. the striking passage on p. 10 about the chaining and the unchaining of the Malthusian "Devil."

8. Keynes's view, and particularly his assertion that "the law of diminishing returns was at last reasserting itself and was making it necessary year by year for Europe to offer a greater quantity of other commodities to obtain the same amount of food in international trade" (*Economic Consequences of the Peace*, p. 25), was challenged by Sir William Beveridge in an address before the British Economic Association (*Economic Journal* [December, 1923], pp. 447–75). Keynes answered the criticisms (*ibid.*, pp. 476–86), and Beveridge came back with an elaborate analysis of import and export statistics in an attempt to show that Keynes had misinterpreted the data ("Mr. Keynes' Evidence for Overpopulation," *Economica* [February, 1924], pp. 1–20). The controversy is enlightening, not as proof or disproof of impending overpopulation, but as revealing the difficulty of arriving at a convincing conclusion from intricate, approximate, and incomplete statistical data of production and trade.

9. Among the more important post-war French books may be mentioned Fernand Aubertin, *La Natalité* (undated, but post-war); A. L. Galeot, *L'Avenir de la Race, le Problème du Peuplement en France* (1917); Henri Lavedan, *La Famille Française* (1917); René Worms, *Natalité et Régime Successoral* (1917); Alfred Krug, *Pour la Repopulation et contre la Vie Chère* (1918); Gaston Rageot, *La Natalité, ses Lois Économiques et Psychologiques* (1918); M. de Roux, *L'État et la Natalité* (1918); G. Dequidt, *Le Statut des Familles Nombreuses* (1923).

10. Some of the more important German books since the war are Franz Hitze, *Geburtenrückgang und Sozialreform* (1917); A. Grotjahn, *Geburtenrückgang und Geburtenregelung* (1921); Johannes Müller, *Der Geburtenrückgang* (1924). Of more theoretical trend are Oscar Wingen, *Die Bevölkerungstheorien der letzten Jahre* (1915); Paul Mombert, *Bevölkerungspolitik nach dem Kriege* (1916); and *Die Gefahr einer Ubervölkerung für Deutschland* (1919); Louis Krafft, *Bevölkerungsprobleme, eine bevölkerungstheoretische Abhandlung über den Begriff der Uebervölkerung und Untervölkerung* (1917); Julius Wolf, *Nahrungsspielraum und Menschenzahl, ein Blick in die Zukunft* (1917); Wilhelm

Schöttler, *Der Nahrungsspielraum Deutschlands nach dem Weltkrieg* (1922). A review by Paul Mombert, "Neuere Erscheinungen zur Bevölkerungslehre und Bevölkerungspolitik," of German population monographs published from 1922 to 1925, may be found in *Archiv für Sozialwissenschaft und Sozialpolitik*, 56 Band, I Heft (August, 1926), pp. 235–45.

11. See the reports of the National Birth-Rate Commission: *The Declining Birth-Rate, Its Causes and Effects* (1917), and *Problems of Population and Parenthood* (1920).

12. "Columbia University Studies in History, Economics, and Public Law," Vol. LXIII, No. 3, 1915.

13. *The Problem of Population* (1923), chap. i.

14. Bureau of the Census, *Birth, Stillbirth, and Infant Mortality Statistics for 1925*, p. 2.

15. *Census of the Commonwealth of Australia*, Appendix A, Vol. I.

16. *Op. cit.*, p. 31.

17. "The Problems of Population, Food Supply, and Migration," *Scientia*, I–XII (1919), 486.

18. "The World-Problems of Population. Part I, The Population Capacity of the Earth," *Scientia*, I–X (1925), p. 250.

19. "The World-Problems of Population. Part II. The Conditions for the Maximum Possible World's Population," *Scientia*, I–XI (1925), 329, 334.

20. "Das Hauptproblem der physischen Anthropogeographie," *Sitzungsberichte der Preussischen Academie der Wissenschaften*, XXII (1924), 242–57.

21. *Mankind at the Crossroads* (1924), chap. iv.

22. *Population and the Social Problem* (1924), chaps. ii, v.

23. "The Adventure of Population Growth," *Journal of the American Statistical Association*, XVIII (March, 1923), 561–74.

24. *Must We Fight Japan?* (1921), chap. xxii.

25. *Standing Room Only?* (1927), chap. i.

26. "The Problems of Population, Food Supply, and Migration," *Scientia*, I–XII (1919), 486.

27. For convenient tables see *Annuaire International de Statistique*, Vol. II, "Mouvement de la Population (Europe)" (The Hague, 1917).

28. Chaps. ii–vii. See also F. L. Hoffman, "The Significance of the Declining Death-Rate," *Proceedings of the First International Conference on Race Betterment* (1914), pp. 23–66; Lilian Brandt, "Facts about the Death-Rate," *New York School of Philanthropy, Studies in Social Work*, No. 7 (December, 1915); G. M. Kober, "Progress of Health Conservation during the Past Fifty Years," *U.S. Public Health Reports*, XXXVIII (April 6, 1923), 725–39; League of Nations, Economic and Financial Section, *Natural Movements of Population during the First Quarter of the Twentieth Century* (1927). For more technical treatment, see Raymond Pearl, *The Biology of Death* (1922), and *Studies in Human Biology* (1924), Part II; R. H. Britten, "Some Tendencies Indicated by the New Life Tables," *U.S. Public Health Reports*, XXXIX (April 11, 1924), 737–49.

29. "The Probability of the Cessation of the Growth of Population in England and Wales during the Next Century," *Economic Journal*, V (December, 1895), 505–15.

30. *Cours d'Économie Politique* (1896–97), I, 196 ff.; *Traité de Sociologie Générale* (1917), II, 33, 34.

31. On Verhulst's work see Raymond Pearl, *Studies in Human Biology* (1924), 569, and G. U. Yule, "The Growth of Population and the Factors Which Control It," *Journal of the Royal Statistical Society*, LXXXVIII (January, 1925), 41 ff.

32. *Essai de Physique Sociale* (1835), I, 275–79; *Du Système Social* (1848), pp. 174, 175.

33. "A Formula for Predicting the Population of the United States," *Quarterly Publications of the American Statistical Association*, II (June, 1891), 278–86.

34. "On the Rate of Growth of the Population of the United States since 1790 and Its Mathematical Representation," *Proceedings of the National Academy of Sciences*, VI, 275–88; Pearl, *Studies in Human Biology* (1924), chaps. xxiv, xxv.

35. G. H. Knibbs, "Laws of Growth of a Population, Part I," *Journal of the American Statistical Association*, XXI (December, 1926), 281–98, and "The Fundamental Elements of the Problems of Population and Migration," *Eugenics Review* (January, 1928); A. L.

Bowley, *Journal of the Royal Statistical Society,* LXXXVIII (January, 1925), 76 ff.; E. B. Wilson, "The Population of Canada," *Science,* LXI (January 23, 1925), 87–89; E. B. Wilson and W. J. Luyten, "The Population of New York and Its Environs," *Proceedings of the National Academy of Sciences,* XI (February, 1925), 137–43; H. Hotelling, "Differential Equations Subject to Error, and Population Estimates," *Journal of the American Statistical Association,* XXII (September, 1927), 283–314.

36. H. B. Woolston, "The Dynamics of Population," *Journal of Social Forces* (January, 1924); "The Limits of American Population," *Social Forces,* IV (September, 1925), 5–16; A. B. Wolfe, "Is There a Biological Law of Human Population Growth?" *Quarterly Journal of Economics,* XLI (August, 1927), 557–94.

37. G. U. Yule, "The Growth of Population and the Factors Which Control It," *Journal of the Royal Statistical Society,* LXXXVIII (January, 1925), 1–58.

38. See Pearl, *The Biology of Population Growth* (1925). For fuller criticism of this aspect of Pearl's work, see A. B. Wolfe, *loc. cit.,* pp. 579–94. For discussion of the distinction between empirical and rational laws—a subject which has important bearing on the question of the validity of bio-statistical methods of studying population—see further, F. C. Mills, "On Measurement in Economics," *The Trend of Economics,* edited by R. G. Tugwell (1924), chap. ii; A. B. Wolfe, "Vital Statistics, Empiricism, and the Mechanism of Nature," *Southwestern Political and Social Science Quarterly,* VIII (September, 1927), 107–26.

39. *The Law of Births and Deaths* (1921), p. 70.

40. *Rassenverbesserung, Malthusianismus und Neumalthusianismus,* 2d ed. (Dresden, 1911), chaps. iii, l.

41. See Dr. Brownlee's evidence before the National Birth-Rate Commission, *The Declining Birth-Rate: Its Causes and Effects* (1917), pp. 149 ff.; also *Journal of the Royal Statistical Society,* LXVIII (January, 1925), 82, 83; "The History of the Birth- and Death-Rates in England and Wales," *Public Health* (June and July, 1916); "Germinal Vitality," *Proceedings of the Philosophical Society* (Glasgow, 1908). For criticisms of Brownlee's idea, see A. Newsholm, *Vital Statistics,* new ed. (1923), pp. 105, 106; Sir William Beveridge, "The Fall of Fertility among European Races," *Economica* (March, 1925), pp. 17, 18.

42. Quoted by Pitirim Sorokin, *Contemporary Sociological Theories* (1928), p. 551, note, from Carli, *L'Equilibrio delle Nazioni* (1920). See also Pignini, *La Biochimia del Cervello* (1915). Pearl seems to share this view. See the *Biology of Population Growth* (1925), pp. 164–67.

43. "Le leggi di evoluzione della popolazione," *Economia* (December, 1924), No. 12; "Decline in the Birth-Rate and the Fecundability of Woman," *Eugenics Review,* XVII (January, 1926), 258–74; "Some Italian Inquiries into Differential Reproductivity," *Proceedings of the World Population Conference* (1927), pp. 157–67.

44. See Pearl, *The Biology of Population Growth* (1925), chap. viii.

45. *Unfruchtbarkeit als Folge unnatürlicher Lebensweise* (Munich, 1926), *Grenzfragen des Nerven und Seelenlebens,* Heft 126.

46. Some of the work cited by Stieve is reminiscent of the "racial poisons" theory current in this country when Stockard was experimenting with the effect of alcohol on guinea pigs, and Saleeby was popularizing the theory in England (*Parenthood and Race Culture,* 1909). It also suggests a possible scientific basis for the "physiological optimum" theories of Pell and Rutgers. Stieve gives a valuable bibliography of German literature bearing on the subject.

PRESENT STATUS AND PROSPECTS OF RESEARCH IN POPULATION*

By Philip M. Hauser

If this paper fulfilled the requirements of the assignment made by President Louis Wirth, it would provide a summary of the state of knowledge, substantive and methodological, in the field of population and an evaluation of the field and its prospects. Let me say at the outset that I am sure that this essay does not meet the bill of specifications that the President of the Society hoped it would.

The subject is worthy of a long and intensive period of research, and calls for a scholarly and carefully documented report. I feel it the better course of wisdom to indicate at the beginning what you will discover by yourselves, that for various reasons this paper is an impressionistic, undocumented essay and not a product of research.

I have attempted to deal with my assignment by answering seven questions about the field of population. So that you may anticipate what is to follow, allow me to list these questions at this point:

1. What are the data?
2. What are the methods?
3. What are the theories?
4. What do we know?
5. What are the important frontiers of research?
6. What is the relation of the field of population to population policy and its implementation, and vice versa?
7. What is the outlook for the field?

Let us, at this point, turn to a consideration of the first of these questions.

What are the Data? The population student has worked primarily, although not entirely, with data about human populations. The most commonly used data, what I shall call the "core" data, include: the number of persons; changes in the number of persons; components in the changes in the number of persons—births, deaths, in-migration and out-migration; family formation and its components—marriage, divorce, separation, widowhood; the composition and characteristics of the population.

The demographer's interest in fertility and mortality has led him to study biological and medical aspects of these phenomena, in addition to their social

* Reprinted from the *American Sociological Review*, 13 (August 1948), pp. 371–382, by permission of the author and the American Sociological Society. Paper read before the annual meeting of the American Sociological Society, New York City, December 28–30, 1947.

aspects. Interest in mortality, for example, has involved the study of related data, particularly morbidity and various phases of public health. Similarly, interest in fertility has included the study of some aspects of the biology of reproduction, of methods of contraception, and of the role of public health and other services in maternal and infant welfare.

The student of population has been concerned with the relation of population to its physical habitat and to its social environment, using both the terms physical and social in a broad way. These interests have involved the use of geographical and ecological data and data relating to resources both potential and exploited. They have also involved the use of cultural, institutional, economic, political, historical, psychological, and anthropological data.

Another field of interest for the population student is to be found in problems relating to the quality of population. This interest has led him to work with the data of genetics—and in recent years with the specialized data of human genetics as contrasted with genetics in general. It has also led him to deal with cultural and social differentials, with problems of social stratification and differential opportunity which has necessitated deep bites into the general field of sociology.

Finally, the population student has also been interested in population policy and action on a local, national and international level and in the effects of policy and its implementation on population phenomena. As scientists, the interest of demographers in policy and its consequences is, of course, an interest in these matters as data for reseach.

Merely to list the wide variety of all of the specific data used by the population student is beyond the scope of this paper, and would not be too profitable. I shall limit myself, therefore, to some brief reflections about problems relating to the sources, availability and quality of the data used at the "core," rather than on what are now the peripheral margins of population study. That is, I shall deal mainly with the data about human populations themselves, on a social-cultural rather than on the biological-medical or other natural science orientated level. (This is not to say that these "peripheral areas" are unimportant or less important than the "core" areas. Rather, it is to recognize that the interest of this audience is primarily in the social-cultural aspects of the problem.) Moreover, although I shall not exclude other regions of the world, I shall, for purposes of convenience, and focus, deal primarily with the situation in the United States.

In general, we are dependent for our "core" data on four basic sources of information: first, a population census, whether on a complete or sample basis; second, a vital records system; third, a registration system, whether permanent or temporary, to meet emergency requirements; and fourth, a flow of by-product statistics emanating from government or non-government administrative agencies. In this country and in the Western world in general, reasonably adequate data have been available from one or more of these sources from, roughly, the beginning of the 19th Century. In contrast, very limited or no basic data of these types are available for the preponderant majority of the world's population, even at this time.

Moreover, the data are by no means available in the quantity or quality desired even in the Western countries or in the United States. In fact, it may be said with reasonable accuracy that the basic sources of even "core" population data are still in an infant and developmental state. In the United States, for example, although we have had a decennial census from the founding of the Nation, there has been a considerable pressure for institution of a quinquennial census. Moreover, as a result of recent developments which have greatly increased the efficiency of sampling human populations, there is some prospect that we shall have annual, or even more frequent, general population data available through sampling surveys. Some very important types of population data are, indeed, now available through sampling for the Nation as a whole, including data on the labor force, which are made available monthly.

With respect to our vital records system, it must be remembered that it is little more than a decade since all states of the Union have qualified for admission to the birth and death registration system. It should also be recognized that we have not yet achieved a flow of national marriage or divorce statistics.

Although registration systems have provided important data for the population student for many decades in some Western countries, for example Sweden and Holland, only limited data have been available from this source in the United States. Such data as have become available from general population registrations have flowed entirely from temporary and emergency registrations of the population incident to mobilization for the past war or earlier conflicts, and have been highly restricted in character.

Finally, with the expansion of government functions necessitated by our complex industrial and urban life, there is becoming available in this country, as in the case of most Western nations, a body of data which will have increasing importance to the population student (particularly the data from the types of agencies which now comprise the Federal Security Administration, from the Bureau of Immigration and Naturalization, from the Internal Revenue Bureau, etc.).

The data which have been made available to the student of population from Census sources have become increasingly enriched in scope, detail, and cross-classification. Of particular importance has been the availability of data in a form which permits the correlation of fertility and mortality phenomena with social and economic characteristics of the population. Similarly, the data which have become available from the vital records system, in addition to embracing the entire Nation, have become more useful as greater attention in tabulation has been devoted to research interests. The tabulations made available by place of residence as well as place of occurrence, the adoption of an urban-rural classification system identical with that employed in the population census, and the greater detail in cross-classifications of births and deaths in relation to characteristics of the mother or the decedent are among the things which have made it possible to extend the frontiers of knowledge about these vital phenomena.

The statistics which have flowed from temporary registration systems such as those connected with the registrations for rationing, the registration of aliens, and the registration for selective service have been particularly important in providing current, even if limited, information for a period of great unsettlement and change. They should contribute materially to the analysis of the impact of the war on vital phenomena in the United States and in other nations, in which the data have been preserved.

The information available as by-products of government administration has perhaps been the least exploited of the data used by the population student. As larger proportions of the population are covered by social security provisions in this country, and to the extent that increasing government interventionism is necessitated by an increasingly complex and interdependent existence, these data may well assume a greater importance for population research purposes.

In respect to these four basic sources of "core" population data, a few brief evaluative observations seem in order.

In respect to population census, it is to be hoped that greater attention will be focused in the future to three basic needs of the population student as regards these data: first, improvement in the quality of the data; second, more frequent reporting; third, an increase in the cross-tabulations of data that have significance for research. In all these respects, the Bureau of the Census in this country has already made great strides forward. It is important, however, to support the Bureau in its efforts in these regards and to maintain close contact so as to assure the continued orientation of the Bureau to research needs. All three of these basic objectives, it should be noted, can be materially advanced through the utilization of the sampling techniques in the development of which the Census Bureau itself has pioneered, and to which it has contributed materially.

In the field of vital statistics the greatest need without question is the need for improving the completeness of birth and death registration. There is also need for greater detail in the cross-classification of birth and death tabulations which, in their present form, although valuable, obscure many important relationships. There is particularly need for the introduction of such items as duration of marriage, parity, characteristics of the father and indexes of social-economic and cultural level as basic controls in the tabulation of births. Similarly there is need for the introduction of various indexes of social-economic and cultural status and of occupation in the tabulation of deaths. Perhaps the most conspicuous need in this area, however, lies in the need for comprehensive coverage in marriage and divorce statistics. I am sure that it seems curious to more than population students that this Nation, which can afford so many things, cannot afford the expenditure required to have these basic data about family formation and disintegration. The achievement of these objectives can in considerable measure also be accelerated and made more efficient by the utilization of sampling techniques. The officials of the National Office of Vital Statistics of the U.S. Public Health Service are not unmindful of these needs, but they also will need support and encouragement if progress is to be made.

There are centers of pressure in this country for the creation of a registration system which would provide "linkage" of all basic vital records. Although valuable information could be obtained from such a system or from a comprehensive and continuing population register, it would hardly be good judgment for the population student to urge the creation of such a register merely to supply him with research data. Although this source of data will undoubtedly continue to be important in some countries and increase in importance in others, I do not think that it will be an important source of data in this country in the foreseeable future, short of a prolonged period of great tension, open internal disorder, or international conflict. I think it correct to say that a population register on a continuing basis is, at this time, regarded as incompatible with our political concepts of individual freedom and democracy.

It is difficult to point to any systematic set of needs in the field of administrative statistics. The data available from this source are necessarily by-products and as by-products, they are determined by administrative rather than research requirements. In general, however, it is clear that data flowing from administrative sources will become increasingly important to the population student, and that there is much to be gained by maintaining close contact with those agencies which can contribute materially to the population field.

For data in what I have referred to as "peripheral" fields of population study, the population student has been in a major way dependent on the products of research of scholars in other disciplines. Many important bodies of data have been developed in these areas of interest, as for example—in human geography, in human genetics and in public health. But for population research many deficiencies are to be found in the "peripheral" data available, and great gaps in even elementary information of this type exist for large portions of the world.

What Are the Methods? The methods of the population student are primarily quantitative in character, although they involve a variety of nonquantitative methods and will probably increasingly utilize experimental methods. Most of the research which has been conducted in the field of population has resulted in quantitative descriptive materials, in which relatively simple statistical methods such as percentage distributions, proportions, and rates have been utilized. Since fertility, mortality and other vital phenomena are greatly affected by the structure of a population, particularly by its age and sex composition, methodological developments have taken the direction of producing measurements which in a scientific sense permit control of these variant structural characteristics. Thus, to control the age and sex composition of a population so as to study, let us say the impact of economic or cultural factors on fertility and mortality, various methods of standardization have been devised to reveal differentials which crude rates tend to distort or to obscure.

In the computation of the various vital rates, the conventional measurements are in a sense substitute measurements for those actually desired. They are in the main compromise measurements—the best the character of the data permit. Thus, although true *a posteriori* probability statements are the desiderata in measuring fertility, mortality, marriage, divorce, and other vital phenomena, few of the rates that can be computed from the available data can actually be described as probability statements. Problems of under-registration and of under-enumeration, problems arising from the lack of current population information, and, usually, the complete absence of information about internal migration tend to make the numerators and denominators of vital statistics rates approximations to the actual measurements desired. In consequence, a considerable portion of the research energy of population students has been devoted to devising methods of "correcting," "adjusting," or "refining" the data so as to improve the quality and precision of the measurements used.

The lack of inter-censal and post-censal population figures has resulted in the development of methods of estimating populations which, although they vary widely in ingenuity, have in common potentially large and unmeasurable error. In consequence, it is possible to say that no adequate methods have yet appeared which permit inter-censal or post-censal population estimates with measurable accuracy, particularly for areas subject to migratory change, short of a complete or adequate sample census.

Perhaps the most interesting and most powerful of the methods developed by the population student are to be found in the series of measurements which reveal the "true" or "intrinsic" vital rates of a population, as contrasted with the actual rates at any given time of observation. The development of the concepts of gross and net reproduction, of the life table and its utilization as a stationary population, and the concept of the stable population must certainly be regarded as among the more ingenious examples of the quantification of complex phenomena by the social scientist.

Other important methodological developments lie in the "projection" of populations, which under stipulated assumptions, tell us what the numbers and composition of future populations would be. There is still considerable confusion, sometimes even among demographers, about the meaning and usefulness of such projections which are all too frequently confused with predictions. In the hands of the skillful student, however, the projections can be useful and have great significance, in providing knowledge about, and showing the policy implications of, population trends.

Another line of development, which has not been highly productive as yet, lies in the application of mathematics, as distinct from statistics, to population phenomena. Although some light has certainly been thrown on some types of phenomena through the use of rational mathematical methods, the most widely known of which is undoubtedly the logistic curve, the value of a pure mathematical approach to population phenomena has yet to be demonstrated.

Although they have much broader applicability, in any listing of the methods of population research, it would be a serious oversight not to mention sampling methods. Development of efficient procedures for sampling human populations has greatly extended the possibility of obtaining basic "core" population and vital statistics with precision and timeliness. Moreover these methods have greatly increased the feasibility of intensive investigations to get at psychological and cultural factors in population dynamics.

The field of population is on the whole in good shape as regards methodology. The methods available to the research student are, in fact, superior to the data with which he must work; and more than a small portion of the methods available have been devised to deal with inadequate data. (I should mention a remark that I heard Gunnar Myrdal make after he heard an impressive paper on population methodology, in which indirect methods for computing gross and net reproduction rates were described. He observed that he was very much impressed with the ingenuity of the methods which were undoubtedly useful in the United States. But he added that those methods were not needed in Sweden where adequate data made simpler methods possible to achieve the same results.)

The deficiencies in the methodology available to the population student are deficiencies which are not peculiar to the field of demography. The relatively recent attention devoted to psychological and social-psychological aspects of population dynamics has made it clear that the population student, like his colleagues in the other social sciences, is dependent on the development of better psychometric and other techniques designed to get at basic attitudes and motivation in human behavior. Similarly attempts to deal with problems of optimum population or, potentially more profitable, with the relationship of population to resources have pointed up the need for better measurements of the aggregate production and components of production of the various nations and areas of the world. In this field, the demographer will undoubtedly continue to be dependent on the developments in other disciplines such as econometrics. Similarly, in other areas in which the interests of the demographer merge with the interests of other disciplines the population student will, in the main, continue to remain dependent on other scholars for methodological advances.

What Are the Theories? I think it is not a gross inaccuracy to say that if it were possible to compute a ratio of theory to data, the field of population would stand very low in an ordering of the sciences with respect to this criterion. I am not sure how the optimum ratio in this regard would be defined, but the limits can be rather easily described and I think agreed upon. A field which contained only theory and no data would not be described as a scientific discipline; a field which contained only data and no theory would, similarly, not merit the appelation of science. The field of population is without question closer to the latter limit than to the former. Moreover, to the extent that theory does exist in the field, it is not too difficult to show that the theory has, on the whole, evolved independently of the data.

There are a number of ways of categorizing the population theories which can be found in the literature. Perhaps the most useful classification lies in the distinction between the "naturalistic" and "institutional" theories.

The classic example of the naturalistic theoretical approach is to be found, of course, in Malthus, although he was by no means the only or the first student to present a comprehensive and embracing theory of population in terms of fundamental natural laws. The classic example of the institutional approach to population theory is to be found in Marx, although here again, Marx was by no means the only or the first student to utilize a cultural or institutional framework in an effort to explain population phenomena. It is worth observing that in the case of both Malthus and Marx the development of population theory as such was, on the whole, incidental to other and more central objectives.

An interesting and more recent variant to the naturalistic approach is afforded by the attempts of some students to describe population phenomena in terms of mathematical "laws" with the implication that the ordering of population phenomena are functions of parameters which at least implicitly reflect fundamental laws of nature. (This interpretation of the mathematical approach to population phenomena is not to be confused with the utilization of mathematics or statistics for purposes of obtaining a more precise description of phenomena.)

The development of population theory has in the main been the work of economists, although the members of this discipline, on the whole, have paid little attention to the field of population for some years. It is difficult, indeed, to say just what the economist's theory with respect to population is at the present time. It seems, on the whole, to be an uncritical adaptation of the Malthusian doctrine at those points where population as an element in the economy cannot be completely disregarded. On the whole, the population problem in economic theory has for some decades been almost completely ignored, although recent developments in "Keynesian" economics point to a revival of interest in the field.

Moreover, the sociologists, who seem to have inherited the field of population by default, have as yet contributed nothing of consequence to the development of systematic and comprehensive theory in this field. The major contribution of the sociologist to population theory to date is an indirect one, and consists largely in placing emphasis on cultural and institutional factors as opposed to biological and genetic factors in dealing with the problem of quality in population. Another area of theoretical development, which I believe promises much, but has not as yet been integrated into population research, is the development of ecological theory.

Various specific theories or hypotheses in segmental areas of the field of population could be enumerated which have had their origin not only among demographers but, also, in the work of biologists, geneticists, mathematicians and others. These theories are in the main narrow in scope, discrete, and not integrated into any uniform framework for dealing with population, either in its structural or dynamic aspects.

There is a basic need, in my judgment, for the development of a framework of integrated theory in the field of population. This is not to say that time or energy should be wasted in looking for a comprehensive general law of population growth along the lines of earlier efforts. On the contrary, it is undoubtedly sounder scientific procedure to assume that there is no single general law to explain complex population phenomena. It will undoubtedly be much more productive to think in terms of variant matrices for alternative patterns of population dynamics. But the denial of the existence of an overall general law of population growth or the decision to assume that there is no such law for research purposes does not negate the need for theory in population research. There is still too much of a tendency among population students to produce discrete, descriptive studies with little or no attention to theoretical framework as a basis for their research orientation or for the formulation of their conclusions.

Perhaps it is just as well that up to this point, while the data have been accumulating, there have been few attempts to develop comprehensive population theory. It would seem, however, that we know enough, or we are on the verge of knowing enough about population phenomena so that the time has come to direct our energies to the development of new theory and to the better integration of theory and data.

What Do We Know? Despite the deficiencies and gaps in data, the absence of comprehensive and integrated theory, the relatively limited facilities for research and the small body of research students with a major interest in population, the population student has amassed a large and significant body of substantive information. Although we are still woefully ignorant about even the size, let alone the composition and dynamics, of most of the populations of the world, we do know a great deal about population numbers, change, components of change, trends and prospects of population in the Western world and in substantial portions of the remainder of the globe.

We have also learned a great deal about the relation of population to resources, about the effect of swings in the business cycle which characterizes our industrial order on short and long run population phenomena, about the effects of war on population. Conversely, we have learned something about the effects of population phenomena on our economy, on our social and political organization, and on international relations and conflict, although in these areas our knowledge is certainly limited and the surface has just begun to be scratched.

Within and among given populations, we have amassed a wealth of information on differential fertility and mortality, and somewhat less on migration. We have certainly reasonably adequately described the significant differentials which are to be found in vital phenomena among the various strata of a society, among the regions of a nation, and among the nations of the world. Similarly, we have traced the relation between divergent forms of social and economic organization, exemplified by urban and rural cultures and by industrial and agricultural economies, and various population phenomena. We have learned some limited things about human genetics.

We have learned much about the characteristics of major segments of the population on which for one reason or other, special attention has been focused. For example, we have discovered much, that was only recently unknown, about the labor force as an important segment of the total population, about its structure and its dynamics in relation to the total population of which it is a part. Similarly, we have learned much about the special characteristics of our "senior" citizens and of youth.

We have learned and demonstrated beyond any reasonable doubt the impotence and limitations of the Malthusian devil. In fact, we are coming to realize, albeit painfully and slowly, that in the complex industrial and urban civilization which we have created, new population devils are emerging of a type never anticipated by Malthus and if anything, more troublesome than that described by Malthus.

This is not the place even to list all of the types of things we know about population, but we have learned at least three types of things about population which, in my judgment, deserve singling out as having profound implications, not only from the standpoint of research interest, but also from the standpoint of their significance to society.

First, I refer to what we have learned about the intrinsic fertility, mortality and natural increase rates of the populations of the Western world. We know that the culture complex we call Western civilization has had a significant effect on the reproductive behavior of Western populations—that the net impact of the elements of our civilization on our fertility and mortality schedules has been so to depress reproductivity that, despite the great declines in mortality, our populations either now, or in the near future, face the prospect of falling short—far short of replacement. This discovery constitutes perhaps the most important single datum made available by the student of population to the world since the days of Malthus. It is, indeed, so startling a discovery that the fact has not only not yet penetrated the consciousness of the masses of peoples in the Western world and particularly in the United States, but I think it can be said with some justification, that its significance has hardly penetrated the consciousness of even population students themselves.

The second fundamental datum to which I refer, the full import of which

has similarly not yet been grasped by our society, is that which we euphe-
mistically refer to as differential fertility and differential mortality. In my
judgment, there are no comparable data in the entire substantive firmament
of the social sciences which tell us so much and so efficiently about the great
differentials in level of living and in opportunity, as do the short tables which
reveal the high inverse correlations between fertility and mortality and almost any measures you wish to choose of social or economic stratification.
Moreover, these data tell an eloquent story about the quality of our contemporary and prospective populations, the significance of which far transcends
the story of the eugenicists which, for easily understood reasons, has received
much more attention.

Third, and of the greatest significance from the standpoint of the international order, the population student, albeit crudely and with many gaps,
has traced the impact of what we call the industrial revolution on population
phenomena as we have experienced it in the Western world. It does not take
an unusually fertile imagination to see the implications of this story for those
areas of the globe which contain most of the world's present inhabitants, as
they increasingly also undergo similar or comparable economic and social
development.

I shall have more to say about this fundamental knowledge which has resulted from the labors of the population student as I discuss the relation of
population research to population policy and its implementation.

What Are the Important Frontiers of Research? The field of population,
more so than some other social science disciplines, is ripe for great advances
in research. The data which have been amassed to date, and the knowledge
we have gained from them, point to the avenues and frontiers of research in
almost dramatic fashion.

For example, we have reasonably fully described patterns of differential
fertility and mortality both within and among populations; we are able to describe present and intrinsic population rates; we are able to describe the impact of industrialization and urbanization on population; but we know relatively little about actual causal relationships, sequences of behavior, basic
attitudes, and human motivations that enter into the patterns we can describe
in relatively precise quantitative terms. One badly needed and important type
of research activity in this area is that which would explore specific problems
of the acceptability and utilization of contraception and other means of voluntary population control. Although this subject is but one of a number of possible social psychological studies, it has such special significance for contemporary and prospective problems relating to population that it seems to me to
be worthy of specific recognition here.

To my mind, one of the most important of the frontiers of research in
population is to be found in the relatively unexplored social psychological
and cultural factors as they are causally related to population phenomena,
particularly to fertility and to migration. New vistas of research opportunity

lie in these fields which few students to date have examined or explored. Research in this area is relatively difficult. It will take much more ingenuity, require improved and new methodologies and, for some time to come, will probably not result in the neat, quantitative formulations which, in the main, characterize other areas of population research. This is the frontier where population comes into contact with psychology, social-psychology, sociology, and anthropology. Research in this area will require laborious inter-disciplinary and cooperative endeavor; but it will be worth the effort.

Another important area for further research, of the type which has recently been pursued both here and abroad, lies in the introduction of further "controls" in the analysis of vital statistics rates. There is a need for supplementing the more conventional controls, namely age and sex structure and sometimes other characteristics, with additional controls closely associated with population phenomena, such as duration of marriage, parity, characteristics of the father, and indexes of social and economic status in studies of fertility; and similarly appropriate characteristics in studies of mortality, and migration. The utilization of such additional controls in the computation and analysis of vital statistics rates would not only throw additional light on the influence of these factors themselves, but, what is more important, would also make it possible to determine with greater precision the impact on population phenomena of "external" factors, namely cultural and other environmental factors.

The introduction of additional controls in the analysis of vital statistics would probably help, also, to clear an area of confusion, not only in the public mind but among demographers themselves. Even the professional student of population seems to have difficulty in distinguishing between cyclical and secular movements in population phenomena as even a cursory examination of the current literature reveals. The wide availability of rates in which the items proposed, among others, were controlled would, I am convinced, help to unscramble cyclical and secular movements and to dissipate at least some of the prevalent confusion.

An important area of research also lies in the more intensive analysis of the labor force in a demographic framework and in relation to general social and economic structure and process. The new data which have recently become available in this country about the labor force indicate that the population student has much to contribute to a better understanding of both the statics and the dynamics of the labor force, and to the exploration of areas which, in the main, have been overlooked by the economists, sociologists, and other social scientists.

Another difficult but promising field of research opportunity lies in more intensive and extended investigations of the relationship between population phenomena and social and economic structure and process. Only the surface of this problem has been scratched by the relatively fragmentary and crude studies of this type now available. A particularly important aspect of this problem, and one of the most promising from the standpoint of rewards for research, undoubtedly lies in the study of population phenomena on a regional, national and international level in relation to international social and economic structure and process.

Perhaps the most significant area of research which lies ahead, significant not only from the standpoint of providing knowledge for its own sake, but also in providing a firm foundation for critical policy decisions which must be made is research directed at providing an answer to the question: How can the areas of the world containing large and impoverished masses of people and constituting over half of the world's total population be subjected to the influences of industrialization and urbanization or comparable advances in agricultural technology without producing population consequences which would completely negate advances in productivity and potentially create serious international confusion or chaos?

This single question embraces many diverse considerations including present and potential relationships between the distribution of the world's population and the world's resources, the patterns of population change which have been experienced in the Western world under the impact of the Industrial Revolution, present and potential patterns of international power relationships, the balance of power among the diverse races of the world, and the general problem of maintaining international order and peace.

Some of the types of research proposed above would help to answer this question. But more frontal attacks are required, particularly on the central problem of whether it is possible for a pre-industrial or primitive culture to receive the benefits of "modern civilization" without producing the cycle of population change experienced by the Western world. More specifically, the question can be stated as to whether it is possible to accelerate the control of fertility so as to cut down the gap experienced in the Western world between decreasing mortality and the decline in the birth rate.

These are critically important questions because it seems clear that the repetition of the experience of the Western world among the great population masses in the East would not only constitute a serious threat to the standard of living of Eastern peoples, but may also conceivably, in light of the present distribution of world resources in relation to population, create literally terrific tensions and prospects of unparalleled international hostility and conflict.

In this area of research, I believe the population student has a great opportunity to make one of the most significant contributions that social science can make to the advancement of the standards of living of the peoples of the world, and to the maintenance of international order and peace. It is a type of contribution of peculiar significance at this stage in human history when the physical sciences, far ahead of the social sciences in their contribution, have made it possible for human beings literally to destroy their civilizations and themselves, unless sound knowledge is available as a basis for social action and great wisdom is exercised in the utilization of such knowledge.

Finally, to conclude this brief and by no means inclusive or exhaustive listing of even the important areas of population research, I should like to mention a field not unrelated to the broad area I have just outlined. I refer to the study of population policy and its implementation as an area which needs more intensive cultivation than it has yet received. Here, also, the research task is relatively difficult but the yield should be great. This consideration naturally leads to an examination of the next of the questions which I have raised, that is:

What is the Relation of the Field of Population to Policy and Its Implementation? Population policy and government action directed at the implementation of policy preceded population research and the development of a science of demography. Population policies and related legislative and administrative decrees can be found, beginning with the records of antiquity, throughout the history of man. Indeed, one is impressed as one reads the record with the repetitive nature of some population policies and actions through the ages, despite their obvious impotence from epoch to epoch. Population policy in the past, and with rare exceptions even in the present, has been, or is being, determined, in the main, independently of a body of knowledge about population phenomena.

In the more remote past, officials of government and other social engineers did not have a sound factual basis for policy determination and governmental action. In the more recent past, however, and at the present time, despite the lacunae in substantive information, there is much more knowledge available than our social engineers—our political leaders, our educators, our clergy, etc. —have either discovered or seen fit to use. But the field of population is not unique in this respect. This same pattern can be observed in the social sciences in general. We have a long way to go in acquiring all of the knowledge and wisdom which is needed as a sound basis for policy and action, but it is indisputable that we already know a great deal more than our society has the intelligence or mechanism to use.

The demographer, like other social scientists, should not, as a scientist, be concerned with the political process and with the solution of problems of the day except as they constitute data for research. The demographer, like other social scientists, however, has been so careful in his efforts to avoid identification with specific political positions or social movements that he has often completely ignored the consideration of such problems even for purposes of research. This, to my mind, is unfortunate because it has undoubtedly contributed to the hiatus between what is known and what is done.

A specific answer to the question of what is the relation between the science of demography and policy and its implementation is, with few exceptions, correctly stated as "very little." The point which I wish to make and emphasize about this relationship is that the population student is failing to perform what seems to me to be an important obligation and missing a great research opportunity in neglecting population policy and mechanisms of implementing policy, particularly in a democratic society, as an important area of research.

The obligations and opportunities of the demographer in this area of activity have become increasingly great with the development of post-war international organization. In the United Nations and the specialized international agencies, there are a number of places in which the demographer can make signal contributions in providing badly needed knowledge as a basis for international and national policy considerations. Special recognition of the international importance of population problems is afforded by the creation of a Population Commission by the Economic and Social Council and the provision for a Population Division in the Secretariat of the United Nations.

Although this may be beside the point for purposes of our present discussion, I am convinced that if competent and adequate knowledge including information about population policies and their efficacy were available, the products of the labors of population students could and would contribute a great deal more to social and human welfare than is now the case.

What Is the Outlook for the Field? You will note that I have deliberately avoided discussing the question of what is the field of population or demography. I see little point in engaging in polemics about the precise boundary lines of this or other specialized scholarly pursuits.

Suffice it to say that population as a field is characterized by the research participation of students of a number of disciplines, including economists, sociologists, medical men, public health specialists, biologists, geneticists, geographers, statisticians, actuaries, and even physicists. The data of population as a field, as has been indicated, are also drawn from a wide number of areas identifiable as separate scientific disciplines in both the natural and social sciences or as arts and professions.

The research interests of the student of population, thus, cut across the interests of the conventionally organized social and natural science disciplines; and the field of population as a field for research is a kind of melting pot for a variety of scientists, on the one hand, and engineers or practitioners on the other. As a focal area for the intermingling of diverse interests the field of population affords a relatively unique opportunity for the cross-fertilization of theory and methods and for the pursuit of inter-disciplinary researches.

History has amply demonstrated that it is on the frontiers of adjoining cultures that the greatest rates of cultural change and development have occurred. Similarly, it has been on the frontiers of the scientific disciplines that many of the great advances in knowledge and method have occurred.

A justifiable criticism of the social sciences in general may lie in their overspecialization, in their adherence to strict boundaries of substantive knowledge and methodology, and in their failure to achieve more effective ways and means of cooperative and complementary endeavor in common areas of interest. In my judgment, the greatest areas of advance in social science in the coming decades will be in those areas where the interests of the various disciplines in the social sciences merge and where inter-disciplinary teamwork characterizes research activity.

Population may be described as a social science research area of this type. The number of students in the various disciplines who have a major interest in the field of population is relatively small. But I think it would be agreed that demographers are a reasonably alert, enthusiastic and active group. To my mind the outlook for the field of population is in most respects an exceedingly favorable one. It is particularly a favorable outlook from the standpoint of opportunity for research, opportunity for opening new frontiers of knowledge and method, and opportunity for contributing badly needed information to guide our policy makers and social engineers. In a word, the outlook for the field of population is good because there is much work and important work to be done and there are competent students who seem willing to do it.

CHAPTER 2

THE ROLE OF THEORY IN POPULATION STUDIES

*I*n this chapter the term "theory" is used in a more specific sense than in Chapters 1 and 3. Theory is here understood to embrace both the construction and use of hypotheses and the transformation of hypotheses, together with what already is known, into models designed to represent reality in relatively simple and comprehensible terms. It is the function of theory to make data meaningful, to reveal what relationships obtain, to disclose what data are important, and to permit economical use of data. The selections included in this chapter describe the various levels at which inquiries may be carried on and indicate in what respects theory may assist the student of population in the conduct of his inquiries.

Every science has to do with some part of reality, with some part of the physical, the animate, or the social world. But few, if any, parts of reality may be studied effortlessly and with ease. Even when direct observation and perception are possible, that part of reality which the scientist is concerned to analyze may be shot through with complex and obscuring detail. When only indirect observation is available to the scientist, the obscuring effect of multiplicity of detail is likely to be intensified. The scientist is compelled, therefore, to do more than merely develop instruments wherewith to select out and observe phenomena and devise tools with which to measure these phenomena and subject them to quantitative analysis. He is compelled to develop or conceptualize abstract models of that part of reality which he is studying, models which are based in part upon what is known and in part upon hypotheses or conjectures.

A model, especially if it depicts a group of interacting individuals (e.g., a business firm, a gang of workers, a growing population), entails simplification of the complex world of social reality that is being represented; for it is designed, in M. Friedman's words, to explain "much by little." A model enables a scientist to determine what is important for his analytical purposes, to organize his data more effectively, and to discover whether additional data are required. If the model adequately represents reality, it reveals how important factors are interrelated, and it permits the scientist to predict what will happen under given conditions. Even if a model is inadequate, use of it may disclose the sources of its inadequacy, lead to its replacement by superior models, and eventually make for a better understanding of reality. Use of a model may also stimulate improvements in a scientist's instruments of observation and in his methods and tools of quantitative analysis.

The student of population is under compulsion, therefore, to make use of theory. He finds it necessary, for example, to hypothesize concerning presumably important demographic relationships, both when information is relatively plentiful and when it is scarce. In the former situation hypotheses may be used to discover order in the data; in the latter, hypotheses may be made also to bridge gaps in the data. The papers of Lorimer, Lotka, and Vance indicate some of the uses to which theory may be put, together with some of the difficulties that attend its use. Other papers included in this volume also illustrate how the student of population employs theory.

The models which the student of population uses may be variously divided. They may be divided into macrodemographic and microdemographic models, much as the models of the physicist are divided into macrophysical and microphysical models and the models of the economist are divided into macroeconomic and microeconomic models. A macrodemographic model has to do with an entire population; illustrative are logistic and other growth models, some of which are described in Chapter 3. A microdemographic model has to do with only a segment of a population, which is studied more or less in isolation from other segments; illustrative are some of the models which are used to study the reproductive behavior of subgroups in a population (see Chapter 8).

Population models may also be classified by the purposes they serve. Thus, models which are formal and mathematical in character (e.g., that of a stable population) are employed to show how characteristics of a population are interrelated and to reveal the manner in which one population depends on another (cp. Lotka's papers in this chapter and Chapter 3). Again, models designed to summarize growth processes may be used to represent the range of ways in which population factors and socio-economic factors are interrelated (see Chapter 3). Yet again, models may be contrived to give direction to specific research. These models, usually called empirical, are designed to enable the student to cope with some portion of the all too complex world of demographic reality. It is the immediate office of an empirical model to facilitate the discovery of functional (i.e., cause-effect) relationships in that part of the world of demographic reality under examination. It permits the population student to maximize the effectiveness with which he assembles and utilizes data. Empirical models may, when it is necessary, allow for interrelations of the sort disclosed by growth and other models.

Construction of an empirical model may pose a dilemma. Other things equal, a simple, easily used model is to be preferred. Yet such a model may prove incomplete, particularly when account must be taken of the fact that population changes have a variety of causes and that effects sometimes attributable to population changes may also have other causes. Under these circumstances a more complicated model may be required, especially if it is likely that otherwise significant factors and conditions will be disregarded and the model will prove inadequate. But such a model is less easy to use.

Inasmuch as various empirical theories may be consistent with given data, the theorist must choose from among the theories available that which is to be preferred. Choice is not always easy. Presumably the most satisfactory measure of a theory's validity is its capacity to predict what will happen as the result of a relevant event or change. The acceptability of a population theory may therefore be made to turn on its capacity to predict what will happen under given conditions.

IS THEORY FOR DEMOGRAPHERS?*

By Rupert B. Vance

Population studies hold high prestige in scientific circles. Each decade multitudes of facts, equivalent in cost to a completely equipped battleship, are gathered at public expense and poured into our waiting calculating machines. Among the social sciences demography has developed some of the most advanced techniques. Our analyses are of the greatest practical use and are eagerly awaited by municipalities, planning boards, and administrators. Empirically and technically, population has gone a long way. And this is no icy perfection. Population has its human interest angle and its materials are much sought after by publicists.

Demography, on the whole, is doing very well these days. We have facts, we have the techniques and we are neatly polishing up our concepts. But there is one area where demography is getting rather poverty-stricken and frayed at the edges. In the realm of high theory we have been living off our capital and borrowing from our associates. It seems some time since we have made any investment of our own in basic theory. As demography comes of age it comes to a point of necessity—the necessity of a closer working relationship between its research operations and basic theory. In theory demography remains relatively unstructured. It lacks, shall we say, a binder for its diverse findings. Moreover some findings which have passed for population research among the laity barely reach the level of description. The actual work, it is apparent, was done by the Census Bureau. It is with this in mind that a leading sociologist once told me that the Decennial Census was the worst thing which had happened to sociology in this country. (And, by the way, if the Civil Service becomes set in the policy of certifying only statisticians to the Census Bureau we may become even less devoted to theory.) There is such a thing as an excess diet of raw data. Undigested, it is very bad for the development of the theoretical muscles. I am reminded of a boner from a student who was oversold on objectivity. Trying to answer the question: Is sociology scientific? he wrote:

The facts gathered are of value and even though they may not prove a point, it must be remembered that the object is to gather the material and not to prove the point.

* Reprinted from *Social Forces*, 31 (October 1952), pp. 9–13, by permission of the author and publisher. (Copyright 1952 by The Williams & Wilkins Company.) Presidential address read before the annual meeting of the Population Association of America, at Princeton, New Jersey, April 25, 1952.

I. There exist today striking differences between demography as a field of knowledge and those disciplines with which it is most closely related. These differences are so great that, for good or ill, they are likely to color the future development of our specialty. The development of theoretical systems at a high level of integration is now apparent in fields which touch on population. In economics, in sociology, in social psychology, in the contribution which psychoanalysis and psychiatry are making to the study of human behavior one has the choice of complex thought systems, sophisticated, rationally articulated, and of the highest importance in the tactics and strategy of science. As the validity of these theories is increasingly subjected to test, hypothesis by hypothesis, assumption by assumption, this body of knowledge assumes increasing importance.

In law there is the *Corpus Juris*—the body of the law. In population the nearest we have to a body of theory is several population texts written for the undergraduate student—admittedly not a high level at which to perform the operations of synthesis and integration demanded for theory. In two texts today I find the implication that it is not the task of the demographer to develop high level theory.

Certainly population is not overrun with the rash of theorists that Colin Clark found when he surveyed the field of economics. Clark wrote that he left the academic world in Britain with dismay at his colleagues' continued preference for the theoretical approach. "There is room," he wrote, "for only two or three economic theorists in each generation, no more. Only men of transcendental powers of reasoning can be candidates for these positions. The rest of us should be economic scientists, content steadily to lay stone on stone in building the structure of ordered knowledge. Instead it seems to be the ambition of nearly every teacher of economics to put his name to a new formulation of economic theory. The result is a vast output of literature of which it is safe to say, scarcely one syllable will be read in fifty years' time."

Among high level theorists we have Malthus to our fathers. He dates from the early Nineteenth Century and falls among the classical English economists for whom Lord Keynes rendered a superb verdict in one sentence: "The characteristics of the special case assumed by the classical theory happen not to be those of the economic society in which we actually live with the result that its teaching is misleading and disastrous if we attempt to apply it to the facts of experience." Undoubtedly in the beginning Malthus intended to analyze the poverty of nations after the fashion of Adam Smith's *Wealth of Nations*. Admittedly the theory now falls far short of explaining poverty in the western world for which it was first written in 1800.

We realize that systematic theory is on the wane. High-level theorists admittedly are lone wolves. In the strategy of science we need one generalissimo of basic theory each generation, whether he is forthcoming or not. Certainly these great theories have not proved cumulative; they are competing and conflicting. After systematic theory what next? The consensus of the future to which we demographers look forward will more likely in Robert Merton's phrase come out of theories of the middle range—"theories intermediate to the minor working hypotheses evolved in abundance during the day by day routines of research, and the all-inclusive speculations comprising a master conceptual scheme from which it is hoped to derive a very large number of empirically observed uniformities of social behavior." It is no secret to tell you that hopes exist that, when all the hypotheses of the Indianapolis Study are finally fused, population will have a healthy young theory of the middle range.

We can not let this occasion pass without some attention to the development of concepts in social demography. Admittedly fertility, mortality, and migration are not concepts in any true sense; they are simply topics we investigate. Further evidence of theoretical weakness in our field is demography's failure, in President Conant's phrase, to use the tactics and strategy adequate to develop new and significant concepts. When we realize, for example, the revolutionary impact of the concept of culture on social science we are tempted to ask to what recent concepts of value can we point? Frankly we have neglected to do the rigorous work required to either establish or disprove some of our seminal ideas. I can think of two concepts now suspended halfway between heaven and earth, the concept of optimum population and the theory of intervening opportunities in migration. Both of these examples remind us that since the establishment of any hypothesis is extremely difficult, the scientist's first duty is to so frame his hypothesis that it is also capable of disproof. Only in this way can we rid the field, piece by piece, of doubtful lumber which otherwise will remain to clutter it up forever. Neither of these valuable hypotheses, I submit, is capable of disproof as now framed. Intervening opportunities can hardly be defined except as potentially different for each migrant, and no equation with that many unknowns can be solved. Similarly in optimum population many students accept the economic optimum as only one of many optima. This will leave the concept forever stillborn. And in the economic optimum one factor, the standard of living, has approximately all the variables of intervening opportunities. Since it is not capable of disproof, neither can it be proved.

Systematic theory, middle range, concepts and hypotheses, we will not build demography until we learn, like the physical scientists, to repeat and repeat. Our smaller studies, those below the middle range, must be focused more and more on specific hypotheses already set up and embodied in these systematic formulations. Like science everywhere, demographic analysis must be made cumulative. Once we get a good hypothesis let us repeat and repeat until we determine whether it stands or falls.

In many of our allied fields alternative theories compete for the support of scientists and we are allowed the hope that research by research these theories of the middle range will either approach the closure characteristic of a complete thought system or else be found invalid and discarded. Aye, there is the rub. When a thought system is invalidated and discarded, a dozen reputations may perish with it. Who wants to take that risk?

II. If there is room in demography for the timid souls, is there also room for the bold and audacious? In science as in poker, we realize we can play it one of two ways. We can play it close to the vest, that is, maximize description and minimize synthesis or we can play it for maximum gains of human knowledge. In other words, as Roger Nett[1] says, the working scientist can be either a tight system builder or a loose system builder. A tight system has high validity and low generality. A line which twists and turns to touch a hundred points in a distribution is worth no more than the hundred points. A line which touches ten points and comes within hailing distance of 90 is usually worth more than the hundred points; it may give the scientist a curve of distribution or an equation of probability for his colleagues to test in a sequence of 100 analyses. "There exists a known tendency for all thought systems to be vulnerable." Accordingly the closer one sticks to his data, the less vulnerable are his generalizations and ofttimes the less important. A loose thought system sacrifices accuracy for the sake of generalization.

In science when one plays for double or nothing, he runs the risk of evolving a system of high generalizations and low validity. Obviously this represents high vulnerability and we are all cautious enough to dread the results. But we should remember there are two forms of maximum error: The first is a system that misses contact with the known facts at every point of observation. The second is no system at all. This is maximum error, for it equates with total ignorance. As a matter of fact, I am willing to make the claim that he who develops a theory capable of being proved invalid makes a contribution. In statistics the disproof of any hypothesis is accepted as a way station on the road to knowledge. Demographers should become brave enough to so state their hypotheses that they are capable of disproof.

Thus far I have been talking about the demographer as a personality, willing or unwilling to take the risks of his profession. As a collectivity, demography should set about organizing its strategy to support shock troops who take calculated risks for theory. In a manuscript which I have been permitted to read in advance of publication, J. J. Spengler demonstrates the extent to which the study of population remains relatively unstructured as to theory and uncircumscribed as to scope. "A variety of scientists," he writes, "have contributed to the development of what currently passes for population theory and their separate contributions have not yet been transfused into an integrated whole."

There is great need for the development of integrated theory of a high order to serve as a "binder" for demography's diverse and particularized findings. Such theory should meet three criteria, says Professor Spengler: (1) It must be dynamic rather than static, (2) it must take account of demographic interrelations as between countries and groups within nations, and (3) it requires a multi-science approach.

I am happy to say I believe the framework for one such theory is now emerging. In concise statement, the transition from high-level deaths and births to the new equilibrium at a low level of vital rates furnishes the population dynamics of the last 300 years in the Western world. The line of succession runs from Dr. Walter Willcox whose studies of world population growth opened up this whole field to Dr. Frank Notestein who has done so much to clinch the analysis. This Demographic Revolution unfolds and diffuses in a manner reminiscent of the Industrial Revolution. Different countries reach different stages of this transition in terms of (1) a time sequence in the West and (2) in terms of culture contacts and time stages as regards non-Western countries. Population status, age, and even sex composition, can then be viewed as stages in this long sequence. Our own low crude death rates and low proportions of natural dependents can be seen as a transitional stage in age distribution which may later level off.

The swarming of Europe is seen as due to the demographic gap which emerged as fertility remained high for 100 years and more after deaths took a sharp decline. Differential fertility emerged in the initial stage of the great decline in birth rates. Outside the West no countries now appear to have the demographic slack which new continents and untapped industrial markets once offered Europe. Demographic movements in succeeding countries, however, are to be judged by economic stages and cultural diffusion as well as the resistance to change within each culture. Such an over-all view can give meaning to the many descriptive population studies now made country by country. If this transition proceeds in orderly sequence it will be the function of demographic studies to classify populations by stage and sequence. But since populations and countries vary, demographers have a choice. They can either explain these variations in the scheme or demolish the basic theory by a critical analysis of succeeding population movements.

It is agreed, I take it, that the function of theory is not to give answers to all the questions which may arise; rather it is to see that in the unfolding of science the "right" questions get asked in the "right" context. Such theories of the middle range in Merton's phrase also serve to set known facts in meaningful context. Demographic fluctuations anywhere can then be tested as short-run movements against the background of this long-run demographic transition. Beginning and ending phases of this great transition, however, will remain unclear: the first because our beginnings run back to inadequate data, the second because closing phases will always remain in the future. An incidental contribution of this scheme is to place the work of Malthus in the perspective of history.

That demography must attend more sharply to its basic theory is indicated in this very field of dynamics. What are long-run and what are short-run phenomena in demography? What is trend and what is a fluctuation? And how long can a fluctuation last before it becomes a trend? Are there reversals in trends?

In fertility analysis it is this problem which caught demographers unprepared. Texts in the hands of our students continued to proclaim decline while the figures showed an amazing upsurge. It is this phenomenon which led Dr. Frank Notestein to the wry comment that to some, demographers now appear as "double distilled false prophets"—prophets who, proven wrong, persist in staying wrong.

Demography can put controversy in its place only as it develops basic theory. Other disciplines have faced this problem and come up with answers based on theoretical models complex enough to encompass alternatives. Techniques in this field can still be used to test broadly stated theoretical systems. Empirical operations without basic theory, no matter how carefully safeguarded, are now proved dangerous. Finally, it is my feeling that these controversies hasten the development of systematic theory.

Such theory—now in process of being filled in—satisfies two of Professor Spengler's requirements: (1) it is dynamic and (2) it takes account of interrelations between countries and classes. It raises, however, the question of a multi-science approach to theory. Interesting to note, the theory of the demographic transition has been the contribution of population specialists developed largely from the consideration of historic changes in the field of vital rates. It did not come out of the theoretical matrix of either biology, sociology or economics. In certain ways the multi-science orientation of demography has operated to delay the development of population theory. Eclecticism is not conducive to the development of unified theory. Biological explanations of changing vital rates have proved immature and completely inadequate; sociologists have not yet developed an adequate theory of social change; economists have often felt obliged to limit their work to direct economic causation. With a theoretical scheme of its own, comparable to its techniques, population study has been able to attain a certain unity of attack.

But as we heard Professor W. F. Ogburn argue so eloquently before the Population Association last year, population study must make its further advances by establishing interrelations and correlations as yet unknown. The dynamics of population need to be integrated with some basic theory of social change. There is no escaping the complexity of the problem of interrelation which demography faces. Population study must seek in the dynamics of culture, the economy, and changing society itself the primary conditions of its own dynamics. And then population change itself operates as a starter. As new demographic conditions emerge—mature age composition, new family size, increasing and then decreasing class differentials, lowered rates of natural dependents—social scientists have the task of seeing how such factors initiate change in the society and in the economy. Truly the work of analysis and theory has just begun if we accept the task of tracing major change through nations and classes from Occident to Orient.

But I forget myself. This is but one theory of many, and I am not attempting here to write the prescription for our theory. I do believe, however, that the best spring tonic demographers can take is a good stiff dosage of theory, adequately compounded. There is a level of complexity to which all our scientific disciplines must aspire or resign their task—namely the creation of valid and significant theory. There is, I take it, work for all. Let us then be about our business.

REFERENCES

1. See Roger Nett, "System Building in Sociology—A Methodological Analysis," in *Social Forces,* 31 (October 1952), pp. 25–30.

POPULATION ANALYSIS*

By Alfred J. Lotka

The various species of living organisms that inhabit our globe are mutually interdependent, so that, strictly speaking, it would be impossible to make a well-rounded study of any one species without taking into account a number of other species that influence it in one way or another.

However, the internal factors (birth rate, death rate, rate of natural increase, etc., etc.) of a population of living beings are connected by a variety of inter-relations which permit, and which in fact call for separate study, without necessitating at each step explicit reference to the influence of the other species inhabiting the same territory.

The study of a population thus singled out for separate consideration constitutes a separate body of research, to the brief consideration of certain examples of which we shall here turn our attention, with special regard to the human population.

Now it is to be noted that the demographic and sociological study of the human species covers a number of relations which, for other living species, either do not exist at all, or play a subordinate role. Thus, for instance, certain statistical and sociological problems peculiar to the human species arise out of the essentially monogamous laws of civilized peoples, and out of the retarded adolescence of the human individual. Thus statistics of the marital state, of sterility and fecundity in marriage, of the family, of widowhood, orphanhood, etc., and the problems which arise from such statistics, exist practically only for our species, although fundamentally they are a particular aspect of the general phenomenon of biological reproduction. Limited to one species as are the applications of certain of these "family" problems, the central position which the human race occupies for us in the scheme of nature lends to these applications prime importance. On the present occasion, if only on account of limitation of time, our discussion will be restricted practically entirely to Population Analysis as applied to the human species.

Population studies can be carried on to some extent on a purely *empirical* basis, as when we investigate, by merely collecting and collating data, the relation (if any) between death rate and population density. Our concern here will not be with such empirical relations, that is relations the physical

* Abstract of a paper presented at a Research Conference on Economics and Statistics held by the Cowles Commission for Research in Economics, July 6 to August 8, 1936. The entire paper, which has not been published, contained a number of examples of results in the field of population analysis. Reprinted from *Colorado College Publication*, General Series No. 208, Study Series No. 21 (1936), pp. 83–85, by permission of the Cowles Commission and Colorado College.

causes or logical reasons for which are unknown to us. We shall here be concerned, not with empirical, but with *necessary* relations between the characteristics of a population. It is this body of *necessary* relations to which the term *Population Analysis* is here to be applied.

It might seem at first sight as if the study of necessary relations must be a sterile occupation, inasmuch as it can never reveal to us any fact of which the truth is not already contained in the premises. To this we shall reply that a truth which for our mind remains "implied" without being recognized is without practical value; and further, that our intellect is more exacting: It asks not merely to be taught a body of facts, but to be shown their inter-relation. And it is precisely this inter-relation that constitutes the subject of study in *Population Analysis,* that is in the investigation of general demography by the deductive method.

As for those who see the justification of science solely in its practical applications, no apology to them is called for on behalf of the study of Population Analysis along deductive lines. For this study enables us, on occasion, to obtain indirectly information for which the direct observational data have not been, or for one reason or another can not be, obtained. And it is hardly necessary to recall that a whole industry of prime importance—life insurance —bases its computations and its practice on relations closely akin to, if not actually borrowed from Population Analysis.

THE DIFFERENTIATION OF LOGICAL LEVELS IN SOCIAL INQUIRY *

By Frank Lorimer

In dealing with population problems and related subjects we necessarily operate on different logical levels. Discussions are commonly confused by failure to distinguish these levels, to appreciate the nature and limitations of each, and to recognize the proper relation of each to others. It is possible to differentiate four distinct levels involving scientific inquiry, beyond the more primitive modes of discourse that still run through a large part of our daily lives. These may be defined as follows:

1. *Science.* Inferences that are rigidly controlled by systems of implication, such as mathematics, and by precise observations.

2. *Technical judgments.* Scientifically informed but nevertheless subjective, intuitive judgments in a field in which a scientist has special competence.

3. *General theories.* Theories that are partially grounded on scientific inferences but that are predominantly intuitive.

4. *Policy designs.* Formulations of possible procedures presented as hypotheses for action.

Science is the product of the fertile union of hypotheses and observations. Hypotheses are the active element in this union. They direct inquiry to significant observations and provide the framework by which observations can be controlled and made precise. Mathematics and other formal systems of implication also provide the necessary framework for the development of empirical inferences, grounded on observation, in systematic scientific theory. The development of scientific theory, in turn, may reveal a need for new hypothetical systems. Hypotheses and observations are thus complementary and dynamic in their inter-action; together they provide that dual control which gives scientific theory its unique value.

A critical test of scientific theory is that any two workers using the same logical apparatus in relation to the same observations must reach identical conclusions. Scientific inferences are, therefore, "objective," in the sense that they are independent of the personal biases that necessarily infect all intuitive judgments. Much confusion can be avoided if we limit the term "science" to such rigidly controlled and therefore strictly objective theory.

Demography as a science has advanced rapidly during the last quarter century. Both of its essential ingredients have been extended and refined.

* Reprinted from the *American Sociological Review*, 12 (October 1947), pp. 507–514, by permission of the author and the American Sociological Society. Presidential address, Population Association of America, Princeton, N.J., May 17, 1947.

There has been a great increase in the volume of data on population and, equally or more important, such data have been improved in precision and in relevance to significant hypotheses. Anyone who has been using American census and vital statistics and related information by public and private agencies in this and many other countries is well aware of this progress.

The demographer today is also equipped with a growing body of appropriate mathematical and logical formulations for the guidance and interpretation of research. Much of this theory has been formed around a central core, the theory of a "stable population," which defines the hypothetical relations between age-specific fertility, age-specific mortality, age and sex composition, and rates of population change. There is documentary evidence that the germ of this system was at work in Lotka's mind at least forty years ago, but it was first presented effectively to population students in 1925. This theory has stimulated many parallel and corollary developments. It is still undergoing extension and modification, as evidenced by Whelpton's recent paper in the *Journal of the American Statistical Association*. It has been a creative force in the development of scientific population theory.[1]

Any interpretation of a concrete situation involves an element of intuitive judgment—at least a judgment that the concrete situation conforms to the conditions specified in an appropriate theory. The most useful interpretation of a social phenomenon, such as population change in a particular situation, often involves a combination of scientific inferences with judgments that can not be rigorously controlled by any logical apparatus. Judgments of this sort which are *in part* intuitive but are nevertheless controlled in large part by scientific inferences constitute a second logical level, here called *technical judgments*.

Technical judgments, when recognized as a distinct logical process, have usually been described as "engineering" or by some other term which implies immediate application to practical ends. But the distinction is equally pertinent in purely theoretical inquiries. Any judgment about the probable future course of the American population, or the economic effects of a declining population, or the genetic significance of differential reproduction, if based in high degree and so far as possible on rigid scientific inferences, would be a *technical judgement* according to this definition. For reasons that I shall now discuss, such judgments must, I believe, form a large part of significant population theory—and more so in the immediate future than in the past.

The empirical value of any scientific theory depends in part on the degree to which relevant *conditions* are explicitly and precisely taken into account in its formulation. For example, the superiority of a system of sex- and age-specific hypotheses in population projection over the logistic or any other global hypothesis is that a system of specific hypotheses includes a formulation of one important set of conditions involved in natural increase. The measurement of fertility in different empirical situations can also be made more precise, as has been shown by Glass and by Whelpton, by taking into account duration of marriage and parity of mother (or birth order), or age and parity and fecundity and frequency of marriage. Sex, age and parity may be regarded as intrinsic factors in the abstract formulation of the dynamics of population; but variation in the frequency of marriage is an extrinsic institutional factor which is here explicitly taken into account. Formulations of natural increase have been or can be made specific in relation to other conditions, such as contraceptive practice, *mores* relating to sex, industrial organization, opportunity for the employment of women outside the home, and general level of employment.

These relevant conditions influencing natural increase are, for the most part, institutional structures, which vary in different societies and at different times. A social institution is in part the product of particular historical conditions and has unique features. In so far as a social situation is unique it can not be precisely described in any scientific system. One can not formulate a rigidly scientific statement of the Republican Party or the structure of the American economy. Yet all social processes exist and operate only within particular sets of institutional structures. One can reduce the risk involved in the empirical application of scientific inferences about human relations by increasing specificity in the statement of conditions; but one can never completely eliminate this risk because it is impossible to specify all the relevant conditions affecting any set of social relations.

It is important to recognize that different situations vary enormously as regards the risk involved in basing empirical judgments on any given scientific theory. So long as the scientific inferences of the demographer, or any other social scientist, are applied within a fairly constant institutional framework, these empirical interpretations may have a high degree of validity, even though many of the relevant conditions are not defined. The empirical value of any scientific formulation of social processes varies *directly* with the specificity of conditions taken into account; it varies *inversely* with the degree to which other relevant conditions are diverse in different situations, or changing within the same situation.

Social scientists who deal with some processes that may superficially appear to be more elusive, such as attitudes or status relations, may have less difficulty in defining the conditions within which their scientific inferences have empirical validity than the scientist who deals with such an aggregate phenomenon as population change. The abstract character of population analysis is deceptive. Population changes, as such, can be precisely measured. Census enumerators reported that there were 486,869 persons in Washington, D.C., on April 1, 1930, and 663,091 persons on the same day in 1940. We know that these figures are not absolutely exact; but their correction would not greatly simplify the problems of interpretation. The point I wish to emphasize is that the precise increase (36.195 per cent) was determined by the interaction of the most complicated and rapidly shifting institutional forces in American society. The relative effect of even the most important institutional factors in this situation can only be appraised in technical judgments involving a large element of subjective intuition. Similarly an interpretation of population trends in the Soviet Union during the last intercensus period that left out of account the operation of the five-year plans, the collectivization of agriculture, the construction of the Turkestan-Siberian railway, the closing of the abortion clinics, and many other institutional changes could have little empirical value.

Most of the scientific inferences of contemporary demographers have been formulated within one broad, stable institutional frame-work—the orderly development of western society, characterized in its economic life by equilibrium among competitive enterprises and in its family life by the gradual diffusion of the pattern of consciously controlled fertility. All this was part of an expanding world economy centered at first in Western Europe and then in Western Europe, the British Dominions, the United States and Japan. Within this institutional framework the mere mathematical formulation of population trends had much empirical value—even without a very complete statement of conditions, because the major controlling conditions themselves were developing in orderly sequence. The profound changes now taking place in European society and the radically different institutional structure of Asiatic society, which is also undergoing revolutionary changes, make any reliable interpretation of world population movements exceedingly complicated.

This is notably the case with respect to fertility. So long as the movement of fertility was largely a function of the diffusion of the pattern of conscious control, a mathematical projection of this movement had predictive value for the future. Such a projection was, at least in large part, really a projection of the diffusion of a culture pattern, although it was formulated in terms of birth frequencies. In so far as this is the case, such a projection ceases to have any empirical value as the control of conception in any population approaches completion. Unfortunately the level of fertility in a society where all families are planned may vary widely in different institutional situations, and must be expected to rise and fall in relation to complex and changing patterns of economic organization, levels of employment, and public policies. Any projection of declining fertility beyond the point at which conscious control becomes generally effective gives results that have exactly the same logical significance as does a projection of fertility below the zero level. The results have immediate validity only in that realm of pure possibility where pink elephants and negative birth rates have logical status. They may, however, have positive theoretical value. A comparison of observed events with such projections provides a clue to the force of new conditions not present in the original situation. Similarly, the effect of various technical judgments or hypotheses about expected population trends can be measured against such a mathematical projection as a theoretical norm.

The demographer is often confronted with a real dilemma in interpreting concrete situations. He may be forced to choose between the mathematical projection of scientific inferences that have doubtful relevance to the actual situation under investigation and the formulation of technical judgments which he believes have greater empirical validity but which are subject to the errors that infect even the most informed intuition. Such technical judgments may take the form of arbitrary adjustments of rigidly scientific inferences. Sometimes when this is done, the hand is the hand of mathematics, but the controlling voice is the voice of intuition; the relationship between these elements may, however, be truly functional. In other cases, a frankly stated technical judgment, or a statement of alternative possibilities with some appraisal of their relative probability, may provide the most useful final formulation—supplemented by an exposition of relevant data, scientific inferences, and hypothetical calculations.

The demographer's lot in some ways is not a happy one. He is acquiring a beautiful set of measuring instruments just as the whole institutional framework in which his material is set is shifting so rapidly that his measurements may have less value in controlling empirical judgments today than results formerly produced with cruder tools. The problems with which he deals are becoming complicated at an even more rapid rate than his scientific apparatus is being developed. This is not to say that his results today would be better if his scientific apparatus were simpler. Quite the contrary, he must use the most precise methods possible in deriving scientific inferences, with careful attention to their logical force and limitations. He must devote a large part of his energy to devising new techniques for the precise formulation of various factors that he could previously ignore with impunity. At the same time, in so far as he seeks to produce results that have empirical value with respect to broad population movements and their social implications, he must, I believe, cultivate greater humility, and frankly recognize that his best services to the community will frequently be the careful formation of technical judgments— at the logical level of the practicing physician. He will, in doing so, properly insist—as does the physician—that such judgments within a field of professional competence, though subject to errors that cannot be rigidly defined, merit much greater confidence than the uninformed judgments of a layman.

The analysis of economic, social and political problems involving demographic factors requires complex judgments in various fields that must be in large part intuitive—*i.e.* operations on the *third* logical level: *general theories*.

Institutional structures in so far as they are unique lie outside the field of the precise social sciences; but they are the most critical elements in modern society. The institutions of industrial nations have been rapidly expanding in *depth* over a long period. The interaction between economic and political and social institutions has become increasingly complex, and these changing complex structures exercise an increasingly powerful influence in the daily life of individuals. Meanwhile social institutions have been expanding *horizontally* in space until, quite suddenly, all nations have become involved in a dynamic institutional network that is charged with high tensions.[2]

Public administrators and diplomats, who are presumed to be most expert in the management of institutional relations, are assumed to function in a democracy as the servants of the people, responsible for implementing the objectives which in theory the citizens of the nation spontaneously evolve. Moreover such officials cannot freely and publicly discuss all the implications of alternative policies. Therefore, the most important leaders in the shaping of public opinion today are probably the radio commentators and newspaper columnists, feature writers and editors. They are citizens who have recognized ability to formulate broad interpretations of public affairs and to present such theories in a style that is appreciated, as edifying or entertaining, or both. They are particularly facile participants in the great forum of which we are all members.

It is commonly said that the scientist as citizen is entitled to participate in the forum of public opinion but that such participation has no relation to his proper function as a scientist (or as a scholar responsible for formulating technical judgments). One of the implications of this idea is absolutely sound. Any formulation of general theory on complex issues in which intuitive judgments are predominant must be sharply distinguished from technical judgments. Any professional worker who presents general theories as science, or even as technical judgments, prostitutes his profession and breeds confusion. One can not too strongly insist on the maintenance of a sharp distinction between these different logical levels.

Another implication of the popular idea which I have just mentioned is, I think, quite fallacious. It is sometimes implied that the process of formulating such general theories on the part of a scientist has no *intrinsic* relation to his work as a scientist. It is said that the same man may "happen" to make useful technical judgments and also to contribute useful general theory. The scientist-citizen according to this interpretation is a schizophrenic personality who carries on two quite uncorrelated types of intellectual activity within the same skin.

I do not maintain that the general theories advanced by social scientists are superior to those advanced by physicists, or physicians, or priests, or business executives, or union leaders, or professional diplomats. I do, however, maintain (1) that theories on a common problem advanced by members of these different professions will tend to have some intrinsic relation to their professional training, their particular fields of experience, and their special interests, and (2) that contributions by social scientists, as well as by persons in other fields, to the formation of public opinion on institutional issues may be a valuable *part* of the total democratic process. The training of any scientist, who is a real scientist as demonstrated by his work on technical problems, will enhance the objectivity of his approach to controversial problems at times when many people may be somewhat hysterical. As regards the relevance of the subjects studied by social scientists to most public issues, the case is perhaps somewhat more dubious. But where one's studies have forced him to deal with the operation of social institutions in a rather broad field, as in the case of those concerned with general population theory, their studies should have some relevance to many major problems. Finally as regards interests, it may be assumed that a scientist—apart from the common interests of every citizen—is likely to be chiefly interested in his own professional advancement and his status among his colleagues; but he is also likely to have acquired some genuine interest in the formulation of coherent theories, in the reconciliation of conflicts, and in the progress of mankind. These interests are at least as proper as the interests of most other citizens. It follows that the demographer, or any other scientist, has a positive responsibility to participate in the formation of general theory in matters of social importance, on which no one is qualified to speak with scientific authority. He must, however, always make clear to himself and to his listeners or readers that such opinions are not science or even technical judgments but merely personal theory, drawn from a particular and partial background of experience.[3]

There is much confusion concerning the relation of values to science and theory. Values combine organic and social preferences with purely intellectual elements. Oranges and melons acquire a positive value because they have pleasant taste and color and have made us feel good after we ate them. They have an established status in our folkways and personal behavior. Recently, scientific inferences in the field of nutrition have caused us spontaneously to reorganize our values with respect to these foods and, in particular, to intensify our positive evaluation of oranges. We don't ordinarily think about this when we reach for oranges; the new valuation now functions more or less as an end in itself. It is, of course, always possible to treat any value as a means to some more final end, and to subordinate this to some still more final end, *et cetera*. We can say that we eat, in order to be strong, in order to earn money, in order to go to Miami Beach, in order to know God and enjoy Him forever. But actually a pure final value is an abstract fiction—so far as most values by which we live from day to day are concerned. These functional values by which we live from day to day are shot through with traditional beliefs, scientific inferences and general theories. The person who believes in heaven, in the Marxist interpretation of history, or in the theory of relativity, will have a different value frame than a person who does not have the same belief.

The scientist may, therefore, change the value frame of society merely by developing scientific inferences, technical judgments, and general theories. Even when he presents such ideas with the intention of influencing the value judgments of other people, he does not function on any different logical level than in formulating and presenting similar ideas as pure theory for theory's sake—provided that he does not use emotionally loaded symbols or other extraneous, affective devices. Such ideas do not involve what are commonly called "value judgments," which are a synthesis of cognitive ideas with organic and traditional preferences.

Propaganda has two principal weapons. One is the use of value judgments disguised as statements of fact or pure theory. Obviously, such behavior is utterly incongruous with scientific work. The other weapon of the propagandist is the use of affective devices, such as emotionally loaded symbols, to influence the value judgments of other people. Propaganda, in this sense, may be either vicious or salutary. I would not minimize the role of moral leaders who can orient the interests of other people around new value designs. But the scientist is more properly concerned with the purely intellectual elements in the formation of values. It would be arbitrary to prohibit a scientist from clothing his contributions with affective appeal; but it seems to me that such behavior is somewhat incongruous with his main responsibility. The introduction of affective elements into controversy tends to destroy that objectivity that is the essence of the scientific spirit.

There is, however, an important intellectual function in connection with the evolution of social policy, beyond that of presenting relevant scientific inferences, technical judgments, and general theories. This is the formulation of *policy designs*, the logical development of their hypothetical implications, and the presentation of such designs as possible patterns for action.

Individuals and societies gradually develop general principles of action to which they subordinate other values and around which they organize their lives. A deadlock between parties whose interests have been centered around conflicting objectives can sometimes be resolved by a new policy design which satisfies the most vital interests of the contending parties. This is the essence of the "diplomatic formula." It is often the major contribution of the conciliator in industrial disputes. Such designs may supply the key to solution of complex social problems. The Myrdals' design of family subsidies in kind as a central principle in democratic population policy is a good example.

Such "creative ideas" and their development have the same logical structure as other hypotheses and systems of implication, but in view of their special role in policy formation, it is useful to refer to them specifically as a *fourth* logical level: the formulation of value designs (or policy designs) as hypotheses for action. Many capable social scientists in the United States today are inhibited from offering such contributions freely by the widespread confusion that surrounds the theory of values. If freed from these inhibitions, social scientists might increase their usefulness by giving greater attention to the formulation of significant policy designs and the development of their hypothetical implications—to be presented purely as hypotheses for action, subject to spontaneous acceptance or rejection in the process of democratic policy formation.

I have described four types of intellectual activity which have different character and functions. It is my thesis that activities on these various logical levels must be differentiated at all times, and that, if they are not confused but clearly differentiated, contributions on these different levels can be and properly are complementary. Their relation to one another is not accidental but intrinsic. Simultaneous complementary advance on all these levels opens to modern man the most promising path to wisdom as the guide of life.

REFERENCES

1. At this point, the audience rose and drank a toast "To Alfred J. Lotka, the father of mathematical demography."

2. The neglect of the significance of unique elements in complex institutional relations damages the otherwise lucid and cogent exposition of the nature of social science recently presented by Lundberg in *Can Science Save Us?* Types of family behavior, many political processes, delinquency, and the formation of attitudes can be sampled and studied experimentally, providing a basis for formulations and interpretations on the first and second logical levels defined above. The illustrations set forth in the early chapters to show the positive achievements and possibilities of social science are drawn from such studies. The author then proceeds in the final chapter to discuss the efficacy of the United Nations Organization, without any explicit recognition that he is shifting to a higher and more precarious level of discourse. "The dominant current faith is a moralistic-legalistic thoughtway, sharply at variance with our analytical attitude toward the rest of nature. The pathetic faith and hopeful trumpetings about so frail an instrument as the United Nations Organization provides a perfect example" (p. 104). The treatment that follows concerning the relative utility of regional and world organizations is intelligently developed and is partially based on rigid scientific inferences. Lundberg's conclusions on this subject may, or may not, be valid; and if valid this may, or may not, be for the reasons set forth. There is, however, no recognition that other equally well-informed social scientists may, and have, come to different conclusions. Only the emotional loading of the language at this point suggests that we have passed beyond those problems which "are to be solved, if at all, by the use of instruments of precision in hands that do not shake with fear, with anger, or even with love" (p. 21). This neglect of the distinction between regular sequences that are the proper subject of science and problems saturated with unique elements that must be intuitively appraised leads Lundberg to disparage political and social history. Historical research is in the main an analysis of unique institutional developments which are never precisely repeated but which do facilitate our intuitive interpretation of present and future possibilities. In giving "undivided faith to science" (p. 115), we must not confuse different logical levels or ignore the rich content of historical studies.

3. The address, as delivered, included a series of observations on population and related social issues which is omitted in this presentation.

CHAPTER 3

THEORY OF POPULATION GROWTH

A great deal of the literature on population has to do with the increase of population aggregates (e.g., the population of France) and some with the actual or potential decrease of these aggregates. Emphasis upon population growth began to dominate literature on population in and perhaps even before the eighteenth century, and it has remained important ever since.

Hypotheses and models employed to describe the growth of population aggregates are of three sorts. There are, first, theories according to which a population aggregate is assumed to grow at a constant, or at a varying rate, for a given period of time. These theories disregard, or at least do not take explicitly into account, the fact that the rate at which a population aggregate can grow is conditioned by the rate at which it can increase its supply of goods and services, together with the average level of consumption it insists upon maintaining. Representative of this type of theory are both hypotheses that population will grow at some geometrical rate and population projections based upon assumed migration and age-specific fertility and mortality rates or rate-patterns. Second, some theories place overwhelming emphasis upon the rate at which the supply of goods and services can be increased, taking virtually for granted that population growth will more or less keep pace. These theories underestimate the role of the forces that shape human aspirations and living standards, and fail to inquire carefully into the extent to which the growth of the supply of goods and services is affected by population growth, technological change, and other factors. There are, third, theories of socio-economic growth, which allow for the fact that the growth of the supply of goods and services depends upon the growth of population even as the latter depends upon the former, and which endeavor to take into account, in varying degree, the divers circumstances that affect, or may affect, both the growth of the supply of goods and services and the level of average consumption. The first and the third types of theory may also allow for the fact that, other circumstances given, the rate at which a population can grow is conditioned by its age and sex composition and by changes therein (cp. Lotka's paper).

While some late eighteenth and early nineteenth century writers were content to subscribe to the second type of theory, others realized that it was not enough to make the growth of population depend upon that of the means of existence, even when variation in the average level of consumption was allowed. It was necessary also to allow for the major factors whereupon the growth of both numbers and the means of existence depended. Accordingly, they formulated the model of growth associated with the names of Malthus, Ricardo, and J. S. Mill and now called classical (cp. Peacock's paper in Chapter 4). In this model three factors are stressed, besides the standard of life insisted upon by workers and (in some degree) by others:

land, whose stock was fixed in amount and subject to diminishing returns; population and the labor force, whose rate of growth was fixed by the level of wages and by the scale of living insisted upon by workers; and the stock of capital, whose rate of growth depended upon the rate of return to capital and (in some measure) upon the disposition of landlords to convert a part of their increasing rent into capital. An increase in population tended to increase the return on capital, to intensify and extend the cultivation of land, and to augment rent. An increase in capital tended to decrease the return thereon, to elevate wages and stimulate population growth, and in consequence to increase cultivation and rent. This growth process would come to a halt when the return on capital no longer stimulated its growth and when the wages received by workers sufficed to maintain but not to increase their number. Ultimately responsible for the halting of the growth process, however, was the tendency of land to yield only diminishing incremental returns to successive applications of labor and/or capital.

A second type of model, the logistic (see Lotka's and Cowgill's papers, and Wolfe's in Chapter 1), dates from 1838 when Verhulst assumed, compatibly with some Malthusian interpretations, that checks to population growth increase in proportion to the population itself, and concluded that a growing population will describe an S-shaped curve, with numbers eventually becoming stationary. This model may be described in summary form as follows: Let b represent a population's biotic potential, or maximum possible rate of increase in the absence of environmental resistance (about .045 today, and about .03 around 1800); K, the maximum population that can exist in a given finite environment under given production and consumption conditions; N, the actual population; and R, the percentage rate of increase per time period in N. N/K may represent environmental resistance to population growth, and $(K-N)/K$, the fraction of the attainable maximum population yet to be realized. The incremental rate of growth is $bN (K-N)/K$; it generates a symmetrical curve, rising to a maximum at $N = K/2$, and then declining to 0 at $N = K$. R becomes $b (K-N)/K$, declining steadily as N increases from an initial relatively low value (approximately zero in some models) to the attainable maximum K. Models resembling the logistic may also be employed.

A third type of theory is that implicit in the transition-growth model, utilized in estimating how much population will have grown in a country with high natality and mortality rates before these rates have descended to a low level and its population has become approximately stationary. It is assumed that mortality falls from its initial high level, at first more rapidly and then less rapidly than natality (cp. Cowgill's Cycle II) until births and deaths balance at a relatively low level and the population becomes virtually stationary. The experience of nations whose populations have nearly completed this transition during the past 100–150 years suggests that their numbers may increase 200–300 or more per cent before it has been completed.

The classical model made explicit the interdependence of socio-economic and demographic growth, but it overestimated the importance of land and underestimated the importance of technological change and the elasticity of the scale of living. The logistic model, though it sometimes describes a country's population growth nicely, fails to specify the conditions, economic and otherwise, which determine the magnitude of the assumed maximum population K; it therefore fails effectively to anticipate changes which may alter the course of R. The transition-growth model similarly disregards factors that may affect mortality or natality and that cause the period and the course of transition to vary significantly from country to country. The postwar upsurge in natality, while consistent with the classical model, is not compatible with the logistic or the transition models. Boulding's paper brings out difficulties involved in the conception and construction of demographic and economico-demographic growth models while suggesting how these models may assist the population student in organizing his materials, findings, and suppositions.

TOWARD A GENERAL THEORY OF GROWTH*

By K. E. Boulding

I. The growth phenomenon is found in practically all the sciences and even in most of the arts, because almost all the objects of human study grow—crystals, molecules, cells, plants, animals, children, personalities, knowledge, ideas, cities, cultures, organizations, nations, wealth, and economic systems. It does not follow, of course, from the mere universality of the growth phenomenon that there must be a single unified theory of growth which will cover everything from the growth of a crystal to the growth of an empire. Growth itself is not a simple or a unified phenomenon, and we cannot expect all the many forms of growth to come under the umbrella of a single theory. Nevertheless all growth phenomena have something in common, and what is more important, the classifications of *forms* of growth and hence of theories of growth seem to cut across most of the conventional boundaries of the sciences. In addition there are a great many problems which are common to many apparently diverse growth phenomena.

It is convenient to start with a threefold classification of growth phenomena. We have first what might be called *simple* growth, that is, the growth or decline of a single variable or quantity by accretion or depletion. In all that follows it should be understood that growth may be negative as well as positive, decline being treated merely as negative growth. In the second place we have what might be called *populational* growth, in which the growing quantity is not regarded as a homogeneous aggregate, but is analysed into an age distribution. Growth is regarded as the excess of "births" (additions to the aggregate) over "deaths" (subtractions from the aggregate), and the analysis of the process is conducted in terms of functions which relate births and deaths to the age distribution. Finally we have what might be called *structural* growth, in which the aggregate which "grows" consists of a complex structure of interrelated parts and in which the growth process involves change in the relation of the parts. Thus in the growth of a living organism, or of an organization, as the "whole" grows, the form and the parts change: new organs develop, old organs decline, and there is frequently growth in complexity as well as in some over-all magnitudes. Problems of structural growth seem to merge almost imperceptibly into the problems of structural *change* or development, so that frequently "what grows" is not the over-all size of the structure but the complexity or systematic nature of its parts. Thus the "growth" of

* Reprinted from *The Canadian Journal of Economics and Political Science*, 19 (August 1953), pp. 326–340, by permission of the author and publisher. (Copyright 1953 by the University of Toronto Press.) Paper presented at the annual meeting of the Canadian Political Science Association in London, June 3, 1953.

a butterfly out of the chrysalis involves an actual decline in over-all magnitudes such as weight or volume, but certainly seems to come under the general heading of phenomena of growth or development.

These three "forms" of growth constitute three different levels of abstraction rather than a classification of actual growth phenomena. Growth phenomena in the real world usually involve all three types. Thus a phenomenon of simple growth such as, for instance, the growth of a capital sum put out to interest, or the growth in the inventory or stocks of a single commodity are in fact part of, and ultimately dependent upon, much more complicated structural processes. Similarly, populational growth as in the case, say, of a human population, never takes place without changes in the organizational structure of the society, that is, in the kinds and the proportions of its "parts"—its organizations, jobs, roles, and so on. Thus all actual growth is structural growth; nevertheless, for some purposes of analysis the structural elements may be neglected and the growing aggregate can be treated as a pure population, and for other purposes even the populational aspects can be neglected and the growth can be treated as simple growth.

II. Turning first then to the analysis of simple growth, the main problem here is that of finding a "law" of growth which will serve to describe the growth curve, that is, which will express the size of the growing variable as a function of time. Perhaps the simplest case of simple growth is growth at a constant rate, for example, the growth of a capital sum at a constant rate of interest. In this case the growth function is the simple exponential $P_t = P_0 (1 + i)^t$, where P_0 is the original sum, P_t the amount into which it has grown in t years at a constant rate of growth i, growth being added at the end of every year. If growth is continuous the function becomes $P_t = P_0 e^{it}$.

Continuous growth at a constant rate, however, is rare in nature and even in society. Indeed it may be stated that within the realm of common human experience all growth must run into *eventually* declining rates of growth. As growth proceeds, the growing object must eventually run into conditions which are less and less favourable to growth. If this were not true there would eventually be only one object in the universe and at that point at least, unless the universe itself can grow indefinitely, its growth would have come to an end. It is not surprising, therefore, that virtually all empirical growth curves exhibit the familiar "ogive" shape, the absolute growth being small at first, rising to a maximum, and then declining eventually to zero as the maximum value of the variable is reached. Many equations for such a curve have been suggested, though none seem to rest on any very secure theoretical foundation. The most familiar is perhaps that of Raymond Pearl, which graphically is a cumulative normal frequency curve. In any such equation the most important constants are (i) one which measures the total amount of growth, that is, the difference between the initial and the maximum value of the variable, and (ii) one which measures the time taken to grow from the initial position to a value reasonably close to the maximum. All that growth equations can do, however, is to describe growth; they are never capable of interpreting or understanding it.[1]

III. Turning now to the second level of growth analysis, that of population growth, we find that fairly detailed and complex analysis are possible. A population may be defined as "an aggregation of disparate items, or 'individuals,' each one of which conforms to a given definition, retains its identity with the passage of time, and exists only during a finite interval."[2] "Birth" occurs when an item begins to conform to the definition which encloses the aggregation, and "death" when the item ceases to conform to this definition. A definition may be thought of as a closed fence: everything inside the fence belongs to the defined population; birth consists in crossing the fence into the enclosure; death in crossing the fence out of the enclosure. The population concept as thus defined is a perfectly general one, and applies not only to human or animal populations, but to populations of automobiles, poems, stars, dollars, ideas, or anything that is capable of definition.

Population *analysis* is only useful in the case of aggregates where birth and death rates can be regarded as some function of the *age composition* of the population. The age composition can be expressed most simply as a series of age groups, $a_1, a_2, \ldots, a_n$, where a_1 is the number of individuals between the ages of 0 and 1 "year," a_r is the number between the ages of $r - 1$ and r "years" old. The "age" of any individual is of course the time which has elapsed since birth. The "year" can of course be made as small as we like: in the limit the age composition reduces to a continuous function. If then the number of births and the number of deaths *in each age group* can be expressed as functions of the age composition, $a_1, \ldots, a_n$, the whole course of the population can be traced as far as patience and arithmetic hold out—or the assumed functions do not change. The simplest "birth function" is $B = b_1a_1 + b_2a_2 + \ldots + b_na_n$. This assumes that each age group makes a specific and constant proportional contribution to the total number of births where $(b_1, \ldots, b_n)$ are constants. Similarly the simplest "death function" is $D = d_1a_1 + d_2a_2 + \ldots + d_na_n$, where the number of deaths in each age group is assumed to be a constant proportion of the numbers in the group. Given such a death function, a "survival function" for any given "cohort" of births can be derived, a "cohort" being all those individuals who have a common "year" of birth. Thus of a number of births B in year 0, Bd_0 will die and $Bs_1 = B(1 - d_0)$ will survive into year 1: of these $B(1 - d_0)d_1$ will die and $Bs_2 = B(1 - d_0)(1 - d_1)$ will survive into year 2; similarly $Bs_{r+1} = B(1 - d_0)(1 - d_1) \ldots (1 - d_r)$ will survive into year $r + 1$. If the population is finite (that is, composed of mortals), we must have $d_n = 1$: that is, none of the oldest age group survive into the next year.

Probably the best way to illustrate the process of population analysis is by an arithmetical example, as the algebraic treatment is both easy and clumsy. Suppose a population of three age groups, a birth function $B = 3a_2 + 8a_3$, and a survival function $s_1 = 1, s_2 = 0.8, s_3 = 0.4$, and suppose we start with a population of 100 in the first age group, 40 in the second, and 10 in the third. The course of the population will be as in Table I.

TABLE I

Year	Births	Age Group 0–1	Age Group 1–2	Age Group 2–3	Total
1	120 + 80 = 200	100	40	10	150
2	240 + 160 = 400	200	80	20	300
3	480 + 320 = 800	400	160	40	600
4	960 + 640 = 1600	800	320	80	1200

Thus in the first year the number of births is $40 \times 3 + 10 \times 8$, or 200; of this cohort of 200 births all 200 survive into year 2, and are then in the first age group: $160 = (200 \times 0.8)$ survive into year 3, and are then in the second age group, and $80 = (200 \times 0.4)$ survive into year 4 and are then in the third age group. Given the number of births and the age composition of year 1 we can get immediately the age composition of year 2; the 200 births of year 1 become the 200 0–1 year olds: the 100 0–1 year olds become the 80 1–2 year olds, and the 40 1–2 year olds become the 20 2–3 year olds. From this age composition we can then derive the birth cohort of year 2 ($80 \times 3 + 20 \times 8$). Similarly from the birth cohort and the age composition of year 2 we derive the age composition of year 3, and from that the birth cohort of year 3. The process can clearly be repeated for an indefinite number of years.

Table I has been arranged so that the population grows exponentially, doubling every year. It will be observed that the birth cohort likewise doubles every year, as does the number in each age group. Such a population may be said to be in "equilibrium exponential growth." If the rate of growth is 1, of course, the population is stationary and exactly reproduces its composition every year. If the rate of growth is less than 1 the population is declining, but the same principles apply. Now, however, suppose that instead of starting with the age composition of Table I we started with a distorted composition, as in Table II.

TABLE II

Year	Births ($3a_2 + 8a_3$ = Total)	Age Group 0–1	Age Group 1–2	Age Group 2–3	Total
1	30 + 800 = 830	10	10	100	120
2	24 + 40 = 64	830	8	5	843
3	1992 + 32 = 2024	64	664	4	732
4	153 + 2656 = 2809	2024	51	332	2407
5	4857 + 208 = 5065	2809	1619	26	4454
6	6741 + 6480 = 13221	5065	2247	810	8122
7		13221	4046	1124	18391

It will be seen that although the underlying laws of development of the population are exactly the same as in Table I, the immediate course of the population is very different. Instead of growing steadily, the population grows in a series of leaps and checks; indeed, from the second to the third years it actually declines, in spite of the fact that the underlying dynamics of the population imply a doubling every year! It will be observed, however, that in the present case the irregularities of the growth rate diminish as time goes on, and the age distribution becomes less distorted. This is because the birth function has coefficients for more than one age group, so that the contribution of the initial age composition gets "mixed" as time goes on. If the birth function only had coefficients for a single age group the "cycle" in the growth curve would perpetuate itself.

A simple algebraic expression of the above principles follows. Let the age composition in year t be $a_1, a_2, \ldots, a_n$, these being the numbers in the age groups 0–1, 1–2, $\ldots$, $(n-1)$–n. Suppose a birth function

(1) $$B_t = b_1 a_1 + b_2 a_2 + \ldots + b_n a_n.$$

Suppose also a series of survival coefficients, $s_1, s_2, \ldots, s_n$, where s_n is the proportion of the births of any year t that survive into the year $t + n$. Then for the year t we have

(2) $$a_1 = s_1 B_{t-1}, \, a_2 = s_2 B_{t-2}, \ldots, \, a_n = s_n B_{t-n}.$$

Combining (1) and (2) we have

(3) $$B_t = b_1 s_1 B_{t-1} + b_2 s_2 B_{t-2} + \ldots + b_n s_n B_{t-n}.$$

Suppose now that we have a population in equilibrium exponential growth (or decline) at a rate g. Then we must have:

(4) $$B_{t+1} = gB_t, \text{ whence } B_{t+r} = g^r B^t.$$

Inserting the appropriate values from (3) and cancelling B_t we have:

(5) $$\frac{b_1 s_1}{g} + \frac{b_2 s_2}{g^2} + \ldots + \frac{b_n s_n}{g^n} = 1.$$

This equation can be solved for g to give the equilibrium rate of growth corresponding to any set of birth and survival coefficients. For a population in stationary equilibrium $g = 1$, and we have

(6) $$R = \sum_1^n b_r s_r = 1.$$

R may be called the "growth potential" of the population; the population must eventually grow, be stationary, or decline according as R is greater than, equal to, or less than 1. If sex ratios are neglected R is the same as the net reproduction ratio of a human or animal population, that is, it is the average number of births which eventually come from a unit of any given cohort of births in a population in equilibrium exponential growth.

Suppose now that the birth function contains only a single coefficient, b_r. If the initial age composition of the population is $a_1, a_2, \ldots, a_n$, births in year t_0 are $b_r a_r$. In year t_r then the rth age group will have $b_r a_r s_r$ individuals in it, and the number of births will be $b_r^2 a_r s_r$. In the year t_{2r} the rth age group will be $b_r{}^2 a_r s_r{}^2$, and the number of births $b_r{}^3 a_r s_r{}^2$. In the year t_{kr} the number of births will be $b_r a_r (b_r s_r)^k$. Similarly in the year t_1 the rth age group will be

$$b_r a_{r-1} \frac{s_r}{s_{r-1}},$$

and the number of births will be

$$b_r{}^2 a_{r-1} \frac{s_r}{s_{r-1}}.$$

In the year t_{kr+1} the number of births will be

$$b_r a_{r-1} \frac{s_r}{s_{r-1}} (b_r s_r)^k.$$

It is clear that the birth cohorts and also the total population will repeat the pattern set up by the first r years, multiplied by the growth factor in all succeeding periods of r years. If however there is more than one birth function coefficient, the effect will be "damped."

The assumption of constant birth and survival coefficients gives us at least a first approximation to the dynamics of human or animal populations. The fact, however, that such an assumption results in exponential growth (or decline) means that it cannot be more than a first approximation for, as we have seen, exponential growth cannot go on forever. In order to achieve growth patterns of an ogive or logistic form it is necessary to assume that the birth or survival coefficients are themselves functions of the total population or of time, one or both eventually decreasing with increase of population, or lapse of time. A period of growth can then be attributed to a rise of

$$R = \sum_{1}^{n} b_r s_r$$

above 1; the ultimate cessation of growth comes about because the growth of the population itself carries R down to 1 again. This is illustrated in Figure 1. We postulate an R-curve rr relating R to the total population. The equilibrium population is OE where $EF = 1$. Suppose now that conditions change—life, say, becomes easier. The R-curve moves to the right to a new position $r'r'$. The equilibrium population is now OE', where again $E'F' = 1$. The exact dynamics of the shift from E to E' of course depend on the nature of the birth and survival functions.

Birth and survival functions need not, of course, be confined to age compositions. In many populations other variables are significant. For instance, for populations of capital goods (e.g., automobiles) we may assume as a first approximation that the object of "births" (production) is to hold the total population either constant, or increasing at a constant rate. In that case the

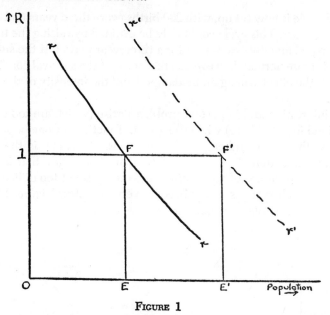

FIGURE 1

number of births in any year will be equal to the number of deaths, plus the number necessary to maintain the desired increase in the total population. On such an assumption within any given pattern of growth of the total population, considerable fluctuations are possible in birth cohorts, if there are distortions in the age distribution. Thus consider the following population table:

TABLE III

Year	Births	Age Composition			Total
		0–1	1–2	2–3	
0	100	100	100	100	300
1	100	100	100	100	300
2	200	100	100	100	300
3	100	200	100	100	400
4	100	100	200	100	400
5	200	100	100	200	400
6	100	200	100	100	400

Here we suppose a population of "one-hoss shays," with three age groups, and survival coefficients of 1, 1, 1, 0: all deaths occur at the end of the third year. We suppose an initial population of 100 in each age group, 300 in all. This is maintained by 100 births every year, as we see going from year 0 to year 1. Now in year 2 it is decided to increase the population to 400, and in order to do this 200 births are "made." In year 3 we then have an age composition of 200, 100, 100. However, only the 100 in the third age group "die," so that only 100 need to be born in year 4. In year 5, however, the 200 that were born in year 2 die, and have to be replaced by another 200. It is clear that a perpetual cycle is now set up, with 200 births every three years and 100 in the intervening years. This cycle could only be avoided by raising the total population by equal amounts each year for a three-year period. If the survival distribution is more normal, however, so that some of the survival coefficients are less than 1, the effect will again be damped and the intensity of the cycle will diminish.

Very interesting and important problems arise (which are too complex to be examined in detail here) when the growth functions of one population depend upon the size of other populations. This, of course, is the theory of œcological interaction. At the level of comparative statics, that is, the comparison of two positions of equilibrium, the theory is not too difficult, but the dynamics of such systems easily become very complex. Figure 2, however, illustrates the principle on which such systems operate.

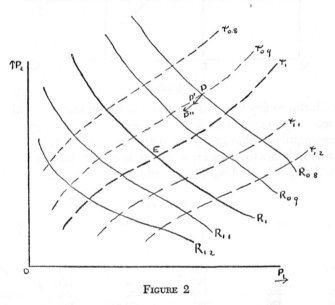

FIGURE 2

We suppose two different populations, P_1 and P_2. Size of population P_1 is measured along the horizontal axis, P_2 on the vertical axis. The solid line R_1 then shows all those combinations of P_1 and P_2 at which the R (growth potential) of population 1 is unity. Similarly the line $R_{1.1}$ shows those combinations for which $R = 1.1$ for population 1, and similarly for the other solid lines. The dotted lines similarly represent those combinations of P_1 and P_2 for which the growth potential of population 2 is 1, 1.1, etc. In the figure as drawn P_2 inhibits the growth of P_1, that is, the larger the population of P_2 the less will be the growth potential of P_1 for each level of P_1 as shown by the family of solid lines. P_2 is a predator or parasite on P_1. Cases in which both populations are mutually competitive, or in which both are mutually co-operative, can be analysed by the same technique. The point E where the R_1 and r_1 curves intersect is the point of general stationary equilibrium, that is, the point at which the populations in equilibrium will coexist without growth or decline of either. Consider, however, the combination of populations represented by the point P. At this point $R = 0.8$, $r = 0.9$. Both populations will therefore decline, unless their age structures are very distorted. P_1 will decline more than P_2, and the two populations will move following the vector PP'. From P' another movement will take place to, say, P'', and so on until the equilibrium is reached. Lines of movement of the populations such as $PP'P''$ may be called "vector lines," and the family of such lines is a good rough description of the dynamics of the system. Examples will be found in my *Reconstruction of Economics,* chapter 1.

IV. The analysis of structural growth is much more complicated than the analysis of populational growth, and is much more difficult to reduce to a neat set of propositions. Structural growth includes such complex phenomena as the growth of crystal structures, the growth, division, and differentiation of cells, the growth of organisms, of organizations, of language and other mental structures, of buildings, and of societies. We would hardly expect such diverse phenomena to reduce themselves to a uniform simple scheme. Nevertheless it is striking how many of the problems which rise to special prominence in one field of study also carry over into others, and it is not impossible to formulate some principles of great generality.

The first of these we may call the principle of nucleation, following a term which comes originally from physics. Any structure has a minimum size, which is its "nucleus." Once a nucleus has been formed, it is not too difficult to understand how additions to the structure are made. The formation of the nucleus itself, however, presents many problems which are quite different from those involved in the growth of an already established structure. Thus there is a minimum size of crystal, depending on its complexity: in smaller aggregations of atoms than this minimum there are not enough components to make up the minimum structure. In the case of the cell the problem of nucleation is almost completely unsolved: as far as we now know, all living matter grows from living matter. We know something about how the complex societies of subordinate structures which comprise the living nuclei can grow, divide, and differentiate as "going concerns." We know practically nothing about how such an immensely complex organization ever came to be established in the first place, and up to the present we have not been able to reproduce that mysterious initial act of nucleation. In the social sciences the nucleation problem also exists; here it manifests itself as the problem of innovation, in the Schumpeterian sense. Once a form of organization is established, whether a type of production or a kind of enterprise, a cult, a school, a party, or any distinct type of institution, it is not too difficult to imitate. The initial innovation, however, is something of a mystery, which does not fall easily within the smooth rubrics of historical necessity. We do not understand very well what it is that makes the genuine innovators—those mysterious individuals who establish religions, cultures, nations, techniques, and ideas. In society as in physics, however, we find that very small amounts of "impurities" (say one Edison per hundred million) produce effects fantastically disproportionate to their quantity, because of the nucleation principle. It is also not perhaps too far fetched to speak of "super-cooled societies," where the external conditions call for change to a new state of society, but where the rate of nucleation is so small that the change does not take place.

Another principle which emerges from the study of nucleation is that the nucleus does not have to be homogeneous with the structure that grows around it; thus the speck of dust at the heart of the raindrop! Consequently *impurity* in a universe is a very important factor in explaining change. Examples of this principle are numerous in society. Colleges nucleate around sects, farm organizations around county agents, trade unions around socially minded priests. One cannot be a student of society for long without observing what I have sometimes called the "Pinocchio principle." Some agent or organization sets up a "puppet" in the form of some other kind of organization. Before long however the "puppet" begins to take on a life of its own, and frequently walks right away from its maker. Here we see the principle of "heterogeneous nucleation" actively at work in society. The principle of nucleation applies even to the learning process, which can be thought of as the growth of a "mental structure." Thus in learning a language it is necessary for the language to "nucleate" in the mind of the learner before it can become anything more to him than an unusable bunch of unrelated words. Even in learning economics the student frequently finds that for the first few months the subject makes practically no sense to him, and then quite suddenly he experiences a "conversion"; what had previously been disconnected parts somehow fall into place in his mind, and for the first time he "sees" the subject as an organic whole. The application of this idea to the phenomenon of religious or political conversion would make a most interesting study.

The second general principle of structural development might be called the principle of non-proportional change. As any structure grows, the proportions of its parts and of its significant variables *cannot* remain constant. It is impossible, that is to say, to reproduce *all* the characteristics of a structure in a scale model of different size. This is because a uniform increase in the linear dimensions of a structure will increase all its areas as the square, and its volumes as the cube, of the increase in the linear dimension. Thus a twofold increase in all the lengths of a structure increases its areas by four times and its volumes by eight times. As some of the essential functions and variables of a structure depend on its linear dimensions, some on its areal dimensions, and some on its volumetric dimensions, it is impossible to keep the same proportions between all the significant variables and functions as the structure grows.

This principle has two important corollaries. The first is that growth of a structure always involves a *compensatory* change in the relative sizes of its various parts to compensate for the fact that those functions and properties which depend on volume tend increasingly to dominate those dependent on area, and those dependent on area tend increasingly to dominate those depending on length. Large structures therefore tend to be "longer" and more convoluted than small structures, in the attempt to increase the proportion of linear and areal dimensions to volumes. It follows therefore that as a structure grows it will also tend to become longer and more convoluted. Architecture and biology—two sciences which are much more closely related than might appear at first sight—provide admirable examples. A one-room schoolhouse, like the bacterium, can afford to be roughly globular and can still maintain effective contact with its environment—getting enough light and nutrition (children) into its interior through its walls. Larger schools, like worms, become long in relation to their volume in order to give every room at least one outside wall. Still larger schools develop wings and courtyards, following the general principle that a structure cannot be more than two rooms thick if it is to have adequate breathing facilities. This is the insect level of architecture (skin-breathing). The invention of artificial ventilation (lungs) and illumination (optic nerves) makes theoretically possible at any rate much larger structures of a "globular" or cubic type, with inside rooms artificially ventilated and lit, just as the development of lungs, bowels, nerves, and brains (all involving extensive convolution to get more area per unit of volume) enabled living matter to transcend the approximately three-inch limit set by the insect (skin-breathing) pattern. In the absence of such devices further growth of the structure involves splitting up into separate buildings (the campus) of which the biological analogy is the termite or bee colony.

The second corollary follows immediately from the first: if the process of compensation for structural disproportion has limits, as in fact seems to be the case, the size of the structure itself is limited by its ultimate inability to compensate for the non-proportional changes. This is the basic principle which underlies the "law of eventually diminishing returns to scale" familiar to economists. Thus as institutions grow they have to maintain larger and larger specialized administrative structures in order to overcome the increasing difficulties of communication between the "edges" or outside surfaces of the organization (the classroom, the parish, the retail outlet) and the central executive. Eventually the cost of these administrative structures begins to outweigh any of the other possible benefits of large scale, such as increasing specialization of the more directly productive parts of the organization, and these structural limitations bring the growth of the organization to an end. One can visualize, for instance, a university of a hundred thousand students in which the entire organization is made up of administrators, leaving no room at all for faculty.

It is interesting to note that the principle of compensation may operate in two very distinct ways—in the direction of an attempt to *solve* the problems posed by large scale or in the direction of an attempt to *avoid* these problems.

Thus the critical problem of large-scale organization is that of the communications system (nerves and blood!). This being a "linear" function tends to become inadequate relative to the "surface" functions of interaction and production as the organization grows. One method of compensation is to increase
the proportion of the organization which is devoted to the communications
system as the organization grows larger (the modern army, David Riesman
has remarked, marches not on its stomach but on the punched card). Another
method however is to diminish the *need* for communication by developing
autonomy of the parts or rigid and ritualistic patterns of behaviour. Thus a
very large church organization, such as the Roman Catholic Church, not only
has to permit a good deal of autonomy to its various parts (in this case, national churches), but can only maintain its structure at the cost of extreme
rigidity in its basic operations. The Pope doesn't have to communicate with
the priest in the wilds of Bolivia because the mass is removed from the agenda
of discussion! In this connection it might be noted also that great size in itself
leads to relative invulnerability, and hence very large organizations do not
face the same problems of uncertainty and adjustment which face smaller
organizations or organisms. The whales and elephants of the universe can
afford to have fairly placid dispositions and insensitive exteriors.

A third principle of structural growth follows somewhat from the second,
but is sufficiently distinct to warrant a separate status. This might be called
the D'Arcy Thomson principle, after its most famous exponent.[3] It is the principle that at any moment the *form* of any object, organism, or organization is
a result of its laws of growth up to that moment. Something which grows uniformly in all directions will be a sphere. Something which grows faster in one
direction than in others will be "long." Something which grows faster on one
side than on the other will twist into some sort of spiral. The shape of an egg
is related to its flow down the oviduct. Examples can be multiplied almost
indefinitely, and the contemplation of these beautiful and subtle relationships
is perhaps one of the most refined delights of the human mind. It is clear that
the principle applies in general not only to organisms, but to organizations,
though its applications here are more complex and perhaps less secure. An
aggressive chairman or department head will cause his department to grow
relative to the total structure. Scientific inquiries follow growth patterns
which are laid down by previous studies and by the interests of scientists.
Economic and technological development follows patterns which in turn determine the structure of an economy. Law grows like a great coral reef on the
skeletons of dead cases.

Growth creates form, but form limits growth. This mutuality of relationship between growth and form is perhaps the most essential key to the understanding of structural growth. We have seen how growth compels adjustments
to changes in relative proportions. It is also true that occasionally growth
stops because of "closure"—because the growth itself seals off all the growing
edges. We see this frequently in the world of ideas where self-contained

ideologies (such as Marxism) exhibit closure in the sense that any development outside the narrow circle of the self-contained system is inhibited. It is often the "loose ends" of systems that are their effective growing points—too tight or too tidy an organization may make for stability, but it does not make for growth. This is perhaps one of the most cogent arguments for toleration in the political sphere; the morbid passion for tidiness is one of the greatest enemies of human development.

There is, I believe, a fourth principle of structural growth, detailed evidence for which it is difficult to find in the biological sciences, but which is clearly apparent in the growth of man-made structures, especially, oddly enough, in building. It may perhaps be called the "carpenter principle." In building any large structure out of small parts one of two things must be true if the structure is not to be hopelessly mis-shapen. Either the dimensions of the parts must be extremely accurate, or there must be something like a carpenter or a bricklayer following a "blueprint" who can adjust the dimensions of the structure as it goes along. If, for instance, we are building a structure out of a thousand identical parts, the tolerable variability of each part would have to be about one thousandth of the tolerable variability of the whole structure, if we were simply adding part to part without making any adjustments on the way. It is only possible, however, to build a brick wall or a wooden house, with bricks and with boards that are in themselves highly variable, if there is exercised during the process of growth a "skill" of adjustment, that is, of adjusting the structure as it grows in conformity with some plan or requirement. It may perhaps be hazarded that the genes perform some such function in the growth of living organisms, though what is the machinery by which these little carpenters of the body operate is still unknown. In social and intellectual structures, however, the principle is of great importance, for the whole development of these structures may be affected profoundly by the existence of a "plan" and of an apparatus by which the growing structure is constantly conformed to the plan. The construction of a building, a machine, or a bridge is an obvious example. The process of academic learning is another example. In the learning of a language, for instance, the existence of a grammar exercises a profound effect on the capacity of the student to develop originality. In any subject, the presence of a textbook exercises somewhat the same influence as a grammar on the process of learning, and the instructor is the intellectual carpenter, trimming the student's mind off at frequent intervals by means of quizzes and examinations. What we have here is essentially a homœostatic process, the divergence which excites action being the divergence at any time between the actual condition of the structure and the "planned" condition.

Even where a detailed "plan" of development is not available the existence of some kind of ideal structure with which present reality may be compared exercises a profound influence on growth, especially in the sciences. One need only cite, for instance, the influence exerted on the progress of chemistry by the existence of the periodic table of elements, an ideal structure which in the beginning had many "holes" (undiscovered elements), but which was gradually filled up as the process of chemical research was directed into filling the obvious gaps in the structure. It may, indeed, be regarded as one of the prime functions of "theory" in any field to set up these ideal structures which are in fact incomplete. In this connection it may be observed that one of the principal advantages which may be derived from interdisciplinary research is the development of a "general theory" which will fulfil this function of the "ideal structure" for knowledge as a whole.

A fifth principle of structural growth emerges fairly clearly from economics, though here also its application to the biological or physical sciences is quite unproved. This may be called the "principle of equal advantage." It governs the distribution of the "substance" of a structure among the various parts of the structure. We assume first that the "atoms" of a structure can be ordered according to a parameter which we label, for want of a better term "advantage," this being defined operationally as a "potential" such that units will tend to flow towards locations of higher, and away from locations of lower, advantage. We then postulate that the advantage of a unit in any location is an inverse function of the relative quantity of units in that location—that is, the fewer the merrier! This implies a concept something like the "demand" for any given location—demand in this case fulfils something of the function of the "plan" under the fourth proposition. We then postulate a principle that "demand" tends to be satisfied, that is, if there are differences in advantage to units ("industries") in different locations, units will tend to move from the low-advantage locations where there are "too many" to the high-advantage locations where there are "too few."

In economic systems the principle of equal advantage, and the fact that the "advantage" parameter can be approximately related to monetary reward, enables us to give reasonably satisfactory explanations of two phenomena which are common in biology, but very little understood. These are the phenomena known as functional substitution and regeneration. If one organ of a living organization is removed, there is an observable tendency for other organs to take over the function of the missing organ. At lower levels of life, also, the organism seems to have a remarkable capacity for the regeneration of lost parts; tadpoles can grow new tails and starfish new limbs. The healing of wounds and of broken bones is an example of the same phenomenon at a somewhat less spectacular level. In the economic system it is possible to observe fairly closely what happens when an "organ" (industry) is cut off, say, by prohibition. In the first place if regeneration of the severed industry is prevented by the cauterizing action of law, other "industries" will begin to take over the functions of the destroyed industry (speakeasies, bathtub gin, etc.). If now the prohibition is removed, the old industry rapidly grows back again into the body economic, under the stimulus of profit (advantage). One may again hazard a guess that biologists will have to look for a variable akin to profit at the level of the cell if they are fully to understand the phenomenon of functional substitution and regeneration.

It is interesting to observe that the "carpenter principle" and the "advantage principle" are to some extent alternative ways of effecting the organization of a society, the first, of course, corresponding to the communist planned economy and the second to the capitalist market economy. In the planned economy, growth is organized by the principle of conformity to the plan: industries which are lagging behind the plan get extra attention to make them catch up, much as a child is taught in an authoritarian educational system. In the market economy, growth is organized by the principle of advantage: it takes place in the directions that "pay off" to the individuals who initiate it or are able to take advantage of its initiation, the "pay off" being derived from "profit," that is, an excess of value of product over cost. There is a certain analogy here perhaps with "progressive" education.

We have not, of course, exhausted a subject so ramified and so universal as growth in five summary propositions, though it may be hoped that there is here presented some indication that general theories of growth are possible. It remains in the compass of a short paper to indicate some of the loose—and therefore growing!—ends of the subject. We have not, for instance, considered the problem of the possibility of equilibrium *rates* of growth in an organism or system such that higher (or lower) growth rates may seriously disturb the functioning of the system even to the point of its collapse and "death." There is evidence in the plant world that too rapid a rate of growth kills the organism; indeed, some very effective weed killers have been developed on this principle, using growth hormones. The growth theories of Harrod and Domar suggest that in the economic system there are "appropriate" rates of growth of a system as a whole which will yield continuous full employment. These theories also suggest, however, that there is nothing inherent in the nature of an unstabilized market economy which will guarantee these appropriate rates of growth. There is a suggestion, indeed, that under some circumstances a continuous equilibrium rate of growth may be impossible, because certain elements, consumption, for example, do not keep pace with the rise in capacity and so force *accelerated* growth on other elements, such as investment, if the system is to maintain full employment. These problems may all turn out to be problems in compensation for structural changes through increasing size, such as we have noted earlier, but particularly where equilibrium seems to require acceleration in certain growth rates some quite peculiar problems may be involved.

The problems of the transition from rapidly growing systems to more or less stationary ones are also very general, and need careful study at many levels. The character of a system frequently has to change not merely because it gets big, but because it stops growing. Thus when a religious movement passes from its initial phase of rapid expansion into the phase of slow or even negative growth it has to make profound adaptations: what is appropriate organization in a "movement" is not necessarily appropriate in a "sect." Any system which passes from a rapidly growing phase to a more stationary one, whether it is a religion, a labour organization, a business firm, a nation, an economic system, or a civilization comes face to face with somewhat the same kind of adjustment. David Riesman makes the growth phase of a culture the principal determinant even of the typical character of its individuals, attributing "tradition-directed" behaviour to low-level, slowly growing, or stationary populations with high growth potential, "inner-directed" behaviour to rapidly growing populations, and "other-directed" behaviour to high-level, slow-growing, or stationary populations. These connections may seem a little far-fetched, but there can be no doubt that the type of growth which any system exhibits will affect most if not all of its major characteristics.

In conclusion one may hazard a guess as to the growth patterns of the sciences. The remarkable universality of the principles enunciated here in regard to a general theory of growth indicate that perhaps there is emerging from the welter of the sciences something like a "general theory," something which is a little less general and has a little more empirical content than mathematics but which is more general and therefore, of course, has less content than the content of specific sciences. Mathematics is itself, of course, a "general theory" in that it applies wherever quantitative concepts and relationships are encountered. The sort of general theory which I have in mind, however, is a generalization from aspects of experience which include more than mere abstract quantity and which are common to many or even to all of the "universes of discourse" which constitute the various sciences. Growth is one such aspect: organization is another; interaction is another. When, and if, such a general theory comes to be written it will be surprising if the general theory of growth does not comprise an important chapter.

REFERENCES

1. My recent acquaintance with the work of Dr. S. A. Courtis suggests that this judgment may be much too severe. An empirical "growth law" which fits many cases has at least the virtue that it calls attention to possible unknown sources of disturbance in cases where it does not fit—just as the law of gravity led to the discovery of the outer planets. Courtis's law ($y = ki^r$) may well be of use in this way. See S. A. Courtis, "What Is a Growth Cycle?" *Growth*, I, no. 3, May, 1937.

2. K. E. Boulding, "The Application of the Pure Theory of Population Change to the Theory of Capital," *Quarterly Journal of Economics*, XLVIII, Aug., 1934, 650.

THE THEORY OF POPULATION GROWTH CYCLES *

By Donald Olen Cowgill

The systematic study of population began with the broad supposedly universal principles enunciated by Malthus. Much of the development of later population theory has been a reaction to these Malthusian principles, largely by way of pointing out specific exceptions to the general principle arising in the last century and a half and attempting to adjust the theory to meet these new facts. This emphasis on events of recent times plus the dearth of population facts for other periods has tended to foster the impression that principles adequate to explain modern phenomena are adequate for all time. One specific area in which this seems to be the case is in the theory relating to population cycles.

The chief cycle theories have been based exclusively upon modern human populations or laboratory experiments with sub-human species. One of the best known is that of Raymond Pearl:

> Growth occurs in cycles. Within one and the same cycle, and in a spatially limited area or universe, growth in the first half of the cycle starts slowly but the absolute increment per unit of time *increases* steadily until the mid-point of the cycle is reached. After that point the increment per unit of time becomes *smaller* until the end of the cycle.[1]

This theory, based first on experiments with the *Drosophila melanogaster* in the limited environment of a milk bottle, was stated as a mathematical law, using a formula for the logistic curve to describe the curve of population growth. This type of curve is illustrated in Figure 1. Pearl found that the same curve could be fitted to the growth pattern of yeast and of chickens, again under the ideal conditions of a spatially limited universe. It may be remarked parenthetically that in all these experiments Pearl started with a limited population in a relatively ample environment—conditions that are seldom approximated in the human population.

Nevertheless, Pearl went on to fit logistic curves to human populations, including the United States, the city of New York, and the city of Baltimore—all recent, modern phenomena. Apparently, like Malthus, he saw no difference in human reasons for decelerating growth as the upper asymptote was approached from the similar phenomenon when found among chickens or fruit flies. Indeed, in the unsuccessful effort to secure an unsophisticated human population that would most closely resemble fruit flies in a bottle, Pearl studied the people of Algeria after their subjugation by the French in the middle

* Reprinted from *The American Journal of Sociology*, 55 (September 1949), pp. 163–170, by permission of the author and the University of Chicago Press. Paper read at the annual meeting of the Midwest Sociological Society, Minneapolis, April 30, 1948.

of the nineteenth century. The analogy was not that the French "bottled" them up in this period but that the pacific condition of the Algerians in subsequent decades permitted expansion of population as the fruit flies expanded in the bottle. Here a reasonably close fit to the logistic curve was obtained, in part due to neglect of the gross inaccuracy of early population data for Algeria.

From this Pearl generalized that "growth occurs in cycles." So far, perhaps, Pearl is on safe ground. It is when he sets forth identical explanations for these cycles, human and subhuman, that he errs.

A somewhat similar cycle theory, though less precise, is that of the Italian, Gini,[2] who mixed his theology, cosmology, and nationalism up with a limited time perspective on population and adduced the theory that a human population has a life-cycle similar to that of the individual, characterized by an early period of rapid growth, a period of maturity and stability, followed by senescence and decline. Gini seems to identify populations with nations and to permit himself the scientific luxury of choosing his starting point in time in such a way that the facts of growth must fit the theory, other periods being ignored. He is also dazzled by the population growth of modern times, especially in Western nations and gains an illusion of universality therefrom. Stripped of metaphysics and nationalistic bias, the part of this theory which treats of the growth phase of the cycle, like that of Pearl, describes cycles that have occurred and may occur. The part of the theory which posits a decline is much more debatable, and illustrations of a decline to the original level are distinctly hard to find.

The purpose of the present paper is not to debate the pros and cons of whether there are cycles of population growth or whether they occur at regular intervals. It is merely assumed that some populations do experience periods of growth approximating the pattern described by Pearl, although these periods of growth show no necessary relation to the chronological life of a nation and do not necessarily occur with any regularity. In fact, it is assumed that, throughout most of human history, growth has been irregular, alternating between periods of growth and plateaus of relative stability.

Assuming, then, that growth cycles may be observed in many and varied populations, and assuming that, in general, such cycles do result in an S-curve of growth, the object of this paper is to examine the mechanics by which such growth takes place. The growth phase of population change is selected for consideration, not because of any illusion of universality on the part of the author but rather as a convenient point of departure and because previous cycle theories to which this paper is a reaction have concentrated upon growth. For purposes of simplicity we shall disregard the effects of migration and treat only of natural increase. It is in regard to the mechanics of the cycle that our cycle theorists come into sharp disagreement. Malthus inferred that any growth cycle would ultimately be curtailed and brought to a close by an increase in the death rate. Gini, Pearl, and Yule see the close of the cycle effected by a falling birth rate. The views of Spencer,[3] Sadler,[4] and Nitti[5] support this latter contention. Interestingly, there is less open or obvious disagreement in explaining the origin of a growth cycle, for the simple reason that the cycle theorists have largely ignored the question. It might be assumed that, as they explain the cessation of growth by a decline in the birth rate, they would ascribe its origin to an increase in the birth rate. However, this is not specifically stated, and the general implication seems to be that they assume the normal situation to be a much higher birth rate than death rate. The highly artificial environmental situation in which Pearl conducted his biological experiments was amenable to this interpretation. In these experiments he was much more concerned with what stopped the cycle than how it started, and it is perhaps not surprising that he carried this emphasis over into the study of human populations. He quotes with approval Yule's treatment of birth-death ratios during a cycle, even reproducing Yule's diagram, which, significantly, depicts a birth rate twice as large as the death rate at the beginning of the cycle.[6] While this may obtain for fruit flies when placed in a bottle or even for human populations suddenly transplanted to an ample environment, it is a logical impossibility for old populations, human or insect, in an already saturated environment. In such conditions the flattening of the curve adjacent to the lower asymptote implies a period of stability. Such stability necessitates a balance of births and deaths at some level. Yule's birth and death ratios would produce Pearl's logistic curve of growth only under the ideal conditions of transplantation of a few individuals into an ideal environment—conditions approximated to a degree in the New World since the discovery of America if we disregard the indigenous American population. Such conditions could not have obtained in Algeria at the beginning of the cycle studied by Pearl. This logical inconsistency is overlooked by Pearl.[7] By contrast, the implication of Malthus appears clear cut; any technological improvement, any new resources, any new territory for exploitation will tend to increase the population by temporarily depressing the death rate.

Here, then, we find implicit and explicit disagreement on how birth rates and death rates behave during a growth cycle of population. What are the mechanics of a growth cycle and are they the same for all cycles?

THEORETICAL CYCLES

Theoretically, a cycle of growth through natural increase could be inaugurated by either an increased birth rate or a decreased death rate and terminated by either a decreased birth rate or an increased death rate. But there is a dynamic relationship between these two variables that requires consideration of the whole cycle.

Four simple theoretical patterns of relationship emerge as possible combinations.

Cycle I.—While the birth rate remains stationary, the death rate falls, then rises again to terminate the cycle (see Fig. 2).

Cycle II.—This cycle is characterized by both falling birth rates and falling death rates; but in the initial stages the death rate drops more rapidly than the birth rate, only to be overtaken by a more rapidly falling birth rate in the later stages of the cycle (see Fig. 3).

Cycle III.—This cycle is initiated by a rising birth rate and brought to a close by a recession of the birth rate, while the death rate remains stable (see Fig. 4).

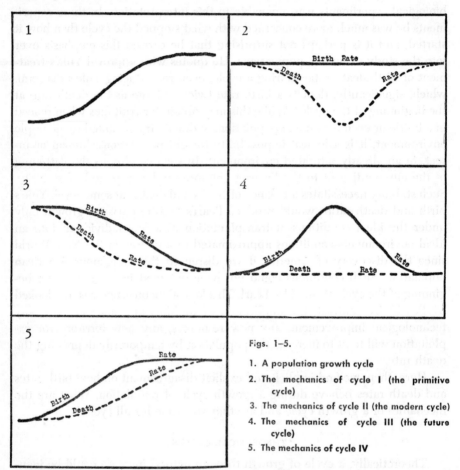

Figs. 1–5.

1. A population growth cycle
2. The mechanics of cycle I (the primitive cycle)
3. The mechanics of cycle II (the modern cycle)
4. The mechanics of cycle III (the future cycle)
5. The mechanics of cycle IV

Cycle IV.—This cycle is also initiated by a rising birth rate but is terminated by a subsequent rise in the death rate (see Fig. 5).

This does not exhaust the possibilities; there are numerous other combinations and permutations that might be remarked. But these will serve as the most obvious and simple pure forms of the cycle. Each of these in the regular form presented above will result in an S-curve of population growth.

Now let us see when and where these different forms of the cycle have occurred.

PRIMITIVE POPULATION CYCLE

Prior to the recent decline in the birth rate in countries affected by the Industrial Revolution and concomitant developments, there is no reliable evidence of growth cycles produced by rising birth rates. Bowen admits of a possible increase in the birth rate during the Middle Ages.[8] However, there is no proof of this development, and the safer generalization is that in the main the birth rate in pre-industrial times was relatively high and reasonably stable. Of this situation Thompson has the following to say:

> Before the development of the more efficient methods of machine production in Western countries and before the accompanying agricultural revolution got under way, steady and rapid population growth was the exception rather than the rule. There was a severe struggle for mere subsistence. When for some reasons conditions were favorable, when there was a series of good crop years, when favorable "runs" of fish appeared, or when disease was less prevalent than usual, there was an increase in population, its rate depending on how favorable these conditions were at the time. But, when dearth and disease came, the death rate rose and population did not grow or even declined.[9]

The inference from this quotation is that the fluctuating variable in these circumstances is the death rate, not the birth rate. A little later Thompson says:

> These facts, coupled with the observations of population growth in the non-industrialized nations of today, lead us to believe that in pre-Industrial Revolution days all death rates were high and averaged very little lower than the birth rates. . . . A violently fluctuating death rate with a very slow increase of population over long periods probably characterized most peoples before the advent of the Industrial Revolution.[10]

Thus we arrive at the hypothesis that cycles of growth in primitive or pre-industrial societies follow the pattern of Cycle I above, i.e., the initial growth is accounted for by a falling death rate, and the cycle closes with a return of the death rate to its previous high level.

There are a number of authenticated cases where this has happened. In Finland between 1810 and 1870 this pattern of growth is evident. In 1810 the death rate stood above the birth rate but, by 1820, was ten points lower than the birth rate. Approximately the same margin was maintained until about 1856, when the death rate rose again to about the same level as the birth rate.[11] Subsequently, of course, Finland has gone into the typical growth cycle which has accompanied industrialization, a cycle which differs in mechanics, as we shall see in a moment.

Recurring famines in many lands induce an appearance of such cycles. India, up to about 1910, gave evidence of alternating patterns of growth and stability or decline, correlated with alternating good crop years and bad. During the limited period for which statistics are available, it appears that the birth rate fluctuated little up to 1910, while the death rate fluctuated widely in the manner described by Thompson.

Again, this is the pattern in China according to Ta Chen:

. . . the data seem to show that Chinese population changes in the past have been cyclical rather than linear and that the cyclical trends may be roughly explained as follows: At the beginning of a new dynasty, when peace and order were maintained, population normally increased by the excess of births over deaths, and cultural development advanced apace through the division of labor. As time went on, the increased density, coupled with the lack of inventions and improvements in farming technology, gradually intensified the struggle for existence by the masses. Nevertheless, population continued to increase until it reached a saturation point, the apex of the cycle. Then came pestilence and famine, symptoms of over-population, until life became increasingly more intolerable and revolution or war broke out. This temporarily relieved the pressure of population and brought a new dynasty into being. Population continued to decrease until it reached the lowest possible level, the bottom of the cycle. Then another cycle began, and the cyclical trends were thus repeated, each lasting several hundred years, the length of time being largely determined by the severity of the population pressure prior to the downfall of the reigning dynasty.[12]

The estimates cited by this author indicate little increase in the Chinese population from the year 2 A.D. to the year 1620. Instead, he postulates periods of growth counterbalanced by periods of loss. While, of course, there are no adequate birth or death statistics for this period, it is significant that Ta Chen cites famine, pestilence, and war as the factors which bring a growth cycle to an end. These are mortality-inducing factors, and the presumption is that a rising death rate closes the cycle. Here again, then, we get the picture of a fluctuating death rate without much change in the birth rate.

The historical and descriptive material dealing with famine and pestilence, all too prevalent in primitive societies, uniformly supports the conclusion that this was the general condition in primitive societies.[13]

The cycle of population increase in primitive society then conforms more closely to Malthus' explanation than it does to the explanation of Pearl, Gini, Spencer, Sadler, Nitti, and others who have believed that the close of the cycle was marked by declining fertility. Pearl's use of the Algerian population as one in which preindustrial conditions would obtain is verging on the ridiculous when he himself notes that the cycle set in after the conquest by the French, who obviously were influenced by the forces of industrialism. Furthermore, if his evidence concerning human populations is of doubtful value, so is that concerning the *Drosophila*. There is no direct evidence in his experiments of the actual birth or egg-laying rate of these fruit flies which would measure their reproductive efforts. The direct evidence is only that of periodic counts of the adult population, i.e., a census. The apparently not excessive mortality among adult fruit flies under conditions of extreme density, coupled with the declining rate of growth of the population, led to the inference that the fertility rate had declined. This is tantamount to disregarding the deaths of infants and children in the human death rate, since the *Drosophila* goes through two stages of development before it emerges as an adult fly. Pearl totally disregarded the possibilities of increased mortality on the part of the larvae and pupae as causes of the declining rate of growth of population in the later phases of the cycle.

It seems likely that he and others have been too much impressed with the obvious decline in birth rates in Western industrial nations in recent times and have tended to give a universal explanation of growth cycles, in terms of the mechanics of this later type, even to the point of imposing the theory upon fruit flies.

THE MODERN CYCLE

It is common knowledge today that population tends to increase with the influences of industrialization, the widening of commercial trade areas, the development of mechanized agriculture, improved medical science, and mass education. Pearl's logistic curve does approximate the growth cycle of most areas subjected to these influences.

The mechanics of this modern population cycle are too well known to require extended treatment. This is the pattern of Cycle II above, with a declining death rate and a declining birth rate but with the birth rate lagging several decades behind the death rate. This cycle is described by Thompson as follows:

The data for Sweden show the pattern of a growing natural increase for several decades after the birth rate began to decline. . . . Here the natural increase—birth rate minus death rate—was greater every decade from 1851 to 1911 than in the corresponding decade a century earlier, although there can be no doubt that Sweden's birth rate had begun to decline as early as 1830. . . .

This period of an increasing margin between birth rate and death rate, or of a rather large but steady margin, as in Finland, is in time succeeded by a period generally shorter but varying considerably in length from country to country, in which the rate of natural increase begins to decline because the birth rate is falling faster than the death rate but during which natural increase still remains quite high.

Thus the modern cycle of population growth in industrialized lands is completed and the population again approaches the stationary or has too few births to maintain itself, as it was in pre-industrial days—although it no longer fluctuates largely between excess and deficit as in earlier days. The failure of population to grow today is not because of the high and fluctuating death rate, as was usually the case in the past, but because of the low birth rate.[14]

Here we have the same pattern of initial reduction in the death rate that characterized the primitive cycle; but, from there on, the pattern is radically different. Instead of a subsequent return to its former height, the death rate remains low—or so it has thus far. Thus the cycle can be concluded only by a reduction in the birth rate, or, more accurately, it is possible to maintain a low death rate indefinitely only if the birth rate is brought under control and reduced commensurately. In any event, the modern cycle shows not only the new feature of a low death rate remaining low but, probably for the first time in history, a secular decline in the birth rate. Both may then tend to become stabilized at a new and lower level.

It seems surprising in the face of the obvious novelty of the influence affecting this cycle, such as scientific medicine and artificial contraception, that anyone could conclude, as Pearl apparently does, that the mechanics of all cycles are the same. It should be noted, of course, that in his late years Pearl gave some recognition to the role played by contraception, but he never fully elaborated its implications for revision of his earlier dogmas.

FUTURE CYCLES

One feature of all the cycles so far discussed is a falling death rate. Are there no cycles characterized by a rising birth rate? With a few limited exceptions, the historical evidence indicates a negative answer to this question. With particular reference to modern times, E. M. East says: "Decreased death rates explain all marked gains in modern populations. Nowhere have birth rates increased—except in very small areas or during short periods of time."[15]

It appears that this statement could be applied as well to ancient as to modern times. As a rule, when such a rare phenomenon appears in the statistical history of a population, it will be found that the rise is due to improvements in recording of births rather than to a real rise in the incidence of birth. For instance, this is the probable cause of the ostensible upward trend in the birth rate in Ceylon from 1850 to 1900.[16]

However, there are instances, as inferred by East, of *short-term* increases in the birth rate. For instances of this kind we need not seek far in space and time. The behavior of the birth rate of the United States since 1933 is a case in point. Here, while the death rate remained nearly stationary, the birth rate responding to economic prosperity and war influences has shown a considerable increase. This suggests the pattern of Cycle III. Although the cycle is not as yet complete, the birth rate has not yet returned to its previous level, but it is dropping, and there is considerable reason to believe that it will continue to drop for some time to come.

A similar phenomenon is apparent in many of the Western countries who were nearing the end of the modern or industrial cycle prior to the depression, i.e., whose birth rates had fallen to a relatively low level by 1930. In most of these areas the low birth rates responded to the influence of prosperity and war and evinced a decided upward trend. This effect, however, was much less apparent in those populations in which the birth rate remained at a high level—say, India and China—areas, that is, that had not yet entered upon the second phase of the modern or industrial cycle characterized by falling birth rates.

From this comes the suggestion that low birth rates are more amenable to increase than are high birth rates. A corollary proposition is that it is an easier matter to lower a death rate of 40 than it is to lower one of 10. In other words, there appears to be a ceiling over birth rates and a floor under death rates. On the latter point Bowen says: ". . . there is an apparent, and presumably inescapable, lower limit which the death rate may approach but never pass, . . . *there is no real lower limit* to the birth rate—or rather, *it is zero.*"[17]

From these propositions we may derive the hypothesis that in Western industrialized areas that have completed the modern population cycle eventuating in both low birth rates and low death rates, any growth cycle in the future will require an increase in the birth rate. Thus we have a reversal of the primitive conditions in which birth rates were high and relatively stable and in which the death rates showed the greatest fluctuation, accounting for any cycles of growth or decline. In the postindustrial phase of population phenomena, it appears that the birth rate must assume the role of greatest freedom and fluctuation, while the death rate becomes relatively stable.

This obviously leads to the further hypothesis that in the postindustrial phase of population, any growth cycle in the future will be of the general pattern of Cycle III and that, as we have labeled Cycle I the "primitive cycle" and Cycle II the "modern cycle," so might we appropriately call Cycle III the "future cycle."

It will be noted, however, that this assumes a continued control of the death rate which would prevent this cycle from assuming the form of Cycle IV. Although a slight upward movement in the death rate is expected in the United States and other countries nearing the end of the modern cycle, there seems to be no precedent in the past for Cycle IV and little prospect of its emergence in the future as a major cycle.

CONCLUSION

In conclusion, then, it may be remarked that, while there have been many cycles of growth that may have approximated the regular and ideal pattern hypotheticated by Pearl, there is no theoretical or historical justification for the conclusion that the mechanics of all population growth cycles are the same. Instead, it appears that in primitive societies cycles of growth are produced by a falling death rate, which subsequently returns to the original high level, while the birth rate remains relatively constant. This general pattern we may call the "primitive cycle." Populations significantly affected by the Industrial Revolution and concomitant factors show a decidedly divergent pattern characterized by both falling birth rates and falling death rates, but with the birth rate lagging behind the death rate in its descent in the first phase, followed by a second phase of a more rapid drop in the birth rate, with the lines ultimately meeting at a low level for both rates. This we have called the "modern cycle." A third pattern is that produced by a rising birth rate which subsequently falls again to a balance with the death rate, which meanwhile remains constant. Some semblance of this pattern has been apparent in many Western countries during the last fifteen years, but otherwise it was virtually unknown in the history of past population growth cycles. However, it is probable that any growth cycles of the future of those populations which have already passed through the modern cycle will manifest this general pattern. For this reason we have referred to it as the "future cycle."

Each of these growth patterns, if regular and symmetrical, would produce a growth curve of the S-form. The mechanics of each obviously differ from one another, and, consequently, so do the conditions producing them. No generalizations ascribing identical causes for all population growth cycles are valid.

REFERENCES

1. *The Biology of Population Growth* (New York: Alfred A. Knopf, 1930), p. 22.
2. Corrado Gini, in *Population* ("Harris Foundation Lectures" [Chicago: University of Chicago Press, 1929]).
3. Herbert Spencer, *Principles of Biology*, II (New York: D. Appleton & Co., 1897), 483 and 501.
4. M. T. Sadler, *The Law of Population* (London: John Murray, 1830), p. 368.
5. F. S. Nitti, *Population and the Social System* (New York: Charles Scribner's Sons, 1894), chaps. ii and iii.
6. Pearl, *op. cit.*, p. 129.
7. *Ibid.*, chap. iii; and G. U. Yule, "The Growth of Population and the Factors Which Control It," *Journal of the Royal Statistical Society*, LXXXVIII (1925), 38.
8. "It is quite probable that birth rates may have had some slight age-long decline. There is, however, the strong possibility of a perceptible upward trend during the Middle Ages" (Ezra Bowen, *An Hypothesis of Population Growth* [New York: Columbia University Press, 1931], p. 169).
9. Warren S. Thompson, *Population and Peace in the Pacific* (Chicago: University of Chicago Press, 1946), p. 22.
10. *Ibid.*, p. 23.
11. Warren S. Thompson, *Population Problems* (New York: McGraw-Hill Book Co., 1935), pp. 123 and 175.
12. Ta Chen, *Population in Modern China*, Suppl. to the *American Journal of Sociology*, Vol. LII (July, 1946).
13. See Thompson, *Population Problems*, chap. xiii.
14. *Population and Peace in the Pacific*, pp. 25–26.
15. *Mankind at the Crossroads* (New York: Charles Scribner's Sons, 1923), p. 271.
16. See Thompson, *Population Problems*, p. 123, for birth statistics of Ceylon.
17. *Op. cit.*, p. 153.

SOME RECENT RESULTS IN POPULATION ANALYSIS*

By Alfred J. Lotka

PHENOMENA EXHIBITED BY THE POPULATION AS A WHOLE.—The study of quantitative demography or population analysis can be undertaken from two points of view or by two methods—the empirical method and the rational or formal method.

The rational method is *possible* through the fact that between the various demographic characteristics there exist certain necessary relations, that is, relations imposed by the laws of physics or the laws of logic.

But the rational method is not only possible, it is *indispensable* if we wish to obtain an entirely satisfactory understanding of population phenomena. Undoubtedly the ideal process is to cultivate both methods side by side. According to our predilections, the empirical data will then be for us concrete illustrations of the abstract principles that mainly interest us; or, on the contrary, the formal relations will serve us as guides in the examination and interpretation of the empirical data which, in that case, will be our fundamental interest.

In what follows, it is proposed to indicate briefly a few examples, among more recent developments, to illustrate the relation between the two methods.

We shall begin by considering a few fundamental types of population, somewhat idealized and yet representing conditions such as are approached in some actual populations. The three types which we will consider are the stationary population, the Malthusian population, and the logistic population in relation to actual populations.

In the chart, Figure 1, there have been plotted two curves of age distribution, first, one corresponding to the stationary population on the basis of the mortality of white females in the United States 1929–1931; and, second, a corresponding age distribution curve, computed on the basis of the same mortality table, but with an assumed constant rate of increase of 1 per cent per annum. Certain points of geometric interest about these curves call for attention. A vertical line has been drawn through the point corresponding to the average age of each population, and a third vertical has been drawn through the point of the intersection of the two curves. The feature to which I wish to draw attention is that to within small quantities of second and higher order the line through the point of intersection lies half way between the two verticals. It can, in fact, be shown that the distance between these verticals is, in close approximation, given by $\frac{1}{2} \sigma^2 r = \frac{1}{2}\lambda_2 r$, where σ is the standard deviation

* Reprinted from the *Journal of the American Statistical Association*, 33 (March 1938), pp. 164–178, by permission of the American Statistical Association. Paper presented at the International Population Congress in Paris, July, 1937.

of the life curve about its mean and r the rate of increase of the Malthusian population.

If instead of drawing the curve for the Malthusian population corresponding to a rate of increase over 1 per cent, we drew a succession of curves of this type with successively diminishing rates of increase, we would obtain a nest of curves, the left hand portion of which would be located at successively

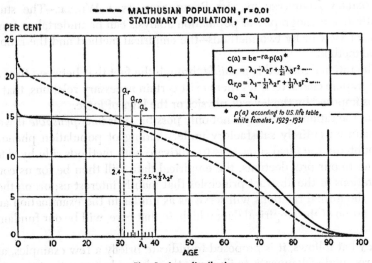

Fig. 1. Age distribution.

lower levels while the right hand portion would be at successively higher levels, as we pass from greater to lesser values of r. This is merely an illustration of the fact that a rapidly increasing population has a relatively high proportion of young persons, and that this proportion of young persons diminishes with a diminishing rate of increase in the population. The general character of these curves may be described by saying that each is produced from the one immediately preceding by a *tilting* movement about a certain point. We may ask what that point is. It can be shown that the *instantaneous center of tilt* as we pass from one of these curves to one immediately following (corresponding to an infinitesimal change in r) is located at the point corresponding to average age of the population. As we pass from curve to curve, this center of tilt moves somewhat slowly from left to right, within relatively narrow limits. So, for example, if we start with a curve corresponding to a rate of increase of $r = 0.01$ and extend the process until we are dealing with a curve with a rate of increase of $r = 0.00$, then the instantaneous center of tilt will be found to have moved from age 31 to 36.

These may at first sight seem to be merely interesting geometric properties. They have, however, a practical bearing. The fact that the center of tilt lies in the neighborhood of the average age of the population implies that, as we pass from greater to lesser values of r, the natural rate of increase, the proportion of the population comprised within the age groups at the young end and at the old end of the curve of the population change materially, but the age group or groups centered about the average age of the population, i.e., essentially the group of productive workers, undergoes relatively small change.

TABLE I

AVERAGE AGE OF THE POPULATION IN UNITED STATES

	1880	1890	1900	1910	1920	1930
1. Males	25.30	26.29	26.93	27.79	28.62	29.89
2. Females	25.01	25.91	26.47	27.27	28.11	29.69
3. Malthusian	24.70	25.46	26.35	27.34	28.38	29.41
4. Malthusian	24.06	24.79	25.67	26.96	28.38	30.17

Note: (1) and (2), Observed values. (3) Values calculated on the basis of (a) the value of r corresponding to the year in question according to the logistic curve of increase in the United States; and (b) the life table for white females, 1919–1920. (4) Values calculated in the same way, but based on a life table as close as possible to the year in question.

While we have recognized these features as special characteristics of the Malthusian age distribution it will be seen from Table I that on the one hand the average age of the actual population of the United States has tended to approach that of a Malthusian age distribution corresponding to the prevailing rate of natural increase; on the other hand, Table II shows that the proportion of persons comprised within the age group 20 to 49 years in the actual population has varied only rather slowly, the extreme limits being 38.6 per cent in 1850 and 44.0 per cent in 1930, an increase of 5.4 in the course of 80 years.

TABLE II

POPULATION OF AGES 20–49 AS PER CENT OF TOTAL POPULATION, UNITED STATES, 1850–1930

Year	1850	1880	1890	1900	1910	1920	1930
Actual	38.6	40.0	41.2	42.2	44.0	43.9	44.0

The Malthusian type of population, being that which prevails when the rate of increase of the population is constant, may be quite closely approached when the rate of increase of the population has been approximately constant for some time. There are several instances of actual populations of this type recorded in the literature. One of these, the population of England and Wales in the period from 1871 to 1880, is exhibited in Table III, taken from one of my earlier publications (1907), together with the correspondingly computed Malthusian ideal type. A similar example was later given by Bortkiewicz (1911), namely the population of Germany in 1910, and quite recently another example by Cramér, namely the population of Sweden in 1935.

These examples lend a certain practical interest to the Malthusian type of population. However, even if no actual case of this type had been observed anywhere, it would still be of serious importance, because it is towards a particular Malthusian type, the "stable" type, that any population, starting from any arbitrary age distribution,[1] would converge, if it were subject to a regime of a constant age schedule of fecundity and mortality.[2]

TABLE III

MALTHUSIAN POPULATION
AGE DISTRIBUTION, BIRTH RATE, DEATH RATE AND RATE OF
NATURAL INCREASE, PER THOUSAND

England and Wales, 1871–1880

Age groups		Male		Female		Both Sexes	
		Calculated	Observed	Calculated	Observed	Calculated	Observed
0– 5		142	139	135	132	138	136
5–10		118	123	114	117	116	120
10–15		107	110	104	104	106	107
15–20		98	99	95	95	96	97
20–25		88	87	86	91	87	89
25–35		150	144	148	149	149	147
35–45		117	112	117	115	117	113
45–55		84	84	87	87	86	86
55–65		57	59	63	61	60	59
65–75		29	31	36	35	32	33
75–∞		11	12	13	15	12	13
Birth rate	b	36.47	36.92	33.74	33.72	35.08	35.28
Death rate	d	22.16	22.61	20.01	19.99	21.07	21.27
Rate of increase	r	14.31	14.31	13.73	13.73	14.01	14.01

Age groups		Germany, 1891–1900		Sweden, 1910	
		Both Sexes		Both Sexes	
		Calculated	Observed	Calculated	Observed
0–10		244	244	218	218
10–20		198	198	185	192
20–30		164	170	155	156
30–40		134	131	129	125
40–50		105	101	107	102
50–60		78	78	86	88
60–70		50	51	65	66
70–80		22	23	40	40
80–∞		4	5	15	13
Birth rate	b	35.90	36.2	—	—
Death rate	d	22.01	22.3	—	—
Rate of increase	r	13.89	13.9	—	—

In the case of a population which has actually attained the stable form, the corresponding stable rate of natural increase is known by direct observation. In any other case it can be found only by computation.[3] In a certain sense this stable rate of natural increase is a purely hypothetical quantity. It possesses no value for purposes of prediction, since the conditions (fertility and mortality) which are assumed constant in its computation, will in actuality rarely be constant. However, in another sense the stable rate of natural increase is anything but hypothetical. It is a very real measure of actually prevailing conditions. If this stable rate of natural increase has a negative value, we know that the existing conditions of fertility or mortality, or both, must be improved if the population is to escape eventual annihilation. The stable rate of natural increase is thus recognized as the measure of an intrinsic quality of the existing population; hence the alternative name "intrinsic rate of natural increase" for this quantity ρ.

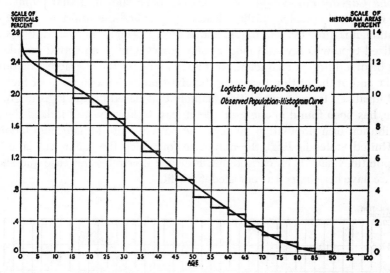

Fig. 2. Age distribution in logistic population compared with native white female population of U.S. 1920.

In its essentially quantitative application the intrinsic rate of natural increase may be replaced fairly satisfactorily by the "Boeckh index" favored by R. Kuczynski, or by the "replacement index" of W. S. Thompson, much used by F. Lorimer. These two measures possess the advantage of being a little easier to compute, although the difficulties of the computation of the intrinsic rate have at times been exaggerated. It is true that the computation of ρ requires a few minutes[4] beyond that of the Boeckh index R_0 (which incidentally is obtained as an intermediate result whenever ρ is computed). But if these few minutes are spent on the extra work, it must be remembered that an additional result is obtained which has the advantage of being directly comparable to the crude rate of natural increase, the crude birth rate and the crude death rate. Furthermore, the particular interest of the intrinsic rate of natural increase lies in the fact that it plays a very important role in a whole system of intertwining demographic relations, as I have set forth in detail in a forthcoming monograph.[5] Among other things it leads directly to an intrinsic birth rate and an intrinsic death rate, which in many cases will differ materially from the corresponding crude rates; of these intrinsic birth rates and death rates the Boeckh index R_0 gives us no indication.

Those who favor the use of the Boeckh index have sometimes remarked that an approximate value of the intrinsic rate of natural increase can be obtained by dividing $1 - R_0$ by the mean length of generation. But it is only fair to draw attention to the fact that this idea dates from the year 1925, the time of the publication of a fundamental article on the intrinsic rate of natural increase. Neither Boeckh, in 1886, nor any of his disciples since had ever suggested this idea or recognized its implications.

The Logistic Population. While, as has been shown, actual populations have on several occasions rather closely approached the Malthusian age distribution, it is quite evident that in actual fact, especially in modern times, the idealized type which would most closely correspond to an actual population must be of a different character, for it must allow for the characteristic downward trend of the birth rate among the civilized nations. In point of fact, the third idealized type of population, namely that based on the logistic growth curve, has been found in one example at least to fit very well indeed the age distribution of a population, namely the native white female population of the United States in 1920, the only case for which the somewhat laborious computations have been carried out. Figure 2 illustrates this case and shows that we have here indeed a very acceptable fit.

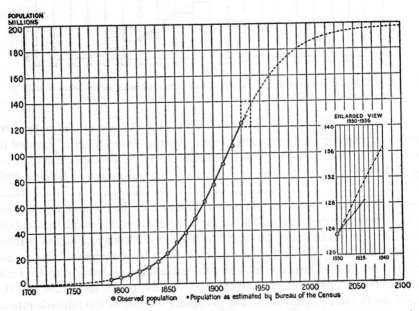

Fig. 3. Logistic growth curve applied to the population of the United States and compared with the population according to census data, 1790–1936.

That the logistic type of age distribution should be found to fit very acceptably the population of the United States, at any rate so far as it is native born, is not surprising, considering that until recently, that is until the date of the last census, 1930, the population of the United States has in its growth followed rather closely the logistic curve. Since that date the growth curve of the United States has deviated quite appreciably from the logistic curve, as shown in the chart, Figure 3. This chart, however, really gives an inadequate idea of the extent of the departure, even though we have used an insert drawn on a magnified scale to bring out recent deviation from the logistic. This deviation is brought into much greater prominence when we compare, not the number of the population, but the annual number of births, as computed according to the logistic, and as actually observed. To this comparison we shall now proceed.

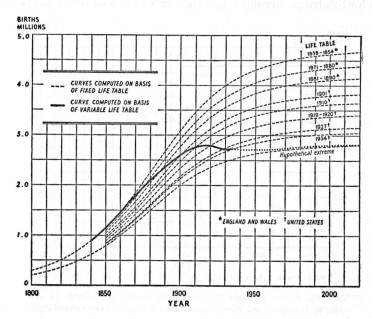

Fig. 4. Annual births computed for a closed population growing according to the logistic law with the characteristic constants of the United States, and according to several life tables.

At a former Congress on population, six years ago, I indicated a method by which it is possible to compute for a closed population growing by the logistic law, on the basis of suitable mortality data, the corresponding curve of annual birth rates. Let me now present a diagram indicating a modified mode of procedure by which, not the curve of the birth rates, but that of the annual births is obtained. If over the whole stretch of time under consideration mortality had been constant it would be a relatively simple matter to compute the course of the annual births corresponding to the logistic curve of growth of the population. So, for example, if the regime had remained unchanged as of the year about 1840, the annual births would have followed essentially the course indicated by the uppermost curve in Figure 4. Similarly had the process taken place entirely under the regime of the mortality of about 1871–1880, the course of events would have been essentially that represented by the second curve from above, etc. Actually, the process has proceeded under the regime of successive mortality rates, and the corresponding annual births, if the population had grown entirely by excess of births over deaths, would have been essentially that represented by the heavily drawn curve which crosses the nest of approximately parallel curves.

An inspection of the heavily drawn curve so obtained brings out an interesting feature. At a certain part of its course, after attaining a maximum about the year 1918, the curve drops downward slightly for several years. The reason for this temporary dip is that the curve of annual births has been com-

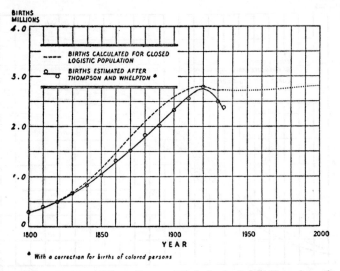

Fig. 5. Comparison of "actual" annual births in the United States (as estimated by Thompson and Whelpton) and curves computed for a closed logistic population.

puted for a series of mortalities improving from year to year, and improving very rapidly in the recent past, with the result that the curves drawn on the basis of recent mortality tables are situated at successively lower levels. However, there is a limit to what we may hope to accomplish further. It is not likely that the mean length of life can be increased much beyond 70 years. The lowermost curve, inserted to complete the diagram, and not by way of prophecy, has been drawn on the basis of a hypothetical[6] life table corresponding to a mean length of life of 70 years. The continuation of the curve of annual births beyond 1934 is indicated in Figure 5 by the dotted curve. This curve represents the lower limit which cannot be crossed by the annual births in a closed logistic population, so long as the mean length of life remains limited to 70 years.

Such would be the course of the annual births in a logistic population possessing certain of the fundamental characteristics of the population of the United States, but growing exclusively by the excess of births over deaths. Actually the evolution of our population has followed a different line, more particularly in that it has received very notable accretions by immigration. Let us then examine how the actual course of events compares with the curve of annual births in a closed population growing according to the logistic law.

The official statistics of births in the United States is of relatively recent origin. It dates only from 1915. However, on the basis of the enumeration of children under 5 years of age in decennial censuses, making due correction for deaths, it is possible to obtain an approximate estimate of the annual births. This is the method employed by W. S. Thompson and P. K. Whelpton,[7] the results[8] of which are indicated by the small circles in Figure 5. The points so plotted have been fitted by the graphic method with a curve shown in full line in the drawing. The curve of dashes in Figure 5 is a direct copy of the curve of logistic births of Figure 4.

TABLE IV

RATE OF INCREASE OF POPULATION IN EMPLOYABLE AGE GROUPS IN RELATION TO
RATE OF INCREASE OF ENTIRE POPULATION, UNITED STATES, 1850 TO 1950

Year	Population, thousands, by Age			Population ages 15–69 as per cent of total	Average annual per cent increase in population from preceding entry			Ratio col. (6) col. (5)
	All ages	15–69	Under 15; also 70 over		All ages	15–69	Under 15; 70 and over	
	(1)	(2)	(3)	(4)	(5)	(6)	(7)	(8)
1950*	141,098	100,458	40,640	71.20	.604	.533	.782	.88
1945*	136,962	97,851	39,111	71.44	.697	.853	.317	1.22
1940*	132,350	93,849	38,501	70.91	.757	1.241	—.335	1.64
1935†	127,521	88,365	39,156	69.29	.774	1.354	—.383	1.75
1930	122,775	82,761	39,920	67.46	1.614	1.980	.944	1.23
1920	105,711	69,085	36,477	65.44	1.494	1.508	1.482	1.01
1910	91,972	60,034	31,769	65.39	2.102	2.535	1.386	1.21
1900	75,995	47,891	27,903	63.19	2.135	2.340	1.798	1.10
1890	62,622	38,811	23,649	62.14	2.486	2.916	1.762	1.17
1880	50,156	30,049	20,107	59.91	3.008	3.197	2.738	1.06
1870	38,558	22,768	15,785	59.06	2.263	2.511	1.964	1.11
1860	31,443	18,198	13,194	57.97	3.558	3.787	3.222	1.06
1850	23,192	13,199	9,979	56.95				

* Estimated on basis of age schedule of mortality and fertility as of 1934.
† Estimated from births, deaths, and migration.

It will be seen that about the beginning of the nineteenth century, the curve of actual births (as estimated by Thompson and Whelpton) fuses with that calculated on the basis of the logistic law. Then comes a period up to about 1920 where the curve of actual births falls a considerable distance below that calculated according to the logstic law for a closed population, which is entirely proper since in actual fact immigrants from abroad have added their numbers to the accessions to the population by births. In late years immigration to the United States has been arrested, and quite recently immigration has actually given way to slight net emigration.

The significant feature strikingly brought out by the diagram is that at the period when the logistic curve of births exhibited a gentle downward dip, the curve of actual births has shown a very sharp decline, and this at the very time when immigration not only touched the zero mark but became a negative quantity.

A little while ago, when we inspected the curve of population growth, we found that since 1930 it had deviated on the short side of the logistic curve, but the deviation in that case began only in 1930, was relatively slight and we had to use an insert drawn on a magnified scale to show it clearly. There is no need of any magnification of the curve of births to show the very strong departure from the logistic which has taken place.

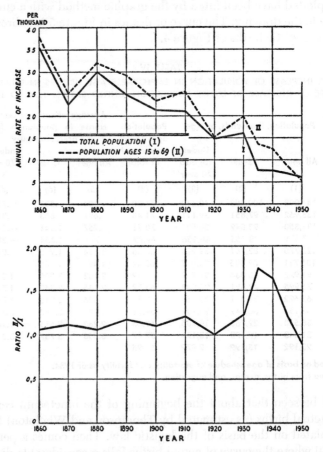

Fig. 6. Comparison of annual rate of increase of the total population and population ages 15 to 69 in the United States.

Differential Growth Rates: The Employable Age Groups. In a population in stable age distribution, all the elements increase at the same per cent rate, and the relative proportion of the several age groups is constant. In the logistic population, on the other hand, older age groups increase more rapidly than the younger, in fact, the youngest age groups actually diminish; there is in consequence, a continual shifting in the proportion of the several age groups. In the actual population of the United States, a similar shifting of the age groups has occurred, with certain important consequences. In Table IV there have been set forth the per cent rates of increase for the total population of the United States, over the calendar period 1850 to 1930, extended to 1950 by estimates; and side by side with these figures the rates of increase of the population between the ages 15 and 69 have been shown. The last column gives the ratio of the increase in the population of ages 15 to 69 to the corresponding increase in the total population at successive decennial dates and in the last three quinquennia. This table brings out a point which may be of very serious interest. Over the early decennia from 1850 to 1930, the ratio of the two rates of increase has not varied very greatly, the lowest value being 1.01 and the highest 1.23. But it will be noticed that from 1930 to 1935 there was a sudden increase in this ratio from 1.23 to 1.75. Here the rate of increase of the population between the ages 15 and 69 is almost twice as great as that of the total population, and judging from the forecast for 1940, that situation will continue essentially until that time. By 1945, this great disparity will again disappear. These facts are brought out graphically in Figure 6.

It is interesting to ponder what effect this situation may have on the opportunity for young persons to obtain gainful employment.

PHENOMENA EXHIBITED BY PARTICULAR UNITS OF THE POPULATION.—Population analysis is concerned not only with the gross phenomena presented by the population regarded as a whole, but comprises within its scope also the consideration of specific phenomena exhibited by unit elements of which the population is composed. Without going to the extreme in this process of particularization, we shall here devote a few paragraphs to a certain aspect of family statistics.

If in a semi-logarithmic system of coordinates we represent the probability p_n or π_v that a new-born child shall, in the course of its life, ultimately have n children or v sons, a series of points is obtained, which, at any rate up to $n = 10$, array themselves essentially in a straight line. In the graph Figure 7 thus constructed on the basis of the statistics of the United States (white persons) a curious circumstance becomes apparent; the probability of having two sons is equal to that of having two children. How does this singular result come about?

The probability of having n children, according to the linear distribution exhibited in Figure 7 is

(1) $$p_n = 0.7358^{(n-1)} p_1$$

or, say

(2) $$p_n = \gamma^{(n-1)} p_1.$$

Let a be the proportion of male births and $\beta = (1 - a)$ be the proportion of female births in the total. Then, by an application of elementary principles of the calculus of probability, we find for the probability π of having ν sons, the expression

(3) $\qquad \pi_\nu = \Gamma^{\nu-1}\pi_1$

(4) $\qquad \Gamma = \dfrac{\alpha\gamma}{1 - \beta\gamma}$

(5) $\qquad = \dfrac{0.515}{1 - 0.485 \times 0.736}$

(6) $\qquad = 0.589$

(7) $\qquad \pi_1 = \alpha p_1 + 2\alpha\beta\gamma p_1 + 3\alpha\beta^2\gamma^2 p_1 + \cdots = \dfrac{\alpha p_1}{(1 - \beta\gamma)^2}.$

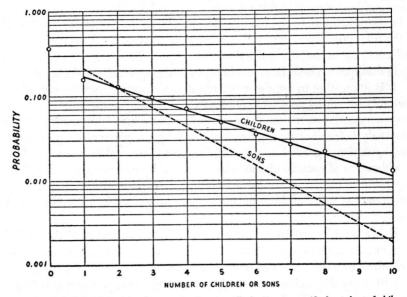

Fig. 7. Probability for a new-born male of eventually having a specified number of children or a specified number of sons.

Let us find the ratio

(8) $\qquad \pi_2/p_2 = \alpha^2/(1 - \beta\gamma)^3 = 0.2652/0.2660 = 0.9971.$

In round numbers this ratio is therefore 1. This arises from the fact that α and β are nearly equal, that is to say, the probability of a male or a female birth is in either case approximately one-half; on the other hand γ has a value of about three-quarters, so that according to formula (8) it follows that

(9) $\qquad \pi_2/p_2 = \tfrac{1}{4}/(1 - \tfrac{1}{2} \times \tfrac{3}{4})^3 = 1.024.$

We have here a statistical curiosity discovered accidentally by the author in dealing with the problem of the probability of extinction of a family.[9]

THE IDEAL AIM OF RATIONAL POPULATION ANALYSIS.—The particularization of the discussion could be carried further. From the consideration of the family as a social unit we could proceed to that of the individual himself. The ideal would be a model which, by its operation, would represent the actions and destinies of the individuals of a typical population. Such a model might consist of a collection of urns which, by a series of drafts conducted according to prescribed rules, would give us a truly representative sample of the characteristics of the population. This ideal, though incapable of realization in all detail, can be approached to within a degree of accuracy which will depend on the one hand on our sources of statistical data and on the other on the pains which we are willing to take in carrying out the task.

Such a model has been actually constructed on the basis of vital statistics of the United States, using, however, in place of inconvenient urns, an equivalent device, a kind of roulette wheel, with discs divided by radial lines into sectors of suitably adjusted angle. Unfortunately it is not possible on a scale suitable for these pages to reproduce the series of discs employed in this model.

REFERENCES

1. Provided only that the age composition of this population were not wholly abnormal, as for instance if it were made up wholly of individuals of one sex, or of individuals beyond the age of reproduction, etc.

2. The author takes this opportunity to correct a faulty enunciation of this principle which has crept into the literature. The principle has been formulated in the words: "a population constantly subject to the same mortality and with a constant rate of increase must *ultimately* become stable, that is to say, have a stable age composition, a stable birth rate and a stable death rate with a constant rate of increase." The fact is that the conditions explicitly stated are insufficient to enable one to make any prediction regarding the further development of the population in question. If we supplement the enunciation in order to render the prediction determinate (by adding the condition which is implicit in the original context, that the population in question is to be subject not only to a constant life table, but also to a constant age schedule of fertility), then it is futile to say that the population will *ultimately* converge to the stable form, for under these conditions it can have none other than the stable form from the start. See A. J. Lotka, *Journal of the Washington Academy of Sciences*, Vol. 27 (1937), p. 299; and *Human Biology*, Vol. 9 (1937), p. 104.

3. Based on statistics not only of mortality but also of fertility.

4. One of my assistants, using a computing machine, carried out the additional steps in eleven minutes.

5. A. J. Lotka, *Théorie analytique des associations biologiques*. Deuxième partie—Analyse démographique. Hermann et Cie. Paris.

6. According to Louis I. Dublin and Alfred J. Lotka, *Length of Life—A Study of the Life Table* (New York: The Ronald Press Company, 1936).

7. *Population Trends in the United States*, 1933, page 262.

8. Thompson and Whelpton's results were, however, for the present purpose, modified by the inclusion of an estimate of colored births, which were not included in the figures of these authors. Also, the number of births for the year 1934 (the last point on the curve in Figure 5) was obtained by a special calculation based on actually registered births; in other words, this particular point is based on more recent data than were available to Thompson and Whelpton at the time they made their estimates.

9. A. J. Lotka, "The Extinction of Families," *Journal of the Washington Academy of Sciences*, Vol. 21 (1931), pp. 377, 453.

CHAPTER 4

POPULATION, RESOURCES, TECHNOLOGY, AND LEVELS OF LIVING

Whereas, prior to the eighteenth century, those who wrote about population tended to stress the political and military aspects of population movements, subsequent writers, in particular those who anticipated or followed Malthus, tended to stress the significance of population movements for the level of living, especially that of the working classes. During the first half of the nineteenth century it usually was supposed that the level of living depended predominantly upon the man-land ratio, or upon the ratio of population to land and other natural resources. This view was qualified somewhat, however, by writers who accepted Adam Smith's emphasis upon the importance of division of labor. They believed that, up to a point, as numbers and population density increase, the division of labor increases, and with it the effectiveness with which a population works and exploits land and other resources at its disposal. Beyond this point, however, advantages attendant upon increasing population density no longer sufficed to offset disadvantages attendant upon increases in the ratio of the population to land and other natural resources. Exception was taken to this emphasis upon the population-resources ratio by most socialist writers (both Marxian and non-Marxian), for they attributed lowness of income, wages, and living standards predominantly to defectiveness of socio-economic organization, a defectiveness that, they asserted, could be removed through collectivization.

Most of the pre-1860 writers underestimated the influence of improvements in technology, improvements which probably played as important a role in bringing about increases in income per head as did the formation of capital upon which great stress was placed throughout the nineteenth century. It was believed, of course, that the growth of numbers should be restrained, since then the pressure of numbers upon land and other natural resources would increase less rapidly, and capital per head could increase more rapidly and thus become a more effective counterbalance to worsening of the population-resources ratio. It was generally assumed, furthermore, that these salutary courses of action were more likely to be pursued under a regime of private property than under one of collectivism, since under the former set of arrangements individuals, because they were held responsible for their actions, would be more disposed to be thrifty and prudent.

In time less importance came to be attached to land and agriculture by English and European writers, for they found in the agricultural products of the New World relief from the impact of diminishing returns at home, and they observed that increasingly, as average income and the standard of living rose, it was the scarcity of goods other than landed products that deterred men from marriage and mutliplication. The role of population-limiting factor, once performed by land, was, for the time at least, being executed by other agents, perhaps by minerals, perhaps by comforts, perhaps even by luxuries.

It came to be assumed explicitly after 1848 that there was a right or optimum density of population for any country, given which average income would be as high as was possible under the existing state of the industrial arts and other relevant circumstances. If a country's population fell short of this optimum number, or if it exceeded it, average income would be less than it would have been had actual density approximated the optimum level. Subsequently, however, it was observed that what constituted the optimum number was not constant; it varied with the state of a country's industrial arts, with its international trading relations, and so on; it had probably risen in the course of the nineteenth century, and it might rise still more, though it could also decline. Accordingly, population maladjustment—i.e., measured by the relative discrepancy existing between actual and optimum density —might change because of a change either in the size of the actual population or in that of the optimum population. Population maladjustment was, however, to be minimized, since maladjustment entailed a lower average income than would otherwise be attainable.

The usefulness of the optimum concept came to be questioned on a variety of grounds, other than those advanced by many nineteenth and twentieth century Marxians. It does not constitute a solution for the population problems of countries which find themselves in a Malthusian situation (see Chapter 6). Some question whether average income is a satisfactory index of the welfare possibilities open to a people, either denying that a satisfactory index can be developed, or asserting that there exist other indexes which are more likely to command universal consent. It is said that it is not possible to determine empirically what is or what will be a country's population optimum, should an index of welfare be agreed upon; and it is added that, even could the optimum be determined, little could be done to modify the size of the actual population accordingly and thereby greatly diminish population maladjustment. These arguments have been directed against the usefulness of the optimum under comparatively static socio-economic conditions. The force of these arguments is considerably intensified in the usual event that dynamic rather than static conditions prevail. For then population maladjustment is avoided, not by removing discrepancies between a population's actual and optimum sizes, but by confining the movement through time of a country's actual population to the optimum path of population change.

Many of these criticisms of the optimum, some hold, overlook the basic source of usefulness of the theory. Optimum theory, it is said, places the burden of proof upon those who urge the advantages of further population growth. Optimum theory recognizes that, population increase having taken place, little or nothing can be done about it even though the population growth in question serves to make average income or welfare, howsoever defined, lower than it would have been in the absence of this increase. Optimum theory, therefore, in so far as it affects social policy or reproductive behavior, exercises a restraining influence upon population growth and makes the range of alternatives open to a community greater than it otherwise would have been.

At the time when social scientists first began to express themselves in terms of the optimum, the capacity of men to regulate their numbers was much less than it is today, the apparatus of state was less adapted than it is today to modification of the levels of age-specific fertility and mortality, and regnant socio-economic philosophy and practice were much less favorable than now to utilization of the apparatus of state for this purpose. There are good grounds for supposing, furthermore, that in many countries there is no net per capita economic advantage to be had from additional population growth, whereas a century ago there were good grounds for supposing that in most countries the advantages attendant upon some additional population growth outweighed the disadvantages. With the progress of industrialization, moreover, and with the advance of per capita income, the absolute magnitude of the demand per head made upon depletable and comparatively non-augmentable natural resources has become very high by even late nineteenth century standards. In consequence, a given increase in population produces a much heavier drain on depletable and non-augmentable natural resources in an advanced than in an underdeveloped country (e.g., in 1950 petroleum consumption per head was about eighteen times as high in the United States as in the remainder of the world.) For these various reasons, some believe that effective regulation of numbers is both more possible and more desirable today than it was in the nineteenth century in those countries in which an agricultural economy gave place to an industrial economy.

The extent to which scarcity of land and natural resources may operate to reduce per capita income as numbers increase is not easy to determine or to forecast. If labor were perfectly substitutable for agricultural land and natural resources, the discomforts of population pressure would not become notable until space had become inadequate. But labor is not perfectly substitutable for land and natural resources; and the increasing scarcity of these elements tends to offset in whole or in part the income-increasing effects of technological progress and extension of division of labor. The impact of this scarcity varies in space and time, however. In the United States raw materials approximated, in value terms, 24.3 per cent of gross national product in 1900, or about 29 per cent of national income. By 1950 these percentages had fallen to 12.7 and 15 even though population had meanwhile doubled, gross national product had increased 272 per cent, and aggregate raw-material consumption had increased about 140 per cent. Apparently raw material consumption per head increases as a society progresses, but less rapidly than gross national product. It is to be expected, therefore, that world raw material production, which in 1950 approximated (in value terms) three-tenths of world income, will for a time grow faster than world population but less rapidly than world income. Eventually, however, it may grow more rapidly than world income, in which event scarcity of land and natural resources will be significantly slowing down the progress of per capita income.

In proportion as this scarcity is felt it will become more difficult for nations to correct imbalance between numbers, per capita income, and desired level of living. For if numbers are so great that realized income is less than desired income, it is almost solely by increasing realized income that a nation can correct this imbalance; and yet this correction will be made increasingly difficult by the growing scarcity of land and raw materials, particularly if numbers continue to increase.

The selections comprising this chapter treat of the optimum and related questions. Ogburn's paper suggests the importance of technology and ownership arrangements. Gottlieb's article clarifies what has been and what may be meant by the optimum concept when applied to countries not engaged in international trade.

Peacock translates Malthusian and modern population theories into economic terms. Spengler's essay indicates a number of ways in which per capita income may be affected by changes in population growth and density. Saunders' discloses how the process of migration and the process of social equilibration are related.

POPULATION, PRIVATE OWNERSHIP, TECHNOLOGY, AND THE STANDARD OF LIVING*

By William Fielding Ogburn

The wealth of nations has been the subject of much distinguished writing. Nowadays we speak of "income" rather than "wealth." And, more recently, in an age of the "welfare" state, much reference is made to the "standard of living"—a less exact term—which usually refers to an economic plane of living in actual existence and not to a moral or spiritual standard.

In this paper four factors that affect differences in the standard of living of peoples will be considered: population, natural resources, organization, and technology. Actually, these factors are interrelated and not independent.

The term "population" refers to quantity, which has meaning only as it is related to the size of an area. The theory is that, if all other factors are constant, generally the greater the population, the lower the standard of living, particularly in agricultural areas; though it is probably true that in some sparsely settled countries an increasing population for a time would have meant an increasing standard of living if other factors had remained the same.

Natural resources vary in quality of soil and variety and extent of minerals as well as in sun, moisture, and temperature. A people with meager natural resources will have a lower standard of living than a people with the same technology and more abundant natural resources.

"Organization" in this context refers to economic organization, though it is tied in with political and social organization. The concept of economic organization is separate from the concept of technology, though actually they are very closely related.

The economic organization of a state may be one in which productive industry belongs to private owners or is owned by government or owned by both in various combinations. It is customary to contrast today these types under the names "communism" and "capitalism." From the organizational point of view, communism and socialism are much alike. "Private capitalism" is not a very satisfactory term, for it implies not only private ownership but also capital goods which are the subject matter of technology. So private capitalism is really a combination of technology and private ownership. These types of organizations, even with the same technology, may affect the standard of living of the people. The economic organization in other cultures than our modern ones, as of hunting peoples, of herders, or of those with a hoe culture, have varying standards of living in the order named, but in these

* Reprinted from *The American Journal of Sociology*, 56 (January 1951), pp. 314–319, by permission of the author and the University of Chicago Press.

cases the technology differs. It is difficult to separate organization from technology.

By 'technology" we mean the knowledge of the production of material goods, and by extension it includes applied physical science. The standard of living is obviously related to the tools of production, that is, technology. For instance, the standard of living of the Stone Age American Indian, two hundred years ago at the foot of Lake Michigan, was lower than that of the present-day Chicagoan, with his advanced machines.

Probably all will admit the validity of the claims for the influence of these variables on the standard of living. But what we should like to know is the degree of influence of each. This question has arisen particularly in a comparison of the effects of communism and of private ownership or free enterprise on the standard of living. In the discussion of this topic it seems to be assumed that communism and private ownership are the main determinants of the standard of living. For instance, in *Time* magazine[1] in an article showing that for seven items of consumption about ten times as many hours of labor were required to earn enough money to purchase them in the Soviet Union as in the United States, the following comment is made: "They . . . prove . . . that 30 years after the Revolution, Russia was still giving its workers 10 percent of what an 'exploited' worker under capitalism got for his labor" (see Table 1). Similar figures have been quoted in newspapers and by speakers, with the suggestion or implication that the reason a Russian worker can buy so much less for an hour's labor than a worker in the United States can is somehow due to a difference between communism and private ownership. Thus a leaflet distributed by the American Telephone and Telegraph Company at the Chicago Fair of 1950 contains the following statement:

America has only 1/16 of the world's population, and about the same proportion of land and natural resources. But America has more than ½ of the world's telephone, telegraph, radio networks; more than ⅓ of the railways, and about ¾ of the automobiles and almost ½ of the radios. Just what is it that has given Americans the highest income, the most goods, the best quality, and the lowest prices on earth? It is free enterprise.

A little reflection, of course, reminds one that there are other things besides organization in the standard of living.

Further consideration suggests that the hours of labor as an index of values might be used to indicate the degree of importance of the four factors just described—population, organization, natural resources, and density— on the comparative wealth of peoples. Accordingly, we chose for comparison five countries: China, India, the United Kingdom, the United States, and the Soviet Union.

China before the war had private ownership of production, with a low technology, abundant natural resources, and a dense population. India's status was much like China's in these respects, but with a somewhat more advanced technology, though one not highly developed. The United King-

dom has about 80 per cent private ownership and is the most densely populated of the five countries, with a highly developed technology, though not
so extensive or so efficient as that of the United States, and with rather good
natural resources. The U.S.S.R. has extensive socialism, is not a very densely
populated country, has excellent natural resources, with a technology somewhat more developed than that of China and India but not so advanced as
that of the United Kingdom and the United States. The latter is favored by
a small population for the size of its territory, a very advanced technology,
abundant natural resources, and private ownership.

TABLE 1

MINUTES OF LABOR REQUIRED TO EARN MONEY TO PURCHASE ARTICLES IN
U.S.S.R. AND IN THE UNITED STATES

Item	In U.S.S.R.	In United States
Rye bread, pound	31	7
Wheat bread, pound	70	7.5
Veal, pound	315	34.5
Butter, pound	642	48.5
Beer, bottle	171	6.25
Cotton dress	1,911	142
Woolen suit	34,815	1,684

Let us see how much an hour's labor will buy of a common list of articles
in each of these countries with varied technology, population density, and
politico-economic organization, as shown in Table 2.[2]

TABLE 2

MINUTES OF LABOR REQUIRED TO EARN ENOUGH MONEY TO
BUY ARTICLES OF CONSUMPTION

Article	United States	United Kingdom	U.S.S.R.	India	China
Cotton cloth, yard	23	45	(276)	96	180
Bread, pound	6	5	30	—	—
Flour, pound	4	5	—	26	(144)
Fish, pound	19	23	170	216	300
Peas, pound	7	17	212	156	170
Sugar, pound	4	9	(140)	(190)	(204)
Rice, pound	8	17	—	84	58
Beef, pound	29	26	(254)	(240)	(280)
Eggs, dozen	27	55	(382)	(348)	(360)
Tea, pound	56	72	(1,506)	(408)	(370)

The low prices in the United States can hardly be due to private ownership of productive industry, since India and China (1937) have private ownership, and their prices are quite high. The industry of India is not highly
developed; yet in the cities theirs is a commercial economy, with private
ownership and a free-enterprise system. Perhaps the influence of private
ownership on prices in India and China may be offset by the large populations of these countries. But it should be remembered that the density of
population is greater in Britain than in India or China, and Britain has low

prices as compared with India and China, though the people of the United Kingdom draw more of their food from an area outside their national boundaries than do the other nations here discussed. Therefore, the concept of density should be qualified for Britain. That these differences in price levels are not caused by population density is further indicated by Russia, which has a low figure for population density, yet rather high prices. Russia's density figures rest in part upon a cold, barren land in the north, and her prices are probably unduly high because of her war-preparation effort, which diverts much income from butter to cannon. Still the Soviet Union, not densely populated like Britain, India, and China, has prices somewhat comparable to those of China and India. Indeed, the density of the Soviet Union is not greatly different from that of the United States, yet her prices are so much higher that it is hard to explain the difference in terms of war effort. If population density were the determining factor, then the prices in the United States and the U.S.S.R. should be more nearly the same.

Since Russia has low population density and high prices, it might be thought that the high prices are due to the politico-economic organization of the Soviet Union. There are no other countries with a long experience in communism or socialism with which to check. Britain has had some socialism for five years, but only about 20 per cent of her industries are governmentally owned. Even so, the prices in Britain are quite low relative to Russia's. But, before drawing conclusions about the influence of state-owned industry in the U.S.S.R. as being a cause of her high prices, we should examine the factor of technology, which is much less developed in the Soviet Union than in the United States and in Britain but somewhat more developed than in India and in China. So the low state of technology in the U.S.S.R. may explain her high cost of living.

The analysis so far fails to indicate that population density is a large factor in explaining the low standard of living; for Britain has a high density and a high standard of living, while Russia and the United States have a low density of population, with Russia having a low standard of living and the United States a high one.

Also organization does not appear to explain the divergencies in the table. For the U.S.S.R. and India, one with communism and the other with private ownership of productive property, have standards of living that are not widely divergent, and the private ownership in the United States and in China has produced very unequal standards of living. So the variation in organization from governmental ownership to private ownership does not vary concomitantly with the standard of living and hardly appears as a controlling factor.

The natural resources are large in all the countries in the table and hence are a constant, approximately.

There remains the factor of technology. When it is found highly advanced with a monetary economy, the products of technology become the capital goods of capitalism. The two countries with advanced technology, the United States and Britain, have high standards of living, even though population pressure and organization differ. And in the three countries where technology is not very advanced—the U.S.S.R., China and India—there are low standards of living even though population pressure and organization vary.

This analysis which has been somewhat winding may be seen in summary in Table 3, which presents numerical measures of the cost of living in these five countries and also measures of two of the factors—population density and technological development. The figures for the cost of living are the sums of the minutes of labor required to buy a pound of bread, flour, or rice, a pound of fish, and a pound of peas. Density is the total population divided by the total area in square miles, and the technological development is the per capita annual consumption of energy of all kinds in hundreds of kilowatt hours. We see from Table 3 that the first and second lines of data, namely, cost of living and density, do not synchronize in the case of Britain and the U.S.S.R. On the other hand, the first and third lines—cost of living and technological development—move up and down together, but in reverse.

The foregoing analysis, then, of the data of prices in terms of labor for five countries indicates that technology is much the most important of the four factors in explaining the variations in the standard of living, though no doubt population density and organization are also factors. Five countries are a small sample, though the extreme variations make them more significant than might be thought from the small number. However, the sample is too small to hold two variables constant while measuring the influence of the third on the dependent variable. That the data indicate the greater influence of technology is probably due to its real importance as a factor. If all three variables had been nearly equal, the small number of countries—only five—would not have indicated such a result.

TABLE 3

COST OF LIVING, POPULATION DENSITY, AND TECHNOLOGY

	United States	United Kingdom	U.S.S.R.	India	China
Cost of living	32	45	412	398	428
Population density	47	521	25	200	209
Technological development	130	71	22	4	2

It is possible to get a larger sample of countries with differing prices, but it is not possible to get a larger sample with a communistic organization in existence for a long time. The *Monthly Labor Review* for December, 1949, publishes for eighteen countries the amount of a list of some forty-one food commodities that could be bought for an hour's labor. The prices of a substantial number of these commodities were found for each of eighteen countries in terms of what an hour of labor of the average factory worker would buy. These countries were the United States, Australia, Austria, Canada,

Chile, Czechoslovakia, Denmark, Finland, France, Germany, Great Britain, Hungary, Ireland, Italy, Norway, Sweden, Switzerland, and the U.S.S.R. The data were for 1948-49. For these same countries it is possible to get an index of the degree of development of technology that seems to be reasonably satisfactory. The ones selected were annual per capita use of energy as measured or translated into kilowatt hours of electricity. This energy may be that used for productive purposes or for all purposes. The data are for 1946. They show that the countries with the greatest use of energy and hence of machines have the highest standard of living, that is, lowest prices as measured in terms of labor.

The coefficient of correlation between the per capita use of energy and the high standard of living, as measured in what an hour of labor will buy, is +.7 for the eighteen states. For comparison, the correlation of the high standard of living with population density (for the total areas) is −.3. These data indicate for a different group of countries that technological development, as measured by use of energy, is a more important factor than density of population.

The comparisons will be better with each of the factors if we hold the other constant. When the data are arranged in a correlation table, the partial correlation coefficient between standard of living and technology, with density held constant, is found to be lowered a little but still about +.7. The correlation between standard of living and density, with the influence of technological variation removed, becomes −.2. The table shows a few far outlying cases, but the coefficients derived from the same data, grouped into only two categories, are approximately the same.

The two sets of data discussed in this paper indicate the great bearing of technology, as compared with population density, on the wealth of peoples, natural resources being approximately constant.

This conclusion of the relatively great importance of technology for the standard of living and hence for the wealth of nations should not be surprising, for productivity may be greatly increased by machines. It would take an American Indian a long time to dig the foundations for a building with his Stone Age tools. Our forefathers with a pick, shovel, and wheelbarrow could dig it much more quickly. But with a steam shovel and a truck, a twentieth-century man could dig it even faster. We have a way of failing to uncover the impersonal technological factor. Thus we often speak of the increased productivity of labor, which is, however, due not to the fact that a laborer works any harder but that he has better tools to work with. The productivity of the American Indian is much less than that of a modern construction worker. Such is the implication of some figures presented by Mills, where he shows that the total annual income in the United States for the forty-seven years from 1899 to 1945 in 1929 dollars was $3,151 billion.[3] But the labor input for each year operating at the 1889–98 level in productivity in 1929 dollars would have created a total of only $1,669 billion, a little more than half. The workers hardly worked any longer or any harder, though the organization may have improved.

While little credit has been given by social science analysts to technological change as a cause of the rise in the standard of living, much has been said about population density as a factor, owing to the remarkable and well-known claims of Malthus.

Then lately we have been attributing much virtue in explaining production, which is the basis of the standard of living, to capitalism and much evil to communism. But capitalism is not wholly private ownership and free enterprise; it means also capital goods, which means technology. Furthermore, communism uses capital goods as well as private capitalism. Again, the technology factor is obscured in favor of human achievement and morals, which are usually quite adequately appreciated.

It is obvious that natural resources are a necessity for a high standard of living, but the question concerns their variability from country to country, not their existence as a factor. Furthermore, technology is needed to use natural resources.

Organization is also closely related to technology. One wonders, indeed, how much difference in economic organization there can be with the same technology, given a sufficiently long time to make adjustments and remove cultural lags.

REFERENCES

1. December 29, 1947, p. 25.
2. The comparisons in Table 2 are in units of the value of an hour's labor of urban wage-earners, usually an average for factory workers. The workers generally comprise some skilled and some unskilled. The prices are for cities, and where there is a variety of kinds of the same item, the ones chosen are those bought by working-class people. It is difficult to find a list of the same articles widely used by the factory wage-earners in all the countries. Thus British wage-earners use little tea or rice, both being imported. Parentheses are used where little use is clearly indicated. The U.S.S.R. has probably restricted the production of consumer goods and is diverting a good deal of income into the heavy industries and hence is unusual. The data are, in general, for 1948 and 1949, except for China, where the data are for 1937, before the war. Obviously, for the comparisons it is not advisable to make them very precise.

The United States data, except for cloth, are from the *Monthly Labor Review*, November, 1949. For the United Kingdom the prices are from the official quotations except for items not controlled as to prices, for which information was obtained in England from stores or from the British Information Services in Chicago. Wages were £6 a week. The wages in Russia were 590 rubles for a month of 204 hours. Prices came from the American Russian Institute and from the State Department and from the U.S. Bureau of Labor Statistics. Prices from China in 1937 are from the Bureau of Social Affairs and were supplied by Professor Ta Chen. The wages were 5 cents an hour in Chinese money. The wages in India were 5 anas per hour, an estimate from the textile, railroad, mining, and government workers. The prices are from the Indian Ministry of Labor, the *Calcutta Municipal Gazette*, and the India Information Service in the District of Columbia.
3. Frederick C. Mills, "Technological Gains and Their Uses: A Review of Some Recent Economic Changes," *Science*, February 28, 1947, p. 221.

THE THEORY OF OPTIMUM POPULATION
FOR A CLOSED ECONOMY *

By Manuel Gottlieb

I. INTRODUCTION.[1] One of the most striking aspects of the growing body of population literature is the widespread disparagement generally accorded both the concept of an "optimum" population and the real problems which that concept was designed to elucidate. The failure of this concept "to gain a prominent place in the literature of economics" and its practical uselessness are generally affirmed even by those who purport to consider themselves as its strong proponents.[2] Effort to project research which would ascertain the optimum or even throw light on its approximate magnitude is lightly dismissed as a fruitless undertaking. And recently even the formal validity of the concept has been challenged, the accusations ranging from comparatively modest assertions that it is "essentially unscientific," "old static analysis," and of "only abstract value" ("nur ideellen Wert") to strident claims that the concept is a "vicious logical circle" or a "will-o'-the-wisp," "one of the most sterile ideas that ever grew out of our science," being merely an "intuitive" or a "strictly value concept," a "speculative construction of little importance for judging actual situations," and "not really entitled to a place in the corpus of theoretical economics."[3]

Formal contempt has been accompanied by neglect of the real problems which the optimum concept was designed to elucidate. The phenomena of population structure, processes, and change have been subjected to comprehensive and illuminating research which has unmistakably demonstrated that the populations of the leading nations of Western civilization are no longer fully reproducing themselves. Almost as large a literature has been devoted to describing the social and economic effects of a change from population increase to stability or decline. The special problem of the connection of the business cycle and secular stagnation with population trends has received close attention by economists.

But a particularly noteworthy feature of the larger part of this literature is the fragmentary, partial, or one-sided treatment given to the problems involved in answering that question which Knut Wicksell once characterized as pre-eminent: "What density of population under given circumstances is most advantageous?"[4] This ominous gap is perhaps best indicated in the comprehensive report on population recently published by the National Resources Planning Board. Every aspect of the process and consequences of

* Reprinted from *The Journal of Political Economy*, 53 (December 1945), pp. 289–316, by permission of the author and the University of Chicago Press.

population trends has been systematically elucidated in this work except the ultimate desirability of that population size which is so meticulously projected.[5] Equally unsatisfactory is a collective volume written by a group of American population specialists and designed to sketch out the main problems of American population policy.[6] All too frequently, this literature, when it does not degenerate into outright tom-tom beating against the "menace" of population decline, endows the cause of larger numbers with a sort of coercive benevolence and legitimacy. An inquisitive probing into the long-run value of large numbers is deemed to be tainted with old-fashioned Malthusianism, which is sharply contraposed to "modern" sociopolitical and economic therapeutics. This point of view is particularly characteristic of the larger part of the literature dealing with the population problems of eastern Europe and Asia.

Yet the optimum concept is one of the culminating points of a large body of tested thought and was explicitly developed as an analytical tool by some of the path-breaking theorists who established the essential foundations of modern economics: Marshall, Sidgwick, Cannan, and—above all—Knut Wicksell.[7] Certainly labeling the theory as a mere rationalization for the cause of population stability or decline or as an "Anglo-Saxon theory" is not acceptable.[8] In its sociological preconceptions the concept indicated the increased secularization of economics and belief in the rational control of social processes for purposes of promoting individualistic-humanistic welfare values.

On the formal side, the concept involved merely the closer application of the "incremental" technique and a more rigorous formulation of assumptions.[9] As for real content, the concept synthesizes a body of doctrine whose essential ingredients have been, each in their turn, the well-established products of a long succession of famous theorists. The notion that larger populations brought with them an enlarged market, a finer division of labor, and, in consequence, a heightened industrial efficiency was known to early British thinkers, brillantly stated by Adam Smith, invested with a historic importance by such figures as List and Henry George, and given its classical elucidation by Alfred Marshall.[10] The other principal ingredient of optimum theory, that of diminishing returns from resources, was clearly expounded by a well-known group of British rent theorists, summarized by Ricardo and later by John Stuart Mill (and Marx), and definitively formulated by Marshall long after it had already become one of the foundation stones of economic theory. These two contrary tendencies were co-ordinated into one doctrine by John Stuart Mill, who pointed out that the raw materials which obey the "law" of diminishing returns are subsequently fabricated by manufacturing trades which are governed by the "law" of increasing returns.[11] In the Marshallian version the co-ordination was improved by the separate consideration of the trend of historical improvements. Thus, the latter-day enunciation of the optimum merely formalized into an unambiguous conceptual tool a large body of accepted doctrine.

While a concern for the integrity of doctrine alone would justify an extended consideration of the optimum concept and the problems which it raises, this is made mandatory by the growing importance of concrete problems of population policy. "Once the decline in numbers becomes apparent," wrote Carr-Saunders recently, "universal interest and concern will be aroused in the population problem. . . . [which] may well assume first place among public questions, and put in the shade these economic and social matters which now occupy attention."[12] Indeed, precisely that has happened in Sweden and, to a lesser degree, in other European countries. For countries of eastern Europe and of the Pacific, population problems have never lost their fundamental importance. Interest in what Keynes once called "the greatest of all social questions" will be revived with possibly greater intensity after the war.[13] All the more necessary will it be to develop a soundly rooted optimum concept without which "population policy is bound to be at sea without rudder or compass.[14]

II. ECONOMIC OPTIMUM FOR A CLOSED ECONOMY AND CONTROVERSIAL ISSUES. We commence, then, with the proposition that in a closed modern economy the size of the population and average man-hour productivity—with all other factors held constant—will have a functional relationship with such properties that a given size of population ("optimum") will result in a maximum man-hour productivity. The characteristics of that relationship are determined by the relative intensities of the downward and upward pulls on man-hour output exerted by two component functions: a decreasing return function for all resource-gathering activities and an increasing return function for all other economic activities. Both functions are persistent, non-reversible, and characterized by divergent rates of intensification. Because of these characteristics, a graphic portrayal of the over-all man-hour productivity function will take the form of an inverted bell-shaped curve with a single optimum point. The kind of calculations required to locate this point has been classically stated by Cannan as follows: "We have to weigh on the one side the advantages which may be expected from the greater possibility of gain from cooperation if people are more numerous against the advantages which may be expected from the greater relative plentifulness of land-surface, natural forces and materials, and man-made material equipment, if people are less numerous."[15] Or, in the more precise formulation of Wolfe, the optimum population is that population size "which furnishes the labor supply which, fully utilized, is necessary to operate the total resources of land, materials and instrumental capital at the point of least (labor) cost per unit of product or income."[16]

This opening hypothesis of optimum theory raises a number of pertinent issues, which are discussed in the remainder of this section. In the following sections an examination is made of problems resulting from an attempt to apply the concept in realistic research: the alleged "statical" nature of the optimum concept, the problem of the "transition" period, the alleged multiplicity of causes and volatility of the optimum, and, lastly, the possibilities for empirical measurement. Throughout this paper the discussion is confined to the theoretical model of a closed economy. The issues raised by "external relations" present, for the larger part, a series of complications embracing an interrelated group of problems which cannot be handled here.

1. It will be noticed that we have used the term "man-hour," rather than "per capita," productivity. The distinction arises because the variation in per capita income which results (hypothetically) from varying population sizes may, by familiar processes of reasoning, affect the amount of labor supplied by the population. Low levels of per capita income have been associated, both historically and to some extent functionally, with longer hours of labor, shorter periods of leisure, and the increased participation of marginal labor strata (aged, women, children, and housewives). However, there is less reason to expect active influence because of changes in age composition. Since we are considering different size populations and *not* populations in process of change, age composition should be treated as comparatively uniform.[17]

2. Various writers have proposed definitions of the optimum in indifferent terms of "economic welfare," "standard of living," "real income," "consumption output," and total of "realized desirabilities."[18] For the purposes of any rigorous formulation it seems desirable to restrict the concept to that of over-all out-put or "real income" (in Marshallian terminology, the "national dividend"). The advantages of this magnitude, as compared with those of "consumption output," were fully elucidated in another connection by Pigou and need not be mentioned here.[19] The use of the term "realized desirabilities," which was seriously proposed by Penrose, confuses the issues involved in establishing, on the one hand, an optimum size population and, on the other, a maximum of welfare within a given size population.[20] Provided that we can assume no self-reversing tendency by which increased per capita income merely wastes itself in unwise expenditures, the problem of a maximum exploitation of income for welfare purposes can be disregarded, since it is equal in importance to all population sizes. To that extent optimum theory is concerned with the general movement of an undifferentiated productivity, or, to use an older term, "productive power," whose enhancement is desirable regardless of the objects upon which it is expended.[21]

The objections to the terms "standard of living" and "economic welfare" do not hinge upon the well-known difficulties involved in objectively defining or measuring these concepts.[22] The objections arise from the circumstance that variations in national productivity must be distinguished, both on conceptual and empirical grounds, from any resultant variations in the "standard of living" or "welfare."[23] It would seem advisable, for that reason, to minimize the strain involved in the elucidation of optimum theory by not invoking any special assumption of identity or of constancy in the relationship between economic welfare and real income. It would suffice, for practical purposes, to utilize the general presumption that the effect of any cause on economic welfare is "*probably* equivalent in direction, though not in magnitude, to the effect on total welfare."[24]

3. In the opinion of some writers the dangers involved in an assumed equivalence in "economic welfare" or "maximum man-hour output" and "welfare" are sufficiently great to invalidate the usefulness of a strictly economic approach to the problem of optimum theory. Among certain circles it has become popular to belittle a "purely economic optimum;" to search for all sorts of possible conflicts between an output optimum and "health," "spiritual," "aesthetic," and "ethnic" factors; and to "deepen" the research with sociological considerations. Warren S. Thompson writes that "one need not give his imagination much headway to see the economic optimum as the chief enemy of a spiritual or personal optimum."[25] Penrose pontifically proclaims that "the view that the economic optimum is the welfare optimum really depends on the assumption that the maximum economic welfare is the maximum satisfaction of actual desires."[26] We are warned that the concept of an economic optimum "is somewhat narrow and partial," "tends to obscure other values," and "fails to appreciate the nature and complexity of human personality and culture."[27] These quotations indicate the attitude and orientation of the "welfare" criticisms which are particularly prominent in the writings of Indian, French, and various European spokesmen.[28]

Only to a very slight extent have the "welfare" criticisms supplied really worth-while contributions to the sociological study of population size.[29] They mostly represent a romanticist and nationalist backwash which seeks protective "scientific" coloration for adherence to conventional or traditional notions. The economic population optimum involves no "subordination" of ethical or moral values to "sordid" material welfare or any postulated "equivalence" of welfare and economics. All that is modestly claimed is that limited productivity universally imposes an actual or potential restraint on economic welfare; that improvements in productivity are desirable; and that the improvements have non-self-reversing effects on welfare. It is not argued that economic productivity cannot be increased by many other means, or that economic welfare cannot be improved with existing productivity, or that the richness and intensity of life could not be raised with constant economic welfare. To this extent the economic population optimum merely becomes one of the many deities—and possibly a minor one at that—in the temple of the social sciences.

4. The development of "optimum" doctrine has been associated with a tendency to deny the validity of the Marshallian distinction between "increasing" and "decreasing" return activities and to substitute therefor a single "law" of "proportional" returns. While much could be said with respect

to the specific details of the argument of such writers as Cannan and Robbins on the subject, it need be emphasized that the controversy chiefly concerns the form and elegance of theoretical formulation.[30] Marshallian terminology is employed in this paper simply because of its heuristic value in organizing the discussion.

5. Early spokesmen for optimum theory were perhaps overhasty in suggesting that in the actual world, as contrasted to a theoretical model, the optimum population would be one specific size ("optimum point"). The later writers have emphasized, with justice, that, in all probability, an index of average man-hour productivity would be relatively insensitive to population changes throughout a middle range of sizes, so that we are concerned more with an optimum "zone" or "area" than with a "point."[31] While this enhances the realism of the concept, it in no way involves an automatic acceptance of the opinion of Gunnar Myrdal to the effect that the curve could "for large spaces have a very level course."[32]

6. Similar observations are in order with respect to other characteristics of the average man-hour productivity curve. It has been generally assumed that this curve will exhibit regularity and "smoothness." While this is a justifiable first approximation, irregularities in inflection and even occasional reverses may be expected because of discontinuities inherent in the economic development which has a "jerky" or "lumpy" character and which (not only historically but functionally) comes in "stages." Thus a certain density is required for the utilization of an elaborate system of railway transport and the improvement of waterways. The development of an iron and steel industry or electrical-power sources, which require a certain minimum density, will unloose a whole series of benefits of the division of labor which would not otherwise be applicable. There is implied a series of optimum "points" corresponding to these exploding "discontinuities." Our curve may have a wavelike tendency characterized by a basic upward and a downward trend and a succession of optima culminating in an *optimum-optimorum*.[33]

7. Optimum theory searches for a maximum output by (hypothetically) varying population size. It must be admitted that this procedure invests the theory with a certain bias which must be corrected. In actual fact, population policy will endeavor to impress its aims on a population which is already in a process of movement and which may only gradually and over the course of a period of time be affected by a given policy. During this prolonged transition, changes in the arts and resources may supervene and easily make it desirable to aim not at a fixed size but at a desirable trend of change, or, to use the phrase of Cannan, a "right movement."[34] The argument of Gunnar Myrdal that "the amount of applicable technical knowledge is changing and increasing all the time" may thus constitute not an insuperable objection to the optimum concept but merely a complication for the practical task of its ascertainment.[35] The problem of an optimum population is, consequently, "not so much that of adjusting a variable population to a given

quantity of land and a given stage of the arts but that of harmonizing its changes with the changes that take place in respect of the latter also." To this extent the theory is, if one chooses, "dynamic rather than static."[36]

8. The concept of the optimum, as elucidated thus far, is framed in terms of a process of active utilization by a variable labor supply of a fixed stock of resources. However, this is—strictly speaking—not true. The modern industrial mechanism both utilizes and *consumes* resources, some of which are available in comparatively limited quantities. The most important of such resources are the fertile and easily mined or wasted top soil; the minerals; the woodland; and the petroleum, oil, and coal reserves.

Measures of conservation, with all their undoubted scope and potential effectiveness, could sharply reduce but could not eliminate this process of depletion. And for the major Western countries, reliance upon the discovery of vast new reserves is somewhat foolhardy. The development of synthetics and improvements in technology would only within certain limits counteract this "fatal tendency."[37]

The connection between resource depletion and optimum theory follows from the self-evident fact that larger population sizes will necessarily be associated with higher rates of resource depletion.[38] The strategic character of many of the depletable resources invests this process with a particularly potent meaning. The celebrated investigations of Jevons concerning the available coal reserves in England and the widespread "conservation" movement in America have stimulated a special literature devoted exclusively to this problem.

Properly speaking, then, the optimum should be conceived of as pertaining to a succession of generations husbanding and consuming a limited and, in part, an exhaustible resource supply. Similarly, the process of diminishing returns from resources involves a tendency for costs to increase as more resources are utilized both spatially and through time.[39]

9. Optimum theory is framed in terms of average product per man-hour— a general productivity of society in utilizing resources. The circumstance, however, that the variable factor—population size—is also the source of the labor supply will inevitably, in a capitalist or free market economy, influence factoral pricing. The entire structure of classical "dynamic" theory was dominated by the belief in the functional character of the relationship between real-wage levels and the quantity of labor. And within the last fifty years it has often been argued that the continuous increases in the labor supply have been, for certain periods, a major factor in depressing real-wage levels.[40]

In developed capitalist countries of a "Western" type it is to be doubted that the shifts in income envisaged by classical theory would actually materialize at the present time. The causal relationship between income distribution to social classes and the purely competitive market forces have been weakened, restricted, and in part superseded by a whole new complex of social controls and institutional agencies. For Eastern and Asiatic countries, however, with comparatively undeveloped or rudimentary forms of social control, the shift of factoral incomes and the general tightening of the market for labor would be one of the most desirable and striking consequences of smaller numbers. In the workings of this process one encounters the major social origin of the widespread popular opposition to smaller numbers: the instinctive realization by employers of labor of their differential social interest in an abundant—and for that reason a cheap and docile—labor supply.[41]

III. OPTIMUM THEORY AS A STATICAL TRUISM. The more rigorous formulation of optimum theory relieved it of the danger of pronouncing a questionable "law" of historical development and fortified its formal accuracy. The theoretical recognition of the long duration of the transition period, during which the population size is adjusted to the optimum, provided room for a certain element of "dynamics" by basing the optimum on a "trend of change" for a "calculable future" rather than on a fixed inventory existing at a prevailing moment.

This revision of the concept, however, only partly meets the charge of "staticism" with which the concept is allegedly infected.[42] To understand that charge, it is only necessary to recall that formal optimum theory impounds into a *ceteris paribus* all the "other factors"—arts of production, technology, social structure, trends of development—when population size is varied. As Robbins emphasized, there is no important variable "in the complex economic life of a community which we do not assume to be unchanging when we postulate the existence of an optimum."[43]

Is this assumption theoretically legitimate? Changes in population size are effected only by means of a complex and prolonged process, which may have a profound effect on the economic system, the arts of production, and the social order. It is for that reason that Cannan characterized the use of the *ceteris paribus* assumption as the "usual cheap expedient. . . . [which] cannot properly be applied to increases and decreases of population." Fairchild has admitted that, rather than a postulated constancy of "other factors" and a one-way dependence between population and output, there exists between these factors "a complex of relationship so intricate and so thoroughly reciprocal that, in a very real sense, any of them may be considered as the result of the other three. . . ." Mombert has emphasized that "in certain conditions the growth of the population becomes an active factor in determining the character of economic life."[44] And distinguished sociologists and economic historians have considered population change and size factors as constituting some of the basic motor forces of economic and social development.[45] In these terms the optimum concept would seem to be inherently tainted with "staticism" because of the assumption of constancy or simple one-way dependency relationships between its component variables. The concept would be "statical" in the very real sense of being useful only under objectively *stationary* conditions.

Any effort to salvage from this assumed wreckage of optimum theory must commence with the proposition that the theory does not logically require, although it freely assumes, *constancy* in the variables frozen in the *ceteris paribus* assumption. Of course, in actual historical development all the frozen variables will change incontinently, cumulatively, and consistently, as Veblen would say. These changes will cover all aspects of the social and economic process: fertility, mortality, and marriage rates; industrial arts; political constellations; location of industry; shifts in tastes and consumption; appearance of new and the disappearance of old resources; climatic changes; etc. However, in order to disclose weakness in the theory, demonstration must be made of a *specific interrelationship* between population size or change and the changes in these variables. That the relationship will frequently be absent is suggested by the fact that societies with different population sizes and with varying rates and directions of population change will exhibit similar kinds of developments, metabolic processes, and social trends. In modern Western societies many changes of even a profound and basic character will occur regardless of demographic phenomena. These changes have social, economic, and political roots of a deep-seated and independent character. So much is necessary in order to avoid the obvious excesses of a purely demographic explanation of all social phenomena.[46]

There would still remain, nevertheless, a large potential area of specific interrelationship between population and "other factors." There is obviously laid open here the task of tracing to its causal origins that complex and still obscure socioeconomic process which is nothing less than the development of Western civilization. We may at once relieve our theory of the burden of postulating a whole system of historical sociology by confining it to *present* periods only. The theory, like the phenomena upon which it is designed to throw light, is forward-looking, and no logical strain is involved in confining its formal application to the current period only. It is very questionable, to be sure, that the development of modern industrialism really required as vast a population increase as that experienced in the past "brief but riotous" century and a half. Given the starting conditions of the nineteenth century, the main outlines of the later development may well be considered independent of any stimulation afforded by rapid population increase. And we can even say that "conditions would have improved still more rapidly if population had grown more slowly."[47] These, however, are historical questions which may be excluded from the corpus of the theory itself.

Doubts concerning the fecundating or inhibiting role of varying population sizes in the past are immensely strengthened in any examination of current prospects.[48] Whatever the original association between the development of industrialism and population density, once industrialism has achieved a certain level, it provides its own foundations. Scientific knowledge and technological improvements now develop virtually on their own momentum.[49] Smaller-size populations may even be expected to stimulate technological improvement by promoting labor "scarcity" and thus further enlarging the scope and usefulness of "labor-saving" devices.

Nor could different population densities bear any clear relationship—other than that flowing from its economic effects—to the "artistic, cultural, and social amenities of life" or to the "beauty and charm of the earth's surface."[50] Only by straining the imagination could a moderate population decline be thought to result in "social loneliness"; nor should one expect increased density to result in "diminution of freedom, more intricate and expensive organization, loss of community self-reliance, and the multiplication of centralized and peremptory social controls."[51] Only as a figure of speech does increased density—again within broad limits—lead to "crowding," i.e., to a "growing difficulty of finding solitude and quiet and fresh air."[52] Urbanization does not vary directly with population size, and the crowded life of the great metropolitan cities of the Western world is not linked up to national size. Problems of political, intellectual, and moral life would continue to be just as vexatious and intractable with larger or with smaller populations. Transitional phenomena, power politics, and past history excluded—and considering only the varying end-product population size—it is probable that the assumption of independence of the "other variables" postulated by optimum theory constitutes a reasonable working hypothesis.

IV. TRANSITION EXPERIENCE. A series of difficulties analogous to those just reviewed arises from the special experience of the transition period during which the size of population gradually becomes raised or lowered to the optimum. The appraisal of the desirability of a given optimum size should, by common admission, not omit consideration of the advantages or drawbacks attached to the process of population change by which it is achieved. Indeed, the popular and almost traditional attitude to population problems is preoccupied with the effects of that process, praising any growth and condemning any decline of population.

This popular attitude has now become officially enshrined as the "modern," "up-to-date" theory in most recent discussions and in the important work of Gunnar Myrdal. The advantages or drawbacks of any given process of change have, in this theory, blotted out any systematic awareness of the cumulative and persistent differential desirability of the resulting population size so achieved. Optimum theory, writes Gunnar Myrdal, "stands mainly as an excuse for and also as an actual inhibition of the proper posing of the problem of the economic effects of population changes." These "economic effects," we are told by Alva Myrdal, are of "paramount importance" and have "little to do with the size of the population; they are mainly caused by the population changes as such." Except where there is "severe overpopulation," writes Frank Lorimer, "the dynamic effects of population growth are more important than the static relation of population to resources."[53]

It would not seem difficult to argue, however, that these "dynamic" effects of change should be considered almost of secondary consequence, since they are inherently so short-lived. They endure for approximately one generation and then disappear, leaving as their single persistent product the solid deposit of a new population size. To increase population for the mere sake of population *growth* or to reduce numbers because of the benefits of a *decline* would seem to require a singular and aggressive shortsightedness. Surely in such matters, which involve the ecological adaptation of the race to its native and acquired habitat, reference should be made to a society envisaged as consisting of a self-renewing succession of generations.[54]

The stress on transitional effects is sometimes reinforced by an assumption which is generally expressed in the form of vague hints and allusions rather than explicit assertion. It is felt that the process of population decline, once established, will become irresistible and thus menace a population with ultimate extinction or at least a dangerously small size. Against this viewpoint Jewkes has made a successful rejoinder. Pointing out that present-day reproductive ratios are already causing a population decline, he asks: "Why would it necessarily be more difficult to do this [stabilize population] at the end of the second generation than earlier?" He answers the contention that habits may become fixed with the assertion of doubt that the "present-day habits," which have already become deeply rooted, "would be any easier" to cope with. The reluctance to experiment with a population decline "implies that public policy regarding population can only work in one of two directions, either increasing or maintaining population." And he correctly concludes that "no reason"can be seen "why a community, if it consciously embarks upon the experiment of allowing the population to fall, does substantially weaken its power to call a halt and to stabilize at a lower level."[55]

It may also be doubted that the transitional effects of population stabilization or decline are so unfavorable as the larger part of the recent literature would indicate. It is hardly our purpose either to summarize that literature or to investigate in detail the issues raised by it.[56] Summary reference, however, might be made to some of the more important problems involved.

The cessation of a trend of population increase and—even more—the advent of a period of population decline will, of course, tend to change the age-composition structure of a population by increasing the percentage share of older people and diminishing the share of the young. This process is frequently described in terms which imply disapproval or dislike. The increasing proportion of old people allegedly results in "an increasing burden on those actively employed"; there will be "fewer toys and more footwarmers."[57] With the fulness of plenary inspiration Gunnar Myrdal speaks confidently of the "loss of daring" and the increased difficulties for youth to advance. "People will get discouraged," "will lose their dynamic interest in working life"; "society will lose the mental attitude that goes with progress." And he concludes with a grand flourish: "Even one who was a socialist in politics but who has felt the pulse of progress in his veins, who has loved free initiative and advance, must feel cheerless before these prospects."[58]

Strictly speaking, the maintenance of both the "aged" and the "young" involves elements of economic burden. The social and individual investment in the nurturing, care, and provision for the "young" has even been subjected to statistical measurement, so that we know approximately how much it "costs" to raise an average child to the age of independence.[59] And the cost involved in the provision for the "aged" has within recent years received careful attention.

It would seem, on first glance, that the two "burdens" tend to balance each other during processes of population decline and growth. The relative increase in the "youth," so characteristic of growing populations, would be offset by a diminution of the "aged." Conversely, the predominance of the "aged" during a period of decline would be offset by the diminution of the "youth." Examination of the relevant statistical data for the United States and England, at any rate, reveals that the proportion of able-bodied is a relatively constant fraction of increasing, stationary, or decreasing populations.[60]

From this point of view the logical aim of a moderately farsighted Western people would be a stationary population—the investment in just enough "youth" to provide a sufficient labor force to staff the workshops to support the "aged." Population increase incurs a burden of investment which probably will not be returned in direct economic satisfaction; and systematic reduction of the "youth" and the avoidance of the "burden" of their nurture would invoke, a few decades later, the stinging penalty of an inadequate support for the "aged." To this extent, any population change for a modern community probably involves slight elements of expense to the generation affected.

The principal grounds, however, for concern with changes of population size relate to the more strictly economic effects of these changes on economic output and conjunctural developments. Disregarding the comparatively minor considerations relating to mobility and "pools" of unemployed resources, attention has chiefly been given to the role of population change as a factor affecting capital outlay. As Reddaway has emphasized, "the influence of the change from an increasing to a stagnating or declining population is exerted mainly through its effect on the amount of national capital . . . per head."[61] We are concerned here with the celebrated problem of "vanishing investment outlets" and with what Pigou once designated as "Mr. Keynes' vision of the day of judgment."

Misunderstanding concerning the role of population change and investment outlets finds its origin primarily in mistaken or narrow conceptions of the real causal interrelationship. Nothing could be more unilluminating, for example, than to search for the effects of population growth on investment outlets by examining such magnitudes as the aggregate of money demand, the intensity of real desires, the quantity of real output, or such partial indices as housing.[62] The basic mechanism at work can be located in a very simple way. New population—or, more strictly, new accretions to the number of workers available for employment in the market economy—must be equipped with capital goods of all kinds in their workshops, in their homes, and for the general process of urban living.[63] The popular conception of vast quantities of "excess facilities" which can absorb large masses of additional workers is based upon exceptional cases and constitutes a mirage. Such "excess capacity" as exists is part of the normal economic life of a free market economy which is afflicted by seasonal fluctuations, industrial changes, and the pressures of monopolistic competition. Only during a period of war is it possible to utilize these reserves by introducing a rigorous tension and strain throughout the economic system.

This thought may be more vividly, and possibly more accurately, expressed in converse form. If the capital accumulation during the past century has objectively fulfilled the function of equipping new population masses with the necessary living and working facilities, the real economic function performed by these new population masses consisted in the utilization and the activization of new increments of capital accumulation. There was a "scarcity" of labor which was as objectively a real factor as the much vaunted "scarcity" of capital. Only by mobilizing the new recruits to the population and by proletarianizing agrarian, craftsman, or previously nonlaboring strata (women and children) could the typical upswing of the nineteenth century achieve its full scope. If, then, it is asked how population growth stimulated investment, we can fitly reply: by providing a large share of the labor force required to man the new capital facilities. And we may refer here to the well-established fact of business-cycle history that one of the contributing factors to the emergence of the downswing is the exhaustion of the labor market as the upswing rounds its peak and the consequent bidding up of wage rates.[64]

Of course, this twofold process of capitalist expansion is predicated upon favorable conjunctural conditions: expansion in the money supply and bank credit, "sound" wage-price relationships, a certain kind of public administration, etc. The sum totality of these conditions constituted the environment of the "upswing" phase of the cycles during the past century, in the same way that the essential mission of the upswing consisted in the installation of innovationary techniques and the provision of capital equipment for new population masses.

It likewise follows that, with the current patterns of income distribution and institutional overgrowth, stabilization or decline of population will tend to impair the ability of the "system" to maintain *for any considerable period of time* the large volume of capital investment upon which a full-employment economy depends. Reduction in long-term interest rates would meet institutional frictions and would have only a limited success in evoking capital investment. And the flow of inventions and improvements—which have a "deepening" character—would either have to be tremendously accelerated or have to obtain an immense new scope at a time when institutional hindrances to the application of inventions have become notoriously widespread. With this "vista" of the future before us the "pessimistic" prognosis of the Keynes-Hansen school seems fully justified. That prognosis elucidates the basic conditioning factors of an entire epoch and may, only with the greatest caution, be used in explaining such localized developments as the depressed "thirties."[65] Moreover, the proportion of the national income used for purposes of accumulation is sufficiently small—averaging around 10–12 per cent—so that the process of capital satiation would be realized only slowly even after a prolonged period of population stability or decline.

It follows from the analysis that the stagnating effects on the conjunctural development—such as they are—are completely due to the institutional overgrowth and have no roots in the economy itself. Remedial policy would have an unhindered area of operations. Cessation of population growth objectively relieves society of the "burden" of mere "extensive" accumulation and makes it possible to increase consumption quotas or develop more efficient and "roundabout" production structures. As Reddaway has emphasized, "the problem is not one of scarcity in any sense (except that of initiative in high places and understanding generally)." Our difficulty "is not to overcome the niggardliness of nature but so to organize ourselves that we can make use of the (relative) abundance which should be available."[66] Larger numbers for the glory of the race, or by the mandate of Providence or the power of the state—the philosophy of the priest or of a dynasty and its gendarmes—is at least understandable and has a historic rationale. But that we "should be reduced to laboriously increasing the number of children in order that we may keep up the level of capital outlay and so avert a slump" is pecuniary logic gone mad—and inverted.[67] And yet, be it noted, that is the unexpressed implication of Gunnar Myrdal's central argument.

The economics of the transition—and that is how a process of population increase or decrease should be envisaged—covers just what the designation implies: the limited operation of comparatively unimportant variables for a transitory period. And it was for this that Myrdal wanted to sacrifice the theory of optimum.

V. MULTIPLICITY OF CAUSES AND VOLATILITY OF OPTIMUM. The classical elucidation of the "laws" of return implied that the forces shaping the optimum point or zone fell into two broad counteracting groups which themselves exhibited a certain historic stability. The discussion by geographers and economic historians had generally postulated a series of characteristic density ratios which were associated with successive stages or types of technical development: hunting; pastoral, simple agriculture, and handicraft; plantation economy; commercial small manufacturing; and massive modern industrialism. These stages or typical socioeconomic structures were considered to be the product of gradual evolutionary development punctuated by major historic upheavals in economic technique and social organization.[68]

In striking contrast to this implied characteristic of relative stability, modern theorists have almost unanimously insisted that the optimum "point" or "zone" is a highly changeable and volatile magnitude. Thus it is stated that the optimum is "perpetually being altered by the progress of knowledge and other changes"; is "never definitely established"; is "continually shifting"; is "likely to be altered at any moment"; is "never the same for two moments together"; and is "always a moving figure."[69] Beveridge seriously asserted that "if the optimum number of the population of Great Britain for the 31st March, 1930, were divinely revealed that night to an economist in a vision, the one thing of which he could feel certain when he waked on 1st April, would be that the number was no longer the same."[70] Dalton and Hansen believe that the optimum is "more sensitive than . . . [actual numbers]to changes in its economic environment," as it "increases rapidly" in periods of prosperity or "rapid economic progress" and "falls sharply" during depressions.[71] Even A. B. Wolfe, whose wise, spirited essays on optimum theory stand out as veritable beacon lights, has joined the chorus and admits that the fundamental determinants of the optimum are "constantly changing, frequently with disconcerting rapidity."[72]

Allied with the theory of volatility, there has developed a doctrine of an "active multiplicity or variety of causes" which are so numerous, interlocking, and dynamic as to "render it highly difficult if not impossible to extricate the effect of gross size of population from the other variables."[73] A characteristic list, which, we are admonished, covers only a "few of the more important" variables, includes sixteen specific factors, ranging from dietary habits to religious taboos.[74] It is further assumed that "any change which takes place in any one of these various factors may modify the proportion existing between the other factors, lead to a new equilibrium and thus create a new optimum."[75]

In terms of the reasoning just reviewed, the optimum becomes a fluctuating magnitude which perpetually oscillates under the impact of innumerable, discrete, impinging forces that displace it in one direction or another. With so forbidding (and puzzling) a vision haunting the theorist, is it any wonder that after a few laudatory words the concept is dismissed as being "too complicated"?[76]

Thus meekly does logical analysis and empirical research surrender what Wicksell rated the "first" and "most essential" task of population research.

It must be emphasized that this view of the optimum is not securely based upon a review of the historic experience of any given country. For all that may be known, the magnitude of the optimum may, in a great number of cases, prove to be—and to have been—the comparatively stable, slow-moving product of that series of major technological revolutions which have produced modern industrial society and the requirements it makes on resources and size. In large part, the factors making for change may, in actual fact, have had only a slight and inconsequential effect on the optimum. Where the effects were more serious, they may have been self-canceling—the indifferent play of random causes. Theorists have been unable to discern a consistent trend in the effects of technical improvements; "it is a matter of the greatest difficulty to formulate even tentative generalizations" or to "classify in advance a whole age of inventions" and "some inventions make a larger population desirable and others a smaller population." These observations would seem to reinforce the thesis of broad stability in the optimum.[77]

It is certainly not our intention to endeavor to sustain the thesis of "broad stability" by mobilizing empirical data. The final determination of the actual complexity and volatility of the optimum will have to await the completion of monographic research, which, in any case, will yield a verdict not of black or white but of gray shaded to various degrees. It is not unlikely that the actual characteristics of the optimum have varied through time and at any given period for different countries. Pending such monographic treatment, however, we may suggest the following propositions, which, it is submitted, are capable of verification and which are designed to serve as so many starting hypotheses for concrete research.

The first proposition is that the fundamental factor by which the optimum size is conditioned has been relatively stable in Western countries for some decades and promises to remain so for the proximate future. Specifically, reference is made to the diverse caliber of resources which must be utilized on their inferior intensive and extensive margin. With respect to almost all of the resource industries, empirical research would, I believe, justify the following conclusions: (1) We are at present and have, for some time, been working on the meager side of inferior margins. (2) Various technical changes, inventions, and discoveries of new resources have lightened the burden on individual kinds but not on the aggregate of resources. (3) While consumption patterns reveal a drift toward commodities and services which do not involve any substantial draft on resources, this secular drift has had only a modest influence.

The second of our propositions is that, while early industrial inventions and discoveries required (and obtained) a large market in order to develop their full effects, the market, once achieved, does not need to be enlarged because of subsequent discoveries and inventions, so that the optimum density preserves a certain stability. That circumstance provides the setting which accounts for the indifferent effect on the optimum of current technological improvements and industrial changes of various types. Thus the inference commonly made that the twentieth century may be expected to follow the example of the nineteenth century and require an increasing density of population would be contrary to reasonable presumption and would need independent empirical support.[78]

Our third proposition is that the single most revolutionary innovation of modern industrialism—that of cheap railway and ocean-going transport— had (and has) the effect of raising the effective economic density of an area. Economic density, as Marx insisted, is relative to the efficiency of transport. "A country with a relatively sparse population which is equipped with a developed network of transportation facilities is more densely ("dichtere") populated than a more numerously populated land with an undeveloped transport system."[79]

VI. MEASURING THE OPTIMUM. The current misunderstanding and opposition to the theory of the optimum and its hypostatization as a nebulous and complex concept have been fittingly accompanied by an extreme pessimism concerning the possibilities of its quantitative measurement. The hopefulness in this direction manifested by a few theorists is lost in an almost universal pessimism.[80] It was the express observation of Wolfe that "practically all serious thinkers" on the subject "have speedily concluded that . . . [it] is purely conceptual and consequently incapable of application in social policy."[81] The thought that there "is no means of determining" the optimum, the "impossibility of expressing [it] in quantitative terms" was "generally agreed" to by the many population specialists collaborating with the International Studies Conference group.[82]

The more modest of the current formulations merely stress the thought that the task of measurement is "difficult, if not impossible"; or that it offers "stupendous—for the present insuperable—difficulty" which cannot be coped with "in the present state of human progress"; or that a given author has "so far . . . discovered no means" of solution. In more strident tones we are told that the task of measurement is "hardly conceivable"; "never possible"; "almost impossible" ("noch als unmöglich"); "so impossible to arrive at any measure that we had best give up trying"; and doomed to failure by "statistical measurement or even by estimates worthy of the name." At the high pitch of pessimism we are warned that the optimum cannot be ascertained "with even modest degrees of precision"; that it is so "unknowable" that we "cannot even say as a rule in what direction the optimum lies, e.g., whether a population increasing at a certain rate is moving toward the optimum or away from it"; and that we not only cannot ascertain an optimum from knowledge of "prevailing conditions" but we cannot "even begin to make such a calculation."[83] With obvious disgust, Gunnar Myrdal complains that "it has, of course, never been possible anywhere to give for any country a quantitatively expressed answer to the practical question of the actual position of this population optimum."[84]

It is somewhat paradoxical that this extreme pessimism with respect to measurement has gone hand in hand with a primitive approach to the concrete task of measurement which at best results in fruitless speculation and which has consistently exerted a harmful influence. That approach essentially consisted in a search for "external signs," "indices," "objective tests," and "visible symptoms," with the aid of which one could "discover" the optimum as one ascertains temperature from a thermometer.[85] The "failure" of the crudest of these "tests"—unemployment, adverse real exchange rates, a comparison of crude or refined density ratios—is generally recognized.[86] One such test, that of the *direction* of per capita real income trends, has been considered worthy of "careful consideration" and has been used despite the incisive and unanswerable critique of Robbins, Dalton, and Hansen.[87] With easy access to income data, judgment has been rendered as to the existence of population exceeding the optimum by ascertaining the adverse or favorable trend of per capita income.[88] Yet it is obvious, on simple reflection, that countries which have substantially exceeded the optimum may still show positive income trends. Conversely, declining or constant output trends may not be caused by overpopulation. A number of other variables—including varying social policy, business-cycle trends, technological improvements, alterations in the foreign economic position, the crudeness and systematic biases of long-time aggregate output statistics—would preclude the automatic use of output-trend data. Real-wage statistics are even more deficient in these respects.[89] To this extent the search for simple "tests" and "symptoms" has been not only fruitless but downright mischievous.

Even if the failure of the "tests" were to mean that the optimum was actually "unknowable" or incapable of quantitative measurement, the optimum concept would not lose validity or even practical usefulness. One need merely refer to the celebrated defense made by Pigou and Böhm-Bawerk of the necessity of constructing "empty economic boxes" or of analyzing the behavior of unknown magnitudes ("das Theoretisieren mit unbekannten Grössen").[90]

Fortunately, however, the argument of "unknowability" can be demolished by simply following it to its logical conclusion: namely, that it is properly a matter of indifference whether populations increase or decrease without assignable limit. In other words, the current viewpoint implies that we have no way of knowing whether a population of 5, 25, 100, 150, or 300 millions in this country would result in varying average man-hour productivity. As early as 1927 Fairchild stated that we could unhesitatingly establish certain empirically verifiable quantitatively expressed limits to the optimum. Even a scanty knowledge of the known density requisites of modern industrialism and the range and caliber of our natural resources would permit the statement that per capita output would be substantially reduced with a population of (let us say) 50 millions and 250 millions. There is, also, no doubt that nobody could ever collect sufficiently exact data to disclose that *the* optimum population was a certain specific figure (let us say 95,750,425). The most fruitful and ingenious research could, at best, hope to emerge with a zone of figures of varying degrees of relevance and probability. A sufficient amount of certainty could only be assured in those cases where, in the words of Dalton, numbers were found to be "seriously out of adjustment with the optimum."[91] We thus see that the whole problem of measurement reduces itself to the task of narrowing, to the greatest possible extent and within relatively manageable dimensions, a broad range of potential optima. Fruitful controversies with respect to measurement must, if they are to be realistic, avoid pretensions of mathematical precision, on the one hand, or a nihilistic absolutism, on the other.

The task of developing quantitative limits to an optimum zone will, of course, require for each specific time and place a vast amount of concrete research and falls necessarily outside the scope of this paper. To that extent the unfortunate jibe of Gunnar Myrdal, who has asked for concrete demonstrations of an optimum, will not be satisfied. While his implied aspersion is hardly merited, it is near enough the mark to carry a sting. After all, forty years of theorizing about the concept might have been accompanied by concrete research work which, to a greater or lesser degree, could assist in the determination of population policy. It may be worth while, for that reason, to sketch out in summary fashion a few considerations indicating the kind of research needed, the difficulties that will be faced, and some of the progress achieved up to date. The problems involved in measuring "real terms of trade" and other problems arising from international relations will be passed over because of their special character.

The first requirement of a research into optimum population is specialized knowledge of the character and diversity of each of the important natural resources and the extent of their utilization on deficient margins of returns. For most countries of the world the continuous research of geographers, geologists, agronomists, and other specialists has accumulated an enormous mass of technical information which is readily usable for purposes of optimum research. This would be disclosed by even a casual glance at standard works on economic geography. Perhaps the most outstanding example of research of this kind is the study by the U.S. Department of Agriculture of the fertility and other characteristics of all the agricultural land of the United States and the classification of that land into five broad categories.[92] The vast descriptive literature on land tenure, soil management, and farm productivity would make it possible to set up schedules of optimum farm sizes for varying rural cultures and regional areas and would be particularly useful for measuring the loss in product caused by intensive utilization of resources of high quality.[93] Information concerning other natural resources—woodland, fisheries, minerals—is also available for most countries of the world.

For countries in which "primary" activities dominate economic life— China, India, southeastern Europe, and other areas—the kind of study outlined above would afford the principal basis for the determination of optimum numbers, supplemented by attention to such factors as the well-known phenomena of agrarian overpopulation resulting from agricultural rationalization and the compensating possibilities for industrial development. Put in these terms, it is obvious that a considerable body of applied economic literature can be utilized with varying degrees of success for purposes of optimum research. To this extent we can say that the outlook for such research is promising indeed.

For the countries or areas with an advanced industrial development, the study of resources will constitute an important starting-point of research, since the tendency of diminishing returns from these resources is now being minimized in importance, as it formerly was overestimated.[94] It would, at any rate, not be difficult to demonstrate in quantitative terms the actual extent and range of that tendency in the United States.[95]

As Colin Clark has emphasized, however, the economic activities of advanced industrial countries are of a "secondary" or "tertiary" type, which are dominated to a greater or lesser degree by tendencies of increasing returns. Our theoretical understanding of these tendencies has been considerably advanced since Adam Smith laid down the "theorem that the division of labor depends upon the extent of the market."[96] This we owe partly to such anti-Malthusians as Friedrich List and Henry George, with their theory of "productive forces"—but principally to Alfred Marshall, whose insight into the economies of large-scale production was almost uncanny. We know that these economies are substantial, omnipresent, and cumulative, ramifying generally into related or collateral industries; and that they are themselves "subject to diminishing returns." For, after an industry has attained a certain size, "the less are the economies to be secured by further growth."[97] It is also plain that we will encounter discontinuities of a "lock-and-key" variety, with the utilization of given technical processes being conditioned by the achievement of a certain size.

But essentially all the later doctrinal developments are nothing but hints and empty formulas which remain in the realm of "vague masses of unspecified fact." Quantitative research has been, with two happy exceptions, virtually nonexistent and would encounter difficulties of a baffling and elusive character. The almost desperate need for quantification is apparent from the wildly divergent estimates which have been thrown out by various writers. It will be recalled that Cannan rebuked John Stuart Mill for his assertion that the English population of 1848 already was sufficiently large for the purposes of industrial development. A generation later R. F. Harrod stated that "the economies of large scale have not yet reached [by 1939] their limit in this country and a contraction of the market would lead to diminished efficiency in many fields." Jewkes replied that his "own impression would be exactly the contrary." It is, he asserted, "difficult to think of any one important industry or public service which could not seize upon the full economies of large scale production with (say) a market of 20 million persons in an area as small as that of Great Britain."[98] Hardly less unedifying, if less uncontroversial, dicta have been pronounced by American writers.[99] It is quite apparent that so far we are dealing with "armchair speculation" which carries no weight "no matter how illustrious are the persons who participate in it."[100]

Any effort to measure the influence of population size upon all nonresource working activities must commence, so it would seem, with a classification of these activities according to their probable responsiveness to size variations. The most sensitive of these activities are undoubtedly those of that considerable segment of the national economy which provides the national overhead services of government, communication, and transportation. Many of the services of government—such as education, local welfare, institutions—would tend to vary with national size; but other services would remain relatively constant. A rough classification of government employment of men and resources into activities of a variable and fixed character, together with coefficients of sensitivity, could be developed on the basis of the voluminous current data. With certain modifications, similar classifications and indices could be developed for the communication and transportation industries, both of which operate with a heavy overhead of equipment and personnel.

At the other extreme must be placed the large mass of activities which provide distributive, personal, recreation, and repair services and small local manufacturing. Reduction or increase of population size—except for extremely large variations—would not sensibly affect the cost of the services provided. These activities are of a duplicative type; and an enlarged mass represents mere agglomeration—more gas stations, grocery stores, drycleaning and laundry plants—without appreciable differentiation or gain. Here, again, analysis of the occupational structure of an economy will reveal the quantitative weight to be assigned.

The third category is a residual makeshift, embracing principally manufacturing activities, which will, to varying degrees, take on the characteristics of the other two classifications. Elusive as is the problem of measuring the influence of size upon these activities, a degree of quantification has already been attained. This may principally be attributed to G. T. Jones, whose ingenious and penetrating analysis, for all its limitations and crudities, constitutes an invaluable starting-point for further research. The analysis was presented in a posthumous publication entitled *Increasing Returns: A Study of the Relation between Size and Efficiency of Industries with Special Reference to the History of British and American Industries, 1850–1910.*[101] Jones subjected to a thorough investigation all the available statistical data with respect to five industries: the American cotton-textile industry, the American pig-iron industry, the British home-construction industry, the British pig-iron industry, and the British cotton-textile industry. His procedure was to select standard competitive products with fixed specifications which remained relatively constant throughout the period studied (1850–1910). It was also ascertained that in these industries no major technological change appreciably affected the continuity of the time series. The selling prices of each product were then averaged and deflated with carefully weighted indices of prices paid for the component raw materials, labor efficiency rates, and overhead and managerial services. The deflated price series thus represents the real cost of the products or that price which would have been charged with fixed factoral unit prices. When the resulting fluctuations in this series are contrasted with a physical-volume series of the product, the tendency for costs to decline as volume expands yields extreme limits to the possible operation of increasing returns.

While the number of products covered by the survey was limited and time (and staff) could have improved the statistical accuracy of almost all the computations, the results of the survey are still very valuable. For the period 1890–1910 the elasticity values (per cent expansion of volume divided by per cent fall in real cost) for the pig iron, cotton textile, and building construction were, respectively, 1, ½, and ⅓; and the analysis of American and British industries emerged with a similar sequence of index values.[102] The extension of similar surveys to other industries, the elaboration of improved indices of the component cost factors, the elimination of the effects of technological improvements not inherently attached to size, the development of an adequate measure of changes in profits, and the coverage of additional standard products—all offer a promising field of optimum research. Other promising avenues for attacking the problem statistically may be provided by comparative studies of similar industries or clusters of industries in different countries.[103] It is not improbable that Soviet economists and industrialists who have had the rare experience of planning and instituting a complex and thoroughgoing industrial development, in many cases starting almost from scratch, will have accumulated rich masses of data bearing on the problem. Finally, the literature on rationalization should yield some concrete suggestions as to the nature of the discontinuities imposed by the size factor.

We thus see that fruitful and realistic optimum research would utilize the findings of a large number of related scientific and descriptive disciplines—industrial, social, and economic. The specific influence of international economic relationships and prospective technological trends would extend the range of inquiry over a still wider field as new and less predictable variables come into play.

It is, of course, manifestly impossible for anyone to "compute" an optimum number as a discrete and unambiguous magnitude. It may even prove difficult to supply a zone of figures sufficiently restricted in range to be useful. It is certain, however, that optimum research could throw its modest light on many of the crucial aspects of the problem. It would, at any rate, be that much easier to dispel the dark counsels of obscurantists and racial chauvinists, whose policy recommendations will, all too frequently, run counter to rational economic calculations.

REFERENCES

1. All references will be fully described at their first citation. Thereafter, the name of the author and date of publication cited will be used for reference purposes.

2. A. B. Wolfe, "The Theory of Optimum Population," *Annals of the American Academy of Political and Social Science* (hereafter referred to as *"The Annals"*), CLXXXVIII (1936), 243. Glenn E. Hoover in his excellent paper on optimum theory expressed his regret that "the quantitative optimum has found so little place in writings on population problems" (G. E. Hoover, "The Quantitative Optimum of Population," *ibid.*, CLXII [1932], 199).

3. The above quotations are extracted in the order quoted from the following works: Benay K. Sarkar, *The Sociology of Population* (Calcutta, 1936), p. 34; Alva Myrdal, *Nation and Family* (New York, 1941), p. 86; Paul Mombert, *Bevölkerungslehre* ("Grundrisse zum Studium der Nationalökonomie," Band XV [Jena, 1929]), p. 242; Pitirim Sorokin, *Contemporary Sociological Theories* (New York, 1928), p. 402; Fergus C. Wright, *Population and Peace: A Survey of International Opinion on Claims for Relief from Population Pressure* (Paris: International Studies Conference, League of Nations, 1939), p. 88; Gunnar Myrdal, *Population: A Problem for Democracy* (Cambridge, 1940), p. 26 (cf. also p. 143); E. B. Reuter, *Population Problems* (2d ed.; New York, 1937), p. 278; paper cited in Wright, 1939, p. 86; L. M. Fraser, "On the Concept of an Optimum in Population Theory," *Population,* I (1934), 42. It hardly needs mentioning that other writers (such as W. S. Thompson, W. Beveridge, J. A. Hobson, I. Ferenczi, and others) have, in varying degrees, opposed the concept but did not sloganize their criticism. Indeed, so low has the status of the concept fallen that in the latest edition of Thompson's standard American textbook on population theory the chapter which had been devoted previously to the subject has been deleted and replaced by a perfunctory short paragraph. Cf. Warren S. Thompson, *Population Problems* (2d ed.; New York, 1935) for a chapter on the optimum population (pp. 422–35), deleted in the 1942 edition.

4. Knut Wicksell, *Vorlesungen über Nationalökonomie auf grundlage des Marginalprinzeps,* I (Jena, 1913), p. 49.

5. National Resources Committee, *The Problems of a Changing Population: Report of the Committee on Population Problems to the National Resources Committee, May, 1938* (Washington, 1938). Members of the Committee were Edwin B. Wilson, David L. Edsall, L. C. Gray, Charles H. Judd, William F. Ogburn, and Warren S. Thompson. The comments of the Committee on the problem of the optimum population are contained in four brief paragraphs (pp. 28–29) and have a stiffly proper noncommittal note ("very little scientific research on the question"). The Committee bent over backward to avoid a welfare appraisal of the population trend, which it analyzed in detail, and stated that "the trend towards cessation of national increase . . . will not necessarily lead to unhappy results." But typically it adds as a precaution that "these changes raise problems that need careful consideration" (p. 8). Elsewhere, however, the Committee indicated a complacent acceptance of the soundness of the 1960 population by asserting that "pressure of total population on natural resources in this country is not so great as seriously to hamper continued economic expansion and a rise in the general level of living, through more efficient economy" (p. 37). This ambiguous formulation indicates the actual disinterest of the Committee in the problem.

6. Frank Lorimer, Ellen Winston, and Louise K. Kiser, *Foundations of American Population Policy* (New York: National Economic and Social Planning Association, 1940). The book represents "a consensus of a larger committee of sixteen members" (cf. Foreword, p. xiii). A program of "positive measures" is recommended for "serious attention" to offset the present trend toward population decrease (p. 141). Presumably the recommendation is based upon the dogmatic assertion in chap. iii, entitled "Labor Supply and Natural Resources," that this country is "no longer threatened" with the "danger" of "excessive multiplication of population" which would lower the resource-population ratio (p. 42), although the problem of "blighted areas" is abundantly recognized (pp. 27–42). Additional considerations are the "disadvantageous aspects" of a population decline,

noted in chap. v, "Population, Investment and Economic Enterprise." Of dominating importance is the openly professed "emotional interest" in the "maintenance of the nation and the enrichment of the national culture" (p. 141).

7. For history of doctrine and the role of Sidgwick, Cannan, and Wicksell see S. S. Cohn, *Die Theorie des Bevölkerungsoptimum: Ein Beitrag zur dogmengeschichtlichen und dogmenkritiken Behandlung des Bevölkerungsprobleme* (Marburg, 1934), pp. 15–22, 81–83; Lionel Robbins, "The Optimum Theory of Population," *London Essays in Economics: In Honour of Edwin Cannan* (London, 1927), pp. 114 ff.; Emil Sommarin, "Das Lebenswerk von Knut Wicksell," *Zeitschrift für Nationalökonomie*, II (1931), 224–25; Alva Myrdal, 1941, pp. 24–26; A. B. Wolfe, "The Population Problem since the World War: A Survey of Literature and Research," *Journal of Political Economy*, XXXVII (1929), 87–93. The concept, of course, even in its explicit formulation, is much older. Thus, Sismondi, Gide, and Effertz have been cited as optimum precursors (cf. Mombert, 1929, p. 241; J. J. Spengler, "French Population Theory since 1800," *Journal of Political Economy*, XLIV [1936], 761 ff.). For a close approximation of the notion see G. Schmoller, *Grundriss der allgemeinen Volkswirtschaftslehre*, I (Leipzig, 1900), pp. 181–84; and the spirited and striking formulation by W. I. King, *The Wealth and Income of the People of the United States* (New York, 1915), pp. 15–41, 238–55. King not only had a clear grasp of the potent role of diminishing returns from resources but even attempted to supply a rough measure of their extent (pp. 15–41). He also had a clear conception of the role of increasing returns (pp. 238–39); and he was aware that these divergent tendencies created a point of maximum productivity. Thus, "Given: a nation with a definite supply of resources and a certain stage of progress in science and the arts, there is always a definite population which can utilize these advantages in such a way as to secure maximum average benefits for all" (p. 238); and "*every nation should maintain its numbers at that point found to give the maximum average real income*" (p. 240).

8. This is the accusation of Gunnar Myrdal ("actually the theory has mostly been utilized to furnish a broad and vague foundation for the opinion that the level should be higher with a smaller population" [G. Myrdal, 1940, p. 144]). It may be noted that when Myrdal in his earlier publication launched the same charge (*Das Politische Element in der nationalökonomischen Doktrinbildung* [Berlin, 1932], p. 64, he quickly added that the same theory "ebenso gut zu einer Propaganda für grössere Familien verdenden" (*ibid.*, p. 65). Cohn commented with perfect correctness that "Wir glauben nicht, dass für die rein abstrakten Ergebnisse der Theorie des Bevölkerungsoptimums die politische Einstellung ihrer Anhänger massgebend war" (Cohn, 1934, p. 85). As a matter of fact, it should be noted that the optimum theory as developed by Cannan and expounded by Robbins and Carr-Saunders was principally aimed against the pessimistic Malthusianism of J. S. Mill and Marshall and became a weapon of the "optimists." For a valuable survey of the dispute between "London" and "Cambridge" theorists in these terms cf. N. Aiyangar, "Some Recent Developments in the Theory of Population," *Indian Journal of Economics*, X (1930), 422–39. The charge of "Anglo-Saxonism" came from Gini (cf. Cohn, 1934, pp. 116 ff., for the criticism and answer). We might note in passing that the charge of "theoretical propaganda" might far more easily be levied against Myrdal. His contemptuous references to optimum theory and the "long-range" study of resources which it involves probably derive from a desire not to embarrass his admirable campaign for the institution of social reforms designed to stabilize population. But why carry into the academic lecture room or scientific writing the workshop habits and tools of a government commission or senate chamber?

9. This has been emphasized in an excellent paper by O. P. Mukerji, "The Optimum in Recent Population Theories," *Indian Journal of Economics*, Vol. XVII (1937), wherein he states that "the very development of economic thought contained within itself a motive power for the drive toward the optimum" (p. 155).

10. For some lively and quaint expressions on the subject from early British thinkers see James Bonar, *Theories of Population from Raleigh to Arthur Young* (London, 1931), p. 55; M. Sadler, *The Law of Population* (London, 1830), I, 120–25.

11. The fact that Cannan and Robbins have by their extreme and one-sided critique of Mill developed the impression that the optimum concept was the special creation of Cannan makes it worth while to cite Mill's passage in full: "As population increases, and the power of the land to yield increased produce is strained harder and harder, any additional supply of material, as well as of food, must be obtained by a more than proportion-

ally increasing expenditure of labor. But the cost of the material forming generally a very small portion of the entire cost of the manufacture, the agricultural labor concerned in the production of manufactured goods is but a small fraction of the whole labor worked up in the commodity. All the rest of the labor tends constantly and strongly towards diminution, as the amount of production increases. . . ." (John Stuart Mill, *Principles of Political Economy* [Ashley ed.: London, 1909], p. 185). See also A. K. N. Sastri, "The Economics of Population—The Optimum Theory," *Indian Journal of Economics,* X (1930), 440–52, for a spirited defense of Mill and Marshall against the critique of Cannan and Robbins. Both Wolfe and Myrdal support the claims of Mill to be considered one of the "founders" of optimum theory. Cf. G. Myrdal, 1940, p. 26; A. B. Wolfe, "The Optimum Size of Population," *Population Problems in the United States and Canada,* ed. Louis I. Dublin (New York, 1926), p. 68, n. 1.

12. Alexander M. Carr-Saunders, "Eugenics in the Light of Population Trends," *Eugenics Review,* XXVII (1935), 15.

13. J. M. Keynes, Preface to Harold Wright, *Population* (New York, 1923), p. vii.

14. B. P. Adarkar, "The Optimum Theory of Population," *Indian Population Problems: Reports and Proceedings of the Second All-India Population and Family Hygiene Conference* (Bombay, 1938), p. 14.

15. Edwin Cannan, *A Review of Economic Theory* (London, 1929), p. 83.

16. Wolfe, 1936, p. 246.

17. Thus, the vivid and even morbid concern of optimum theorists in age composition —except as a transition phenomenon of a population in the process of change—introduces unnecessary complications. For examples of this concern see Paul Mombert, "L'Optimum de population," *Revue économique internationale* (Brussels, 1935), p. 529, who says that "la question de l'optimum de population ne se ramène pas seulement à une question de nombre, mais aussi à une question de structure naturelle de la population." See also Cohn, 1934, p. 143; Imre Ferenczi, *The Synthetic Optimum of Population* (Paris: International Studies Conference, 1938), p. 48; Alfred Plummer, "The Theory of Population: Some Questions of Quantity and Quality," *Journal of Political Economy,* XL (1932), 624 ff.

18. Early writers (e.g., Sismondi and Sidgwick) referred to levels of "happiness." Henry Pratt Fairchild in his latest work continues to use the concept of "living standard," or "levels of living," which he presented in his famous exposition of optimum theory at a conference of population theorists in 1927. (See *People: The Quantity and Quality of Population* [New York, 1939], pp. 64–70), and "Optimum Population," *Proceedings of the World Population Conference, 1927,* ed. M. Sanger (London), pp. 76 ff. A. B. Wolfe has consistently championed the measurement of productivity in terms of "per capita income of consumers' goods," and he actually proposed an "index of the inventory of consumers' goods produced each year" (Wolfe, 1928, p. 87; Wolfe, 1926, p. 71). Cf. E. F. Penrose, *Population Theories and Their Application* (Stanford University, 1934), pp. 47–91, particularly pp. 74 ff. for use of "realized desirabilities."

19. Cf. A. C. Pigou, *The Economics of Welfare* (2d ed.; London, 1924, pp. 34–37), for the advantages of conceiving of the "national dividend" as the flow of goods and services which are "produced during the year."

20. Penrose summarized his concept in a prolix chapter, entitled the "Welfare Optimum," as follows: "The per capita welfare optimum population for any area is that population in which per capita income stands at a maximum when it is spent in the consumption of the composite commodity that, in the light of existing scientific knowledge, makes a greater contribution to welfare than, in the existing state of the arts, can be made by any alternative composite commodity" (Penrose, 1934, p. 84.). Penrose' book was hailed in a review as "one of the best books on economic-demographic conditions published in a decade" (cf. *American Economic Review,* XXV [1935], 372).

21. Thus Henry George framed the question: "Does the relative power of producing wealth decrease with the increase of population?" He continually refers to the general "productive power," "power of the human factor," and "productive power of labor" (Henry George, *Progress and Poverty* ["Modern Library" ed.; New York, n.d.], pp. 143, 149, 232, and *passim*).

22. For a rigorous probing of the weaknesses of Fairchild's definition, cf. Cohn, 1934, pp. 69–70.

23. The grounds for the distinction are sufficiently well known and in the optimum

literature have been reviewed by a number of writers: Cohn, 1934, p. 70; G. Raghana Rao, "The Optimum Population," *Indian Journal of Economics*, XIX (1939), 443, states that "while income per capita is what people get, their standard of life depends—within the limits defined by their income—on what they spend and how they spend it"; and the various writings of Radhakamal Mukerjee, the Indian sociologist-economist (for the most pertinent, see his rejoinder to A. B. Wolfe, "On the Criterion of Optimum Population," *American Journal of Sociology*, XL [1934], 344–48). But for the classical statement of the problem see Pigou, 1924, pp. 12 ff.

24. Pigou, 1924, p. 20.

25. Thompson, 1935, p. 429. He raises such totally irrelevant considerations as the following: "One can easily imagine a social order in which men would prefer relatively modest security to abundance" (*ibid.*); "the acceptance of the economic optimum as the goal toward which population policies should be directed would tend to introduce a uniformity of social organization among all peoples of the world" (p. 431); and the necessary "implication" of an economic optimum "that all other values must be assessed in the light of their consequences upon the economic productive efficiency of a population" (*ibid.*). And he complains of the "complete subordination of personal and spiritual values which appears objectionable in the current theory of the optimum population" (p. 432). Hence he concludes that the economic optimum is "indeed not the optimum in which we as human beings are primarily interested" (p. 430).

26. Penrose, 1934, p. 73.

27. Reuter, 1937, pp. 279–80.

28. See, in addition to the already cited works of Mukerjee, Fraser, Ferenczi, Wright, and the *Proceedings* of the 1927 Population Conference, the following: E. Dupréel, "L'Optimum de population et ses critères," *Revue de l'Institut de Sociologie*, VIII (1928), 1–34; H. Sonnabend, "Some Notes on the Optimum Size of Population," *South African Journal of Economics*, I (1933), 291–99; David A. McCabe, Richard A. Lester, and Burnham N. Dell, *Population, Labor, and Social Reform* (Boston, 1937), pp. 88 ff.

29. See A. B. Wolfe's excellent paper, "On the Criterion of Optimum Population," *American Journal of Sociology*, XXXIX (1934), 585–99; Wolfe, 1936, pp. 244 ff.; Cohn, 1934, for his comments on Mukerjee (pp. 56 ff.), on Dupréel (pp. 103 ff.), on Gini (pp. 109 ff.); Adarkar, 1938, pp. 15 ff.; and finally, Pitirim Sorokin, who attempts to give a serious appraisal of the sociological aspects of population density (Sorokin, 1928, chap. vii, pp. 357–432).

30. For a striking defense of the classical version as stated by Mill and Marshall against the one-sided critique of Cannan and Robbins, see the incisive paper of Sastri, 1930, pp. 440–52. As Sastri pointed out, Cannan "denies the existence of a tendency to diminishing returns in agriculture in any sense in which it is not present in manufacturing" (p. 544).

31. Thus we have optimum zone of Gini ("Zona di optimum," cited in Cohn, 1934, p. 112); the "plateau" of Penrose (Penrose, 1934, p. 57: "the part of the curve in which the ordinates had their maximum value would give the appearance of a plateau rather than a peak"); and the optimum "area" of Fairchild (Fairchild, 1939, pp. 87–88).

32. G. Myrdal, 1940, p. 142.

33. The term itself, with a somewhat similar usage is attributable to Gini (Cohn, 1934, pp. 112 ff.). For an interesting elaboration of the "discontinuities" referred to in the text see Roy Glenday, *The Future of Economic Society* (London, 1944), pp. 63 ff.

34. This new thought was introduced by Cannan in the third (London, 1928) edition of his *Wealth:* "Population is not so agile in its movements as to be able to follow every shifting of the point of maximum return immediately. . . . An increase of workers will only follow from an increase of births after an interval of more than a decade while deaths cannot be accelerated or retarded. The population of any moment is dependent for its magnitude on the population of the past, and will in its turn affect the population of the future. . . . [So] we have to treat the ideal or optimum in regard to population as being the right movement (i.e. increase or decrease) of population rather than define it in reference to one particular point of time" (pp. 60–61).

35. G. Myrdal, 1940, p. 143.

36. Rao, 1939, p. 444. Cohn also approves of the element of dynamics infused into optimum theory by Cannan. "Damit ist das dynamische Element als wesentlicher Faktor zur Beurteilung des Optimums eingeführt" (Cohn, 1934, p. 21).

37. J. J. Spengler, "The Social and the Economic Consequences of Cessation in Population Growth," *Proceedings of the International Congress for Studies on Population,* ed. C. Gini (Rome, 1933), IX, 37. See the caustic comments of Wolfe (1926, p. 66), on the "naïve faith" that invention will "'set aside' and 'indefinitely postpone' the law of diminishing returns."

38. "With a stationary population, replaceable natural resources are exhausted at a less rapid rate" (Spengler, 1933, p. 34). In Spengler's later book, *France Faces Depopulation* (Durham, N.C., 1938), p. 260, he has expressed himself more forcefully: "From the longer run point of view none of the factors and conditions mentioned is as significant as the rate at which the supply of exhaustible resources is being diminished." See also Wolfe, 1928, pp. 549–59; and the excellent discussion by Radhakamal Mukerjee, *The Institutional Theory of Economics* (London, n.d.), pp. 44 ff.

39. This, it seems, is the answer to Dalton's question: "What is the relation of time to the optimum?" (Hugh Dalton, "The Theory of Population," *Economica,* VIII [1928], 43). An answer to one of his other questions ("And over what range of time . . . ?") is more perplexing. Presumably, in as many generations as we are interested.

40. With reference primarily to the behavior of real-wage rates during the twenty years preceding the first World War, see King, 1915, pp. 176–207; Frank Fetter, "Population or Prosperity," *American Economic Review,* Suppl., III (1913), 16; F. W. Taussig, *Free Trade, the Tariff, and Reciprocity* (New York, 1920), pp. 93 ff. Knut Wicksell did not hesitate to declare that the "relatively slight, and in many cases very doubtful, improvement in the conditions of labor" during "the last two centuries" found its "primary cause" in the "one-sided increase in one factor of production, namely, labor" (Knut Wicksell, *Lectures on Political Economy,* trans. E. Classen [London, 1934], I, 143).

41. The fifty-year struggle for the restriction of immigration into the United States provided abundant and explicit "unveiling" of the social origins of the "population-growth" school of thought. Early economists were comparatively frank in recognizing a differential class interest in promoting population growth. See E. A. J. Johnson's chapter on "Land and Labor" in his *Predecessors of Adam Smith* (New York, 1937), pp. 237–59; Edgar S. Furniss, *The Position of the Laborer in a System of Nationalism* (Boston, 1920); and E. A. Ross, *Standing Room Only?* (New York, 1927), pp. 204 ff., 314 ff.

42. Professor A. W. Marget has gone a long way toward clarifying the methodological and substantive issues involved in the general problem of "statics versus dynamics"; and our discussion, in part, is based upon his analysis (A. W. Marget, *The Theory of Prices,* I [New York, 1938] 39–101; II [1942], 450–58.

43. Robbins, 1927, p. 123.

44. Cannan, 1929, p. 81; Fairchild, 1927, p. 75; Mombert, 1935, p. 536. Or, as Cohn stated, "Die besondere Schwierigkeit unseres Problems liegt dahin, dass Sozialprodukt und Bevölkerung sich nicht unabhängig voneinander entwickeln, sondern sich gegenseitig beeinflussen" (Cohn, 1934, p. 125).

45. See the exposition of the views of Adolphe Coste, Maxim Kovalevsky, and A. Loria in Sorokin, 1928, pp. 359–70, 388–403. Coste stated that "the numerical increase of the members of a society is the primary cause of its whole evolution" (*ibid.,* p. 364). See also Ross, 1927, pp. 177 ff.

46. See particularly Sorokin's criticisms of the "demographic school" (Sorokin, 1928, chap. vii, and *passim;* and Ross, 1927, pp. 179 ff.).

47. Hoover, 1932, p. 200.

48. "So however it may have been in the past, there is now no need of conserving population pressure as a whip to lash us into utilizing the resources of the globe" (Ross, 1927, p. 183).

49. See J. J. Spengler, "Population Movements, Employment and Income," *Southern Economic Journal,* V (1938), 137, for references to the thesis that "in general the relative amount of inventiveness seems to be virtually independent of population growth."

50. Thus H. Sonnabend, 1933, p. 297, states that "literature, art, science, etc., can exist and prosper only under conditions of an adequate density of population. . . . A big population creates both the demand and the supply of a variety of institutions for social entertainment and pleasure . . . [and] may increase the artistic, cultural and social amenities of life." And this after the American experience which, as far as "variety" goes ("a million drops and every one the same"), is a living demonstration of the contrary. The other

quotation is from Dupréel (1928, p. 15), who asserts that "l'aspect, la beauté, le charme de la surface terrestre n'est pas independant du nombre des êtres vivant qui l'occupent. . . ." It must be noted that the "economic effects" mentioned in the text will, of course, influence social, moral, and aesthetic life both by their direct influence on the standard of living and through the increased utilization of forest land, wild life, etc.

51. For adumbrations on "social loneliness" see Fraser, 1934, p. 40. The other quotation is from Wolfe, 1926, p. 73.

52. These terms are borrowed from Alfred Marshall, *Principles of Economics* (8th ed.; London, 1927), p. 321.

53. G. Myrdal, 1940, p. 27; Alva Myrdal, 1941,p. 86; Frank Lorimer, "Issues of Population Policy," *The Annals*, CCXXXVII (1945), 196. See the suggestive paper of J. Jewkes, "The Population Scare," *Manchester School*, X (1939), 105, where the author emphasizes that "in most present-day discussions of population, no distinction is made between the alleged drawbacks of the actual process of a fall in population and the alleged drawbacks of a smaller, as against a larger, population."

54. At least this will be the case for those who believe with Viner that the economist "is the special custodian for society of the long view in economic matters, and that even in troubled periods that view is entitled not to undisputed dominance but to a full hearing" (Jacob Viner, "Short and Long View in Economic Policy," *American Economic Review*, XXX [1940], 9).

55. Jewkes, 1940, pp. 105–6. Cf. Wicksell, 1913, p. 52.

56. Bibliographies, as well as good summaries of the literature, are available in Thompson (3d ed.), 1942, chap. xviii; J. J. Spengler, "Population Movements and Economic Equilibrium in the United States," *Journal of Political Economy*, Vol. XLVIII (1940); Allen Sweezy, "Population Growth and Investment Opportunity," *Quarterly Journal of Economics*, Vol. LV (1940). For the earlier German literature see Cohn, 1934, pp. 42 ff., 93 ff., 152 ff.

57. For characteristic examples see R. F. Harrod, "Modern Population Trends," *Manchester School*, X (1939), 17; L. Robbins, "Notes on Some Probable Consequences of the Advent of a Stationary Population in Great Britain," *Economica*, IX, No. 25 (1929), 76, 79.

58. G. Myrdal, 1940, pp. 165–66.

59. The available literature was reviewed and ably summarized by Howard Bowen, "Capital in Relation to Optimum Population," *Social Forces*, XV (1936–37), 346–50. The amount of the investment in a child was found to be so great that, in Bowen's opinion, "investment in new population is at least partially at the expense of investment in capital" (p. 348). See also Alva Myrdal, 1941, pp. 66 ff. As a result of Jewkes' sharp critique, R. F. Harrod admitted that "it is not denied that the reduction in the size of the family, which occurs during a period of decline, is an advantage to be set off against the evils caused by the transition" (Harrod, "A Rejoinder," *Manchester School*, XI [1940], 53). That the problem is of no small importance may be gauged by the heavy social burdens incurred by the Soviet people in providing for their large "children supply."

60. See, e.g., the table of age distributions for various estimated 1980 populations in this country in Thompson (3d ed.), 1942, p. 282. The percentages of the total population between the ages of twenty and sixty-five are practically constant, fluctuating between 58.7 and 62.7 per cent of the total population. The estimate projecting the quickest stabilization point and decline exhibits practically a constant percentage ratio of adults between the ages of twenty and forty-four from 1850 through an estimated 1980. This also was the conclusion of W. B. Reddaway. See his *The Economics of a Declining Population* (London, 1939), pp. 142 ff., 254 ff., on the basis of an examination of the British data.

61. Reddaway, 1939, p. 136.

62. These were discussed by Joseph A. Schumpeter, *Capitalism, Socialism, and Democracy* (New York, 1942), pp. 113 ff.

63. This was most clearly stated by Cassel, who developed the point with special emphasis: "Primarily, and generally, this means the building of new houses for the newcomers; but under modern conditions it also means equipping the economy with means of transport, factories, machinery, etc., in proportion to the growth of population" (Gustav Cassel, *The Theory of Social Economy*, trans. Joseph McCabe [New York, 1924], p. 42).

64. This, of course, is the essential and irrefutable message of Keynes and Hansen in their essays on the subject, which such critics as Pigou, Schumpeter, and Ellis apparently

refuse to grasp. Stating the problem in this way clears up the "skepticism" of those who "feel" that "population growth would be powerless by itself to reverse a general downswing" (Sweezy, 1940, p. 69). Of course, it would be powerless to avert a downswing but it would give new scope and power to an upswing. That is why "additional people," to quote Sweezy again, are a "stimulus to investment . . . instead of a problem for the relief administration" (p. 65). Again this does not mean that an accession of new workers will automatically breed a new upswing. A condition of "extensive" growth that "early capitalism" could absorb in its stride and yet flourish upon may strain the capacity of a "high" capitalism which has, to a considerable extent, lost its creative and accumulative powers.

65. Hence there is much soundness in the skepticism of those who refuse to accept the Keynes-Hansen explanation of the thirties. See, particularly, the comments by Hans Staudinger, Emil Lederer, Leland R. Robinson, Rufus S. Tucker, and Alexander Sachs in the symposium on "secular stagnation" conducted in 1939 by the Graduate Faculty of the New School for Social Research, *Social Research*, VI (1939), 143, 157, 165, 172, 174; and Howard Ellis, "Monetary Policy and Investment," *American Economic Review*, Suppl., XXX (1940), 27–39.

66. Reddaway, 1939, p. 230.

67. Reddaway, 1939, p. 120. Cassel, again, may be cited for his clear recognition of the basic fact that capital accumulation destined for the provision of new population increments results in a withdrawal of "productive forces" from the "satisfaction of current wants, and therefore this satisfaction of wants will at any moment be scantier than need be if there were no increase of population." This, he states, "is interesting insofar as it shows that the growth of population costs something more than the bearing and rearing of those children which make up the increment of population" (Cassel, 1924, p. 42).

68. See Schmoller, 1900, I, 181, for a discussion of the cultural and technological revolutions which determined "suitable" population densities. Also, E. Levasseur, *La Population française* (Paris, 1889–92), III, 473–78, describes five historic density ratios. A set of optimum density ratios for the many kinds of agricultural production was computed by Ratzel, the famous economic geographer, and these ratios have been cited or adapted frequently. See Karl Kautsky, *Vehrmehrung und Entwicklung in Natur und Gesellschaft* (Stuttgart, 1910), p. 89; W. G. Sumner and A. G. Keller, *The Science of Society* (New Haven, 1927), I, 46–63.

69. E. Cannan, *Wealth* (2d ed.; London, 1916), p. 69; E. Maurette, "Comments," *Proceedings of the World Population Conference, 1927*, p. 93; Robbins, 1927, p. 111; L. M. Fraser, 1934, p. 407; William Henry Beveridge, *Unemployment: A Problem of Industry* (2d ed.; London, 1930), p. 376; Fairchild, 1939, p. 165.

70. Beveridge, 1930, p. 379.

71. Dalton, 1928, p. 37; Alvin Hansen, *Economic Stabilization in an Unbalanced World* (New York, 1932), p. 220.

72. Wolfe, 1936, p. 246.

73. *Ibid.*, p. 247; Thompson, 1935, p. 424. Even economic geographers catch the idiom of current discourse, for Erich W. Zimmerman, *World Resources and Industries* (New York, 1933), p. 137, states that the optimum depends on a "relationship . . . so complex and dynamic that predictions of future trends seem folly."

74. Thompson, 1935, p. 424. The actual list is as follows: the sex and age composition of a population; the habits of work that have developed the efficiency with which it uses its tools and machines; the housing of the people; their dietary habits; the climate of the country; the use made of leisure time; the form of the social organization; the motives dominant in determining the objects for which people will work; the distribution of wealth among the different classes in the community; the religious taboos against the use of certain resources or the employment of them; the effects of the density and size of the population upon the course of inventions; the consumption habits of people and their effects upon the social and economic structure; the rate of the accumulation of capital; the relative amounts of labor spent upon the production and distribution of goods; the amount and the form of taxes; the rewards bestowed by the social system upon different kinds of economic and social activity; and a host of other social and economic factors all of which have an effect upon the productive processes of the community. Similar lists, although less extended, were developed by Mombert, 1929, p. 243; Hansen, 1932, p. 219.

75. Ferenczi, 1938, p. 48.

76. McCabe and Others, 1937, p. 88. For similar confessions see Ferenczi, 1938, p. 48; and Robbins, 1927, p. 128.

77. Robbins, 1927, p. 129; Plummer, 1932, p. 620. Both writers pondered the question seriously.

78. One of Wicksell's followers in Sweden, Dr. B. W. Silverstope, speaking at the 1927 Population Conference, expressed the point very clearly: "But it is not true that every new invention means a moving up of the optimum point, for, once the division of labor has been fully developed, it is possible to profit by new inventions and new methods of production without any further increase of population" (*Proceedings of the World Population Conference, 1927*, p. 100). We might add that many new inventions or discoveries are displacing in type (one mechanized industry displacing another).

79. Karl Marx, *Das Kapital* (Marx-Engels-Lenin Institut ed.; Moscow, 1932), p. 370. For the same thought see Zimmerman, 1933, p. 137; Silverstope, 1927, p. 100; Mombert, 1935, p. 539.

80. We do not have primarily in mind the "hopefulness" of an earlier generation of population theorists for whom the search for the optimum took the form of an analysis of conditions of "overpopulation." Nor should we, perhaps, utilize the optimistic statements of such optimum "pioneers" as Wicksell and King. Attention is called to recent utterances by writers who may be presumed to be fully aware of the complexities of measurement. Thus J. J. Spengler, who, in his *France Faces Depopulation*, pp. 256 ff., made an admittedly sketchy but suggestive analysis of optimum conditions in France, stated the following in his paper before the Population Congress in 1933: "To assert, as some writers do, that the concept of an economic optimum is meaningless because optimum density cannot be measured with precision indicates that the writers do not know what is meant by the law of diminishing returns or that they are unclear as to what gives meaning to concepts" (Spengler, 1933, p. 41, n. 1). The well-known English statistician-economist, P. Sargent Florence, declared that the determination of an optimum "should be amenable to a statistical answer," although he declared that "no statistician, so far as I am aware, has given it serious attention" (Florence, *Overpopulation, Theory and Statistics* ["Psyche Miniatures," No. 2 (London, 1926)], p. 15). Rao stated that the concept presents "one of the unsolved but nevertheless soluble problems of economics" (Rao, 1939, p. 447).

81. Wolfe, 1936, p. 247.

82. Wright, 1938, pp. 83–85.

83. In the order of their appearance, the above citations are extracted from McCabe and Others, 1937, p. 89; Fairchild, 1927, p. 80; Ferenczi, 1938, p. 111; Dalton, as cited in Cohn, 1934, p. 33, n. 118; Penrose, 1934, p. 66; Mombert, 1935, pp. 558–59 ("Jamais il n'est possible de déterminer si et quand l'optimum est atteint dans un pays"); Cohn, 1934, p. 83; Thompson, 1935, p. 424; Zimmerman, 1933, p. 136; Sarkar, 1936, p. 34; Beveridge, 1930, p. 376; A. M. Carr-Saunders, *World Population: Past Growth and Present Trends* (Oxford, 1936), p. 137.

84. G. Myrdal, 1940, p. 143.

85. The quoted words are from Wright, 1938, p. 84; Ferenczi, 1938, p. 49; Dalton, 1928, pp. 34 ff. Robbins, Carr-Saunders, Beveridge, and others were all engaged in a similar search and examination of "signs," "tests," and "symptoms." Already in 1927, however, Ross had declared that, "unlike the pressure of the atmosphere or of a confined gas, population pressure cannot be measured upon one simple scale, for it manifests itself in various ways and enters into many concrete forms and situations" (Ross, 1927, p. 127).

86. Dalton, Robbins, Ferenczi, Röpke, Wright, and Mombert have revealed the weakness of these "indices."

87. The quoted words are from Carr-Saunders, 1936, p. 330: "Of the various tests for the existence of overpopulation which have been proposed, one only deserves careful consideration, namely movements of real income." For the same thought see Penrose, 1934, pp. 51 ff.; Beveridge, 1930, pp. 377 ff. None other than Allyn Young was responsible for the statement that he "should go along with Professor Carr-Saunders . . . so far as to hold that so long as increasing population is accompanied by increasing average real income there is ground for the presumption that no overpopulation exists." See his review in *Economica*, VIII (1928), 115. So widespread has the notion become, that one writer observed that "the measure for overpopulation emphasized by holders of the income-optimum concept is the rise or decline of real income per capita" (Allan B. Cole, "Japan's

Population Problems in War and Peace," *Pacific Affairs*, XVI [1943], 406). For criticisms see Robbins, 1927, pp. 124–28; Dalton, 1928, pp. 40 ff.; Hansen, 1932, pp. 220 ff.

88. Particular sinners who may be noted here are Penrose, 1934, p. 53, who applied the "index" to Japan; and Carr-Saunders, 1936, pp. 140–44, who applied it to the various countries of western Europe.

89. Mombert defended the use of real-wage data as an acceptable measure of productivity trends: "Si l'on veut déterminer de la façon la plus directe si la rendement de l'économie et, par conséquent, le bien-être de la population sont en hausse, il n'est pas de moyen plus simple que d'étudier les ressources réelles de la population, par tête, ainsi que l'évolution des salaires réels" (Mombert, 1935, p. 556). The English figures cited were, however, cautiously interpreted in this ingenious and thoughtful article.

90. See Pigou, 1924, pp. 199 ff.; Marget, 1938, I, 64, n. 65, for the reference to Böhm-Bawerk.

91. Dalton, 1928, p. 34. Mombert expressed the thought differently by insisting that, even if we could never ascertain the precise optimum, we could ascertain whether we were approaching or drawing away from it: "Tout ce qu'il sera possible de faire, c'est d'indiquer si l'évolution se rapproche de cet optimum ou si elle s'en éloigne" (Mombert, 1935, p. 559).

92. National Resources Board, *A Report on National Planning and Public Works in Relation to Natural Resources, and Including Land Use and Water Resources . . .* (Washington, 1934), Part II, pp. 126–27; U.S. Department of Agriculture, *Yearbook of Agriculture, 1938, Soils and Men* (Washington, 1938), pp. 979–1161.

93. For countries of the Pacific a considerable amount of information has been collected by the Institute of Pacific Relations. See Karl J. Pelzer, *Population and Land Utilization*, Part I of *An Economic Survey of the Pacific Area*, ed. F. V. Field (New York: Institute of Pacific Relations, 1941). For an example of how *not* to use data of this type to uncover tendencies of diminishing returns, see Ryoichi Ishii, *Population Pressure and Economic Life in Japan* (Chicago, 1937), pp. 148–53. He manages to conclude that "there is no factual basis" for the opinion that "Japanese agriculture is now being operated at the stage of a decreasing marginal return" (p. 148). Again, comparisons of crude indices of farm productivity of different countries with agrarian density ratios are only loosely suggestive and should not replace a direct analysis of the peculiar features of each country's own situation. For a development of an interesting series of indices of the type mentioned, see E. Huntington, "Agricultural Productivity and Pressure of Population," *The Annals*, CXCVIII (1938), 73–92.

94. Jewkes, 1939, pp. 110–11.

95. Again, a large part of the essential material has been collected: by the National Resources Planning Board in its various publications; in the large literature on our "depressed" areas (e.g., Carter Goodrich and Others, *Migration and Economic Opportunity* [Philadelphia, 1936]); and in standard works on "conservation" in the various resource industries.

96. Allyn Young, "Increasing Returns and Economic Progress," *Economic Journal*, XXXVIII (1928), 529.

97. E. A. G. Robinson, *The Structure of Competitive Industry* (New York, 1932), p. 135.

98. Harrod, 1939, p. 17; Jewkes, 1939, pp. 109–10.

99. Sumner H. Slichter, *Modern Economic Society* (New York, 1928), p. 338, says that, "taking the country as a whole, the present population of 120,000,000 appears to give us the principal economies of large-scale production." See also King, 1915, p. 239.

100. Hoover, 1932, p. 203.

101. Cambridge, 1933. Colin Clark has also attempted to apply statistical research to the problem (see his *The Conditions of Economic Progress* [London, 1940], pp. 291–316). His technical measures are far cruder and much less illuminating than those of Jones. See, however, his two tables on pp. 297 and 305, especially the latter, with its correlation between volume of output and output per head.

102. The index represents: per cent of volume expansion/per cent fall in real costs.

103. The U.S. Tariff Commission has published the results of many studies involving comparisons of domestic and foreign industries (see, e.g., Report No. 139 [2d ser., 1940]: *Silverware*; Report No. 60 [2d ser., 1933]: *Blown Glass Tableware*).

THEORY OF POPULATION AND MODERN ECONOMIC ANALYSIS*

By Alan T. Peacock

I. In recent years, the fashioning of new tools of economic analysis has been accompanied by their application not only to the development of current theories but to the reformulation of earlier theories. In the case of the latter application, this has even resulted in the rehabilitation of earlier theories as working hypotheses.[1] It is interesting to inquire, therefore, what modern economic analysis has to offer in the way of a rehabilitation of Malthusian theory, if, indeed, there is any need to rehabilitate a theory of population which has never been wholly rejected even by economists and which still captures the imagination of social philosophers.

A reformulation of the Malthusian theory can serve two useful purposes. Firstly, in keeping with the whole trend in modern economic analysis, the political judgements can be separated entirely from the logic of the analysis. This is not to say that recent theories have not been used to justify particular modes of social and political policy. A good example is surely that of the Keynesian analysis. The general thesis of the *General Theory of Employment, Interest and Money* is difficult to divorce from the famous 'Notes on the Social Philosophy to which the General Theory might lead,'[2] which concluded Keynes's *magnum opus*. Nor is this to say that complete divorce of economic theory and social philosophy is desirable even on scientific grounds. As Lange has reminded us,[3] while economic analysis developed by resolving disagreements over the fact, logic and systems of values, it is often precisely because of the particular political bias of the social scientist that theories of significance are conceived. Keynes's work is surely testimony of this, not to mention the *Essay on Population* or the *Wealth of Nations*. Nevertheless, while one may agree to differ over political judgements, there need be no grounds of dispute if assumptions are made clear, the logic is closely scrutinized and facts can be established. There is a remarkable agreement among economists about the general method of approach of Keynesian analysis which is divorced entirely from the policy recommendations of particular economists. 'We are all Keynesians now' in the methodological sense. I cannot make the same claim for Malthusian theory so far as methodology is concerned, as I hope to show later, but I shall attempt to prove that the theory is a much more general one than is sometimes supposed and can be divorced entirely from any particular system of values.

* Reprinted from *Population Studies*, 6 (November 1952), pp. 114–122, and 7 (March 1954), pp. 227–234, by permission of the author and the Population Investigation Committee, London School of Economics and Political Science.

The second reason which justifies reformulation is concerned with the development of the scientific analysis itself.

New modes of expression often highlight assumptions of analysis which may not have been clearly enunciated. The same old wine may merely be being poured into new bottles. But the shape and colour of the bottles give a different perspective to its contents. There are countless examples of this in economic theory, such as the reformulation of the classical theory of value in terms of indifference curve analysis. This often shows that the original investigation of a particular economic phenomenon has considered a special case of a more general theory. We shall consider this point in more detail when we come to deal specifically with the Malthusian theory.

The method of approach in this article follows very strictly that used in modern economic analysis. First, I shall build a 'model' of the Malthusian theory based on particular assumptions, then I shall consider the functional relationships between the main variables which can hold for the assumptions given, independently of the specific Malthusian assumptions. Then I shall go back to consider the assumptions in detail and conclude with some remarks on the relevance of the Malthusian theory for present-day economic systems.

II. We must start, then, by building a model of the Malthusian theory in the same way as an economic theorist would build a model of the business cycle.

Certain simplifying assumptions are made about the environment in which population changes are to take place: (a) we are concerned with a closed economy without international trade; (b) only one commodity is being produced which is a gauge of living standards (in the Malthusian analysis it is, say, corn, which symbolizes food); (c) all productive forces are fully utilized, i.e. there are no unemployed resources; (d) for every level of population a conventional subsistence minimum is given; (e) the supply of land and capital is fixed; (f) the units of labor applied to the fixed stock of land and capital are homogeneous. Certain functional relationships are supposed to have been established by empirical observation: (a') that population is an increasing function of the average output per head of population, the latter being determined by the ratio $\dfrac{\text{total product}}{\text{total population}}$; (b') that the supply of labour is an increasing function of the level of population; (c') that the application of successive increments of labour to the fixed supply of capital and land will, after a certain point, result in a decline in both the marginal and average product per head of population.

From these assumptions (a)–(f) and these observations (a')–(c'), it can be proved that the level of population tends always to the level which will just be supported at the given subsistence minimum.

We can show this more clearly diagrammatically with the use of the four-quadrant system (Fig. 1) now commonly used in modern economic analysis in order to illustrate problems in statics and comparative statics.[4]

Contrary to the usual geometrical convention, all axes x, x' and y, y' are positive. The functions in each quadrant are drawn to correspond with our empirically determined propositions.

In the north-west quadrant we relate population to the standard of living (corresponding to observation (a')) by drawing a straight line from O at an angle which determines the subsistence minimum. For instance, given total product $OA(=PQ)$ is just sufficient to provide subsistence for population OP $(=AQ)$, then the subsistence minimum is OA/OP. Provided that the subsistence minimum does not vary with the level of population and output, OQ is linear. This is the essentially Malthusian proposition. As total product rises, population rises, either through increasing fertility or declining mortality, but at a rate faster than the rise in productivity per head of population. Although there is no real statement of the law of diminishing returns in the *Essay*, the law is implied in the famous 'ratios'.

In the south-east quadrant we draw the function relating population and the supply of labour. In part, this must be a 'demographic' function. The shape of the function will depend upon whether population growth is caused predominantly by increasing births or declining mortality, and thus upon the relation between population growth and age composition. In part, it may be determined by law and custom; in developed economies, for instance, by the legal school-leaving age and the customary age of retirement. It does not seem unreasonable to suppose that the sum of children and old people bears a fairly fixed relation to the whole population and, as a first approximation, we can illustrate this by a linear function.[5]

Corresponding to (c') we draw the total product curve in the north-east quadrant so that it expresses the law of diminishing returns; and this function, if not characteristic of the Malthusianism of Malthus, is so of the Malthusianism of J. S. Mill and most neo-Malthusians.[6] The point of 'maximum average return' is the point of tangency of a straight line drawn from the origin to the total product curve, so that the maximum average return per unit of labour is equal to tan θ.

Calling total product π, population p, the subsistence minimum S, and the supply of labour l, then the conditions of equilibrium are

$$\frac{\pi}{p} = S, \quad l = ap, \quad \frac{d^2\pi}{dp^2} < 0,$$

where obviously $a < 1$. If for any reason p is higher than the equilibrium level, then l will rise and, although π will rise, it will be insufficient to cover subsistence needs, so that population falls and with it the supply of labour, until equilibrium is re-established. In terms of our graph, equilibrium is demonstrated by the 'closed circuit' $PP'LMAQP$.

Before we consider some of the characteristics of this approach in a little more detail, we can demonstrate clearly with this presentation the condition where the 'optimum' level of population is reached, the optimum being defined here as the point of maximization of product per head of population.

At this stage of analysis, this is purely a question of definition. This point is reached when

$$\frac{F(p)}{p} = f'(p), \quad l = a\,p.$$

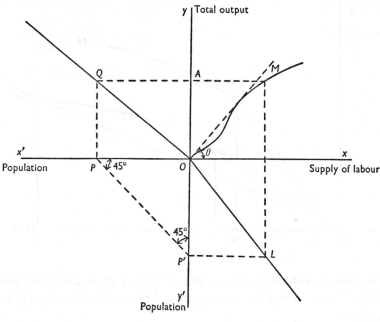

Fig. 1

It is to be noted that the point of maximum return per head of supply of labour and per head of population coincide unless the condition is fulfilled that the supply of labour is a given proportion of the population. This can be demonstrated by a simple graph.

In this graph the optimum level of population is determined in much the same way as the point of maximum average receipts per unit of product in the analysis of the individual firm in economics. The subsistence line corresponds to the 'total cost curve', and the total product curve to the 'total revenue curve'. In fact, the analogy is a striking one, for the subsistence theory of wages which is closely connected with population theory visualized wages as being just that cost which would be necessary to maintain the wage-earner in a condition to work at a given level of efficiency. First we draw our original total product curve OM related to the supply of labour. In the same quadrant we draw the curve relating total product to population. Our first equilibrium condition is fulfilled when population level is OP and the average and marginal product per head of population are equal. Our second condition is fulfilled when the supply of labour is OL, and thus $OL =$

a (OP). The fact that a expresses the linear relationship between population and the supply of labour means that where $\dfrac{F(p)}{p} = f'(p), \dfrac{F(l)}{l} = f'(l)$. In Fig. 2 the latter relationship is shown at the point R.

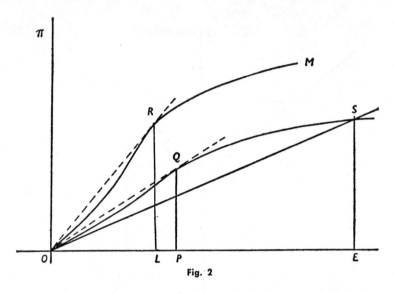

Fig. 2

III. There are two characteristics of this method of approach which must be considered in some detail before we proceed to examine the assumptions of the analysis.

First of all, as presented so far, the theory is a static one in the sense that we cannot use it to analyse continuous changes in the economy within its framework. However, the word 'static' has unfortunate emotional associations, which suggest that in some way, not often precisely defined, 'dynamic' analysis is superior. It is true that the equilibrium conditions presuppose that the functions remain stable throughout the period of adjustment towards the stationary state where the total product curve and subsistence line intersect (point S in Fig. 2), but this is not to say that the adjustment is assumed to be instantaneous. Time elements can be incorporated into the analysis by the assumption of 'lagged' adjustment;[7] for instance, we can assume that the population adjusting itself to the subsistence minimum is a function of output of a previous period of time, and likewise that the supply of labour is a function of population increase of some previous period. However, the time periods here may be extremely difficult to define. 'Lagged' adjustment really only shows us the path towards equilibrium or from one equilibrium position to another, given the shape of the functions we have drawn and assumptions about the length of the time period.

However, it does less than justice to Malthus himself to treat his theory as an equilibrium theory of population. It is clear from Book I, Chapter II of the *Essay on Population* that population is assumed to oscillate about the level which is sanctioned by the subsistence minimum.[8] Not only that; this 'sanctioned level' may alter over time. Let us assume that the 'sanctioned level' increases, as would be the case when the total product curve shifted to the right. According to Malthus, the rise of the average total product above the subsistence level would cause an increase in population through earlier marriages; in time labour supply would increase and its supply price would fall; in consequence population would have increased faster than the means of subsistence (as demonstrated by the shape of the total product curve), and this would bring into operation the preventive check. In certain circumstances, which we shall demonstrate shortly, this would produce, not the stationary level of population sanctioned by the increase in productivity but an oscillation about the new equilibrium point.[9] It is a travesty of the Malthusian theory to argue as if the positive checks and not the preventive check were more important and to use this assertion in order to prove that the Malthusian theory must lead to the conclusion that population just increases up to the limits sanctioned by the population minimum and stays there.[10]

We can demonstrate the Malthusian 'oscillation' by using our graphical analysis. A shift in the total product curve takes place. In period 1 the change in output per head takes place, inducing an expansion of population in period 2 on the assumption that there is no change in total output. These expectations are not fulfilled in period 2, so that in period 3 there is a fall in population in order to better the circumstances of the wage-earner in accordance with Malthus's preventive check. This fall in population in period 4 increases returns per head, and the cycle continues until the conditions of production alter again. It is to be noted, however, that this Malthusian oscillation can only occur if it is assumed that an increase in population actually promotes a fall in *total* output, not merely average output, and then only because of the particular shape of the two curves. Where total output rises with an increase in population, it is clear that population will be stationary at the new level. However, the time periods are likely to be so long that, throughout the whole process, the functions themselves may be altering. All we can show here are the forces at work, and only certain forces at that. We shall have good reason to question the general validity of the Malthusian assumptions at a later stage.

The second feature of this approach is that, although we have used what might be described as the Malthusian analytical framework, there is no reason why we should necessarily accept the Malthusian assumptions.

To take a modern parallel, the Keynesian analysis of income determination in its simplest form assumes that the saving of a community is an increasing function of the level of real income and that investment in the short period is autonomous with respect to real income. The intersection of the

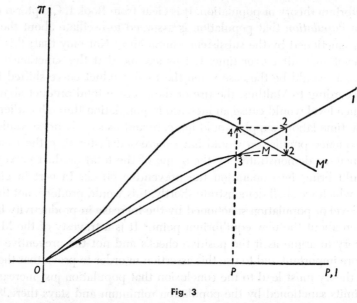

Fig. 3

corresponding saving and investment schedules give us, therefore, an equilibrium level of real income. Now no economist would deny that there is a functional relationship of some sort relating income and saving and income and investment. What he would deny, however, is that the *shape* of the functions is necessarily of the type envisaged by Keynes. It would be agreed that, even allowing for other influences on the level of saving and investment and thus on income, the Keynesian conclusion of under-employment of resources would follow from the assumptions, but it would be denied that these are the only assumptions. Thus investment is often assumed in economic analysis to be an increasing function of income (or of the rate of change in income, as in the famous 'acceleration principle'), and the shape of the saving function is often assumed to be linear.

Now the central variable in our analysis is population, and we have assumed it to be a function of the level of output, the latter in turn being indirectly a function of the level of population. No one could deny that, ultimately at least, some functional relationship exists between output and population, but this relationship need not be the one postulated by Malthus and Malthusians generally.

Let us consider an example. The functional relationship between population and total output denoting the subsistence conditions need not be a straight line. It is quite conceivable that a rise in output per head and thus in total output prior to the point where average returns begin to diminish may be associated with a continual revision of the subsistence minimum. Population may conceivably be a decreasing function of total output and may even decline absolutely. Historically this is borne out by the experience of western countries where population, while it has grown absolutely over

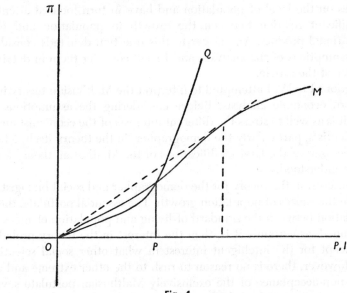

Fig. 4

the last 70 years, has done so at a decreasing rate, while total real output has grown remarkably. Sir Charles Darwin's symbolic aphorism—'the prospect of owning a motor car is a sufficient bribe to sterilize most people'—is the modern counterpart to Senior's assertion that 'as a nation advances in civilization and opulence the positive checks are likely to be superseded by the preventive'.[11] Accordingly, our modification can be regarded as being quite in keeping with the classical analysis. Again, the relation between the supply of labour (and thus population) and total output need not necessarily express the law of diminishing returns over the relevant range. Let us combine these two modifications to illustrate what might be a rather unusual case. The reason for choosing this example will be made clear in a moment. We draw the subsistence line in accordance with the statement in the previous paragraph and so that it intersects the total product curve at a point below the point of maximum return. Accordingly, in this case the equilibrium level of population is below the optimum level as defined in § II. While it is true, as Myrdal has stressed, that the optimum theory of population has been associated with neo-Malthusianism and thus with the demand for a smaller population on policy grounds,[12] there is no *logical* reason why this need be so. However, we are far from being in a position where we can safely suggest what the implications of policy recommendations with respect to population may be.

IV. The model we have elaborated from the Malthusian theory is still based upon the same or similar assumptions to the original analysis. Whatever changes we have made in the shape of the various functions, we have still to answer the question whether we have really singled out the *significant* influences on the level of population and have in turn focused attention on the significant relation between the growth in population and changes in the national product. An answer to this question demands consideration of the assumptions of the analysis, and I shall consider them in detail in the remainder of the article.

V. In sections I to IV, I attempted to interpret the Malthusian theory in terms of modern economic analysis. Before considering the assumptions of the analysis it is as well to stress the different interests of the economist and other social scientists, particularly the demographer, in the theory itself. I feel that this is necessary if the later modifications of the Malthusian theory are to be correctly understood.

The interest in the theory for the demographer and social biologist, I suppose, is in the *causes* of population growth. The essential postulate, therefore, is the relation between the standard of living and population changes. If this is questioned, as certainly it is, then the interest in the theory probably declines except for the intelligent interest in what other social scientists are doing. However, there is no reason to rush to the other extreme and assume that the non-acceptance of the exclusively Malthusian postulate severs the nexus between material conditions and population changes. In fact, the developments since Malthus's day perhaps give added significance to the economic factor. In the absence of preventive checks, the rate of growth of population is based purely on physical necessity—'the passion between the sexes' remaining constant. With the introduction of preventive checks, the question of choice in the procreation of children becomes important. The motives for having children are reflected in economic choices, the cost of children being measured in terms of the alternatives foregone. The economist would not be prepared to answer the question as to how far the alternatives can be weighted for typical cases; that is a matter of sociological investigation. He would merely say that the ultimate sanction in choice is the problem of relating competing ends to limited means, a prospect not considered relevant in a situation where children were the necessary consequence of sexual intercourse. But while the Malthusian theory does, as it were, not allow for the 'substitution' effect in the allocation of income, this is not to say that its stress on the 'income' effect is to be forgotten. While in the long-run there is a marked correlation between growth in real income and in the decline in birth rates in Western countries, there are very pronounced short-run variations in birth rates and marriage rates over the period of the business cycle. It may be, however, as Spengler points out, that income effects may become less important with the disposition of states to maintain the level of employment and to provide social security support for the reproduction and rearing of children.[13]

To the economist, on the other hand, the Malthusian theory stands or falls by its attempt to explain economic development. He is not so interested, therefore, in the causes of population changes, but more in the *consequences* of these changes. The fact that these changes themselves, that is to say the change in total product and thus average product per head, bring about population changes is interesting, but it is not this fact alone which influences the economist in singling out the important variables. The test of the theory therefore becomes that of proving that only these two variables, total product and population (or, more accurately, the supply of labour), are the significant ones, and that the relations between them are correctly interpreted. This is to say that the remainder of this analysis is taken up with problems of economics, and not with demography. In this respect I am aware that I run the risk of employing a method which is open to criticism[14] by my professional colleagues and of disappointing those whose conception of what a population theory should do is of a different kind. Perhaps, however, it is of interest to consider why it has come about that, despite the modifications in the analysis produced by the possible alternative assumptions to be used (and which I am about to discuss), the Malthusian doctrine has never been entirely removed from the text-books on economics.

VI. The first major assumption is that the theory as stated assumes a closed economy. Thus national output is identical with the domestic product, and the supply of labour is solely determined by the birth rate and death rate. There is no reference, therefore, either to movements of goods across national frontiers or movements of factors, and more particularly labour. Now it is conceivable that the world is a closed economy in this sense, but to talk of the world economy is to make nonsense of the practical application of the Malthusian theory and to divorce it entirely from its original setting. Let us therefore consider the case of a country with either movements of goods or movements of factors.

Let us consider movements of goods. Obviously, then, in any given period, the relevant magnitudes for the calculation of disposable product are equal to national product plus the volume of imports minus the volume of exports. Of course, it makes nonsense also of the assumption of one commodity, unless we assume that we value all goods in terms of money and forget about index-number problems in the weighting of the different items comprising national product. These changes can easily be *expressed* in our original diagram by re-drawing our total product curve to allow for changes in the real terms of trade, i.e. in the volume of imports received for a given volume of exports. Beginning with a situation where exports equal imports in real terms, a favourable change in the real terms of trade would be represented by an upward shift in the product curve, and an unfavourable change by a downward shift. But while these changes can be expressed, what is their relevant expression? In other words, what conceivable relation is there between changes in the real terms of trade and population changes? For those particularly interested in the 'optimum' theory, this is a crucial question which requires a definite answer, for otherwise it is impossible to determine the point of maximum product per head.

It is exceedingly unlikely that one will ever be able to produce a general answer to this question. At the highest level of abstraction with the demand and supply schedules of exports and imports known, with no barriers to trade, and so on, Mr. Gottlieb[15] produces a bell-shaped curve which purports to show that, as a first approximation, a growing population will first of all be associated with worsening real terms of trade and then an improvement. Mr. Gottlieb's reasoning, even at this level of abstraction, is hardly rigorous. There is nothing in the nature of the argument at this level of abstraction which demands that, even if the supply and demand schedules for exports and imports are known, a bell-shaped curve will result. It turns out, however, that Mr. Gottlieb is really thinking of a simple subsistence economy which has to import all its manufactures and in which the pattern of economic development postulated—gradual industrialization and exploitation of natural resources previously imported—is, to say the least, rather arbitrary. Nor is the theory complete. If we adapted our total product curve in order to allow for the changes postulated by Mr. Gottlieb, are we to hold that the analysis is reversible, that a decreasing population will first lead to a deterioration, and then an improvement in the terms of trade?

A simpler approach is surely to recognize the difficulty, and to remember that in any prediction involving population changes and terms of trade, *some* assumption has to be made. But the terms of trade are a function of so many different variables that it seems inconceivable that one can produce a general case. What we can say is that, given the likely changes in the terms of trade whatever their cause, we must take these changes into account in any relation between numbers and resources. Thus a policy recommendation which neglected this factor altogether, say, in Malaya, which is heavily dependent on its export trade, would be worthless. But so also would one be which assumed that over the period of population growth the supply and demand conditions for imports and exports for a given country would remain stable.

About the assumption of no factor movements, I need say little. At this stage, with the relaxation of only one assumption, the only variable factor we have is labour. Again, if we wished to introduce immigration or emigration, we could consider this in a dynamic version of the analysis. What I mean by this is that if, for instance, a rise in total national product is associated with net immigration, then in an economy on the path towards equilibrium, the addition to the working population at some stage of development will hasten the movement towards equilibrium just as any 'autonomous' rise in population would do. Of course, when we regard the subsistence minimum as a psychological and not a physiological phenomenon, then immigrants with a definite pattern of living may have different conceptions of minimum standards. With large immigration this would imply a modification in the subsistence line as well, and where immigration is in response to higher living standards in the receiving country, the line might be pivoted towards the right. Theoretically it is conceivable that this modification would result in higher returns per head, provided the original intersection of the subsistence line and the total product curve was to the left of the point of maximum returns per head. Again, however, it would be futile to try to provide a general case, but to work with alternative assumptions for the individual cases studied.

At this stage of the analysis, the reader may well be appalled at the level of abstraction. We demonstrate once again the well-known paradox, that the attempt to proceed by successive approximations towards reality seems to take us away from reality altogether. We are prepared to accept the broad strokes of the Malthusian brush to rivet our attention on a fundamental problem, but once we modify the picture with the details required by actual conditions, we seem to lose sight of the significant problem.

VII. But the next problem is a really formidable one. In our analysis, the level of production depends on the productivity of labour with a given quantity of the other factors of production.

A succession of well-known writers were prepared to argue that an increasing population would successively modify the level of the total product curve by the effect on productivity of a highly mobile labour force, and by the advantages of large populations for the division of labour. I can assume that these arguments are well known, and in any case they can be allowed for in the analysis quite easily. What really conspires to remove the population problem altogether from the economist's text-books is the modern theory of output and employment. The argument of this theory, the level of real national output, is a function of the demand for consumption and investment goods, and not merely of productivity of labour and other factors. Thus, there is a missing link in the chain of reasoning which postulated an automatic relation between labour inputs and total output.

It is now sufficiently well known that Keynes claimed Malthus's support for a theory of output and employment based on under-consumption.[16]

However, there is little to show, in the scattered references given by Keynes, that Malthus saw the implication of under-consumption for his theory of population. The one reference to population within the context of his discussion of under-consumption is an *obiter dictum* regarding the difficulty of employing an increasing population when excessive capital accumulation leads to a fall in profits and thus in further accumulation.[17]

It is clear that this statement is not by any means a contradiction of his views on population, but it does suggest that the popular supposition that an increasing population will also exacerbate the unemployment problem is correct.[18]

On the other hand, precisely the opposite conclusion has been drawn by Keynes himself and by Hansen and Sweezy as the protagonists of the theory of 'stagnation'. Thus it is argued by Sweezy that 'it does seem clear that, given *otherwise favourable conditions*, population growth widens the scope of profitable investment opportunity. . . .'[19] In other words, population increase will be a motive force in shifting the total product curve up, and not in dragging it down.[20] If this argument has any substance, then for countries likely to suffer long-run chronic under-employment of resources, the Malthusian question would appear to have no relevance.

However, all depends on the 'otherwise favourable conditions'. It is certainly true that the existence of a growing population suggests growing needs, but this is not to say that it means growing effective demand. To this objection the more subtle version of the argument[21] puts forward another answer.

An increase in the absolute increment of population will result in a *redistribution* of effective demand towards the purchase of investment goods, particularly housebuilding and public utilities, and in this way the level of aggregate output and employment will be fostered. An even more subtle variant is provided by Higgins,[22] who argues that the level of consumption will be increased at the expense of saving, because of the redistribution of income between wage-earners and their dependants.

There is still a large body of opinion which thinks otherwise, and the Hansen thesis is still simply an unverifiable hypothesis because of the other influences operating on effective demand. It is still thought conceivable that Malthus's contention about the difficulty of employing an increasing population when there is over-saving is a possibility. In fact, Jørgen Pedersen argues that population growth in the nineteen-thirties in the United States was accompanied by unemployment precisely because of low aggregate demand and argues that a country with an expanding population and the threat of under-employment must consider the possibility of a continual lowering of the long-term rate of interest and budget deficits or a suitable combination of both.[23]

No theory of economic development, therefore, can afford to neglect the influence of aggregate demand on output as well as productivity changes. It would, indeed, be a diverting paradox if we could stand the Malthusian population theory on its head and could hold that population increases are necessary to offset and not to fulfil the operation of diminishing returns. However, it would be a travesty of present opinion in economics to give other social scientists the impression that this thesis is universally accepted, not the least because it is applied largely to capitalist economies at a mature stage of development.

VIII. We can apply two tests to the analysis we have developed in the preceding sections. The first test is its general interpretative value. We can observe, for instance, how far it clarifies the issues in contemporary controversy over the economics of population. The second test is a more formidable one—its use for prediction purposes. This implies some discussion of methodology in economic analysis.

The analysis comes off quite well so far as the first test is concerned. With it we can state the issues in the present so-called Malthusian controversy succinctly and clearly. The main controversy is conducted in terms of the world economy, and this must inevitably mean that the analysis is highly abstract, for we must imagine to ourselves some sort of world production function coupled with some relation between average income per head of the income of the world and population growth. But at this level of abstraction there is not even unanimity about the facts themselves.[24] Nevertheless, the analysis provides a neat way of classifying these disagreements. Thus the 'optimists' visualize a situation in the world economy in which the total product curve is continually shifting to the right because the assumption of fixed land and capital is not accepted and/or one in which the subsistence line is pivoted upwards to the left because the subsistence minimum is revised as incomes per head rise. Thus the subsistence level is never reached because the functions are not assumed to be stable in time. The 'pessimists' assume that something approximating to the Malthusian special case is fulfilled, because capital and land are regarded as scarce relatively to labour and/or it seems to them a reasonable hypothesis that population increase is a function of living standards, not necessarily because of increasing birth rates but because of declining mortality rates. We can only clarify disagreement at this level of the controversy, and the disagreement will never be resolved so long as the facts are disputed. Even on the basis of alternative hypotheses, it is impossible to specify more than the likely stages of world economic development, but no guidance is given to the time periods involved. My own view is that the dominating factor in the short run is the prospect of declining mortality rates in consequence of shifts in the world production function which increases living standards in areas such as the Asiatic countries.

This brings me to the second field of application of the analysis. Not even the most confirmed optimist would deny the applicability of the special Malthusian case, at least in the short run, to certain areas. Even given no world food shortage in the sense that incomes per head *could be* well above subsistence levels, the distribution of world resources, and therefore the distribution of wealth and incomes makes nonsense of an argument which assumes that we all eat at the same table. The assumptions of the special case are largely fulfilled in the analysis of, say, the area comprising the Indian subcontinent, Malaya, Burma and Japan. There is a scarcity of capital and land relatively to labour. The prospect of large-scale emigration is remote—a striking contrast to the situation in the nineteenth century, which allowed Europe to solve her problem at least partially in this way. While fertility rates for different ages are not so very much higher than, say, in the United States, the age of marriage is earlier and mortality rates have a long way to fall. The main problem of economic policy is inflationary conditions and not chronic underemployment. Some economists have gone so far as to argue that the terms of trade of the primary producing part of these areas are undergoing a secular decline. Our analysis provides the diagnosis and suggests the remedies, but the choice of remedies is not dictated by the analysis. It is unnecessary to accept the Malthusian remedies along with the Malthusian analysis.

But can we go further than this, and predict more precisely what is going to happen, say, in the areas we have just mentioned? This would be the real test of our analysis. Here we are faced with a most difficult methodological problem, and it is one which besets all attempts at economic prediction, particularly those attempts which must necessarily involve forecasting the decisions of political institutions.

The problem can usually be avoided altogether by strict *ceteris paribus* assumptions. Thus a common method in the economic analysis of population problems is merely to argue that given the continuation of present conditions, in this case capital scarcity, emigration barriers, etc., population is likely to approach the level which will reduce incomes per head to subsistence levels. It is then left to the politicians to take their choice of alternative policies in order to avoid the problem, e.g. through foreign capital imports, propagation of birth control methods, etc. One can thus be non-committal or merely hopeful, and say that the realization of the problem will bring its own solution.

The problem has to be faced, however, when anyone is bold enough not merely to state what appears to be desirable or possible, but what they think will actually happen.[25] The trouble with this method is not only the inherent difficulty of forecasting what policies will in fact be introduced which must involve some theory of governmental action, however crude; but it involves the curious phenomenon which besets all economic forecasting, namely, that the prediction itself may alter the data on which it is based. If the British government in the *Economic Survey for* 1949 had blandly announced that they expected that the devaluation of the pound was expected to occur in 1949, then it is quite conceivable that devaluation would have been forced upon them because of the flight from Sterling which the original prediction might have precipitated. If a United Nations report stated that it did not anticipate that Great Britain would acknowledge any obligations laid down in the Colombo Plan and would not be prepared to make any contribution to the capital requirements of underdeveloped countries with a population problem, it is quite conceivable that such a statement might radically change the stated policy itself because of the reaction of world opinion. Thus those who are in ignorance of official intentions can only guess, and those whose job it is to make official predictions are not in a position to disclose them for fear that the revelation may make nonsense of the predictions themselves. Perhaps it is as well not to drive the method too far, and to stick to the *ceteris paribus* method. It suggests, if it does not approve alternative possible courses of action.

Most social scientists would probably be content to confine prediction to the relatively short run, if only for the very good reason that this is the period that interests policy makers. But the strict Malthusian theory of the original *Essay* of 1798 has been applied to the very long run, as the title of Sir Charles Darwin's book, *The Next Million Years*, suggests. In arguing that the original Malthusian prediction is essentially correct, Sir Charles relies on a purely biological interpretation of human behaviour which ignores the power of human institutions altogether. In this way he avoids altogether the problem of human reactions discussed in the preceding paragraphs. This approach is, I suppose, defensible, on the grounds that human institutions and values change. Perhaps over a sufficiently long period we might find in the future cycles in human populations comparable with those found in animal populations. There is no space to consider these problems here. It is sufficient to mention, perhaps, that it would be contrary to our whole experience of human population problems if population growth and with it economic development were not to be influenced by sociological factors. Thus, our very awareness of the dangers which Sir Charles says are impossible to avoid, might prevent them from ever arising at all.

IX. Our conclusion is that the Malthusian theory of population considered as a theory of economic development is a much more general one than is often supposed. Different patterns of assumptions about the relation between population growth and living standards can be considered within the framework of its analysis. There is also reason to believe that, so far as the world economy is concerned, the original assumptions of the analysis are highly relevant. However, whatever alternative sets of assumptions are used, the analysis does not commit anyone in any way to the policy prescriptions of Malthusian social philosophy.

REFERENCES

1. As found, for instance, in the revival of interest in Ricardo sponsored by R. F. Harrod in his *Towards a Dynamic Economics*.
2. The title of the final chapter of the *General Theory*.
3. Oscar Lange, 'The scope and method of economics,' *Review of Economic Studies*, vol. XIII, 1945.
4. Diagrammatic illustration of population theory has been used recently by a number of writers. The exposition here is most closely related to Baumol's analysis in his *Economic Dynamics*, chapter 2, except that we have found it necessary to treat the supply of labour as a separate variable. See also the recent treatment of Alfred Sauvy in his *Théorie Générale de la Population*: (1) *Economie et Population*, and that of Kenneth Boulding, *Economic Analysis* (revised ed.), pp. 657–60.
5. A more extensive analysis of this assumption is provided by M. Sauvy, op. cit. Chapter VIII.
6. Following Cannan's familiar distinction in his *Production and Distribution Theories*.
7. It can therefore be 'dynamic' in the sense in which the word is employed by Prof. Hicks. See J. R. Hicks, *Value and Capital* (2nd ed.), p. 115. For a thorough discussion of the economist's use of the terms static and dynamic, see W. J. Baumol, op. cit., chapter 1.
8. 'During . . . (the) season of distress, the discouragements to marriage and the difficulty of rearing a family are so great that the progress of population is retarded. In the meantime, the cheapness of labour, the plenty of labourers, and the necessity of an increased industry among them encourage cultivators to employ more labour upon their land, to turn up fresh soil, and to manure and improve more completely what is already in tillage, till ultimately the means of subsistence may become in the same proportion to the population as at the period from which we set out. The situation of the labourer being then again tolerably comfortable, the restraints to population are in some degree loosened; and after a short period the same retrograde and progressive movements, with respect to happiness, are repeated.' *Essay on Population* (6th ed. 1926), p. 11.
9. Equilibrium point in the sense that, given *instantaneous adjustment* from the previous equilibrium point, the population level would increase and then remain stable.
10. This criticism was made by L. v. Bortkiewicz of those German theorists who main-

tained that Malthus envisaged a situation of continual overpopulation. See his whole argument in pp. 21–7 of his article 'Bevölkerungstheorie' in *Die Entwicklung der deutschen Volkswirtschaftslehre im neunzehnten Jahrhundert* (ed. by Gustav Schmoller), Duncker und Humblot, 1908. I repeat it because this appears to be the burden of Kenneth Smith's argument in his article 'Some observations on modern Malthusianism,' *Population Studies,* vol. VI, no. 1, July 1952, p. 92. While it is true that some modern Malthusians interpret the Malthusian theory in this way, it is not always clear whether Mr. Smith is discussing their views or those of Malthus himself. If he is discussing Malthus, then it is difficult to see how this interpretation can be made of the *Essay on Population.*

11. Charles Galton Darwin, *The Next Million Years,* 1952, p. 136, and Nassau Senior, *An Outline of the Science of Political Economy* (Library of Economics Edition), p. 42.

12. Gunnar Myrdal, *Population; A Problem of Democracy* (1940), Lecture VI. See, however, the criticism of Myrdal's view of the history of optimum theory in M. Gottlieb's article, 'The theory of optimum population in a closed economy,' *Journal of Political Economy,* vol. LIII, December 1945.

13. Joseph J. Spengler, *Population Theory* (Survey of Contemporary Economics, vol. II. Edited by Bernard Haley, especially pp. 99–106). The article has an excellent bibliography of the literature on the relation between birth rates and economic activity.

14. Compare the short discussion on the methodology of economic analysis of population in para. 5, Report of the Economics Committee (*Papers of the Royal Commission on Population,* vol. III).

15. M. Gottlieb, 'Optimum population, foreign trade and world economy,' *Population Studies,* vol. III, no. 2, September 1949, pp. 151–69.

16. Keynes, *General Theory of Employment, Interest and Money,* London, 1936, pp. 362–5.

17. See the passage quoted by Keynes, op. cit., p. 363.

18. It is a short step from this to the argument that the presence of unemployment denotes 'over-population' in the sense used by optimum theorists. This was a common view in the nineteen-thirties and it is echoed in the *Report of the Inter-Departmental Committee on Migration Policy,* 1934. There are several references in this report to an over-populated United Kingdom, and in para. 85 it is stated that 'the volume of migration since the war (1914–18) has fallen short of the volume of migration in the corresponding period prior to the war by a number equivalent to the total present number of persons unemployed in this country; whence the conclusion is drawn that if migration from the United Kingdom had continued at the same rate since the war, there would be no unemployment in the United Kingdom today (1934)'(!).

19. Alan Sweezy, 'Declining investment opportunity' (Chapter XXXII of the *New Economics,* p. 343, edited by Seymour Harris). The italics are mine. See also A. Hansen, *Fiscal Policy and Business Cycles,* Chapter XVII, for more detailed argument.

20. Note, however, that this is a long-run argument and thus involves the consideration of a further assumption of our statement of the Malthusian view, namely that the supply of capital and land is fixed.

21. A. Hansen op. cit., pp. 354–61.

22. B. Higgins, 'The theory of increasing under-employment,' *Economic Journal,* June 1950, p. 273.

23. J. Pedersen, 'Interest rates, employment and changes in population,' *Kyklos,* vol. II, 1948. He concludes that 'The popular view of the relationship between population growth and the degree of employment is confirmed as to its tendency but not as to the mechanism by which the tendency is brought about. An increase in the population of working age does cause unemployment if steps are not taken to prevent it. The reason is that the additional numbers could not be absorbed into employment, unless demand for labour is increased, and *there is no mechanism connected with the increase that produces such additional demand.*' (Italics mine.) A similar argument is to be found in Mrs. Robinson's recent discussion of the long-run application of Keynesian theory to the long-run economic situation. See her *Rate of Interest and Other Essays,* pp. 107–11.

24. For a useful summary of the controversy over world food supplies, see 'The world's food,' *Planning,* vol. XVIII, no. 340, 7 April 1952.

25. Thus Prof. Viner attempts this in his chapter on 'The economics of development,' *International Trade and Economic Development,* 1953.

POPULATION AND PER CAPITA INCOME*

By Joseph J. Spengler

Our main purpose in what follows is to trace the effect of population changes upon economic conditions as measured by per capita income. Inasmuch as the subject is complicated simplicity of treatment is achieved at the expense of rigor.

"Nothing is . . . gained . . . by pretending that [Nature's action] is simple."[1] The relationships between the population factor and other of the variables making up the societal universe can be treated in terms of one-at-a-time analysis, but not with as much completeness as one would like. For the societal universe is a system of mutually interacting variables, acted upon also by external conditions not readily comprehensible within such a system. Each of these variables, of which the population factor is one, is both a cause and an effect. A change in any one mode (e.g., natality, mortality) of the population factor, if not counterbalanced by a change in external conditions, will be accompanied by a compensatory change in some other mode of the population factor, or by a change in other of the variables composing the system, or by a combination of such changes. The change, or changes, consequent upon an initial modification of the population factor, therefore, will react upon the population factor itself. Repercussions will end when the system has ingested the initial change and its consequences.

Suppose we consider the functional relationship between population factor a and some other variable b. If a is modified, action will be exerted upon b through a number of paths, some direct and some circuitous and not readily perceptible. Moreover, b, having been modified in consequence of the assumed initial modification of a, acts in turn through a number of paths upon a and produces further modification in a. One-at-a-time analysis cannot serve, therefore, to disclose completely the functional relationship existing between a and b because the *ceteris paribus* assumption does not and cannot be made to hold. Whence the "effect," which the social scientist pretends to trace to an initial modification of a, may differ markedly from that which in reality was produced—particularly if he ignores interactions between the given societal system, defined as coterminous with a given geographical area, and other societal systems coterminous with other geographical areas. Moreover, even if the "effect" is traced with considerable

* Reprinted from *The Annals of The American Academy of Political and Social Science*, 237 (January 1945), pp. 182–192, by permission of the publisher. (Copyright 1945 by The American Academy of Political and Social Science.)

accuracy, it by no means follows that upon a subsequent occasion an identic modification of *a* will set up an identic chain of repercussions.

Real income (or net output) *per caput* is governed, in a given economy, by a number of interrelated factors, subject to the influence of the population factor, of which we shall discuss the following: ratio of population to the productive factors (i.e., equipment, land, and natural resources) used jointly with labor in the creation of goods and services; occupational composition of the population; pattern of consumer demand; the extent to which the economies associated with improved organization, with specialization and the division of labor, with large-scale production, and with agglomeration, are being realized; trading relations with other economies; age composition of the population; and fullness of employment.[2]

RATIO OF POPULATION TO PRODUCTIVE FACTORS.—An increase in the ratio of labor[3] to the complex of productive factors used jointly with labor is accompanied, when the whole of this complex has been set to work and other conditions remain unchanged, by a diminution in the average output per unit of labor input, and, therefore, by a corresponding relative diminution in income *per caput*.[4] For since production is a joint and co-operative process to which both labor and other productive factors contribute, and labor is not, directly or indirectly, a perfect substitute for the other factors of production, labor becomes less well equipped when it increases faster than the (first-grade) factors used in combination with it: whence average output per unit of labor input falls. If labor were a perfect substitute for the other factors, production would not be a joint process, and average output per unit of labor input would not fall. If, on the contrary, labor were not, within limits, an imperfect substitute for the factors combined with it, additional increments of labor would be employable and productive only on condition that additional increments of the complex of nonlabor factors were available for combination with the additional increments of labor.

The complex of productive factors used jointly with labor may be divided roughly into five categories: (1) land, measured in terms of area and viewed as a situs for habitation and for agricultural and other productive activities; (2) nondepletable natural resources whose supply is essentially fixed; (3) depletable and nonreplaceable natural resources; (4) natural resources which are replaceable and whose supply is augmentable; and (5) equipment —i.e., machinery, buildings, etc.

The supplies of (1) and (2), in use and/or available for use, are practically fixed quantities in any given economy; that of (3) is a diminishing quantity; those of (4) and (5) are susceptible, within limits, of increase. Land, measured in terms of productive power, is augmentable, within limits, through conversion into it of labor, of resources with which labor has been mixed (e.g., fertilizers), and of fixed and circulating capital consisting in part of labor (e.g., drainage and irrigation systems, counter-agents to erosion, improvements in terrain, and so forth).[5]

If the labor supply continues to grow after the whole of the complex of factors used with labor has been brought into use, average output per unit of labor input will fall. The rate of fall will depend upon (a) the *substitutability* of labor for the factors with which it is combined, and the rate of decline in this substitutability, and (b) the *convertibility* of labor into the factors with which it is used, and the rate of decline in this convertibility. Of course, given perfect substitutability, recourse to convertibility is unnecessary.[6]

Substitutability of labor. The rate at which average output per unit of labor input falls as labor input increases depends upon the rate at which the marginal output of labor falls, and this depends upon the substitutability, direct or indirect, of labor for the factors with which it is combined. In agriculture the direct substitutability of labor for the factors (especially land) used jointly with it appears to be less, and more subject to decline,[7] than in manufactures; it falls to zero when the ratio of labor to land passes a certain point.[8]

Labor may also be substituted indirectly for the factors used with it in agriculture by converting it into capital, or by substituting it for capital, and in turn substituting the capital for (say) land. While indirect substitutability is subject to limitations, it may be more effective than direct substitutability in slowing down the fall in output per worker in agriculture. In American manufactures as a whole, about three-fourths of the output of which is imputable to labor, labor is directly substitutable for equipment, and substitutability falls slowly; a one per cent increase in the ratio of labor to equipment is accompanied by a decline of one-fourth of one per cent in the average output of labor.[9] If, with other conditions and assumptions the same, only one-half of the output were imputable to labor, the corresponding decline would be one-half of one per cent; while if nine-tenths were imputable to labor, the decline would approximate one-tenth of one per cent. For a closed economy as a whole, factor supplies being given, substitutability is governed primarily by the ruling technical conditions and by the over-all pattern of consumption.

Convertibility of labor. The supply of each of the five factors used with labor may be increased, within limits, by converting labor into it. This convertibility diminishes, however, with the increase in the relative supply of labor, if other limitations become operative. For example, while labor is not very convertible, directly or indirectly, into landed area, it is convertible, especially indirectly, into landed productive power; for it may be embodied in equipment, or mixed with resources, that are transformable into land. The fixity of landed area, however, limits this convertibility and subjects it to diminution. Labor does not appear to be significantly convertible into the factors included in categories (2) and (3). But it is readily convertible into equipment, something like three-fourths of whose cost in this country consists of labor; and it is convertible, in lesser measure, into augmentable natural resources. It is to be noted, however, that an increase in the supply of any factor, accomplished by converting labor into it, is purchased at the expense of current *consumable* output, if the labor so used could have been employed in the creation of *consumable* goods and services.

Analysis along preceding lines suggests that continued growth of population exercises greatest pressure upon output per worker in realms of production founded predominantly upon land and upon nonreplaceable or nonaugmentable natural resources. It exercises least pressure in realms of production in which the role of land, natural resources, and equipment is small, and intermediate pressure in those in which the principal agent other than labor is equipment. The occasional tendency to increasing returns, and the constant tendency to progress technologically, apparently do not operate to eliminate these differences in sensitivity to population growth; they may, if they operate with greater force in some than in other realms of production, increase or decrease these differences in sensitivity. If an economy can overcome, by external exchange or other means, the restraints imposed by land and natural resources, it can free itself in considerable measure of the income-depressing influence exercised by population growth. If an economy experiences a diminution in numbers and labor supply, and in consequence can abandon *inferior* land and resources and reduce the ratio of labor to the complex of factors used with labor, it should also experience, after productive processes have been appropriately reorganized, an increase in output *per caput*.

OCCUPATIONAL COMPOSITION.—Labor is not, as we have heretofore assumed, a homogeneous factor. It consists of subfactors, which are, at best, imperfectly substitutable, one for another. In the longer run and within the limits set by qualitative interpersonal differences, the quantity of any one such subfactor can be augmented, through training and recruitment, at the expense of other subfactors. The composition of the total labor supply can thus be kept adjusted to the requirements of the economy.

Differential natural increase may depress output per worker by increasing interoccupational imbalance. Average output is at a maximum when the respective marginal product of each labor subfactor, and of each factor used with labor, is the same in all uses. If natural increase is higher in population groups whence come most of certain labor subfactors, and if at the same time worker training and redistribution programs do not suffice properly to distribute this excess, the actual productivity of these labor subfactors falls below what it otherwise would be. Moreover *ceteris paribus*, the greater the difference in group rates of natural increase, the greater is the cost of attaining the appropriate distribution of workers among occupations. Generalizing, other things equal, that set of differences in natural increase which, given as desideratum the maximization of average output, minimizes the cost of labor redistribution and recruitment, is the most advantageous on *purely economic* grounds.[10]

Disguised unemployment may be said to exist when labor subfactors are employed less advantageously than they are capable of being employed, given their training and aptitudes; it varies, therefore, with the time allowed for adjustment. It originates primarily in restraints upon competition and mobility, and secondarily in general population pressure and in uncompensated and marked intergroup differences in natural increase. It depresses output *per caput*. Its net effect upon population growth, if depressive, is much less depressive than that of complete unemployment, and varies with time and country.

With the progress of an economy in per capita income, secondary industry becomes more important than primary, and, eventually, tertiary industry may become more important than primary and secondary.[11] This trend, which, while largely traceable to consumption tendencies, is influenced also by differences in the ease with which specific employments may be entered, is of significance for population study. First, since equipment and/or land and resources are relatively less important in tertiary than in secondary industry, and less in secondary than in primary industry, population growth exercises a less and less depressive effect upon income *per caput* as a nation's occupational and industrial structure becomes less primary in character (see Ratio of Population to Productive Factors, *supra*). Second, since tertiary products are largely consumed at home, the external trading relations of an advanced economy, unless it is dependent upon imported foodstuffs and raw produce, decline in relative importance (see External Trading Relations, *infra*). Third, since production becomes less resource-oriented, the location of complexes of economic activities and population is attended by an increase in freedom (see Economics of Specialization, *infra*). Fourth, since higher fertility is associated with primary rather than with secondary and tertiary occupations, the net effect upon fertility is depressive, other things equal.

PATTERN OF CONSUMPTION.— The pattern of consumption, within an economy, becomes adjusted, in some measure, to its resources and population pattern; for, insofar as circumstances permit, a population tends to consume more largely of goods that are relatively plentiful and, therefore, relatively low priced. This consumption adjustment becomes less significant as income *per caput* rises, for in consequence consumer freedom of choice increases, and the population comes to view more of the "cheap" goods and services as "inferior," and to curtail their consumption. In theory, modification of the pattern of consumption offers relief to economies in which the ratio of labor to the factors employed with labor is high; for shifts from goods and services embodying relatively little labor to those embodying relatively much labor operates to raise output *per caput* and to decelerate its decline as the relative amount of labor increases. In reality, however, densely populated *closed* economies are not free to make such change, and when they do, it is generally to *waste* labor;[12] for they must first satisfy their more pressing requirements which cannot be fashioned largely out of labor. Wealthy economies, in contrast, can indulge in such consumption. To them that hath shall be given.

Consumption and population are related in other ways. Thus the consumption pattern of a population is conditioned by its age composition. Again, when the consumption pattern is making for a small family system, the latter in turn generates changes in the consumption pattern which re-enforce the trend toward small families. And again, when because per capita income is high, consumer freedom of choice is great, a larger portion of consumer demand is volatile and hard to anticipate than when consumer freedom is restricted; in consequence existing tendencies to unemployment are strengthened, other things equal.[13]

ECONOMIES OF SPECIALIZATION.—Population growth serves, up to a point, to provide a larger market for goods and services, and, therefore, to make possible in greater measure division of labor and specialization, realization of economies of scale and improved organization, and development of inventive tendencies implicit in such expansion. Consequently, in industries which benefit from such expansion, the resulting increase in output per over-all unit of input more than counterbalances the diseconomies which are occasioned in other industries. Population growth exercises this efficiency-increasing effect only up to the point where numbers, together with income, provide a market sufficient to permit both the realization of these economies and a more economic interindustry fit. The population required will be large or small, other things equal, as optimum-size industrial and plant units are large or small. What the economically desirable number of people is, we do not know with precision. There is every reason to suppose, however, that we have long since passed it in the United States and in the larger European economies. Any increase beyond this number tends, under most conditions, to reduce income per caput, or to counterbalance in whole or in part the income-increasing forces at work in the economy; if it does not have this effect immediately, it does endanger future income by hastening the depletion of nonreplaceable resources.

Increases in per capita income issue also, up to a point, out of the geographic concentration of population which permits realization of the economies and waste-avoidance associated with the agglomeration of economic activities. Complexes of economic activities may be resituated or newly established; but they remain complexes and force concentration of numbers. And in so doing they generate conditions unfavorable to natural increase—conditions for which, as yet, satisfactory counterbalancing social arrangements have not been discovered.

EXTERNAL TRADING RELATIONS.—If, in an economy, the substitution ratio between (say) labor and land, or between capital and land, is unfavorable to labor and to capital, it may be improved, other than by technological progress, in one or both of two ways. If labor emigrates, the economy's requirement of landed products is reduced, the pressure of labor and of capital upon land is relaxed, and the substitution ratio is improved, with the result that output *per caput* increases. If labor does not or cannot emigrate in person, it may emigrate by proxy in the form of exports embodying relatively large amounts of labor. It may be converted into or substituted for equipment, in conjunction with which it is employed to fabricate goods and services which are exchanged for the landed products of economies relatively better supplied with land. The substitution ratio of labor for land is thus improved and output *per caput* rises. If there is opportunity neither for emigration nor for trade with other economies, relief may be obtained, if at all, only through technological progress. If, on the contrary, land and/or natural resource deficiencies are resolved, and the economy is large enough, in terms of territory and population, to permit full realization of economies of scale, etc., the income-increasing effect of additional increments of external exchange declines.

AGE COMPOSITION.—Output *per caput* is affected in at least four ways by the age composition of a population, and so long as a population's age composition has not become stabilized, by the changes taking place in that age composition. (1) As the rate of population growth falls, potential productive capacity *per caput* increases, other things equal, up to the point where the relative number of persons of productive age, weighted by age and occupational attributes, is at a maximum. (2) As population growth falls, it may become more difficult to maintain inter-occupational balance because the ratio of new workers to the existing labor force falls. But this difficulty is easily surmounted, even in a declining population, given planning. For short-run population changes are predictable with precision. And, given a satisfactory occupational composition, little interoccupational transference of workers is necessary since, if new recruits are not added, the number of workers attached to any given occupation usually declines (through death and retirement) more than three times as fast as the total population by which the demand for the occupation's services is conditioned. (3) Because of changes under way in the age composition of the working force proper, present methods of job allocation and remuneration are in need of modification, lest absolute or disguised unemployment ensue. (4) The methods employed to select economic and political leaders must be modified in a manner suited to allow, in the future, a sufficient number of places to those under (say) fifty; otherwise, given *both* present methods of selection and prospective changes in age composition, too much power may pass into the hands of gerontocrats with a Struldbruggian incapacity for fashioning or selecting economic and political policies suited to the needs of the times.[14]

FULLNESS OF EMPLOYMENT.—Population growth acts upon three factors by which the level of employment is conditioned: the degree of equality with which income is distributed; the nature and volume of offsets to savings; and the consumption-investment structure of the economy.[15]

Equality in distribution of income. When a population is growing slowly, or not at all, while some of the factors used jointly with labor are increasing more rapidly, the imputed product of labor rises. If it rises sufficiently, and the distribution of output is based upon productivity, the relative share of income going to labor increases. Under these circumstances, and with income and property ownership distributed much as at present, income tends to become distributed more evenly. And when income is distributed more rather than less evenly, it is easier, as a rule and within limits, to maintain practicably full employment.

Volume of offsets to savings. Suppose real income, consumption, and saving to vary in relation to one another as follows:

Income	50	60	70	80	90	100
Consumption (1)	52	58	65	71	76	80
Saving (1)	-2	2	5	9	14	20
Consumption (2)	55	59	67	74	80	85
Saving (2)	-5	1	3	6	10	15

Suppose, also, that the level of employment corresponds with that of income, and that 100 represents the attainable maximum for income and employment. Given income = 100, and the corresponding Consumption (1) = 80, an offset (largely investment) of 20 is required to restore to the income stream the associated saving of 20, whereas, given Consumption (2), an offset of but 15 is required to balance saving; if the offset falls short of the saving associated with an income of 100, income will fall to the level at which the consequently lower amount of saving is offset.

In the nineteenth century, when population was growing rapidly, the equipping of new increments of population absorbed something like one-half of the then volume of savings, Hansen has estimated. Today, with a rate of population growth that is much lower and that is approaching a zero or a negative value, a smaller and diminishing amount of investment is required to equip the smaller and diminishing increment of population. Accordingly, given the rate of (investment-stimulating) invention and the rates at which money may be borrowed, the maintenance of employment calls for one or the other, or a combination, of two policies: (a) private and public enterprise must provide new offsets to savings to take the place of those which heretofore have been supplied through the provision of physical capital for additions to the population; (b) income *after taxation* must be distributed more evenly, or increased consumption must otherwise be facilitated; for then a smaller proportion of income is saved and, consequently, a smaller volume of offsets is required to return savings to the income stream.[16] For example, suppose that, in our numerical illustration above, the offsets associated with an income of 100 fall from 20 to 15 in consequence of a fall in population growth. Either 5 additional units must be added to the 15 in order that the 20 units of saving may be offset; or, through the introduction of changes in consumption pattern and greater equality of income distribution, Consumption (2) may be substituted for Consumption (1), with the result that saving falls to 15 units, which amount the 15 units of offsets can absorb. It is, of course, silly to suggest that, unaided by increased work on the part of the stork, an economy cannot maintain employment at a practicable maximum level. Even if increased activity on the part of the stork might serve temporarily to push up the level of employment, it could no longer accomplish this effect when the population of the economy had been carried to the maximum level, a level of which few populations today fall far short.

Consumption–investment structure. The bulk of the net output of an economy may be divided roughly into four parts: (a) that devoted to *current* necessary consumption; (b) that devoted to current consumption which, according to prevailing cultural standards, is considered less necessary or unnecessary to individual welfare; (c) that devoted to shorter-lived durable consumer goods, some of which resemble (a) in terms of necessity, and some of which resemble (b); and (d) that devoted to producers' durable capital and to longer-lived consumers' durable goods (e.g., housing). In an economy in which per capita income is high and the population is growing slowly or not at all, (d) will tend to be relatively smaller than in an economy in which population is growing and population pressure is not great enough to restrict the formation of (d) to a very small fraction of total output. The production of (d) is subject, especially in an economy in which the distribution of (d) through time is not carefully planned, to considerable fluctuation, the effects of which are transmitted primarily to (b) and (c). It is probable, therefore, that as population growth falls to zero and in consequence (d) diminishes in relative magnitude, the tendency to unemployment will be less[17] than when population was growing; that the economy will be more stable; and that consumable income will constitute a larger fraction of total output.[18]

CONCLUSION.—Our analysis in the preceding section suggests that, if man could free his productive activities of the restraints imposed by land and most natural resources, he would be free of a considerable part of the depressive effect exerted by population growth upon *over-all* per capita income, and of a somewhat smaller part of the depressive effect exerted upon currently *consumable* output per capita. In this man has not generally succeeded, for science has not yet completely broken the fetters imposed by the niggardliness of nature; it has not delivered man and his growth from the restraints imposed by agriculture, nor has it freed modern industry of dependence upon those natural resources whose supplies are fixed or being depleted.

Nor has cultural change everywhere clipped the wings of the stork and released mankind from the clutches of the Malthusian Devil. Income data, supported by nutrition studies, suggest that the incomes of more than half the world's population are in the neighborhood of bare subsistence. The population of the world falls, Thompson finds, into three groups: I, comprising 21 per cent, has natality and mortality under control; II, comprising 21 per cent, is bringing natality and mortality under control; III, comprising 58 per cent, has neither mortality nor natality under "reasonably secure control." In 1925–34, C. Clark's studies suggest, group I received about 58 per cent of the world's income; II, about 24 per cent; III, something like 18 per cent.

The security of the food supply, even of some of the better situated nations, may be endangered by population growth. About three-fifths of the population in group I have to import part of their agricultural raw materials and food requirements. With a minor exception, all of the peoples in group II were able, before 1939, to produce, in terms of product value, either more agricultural products than they consumed, or nearly as much as they required. If, however, population continues to grow in these countries, and consumption standards improve, agricultural export surpluses will shrink and, in a number of instances, disappear. In group III we find the countries of Asia (other than Japan and Russia), much of Africa, and the Western Hemisphere (except Canada, the United States, Brazil, Uruguay, and Argentina). Here population growth and the need for greater per capita consumption, together with limitations imposed by climate and disease, may operate to prevent the development of great agricultural surpluses for export; at worst, increased consumption may wipe out such surpluses as exist.

Gradual redistribution of the occupied population of the world among employments could increase per capita income considerably. At present, about three-fifths of the world's occupied population is engaged in primary industry. Given technological knowledge, equipment, and organization such as are found in the most advanced countries, this proportion probably could be reduced without loss of output to about one-fourth, thus releasing about one-third for employment in secondary and tertiary industry. Yet, even granted the capital formation and other conditions prerequisite to such gradual shift, widespread misery will persist unless population growth is brought under control, especially in group III countries, and the increase, diffusion, and spread of technological knowledge continues. For the arable land of the world probably cannot, under present conditions, support in comfort much more than 2.5 billion (if that many), to which level the present 2.1 billion would soon grow, were the reproductive potentials of group III countries allowed free rein. The countries composing groups I and II, especially the former and selected countries in the latter, therefore have a common interest in the imposition of effective restraints upon these reproductive potentials, an interest which should find expression in any plan for world economic and/or political organization.

REFERENCES

1. A. Marshall, *Principles of Economics* (8th ed.; London, 1920), p. x.
2. Lack of space prevents consideration of the effect exercised upon income by political and cultural progress, the qualitative composition of the population, and the state of

the industrial arts, of which the last two are among the most important of the determinants of income. Each of these factors is related to the population factor.

3. It is assumed, here and elsewhere unless otherwise indicated, that determinants of income other than the one under examination are unaffected; that labor and the factors used with it are homogeneous; and that the labor force constitutes a fixed fraction of the population.

4. Sufficient factor divisibility to exclude an initial stage of increasing average returns for labor is assumed. Accordingly, average output per unit of labor input does not fall until all first-grade factors, employable with labor, have been brought into use, and part of the total net product is imputable to these factors.

5. Technological progress (i.e., improvement in the state of the industrial arts) may augment (3) by rendering utilizable that which has not been utilizable; or it may increase the efficiency with which (3) is used. In general, it operates to break the fetters imposed upon production either by the limitedness of resources, or by restrictions upon competition. It may operate also to increase the rate at which (3) is used up. In sum, it participates on both sides in the race between exhaustion of resources, on the one hand, and the replenishment of resources through discovery and recovery, on the other.

6. If only one of the factors used with labor, say land, has been brought fully into use, the deficiency in its supply may be relieved in part by substituting for it, or converting into it, units of other factors (e.g., equipment, chemical compounds) not yet fully in use. Moreover, an increase in numbers may be offset in part by increasing the rate of consumption of category (3) natural resources; such offset, however, is purchased *ceteris paribus* at the expense of a subsequent reduction in output and income.

7. Satisfactory data are lacking, but the following figures are suggestive. Suppose the return on $100 of capital in manufactures, or of agricultural property in agriculture—i.e., the "marginal product"—is $6. In 1929, in manufactures, the ratio of average remuneration per employee ($1,492) to this supposed $6 "marginal product" was 249 to 1. In agriculture, per worker net product *imputable to labor* (i.e., net output per worker minus the assumed 6 per cent allowance on agricultural property used per worker) was $581; the ratio of this per worker rate of return to the assumed rate of return on property was 95 to 1. The corresponding ratio was 132 to 1 in the Pacific Coast area where agricultural property per worker approximated $9,670; and 62 to 1 in the East South Central states where agricultural property per worker approximated only $1,920. These data are taken or computed from C. A. Bliss, *The Structure of Manufacturing Production* (New York, 1939), p. 19, and John D. Black, "Agricultural Population in Relation to Agricultural Resources," *The Annals*, Vol. 188 (Nov. 1936), pp. 205–17.

8. In densely populated China, J. L. Buck's data suggest, the marginal product of labor falls to zero when the ratio of labor to land is increased beyond 0.25 man per acre. See *Land Utilization in China* (Chicago, 1937), Chap. IX, Tables 9, 11, 12, 16. C. Clark finds output per agricultural worker to vary inversely with the square root of the number of agricultural workers per unit of farm land. See *The Economics of 1960* (London, 1942), pp. 35–36.

9. See P. H. Douglas, *The Theory of Wages* (New York, 1934), pp. 143–58; also C. Clark, *Conditions of Economic Progress* (London, 1940), Chap. XI.

10. Differential increase may affect the qualitative composition of the population through the media of biological and/or cultural heredity. Qualitative composition exercises more influence upon income in a complex than in a simple economy. At one extreme, policy formation and the effectuation of technological progress appear to require sharper and better trained minds than formerly. At the other, the increase in the complexities and responsibilities attendant even upon simpler occupations is rendering more difficult the employment of low-grade individuals.

11. Agricultural, pastoral, forest, fishing and hunting industries are included under primary; manufacture, electric power production, mining, building and construction, under secondary; other economic activities, under tertiary. See C. Clark, *The Economics of 1960* (London, 1942) and *Conditions of Economic Progress* (London, 1940).

12. E.g., see H. G. Moulton, *Japan* (Washington, 1931), pp. 398–99.

13. See also Fullness of Employment, *infra*.

14. See Joseph J. Spengler, "Population Movements, Employment and Income," *Southern Economic Journal*, Vol. V (1938), pp. 142 ff.; "Some Effects of Changes in the

Age Composition of the Labor Force," *ibid.*, Vol. VIII (1941), pp. 157 ff.; "Population Trends and the Future Demand for Teachers," *Social Forces*, Vol. XIX (1941), pp. 465 ff.

15. The level of employment, in turn, affects the rate of population growth, inasmuch as natality and nuptiality are higher, other things equal, when employment is great than when it is low.

16. Inasmuch as the supply of human effort is governed by the elasticity of the demand for income in terms of effort, the system of taxation must take this into account. Otherwise the diminution of unemployment will be purchased at the expense of a diminution of effort, especially on the part of those possessed of rarer talents.

17. This diminution in tendency to unemployment may be offset somewhat by increases in the magnitudes of (b) and (c) in relation to that of (a), since the demand for and production of (b) and (c) are more volatile than the demand for and production of (a). However, with the passage of time, greater proportions of the output presently included under (b) and (c) may take on the necessitarian character of (a).

18. This result will become manifest only after transition of the population from a growing to an essential stationary state; for during the transition period, adjustment to a lower level of investment, together with the effect of the operation of the deceleration principle and the transient worsening of expectations, will increase tendencies to unemployment. See Joseph J. Spengler, "Population Movements, Employment, and Income," *op. cit.*; "Some Effects of Changes in the Age Composition of the Labor Force," *op. cit.*; "Population Trends and the Future Demand for Teachers," *op. cit.*; and "Population Movements and Economic Equilibrium in the United States," *Journal of Political Economy*, Vol. XLVIII (1940), pp. 153 ff.

HUMAN MIGRATION AND SOCIAL EQUILIBRIUM *

By Harold W. Saunders

When the present hostilities cease and the representatives of the victorious nations assemble around the peace table to consider matters of postwar reconstruction, the question of migration, or spatial redistribution of world population, is almost certain to be one of the problems discussed. Population phenomena are so intimately related to international frictions and international welfare that they will hardly be permitted to escape consideration. Most intelligent national leaders realize that differentials in population pressure, rates of population growth, and rates of natural increase among the various nations or peoples of the earth produce "danger spots" in world social organization, *i.e.* contribute to international insecurity, apprehensiveness, and general belligerency. The continued existence of such situations in the postwar world economy would endanger any set of political arrangements, no matter how carefully devised and established otherwise, unless adequate provision were made for their rapid and effective control or elimination. It seems that a realistic facing and evaluation of these factors is virtually inescapable.

When mechanisms or programs for the alleviation of population pressure are up for consideration, migration will probably be suggested as the proper method for providing relief to distressed areas. Such a recommendation will unquestionably provoke much opposition in certain quarters inasmuch as many nations, including the United States, have well established restrictions on immigration, emigration, or both. Our own nation not only operates on a "quota" basis but also includes as part of its immigration policy a provision for the exclusion of all migratory Orientals as prospective permanent residents and citizens. Any suggestion that this policy be abolished in the interests of future international harmony would undoubtedly result in a storm of protest.

In view of the foregoing possibilities or, rather, probabilities, such questions as the following are extremely pertinent: Would free or unrestricted migration materially reduce population pressure in those areas which constitute "danger spots" in world population? Does migration operate to reduce the population size of the population "exporting" area in the long run? If so, under what conditions? Does the efficient functioning of the world economy demand or necessitate the free movement of people as well as the free movement of goods, capital, and ideas?

* Reprinted from the *Journal of Business, University of Iowa*, 23 (March 1943), pp. 5–6, 11–15, by permission of the author and the State University of Iowa.

The remainder of this article is devoted to an attempt to cast some light on these fundamental but obstinate questions. The material which follows, however, will by no means provide dogmatic answers to these troublesome queries. Nevertheless, since the bulk of the subsequent analysis and discussion constitutes an endeavor to formulate a systematic exposition of basic principles relative to the nature and role of human migration in the economic and social affairs of nations, such a presentation is seemingly apropos. Unless such basic principles are given due consideration, public opinion and public policy with respect to matters of population will rest upon a much too precarious ideological foundation. If the long run interests of the American people are to be rationally and consistently pursued, basic issues need to be relentlessly and intelligently isolated, analyzed, and discussed. The following formulation and analysis is presented in the hope and expectation that some contribution, no matter how slight, can be made to the formation of an intelligent and enlightened approach to the disturbing problems which World War II will inevitably leave in its wake.

Migration is one of the indices or symptoms of population pressure, population pressure referring to the intensity of the competitive struggle going on within the limits of any given population. The degree of pressure seems to be directly proportional to the size of the discrepancy between the group's scale of living and its standard of living.

By *scale of living* is meant the actual per capita flow of goods and services produced and consumed by the members of a given population in some standardized unit of time such as a year. *Standard of living*, on the other hand, refers to that per capita flow of goods and services to which the members of the population aspire and for which they stand ready to expend time and energy. The former is a level of achievement; the latter is a level of aspiration, what the group members consider a decent level of living.

Competition is a struggle on the part of human beings to close the gap between their scale of living and their standard of living. Mechanisms and processes are in constant operation which tend to reduce population pressure within any given area to zero. This result is achieved either by raising the scale, lowering the standard, or a combination of each, usually the last. Competition is the basic force which compels people, in the long run, to utilize their scarce resources to maximum advantage and, thereby, to attain the highest possible scale of living under the circumstances. However, when resources are being used as efficiently as possible and a gap between scale and standard continues to exist, people are forced to lower their level of aspiration. The process of lowering the standard is one involving a "weeding out" of all wants of lesser relative importance through some form of rationalization.

Control over population size is a common and necessary technique for removing the discrepancy between scale and standard. Moreover, if any population is to maintain, in the long run, a scale of living appreciably above the level of mere subsistence, population size must be so regulated as to approach the "optimum:" that size of population, given the natural resources and the state of the industrial arts, which maximizes the scale of living. A population either larger or smaller than the optimum size would result, under the circumstances, in a lowered scale of living. The optimum size is decidedly smaller than the maximum size. The latter represents such an imbalance between size of population and economic resources that the scale of living hovers around the bare level of subsistence.

Human migration refers to those spatial movements whereby people, individually or collectively, change their place of abode. It is a process by which people relinquish one habitat in order to live in another; as such, it involves uprooting, spatial movement, and resettlement. It begins with the severance of those bonds or connections representing adjustments to one habitat and it ends with the establishment of a new set of bonds or connections representing adjustment to a new habitat.

Obviously not all spatial movement of people is migration, in the sense just indicated. Movements of various sorts occur that do not involve change of abode and the working out of a life adjustment to a new habitat.

Migration, or movement, is closely associated with and dependent upon mobility, but is not to be, for that reason, confused with it. Mobility refers to the capacity for free movement, the quality of being movable. It involves both a physical and a psychological condition. Any change in the technology of transportation is likely to affect the ability of individuals or groups to move at greater speed over wider areas at less cost. Any change which weakens or dissolves man's habitual attachment to his habitat at once frees him for movement and makes him psychologically ready for movement. Improvements in the technology of transportation widen the area of contact and communication and, even without actual migration, result in expanded spatial horizons. They make possible a wider range of choice in the selection of a habitat in which to dwell.

Population pressure, by making people dissatisfied with their habitat, results in a readiness to move. A corollary of this is that the greater the pressure of population, the greater the readiness to move (the more excited and restless the population becomes). Mobility is, then, in great part, produced by population pressure, which serves to make people unadjusted, to uproot them, to make them psychologically ready for movement.

When the ability to move is associated with readiness to move, the expectation of enhancing one's competitive position by changing habitats results in migration. In other words, mobility is translated into migration whenever people see the opportunity of closing the gap, in whole or in part, between their scale of living and their standard of living by changing their spatial position, i.e., their habitat.

This conception of the causes of migration implies both "push" and "pull," or, rather, two sets of forces: (1) one set of forces tends to produce the evacuation of the habitat already occupied; and (2) one set of forces attracts the prospective migrant toward an alternative habitat. Before migration actually takes place, there normally occurs a period in which the relative opportunities offered by the present and the anticipated habitat are compared. If the balance is on the side of the anticipated habitat, the person or group migrates unless prevented by external barriers. Migration has always these two aspects; both the pushes and the pulls must be in operation if it is to occur.

It is conceivable, of course, that migration may take place in the absence of known alternative opportunities: when competition reaches the brute level of a mere struggle for continued existence, because the previous supporting capacity of an area has disappeared, people may forsake that area for a blind adventure into unknown areas. Often, in desperation, such movements do take place because some people would rather starve on the move than just give in to circumstance. The risks being great in either case, they stake their chances on the great adventure. It is perhaps true, however, that even in such cases, where no knowledge of alternative habitats is available, some adventitious circumstance precipitates actual movement and gives it direction.

From the foregoing analysis it appears, then, that migration is a way of competing, a means for removing the discrepancy between the scale of living and the standard of living. As one writer puts it: "Migration is a process of social osmosis. It is one of the means which man has always used to establish a more satisfactory relation between his wants and his fulfillment of them. It is an attempt to equalize as best he can what he feels to be the unequal pressure of environment on individuals and groups."[1] Where no such discrepancies exist there are no potential migrants; the population is immobile. Mobility may develop, however, in either of two ways: (1) through a decline in the scale of living; or (2) through a rise in the standard of living. Of course, both changes may occur together and thereby give accentuated impetus to the development of a condition of mobility.

A decline in the scale of living occurs in economies that are retrogressing because of depleted natural resources, excessive consumption of capital, economic "depression," etc. The present so-called "dust bowl migration" from the Great Plains of the United States is a case in point. A rise in the standard of living occurs as an area is touched by the forces of an expanding civilization. A case in point here is that of Japan following the establishment of trade relations with the Western World. The territorial spread of Western Civilization has everywhere created much population pressure and consequent mobility in the "culturally undeveloped areas" by raising their standards of living to a level nearly equal to that of Europe and America. These areas have become great sources, actual and potential, of intercontinental migration. The potential migration has greatly exceeded the actual because of the existence of strong impediments, especially the national restrictions on immigration established by the potential receiving areas.

When the statement is made, however, that every person who has a discrepancy between his scale of living and his standard of living is a potential migrant, it must not be inferred that he will move if the money income obtainable elsewhere is greater than the money income he is receiving in the area in which he is located. It must be kept in mind that the determining factor is a matter of real income; also, it must be remembered that part of the real income of every individual or family consists of goods or services, especially the latter, not for sale "on the market," or, at least, not in the usual sense of that term. Part of everyone's real income consists of psychic income, things immaterial and intangible which may be more or less indigenous to an area and not found elsewhere. They may be such things as the local scenery, climate, intimate association, or the security and domestic tranquility of a rural area. Inasmuch as these values are scarce (limited to a particular area and not available elsewhere), they enter into the balancing of alternative opportunities when decisions are made relative to spatial relocation, even though they do not usually enter the pecuniary calculus of the market place. These factors are integral parts of both the scale of living, and the standard of living and, hence, partially determine all decisions relative to migration.

With these qualifications, it may be said that migrations occur in response to differentials in economic opportunity. These differentials are variations in the scale of living obtainable in the various areas; they exist or appear because economic resources are inequitably distributed over the face of the earth. The relative scarcity of labor in one such area produces a relatively greater demand for population in that area; this greater relative demand is reflected in the earnings of labor and produces discernible differentials in economic opportunity. These differentials then become attractions and the area with the higher scale of living tends to receive population from the areas with the lower scales of living.

"This unequal distribution of economic opportunity has always been the chief cause of migration. It is true that most men were long ignorant of, and many men still imperfectly aware of, informed of, the existence of greater opportunity elsewhere. But given knowledge of the situation and other cultural factors, men seek higher levels of economic well-being, almost as surely as water seeks a lower geographical level. Moreover, such a tendency we call 'natural'."[2]

The relative economic opportunities which determine the direction and rate of flow of migratory movements are matters of the proportionality of the factors of production: land, labor, and capital. Land is relatively fixed and immobile, whereas labor and capital are not. Hence, spatial movements of labor and capital occur so as to transfer these factors from those areas in which they are relatively abundant to those areas where they are relatively scarce. Such movements continue until the relative proportions of the factors are the same in all of the interconnected areas, as manifested by the fact that areal differentials in the scale of living disappear. When this state of affairs is realized, migration ceases.

Foreign trade and capital movements operate as surrogates for the immobility of natural resources along with migration. The three in combination, when operating freely, serve to maintain the same proportionality of economic resources in all interconnected areas and, thereby, operate to maintain an equal distribution of economic opportunity in space.

Such an equilibrium condition, if ever fully attained, rarely remains undisturbed for any length of time. It may be disturbed by (1) differential rates of reproduction in the various interconnected populations; and (2) differential rates of change in the economic resources of the areas—that is, in (a) the accumulation of capital, or (b) the exploitation of natural resources. If one population remains stable while the others either increase or decrease, or if one population either increases or decreases more slowly or more rapidly than the others, the spatial distribution of people (that is, labor) would again be in a state of imbalance, the economic resources other than labor remaining unchanged. Discrepancies in the scales of living of the interrelated areas would again appear, with the areas now having a relative abundance of labor as a result of differential rates of change, experiencing relatively low scales of living and again becoming sources of emigration to the other areas. These new migratory flows, in turn, would continue until the discrepancies were removed and equilibrium was restored.

As Taeuber says, "a mobile population is essential to the maintenance of an effective balance between population and resources in a nation characterized by marked differentials in rates of reproduction and in employment opportunities."[3]

Migration, however, does not always flow so nicely as to maintain such a state of equilibrium, even when sufficient time is given for the expected results to occur. This disjunction between the general theory and observed facts necessitates some subsidiary postulates. It necessitates a more comprehensive statement of the conditions under which migration would occur, as stated above, and under what conditions it would not.

Underlying the theory as just stated is the basic assumption of complete or "perfect" mobility, of ability and readiness to move in response to an opportunity for improving one's competitive position. However, in actuality, perfect mobility is never attained; it is only approximated. Perfect mobility would rest upon (1) perfect transportation facilities, (2) perfect communication facilities, (3) the dissolution of all habitual ties that produce inertia on the part of potential migrants, and (4) the absence of external restraints imposed by persons or groups in control of power and desirous of restricting migration in order to preserve preferential positions. All of these conditions are fulfilled only in part in particular historical circumstances. "Frictional" factors are in constant operation and prevent the "ideal" results from being realized in concrete cases.

The first precondition, perfect transportation facilities, is a matter of time-cost. When a great amount of time is necessitated in movement a sacrifice occurs, since the time lost in the process of transportation could have been spent in procuring the goods of life. Along with the fact of mere time is that of the cost of the facilities themselves. The equipment, food, etc. utilized in or during migration demands an investment, larger or smaller, depending on the nature of the prospective movement. The time lost and the outlay necessary to procure the facilities together are significant and vary directly in significance with the distance traversed. This also includes the time necessary to "work up" to the job desired and available. Every migrant needs a longer or shorter period in order to make adjustments to the new conditions of life. These adjustments are preliminary to achieving the opportunity visualized prior to migration.

The expected increase in earning power must be more than large enough to cover the necessary total sacrifice or investment. But many potential migrants do not have the funds to invest in such a spatial movement; or they do not have large enough incomes to save up for a future movement. The "time preference" of many is such that they do not care to sacrifice present income which is certain, for a larger but uncertain future income.

Every improvement in the technology of transportation, however, reduces the time-cost of migration and serves to reduce this barrier or friction to a minimum. Such advances allow for an ever closer approximation of the "ideal" situation as stated theoretically.

The second precondition, perfect communication, is necessary to accurate and complete knowledge concerning the relative opportunities. Many persons in a state of unrest, because of the existence of a considerable gap between their scale and standard of living, are unaware of the existence of relatively better opportunities elsewhere. When the necessary information is lacking, the attraction of the alternative area cannot produce the resultant effect, migration. Or, as often happens, disequilibrium is accentuated because of "wasted" migration, because false or misleading reports on relative opportunities result in movements into areas where the scale of living is actually lower. Under these circumstances migrants return if possible, or wander aimlessly, or stay where they go, disillusioned. When such wasted movements become known to other potential migrants, they serve to produce inertia and impede further movement.

The lack of adequate information relative to alternative possibilities produces a risk factor which must be covered if people are to move. The anticipated gains must be at least sufficient to cover the necessary "insurance" if persons with foresight are to forsake a habitat to which they are partially adjusted.

Added to this risk, or included in it, is the fact that the expected gains in the scale of living to be obtained through movement may prove too short-lived because of the uncertainties in the area of immigration. Periodic economic crises operate to increase the potency of this barrier to migration, especially for all people who value security highly. Inadequate and imperfect knowledge concerning the existence and certainty of economic opportunities probably constitutes the major factor impeding internal migration in the United States.

The third precondition implies a flexibility of habits, attitudes, and social obligations that is by no means common. Many potential migrants are not mobile because they are bound by routine, lack initiative or adventuresomeness. They want things they do not have; but they cannot put forth the energy necessary to obtain them. Often they have personality conflicts, are afraid and do not trust their own abilities. Many have obligations, familial or otherwise, which impede their freedom of movement. Married persons with children not only have a much greater expense involved in movement, but hesitate to risk the welfare of the whole family group on a migratory enterprise. There is often conflict within the family as to the desirability and direction of movement. This third set of factors is evidenced by the fact that migration is predominantly a matter of young unmarried males when the distance is great, the new area strange, and the risks considerable. The social ties impeding such persons are at a minimum.

The absence of the last precondition is perhaps the most important barrier at the present time impeding intercontinental migration. The imminence of war and the resurgence of nationalism have led to the imposition of many legal barriers to the movements of people from one national economy to another.

The national restrictions on the movements of capital and the movements of goods have been likewise severe. The attempt, since 1918 particularly, to regain national self-sufficiency has seemed to greatly accentuate economic disequilibrium.[4]

Some of these barriers have been absolute in their nature (such as the complete exclusion of Orientals from permanent residence in the United States); others have been partial restrictions (such as the United States quota law for Europeans). Many nations restrict the influx of migrants in order to preserve scales of living comparatively high because of a partial monopoly on world resources. Other nations, attempting to become militarily powerful, have prohibited emigration in order to maintain a cheap labor supply and an abundant reserve of "cannon fodder," in spite of "overpopulation." Moreover, these legal barriers have not been limited to nations; even the smaller constituent units of nation-states have utilized this monopolistic technique.

Many local areas in the United States utilize the technique of denying relief to migrants by setting up residence requirements. Many states set up "border-blockades."

Since there are many attractions and impediments which serve to keep people spatially located where they already are, it takes more than a slightly higher scale of living elsewhere to induce them to move. The size of the differential to be obtained through movement must be sufficiently large to offset the sacrifices and inconveniences which migration necessitates. Hence the general principle that the volume of migration varies directly with the size of the differentials existing in interconnected areas seems to be a close approximation to the truth.

If this general principle is true, the supply of migrants is similar to the supply of any commodity or service. Shown graphically, it is a curve which ascends from left to right (when the size of the gain in the scale of living to be obtained through migration is expressed on the vertical axis of a graph, and when the number of migrants is expressed on the horizontal axis.)

Population equilibrium is the same regardless of the source from which population is drawn. An area could maintain its population forever through migration as long as it had another area (or other areas) from which to obtain population. Of course, in the long run, this would be possible only if an area supplying migrants produced more than sufficient children to maintain its own areal equilibrium.

Modern cities, at present, rely in great part upon rural-urban migration to maintain their equilibrium, precarious as it is. It is possible that national population stability could be maintained by having the rural areas "specialize" both in the production of food and "human raw material."

If the foregoing analysis of the causes of migration and of the factors operating to restrain it is correct, the effects of migration upon population pressure cannot be reduced to a simple dogmatic statement. These effects will vary with the conditions existing in the various interconnected areas when migration occurs. Nevertheless, it can be said that migration is: (1) the process for maintaining a sort of short-run population equilibrium, because the long run process of balancing births and deaths moves so slowly, although inexorably; and (2) the process for taking advantage of the shifting territorial organization of an economy when changing effective natural resources or changing technology occasion it.

The first process (that which operates to maintain short-run population equilibrium) is initiated when population growth, because of the inability to control it properly, is such as to produce general overpopulation, in the sense that all interconnected areas are past the optimum point (a condition of "closed resources" or decreasing returns). Under these conditions, migration merely serves to shift the incidence of population pressure by equalizing it, since movement occurs as long as differentials in scales of living exist. Migration operates to keep the scales of living in all the interconnected areas somewhere in the proximity of one another.

The equalization of the scales of living among the interconnected areas is not sufficient, however, for the equalization of population pressure, since the standards of living must also be taken into account. Nevertheless, areas that are connected by bonds of communication, among which isolation is relatively absent, tend to possess a common standard of living. They tend to be assimilated to a common cultural pattern, or a common mode of life, and this means not only that they use a common technology, but also that they share the same values, the same wants, desires, and aspirations. Migration operates to equalize the spatial distribution of economic resources, or economic opportunity, and to equalize the spatial distribution of wants, as one important aspect of culture, since migration promotes culture contact and cultural assimilation. If interconnected areas tend to possess a common standard of living, and if migration tends to eliminate differentials in their scales of living, then migration shifts the incidence of population pressure and equalizes it throughout a far flung ecological community. A greater incidence of population pressure in some areas than in others may result either from impediments restricting migration (or capital movements and foreign trade) and the equalization of economic opportunity, or from resistances in the channels of communication restricting the spatial dissemination of living-standards.

The second process (that which operates to produce a new territorial division of labor) is initiated when economies are expanding, when new natural resources are being discovered and exploited, or when new technologies of production are being invented and exploited. Under these conditions, migration may actually relieve population pressure, not merely equalize it.

If new natural resources are discovered where sufficient people to utilize them fully do not exist, their proper exploitation awaits the arrival of migrants capable of putting them to efficient use. As this migration occurs and efficiency in the use of the new resources increases, the general scale of living rises and the general demand for population increases. Such a spatial redistribution of population reduces the gap between the scale of living and the standard of living for all interconnected areas, or reduces the general incidence of population pressure.

Improvements in technology operate toward the same result. New techniques of production necessitate, usually, the spatial rearrangement of the labor supply, if they are to be completely assimilated into the economic organization.

Such a spatial rearrangement of the labor supply seems to be the function that rural-urban migration has performed. The Industrial Revolution created the modern city and necessitated a redistribution of population. If people were to enjoy the rising scale of living possible with new techniques of production the labor supply had to be concentrated, in part, at the points where the new goods and services were to be produced, namely, in the cities.

Such improvements are adopted because they reduce production costs and increase the scale of living. Hence, they reduce the intensity of the competitive struggle by diminishing the discrepancy between scales of living and living-standards.

In other words, an expansion of economic resources in an area (resulting from the discovery of new natural resources, the invention of new production techniques, or a combination of the two) changes the economic situation of that area from one of "closed resources" (or decreasing returns) to one of "open resources" (or increasing returns). The new scarcity of labor in this area results in a rising wage level which, in turn, serves to attract migrants from other areas having "closed resources," or lower wage rates. The influx of population into the economically expanding area allows it to raise its scale of living by exploiting the new resources. The outflow of migrants from the economically stable (or declining) areas allows them to raise their scale of living, by bringing the size of population closer to the optimum point. This all around increase in scales of living serves, therefore, to reduce the general incidence of population pressure and not merely to reduce it in some areas by intensifying it in others.

In the long run, however, this reduction in population pressure may prove mainly temporary. If the possibilities of birth control are very limited, practically all the new productivity will ultimately go into the maintenance of a larger population. Under these conditions, the intensity of the competitive struggle may be reduced only slightly, when sufficient time is allowed for population to catch up. Increased economic opportunity, and the consequent spatial redistribution of population, result in a permanent reduction of population pressure only when reproduction is so controlled as to allow for a rising scale of living rather than a mere increase in size of population.

Migration is a secondary phenomenon; reproduction is the basic process of the two. In the long run, total population size, for all interconnected ecological areas, is a matter of the balance of births and deaths, of the demand for and the supply of population. Migration serves to increase population size only when it makes possible a more efficient use of economic resources and, thereby, results in an increased demand for population, without a correlative offsetting increase in the standard of living and its consequent decrease in the supply of population.

REFERENCES

1. Thompson, Warren S., *Research Memorandum on Internal Migration in the Depression*, Social Science Research Council Bulletin No. 30, p. 7.
2. Taft, Donald, *Human Migration: A Study of International Movements*, pp. 555–6.
3. Taeuber, Conrad, "Migration and Rural Population Adjustment," *Rural Sociology*, 5: 399–410, (Dec. 1940).
4. Mander, Linden A., *Foundations of Modern World Society*, pp. 408–27.

CHAPTER 5

POPULATION AND LEVEL OF ECONOMIC ACTIVITY

Throughout the nineteenth century and the early decades of the present century it was supposed that the level of economic activity obtaining in a country was independent of the density of its population, or of variations in its rate of population growth. Capital and land, it was supposed, were sufficiently variable and adaptable to permit their nice adjustment to the labor force, be that force relatively large or small in comparison with the stock of capital and land. Unemployment from a shortage of land or capital was not to be expected, therefore; such shortages manifested themselves only in the form of low capital—man and low land—man ratios with which low outputs, incomes, and wages were associated. Nor did unemployment tend to arise from a deficiency in the aggregate demand for labor, occasioned by increases or by diminutions in the rate of population growth. Supply, so it was believed upon the authority of Mill and Say, created its own demand, with the result that the aggregate demand for labor always sufficed to absorb those seeking employment at the ruling wages, be they immigrants, workers from the countryside, the products of natural increase, or others. While unemployment might manifest itself in particular occupations that had become relatively overcrowded, it tended to disappear since surplus workers attached to these occupations could and would find work in occupations comparatively short of workers. Finally, while unemployment manifested itself during business recessions and depressions, it was not to be attributed to variations in population growth or to other population movements. It followed, in the light of what has been said, that increases and decreases in population were significant for the movement of average income only because of their effects upon the ratio of numbers to resources, together with the division of labor; variations in the rate of population growth as such did not affect the level of economic activity and employment and therewith the level of average income.

After the great depression that began in 1929 these views, often but ineffectively challenged, underwent marked modification as the case for public works and public investment was developed. It was no longer accepted, in accordance with Say's Law, that supply always generates its own demand, or that the aggregate demand for labor adjusts itself readily and nicely to variations in the rate of population growth and in the rate of increase of the labor force. The aggregate demand for labor might be inadequate to afford employment for all members of the labor force; and it could be so great as to make for wage and price inflation. Furthermore, variations in the aggregate demand for labor might be attributable, and in fact often were attributable, to variations in the rate of population growth occasioned by variations in natural increase and migration. Whence it followed that, contrary to the view which had formerly prevailed, the magnitude of average income in a country depended, or at least might depend, upon the manner in which its population was growing as well as upon its capital–population and land–population ratios.

It came to be argued that a decline in the rate of population growth tended to diminish the average propensity to consume and to increase the average propensity to save without at the same time augmenting the rate of planned investment. It was concluded, therefore, that there would tend to be insufficient offsets to saving, when employment was full, to permit continuation of full employment. Underemployment equilibrium might therefore result.

Minor emphasis was given to the proposition that the average propensity to consume is higher in a relatively growing than in a comparatively stationary population, in part because in the former the relative number of dependents tends to be somewhat higher. This statement could hold, of course, only for disposable personal income; it would not be applicable to undistributed corporate income. It would be most pertinent to disposable income in the hands of individuals with dependents; for, as the number of dependents per family rises, an ever smaller fraction of income tends to be saved and an ever larger fraction tends to be devoted to nondeferrable expenditures.

Major emphasis was placed upon variations in the demand for investment goods supposedly produced by variations in the rate of population growth, together with the secondary influences upon consumption and investment demands thereby set in motion. For, it was supposed, something like half of a community's outlay upon net capital formation (which in the United States approximated somewhat more than a tenth of net national product [defined as gross national product less current consumption of durable capital]) was directly and indirectly occasioned by population growth (see Hansen's paper); and it was inferred that if the rate of population growth fell, or fell sufficiently, annual outlay upon net capital formation would decline relatively and perhaps absolutely. National income and expenditure would, in consequence, be lowered by an amount approximating 2–3 times the diminution in annual outlay upon net capital formation, because of the secondary or multiplier effects attendant upon increases or decreases in the annual rate of capital formation. The aggregate demand for labor would diminish accordingly, unemployment would increase, and both output and consumption per capita would decline. For example, if a decline in the rate of population growth occasioned a decrease in outlay upon net capital formation amounting to 5 per cent of net national product when employment was full, the total decrease in net national product might amount to 10–15 per cent, with the result that employment would be diminished by a roughly corresponding relative amount. Should the accelerator effect be operative (see Spengler's paper), a somewhat greater decline in employment might result. Trade-cycle influences traceable to population movements might also intensify the longer-run effects of population growth (see Lösch's paper).

An increase in the rate of population growth would tend to produce an opposite set of effects. It would, as has already been implied, make for a reduction in the proportion of disposable income that was saved, and, given appropriate monetary conditions, for an increase in offsets to savings. Capital outlay would increase, and with it both the demand for consumption goods and the aggregate demand for labor. This increase would be intensified if the accelerator principle came into operation. Something like full employment would prevail, and the aggregate demand for labor might even become so great, in the absence of restrictions upon the increase of money and credit, as to bring about wage and price inflation. It followed that population growth, in particular an increase in the rate of population growth, was a source of prosperity, often tending to make even per capita income and output greater than it otherwise would have been. By the same reasoning a decline in the rate of population growth might be a cause of recession or depression.

Various criticisms have been directed against the line of reasoning described (see Brockie's paper; also Barber's, wherein it is shown, among other things, that it is the percentage rather than the absolute rate of population growth that is most relevant to the argument). It has been found that increases in family size serve only within limits to increase the demand for residential construction; beyond a point increase in quantity of construction is offset by decrease in quality. It has been observed that periods characterized by declines in the rate of population growth have not necessarily been periods of marked unemployment. More generally, it has been noted that, since the aggregate demand for labor is made up of governmental expenditures and of private expenditures upon consumer goods and investment goods, relatively small upward adjustments in governmental outlays and in private consumption expenditures may serve to counterbalance any diminution in private outlay upon capital formation occasioned by a decline in the rate of population growth. Thus, if net capital formation has been approximating 10 per cent of national income, a decline in this rate by one-half would be offset by an increase of one-eighteenth in consumption; or if gross private investment has been approximating one-seventh of gross national product, a decline in this fraction by one-half would be offset by an increase of one-twelfth in private consumption and governmental expenditures. It has been inferred, therefore, that in economies in which governmental expenditure is relatively large, such counterbalancing action would be expected. Difficulties would be likely to arise only during a period of transition when the rate of population growth was moving from a relatively high to a relatively low level, and some redistribution of labor and other factors of production among occupations was proving necessary.

Because of the depressive effect continuous population growth eventually exercises upon per capita capital-formation, resource-use, and related income-elevating changes, it is evident that population growth cannot long be relied upon to occasion full employment by generating investment. It has been remarked that only under certain conditions do increments in the labor force get employed. It has been noted, furthermore, that one does not encounter in all countries the mechanisms through the medium of which variations in the rate of population growth may, on the line of reasoning outlined, significantly affect the level of activity and employment. It has been observed also that jobs can be provided for all members of a country's labor force only if a sufficient amount of equipment or capital per head can be made available, and that this may prove impossible when the rate of population growth rises above a level critical for the country in question.

While it is generally admitted that an increase in the rate of population growth intensifies the tendencies to overemployment and/or inflation present in countries undergoing rapid development, it is also recognized that it is easier to control booms of this sort than it is to get rid of disguised and related forms of unemployment. When such inflation is permitted to flourish, it is because planned investment is deliberately allowed to exceed planned saving, or because a nation's fiscal instruments are defective.

The selection from the Papers of the British Royal Commission, included in Chapter 9, might well have been included in this chapter and should be consulted on the possible impact of a decline in numbers. At present, with population growing in most countries, much less attention is being given to possible effects of a decline in numbers, a decline that appeared imminent in the 1930's when three of the selections included in this chapter were written. Presumably this subject will again command attention if the rate of growth declines markedly and threatens to become negative. Discussion of the subject will have to take into account the economic-institutional structure of society then obtaining, however, since the nature of the response of an economy to a decline in numbers is very much conditioned by this institutional structure.

It has been shown that full employment tends to persist only when an economy's output increases rapidly enough to generate a sufficiently high rate of investment. It has not been shown, however, that a sufficiently high rate of growth can be achieved only when population is growing appreciably, since what constitutes an adequate rate depends upon a number of circumstances, of which the rate of population growth is but one.

POPULATION MOVEMENTS, EMPLOYMENT, AND INCOME*

By Joseph J. Spengler

Throughout the world at present interest in the economic consequences of demographic movements and in state policies designed to control such movements is developing. In view of this growing interest, and in view of the fact that many tentative and actual state demographic policies are founded upon questionable economic presuppositions, it is not amiss to indicate, even though in an incomplete form, certain effects of population movements upon employment and income levels.

Inasmuch as the relationship between money (or physical) income per person and "welfare" per person is governed, assuming a given level of culture and pattern of tastes, by the prevailing degree of inequality in income distribution, and by the extent to which personal expenditure is "economic" and in line with the prescripts of "science,"[1] we shall not employ the term "income" in the "welfare" sense. We shall simply treat the term "income" as synonymous with "output" and assume, since other conditions are postulated to be constant, that any increase in the current per capita output of goods and services constitutes an increase in per capita income and per capita welfare as of the present and/or proximate future.

I

Population movements—i.e., variations in the rate of growth of the total population, and in relative rates of natural growth by class or sub-region— within a closed economy influence per capita income through their effect upon the determinants of per capita income: (1) *fullness* of employment; (2) geographical distribution of population; (3) supply of resources per head; (4) efficiency with which resources are used.

Full employment of labor prevails in an economy when, other things equal, everyone who desires to work not only is occupied a specified number of hours per week or per year (say 40 or 2000), but is so employed that, given his training, aptitudes, and preferences, and the tastes and demands (actual and/or realizable) of the community, he is earning as much as, or more than, he could earn in any other employment persuable by him and acceptable to him. For since (other things equal) the utility and demand functions of specific goods and services fall with an increase in their relative supply, and

* Reprinted from *The Southern Economic Journal*, 5 (October 1938), pp. 129–157, by permission of the publisher. (Copyright 1938 by the Southern Economic Association.)

the per capita productivity function within any given occupation eventually tends to fall, given an appreciable increase in the relative number engaged therein, it follows that some distribution of workers among occupations will make possible a greater overall per capita productivity than any other alternative distribution. Therefore, other things equal, labor income will be greatest when employment is *full*. Per capita income will be at a maximum when all factors of production are *fully* employed: i.e., when all factors are so occupied that the marginal productivity of each factor in any one employment is the same as in any other employment (pain costs and costs of factor-transfer being ignored), and the ratio of the marginal productivity of any one factor to that of any other factor is the same in all employments.

What constitutes the best, or *optimum*, distribution of factors among employments, varies with the period of time allowed for the adjustment and transfer of factors. The short run optimum will have been achieved when, given prevailing educational and training levels, no owner of any production factor can, by shifting the said factor from one employment to another, increase its rate of remuneration sufficiently to offset the psychic and non-psychic costs of making the shift. (Presumably, correct cost accounting under the circumstances assumed requires the owner of the factor of production to allow for indirect as well as direct changes in factor income attendant upon such a shift.) The longer run optimum will have been realized when, assuming easily achievable upward adjustments of educational and training levels, an analogous equilibrium will have been established.[2] (Obviously, any change in tastes, technology, income distribution, resource supply, etc., will alter the short and the long run optima.)

It follows from what has been said that human employment, or unemployment, may range from zero to 100 per cent. When no one is employed, employment is zero, unemployment is 100 per cent. If everyone is so employed that, given his training and inclinations, he could not earn enough more in any other occupation to induce his shifting thereto, employment is 100 per cent, unemployment is zero. If, given the same conditions, not everyone is employed, or some persons are so employed that they are earning less than they could earn if they shifted to other occupations wherein they are willing and able to work, employment is less than 100 per cent. In short, the coefficient of unemployment, to be accurate, must measure both absolute unemployment and what Joan Robinson has called "disguised unemployment."[3]

II

Whereas changes in the rate of population growth may give rise, as we indicate below, to absolute unemployment, variations from occupation to occupation and from sub-region to sub-region tend to swell the relative volume of disguised unemployment. For when such variations exist, the social agencies whose function it is to distribute correctly among occupations the annual increments of as yet uninitiated young workers find themselves unable to effect a proper distribution: the number of workers requiring re-distribution proves relatively too large.[4]

In theory, given free and effective competition and suitable labor distributing agencies (schools, labor exchanges, etc.), new increments of labor can be properly distributed among various occupations. In practice, however, the redistribution of the new increments of labor prerequisite to the preservation or restoration of an optimum or employmentless balance among occupations is not realized. Conditions of imperfect competition[5] prevail. Moreover, children tend to pursue occupations resembling those followed by parents and adult acquaintances; for the home, social, and educational media within which children move (and these are relatively unfavorable in larger families in economies wherein family size is not an important determinant of income) largely shape their personal inclinations, attitudes toward occupations, acquired aptitudes, etc.[6] Consequently, since natural increase not only varies from occupational group to occupational group, but also varies in the direction opposite that in which it needs to vary to preserve an optimum and full-employment balance among occupations, prevailing variations from occupation to occupation in natural increase constitute an important cause of disguised unemployment.

The effects of variations in the geographical distribution of the population throughout a region may be dealt with in a manner analogous to that employed in treating occupational distribution. In general it may be said that an optimum geographical distribution of the population has been achieved if, assuming tastes, income and resource distribution, etc., as given and constant, no one, given his training, aptitudes, and inclinations, can increase his income sufficiently to justify his changing his geographical location. So long as changes of this sort are justifiable the geographical distribution of the population is at a sub-optimum level, and average per capita real income can be augmented through migration.

Subregional disparities in the rate of natural increase may augment or diminish the geographical maldistribution of the population. For an optimum geographical distribution of the population does not exist until it is impossible for anyone, given his training and inclinations, and the tastes, income distribution, and resource pattern of the community, to increase his income sufficiently, through a geographical transfer of his services, to justify such a change. So long as the geographical distribution of the population is at a sub-optimum level, such transfers serve to augment overall per capita income, inasmuch as intersubregional trade is but a partial counterbalance to geographical maldistribution. Whenever subregional variations in natural increase are not counterbalanced by variations in the subregional supplies of wholly or partially unutilized resources, geographical maldistribution increases; given opposite conditions, geographical maldistribution decreases. In practice the unemployment which is associated with geographical maldistribution of population is disguised rather than absolute, tending to assume the guise of occupational maldistribution. When, as in the United States, frontier areas become settled, and in consequence the struggle of man with nature becomes transformed into a struggle between man and his fellows, both occupational and regional disparities in natural increase tend in a more marked degree to give rise to disguised unemployment.

Although occupational and regional disparities in natural increase give rise primarily to disguised unemployment, they may aggravate cyclical tendencies to unemployment. For overcrowded regions and occupations constitute enclaves of industrial reserve armies that may be hired at less than their marginal productivities by entrepreneurs in other subregions and employments. Wherefore these entrepreneurs may enjoy "supra-normal" profits and be motivated thereby to seek larger volumes of credit and expand their activities to a supra-equilibrium level which cannot be preserved. Both the latter stages of the expansion period and the several stages of the contraction period within the industries in question will exercise a depressive effect upon the remainder of the industrial structure.

III

Per capita income is primarily dependent upon the supply of resources being utilized per worker and upon the efficiency with which this supply is utilized. In this and the ensuing section we shall treat the relations between population growth and resource supply, occupational and geographical distribution, age composition, and relative number employed being assumed to remain constant. The term resources denotes both things existing wholly or largely independently of man's past and present efforts, and instruments produced predominantly by human effort, from which utilities flow directly and/or indirectly. Current income flows only from resources actually in use, unused and partly used resources constituting a fund whence future income may flow.

The total supply of resources *available* to man is not fixed through time. Man can increase the present effective supply of depletable and non-replenishable resources (e.g., mineral supplies) by reducing the waste involved in their utilization. He can increase the effective supply of depletable but replenishable resources (e.g., timber supply) both by reducing the waste involved in their use and by increasing the rate of replenishment. (In practice, such replenishment is generally in part at the expense of depletable non-replenishable resources.) Man can increase the resource supply by bringing within the circuit of human use things which otherwise would be valueless or of lesser value (e.g., minerals, etc., in ocean waters; solar energy; herbs; etc.), and by changing communal patterns of tastes and the income distribution which helps to transmute tastes into effective demands.[7] The amount of resources utilizable per time period per worker in a community with a given supply of resources as already defined is governed by the level of technologic knowledge and the degree of its diffusion through and use in the population. (E.g., the invention of the combine as a substitute for simple reapers and threshers increased the amount of resources manipulatable per person.)

If the term, efficiency of use of resources, is understood to refer to the amount of net utility obtained from given resources per unit of human effort, it may be said that such efficiency will depend upon organizational aspects of the economy, some of which are referred to below, and upon the personal quality of the population. The latter depends upon genetic make-up, upon the quantity and nature of educational and similar stimuli impinging on the population, and upon the extent to which the application of principles of scientific management conserves and economizes human energy independently of the state of technology and per worker resource supply. (The relative amount of human and non-human resources required to impart the economically desirable quantum of educational stimuli will vary inversely to the genetic composition of the population.)

Although, as we indicate in the next section, populations of given sizes are necessary, other things equal, to permit the utilization of the best industrial techniques and interindustrial fits, population growth in a given region tends to diminish per capita *utilizable* resource supply. If population grows sufficiently, recourse to second, third, and lower grade resources (depletable and non-depletable) becomes necessary, and the supply per worker and per inhabitant falls below the level susceptible of current utilization. Moreover, the larger the population, other things equal, the greater the rate of depletion of both non-replenishable and replenishable depletable-resources, and the lower, after given periods of time, the per capita and per worker supply of such resources. Whenever the supply per worker and per inhabitant falls below the maximum utilizable level, per capita income falls, other things equal.

While it is possible that the intensification of interaction which accompanies increases in population density may stimulate technologic progress and cultural changes that serve to augment the total *available* supply of resources,[8] this proposition appears to be valid only for sparsely populated countries. All that is necessary to increase the relative amount of inventiveness to a maximum, given existing means of communication, is such a geographical distribution of the population as will allow a few local points of a density sufficient to permit cultural set-ups favorable to invention. In general the relative amount of inventiveness seems to be virtually independent of population growth. At any given time the quantity of inventiveness may be taken as fixed, just as the quantity of any other factor of production may be taken as fixed; and the social gain derivable from inventiveness may be taken as at a maximum when inventiveness is correctly allocated among industrial and other employments.[9]

IV

Per capita output within a region depends (the resource supply, occupational and geographical distribution, and state of the arts being given) upon the extent to which optimum (i.e., minimum cost) scales of production are attained within each industry and within the economy as a whole. The extent to which optimum scales of production are attained within given industries (or layers of the economy) and within the economy as a whole is governed, other conditions remaining constant, by the size of the population.

It is evident that since factors of production are not infinitely divisible and therefore are not susceptible of being combined in fixed proportions on any desired scale, some scale of output for any given technique will permit lower per unit normal costs than any other scale, and some technique will permit lower per unit normal costs for a given output than any other technique. Let us call the minimum per unit cost scale of a producing unit in a given field of production or distribution the optimum scale, and let there be one optimum for each possible technical pattern of production. Let us assume three techniques, I, II, III, with respective optimum outputs of 5,000, 10,000, and 20,000. We might then have a situation such as is depicted in Table I, where it is evident that I, II, and III would permit minimum per unit cost, respectively, given market demands of 5,000, 10,000, and 20,000. Other things equal, the cost and price per unit of output would be lower, and per capita output and income (in so far as per capita output and income in general are influenced by the condition of operation within the industry described in Table I) would be higher, given a population with a demand of 20,000 (or some multiple thereof) units than given populations with demands of 5,000, 10,-000, or 15,000.[10]

Inasmuch as the populations which express effective demands for the optimum scale output (or some multiple thereof) within any one industry do not necessarily correspond in size with the populations that express effective demands for the optimum scale output (or some multiple thereof) of any other particular industry, only populations of certain sizes enable the entire industrial structure of a closed economy to operate at optimum scale. Given a population of such size, an optimum *fit* of producing units, one into another, may be said to exist.

TABLE I

Units Produced	Normal Per Unit Production Cost, Given Designated Technique and Quantity		
	I	II	III
5,000	$1.00	$1.25	$1.50
10,000	$1.00	.90	1.10
20,000	$1.00	.90	.80

The most efficient or optimum *fit* among the producing units in the various lines of production within a region is that fit which would permit each industry to consist of one or more units employing technique III, as in Table I. Such a fit would be possible, given certain but not all sizes of population within a region. Let us assume there are four stages of production, A, B, C, D, goods flowing from A through B and C to D wherein they are made ready for, and delivered to, the consumer. If the lowest per unit cost scale in each stage were III (see Table I) and each stage took 20,000 units from the preceding stage, then the lowest cost per unit finished good and therefore the greatest per capita income would be realized (other things equal) if the producing and consuming populations corresponded to one necessary to produce and consume 20,000 (or some multiple thereof) units of goods flowing from D. If the population were appreciably less than this size, the best fit would be obtained through use of the less productive techniques I or II or a combination thereof. If the optimum scale for III were 40, 30, 20, and 10 thousands respectively in stages A, B, C, and D, and each unit of production in a given stage absorbed one unit of production from the preceding stage, there would have to be produced in stage D 120,000 (i.e., the L.C.M. of the four optima) units if production in each stage were to be carried on at the lowest possible per unit cost scale. We should then have 12, 6, 4, and 3 producing units in D, C, B, and A. If less than 120,000 were produced in stage D, part of the output in some of the prior stages would have to be produced through use of the more costly techniques I and II, or through use of III in a state of undercapacity. Per capita income then would be less, and "abnormal" profits (or rents) would manifest themselves in those producing units in the prior stages operating with technique III.

In view of what has just been said, it is evident: (a) that given any particular technique, populations of given size are necessary if the best possible fit and highest per capita income are to be obtained; (b) that any invention which increases the divisibility of the factors and makes possible smaller scales of operation frequently but not necessarily tends to reduce the size of population necessary to achieve a given per capita income; (c) that trading relations with other regions which absorb the "excess" output of certain stages in a given region may enable a smaller population in the latter region to obtain a given per capita income.[11] The highly simplified illustration here employed must be corrected for the following: (a) that the effort to obtain the best *fit* through population growth may push production in some stages so far that *inferior* resources have to be used, thus altering the data as given in Table I; (b) that a given stage may feed several later stages (e.g., coal mining); (c) that the transportation factor must be fully taken into account.

V

The major longer-run effects of continued population growth, assuming a given geographical and occupational distribution of the population and similar rates of natural growth in the various occupational and geographical sectors of the population, are three in number: (a) the resource supply per worker in some or all fields of production falls below the amount necessary to permit maximum possible output per person, the ultimate fixity of the total supply of first class resources compelling either their use under less favourable circumstances or recourse to the use of inferior order resources;[12] (b) the *fit* among producing units is improved, or worsened, thus counterbalancing or aggravating the effect noted under (a); (c) the rate at which depletable resources are being exhausted is increased, with the result that over time per capita income may be depressed. It follows that if maximum per capita income over time[13] were the desideratum, and the supply of resources of first order were sufficiently great, the desirable or *optimum* population would be the *smallest* number of persons necessary to permit an optimum *fit* of all industries. Since, however, the supply of resources of first order does not tend to correspond with that required by the preceding proposition, per capita income over a designated period of time will be at a maximum only if an appropriate compromise is struck between the worker: resource ratio and some approximation to optimum *fit* among industries, each of which variables is a function of the size of the population and not readily measureable.[14]

Our analysis has thus far presupposed a closed regional economy. Such an assumption is unreal, however, for it is generally true that in the absence of interregional trade the ratio of the prices of some productive factors to the prices of other productive factors will vary from region to region, giving to each region a differential advantage in the production (within limits) of such goods and services as require for their production relatively large amounts of the productive factors abounding in said region. For seldom do the relative proportions in which the population of a region demands the various productive factors found in that region just match the relative proportions in which such factors are available and thus cause the factor price structure in that region to be the same as the factor price structure in other regions in which productive factors occur in different proportions. Wherefore interregional trade usually pays, its establishment adding to, or subtracting from, the domestic demand for specific classes of productive factors found within a region. Accordingly, the exchange value of some of the productive resources becomes less than it would be in the absence of trade; the exchange value of others increases. The total exchange value is greater. What constitutes the best geographic and occupational distribution of the population differs from what it would have been in the absence of trade and becomes dependent upon extra- as well as upon intra-regional changes in tastes, income distribution, technologic progress, etc. Given trading relations; (a) per capita income will be greater with a given population than in the absence of trade; (b) the regional population permitting the greatest possible continued per capita income (i.e., the income *optimum* population) may be larger or smaller than it would be in the absence of trade, but the maximum possible income will be greater.[15]

TABLE II*

| Period | Per Cent Decrease in Population | | | | Per Cent Decrease in Males 20–64** | | Quinquennial Per Cent Decline in Original Cohort of Males Aged 20–64*** | | | |
| | Estimate 1 | | Estimate 2 | | | | | | | |
	Total	Male	Total	Male	Estimate 1	Estimate 2	1935_1	1935_2	1960_1	1960_2
1935–40	+0.653	+0.817	+0.227	+0.390	11.107	10.751	11.107	10.751	12.232	10.964
1940–45	+0.118	+0.265	+0.647	0.512	11.287	10.624	12.667	11.960	15.419	14.182
1945–50	0.484	0.325	1.550	1.404	11.152	10.296	14.482	13.477	17.693	16.722
1950–55	1.158	0.964	2.487	2.316	11.296	10.276	16.922	15.564	20.471	19.458
1955–60	1.838	1.607	3.445	3.231	11.466	10.240	20.062	18.271	23.180	22.011
1960–65	2.442	2.172	4.386	4.107	12.232	10.964	25.539	23.295	31.939	31.274
1965–70	3.015	2.798	5.620	5.347	14.025	13.075	36.780	34.685	38.764	38.473
1970–75	3.495	3.263	6.911	6.683	14.298	14.152	53.679	52.022	54.417	55.831
1975–80	3.951	3.766	8.251	8.100	14.444	14.943	100.000	100.000	100.000	100.000
1980–85	4.357	4.215	9.599	9.530	13.982	15.160				
1985–90	4.673	4.561	10.844	10.825	15.814	18.840				
1990–95	4.880	4.798	12.116	12.165	14.778	19.029				
1995–2000	4.987	4.931	13.478	13.600	14.509	20.593				
2030–2035	5.000	4.991	20.598	20.602						

* Computed from Charles, op. cit.

** Computed as follows: Males aged 25–64 in given year (say 1940) divided by males aged 20–64 five years earlier (say 1935) and subtracted from 100.

*** Illustration: A cohort of males, 20–64 in 1935, declines 11.107 per cent in 1935–40, 12.667 in 1940–45, on assumption 1; a cohort of males, 20–64 in 1960, declines 10.964 per cent in 1960–65, 14.182 in 1965–70, on assumption 2.

VI

In the remainder of this paper we shall deal briefly with the effects of a long-continued decline (or increase) in natural increase of population upon the *fullness* of employment. Inasmuch as the precise effect of such a decline will depend, other things equal, upon the nature of the changes in mortality, several observations are necessary. First, if fertility and mortality rates become constant, after a decrease (or increase) in fertility rates and a decrease (or increase) in mortality rates, the population finally becomes stable in age composition and the rate of natural decrease (or increase) becomes constant. If, on the contrary, fertility rates continue to fall (or to rise) relative to mortality rates (which shall be assumed to be falling), the age composition will not become stable, and the rate of decrease (or increase) will not become constant: the relative number of older persons will continue to increase (or decrease), and the rate of increase will continue to fall (or rise) within determinable outside limits.[16]

For purposes of illustration use is made of two estimates of the future population of England and Wales: (1) based on the assumption of the continuation of the fertility and mortality rates of 1933, at which time the net reproduction rate was 0.734; (2) based on the assumption of a continuation of the past decline in fertility and mortality rates.[17] The relevant characteristics of the types of decrease are given in Tables II and III. On the former assumption the age composition and the rate of decrease become stable about 1995. On the latter assumption, the percentage of the population aged 0–15 steadily decreases; that 60 and over steadily increases; that 15–60 increases to a maximum about 1960 and then steadily decreases; the rate of decrease steadily rises. In columns 6–11 of Table II are given the rates of decrease, in the absence of the addition of new recruits, in a cohort of males initially aged 20–64 (i.e., of working age). Within any given five-year period (cols. 6–7) death and age reduce such a cohort by 10+ to 20+ per cent, and this rate of decrease steadily increases (cols. 8–11).

TABLE III*

Age Distribution, in Per Cent

Year	Estimate 1				Estimate 2			
	0–4	15–19	20–59	60 +	0–5	15–19	20–59	60 +
1871–80	13.80	9.70	46.60	7.40	13.80	9.70	46.60	7.40
1935	7.05	7.46	56.84	12.45	7.05	7.46	56.84	12.45
1950	6.30	6.74	58.44	15.81	4.46	6.96	60.62	17.01
1960	5.83	6.40	57.86	17.50	3.23	5.37	62.13	20.69
1980	5.38	5.98	55.27	22.18	1.56	3.25	58.07	32.63
1995	5.32	5.94	53.92	23.60	1.12	2.15	49.81	43.83
2010	5.32	5.95	54.27	23.31	0.88	1.77	43.64	51.22

* 1935–2010, from Charles, op. cit.

Assuming tastes, income distribution, and income levels to remain unchanged except in so far as they are governed by changes in the rate of increase and in the age composition, the relative amount of absolute and/or disguised unemployment is fixed in part by changes in the rate of population growth; for, given imperfect mobility of the factors of production and imperfect knowledge on the part of entrepreneurs and of factor-owners relative to the utilizability of the factors of production, re-distributions of productive factors appropriate to changed demographic conditions are not made.

Let P = the total population; D = the total demand for the services of employables; E = the total number of employables; $d_1, d_2, \ldots d_n$ = the respective demands for labor in employments 1, 2, ... n; $e_1, e_2 \ldots e_n$ = the number of employables affiliated with employments 1, 2, ... n; C = the coefficient of *fullness* of employment, expressed as a relative ranging between zero and 100.[18] Let $D = \Sigma \, d_1 \ldots d_n$; $E = \Sigma \, e_1 \ldots e_n$. Changes in P, or in the rate of growth of P, may be accompanied by changes in C, if changes in P, or in the rate of growth of P, are necessarily accompanied by changes in the mobility of labor, in $\dfrac{D}{E}$, or in $\dfrac{d}{e}$.

The mobility of labor and $\dfrac{D}{E}$ both undergo change in consequence of the changes in age composition which accompany changes in the rate of natural increase. Let m = the coefficient of mobility of labor; r = the percentage of the population just short of the age of employability, say in the age group 15–19; let E = the percentage of the population in the age group 20–59, or in that 20–64. Presumably, other things equal, $m = \dfrac{r}{E}$; for the greater the relative number of as yet unspecialized workers, the greater the facility with which a given change can be made in the proportions in which workers are distributed among various employments. m falls in value as the rate of natural increase falls, continuing to fall until the age composition becomes stable. The values for m, according to the data in Table III, are: 1871–80, 0.208; 1935, 0.131; 1960_1, 0.111; 1960_2, 0.086; 1995_1, 0.110; 1995_2, 0.043; 2010_1, 0.110; 2010_2, 0.042. If C varies directly as m, it follows that, other things equal, a decrease in the rate of increase in P will be accompanied by declines in m and C until the age composition of the population becomes stable. In view of our subsequent analysis it will become evident that every possible effort must be made, given a falling population, to improve educational institutions, employment exchanges, and so on, in order that the effects of a decline in $\dfrac{r}{E}$ may be counteracted.

Let E = the percentage of the population aged 20–59; U = the percentage in the unemployable age groups, 0–19 and 60+. The demand ($=D$) for the labor of E derives immediately from the purchasing power—itself *in the long run* the product of the goods and services created by E in conjunction with non-human factors of production—in the hands of $E + U$ ($= P$). Wherefore, given present capitalistic institutional and monetary arrangements, it is probable, but not necessary, that an increase in $\dfrac{E}{E + U}$ (i.e., in $\dfrac{E}{P}$) will be accompanied by a diminution in the value of $\dfrac{D}{E}$ and that a decrease in $\dfrac{E}{P}$ will be accompanied by an increase in the value of $\dfrac{D}{E}$.[19] Assuming that C varies directly with $\dfrac{D}{E}$, it is evident that per capita income will fall if $E \times C$ falls, and rise if $E \times C$ rises. On a priori grounds it appears unlikely that any given small relative change in E will be accompanied by a change in C sufficiently great to offset or more than offset the change in E. Whence it is highly probable that an increase in $\dfrac{E}{P}$ will be accompanied by an increase in per capita income and a decrease in the relative amount of employment (i.e., in C); a decrease in $\dfrac{E}{P}$ will be accompanied by a decrease in per capita income and an increase in the relative amount of employment (i.e., in C).

Substitution of values in Table III (cols. 4, 8) for $\dfrac{E}{P}$ indicates that, assuming other conditions than age composition[20] to be constant: (a) per capita income and unemployment will be at a maximum in 1950–60; (b) unemployment will fall less rapidly, given estimate 1 than estimate 2; (c) per capita income will become stable about 1995, given estimate 1, but will steadily fall, given estimate 2. Whence it follows that, should it prove impossible to elevate fertility and bring about the establishment of a stationary population, it is highly desirable that fertility rates be stabilized and that the population, though declining, be made to assume a stable age composition.

VII

A given relative decline in P will be accompanied at least temporarily by a decline in C, if such a decline in P, and the correlative declines in the numbers of employables in given employments (say $e_1 \ldots e_{20}$), are accompanied by declines of greater magnitude in the demands (say $d_1 \ldots d_{20}$) for the services of said groups of employables (i.e., $e_1 \ldots e_{20}$), and unaccompanied by *simultaneous* or *prior* offsetting increases in the demands (say $d_{21} \ldots d_{40}$) for the services of other groups of employables (i.e., $e_{21} \ldots e_{40}$). For, given such offsets, it is conceivable, despite the imperfect mobility of labor, that the incipient surplus of workers in $e_1 \ldots e_{20}$ will be drawn at once into $e_{21} \ldots e_{40}$. In practice a decline in P may be accompanied by an at least temporary fall in C for at least one of three main reasons: (i) changes in age composition; (ii) the nature of inter-employment relationships; (iii) the partial dependence of investment upon demographic trends. [21] The actual effect of (i), (ii), and (iii) upon C will be governed, other things equal, by the state of entrepreneurial (individual, institutional, or governmental) expectation or anticipation with respect to the future. If, for example, this state is characterizable as "pessimistic," the depressive effect of (i), (ii), or (iii) upon C will be greater than if this state is characterizable as "optimistic." For purposes of analysis varying values may be assigned to the "state of entrepreneurial expectation," —a state determined in part by nondemographic sociological and institutional conditions and therefore in large part independent of the variables that are being discussed here—and employed to correct conclusions reached on the basis of a given "state of entrepreneurial expectation."

(i) Given declines in P are accompanied, until age composition becomes stable, by relatively greater declines in the younger age groups and by relatively smaller declines in the higher age groups (see Table III). If any d is a function of age composition, it will change by greater or lesser relative amount than P so long as age composition is not stable. Let us suppose that $d_1 \ldots d_3$ vary directly and proportionally as the age group 0–4; that $d_4 \ldots d_6$ vary directly and proportionally as the age group 60+; and that $e_1 \ldots e_6$ vary directly and proportionally as P. Given estimate 1, $d_1 \ldots d_3$ decline 19.6 per cent in 1935–50, $d_4 \ldots d_6$ increase 37.5 per cent, and $e_1 \ldots e_6$ decline 2.7 per cent. A surplus will have developed in $e_1 \ldots e_3$; a deficit in $e_1 \ldots e_6$. A transfer of workers from $e_1 \ldots e_3$ to $e_4 \ldots e_6$ will eliminate the unemployment in the former occupations.

If the decline in $d_1 \ldots d_3$, and the increase in $d_4 \ldots d_6$ are anticipated; and if it is customary to recruit given employments in so far as possible from the offspring of persons enrolled in such employments, the bulk of the offspring of persons engaged in $e_1 \ldots e_3$ may be shunted into $e_4 \ldots e_6$. For example: in 1935–40, the number aged 0–4 declines 6.01 per cent; the number engaged in $e_1 \ldots e_3$ would be reduced by death and age, assuming no recruits, by 11.1 per cent (Table II, col. 6), and increased, assuming the recruiting of all offspring, by 1.64 per cent. Balance is preserved on condition that 40 per cent of the offspring (of persons in $e_1 \ldots e_3$) ageing into employability, are directed into $e_1 \ldots e_3$, and the remaining 60 per cent are directed into $e_4 \ldots e_6$ which, in the absence of outside recruiting, will be too small. Should there develop complications, such as arise because of conditions described in (ii), further corrections will be necessary; but the indicated procedure remains the same.[22]

(ii) It is generally accepted that, given appropriate qualifications, a decline in the rate of increase in the consumption of a given service will be accompanied by an absolute decline in the consumption of durable and/or producers' goods whence this service flows, provided that the replacement needs for such goods do not expand sufficiently per time period to offset the decline in the need for *additional* goods.[23] A decline in the rate of population growth will not only diminish the rate of increase for given services, but will eventually bring about an absolute decrease in the demand for given services, and corresponding or greater relative decreases in the absolute demand for durable and/or producers' goods. In other words: given declines in the rate of natural increase, if continued for a long enough period, will diminish not only the rate of increase in the demand for given services, but also the absolute demand for such services. The absolute demand for durable and/or producers' goods whence flow such services will be depressed even more, at least temporarily. In brief: given declines in P will be accompanied by relatively greater declines in some d's; wherefore surpluses of workers will develop in some e's unless the recruiting of said e's is checked.

Let each e and d_1 vary directly and proportionally as P. Suppose: (a) that per time period t, one mechanical unit M_1 produces 1000 units of goods 1, one M_2 produces 100 M_1 and one M_3 produces 10 M_2; (b) that replacements per time period $t = 25$ per cent of the number of mechanical units in use in the preceding time period; (c) that P declines after a long period of stationarity. The results are given in Table IV. Given a constant rate of decline in P (col. 6), d_{M1}, d_{M2}, and d_{M3} decline at a constant rate after a lapse of one, two, and three time periods respectively. In t_2 a labor surplus of three units develops in e_{M1}; in e_{M2}, a surplus of 15 in t_2 and 5.85 in t_3; e_{M3}, a surplus of 63 in t_2, a deficit of 21.04 in t_3, and a surplus of 8.5563 in t_4 (cols. 7–9). Provided that these surpluses are transferred to other relatively expanding e's, continuation of the constant rate of decline in P will occasion no further surpluses in e_{M1}, e_{M2}, and e_{M3}. If, however, P declines at an increasing rate (col. 2), d_{M1}, d_{M2}, and d_{M3} will fall at slightly greater rates. Wherefore continually recurring labor surpluses will develop in e_{M1}, e_{M2}, and e_{M3}—surpluses which can be avoided only by shunting a sufficient proportion of the offspring of persons in these employments to other relatively expanding employments.

Let us substitute for assumptions (a), (b), and (c) the following postulates, and retain the assumption that each e and d_1 vary with P: (d) M_1, M_2, M_3 are put into use in the time period following that of their construction and become absolutely useless upon the completion of the fourth period of of use, whether actually used or not; (e) that M_1, M_2, and M_3 are produced respectively in the time period preceding their use; (f) that P decreases, or increases, after having been stationary. The introduction of condition (d) produces periodic fluctuations in d_{M1} and marked fluctuations in d_{M2} and d_{M3} which are greatly influenced by past irregularities in the volume of their construction (see Table V). Whereas deaths, age changes, and minor transfers of workers out of or into e_{M1} will adjust e_{M1} to d_{M1} (cp. cols. 2 and 3; 6 and 7) large periodic transfers are required to adjust e_{M2} (cols. 4, 8) and unmanageable transfers to adjust e_{M3} (cols. 5, 9). If, however, one substitutes for assumption (d) the assumption that M_2 and M_3 may be used 4–6 years, given extra allowance for wear and tear, the production of M_2 and M_3 may be evened out and made to behave somewhat as in Table IV.

When the supposition that any e varies directly and proportionally as P is adjusted to reality, it becomes evident that, given conditions at all similar to those depicted in Table IV, no inter-employment transfer of workers is necessary to preserve full employment. It is but necessary that workers just aged into the employable age group (say 20–24) be distributed among the various employments in different proportions than older workers already employed. For, as we have indicated (cp. cols. 6–11 with cols. 2–5 in Table II), death and age alone will diminish the number originally in any employment e much more rapidly than an excess of deaths diminishes P, or economic changes associated with declines in P depress any particular demand d. In fact, so great is the incidence of death and age, that some new recruits are needed in almost all employments to adjust d to e. Wherefore it is evident, as has been indicated already, that proper occupational guidance and direction of youth will be far more important in a falling than in a growing population.

TABLE IV

Time period	Index of population	Index of demand for			Index of population	Index of demand for		
		M_1	M_2	M_3		M_1	M_2	M_3
t = 0	100	100	100	100	100	100	100	100
1	100	100	100	100	100	100	100	100
2	99	96	84	36	99	96	84	36
3	98	95	92	116	98.01	95.04	92.16	116
4	97	94	91	88	97.0299	94.0896	91.2384	88.4736
5	96	93	90	87	96.059601	93.148704	90.326016	87.588864
6	95	92	89	86	95.09900499	92.21721696	89.42275584	86.71297536

TABLE V

Time period	Population index	Index of demand for			Population index	Index of demand for		
		M_1	M_2	M_3		M_1	M_2	M_3
t = 000	100	100	100	100	100	100	100	100
00	100	100	100	36	100	100	100	164
0	100	100	84	164	100	100	116	36
1	100	96	100	100	100	104	100	100
2	99	96	100	100	101	104	100	100
3	98	96	100	0	102	104	100	292
4	97	96	68	200	103	104	132	0
5	96	92	100	100	104	108	100	8
6	95	92	100	100	105	108	100	100
7	94	92	100	0	106	108	100	420
8	93	92	52	200	107	108	132	0
9	92	88	100	100	108	108	84	0
10	91	88	100	100	108	104	100	0
11	90	88	100	0	107	104	100	528

VIII

(iii) The long-run trend in population growth influences investment and the level of employment, not as an independent factor but as a factor serving either to re-enforce or to counterbalance shorter-run cyclical determinants of investment and employment. Early in the present century Pohle found in population growth, despite its not highly variable character, a periodically disequilibrating factor.[24] Recently Lösch has sought to show that production and business activity have co-varied closely with fluctuations in the annual rate of population growth,—fluctuations largely traceable in turn to the immediate effects of great wars. For fluctuations in the annual rate of increase give rise to fluctuations in the supply of labor and in the rate of growth of *reliable* markets for old and tested types of goods, in particular for buildings and for machinery to be used in conjunction with the new labor supply. The resulting business optimism, coupled with the increased availability of labor, at times may serve also to encourage innovators and intensify their activity. When, on the contrary, the absolute and relative amount of natural increase falls below the previously prevailing level and therefore below the level pre-supposed by business, a crisis develops, particularly in the capital goods industry, a large part of which in the past has been engaged in making provision for new increments of population and labor.[25]

When population growth began to taper off, business cycle theorists, who found the main source of economic fluctuation in variations in the rate of investment or in the production of fixed capital, predicted that business conditions would become more stable as population leveled off, inasmuch as the highly fluctuating capital-producing industries would decline in relative importance and therefore in capacity to dominate the economic situation.[26] With depopulation in the offing, however, other writers now predict that a decline in numbers may tend to augment the relative amount of unemployment, either because the modern want pattern tends to become less favorable to investment as numbers decline, or because the anticipated return on investment is too low, in consequence of the decline in population, to induce sufficient investment to assure full employment.

According to the Keynesian theory of investment and employment—the most full-bodied of contemporary investment theories—a decline in population will depress the rate of investment and reduce the level of employment.[27] For at any given time the fullness of employment and the level of income are governed by the desire to save and the rate of investment. If, given the current level of thrift and the current rate of interest, entrepreneurs are unwilling, in light of the prospective earnings of capital, to invest at the same rate as the population saves (i.e., does not spend upon current consumption), given the level of income associated with full employment, income and employment must fall to that level at which the rate of investment equals the rate of saving; for the rate of saving and the rate of investment must of necessity be equal. If, however, entrepreneurs stand ready to invest whatever portion of the communal income is saved at the level of full employment, full employment equilibrium will prevail. But it cannot prevail for long, in the absence of appropriate adjustments in the interest rate, the thriftiness of the community, and the technique of production; for capital accumulates, the prospective earnings of capital fall, and (assuming no adjustments) employment and income fall to a level at which investment and saving are equal. Long-period full employment equilibrium can prevail, other conditions remaining constant, only on condition that net saving is zero.

If, assuming that long-period full employment equilibrium has prevailed, population declines and, in consequence, the prospective earnings of capital fall, disinvestment sets in and, through the operation of the multiplier, produces unemployment in both the capital goods and the consumption goods industries and a fall in the level of per capita income. (Presumably, disemployment of this sort will always outstrip in rate the decline in the number of employables.) It follows, on the Keynesian premises, therefore, that given a declining population, employment and per capita income can remain at the theoretically maximum level only on one or both of two conditions: (a) that the rate of interest be kept low enough to induce entrepreneurs to effect great changes in the technique of production, and consumers to consume much larger relative quantities of goods involving a larger relative amount of capital; (b) that institutions and the distribution of income be altered in ways that strengthen the propensity to consume and reduce the portion of income that is saved. Otherwise investment and saving will be equal only at a level of employment and income far below the theoretically attainable maximum. Inasmuch as most of the Keynesians, in contrast with other interest theorists,[28] consider it improbable that a sufficient fall in the interest rate can or will take place, they must place major emphasis upon condition (b).[29]

The difficulties involved in preserving something like a full-employment equilibrium between investment and saving in a declining population are enhanced by conditions peculiar to the present-day as contrasted with the century-ago want pattern. On the one hand, certain conditions are more conducive to thrift. The propensity to consume is less pronounced in small than in large families,[30] and in practice this propensity can be varied appreciably, inasmuch as a large proportion of the commodities consumed today are more or less durable and therefore utilizable for longer or shorter periods of time at the discretion of the consumer. The propensity to consume is checked likewise by the fact that the primary desideratum of the representative person today is economic security, and by the belief that, were full employment attained, it would not long continue. On the other hand, certain conditions are unfavorable to the expansion of investment. Since little if any increase is to be expected in the demand for simple and basic commodities requiring little entrepreneurial ingenuity for their production and distribution, a hitherto ever-present stimulus to investment will have disappeared. Instead, many of the goods and services, the demand for which as a group is certain to prove quite expansible, do not appear very susceptible of production by individual entrepreneurs for sale to individual consumers, or are likely, in so far as the production and distribution of any one member of the group is concerned, to be heavily loaded with risk and uncertainty.[31]

Whether or not the Keynesian analysis is accepted, it is evident that adjustments of the sort thereby indicated as necessary will have to be made as the crude rate of population growth approaches and falls below zero. In the 1920's business and construction capital expenditures helped to initiate and sustain the level of business activity and consumption in the United States. In the post-1928 era the decline in the rate of population growth apparently contributed to the restriction of capital expansion.[32] In the immediate future monetary savings are likely to approximate $11–13 billion in contrast to estimated capital requirements of $8–9 billion.[33] Whence it is evident that if the level of employment and income in the United States is to be elevated appreciably, the conditions on which money is lent must be sufficiently relaxed to permit an appreciable increase in the rate of investment—an increase that should prove easy of attainment, given the continued drift of population from capital- and utility-lacking rural areas to capital- and utility-requiring urban and suburban developments, and the present backlog of technological change. When population shall have begun to decline (probably shortly after 1950 in the United States) capital requirements, on the basis of the premises underlying the above estimates, will fall far short of $8–9 billion.

It is evident, regardless of what may be the specific theory of investment to which one subscribes, that as population passes from a positive through a zero into declining state of growth, full employment and maximum per capita income (exclusive of voluntary leisure which will increase) will prove attainable only in proportion as the economy is progressively adapted to the following structural changes which are certain to accompany a decline in population: (1) a diminution in the relative importance of those capital and durable goods industries, a large part of whose function in the past has been to provide for new increments of population; (2) an increase in the relative importance of those capital and durable goods industries suited to supply goods and services falling within the higher comfort and luxury categories; (3) a diminution in the relative importance of industries, such as agriculture, engaged in the production of consumer goods marked by a nonexpansivity of demand; (4) a very marked increase in the relative production of consumers' goods and services other than those falling in the preceding category. Moreover, since it is unlikely that the economy will be voluntarily adapted to changes (2) and (4), the state will have to adopt tax and fiscal policies suited to redistribute income, and (assuming private collective investors fail in this regard) steadily expand its investment in instruments suited to produce goods and services collective in nature (e.g., recreational centers), new in type and/or risky in character. Given these policies and a dissolution of union- and industrial-monopoly barriers to the mobility of capital and labor, the decline in numbers, assuming it is stable, should not augment unemployment. If the decline is at an increasing rate (see Table III), per capita income will be greatly depressed even though employment becomes full.

IX

Whatever be the economic benefits accruing to man in consequence of a diminution in occupational and sub-regional fertility differentials, and of an improvement in the population: resource ratio (see secs. I–V above), it is certain, as H. D. Henderson has observed, that "the declining trend of population will prove the central economic and social issue of the next generation."[34] The "declining trend" will do more than precipitate discussion: it will re-enforce in a two-fold manner the collectivistic tendencies in modern economies. For, as we have shown elsewhere,[35] short of an extreme redistribution of income, it is highly improbable that any occidental capitalistic population will or can replace itself. And, as we have indicated in the latter part of this paper, it is highly improbable that a free enterprise economy, however successful in a demographically expanding world, will prove at all equal to the employment problems precipitated by a continuous decline in numbers. Perhaps the redistribution of income and the collective provision of security prerequisite to the re-establishment of fertility on a replacement level will prevent the unemployment-causing oversaving feared by the Keynesians and enable a highly circumscribed private enterprise economy to function at a fairly full level of employment under conditions of approximate stationarity of population.

REFERENCES

1. The writer has treated relationship of "output" and "income" to "welfare" in *France Faces Depopulation* (Duke University Press), Chap. XI, Sec. II.

2. For example, the longer run optimum will not have been attained until investment in education is carried to the point where the marginal product of education, given the capital supply of the community, is equivalent to the marginal product of capital invested in other employments. Although, given present conditions of social cost accounting, investment in education beyond the point indicated may be deemed advisable, the above proposition is valid without qualification if communal and private cost accounts are extended and consolidated to include, in economic form, sufficient allowances for all types of investment justified on so-called "non-economic" grounds.

3. "Disguised unemployment" exists, Mrs. Robinson states (*Essays In The Theory of Employment*, pp. 82 ff.), whenever it remains possible for a worker to transfer part of his time from the occupation in which he is engaged to another occupation in which the productivity of his time is higher. In the writer's opinion the concept of *disguised unemployment* should be geared to *time*, inasmuch as the passage of given time periods enables new net-employment-increasing shifts of labor. The concept is equally applicable to the other factors of production, as has been indicated.

4. For example: assume a community to consist of four occupational groups and postulate that each group recruits itself solely through natural increase. If, between time periods I and II, each group increases or decreases as in Table A, and if in period II the optimum balance among occupations remains as in period I, 300 workers must be transferred from

occupational groups C and D to A and B. Were the rates of increase by occupation identical, no transfer would be necessary.

TABLE A

Time Period	Number in Each Occupational Group in Each Time Period				
	A	B	C	D	All
I	1,000	1,000	1,000	1,000	4,000
II	800	900	1,100	1,200	4,000
Difference	—200	—100	+100	+200	0

5. When competition is imperfect, employment is less fully extended in industries marked by conditions of imperfect competition than it would be, were competition perfect. Moreover, in so far as the labor supply of imperfectly competitive industries is drawn from trade union groups able to set wages above the "competitive" level, trade union policy further reduces the volume of employment offered by imperfectly competitive industries.

6. E.g., see P. E. Davidson and H. D. Anderson, *Occupational Mobility In An American Community*, especially pp. 170, 172–73, 186, 188; also L. Hogben, ed., *Political Arithmetic*.

7. For example, if, in a region where because of the tastes and income distribution little use was being made of land well suited to cotton production, tastes and income distribution were suddenly to become favorable to cotton consumption, real income per person would rise, provided the assumed change were not completely counterbalanced by a fall in the demand for some other resource of comparable size and quality within the region. A change in tastes (or income distribution) such as we have postulated would probably have more significance for income over a time period than for income at the moment, provided that the change in tastes involved a shift to the use of resources more or less depletable or more or less subject to rising costs as a result of partial depletion.

It should be noted that tastes and techniques are not wholly independent of each other or of the distribution of actual and potential resources throughout a region. Tastes, in part determined by technique, adapt themselves more or less to a region's resource pattern. Improvers of technique concentrate upon two things: (a) how to exploit the type of resources available; (b) how to overcome relative factor scarcity occasioned by regional resource and taste patterns.

8. For a summary of this thesis see P. A. Sorokin, *Contemporary Sociological Theories*, Chap. VII, especially pp. 364, 388–91, 397–98, 403.

9. Presumably, if maximum economic use is made of the given quantity of inventive capacity, it will be employed to counterbalance the scarcity of those factors relatively least abundant and most expensive. Accordingly, since the relative scarcity of non-human factors is influenced in part by the size of the population, the particular uses to which inventive capacity may be put most economically will depend in part upon the size of the population. (For a discussion of the determinants and effects of inventiveness see R. K. Merton, *Scientific Monthly*, XLIV, pp. 165–70; Spengler, *Southern Economic Journal* [July, 1936], pp. 20–21.) While some would say that the economic exploitation of a given quantity of inventiveness will be greater in a growing than in a non-growing population, it seems to the writer that invention-exploiting entrepreneurial ability is as independent of population growth as is inventiveness.

10. The average per unit cost of producing 25,000 units under the conditions assumed will range between 84 and 94 cents, according as the extra 5,000 units are produced by plants employing technique I, II, or III. The minimum price necessary to call forth the extra 5,000 units supply is $1.00. If, however, the supply being taken were many times 20,-000, the production of an additional quantity less than 20,000 would occasion no change in technique and only a very slight increase in marginal cost and price. For example: if 500 plants utilizing technique III were supplying 10,000,000 units at a cost and price of 80 cents per unit, and demand were to increase to 10,012,000 units at 80 cents, price would rise slightly above 80 cents, and each of the 500 plants would produce slightly less than 24

additional units at a marginal cost slightly in excess of 80 cents. In sum, the closer the number of producing units approximates the number necessary to insure perfect competition, the less significant becomes the problem under discussion.

11. Much of the treatment of optimum size in producing units is rendered inaccurate by the failure of economists to recognize the problem of *fit* and the need to include every necessary type of producing unit, whether governmental or private. The problems of intra-plant and inter-plant coordination are closely related, but not necessarily identical. Thus if one were to conclude from an analysis of the determinants of intra-plant coordination that a smaller scale of operation might be preferable, one might ignore the fact that the social costs of coordinating a larger number of smaller producing units might more than counter-balance the seeming economies of smaller scale operating units. These inter-plant co-ordinating costs would manifest themselves in the form of greater governmental or trade association or similar costs. It is therefore necessary to distinguish intra- and inter-plant coordinating costs, determine the functional relation between them, and correct the intra-plant solution accordingly; or to reduce all inter-plant coordinating costs to intra-plant form and then ascertain under what conditions per unit costs will be at a minimum for each type of activity necessary to the creation and distribution of goods and services.

12. The rate of accumulation of capital, as distinguished from "natural" resources, is checked, other things equal, by natural increase. See H. Bowen, *Social Forces*, XV (1937), pp. 346–50.

13. For a treatment of the time factor in economic and sociological analysis, see the writer's article in the *International Journal of Ethics* (April, 1934), pp. 319–26. On the "economics of exhaustible resources" see H. Hotelling, *Journal of Political Economy*, XXXIX (1931), pp. 137–75.

14. Concerning measures of "overpopulation" see H. Dalton, *Economica*, VIII (1928), pp. 28–50. It is not our intention here to discuss the theory of the *optimum* population, points concerning which are discussed in our *France Faces Depopulation*, Chap. XI.

15. For statements of the argument that some protection may increase population capacity of a given region at a given income level see J. B. Brigden *et al.*, *The Australian Tariff*, especially p. 84; D. B. Copland, *Economic Record Supplement* (March, 1935), XI, pp. 33–34. For criticism see G. Haberler, *The Theory of International Trade*, pp. 277, 286–89.

16. See A. J. Lotka, *Journal of American Statistical Association*, XX (1925), pp. 329 ff. and references; R. R. Kuczynski, *Fertility and Reproduction*; B. Karpinos, *Human Biology*, VII (1935), pp. 514–38.

17. E. Charles, Royal Economic Society *Memorandum No. 55* (December, 1935), pp. 2–19. We shall employ the subscripts 1 and 2 to designate estimates according to assumption 1 and 2.

18. D, d, E, and e are assumed to be functions of all pertinent prices, but are not so described in the text inasmuch as such description would unduly complicate the discussion.

19. It is not our thesis that, given some particular desire scale for leisure, it is impossible to employ E fully when $\dfrac{E}{P}$ is high; but rather that it is more difficult to secure full employment of E when the value of $\dfrac{E}{P}$ is high than when it is low. In theory, a full employment distribution of E among employments can be obtained whatever be the value of $\dfrac{E}{P}$.

20. The effect of any given change in age composition upon per worker and per capita productivity depends, other things equal, upon the occupational composition of the population. In some occupations (e.g., tap dancers, boxers) maximum productivity is reached at an early age and thereafter declines rapidly; in other occupations (e.g., carpenters, mechanics) maximum productivity is reached at a later age and maintained for many years.

21. Other reasons than those indicated may be mentioned but cannot be treated in the space available. E.g.: the elasticity of demand may be altered by demographic changes; the complex of monetary price levels may be influenced by demographic change; disparities between actual and appropriate levels of remuneration of productive factors may develop in consequences of demographic change. Moreover, assuming changes in tastes and

technology, the relative amount of factor transfer prerequisite to full employment tends to be greater in a declining than in a growing population. On some of these points see the writer's discussion in *Harvard Business Review*, XII (1934), pp. 204–21, and in references cited in notes 1 and 9 above.

22. For a treatment of certain possible complications see M. Mitnitzky, *Social Research*, I (1934), pp. 198–218.

23. See R. Frisch, *Journal of Political Economy*, XXXIX (1931), pp. 646–54, and ensuing controversy with I. M. Clark, *ibid.*, XXIX–XL; J. M. Clark, *Strategic Factors in Business Cycles;* G. Haberler, *Prosperity and Depression;* S. Kuznets, in *Economic Essays in Honor of Wesley Clair Mitchell*, pp. 209 ff.; W. Röpke, *Journal of Political Economy*, XLIV (1936), pp. 318–38; J. Tinbergen, *Economica*, n.s., V (1938), pp. 164–76; also A. H. Hansen, *Business Cycle Theory*.

24. See L. Pohle, *Bevölkerungsbewegung, Kapitalbildung und periodische Wirtschaftskrisen*.

25. *Bevölkerungswellen und Wechsellagen; Schmollers Jahrbuch*, LX, Heft 6, 1936, pp. 37–45, LXI, Heft 4, 1937, pp. 71–76; *Quarterly Journal of Economics*, LI (1937), pp. 649–62. Although Dr. Lösch does not deal specifically with the problem of a declining population, his analysis seems to imply that were the rate of population growth stable, or zero, business fluctuation would be less pronounced; and that were numbers to decline, the capital goods industries would tend to be more depressed through time than when numbers are growing.

26. G. Cassel, *Theory of Social Economy*, pp. 646–47; A. H. Hansen, *Journal of Farm Economics*, XIV (1932), p. 66; *American Economic Review Supplement*, XXI (1931), pp. 200–201; also J. M. Clark, *Strategic Factors . . .* , p. 225.

27. See J. M. Keynes, *General Theory of Employment, Interest, and Money;* also article in *Eugenics Review*, XXIX (1937), pp. 13–17; Joan Robinson, *Essays In The Theory Of Employment*, and *Introduction To The Theory Of Employment;* also J. R. Hicks, *Economic Journal*, XLVI (1936), pp. 238–53, and R. F. Harrod, *The Trade Cycle*.

28. See Spengler, *Southern Economic Journal*, III, pp. 7 ff.; also F. Knight, *Journal of Poltical Economy*, XLIV, pp. 433 ff., 612 ff.

29. Needless to say, problems associated with government and other debt burdens will be aggravated by a decline in numbers unless appropriate counter-remedies are taken.

30. Each child increases by 10–20 per cent the non-deferrable expenses of a family. Therefore, other things equal, the smaller the family, the less the pressure of non-deferrable expenses. It is quite possible, however, that in the long run the spread of the small family system will not be accompanied by a decline in the propensity to consume. For as the pattern of living changes, and the absolute amount of non-deferrable expenses per person increases, and other conditions cease to remain equal, the propensity to save declines.

31. See W. B. Reddaway, *Economic Journal*, XLVII (1937), pp. 297–307; also article by writer, *Southern Economic Journal*, III (1936), pp. 10–13, and relevant references there cited.

32. See testimony of A. H. Hansen, in *Hearings On Unemployment And Relief*, pursuant to S. Res. 36, seventy-fifth Congress, third session, 1938, II, pp. 960–65.

33. G. Colm and F. Lehmann, *Economic Consequences of Recent American Tax Policy, Social Research Supplement*, I (1938), pp. 10–23.

34. *Economic Journal*, XLVII (1937), p. 87.

35. *France Faces Depopulation*, Chap. XI.

ECONOMIC PROGRESS AND DECLINING POPULATION GROWTH*

By Alvin H. Hansen

The main papers and the round tables in this year's program, like those of a year ago, concern a single, though broadly inclusive, subject. A year ago we considered the various factors which influence *fluctuations* in the rate of investment, income and employment. In selecting the topic for this year we have turned away in large measure from the ever-present and all-absorbing problem of cyclical fluctuations and have set ourselves the task of probing the problems of structural change in our economy, involving among other things also how these structural changes in various countries have affected the cycle itself. In the main sessions and in the round-table discussions various aspects of "The Changing American Economy" are considered—changes in the structure and functioning of our economic institutions. The topic is, however, so vast that even in a meeting as large as ours it is quite impossible to include all aspects pertinent to the subject; and doubtless many members will feel that important segments of the problem have been overlooked by our program committee.

One may ask: "Is there any special reason why in the year 1938 we should devote our attention as economists to the general subject "The Changing Character of the American Economy"? Throughout the modern era, ceaseless change has been the law of economic life. Every period is in some sense a period of transition. The swift stream of events in the last quarter century offers, however, overwhelming testimony in support of the thesis that the economic order of the western world is undergoing in this generation a structural change no less basic and profound in character than that transformation of economic life and institutions which we are wont to designate loosely by the phrase "the Industrial Revolution." We are passing, so to speak, over a divide which separates the great era of growth and expansion of the nineteenth century from an era which no man, unwilling to embark on pure conjecture, can as yet characterize with clarity or precision. We are moving swiftly out of the order in which those of our generation were brought up, into no one knows what.

Overwhelmingly significant, but as yet all too little considered by economists, is the profound change which we are currently undergoing in the

* Reprinted from *The American Economic Review*, 29 (March 1939), pp. 1–15, by permission of the author and publisher. (Copyright 1939 by the American Economic Association.) Presidential address delivered at the Fifty-first Annual Meeting of the American Economic Association, Detroit, Michigan, December 28, 1938.

rate of population growth. In the decade of the nineteen-twenties the population of the United States increased by 16,000,000—an absolute growth equal to that of the pre-war decade and in excess of any other decade in our history. In the current decade we are adding only half this number to our population, and the best forecasts indicate a decline to a third in the decade which we are about to enter.

Inadequate as the data are, it appears that the prodigious growth of population in the nineteenth century was something unique in history. Gathering momentum with the progress of modern science and transportation, the absolute growth in western Europe mounted decade by decade until the great World War; and in the United States it reached the highest level, as I have just noted, in the post-war decade. The upward surge began with relatively small accretions which rapidly swelled into a flood. But the advancing tide has come to a sudden halt and the accretions are dwindling toward zero.

Thus, with the prospect of actual contraction confronting us, already we are in the midst of a drastic decline in the rate of population growth. Whatever the future decades may bring, this present fact is already upon us; and it behooves us as economists to take cognizance of the significance of this revolutionary change in our economic life.

Schooled in the traditions of the Malthusian theory, economists, thinking in terms of static economics, have typically placed an optimistic interpretation upon the cessation of population growth. This indeed is also the interpretation suggested by the National Resources Committee which recently has issued an exhaustive statistical inquiry into current and prospective changes in population growth. In a fundamental sense this conclusion is, I think, thoroughly sound; for it can scarcely be questioned that a continued growth of population at the rate experienced in the nineteenth century would rapidly present insoluble problems. But it would be an unwarranted optimism to deny that there are implicit in the current drastic shift from rapid expansion to cessation of population growth, serious structural maladjustments which can be avoided or mitigated only if economic policies, appropriate to the changed situation, are applied. Indeed in this shift must be sought a basic cause of not a few of the developments in our changing economy.

Adam Smith regarded growth of population as at once a consequence and a cause of economic progress. Increasing division of labor would, he argued, bring about greater productivity, and this would furnish an enlarged revenue and stock, from which would flow an enlarged wages fund, an increased demand for labor, higher wages, and so economic conditions favorable for population growth. Now a growing population, by widening the market and by fostering inventiveness, in turn facilitated, he thought, division of labor and so the production of wealth. Thus he arrived at an optimistic conclusion. Population growth, he held, stimulated progress and this in turn stimulated further growth and expansion. In contrast, the pessimistic analyses of Malthus and Ricardo stressed the limitation of natural resources and the danger of an increasing population's pressing down the margin of cultivation to a point at which real income would be reduced to a bare subsistence level. In this static analysis the more dynamic approach of Adam Smith was quite forgotten. If we wish to get a clear insight into the economic consequences of the current decline in population growth, it is necessary to return to the suggestion of Adam Smith and to explore more fully the causal interconnection between economic progress, capital formation and population growth.

Economic analysis from the earliest development of our science has been concerned with the rôle played by economic progress. Various writers have included under this caption different things; but for our purpose we may say that the constituent elements of economic progress are (a) inventions, (b) the discovery and development of new territory and new resources, and (c) the growth of population. Each of these in turn, severally and in combination, has opened investment outlets and caused a rapid growth of capital formation.

The earlier economists were concerned chiefly with the effect of economic progress upon the volume of output, or in other words, upon the level of real income. For them economic progress affected the economic life mainly, if not exclusively, in terms of rising productivity and higher real income per capita.

Not until the very end of the nineteenth century did an extensive literature arise which stressed the rôle of economic progress as a leading, if not the main, factor causing fluctuations in employment, output, and income. Ricardo had indeed seen that there was some relation between economic progress and economic instability; but it was left for Wicksell, Spiethoff, Schumpeter, Cassel, and Robertson to elaborate the thesis that economic fluctuations are essentially a function of economic progress.

More recently the rôle of economic progress in the maintenance of full employment of the productive resources has come under consideration. The earlier economists assumed that the economic system tended automatically to produce full employment of resources. Some unemployment there was periodically, owing to the fluctuations incident to the business cycle; but in the upswing phase of the cyclical movement the economy was believed to function in a manner tending to bring about full recovery—maximum output and employment. This view was inspired by a century in which the forces of economic progress were powerful and strong, in which investment outlets were numerous and alluring. Spiethoff saw clearly that technological progress, the development of new industries, the discovery of new resources, the opening of new territory were the basic causes of the boom, which in turn was the progenitor of depression. Indeed he believed that once the main resources of the globe had been discovered and exploited, once the whole world had been brought under the sway of the machine technique, the leading disturbing factors which underlie the fluctuations of the cycle would have spent their force and an era of relative economic stability would ensue. But he did not raise the question whether such stability would be achieved at a full-employment and full-income level.

The business cycle was *par excellence* the problem of the nineteenth century. But the main problem of our times, and particularly in the United States, is the problem of full employment. Yet paradoxical as it may seem, the nineteenth century was little concerned with, and understood but dimly, the character of the business cycle. Indeed, so long as the problem of full employment was not pressing, it was not necessary to worry unduly about the temporary unemployment incident to the swings of the cycle. Not until the problem of full employment of our productive resources from the long-run, secular standpoint was upon us, were we compelled to give serious consideration to those factors and forces in our economy which tend to make business recoveries weak and anaemic and which tend to prolong and deepen the course of depressions. This is the essence of secular stagnation—sick recoveries which die in their infancy and depressions which feed on themselves and leave a hard and seemingly immovable core of unemployment.

In every great crisis the struggle of contending groups maneuvering for an advantageous position amidst rapid change whips up the froth and fury of political and social controversy. Always there is present the temptation to explain the course of events in terms of the more superficial phenomena which are frequently manifestations rather than causes of change. It is the peculiar function of the economist however to look deeper into the underlying economic realities and to discover in these, if possible, the causes of the most obstinate problem of our time—the problem of under-employment. Fundamental to an understanding of this problem are the changes in the "external" forces, if I may so describe them, which underlie economic progress—changes in the character of technological innovations, in the availability of new territory, and in the growth of population.

The expanding economy of the last century called forth a prodigious growth of capital formation. So much was this the case, that this era in history has by common consent been called the capitalistic period. No one disputes the thesis that without this vast accumulation of capital we should never have witnessed the great rise in the standard of living achieved since the beginning of the Industrial Revolution. But it is not the effect of capital formation upon real income to which I wish especially to direct attention. What I wish to stress in this paper is rather the rôle played by the process of capital formation in securing at each point in this ascending income scale fairly full employment of the productive resources and therefore the maximum income possible under the then prevailing level of technological development. For it is an indisputable fact that the prevailing economic system has never been able to reach reasonably full employment or the attainment of its currently realizable real income without making large investment expenditures. The basis for this imperious economic necessity has been thoroughly explored in the last half century in the great literature beginning with Tougan-Baranowsky and Wicksell on saving and investment. I shall not attempt any summary statement of this analysis. Nor is this necessary; for I take it that it is accepted by all schools of current economic thought that full employment and the maximum currently attainable income level cannot be reached in the modern free enterprise economy without a volume of investment expenditures adequate to fill the gap between consumption expenditures and that level of income which could be achieved were all the factors employed. In this somewhat truistic statement I hope I have succeeded in escaping a hornets' nest of economic controversy.

Thus we may postulate a consensus on the thesis that in the absence of a positive program designed to stimulate consumption, full employment of the productive resources is essentially a function of the vigor of investment activity. Less agreement can be claimed for the rôle played by the rate of interest on the volume of investment. Yet few there are who believe that in a period of investment stagnation an abundance of loanable funds at low rates of interest is alone adequate to produce a vigorous flow of real investment. I am increasingly impressed with the analysis made by Wicksell who stressed the prospective rate of profit on new investment as the active, dominant, and controlling factor, and who viewed the rate of interest as a passive factor, lagging behind the profit rate. This view is moreover in accord with competent business judgment.[1] It is true that it is necessary to look beyond the mere *cost* of interest charges to the indirect effect of the interest rate structure upon business expectations. Yet all in all, I venture to assert that the rôle of the rate of interest as a determinant of investment has occupied a place larger than it deserves in our thinking. If this be granted, we are forced to regard the factors which underlie economic progress as the dominant determinants of investment and employment.

A growth in real investment may take the form either of a deepening of capital or of a widening of capital, as Hawtrey has aptly put it. The deepening process means that more capital is used per unit of output, while the widening process means that capital formation grows *pari passu* with the increase in the output of final goods. If the ratio of real capital to real income remains constant, there is no deepening of capital; but if this ratio is constant and real income rises, then there is a widening of capital.

According to Douglas[2] the growth of real capital formation in England from 1875 to 1909 proceeded at an average rate of two per cent per annum; and the rate of growth of capital formation in the United States from 1890 to 1922 was four per cent per annum. The former is less than the probable rate of increase of output in England, while the latter is somewhat in excess of the annual rise of production in the United States. Thus, during the last fifty years or more, capital formation for each economy as a whole has apparently consisted mainly of a widening of capital. Surprising as it may seem, as far as we may judge from such data as are available, there has been little, if any, deepening of capital. The capital stock has increased approximately in proportion to real income. This is also the conclusion of Gustav Cassel;[3] while Keynes[4] thinks that real capital formation in England may have very slightly exceeded the rise in real income in the period from 1860 to the World War. If this be true, it follows that, in terms of the time element in production, which is the very essence of the capital concept, our system of production is little more capitalistic now than fifty or seventy-five years ago. It requires, in other words, a period of employment of our productive resources no longer than formerly to reproduce the total capital stock. The "waiting," so to speak, embodied in our capital accumulations is no greater today than half a century or more ago. Capital has indeed grown relative to labor. Thus the technical coefficient of production, with respect to capital, has increased. While this indicates a more intensive application of capital relative to the other factors, it does not necessarily imply any deepening of capital.

In important areas the capital stock has not increased significantly even in relation to population. This is notably true in the service industries. Moreover, in the field of housing real capital has little more than kept pace with population growth. In manufacturing as a whole it is certainly true that real capital formation has not only far outstripped population but has also risen more rapidly than physical product. The studies of Douglas for the United States and Australia show that real fixed capital invested in manufacturing increased more rapidly than physical output of manufactured goods. On the other hand, Carl Snyder's[5] data, which run in terms of value of invested capital and value of product, indicate that for important separate industries, such as textiles, iron and steel, and petroleum, capital has grown little or no faster than output since about 1890. With respect to the automobile industry, according to his findings, capital investment has risen no more rapidly than value of product, while in the electrical industries, invested capital increased at a slower rate than output after 1907. Considering the economy as a whole, including fields of economic activity other than manufacturing, there is no good evidence that the advance of technique has resulted in recent decades, certainly not in any significant measure, in any deepening of capital. Apparently, once the machine technique has been developed in any field, further mechanization is likely to result in an increase in output at least proportional to and often in excess of the net additions to real capital. Though the deepening process is all the while going on in certain areas, elsewhere capital-saving inventions are reducing the ratio of capital to output.

In order to get some insight into the effect of population growth upon capital formation, it is necessary to consider the rôle it plays in conjunction with other factors in the widening and deepening process. The widening of capital is a function of an increase in final output, which in turn is due partly to an increase in population and partly to an increase in per capita productivity, arising from causes other than a larger use of capital per unit of output. On the other hand, the deepening of capital results partly from cost-reducing changes in technique, partly (though this is probably a much less significant factor) from a reduction in the rate of interest, and partly from changes in the character of the output as a whole, with special reference to the amount of capital required to produce it.

Now the rate of population growth must necessarily play an important rôle in determining the character of the output; in other words, the composition of the flow of final goods. Thus a rapidly growing population will demand a much larger per capita volume of new residential building construction than will a stationary population. A stationary population with its larger proportion of old people may perhaps demand more personal services; and the composition of consumer demand will have an important influence on the quantity of capital required. The demand for housing calls for large capital outlays, while the demand for personal services can be met without making large investment expenditures. It is therefore not unlikely that a shift from a rapidly growing population to a stationary or declining one may so alter the composition of the final flow of consumption goods that the ratio of capital to output as a whole will tend to decline.

In the beginning stages of modern capitalism both the deepening and the widening processes of capital formation were developing side by side. But in its later stages the deepening process, taking the economy as a whole, rapidly diminished. And now with the rapid cessation of population growth, even the widening process may slow down. Moreover it is possible that capital-saving inventions may cause capital formation in many industries to lag behind the increase in output.

An interesting problem for statistical research would be to determine the proportion of investment in the nineteenth century which could be attributed (a) to population growth, (b) to the opening up of new territory and the discovery of new resources, and (c) to technical innovations. Such an analysis it has not been possible for me to make, and I shall venture only a few rough estimates together with some qualitative judgments. With respect to population growth some insight into the problem may perhaps be gained by considering first the rôle of population growth in the rise of aggregate real income. The various estimates agree that the annual rate of growth of physical output up to the World War was roughly three per cent in western Europe and nearly four per cent in the United States. Of this average annual increase something less than half of the three per cent increase in western Europe can be attributed to population growth, while something more than half of the annual increase in the United States can be assigned to the increase in the labor supply. Thus it appears that per capita output has increased both in western Europe and in the United States at approximately one and one-half per cent per annum. This increase can be attributed mainly to changes in technique and to the exploitation of new natural resources.

We have already noted that capital formation has progressed at about the same rate as the rise in aggregate output. Thus, as a first approximation, we may say that the growth of population in the last half of the nineteenth century was responsible for about forty per cent of the total volume of capital formation in western Europe and about sixty per cent of the capital formation in the United States. If this is even approximately correct, it will be seen what an important outlet for investment is being closed by reason of the current rapid decline in population growth.

Obviously the growth of population affects capital formation most directly in the field of construction, especially residential building. From decade to decade the increase in the number of dwellings had maintained a close relation to the increase in population. In the decade of the twenties, however, the increase in houses ran about twenty-five per cent in excess of previous decennial increases in relation to population. According to Kuznets, during the seven prosperous years 1923 to 1929, a quarter of the net capital formation was residential building. But the effect of population growth on capital formation is, of course, felt in other spheres as well. This is notably true of all the various municipal and public utilities, and also of the manufacture of essential consumers' goods.

An interesting excursus would lead us into a consideration of the problem how far an increase in population itself contributed to a more efficient technique and so was in part responsible for the rise in per capita real income. According to the older Malthusian view, the growth of population would act counter to the effect of technological progress upon per capita productivity, and would thus slow down the rise in per capita real income. If this were correct, population growth considered by itself alone would tend to check the rise in per capita consumption, and this in turn, *via* the so-called *Relation,* would affect the volume of capital formation. According to the optimum population theory, however, it may not infrequently be the case, and indeed probably was during the greater part of the nineteenth century, that population growth itself facilitated mass production methods and accelerated the progress of technique. If this be correct, population growth was itself responsible for a part of the rise in per capita real income, and this, *via* the influence of a rising consumption upon investment, stimulated capital formation. Thus it is quite possible that population growth may have acted both directly and indirectly to stimulate the volume of capital formation.

It is not possible, I think, to make even an approximate estimate of the proportion of the new capital created in the nineteenth century which was a direct consequence of the opening up of new territory. The development of new countries was indeed so closely intertwined with the growth of population that it would be difficult to avoid double counting. What proportion of new capital formation in the United States went each year into the western frontier we do not know, but it must have been very considerable. Apparently about one-fourth of the total capital accumulations of England were invested abroad by 1914, and one-seventh of those of France.

These figures, while only suggestive, point unmistakably to the conclusion that the opening of new territory and the growth of population were together responsible for a very large fraction—possibly somewhere near one-half—of the total volume of new capital formation in the nineteenth century. These outlets for new investment are rapidly being closed. The report on *Limits of Land Settlement* by President Isaiah Bowman and others may be regarded as conclusive in its findings that there are no important areas left for exploitation and settlement. So far as population is concerned, that of western Europe has already virtually reached a standstill; but that in eastern Europe, notably in Russia, is still growing, and so also is that in the Orient. And much of this area will probably experience a considerable industrialization. But it is not yet clear how far the mature industrial countries will participate in this development through capital export. Russia still has a long way to go before she becomes completely industrialized; but foreign capital is not likely to play any significant rôle in this process. India will offer some opportunity for British investment, but the total is likely to be small relative to the volume of British foreign investments in the nineteenth century. China and the Orient generally offer, in view of the present and prospective turmoil in that area, relatively meager investment opportunities. At all events, no one is likely to challenge the statement that foreign investment will in the next fifty years play an incomparably smaller rôle than was the case in the nineteenth century.

Thus the outlets for new investment are rapidly narrowing down to those created by the progress of technology. To be sure, the progress of technology itself played in the nineteenth century a decisive rôle in the opening of new territory and as a stimulus to population growth. But while technology can facilitate the opening of new territory, it cannot create a new world or make the old one bigger than it is. And while the advance of science, by reducing the death rate, was a major cause of the vast nineteenth-century increase in population, no important further gains in this direction can possibly offset the prevailing low birth rate. Thus the further progress of science can operate to open investment outlets only through its direct influence on the technique of production.

We are thus rapidly entering a world in which we must fall back upon a more rapid advance of technology than in the past if we are to find private investment opportunities adequate to maintain full employment. Should we accept the advice of those who would declare a moratorium on invention and technical progress, this one remaining avenue for private investment would also be closed. There can be no greater error in the analysis of the economic trends of our times than that which finds in the advance of technology, broadly conceived, a major cause of unemployment. It is true that we cannot discount the problem of technological unemployment, a problem which may be intensified by the apparently growing importance of capital-saving inventions. But, on the other side, we cannot afford to neglect that type of innovation which creates new industries and which thereby opens new outlets for real investment. The problem of our generation is, above all, the problem of inadequate private investment outlets. What we need is not a slowing down in the progress of science and technology, but rather an acceleration of that rate.

Of first-rate importance is the development of new industries. There is certainly no basis for the assumption that these are a thing of the past. But there is equally no basis for the assumption that we can take for granted the rapid emergence of new industries as rich in investment opportunities as the railroad, or more recently the automobile, together with all the related developments, including the construction of public roads, to which it gave rise. Nor is there any basis, either in history or in theory, for the assumption that the rise of new industries proceeds inevitably at a uniform pace. The growth of modern industry has not come in terms of millions of small increments of change giving rise to a smooth and even development. Characteristically it has come by gigantic leaps and bounds. Very often the change can best be described as discontinuous, lumpy, and jerky, as indeed D. H. Robertson has so vividly done. And when a revolutionary new industry like the railroad or the automobile, after having initiated in its youth a powerful upward surge of investment activity, reaches maturity and ceases to grow, as all industries finally must, the whole economy must experience a profound stagnation, unless indeed new developments take its place. It is not enough that a mature industry continues its activity at a high level on a horizontal plane. The fact that new railroad mileage continued to be built at about the same rate through the seventies, eighties and nineties was not sufficient. It is the *cessation of growth* which is disastrous. It is in connection with the growth, maturity and decline of great industries that the principle of acceleration operates with peculiar force. And when giant new industries have spent their force, it *may* take a long time before something else of equal magnitude emerges. In fact nothing has emerged in the decade in which we are now living. This basic fact, together with the virtual cessation of public investment by state and local governmental bodies, as indicated by a decline of $2,000,000,000 in their net public debt since 1932, explains in large measure the necessary rise in federal expenditures.[6]

Spiethoff was quite right when he argued that a vigorous recovery is not just spontaneously born from the womb of the preceding depression. Some small recovery must indeed arise sooner or later merely because of the growing need for capital replacement. But a full-fledged recovery calls for something more than the mere expenditure of depreciation allowances. It requires a large outlay on new investment, and this awaits the development of great new industries and new techniques. But such new developments are not currently available in adequate volume. It is my growing conviction that the combined effect of the decline in population growth, together with the failure of any really important innovations of a magnitude sufficient to absorb large capital outlays, weighs very heavily as an explanation for the failure of the recent recovery to reach full employment. Other factors are certainly significant and important, particularly our failure to control the cost structure and to grapple effectively with specific situations, such as those presented by the railroads and by building construction.

We have noted that the approaching cessation of population growth and the disappearance of new territory for settlement and exploitation may cut off a half or more of the investment outlets which we were wont to make in the past. We are thus compelled to fall back upon that measure of capital formation which is associated with the advance of technique and the rise in per capita output. But current institutional developments are restricting even this outlet. The growing power of trade unions and trade associations, the development of monopolistic competition, of rivalry for the market through expensive persuasion and advertising, instead of through price competition, are factors which have rightly of late commanded much attention among economists. There is, moreover, the tendency to block the advance of technical progress by the shelving of patents.

Under vigorous price competition, new cost-reducing techniques were compulsorily introduced even though the scrapping of obsolete but undepreciated machinery entailed a capital loss. But under the monopoly principle of obsolescence new machines will not be introduced until the undepreciated value of the old machine will at least be covered by the economies of the new technique. Thus progress is slowed down, and outlets for new capital formation, available under a more ruthless competitive society, are cut off. Capital losses which could not be avoided under rigorous price competition can be and are avoided under an economic system more closely integrated by intercorporate association and imperfect competition. If we are to save the one remaining outlet for private capital formation, deliberate action of a far bolder character than hitherto envisaged must be undertaken in order to make the price system and free enterprise sufficiently responsive to permit at least that measure of capital formation to which the rate of technological progress had accustomed us in the past.

Yet even though this much were achieved, it is necessary to recognize that such a rate of progress would not provide sufficient investment outlets to give us full employment of our resources. With a stationary population we could maintain as rapid a rise in per capita real income as that experienced in the past, by making annually only half the volume of new investment to which we have been accustomed. A volume of investment adequate to provide full employment could give us an annual percentage increase in per capita output greatly in excess of any hitherto attained.

Various measures have been offered to maintain full employment in the absence of an adequate rate of technological progress and of the development of new industries. Consumption may be strengthened by the relief from taxes which drain off a stream of income which otherwise would flow into consumption channels. Public investment may usefully be made in human and natural resources and in consumers' capital goods of a collective character designed to serve the physical, recreational and cultural needs of the community as a whole. But we cannot afford to be blind to the unmistakable fact that a solution along these lines raises serious problems of economic workability and political administration.

How far such a program, whether financed by taxation or by borrowing, can be carried out without adversely affecting the system of free enterprise is a problem with which economists, I predict, will have to wrestle in the future far more intensely than in the past. Can a rising public debt owned internally be serviced by a scheme of taxation which will not adversely affect the marginal return on new investment or the marginal cost of borrowing? Can any tax system, designed to increase the propensity to consume by means of a drastic change in income distribution, be devised which will not progressively encroach on private investment?[7]

As so often in economic life, we are confronted by a dilemma. Continued unemployment on a vast scale, resulting from inadequate private investment outlets, could be expected sooner or later to lead straight into an all-round regimented economy. But so also, by an indirect route and a slower process, might a greatly extended program of public expenditures. And from the standpoint of economic workability the question needs to be raised how far such a program can be carried out in a democratic society without raising the cost structure to a level which prevents full employment. Thus a challenge is presented to all those countries which have not as yet submitted to the yoke of political dictatorship. In one of our round tables we are discussing divergencies in the success of governmental spending in democratic countries and in totalitarian states. Totalitarian states have the great advantage that they can rigorously check the advance of costs, including wage rates, while engaging in an expansionist program of public investment. Democratic countries cannot in modern times escape from the influence exerted by organized groups upon the operation of the price system. From the standpoint of the workability of the system of free enterprise, there emerges the problem of sovereignty in democratic countries confronted in their internal economies with powerful groups—entrepreneurial and wage-earning—which have robbed the price system of that impersonal and non-political character idealized in the doctrine of laissez-faire. It remains still to be seen whether political democracy can in the end survive the disappearance of the automatic price system.

Thus we are confronted with various alternatives. On the one side, there is the proposal to risk a negative governmental policy in the expectation that the recuperative forces to which we have long been accustomed will, in the absence of political interference, re-assert themselves. On the other side, there is the proposal to go forward under full steam with unrestrained governmental expansion until full employment has been reached. Those who have no doubts whatever about the correctness of their economic analyses will not hesitate to make a bold choice of policy. But others, impressed with the stubborn economic realities of a rapidly changing world, on the one side, and the frailties of human nature in its power to make the appropriate adaptation to change, on the other, will not be so sure, and may prefer to take a course that risks neither a negative policy nor a breakdown of collective management.

The objection will almost certainly be raised that the argument which I have directed against continued governmental spending to the point of full employment, could equally well be directed against private investment, once the upper danger zone has been reached. I should doubt the validity of this criticism. If the government continues to pour out funds at a lavish rate, wage-earners and employers alike are prone to take the easy course which leads to higher costs and higher prices. But if reliance could not be placed upon a stream of purchasing power external to business itself, we could expect, I think, a more vigorous resistance to uneconomic cost-raising demands. Public spending is the easiest of all recovery methods, and therein lies its danger. If it is carried too far, we neglect to attack those specific maladjustments without the removal of which we cannot attain a workable cost-price structure, and therefore we fail to achieve the otherwise available flow of private investment.

There are no easy answers to the problems that confront us. And because this is true, economists will not perform their function if they fail to illuminate the rapidly shifting course of economic development, and through such neglect unwittingly contribute to a dangerous lag in adjustments to change. Equally they will not perform their function if they fail to disclose the possible dangers which lurk in the wake of vastly enlarged governmental activities. Choices indeed must be made, and scientific analysis and painstaking research can aid by exploring the probable consequences of alternative choices. The problems which I have raised offer a challenge to our profession. The great transition, incident to a rapid decline in population growth and its impact upon capital formation and the workability of a system of free enterprise, calls for high scientific adventure along all the fronts represented by the social science disciplines.

REFERENCES

1. Cf. J. E. Meade and P. W. S. Andrews, "Summary of Replies to Questions on Effects of Interest Rates," Oxford Econ. Papers, no. 1; also J. Franklin Ebersole, "The Influence of Interest Rates upon Entrepreneurial Decisions in Business—A Case Study," Harvard Bus. Rev., vol. xvii, pp. 35–39. The indirect effect on valuation is perhaps overlooked.

2. Paul H. Douglas, The Theory of Wages, Macmillan, 1934, pp. 464–5.

3. Gustav Cassel, On Quantitative Thinking in Economics, Oxford, 1935, chapter 6.

4. J. M. Keynes, "Some Economic Consequences of a Declining Population," *Eugenics Review*, April, 1937.

5. Carl Snyder, "Capital Supply and National Well-Being," *Am. Econ. Rev.*, June, 1936.

6. *Debts and Recovery 1929 to 1937*, The Twentieth Century Fund, 1938, p. 230.

7. Joseph J. Spengler, "Population Movements, Employment, and Income," *Southern Econ. Jour.*, Oct., 1938.

POPULATION GROWTH AND THE RATE OF INVESTMENT*

By Melvin D. Brockie

I

Arguments concerning some phase or phases of the problems of overpopulation, underpopulation, optimum population, "race suicide," and the declining rate of population growth are to be found in some measure in almost all the literature of economics since at least the years of Adam Smith. Smith was interested in population increase and division of labor, the opening up of new markets, and the prospects for economic progress.[1] The literature on the subject continues down through Malthus,[2] Ricardo, Mill, Marx, Keynes, Myrdal, and Hansen. Most recently, two books[3] have been published which have alarmed a few educators and many laymen with the spectre of overpopulation and the impairment of our natural resources.

Among professional economists, the names of Keynes, Hansen, and Myrdal probably carry more authority. Keynes, of course, did not systematically develop a theory of stagnation, but he did succeed in arousing the further interest of Myrdal and Hansen regarding the population problem. It is with these last two gentlemen that our analysis begins. For Mr. Myrdal, new investment demand is very closely allied with population growth. He writes:

. . . the expansionist capitalistic system of private enterprise had as one of its prerequisites a progressive population. A declining population will increase investment risks all around and, even apart from that, will lessen the demand for new investment.[4]

Professor Hansen is the most articulate of all in the matter of population and investment. In his 1938 presidential address to the American Economic Association, he said:

. . . the constituent elements of economic progress are (a) inventions, (b) the discovery and development of new territory and new resources, and (c) the growth of population. Each of these in turn, severally and in combination, has opened investment outlets and caused a rapid growth of capital formation.[5]

Continuing, he observed that

. . . the approaching cessation of population growth and the disappearance of new territory for settlement and exploitation may cut off a half or more of the investment outlets which we were wont to make in the past.[6]

Or,

. . . as a first approximation we may say that the growth of population in the last half of the nineteenth century was responsible for . . . about sixty per cent of the capital formation in the United States.[7]

* Reprinted from *The Southern Economic Journal*, 17 (July 1950), pp. 1–15, by permission of the author and publisher. (Copyright 1950 by the Southern Economic Association.)

An earlier, and perhaps more familiar, dictum of Professor Hansen appeared in 1938; it reads:

A society which saves . . . can escape a progressive fall in income and employment only through the continuous development of new investment outlets, such as are created by technological progress, the rise of new industries, the discovery of new resources, the opening up of new territory, and the *growth of population.* [Italics mine.][8]

Replies and rebuttals to the stagnationist dicta were not long in coming. Professor Ellis disagreed with Professor Hansen, arguing that if a society

. . . can successfully cope with institutional obstacles, new investment outlets exist in adequate volume in known but unexploited techniques without the necessity of the various creations [in Professor Hansen's list].[9]

Dr. Ellis actually attacks the theory of created outlets (technological progress, new industries, new resources, and new territory) and asks whether ". . . we propose to cure unemployment by encouraging the birth rate."[10]

Professor B. M. Anderson replied that a more slowly growing population would affect investment only in the sense that ". . . any violent shift in the economic situation creates for a time the problem of adaptation."[11] The adaptation would be necessary, for example, to compensate for a larger old age segment of the population. The structure of demand for consumer goods would be altered. Proportionately more wheel chairs and proportionately fewer rattles would be demanded; relatively more radios and fewer cribs. Herein lies the nature of the adaptation which would be required.[12]

II

The concept of population as contracting, expanding, or stationary, as carried over into concepts of production and investment, tends to apply a bias or fit which may not be justified. The relative fluctuations in population data[13] should perhaps not be too literally correlated with alterations in the economic components which characterize our national level of well-being.[14] A correlation of recent trends of population growth and production would lead some analysts to the conclusion that stagnation of a permanent nature is with us and that the only solution is to find adequate "offsets" to counterbalance the diminishing importance of population growth as an outlet for savings.

However, even Marx would not agree that stagnation or maturity is permanent. Marx's theory of the falling rate of profit tells us, writes Klein, that

Capital accumulation implies a rising organic composition of capital and, hence, a falling rate of profit . . . It was the capital accumulation of the twenties [resulting from a good and persistent profit outlook in automobiles, housing, utilities, etc.] which led to the fall in the rate of profit and the consequent stagnation of the thirties. The theory does not say that the stagnation or maturity is permanent . . . However, the theory indicates specifically that . . . capital expansion will not continue indefinitely. Once a large stock of capital has been accumulated . . . the mature-economy doctrine should predict another stagnant period of a decade or more.[15]

This interpretation is at least more optimistic than some of the more popular current dogmas which are singularly depressive when thought is taken of events since 1940. Observers have of course been watching population trends and social progress for many decades, but at no time has the literature published by authorities like Dr. Hansen been more pessimistic than now.[16] It seems to stem in part from a fear that sometime in the "fifties" we will experience another secondary post-war depression which will be explainable in the stagnationist terminology of the thirties.

Even the idea of an optimum population has been shunted aside for the most part by all except a minority of our population theorists.[17] Professor J. J. Spengler still gives attention to the proposition in his trenchant writings on the issues of human numbers, but he is not followed by very many of the other economists in this matter.[18] Optimum population is implicit in the writings of men like Dr. Hansen who nonetheless devote most of their energies to an explanation of the mutual interdependence of territorial expansion, technological expansion, and expansion of the population. Professor Hansen does not always argue that population must continue to grow unless the economy is to encounter grave difficulties. He has postulated that ". . . it can scarcely be questioned that a continued growth of population at the rate experienced in the nineteenth century would rapidly present insoluble problems."[19] If both overpopulation and underpopulation are possible, what is the middle ground? Is it a stationary population, or an optimum population?[20]

H. D. Henderson, while noting that a declining population in absolute terms entails disadvantages which outweigh the advantages, tells us that

. . . a slowly growing or *stationary* [italics mine] population is, on balance, more favorable than a rapidly growing population to the economic welfare of society. From the economic standpoint,[21] therefore, we have reason to welcome the fall of the birth rate down to the point at which it is compatible with a stationary population.[22]

Somewhat opposed to this view is the attitude of Professor Spengler in 1938 when he thought it improbable that a free enterprise economy could solve the problems of a declining population unless perhaps redistribution of income, and fertility at a replacement level could provide an adequate offset.[23] This comment was made at a time when the population problem was foremost in the minds of those persons who were wrestling with the task of integrating Keynes' analysis into a societal structure which had recently revealed a striking tendency to stagnate, or at least to "run down" for a time. The decade since that time has provided us with the opportunity to scrutinize more carefully the implications of the "shortage of investment outlets" proposition.

By taking a somewhat more comprehensive view of the social milieu, Professor Spengler has recently concluded:

Given present technological prospects, together with the current world income and resource situation, a speedy cessation of world population growth appears to be essential to the gradual alleviation and removal of widespread poverty. Social and economic programs which fail to take this condition into account are almost certainly doomed to fail . . .[24]

Thus, for some theorists, a re-examination and re-appraisal of the population factor has led to modifications of past tenets. Moreover, these modifications are not always in the same direction inasmuch as Professor Hansen has moved away from a rather optimistic position as of 1932 to a decidedly anxious state of mind in the present.[25] In other words, the same set of socio-politico-economic factors has produced varying mental patterns among those scholars who have witnessed human "progress" since 1930, and, furthermore, the areas of disagreement are just as boundless today as they were then except for the rather singular fact that the protagonists to some extent have been re-shuffled.

III

Despite the fact that a pulsating population in terms of numbers is a theoretical possibility, let us examine more closely the evidence bearing on growth of population and its effect upon consumption[26] and investment in the short-run when the rate of growth is decreasing. A preliminary observation might be made to the effect that population growth would tend to stimulate production and investment if such growth increased the average and/or marginal propensity to consume. To one authority, thinking in over-all terms, can be attributed the remark that the evidence does not indicate any stimulating effect of population growth on production.[27] Furthermore, after pointing out that the evidence reveals a higher marginal propensity to consume among "old stock" population than the average propensity to consume of additional consuming units, Professor Fellner adds:

This surely contradicts the thesis that population growth, in general, tends to raise the marginal propensity to consume. This assumption is contradicted also by the circumstance that the consumption function for the aggregate population tends toward linearity with minor oscillations that seem to be unrelated to changes in population growth.[28]

It is worth remarking that past periods of population growth, while revealing a total increase in consumption expenditure, also show a marked increase in per capita consumption—in fact a large fraction of the total increase in consumption can be so explained.[29]

Kuznets' statistics reveal a negative relationship between the amount of investment and percentage growth of population,[30] but Professor Fellner's conclusion is that ". . . it is impossible to verify or refute statistically a hypothesis that would postulate a significant relationship between the two [population growth and investment],"[31] and that previous experience does not substantiate the causal nexus between the simultaneous decline in population growth and investment in the thirties.[32]

The most one of the early authors would concede on this relation of population growth, investment, and wealth is that growing populations facilitated the development of the means of transport and made mass production feasible.[33] He then admits to the impossibility of determining with any precision the effect of an increasing population on the progress of civilization and the accumulation of wealth. For him the most sweeping economies to be derived from increasing numbers had already been attained in industrialized Europe and the United States, and the concomitant increase in wealth and population before World War I did not preclude the possibility of a still faster increase in per capita wealth if only the population had not grown so rapidly.[34] His final statement reads:

> From the economic point of view, at all events, there seems no reason to bemoan the slowing down of the rate of growth of the population of the Western World which has alarmed some English bishops and French patriots in recent years.[35]

In much this manner the literature on economic maturity builds up each year and the residues and overtones of past decades still linger on.[36] Much of it is of course necessary in order to stimulate thinking on economic problems of this nature which so well characterize the degree of indeterminateness to be found in economic science even though we have the money measure!

IV

The older theory of investment postulated that *intensive* investment and *extensive* investment were incompatible in the sense that investment of savings in capital "widening" would take place at the expense of proposed capital "deepening" projects. Professor Hansen's group, wrestling with the spectre of stagnation, believe both forms of investment to be necessary for the absorption of the current level of savings.[37] Nonetheless, the "younger" Hansen was not so concerned with population growth as one of the three channels of investment open for the dissipation of savings. More precisely, he was not at all alarmed at the prospect of a stationary population. In 1932 he opined:

> . . . a stationary society will produce relatively more consumer goods and less producer goods than will a growing society . . . [and] if we may assume that a stationary population will not enjoy any more rapid discoveries of new products, it is reasonable to suppose that it will have reached sufficiently near the saturation point with respect to many material goods so that the demand for these commodities will have become relatively inelastic. The business man is likely to bemoan this as an evil, but this is only because he is accustomed to think of production purely in terms of material goods.[38]

Dr. Hansen offers as an alternative the production of personal services—the term personal services being used in its broadest sense to include all spiritual wants.[39] The stationary population, as he envisions it, will achieve a relatively higher standard of living, and will have the added advantage that the workers will be burdened by a smaller number of dependent children.[40] The increased tendency to save for old age via insurance, endowments, and pensions will be offset by the heavier burden of taxes and additional social responsibilities of the wealthy.[41] The conclusion is:

> On balance there is likely to be less saving per capita rather than more. But fortunately there will also be less need for saving[42] . . . it will not be necessary to provide houses and capital equipment for a growing population.[43]

Now this statement concerning the amount of per capita saving forthcoming in a state with a stationary population is especially significant inasmuch as Dr. Hansen has inspired others to write on the volume of saving to be expected in such a situation and the results have partially supported this earlier a priori formulation. After analyzing the 1871–1911 period in France, Mr. Goldenberg decided that France saved a smaller share of her national income than Great Britain or Germany. Nevertheless, a capital abundance still existed, and over one-half of this capital was forced to seek employment abroad.[44] Yet in 1940 Professor Hansen spoke of statistics which indicated that small families save more than large, and that the relatively higher standard of living which couples with few or no children would enjoy could not entirely offset that part of income which larger families would spend to maintain a more moderate standard of living for their extra children.[45]

Habits of consumption display such variable patterns that an evaluation of the last statement is inordinately difficult. The determining factors of capacity to consume have been enumerated as wants, goods and services available, time and energy, and purchasing power.[46] The inclusion of time and energy in the enumeration supplies us with a factor which must certainly provide some appreciable offset to the expected savings of the smaller family. Historically, most saving has been done by the higher income families which also are the particular families which do not reproduce their numbers. These particular families have reproduced in this manner for several decades—the occurrence is not unfamiliar.[47] Nonetheless, the population factor has not been overworked until recently.

The sharp decline in the rate of population growth in the thirties brought with it a significant amount of protest, yet the depression itself was probably more cause than effect in this matter of cessation. Young wives tended to work at income-bearing tasks rather than at the tasks of childbearing. Emigration became more important numerically than immigration. Many marriages were postponed until economic difficulties could be resolved. This behavior pattern is not uncommon; long ago "Pareto concluded . . . that the 'economic factor exercises a very considerable influence' upon numbers, and that in a given society population movements vary with economic movements."[48]

Reversing the causal nexus, however, has recently become a popular notion because of the ease with which such a formulation can be integrated with the savings-investment schema.[49] The traditional model of the interest rate, prospective profit, and investment[50] has been embellished with the population growth element. Dr. Hansen admits he is ". . . increasingly impressed with the analysis made by Wicksell who stressed the prospective rate of profit on new investment as the active, dominant, and controlling factor, and who viewed the rate of interest as a passive factor, lagging behind the profit rate,"[51] yet Professor Hansen can deal with prospective profit on new investment as though it were significantly dependent upon population growth.

Population increase is all very well, especially if considered from the vantage point of a particular religious or political bias, but conditions must be exacted. Will not our economic problems tend to multiply? Do we propose to solve the problem of unemployment by encouraging an increase in the rate of population growth?[52] One would imagine that if newcomers to the population would provide investment outlets, so should the seemingly superfluous members of the labor force who are unemployed.[53] The answer surely cannot be found by examining the purchasing power of the two groups. Newcomers don't have any purchasing power except that which they receive indirectly from parents or guardians. The unemployed suffer from a paucity of purchasing power, but their needs are not thereby lessened. Nor does one untie this Gordian knot by bringing in time period analysis. As the newcomers mature, most of them *become* both producers and consumers. But this producer-consumer coexistence is also the status of the unemployed. Perhaps the difference is that the newcomers receive a better education and training for productive labor. How so, when most of the newcomers are born into lower-income families? To be sure, a gradual improvement is occurring in this matter, but not of the magnitude necessary to serve as a satisfactory explanation.

Newcomers do not really demand any appreciable investment outlay until they are mature enough to serve also as producers.[54] Their consumption of food, clothing, and miscellaneous items does react to some extent on higher order goods simply because such demands are part of the composite demand for consumers' goods, which in turn affects the level of activity in the market for investment goods. These induced changes, however, result from the composite demand—the newcomers are responsible for so minor a portion of the composite[55] that no amount of imputation could ever produce the slogan: "the babies call the tune."

Admitting some effect of newcomers on the level of investment,[56] do we always need a few more potential workers to keep the mature workers employed? Are we just one step ahead of stagnation? This position would involve our economy in sort of a Charybdis and Scylla drama. A stationary or slowly growing population would mean secular stagnation, and a rapidly growing population would present "insoluble problems."[57] Certainly the future of capitalistic progress is more secure than this thesis would indicate.

The rate of investment is dependent upon the relationship between the interest rate and the anticipated earnings to be derived from a specific allocation of funds.[58] The old profit-prospect theory of Lescure and, later, Wesley Mitchell considered this "expected earnings" proposition to be most germane. Analysis could then be directed to those variables which altered the prospect for profit. The growth of monopoly would constitute a variable of this nature.[59] Absence of supply and demand rigidities would make possible a positively sloped trend of economic progress. Contemporary theory has amplified the older postulates; C. R. Noyes concludes that the growth of business and the standard of living at a rate equal to that prevailing during the period 1919–1930 might only be achieved by involuntary saving, changing the income tax structure, diverting the savings of small savers into new equity capital for business through governmental intervention, or a radical alteration in customary practice.[60]

The control of savings appears to be basic to the argument. However, a stationary population would tend to save less in any case inasmuch as the working population would constitute a relatively smaller portion of the aggregate population. The greater demand for personal services by the older segment of the population would require less investment, but the concomitant increase in the propensity to consume is equally satisfactory as an explanation of how savings and investment can be equilibrated at a high level of employment. Also, entrepreneurial expectations would tend to be more stable in the instance of a stationary population since a zero net increase in population would mean that errors in calculating future demand would tend to decrease because of the one less variable to be considered.

Errors would continue in appreciable number, however, because mistakes can be made in capital deepening projects as well as in capital widening. Qualitative improvements in both consumers' and producers' goods would be more important than quantitative duplication. John Bates Clark stressed the qualitative aspects of investment more than sixty years ago, yet this type of investment would also be of primary importance in offsetting the somewhat smaller volume of savings forthcoming from the stationary population of the future.

Admittedly, the rapid growing population of the past has facilitated the development of mass production methods and techniques. A large population is necessary as a market for the products of capitalistic industry. Capital widening has occurred on a vast scale. Nonetheless, some capital widening would occur in satisfying the demands of a stationary population. Two and three car families would become more prevalent as incomes shifted from meeting the expenses of parenthood to meeting the demands of a higher material standard of living. More young couples would purchase a home of their own—more old couples would acquire their own house to serve as an insulator against the outside world. Furthermore, the shift from a young to a relatively more mature population would tend to entail a larger volume of investment simply because the adults' demands, besides being quantitatively greater, are more sophisticated and expensive to satisfy. In general, golf courses, bowling greens, opera houses, and symphony orchestras would provide investment outlets for a relatively older population enjoying a rising real income which would perhaps more than offset the decreased investment in day nurseries, play pens, and harmonicas, especially since numerous assets like parks, hospitals, and playgrounds are necessary for oldsters as well as for youngsters.[61]

Returning to the question of short and long-run population growth, one must acknowledge that some sort of compromise is essential. If it be assumed that a progressive rate of increase in population growth is necessary to serve as an investment outlet,[62] the short-run effect is desirable; yet the long-run result will be that our numbers will far exceed the optimum. Many countries have already reached such a stage of overpopulation. Certainly Germany, Italy, Japan, and England are striving to maintain populations which have gone beyond any standard or optimum. If these populations, which at one time were rapidly expanding, were responsible for the largest percentage of historical capital formation, the price has been enormous and it is daily growing larger.

It is entirely possible that capital formation, both in these foreign countries and in the United States, could have been similarly great in the absence of such astonishing increases in human numbers. The flow of savings into investment channels destined to satisfy an enlarging population does not alter the possibility that these savings would have flowed elsewhere in the absence of such growth. Savings have tended to gravitate toward the most remunerative undertakings—namely, those projects dependent upon a numerical increase of inhabitants. The savings could have been used for qualitative improvements and a higher standard of living, but were in large part diverted away from these outlets by the still more enticing profit-prospects which existed in the latter half of the nineteenth century.

During this same period, rate of increase in our population growth was decreasing just as it is today, but investment continued at a high level. It was not until the thirties that declining growth rates were causally connected with economic depression. Today the arguments for stagnation are more formalized and more widely disseminated. Yet they fail to emphasize what the alternatives could be. For example, consider the position of the investor in 1870 with his position in the present. Savings freely flowed into investments in 1870 because barriers to capital formation were not as prevalent as they are now. There were no complicated registration certificates, prospecti, margin requirements, and stringent federal regulations enforced by administrative commissions. Both the buying and selling of securities were unfettered. For the most part, this state of affairs continued until the thirties. Today the barriers to capital formation are so formidable that the institutional structure of our security markets is undergoing a remarkable transformation. Stock and bond salesmen are principally members of the older generation—young men are not now attracted to the security business as they were in the twenties.

Investment bankers are being shunted aside in many instances where a direct placement of securities is made via insurance company purchases, for example, in order to avoid a share of the federal regulations pertaining to security issuance. Security markets are "thinner," and no longer are they as accurate as they once were in reflecting the underlying values in our shifting economic structure. The result has been disagreeable to most of the parties concerned. Only recently a nation-wide good will and information campaign has been utilized by the security exchanges in an endeavor to channel the vast savings of the past decade into investment.

The process of saving has not changed appreciably in the past eighty years, but the problems of investment have. In addition to the federal regulations governing the issuance and trading of securities, the potential investor must wrestle with fears engendered by two great wars, the most severe depression in our history, and the national and international struggle between the proponents of collectivism and individualism. The conservative economic and political bias which is characteristic of most investors has been simultaneously assaulted and reinforced by the political and economic forces which have been reconstructing the world since 1929. The economic climate in this country since that time has not impressed the typical capitalist with its wholesomeness. He has been fearful and, right or wrong from the "objective" viewpoint, he has not promoted capital formation on a scale commensurate with the past.[63] This state of affairs might well be transitory. It does not lead inevitably to secular stagnation. The investor could either reconcile himself to the realities of current economic life, or perhaps the realities themselves might be altered sufficiently to restore confidence in the mind of the conservative.[64]

V

In summary, one might aver that although population growth historically has provided broad investment opportunities for saving, a stationary population need not be the prelude to secular stagnation. Alternative investment outlets exist today and have existed for generations; population growth of the past simply created opportunities which were more lucrative at a particular time. Savings could just as easily have gravitated toward qualitative improvements and a furtherance of the standard of living of already existing numbers.

As for the future, a stationary population will not only demand these qualitative improvements and a higher standard of living, but in addition will provide offsets to oversaving. Smaller families will spend more on housing, cars, clothing, and miscellaneous goods in order to increase their standard of living, but at the same time they will be reducing the expected volume of saving forthcoming from a given level of income. More families will own their own homes, and the increasing percentage of mature and older population will demand goods requiring more investment. Moreover, they will not tend to save as great a proportion of their income, primarily because the economy will tend to be more stable, the future more certain, and the need for investment outlays less acute.[65]

Parenthetically, there appears to be little validity to the argument which concerns itself with increasing numbers as a device for keeping the mature population employed. Beyond the fact that even the stagnationists agree that the tribulations of overpopulation are perhaps more severe than the trials of underpopulation, there seems to be no logical reason why we need still more people to keep the oldsters employed when one of the perplexing questions of capitalism is how to keep the existing population employed. Has our material progress of the past one hundred and fifty years merely been an economically serious, hybridized version of leapfrog and musical chairs? Surely our population has at least one more "good" place to go.

Our progress will be implemented, and our journey more pleasant if we remove part of the barriers to capital formation which in the future will, as they do now, impede the flow of savings into investment. We have noted the influence of monopoly and found it acting as an investment deterrent. Government intervention in, and control of, economic affairs, especially those in which the government appears to be encroaching upon private entrepreneurship, retard the movement of savings into investment because of the dampening effect exerted upon entrepreneurial psychology. Expectations are altered for the worse, and private projects are postponed while savings accumulate. Coupled with this, are the general supply and demand rigidities, often causally connected with the aforementioned barriers, which permeate the economic structure in its totality. Restrictive policies of both management and labor serve as examples of this last condition. Thus, the long-run aspirations of our citizenry for full employment and material progress cannot be reconciled or resolved satisfactorily with the motives of the all too plentiful variety of "profit-seeker"[66] who apparently is largely impelled to act by the command of a reasoning mechanism which oftentimes is ostensibly devoid of reason. The future of capitalistic progress will be determined principally by the proportionate success or failure we achieve in our attempt to unearth the common denominators requisite for a reconciliation and resolution.

REFERENCES

1. Adam Smith looked upon growth of population as both a consequence and a cause of economic progress because of division of labor.

2. Malthus related population to demand theory and overproduction. For a review of Malthus' "glut" theory that goods are not always exchanged for goods, but frequently are exchanged for labor, and that goods are objects of human consumption owing their whole character to human wants and are therefore not merely to be treated as mathematical symbols, see J. Bonar, *Malthus and His Work*, pp. 282–302.

3. F. Osborn, *Our Plundered Planet;* and W. Vogt, *Road to Survival*.

4. G. Myrdal, *Population, A Problem For Democracy*, p. 164.

5. A. H. Hansen, "Economic Progress and Declining Population Growth," *American Economic Review*, Pt. 1, March 1939, p. 3.

6. *Op. cit.*, p. 11.

7. *Ibid.*, p. 8. For two articles resulting from this speech, see H. L. Reed, "Economists on Industrial Stagnation," *Journal of Political Economy*, April 1940, pp. 244–250; and A. H. Hansen, "Extensive Expansion and Population Growth," *Journal of Political Economy*, August 1940, pp. 583–585.

8. A. H. Hansen, *Full Recovery or Stagnation?*, p. 296.

9. H. S. Ellis, "Monetary Policy and Investment," *American Economic Review*, Pt. 2, Supplement, March 1940, p. 37.

10. *Ibid.*, p. 37.

11. B. M. Anderson, "Governmental Economic Planning," *American Economic Review*, Pt. 2, Supplement, March 1940, p. 249.

12. More will be said of this later.

13. It is not gratuitous to assume a concept of a "pulsating" population which expands and contracts with changes in religious beliefs, political institutions, teleological factors, and the various socio-economic institutions of society. The downward trend of current population growth might well be a temporary phenomenon. The short-run movement of a variable like population could well last for several generations and indicate a declining tendency, only to reveal in the long-run a reversal which would present a pulsatory pattern for the entire period. There is little reason to believe that future societal structures would make such a pattern impossible.

14. An early study revealing a correlation between population growth and production was made by A. Lösch, "Population Cycles as a Cause of Business Cycles," *Quarterly Journal of Economics*, August 1937, pp. 649–662. An authoritative study of methods and results of measuring population growth has been the contribution of R. R. Kuczynski, *The Measurement of Population Growth*.

15. L. R. Klein, "Theories of Effective Demand," *Journal of Political Economy*, April 1947, pp. 127–128.

16. For selected essays on the population problem before the stagnation argument became popular, see J. A. Field, *Essays on Population*. For early discussion of the problems of a declining birthrate and social progress, see E. M. East, *Mankind at the Crossroads*, Chapters IX and X, pp. 252–317; E. A. Ross, *Standing Room Only?*, Chapter XV, pp. 177–183; and H. Cox, *The Problem of Population*, Chapter IV, pp. 111–146.

17. A discussion of the theory of optimum population and the problems connected with such an optimum has been worked out by M. Gottlieb, "The Theory of Optimum Population for a Closed Economy," *Journal of Political Economy*, December 1945, pp. 289–316.

18. A long and splendid article on population doctrines as developed in the United States by those authors who labored under misconceptions regarding the theories of Malthus and Ricardo, versus those authors who understood Malthusianism, is another contribution of Professor Spengler. Cf. J. J. Spengler, "Population Doctrines in the United States," *Journal of Political Economy*, August 1933, pp. 433–467; and *op. cit.* October 1933, pp. 639–672.

19. A. H. Hansen, "Economic Progress and Declining Population Growth," *American Economic Review*, March 1939, p. 2. Some authorities think much of the growth to the present has been wasteful and discouraging, e.g. J. R. Hicks, *Value and Capital* (2nd ed.), p. 302, n. 1.

20. Dr. Hansen has further enhanced the dilemma by asserting that ". . . the difficulty of determining definitely whether a society is actually economically underpopulated would always make possible a difference of opinion as to the policy that would be genuinely desirable socially." Cf. A. H. Hansen, *Economic Stabilization in an Unbalanced World*, p. 224.

21. Also, from the *social* standpoint in England, say Glass and Blacker, "When we survey the picture of social life in England today, we are impressed with the number and the excellence of the reasons why married couples should have few children." See D. V. Glass and C. P. Blacker, *Population and Fertility*, p. 101. This is not simply confined to England. For example, consult the survey of international opinion on claims for relief from population pressure by F. C. Wright, *Population and Peace;* and population studies of East Asia by G. F. Shirras, "The Population Problem in India," *Economic Journal*, March 1933,

pp. 56–73; J. B. Condliffe, "The Pressure of Population in the Far East," *Economic Journal*, March 1932, pp. 196–210.

22. H. D. Henderson, "Economic Consequences," *The Population Problem*, p. 104.

23. J. J. Spengler, "Population Movements, Employment, and Income," *Southern Economic Journal*, October 1938, p. 157.

24. J. J. Spengler, "Aspects of the Economics of Population Growth—Part II," *Southern Economic Journal*, January 1948, p. 265. A worthwhile article on population growth and cultural, rather than economic and biological, phenomena has been written by E. T. Hiller, "A Culture Theory of Population," *Journal of Political Economy*, October 1930, pp. 523–550. For a summary of the social and economic implications of a declining population, see D. V. Glass, *Population Policies and Movements in Europe*, pp. 363–373.

25. An example of Hansen's earlier position is presented later.

26. For the age distribution of consuming units, consult W. S. Thompson and P. K. Whelpton, *Population Trends in the United States*.

27. W. Fellner, *Monetary Policies and Full Employment*, p. 55. This conclusion is in accord with Mr. Terborgh's who summarizes his position by noting that ". . . there is no evidence that countries with high rates of population growth have had in general any more rapid rise in their per capita production than others with slow population growth." Cf. G. Terborgh, *The Bogey of Economic Maturity*, p. 40. Moreover, ". . . it is evident . . . that fluctuations in the rate of advance in per capita production must be due largely or wholly to factors other than changes in population growth." *Ibid.*, p. 43.

28. *Ibid.*, p. 59.

29. *Op. cit.*, p. 70.

30. *Ibid.*, p. 70.

31. *Ibid.*, p. 70.

32. *Ibid.*, pp. 72–73.

33. H. Wright, *Population*, p. 69.

34. *Op. cit.*, pp. 69–70.

35. *Ibid.*, pp. 69–70. The most extraordinary feature of this book is that J. M. Keynes wrote a glowing preface to the work.

36. The issues of whether economic maturity actually exists and whether or not it is important have been dealt with by W. I. King, "Are We Suffering from Economic Maturity?," *Journal of Political Economy*, October 1939, pp. 609–622; and G. Colm, "Comments on W. I. King: 'Are We Suffering from Economic Maturity?,'" *Journal of Political Economy*, February 1940, pp. 114–118.

37. This is treated by Terborgh, *op. cit.*, p. 45.

38. A. H. Hansen, *Economic Stabilization in an Unbalanced World*, p. 232.

39. *Op. cit.*, p. 232.

40. *Ibid.*, p. 233.

41. *Ibid.*, pp. 233–234.

42. This doesn't sound like the Alvin Hansen of today. In this passage he seems almost relieved that we would have enough saving to satisfy a meager minimum of capital replacement and extension.

43. *Op. cit.*, p. 234.

44. L. Goldenberg, "Savings in a State with a Stationary Population," *Quarterly Journal of Economics*, November 1946, pp. 40–63. For a criticism of this article, see H. W. Arndt, "Savings in a State with a Stationary Population: Comment," *Quarterly Journal of Economics*, August 1948, pp. 623–628.

45. A. H. Hansen, "Extensive Expansion and Population Growth," *Journal of Political Economy*, August 1940, p. 583, n. 1.

46. A. Cornish, "Capacity to Consume," *American Economic Review*, June 1936, p. 292.

47. Moreover, the income differential which bestows such status as these families might enjoy is not transient. Professor Copeland has expressed it in more precise terms: "Various factors [relation between income inequality and inequality of investments owned, nepotism, superior education of children of opulent] tend to make income inequality persist once it has been established. . . ." Cf. M. A. Copeland, "The Social and Economic Determinants of the Distribution of Income in the United States," *American Economic Review*, March 1947, pp. 74–75. With regard to urban incomes, he observes: "Urban

communities appear to differ in price structure in such a way that income inequality increases as the size of the community increases." *Ibid.*, p. 74. As to the effect on national output, he concludes: "We cannot say that altering the existing pattern of income distribution would necessarily have an adverse effect on national output." *Ibid.*, p. 75.

48. J. J. Spengler, "Pareto on Population," *Quarterly Journal of Economics*, Aug. 1944, p. 578.

49. An incisive article on population growth and investment has been contributed by S. C. Tsiang, "The Effect of Population Growth on the General Level of Employment and Activity," *Economica*, November 1942, pp. 325–332.

50. For a discussion of the interest rate and investment, see F. H. Knight, "Some Issues in the Economics of Stationary States," *American Economic Review*, September 1936, pp. 393–411.

51. A. H. Hansen, "Economic Progress and Declining Population Growth," *American Economic Review*, March 1939, p. 5.

52. Cf. Ellis, "Monetary Policy and Investment," p. 37; and A. R. Sweezy speaking at "Round Table on Population Problems," *American Economic Review*, Pt. 2, Supplement, March 1940, p. 397. Dr. Sweezy then goes on to answer partly the question. This entire round table discussion is worth reading: *ibid.*, pp. 383–398.

53. A degree of labor superfluity will probably always exist because of technological unemployment. As Neisser has written: "There is no mechanism within the framework of rational economic analysis that, in any situation, would secure the full absorption of displaced workers and render 'permanent' technological unemployment in any sense impossible." Cf. H. P. Neisser, "Permanent Technological Unemployment," *American Economic Review*, March 1942, p. 71.

54. The principal exceptions would be their demand for schools and hospitals. Comments on other effects of population growth and investment may be found in M. M. Rosen, "Population Growth, Investment, and Economic Recovery," *American Economic Review*, March 1942, pp. 122–125; and C. O. Hardy, "Fiscal Policy and National Income: A Review," *ibid.*, pp. 106–108.

55. Actually, in the majority of families the first baby would exert the largest amount of influence on consumption and investment, inasmuch as parents tend to "overbuy" for the first one, and because items like the nursery, highchair, crib, and clothes are handed down to the next in line.

56. The effect is on the increment of investment which in turn reacts on income. As Domar puts it: ". . . an increase in income is not a function of the amount of investment; it is a function of the increment of investment." Cf. E. V. Domar, "Expansion and Employment," *American Economic Review*, March 1947, p. 47.

57. Hansen, *loc. cit.* He referred to nineteenth century growth.

58. This general statement is complicated by the fact that some investments are made without strict regard for the element of pecuniary gain (e.g., a wealthy person purchases a new library for a university).

59. Recently, Mr. Abramovitz has declared that strong arguments support ". . . the notion that the destruction of monopoly controls will make for a higher rate of new investment, both immediately and in the long run." Cf. M. Abramovitz, "Savings and Investment: Profits *vs.* Prosperity?," *American Economic Review*, Supplement, June 1942, p. 85.

60. C. R. Noyes, "The Prospect for Economic Growth," *American Economic Review*, March 1947, pp. 31–33.

61. Cf. Anderson, *loc. cit.*

62. War would appear to be just as large an outlet. Is it omitted simply because it is not "acceptable" as an investment oulet?

63. This was apparent in 1937 when such important representatives of private enterprise as Clarence Francis (President of General Foods Corporation), Henry Ford, Francis E. Frothingham (Investment Bankers Association of America), Alfred P. Sloan, the President of du Pont, Tom M. Girdler (Chairman of Republic Steel Corporation), and William S. Knudsen (President of General Motors Corporation) were condemning the federal government for its "undue interference" in the private sector and its creation of fear and uncertainty in the minds of private enterprisers and investors. In the main, these capitalists called for more private and less government activity, and predicted increasing private investment if the government would decrease its "interference." See *Commercial and Finan-*

cial Chronicle, Nov. 27, 1937, p. 3432; *ibid.,* Dec. 4, 1937, p. 3588; *ibid.,* p. 3593; *ibid.,* p. 3591; *ibid.,* Dec. 11, 1937, p. 3754; *ibid.,* Dec. 18, 1937, p. 3410; and *ibid.,* Jan. 8, 1938, p. 194. All this occurred despite the fact that short and long-term interest rates were down to levels comparable to those prevailing today.

64. The latter possibility seems to me to be most unlikely.

65. Keynes' point that saving and investing are done in the main by two different groups who are responding to different stimuli does not damage this statement. Both savers and investors are affected in this particular case, which the more general theory does not consider.

66. The term "profit-seeker" is used in the broad sense to include both employer and employee.

POPULATION GROWTH AND THE DEMAND FOR CAPITAL*

By Clarence L. Barber

In discussions of the stagnation thesis economists still disagree about the relative significance of a decline in the percentage rate of population growth and a decline in the absolute rate of growth. A number of supporters of the stagnation thesis attach a special importance to the absolute rate of growth apparently on the grounds that the acceleration principle is based on the absolute rather than the percentage rate of growth in final demand. Thus Benjamin Higgins states: "Speaking generally, the absolute rate of growth is the more important concept, and a falling percentage rate of increase is significant mainly as a harbinger of a later drop in the absolute increase. . . . For that part of the argument based upon the acceleration principle, the absolute rate of increase is clearly more important."[1] Similarly A. H. Hansen, after a reference to the long-run effect of the percentage rate of population growth upon capital formation, states: "The business depression in 1929 was the first one in our history in which a drastic decline in the absolute increment of population growth occurred. Now we all know that the acceleration principle in business cycle theory is based on the absolute increment of growth of final demand and not on percentage increase. Here was a wholly new factor that contributed to the severity of this depression."[2] Likewise, H. A. Adler states: "The reason for emphasizing the absolute increment in population growth with respect to the 1930 depression lies in the working of the acceleration principle."[3] The opposite view to this has been summed up by George Terborgh in his terse remark that, to say the absolute decline in population growth is more important than the relative decline "is like saying that a pound of growth on a dog has the same significance as a pound on an elephant."[4]

None of the writers who stress the importance of the absolute rate of growth state exactly why or to what extent the acceleration principle supports their argument. If their conclusions are based on a belief that this principle applies only to the case of absolute growth, they have fallen into an error. The acceleration principle can be applied either to a percentage rate of increase or to an absolute rate of increase in population or of final demand. Its basic assumption is that there is a fixed ratio between the level of income or consumption and the quantity of capital. It is true that textbook illustrations often state the principle in terms of absolute increments of final demand but

* Reprinted from *The American Economic Review*, 43 March 1953), pp. 133–139, by permission of the author and publisher. (Copyright 1953 by the American Economic Association.)

this does not mean that it cannot also be applied to percentage increments. It seems more probable that these writers have been thinking of the fact that, neglecting replacement demand, an absolute fall in the volume of investment will occur when the absolute increments in final demand begin to fall. But the significance of this conclusion may be more limited than has been generally realized. Since there has been some confusion on this matter, it will be useful to state these relations more precisely. The application of the acceleration principle to the cases of absolute and relative growth in population will be considered in turn. For simplicity it will be assumed initially that the level of per capita real income remains constant. The effects of replacement demand are neglected throughout.

Let us suppose that population is increasing by equal annual increments which we will designate by p. Let k represent the amount of increased investment measured in dollars of constant purchasing power that is called forth by the addition of one person to the population. Accordingly, the total amount of investment due to the working of the acceleration principle in relation to population growth (hereinafter called population investment) will be $k \cdot p$ and this will remain constant as long as population continues to grow by equal annual increments. Now it is clear that if per capita real income remains constant the total national income must rise as the population grows. If savings are a constant percentage of income, the total amount of savings will rise also. Thus as the population grows at a constant absolute rate, population investment will become a successively smaller percentage of national income and of total savings. A gradually increasing percentage of the total investment required to offset current savings will have to come from other sources. Hence even when population is increasing by equal annual increments, there is need for a rising volume of investment from sources other than population growth if chronic underemployment is to be avoided.[5]

Let us now assume that population, instead of growing each year by constant absolute amounts, grows at a constant percentage rate which we will designate p'. Assume as before that the amount of investment called forth by the addition of one person to the population is k. Then, if we denote by P_n the population at the beginning of any year n, the absolute growth in population for the year n will be $p' \cdot P_n$ and the absolute amount of population investment will be $k \cdot p' \cdot P_n$.[6] From this it follows that the ratio of population investment to national income for any year n will be equal to:

$$\frac{k \cdot p' \cdot P_n}{P_n(1 + p')\frac{y}{2}},$$

where $P_n(1 + p')\frac{}{2}$ is the population at midyear and y is the level of per capita real income. Since P_n cancels out of both the numerator and denominator we are left with an expression in terms of k, p', and y, all of which are constants by hypothesis. This means that, where population is growing at a constant percentage rate, population investment will remain a constant percentage of income. If, in these circumstances, saving is a constant percentage of income, population investment will absorb a constant proportion of total savings. It also follows from this expression that a decline in the percentage rate of population growth will cause the ratio of population investment to national income to decline.[7] One particular form of a decline in the relative rate of population growth is a population which increases by constant absolute amounts.

Finally, let us drop the assumption that the level of per capita income remains constant and assume instead that it is gradually rising. It seems reasonable to suppose that any growth in per capita income would cause k to increase also.[8] If each person in the population enjoys a higher standard of living, it is not unreasonable to expect that the capital required to produce this higher standard will be larger also. If the ratio of k to y remains constant, which will be true if the capital-output ratio remains constant, the conclusions reached above are unaffected. In this particular case the ratio of population investment to national income will remain constant as long as population grows at a constant percentage rate even though the level of per capita income is rising. Only if k and y grow at different rates is it impossible to state definitely what will happen to the ratio of population investment to national income. However, unless the size of the ratio k/y is inversely affected by the rate of population growth, it will still be true that the ratio of population investment to national income will decline more slowly (or grow more rapidly) when population grows at a constant percentage rate than when it grows at a constant absolute rate.

In view of these conclusions why have a number of economists placed so much emphasis on the absolute rate of population growth? For with a constant absolute rate of growth one can expect a steadily declining ratio between population investment and national income. As was suggested above, it seems likely that the economists in question have been thinking too much in terms of a static economy in which it might be reasonable to assume that a constant absolute volume of investment would maintain an acceptable level of employment for an indefinite period of time. Needless to say, we live in a rapidly growing economy and in these circumstances we are likely to need a growing volume of investment. There can be little question then that the percentage rate of growth in population is a much more relevant concept than the absolute rate of growth.

The argument advanced here is essentially similar to that given by a number of economists who have discussed the dynamic growth aspects of capital investment.[9] The principal difference is that these economists have been primarily concerned with the relation between capital investment and the rate of growth in output as a whole whereas my argument has been restricted to the relation between population growth and capital requirements.

In both instances the basic assumptions are that the capital-output ratio and the average propensity to save remain constant. Given these assumptions Harrod, Domar and others have shown that a constant proportionate (not absolute) rate of growth in output is required to induce sufficient capital investment to offset the amount of saving that would be forthcoming at a full-employment level of income. The required rate of growth is equal to the average propensity to save multiplied by the reciprocal of the capital-output ratio.[10] I have shown that under similar assumptions a constant proportionate rate of growth in population is necessary if population investment is to remain a constant proportion of national income and total saving.

While I have demonstrated that under certain assumptions a constant percentage rate of population growth will induce a level of investment that will remain a constant proportion of national income, this still leaves unanswered the further question of whether one constant percentage rate of growth is better or worse than another. I should like to suggest that for any country at any point of time there is some optimum rate of population growth.[11] An optimum rate of population growth can be defined as that rate of growth which is most conducive to the maintenance of a high level of employment and a rapid rate of economic progress (where economic progress is defined as increase in output per capita). A more rapid rate of growth than this might slow up the rate of economic progress by reducing the average propensity to save, because of the high consumption rate associated with large families, thus in turn reducing the amount of capital investment.[12] A slower rate of growth might induce less capital investment and thus be less favorable to both the maintenance of a high level of employment and the rate of economic progress.

It seems likely that the optimum rate of population growth would change over a period of time as the ratio between a country's population and its natural resources changed. In effect, this means that the optimum rate of population growth would vary as the position of a country's population changed with reference to its optimum population.[13] It would also vary as the volume of opportunities for investment arising out of growth in per capita output changed. When the population is below an optimum level, a high rate of population growth will mean a rapid approach towards the optimum. This movement of the population towards an optimum will cause an increase in output per capita because of the more favorable ratio of total population to resources. On the other hand, with a lower rate of population growth a larger proportion of total savings will go into forms of capital investment which help to raise the level of output per capita. Under these conditions the minimum acceptable rate of population growth would be the rate which, given the average propensity to save and the opportunities for investment related to growth in output per capita, was just sufficient to maintain full employment. A maximum acceptable rate would be a rate so rapid that any further increase in the rate of population growth would cause a slowing up in the growth of output per capita either because it reduced the community's propensity to save or because the total supply of capital equipment did not keep pace with the growth in population. Within the limits set by this maximum and minimum, a range which could be substantial, it might be difficult to determine an optimum position.

In contrast, when a country's population is beyond its optimum, any increase in the rate of population growth above the minimum rate necessary to induce sufficient investment to maintain full employment will be clearly undesirable for it will result in a less favorable ratio of population to resources and a lower level of per capita output. Thus, where a country's population is beyond the optimum, the optimum rate of population growth will depend primarily on the opportunities for investment related to growth in output per capita. In fact, if growth in output per capita alone would induce sufficient capital investment to maintain full employment, the optimum rate of population growth would be zero. As Fellner has shown, given a constant average propensity to save (s) and a constant capital-output ratio (R), the required over-all rate of growth necessary to induce sufficient capital investment to maintain full employment is a constant percentage rate of growth of $\dfrac{(s)}{R}$.[14]

When a country's population has exceeded the optimum, the more of this required rate of growth which can be made up by growth in per capita output the lower will be the optimum rate of population growth. When a country's population is below the optimum, it may be difficult within certain limits to determine the best combination of population growth and growth in output per capita needed to meet this required rate of growth.

In practice the concept of an optimum rate of population growth is difficult to apply. Consider, for example, the changes that have occurred in the percentage rate of population growth in the United States over the period 1790 to 1950. The relevant data are given in Table I.

TABLE I
PERCENTAGE GROWTH IN POPULATION, BY DECADES,
THE UNITED STATES, 1790 TO 1950

Decade	Percentage Growth	Decade	Percentage Growth
1790–1800	34.8	1870–1880	26.0
1800–1810	36.4	1880–1890	25.5
1810–1820	33.1	1890–1900	20.7
1820–1830	34.1	1900–1910	21.4
1830–1840	32.7	1910–1920	15.2
1840–1850	35.9	1920–1930	15.6
1850–1860	35.5	1930–1940	7.2
1860–1870	26.6	1940–1950	14.9

Source: U. S. Bureau of the Census, *Historical Statistics of the United States, 1789–1945* (Washington, 1949) and *Survey of Current Business,* July 1951.

If we exclude the decade 1930 to 1940, rates of growth over the period 1790 to 1950 fall into four groups. From 1790 to 1860 population grew at the rate of about 33 to 36 per cent per decade. A sudden decline in the rate of growth occurred about 1860, and thereafter population grew at a rate of about 26 per cent per decade from 1860 to 1890. A further decline in the rate of growth occured at this time and population grew at about 21 per cent per decade from 1890 to 1910. Finally, with the exception of the 'thirties, population has grown at the rate of about 15 per cent per decade since 1910. Thus there has been a regular step-like decline in the percentage rate of population growth since 1860.[15] A detailed study would be necessary to determine whether these declines in the rate of population growth were accompanied by corresponding reductions in the optimum rate of growth. However, a few observations appear justified. It seems reasonable to suppose that the optimum rate of population growth would be higher during the earlier part of this period when the ratio of population to land and other resources was extremely low and the total population was well below an optimum. Further, the inflow of foreign capital during the first part of this period would raise the optimum rate of growth for that period. It is also possible that the rate of population growth during part of this period may have exceeded the optimum by a substantial margin.

More recently, the population of the United States has probably approached an optimum and may well have passed it. Accordingly it seems probable that the optimum rate of growth is now substantially lower than it was during the earlier part of the period, say before 1900. Some economists, in particular those of the secular stagnation school, are inclined to believe that the rate of growth in recent decades has been below the rate necessary to maintain a high level of employment. However, the occurrence of two world wars and a great depression makes the period since 1910 difficult to interpret and a more detailed study will be needed to determine whether the optimum rate of growth has declined more or less than the actual rate of growth in recent decades. In fact, the whole problem of the relation of population growth to the demand for capital merits more detailed attention than it has yet received.

In view of the recent emphasis that has been placed on the "amazing population upsurge" in the United States it may be useful to note by way of conclusion that although the absolute growth in the population of the United States during the decade ending in 1950 was the largest on record, the percentage rate of growth for this decade was slightly smaller than that of the decade ending in 1930.

REFERENCES

1. "Concepts and Criteria of Secular Stagnation," *Income, Employment and Public Policy* (New York, 1948), p. 99. Higgins also notes certain circumstances where he believes that the percentage rate of growth is the more important concept.

2. *Economic Policy and Full Employment* (New York, 1947), p. 300.

3. "Absolute or Relative Rate of Decline in Population Growth?," *Quart. Jour. Econ.* (Aug. 1945), LIX, 631.

4. "Dr. Hansen on 'The Bogey of Economic Maturity'," *Rev. Econ. Stat.* (Aug. 1946), XXVIII, 170.

5. This analysis has an application to a famous discussion in the literature of the acceleration principle. Ragnar Frisch has shown that under certain circumstances a decline in the rate of increase in consumer-taking need not lead to an absolute fall in the level of investment. This would be true if the rise in the replacement demand for equipment were sufficient to offset the fall in the expansion demand for capital equipment. But even in this special case Frisch's argument fails to note that the volume of net investment would fall and that the volume of gross investment, even though constant, would be a declining percentage of national income. See R. Frisch, "The Interrelation between Capital Production and Consumer Taking," *Jour. Pol. Econ.* (Oct. 1931), XXXIX, 646–54, and the discussion with J. M. Clark in subsequent issues.

6. This assumes a constant percentage growth compounded annually.

7. The proof is as follows. Assume another rate of growth p'' such that $p' > p''$. It is required to prove that

$$\frac{k \cdot p'}{y + \dfrac{p'}{2} \cdot y} \Big\backslash \frac{k \cdot p''}{y + \dfrac{p''}{2} \cdot y}$$

If we divide both sides by k, multiply through by y and then multiply both sides by the product of the remaining denominators we obtain $p' + \dfrac{p'p''}{2} > p'' + \dfrac{p'p''}{2}$, which must be true if $p' > p''$.

8. It should be noted that I am concerned here only with the effects of rising per capita income on the amount of investment induced by population growth. This growth in per capita income will, of course, induce additional investment if the capital-output ratio is to remain constant.

9. See, in particular, R. F. Harrod, *Towards a Dynamic Economics* (London, 1948); E. D. Domar, "The Problem of Capital Accumulation," *Am. Econ. Rev.* (Dec. 1948), XXXVIII, 777–94; and W. Fellner "The Capital-Output Ratio in Dynamic Economics," *Money, Trade, and Economic Growth* (New York, 1951); and the references given by Fellner on p. 106.

10. Fellner, *op. cit.* pp. 111–12.

11. Higgins has suggested the need for such a concept. See *op. cit.*, p. 106.

12. This introduces the question of the possible effects of population growth on the propensity to save, a difficult problem and one beyond the scope of this note. It also assumes that the amount of investment is limited by the amount of voluntary saving, that inflation and forced saving are prevented by monetary controls.

13. The difficulties of defining an optimum population have been carefully discussed by J. R. Hicks. See J. R. Hicks and A. G. Hart, *The Social Framework of the American Economy* (New York, 1945), pp. 240–43. I would suggest that the optimum population be defined with reference to the amount of capital equipment, the opportunities for foreign trade and the state of technical knowledge at a given time and that we recognize that this optimum will change over time with changes in these factors.

14. Fellner, *op. cit.*, pp. 111–12.

15. These data give little support to Hansen's contention that "the percentage decline in population in the United States was not marked until after World War I." See *op. cit.*, p. 299.

POPULATION CYCLES AS A CAUSE OF BUSINESS CYCLES*

By August Lösch

Most of the more important factors by which economic life is determined
have been pretty satisfactorily dealt with. We have a fairly well established
stock of knowledge of these relations. Some matters, however, are less clear.
Population, for example, is usually included among the main factors of economic consequence. But how well do we understand it?

The prevailing opinion still regards changes in population as *results* of
economic developments, as Malthus did, and as all those do who point to
such facts as the familiar one that marriages and births reflect the business
cycle. No doubt there are such reflections, but their range of size makes
most of them negligible. The thesis of the present paper is that the relation
between population and business is just the other way around: changes in
population are among the main *causes* of economic changes. Let us disregard
the secular movements of population and confine ourselves to the last hundred years, or even to the problems of our own times. In this sphere there are
three developments of population that concern our economic situation most
deeply. These are (1) the increase in the expectation of life, which has nearly
doubled within less than a century, raising many economic problems, of
which the burdens for old-age pension systems are but a foretaste; (2) the
increase in birth control, with its sweeping effect on the capital market; and
(3) fluctuations in the increase of population. It is upon this last point that I
wish to enlarge here. I maintain that, at least in Germany, these fluctuations
were the main cause of business cycles. The proof of this will be in three
steps: first that large cycles of population movement exist, secondly that they
fit fairly well with production series, and thirdly the explanation of this co-
variation.

I

POPULATION CYCLES.—While the movement of population shows unimportant and irregular fluctuations which seem to be mere reflections of economic, sanitary and other conditions, we find quite clearly great waves,
the main cause of which are the great wars. The deficit of births during
a war and the surplus of births in the immediate postwar period repeat
themselves about thirty-three years later, when the new generations are at
their time of highest fertility. For the same reason thirty-three years later

* Reprinted by permission of the publishers from *The Quarterly Journal of Economics*,
51 (August 1937), pp. 649–662. (Cambridge, Mass.: Harvard University Press, Copyright
1937 by The President and Fellows of Harvard College.) Paper read at the annual meeting of the Econometric Society in Chicago, December 1936.

a third wave occurs. Of course these subsequent waves become broader and broader, flatter and flatter, and after a hundred years entirely interfere with each other, so that it may roughly be said that a war calls forth a set of three full cycles of a hundred years duration in all. Two things usually happen to these cycles: they are either reinforced or disturbed by cycles resulting from later wars. For the first possibility Sweden is an excellent example. There it happened again and again that at the end of a cycle a new great war renewed the waves, with the result that there was a continuous succession. The regularity is so great that in each century about the same quinquenniums fall into the same phase. There was for instance a peak of births in 1720–25, 1820–25; 1920–25; again in 1650–55, 1750–55, 1855–60; few children were born around 1635–40, 1735–40, 1835–40, and probably around 1935. In other cases cycles interfere with each other, so that shorter fluctuations arise. A good example of

GROWTH OF THE GERMAN POPULATION

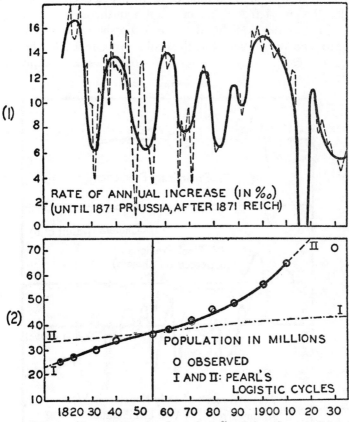

Sources: Chart 1: Free hand trend. Original data from A. Lösch, Bevölkerungswellen u. Wechsellagen (1817–1910), and Statistiches Jahrbuch für das Deutsche Reich (1911–1935).

Chart 2: Pearl, Biology of Population Growth, 1952, pp. 21 and 221.

this is the development of the German population after the Napoleonic Wars, which is shown on the first graph, on page 293.

It may be of some interest to compare this with Mr. Pearl's logistic curve of population growth. In Mr. Pearl's opinion[1] the German population received an impulse towards increase twice during the last century, each increase following a logistic curve as on chart 2. He draws the dividing line around 1855. But a comparison with chart 1 makes it clear that the downswing of the increase in population preceding this dividing year was just a repetition of another downswing thirty-three years before which was due to bad harvests and above all to the war of 1813. In Mr. Pearl's interpretation, however, this low rate of increase from 1846–57 would be a sign that economic possibilities were close to being fully used—an explanation which seems to me to be more difficult and harder to support. As in Pearl's theory the fact that our means of living are limited results in diminishing the rate of population growth, so in Corrado Gini's theory[2] a decrease in reproductive powers has the same effect. Whether or not both these most stimulating ideas are right, most of the available data cover too short a period of time to be sufficient for the verification of such secular laws. It is still very difficult to separate satisfactorily the secular trend, to which these laws apply, from those

VERIFICATION

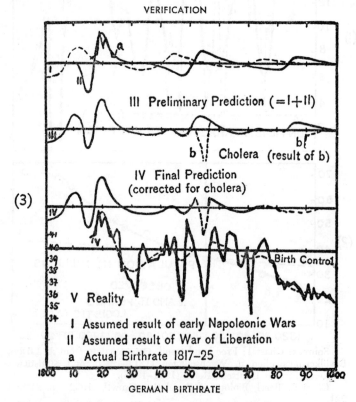

(3)

Source: A. Lösch, Bevölkerungswellen u. Wechsellagen, Jena 1936.

fluctuations due to wars, and for the last decades also from some other disturbances. Mr. Pearl will find it hard to prove that the trough of the 'fifties
is more than a mere repetition of a previous trough. And so too Mr. Gini's
task of showing that reproductive powers are definitely declining is rendered
difficult by the fact that not only age distribution[3] but, strangely enough,
specific fertility as well is fluctuating in consequence of the wars.

In order to determine whether the somewhat complicated movement of
the German birth-rate during the last century can be sufficiently explained
as a result of the Napoleonic Wars I took the actual figures from 1817–25
(curve a on chart 3), together with the history of those wars, and made an
extrapolation on this basis for the rest of the century. Curve I shows the
fluctuations of the birth rate as they ought to have resulted from the early
Napoleonic Wars—if the theory is correct. Curve II shows similar fluctuations
following the war of 1812–15. By adding both curves we get a preliminary
forecast represented by curve III. Its troughs and crests coincide fairly well
with those of the actual series, with two exceptions: the great cholera epidemic in the 'fifties and the widespread birth control since the 'eighties could
not possibly be foreseen. But on the whole it seems to be well established that
the great wars are the main cause of the large fluctuations in the increase
of population. There may be some minor disturbances too, such as the cholera
epidemic just referred to, but very few are primarily economic, and this is
my main point. More especially, the fluctuations of marriages during the
business cycle, which are so often pointed out, are usually not important
enough to have any considerable effect on the birth rate. Even the heaviest
drop in marriages, which occurred during the depression of 1902, was only
4 per cent of the couples married at the peak of the preceding boom, and it is
doubtful whether the birth rate was at all affected by this factor. In comparison with this the world war cut down marriages by nearly 50 per cent and
births even more. This makes it clear that the effects of business fluctuations
on population are, at least before the great war, negligible. Hence the waves
of population may be compared as a nearly independent series with the
waves in business activity, and I shall make that comparison in the second
part of my paper.

II

CO-VARIATION WITH BUSINESS CYCLES.—All the time series which I am going to compare represent the annual rate of variation that is derived from the
original data. Before Germany entered the highly capitalistic stage, its labor
supply[4] (which approximately reflects the fluctuations of the total population)
and its crops had every important trough and peak in common. I am confining myself, however, to industrial cycles. The co-variation between building
and existing marriages is not surprising, and the only comment I wish to
make is that it is not the variations in weddings but only the variations in the
number of families—not necessarily the same—which are of consequence for
building activity. Even more remarkable is the co-variation between labor

CO-VARIATION OF POPULATION AND PRODUCTION IN GERMANY

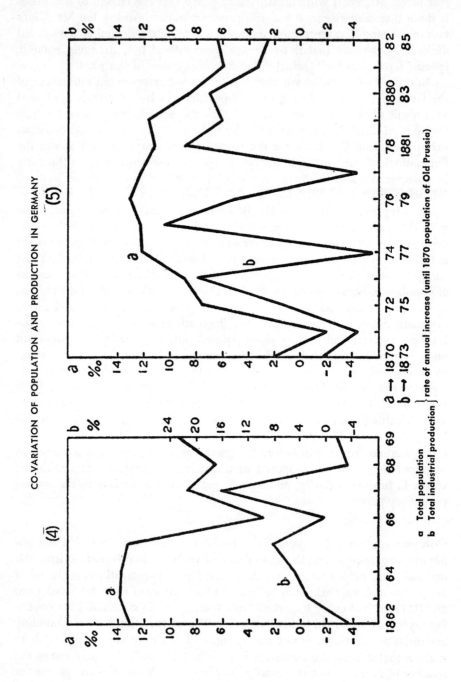

(4)   (5)

a Total population
b Total industrial production

$a \rightarrow$ 1870
$b \rightarrow$ 1873 } rate of annual increase (until 1870 population of Old Prussia)

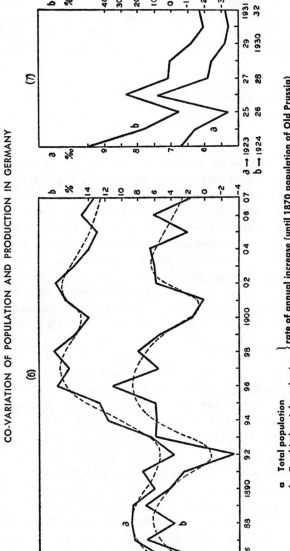

CO-VARIATION OF POPULATION AND PRODUCTION IN GERMANY

a   Total population   } rate of annual increase (until 1870 population of Old Prussia)
b   Total industrial production

supply and producers' goods. Most striking, however, is the simple co-variation between total population and total industrial production which is shown on graph 4–7. This shows only two time-lags of similar origin between 1862 and 1932: the war of 1870 and the severe crisis of 1873 break the connection for a time, and only after a three years' lag do the facts of population movement make themselves felt again. And there is a one year's lag after the world war; again population is going ahead, and it is production that follows. But during the rest of the period there is a parallel tendency, not only on the whole but from year to year as well: both series rise and fall concomitantly, altho to a different degree. Hence a pretty close correlation between population and production cannot be denied, and I shall next endeavor to explain this striking fact.

III

EXPLANATION.—Whereas an increase in labor supply led directly to higher activity in the pre- and early capitalistic period, the effect of population movements on industrial cycles is an indirect one. The economic development of growing nations consists essentially in making it possible to increase population by providing the necessary capital goods and corresponding consumers' goods. In such an economy, which is primarily adapted to extensive growth, and only in a secondary way to expansion by means of technical progress, it is natural that the rhythm of population should govern the rhythm of business. It is natural that business leaders should take courage again just when a great increase in population guarantees them cheap labor and a reliable extension of markets, especially for buildings and machinery.

Most people will find it obvious that an increase in population stirs up building activity. But why should an addition to the labor supply increase anything else but unemployment? Why should it stir up the activity of the firms producing tools and machinery? The answer is that the situation is exactly the same as for building. Just as it is a pretty safe guess that the additional population will not live in tents, so it is equally unlikely that they will go barefoot. If, therefore, the producers of additional houses see a fair chance of selling them profitably, the same must be true for the producers of additional shoe machines. By building the houses and by producing the machines they create the purchasing power which is needed to pay for the shoes and to hire the apartments, thus justifying their production. It is essential to see that unemployment among the old population, whose capital equipment already exists, is an entirely different thing from the case where there comes an increase in labor supply for which buildings and machines must first be constructed. The former is simply a sign of depression; the latter, however, is a stimulus to recovery.

Once the upswing has begun the entrepreneurs also venture upon new methods and new goods, but the very essence of my argument is that it is the upswing of population which sets the pace. For compared with technical progress and with the opening of new markets, which likewise expand production, the absorption of the increase in labor involves a smaller risk. It requires neither adjustment for new goods and new methods (as technical progress does) nor exploring unknown markets (as may be necessary in order to increase exports). It requires nothing but expanding along the old lines, nothing but producing for a highly probable increase in demand. No exceptionally capable entrepreneurs are necessary for this, tho it does not exclude the importance of the pacemaker in the sense Spiethoff and Schumpeter imply. It remains a question of fact whether the leading entrepreneur does venture upon his bolder projects, which give the swing proper to the revival, before he has a certain indication and strong position in the optimism of the average; or, if he goes ahead, whether he does carry the bulk of the entrepreneurs along with him before they see possibilities suitable for *them*, that is to say, less difficult and less risky ones. In any case, an unusual increase in the labor supply is likely to bring about an upswing of business activity for two reasons: because it offers more and safer possibilities to the producers of capital goods.

It is one of the best established results of research that the capital goods industry is much more affected by the business cycle than the consumption goods industry. My theory easily explains this. Let us take a yearly increase in the labor supply of 100,000 men, and let us assume their average yearly income to be 1,000 dollars, and the average capital equipment for each additional worker to amount to 10,000 dollars. Then total consumption increases by 100 millions, and capital goods by 1,000 millions.

If in the following year labor increased by 120,000 men, in the third year by 140,000 men, and in the fourth year by 160,000 men, most people would conclude that the increase in the fifth year was likely to be 180,000 men, and that is just what the entrepreneurs do. If the *actual* increase in the fifth year is only 90,000 men, then breakdowns must follow. Of course a question arises here. Are the fluctuations really so large; and even if the increase in labor supply is cut by a half, will the difference be of sufficient importance to bring about a crisis for the capital goods industry? My answer is in the affirmative for several reasons. First of all, as Professor von Haberler has pointed out, business is so sensitive at the end of the upswing that it will react even to comparatively small disturbances. The fluctuations in new labor supply are, moreover, sometimes very considerable. It has happened more than once that the annual rate of increase dropped by more than 50 per cent within a few years. And, above all, nearly half of the German capital goods industry has so far been entirely dependent upon the increase in population, and only the remainder was working for replacement and technical progress. For this very reason technical innovations alone are as a rule unlikely to bring about an upswing or to support it any longer in face of a decrease in new labor supply. For this decrease in population growth results in heavy losses for nearly half of the capital goods industry. If the firms concerned could foresee this turn in population, they might perhaps be able to change their line of production in time and work for technical progress instead of producing houses and old-fashioned machinery. Unfortunately, however, they do not become aware of the *decrease* in new labor supply until they try to sell the equipment for an *increase* in labor that turns out to have existed only in their imagination. No prospective increase in population can change the crisis that results from its present stability. No transposition can make good the losses that result from this mistaken investment that has already occurred. Even if such a transposition were possible, which in many cases it is not, it would mostly come too late. Failures have already begun; the depression has started.

These are the outlines of my explanation of the business cycle. I am, however, well aware of the fact that there are limitations to its validity. First, the argument has been intentionally simplified by not mentioning the well known, tho in my opinion only supplementary, rôle played by the rate of interest and by wages, in so far as they are likewise affected by the fluctuations in labor. Secondly I do not know if my explanation holds true for other countries besides Germany. Yet the fact that all European states must have in common a similar movement of population, since all of them were involved in the Napoleonic Wars, would be in my favor and could help to explain why Europe shows more or less the same fluctuations in business activity. As for the United States there is little hope of getting reliable annual data for the natural rate of population growth, and more particularly for the increase in labor supply. But if any fluctuations in natural growth exist at all, they are very likely to be by far surpassed by the fluctuations in immigration. These have hitherto been regarded as a *result* of the changes in business activity. But there is much similarity between the German increase in labor supply, which accumulates in the villages until it is large enough to encourage the entrepreneurs, and the potential European emigrants, who accumulate there until American business recovers, at least partly *in anticipation of new immigration*. The production of capital equipment for these additional workers helps to bring about revival in both cases, and parallel to it these additional men immigrate into the United States as they do into the German towns. While this immigration seems to follow revival, it really is its *cause*. Yet there may be one important difference between Germany and the States. It is true that a large part of the American durable goods industry is engaged in producing the capital equipment for additional workmen and settlers, and hence depends upon immigration; but we do not know to what extent the fluctuations in American immigration are due to fluctuations in European business activity and population growth. If this connection is unimportant, if the European reservoir could supply a pretty constant stream of immigrants, the conclusion would be that (just the reverse of the German situation) it may be intermittent possibilities of technical progress, or whatever else may be regarded essential, which give the lead to American business activity. Immigration, tho still one cause of growing optimism, would in this case not turn the scale, or at least not as decisively as in the German industrial centers. It would merely strengthen the effects brought about by technical progress.[5] However, our knowledge of the facts is insufficient to make clear the rôle played by population in American business cycles. This involves a third limitation of my theory. Professor Spiethoff in Bonn, who suggested this investigation of mine, always stresses the point that altho all the business cycles of which we know have their important features in common, they differ widely in their details. The beginning of a boom, for instance, is necessarily characterized by an increase in the demand for capital goods. This demand may result from innovations, large replacements, the developing of backward countries. I merely add to this list population, not claiming that it is the only cause of the cycles. All I maintain is that the timing and the form of most of our German business cycles have been determined primarily by waves in labor supply. Limited as this result is, it strengthens the proposition that among the most decisive factors in the economic life of a country is its population—its people, their number and quality.[6]

REFERENCES

1. R. Pearl, Biology of Population Growth, 1925, p. 20.
2. C. Gini, The Cyclical Rise and Fall of Population, in Population Problems, Harris Foundation Lectures, Chicago, 1930.
3. The first to explain a wave in age distribution by war was, as far as I know, Eifert Sundt in his book, Om Giftermaal i Norge, Christiania 1855.
4. My method of calculation was roughly this: Before 1871 I took the number of male Prussians between fifteen and sixty-five years of age as representative. From 1871–1910 I figured out the German population for each year, classified by age and sex, on the basis of the annual number of births and deaths, and making allowance for emigration. The census of 1882, 1895, 1907 shows the percentage of each age group and sex that was willing to work at that time. The interpolation of these percentages for the intermediate years gives far less cause for discussion than one might expect. By multiplication I got the employables for each year. Their number—as calculated—depends upon births, deaths, marriages, migration, willingness to work. Wars are consequently only one, altho a main, factor influencing this number. For some of the items mentioned economic conditions are obviously of some consequence. However, they belong either to a former date, or a foreign country, and insofar as they belong to the country and time in question (marriages and business cycle), they are of little importance. This alone is vital, that population be independent of that business cycle which it should explain. For details see August Lösch, Bevölkerungswellen und Wechsellagen, Jena 1936, where I tried to show the importance of each factor separately. A summary of the theory involved is given in my paper "Wirtschaftsschwankungen als Folge von Bevölkerungswellen" in Schmollers Jahrbuch, Jahrg. 60, 1936.
5. Factors that work intermittently of course have the precedence in the explanation of business cycles. May I add, however, that even where no such factors determine human optimism, business cycles are quite conceivable. The mere fact of population growth, even if it were at a constant rate, is likely to involve economic fluctuations.
6. I wish to call attention to a forthcoming book by Mr. Constantine E. McGuire who confirms the point of view presented here.

CHAPTER 6

POPULATION GROWTH AND ECONOMIC DEVELOPMENT

What constitutes an underdeveloped country turns on the meaning assigned the term "economic development." In some respects every country may be described as underdeveloped, for no population makes as efficient use as it might of the resources and skills at its disposal. As a rule, however, the term "underdeveloped" is restricted to countries wherein per capita income falls below a certain level. If this level is put at $100, as of 1949, most of Asia and Africa and portions of Oceania and Latin America are describable as underdeveloped. If the level is moved nearer to $200, all of Asia (except Soviet Asia, Israel, and possibly Japan), most of Africa (except South Africa), most of Latin America, and small parts of both Europe and Oceania appear underdeveloped.

Characteristics of the underdeveloped countries and their populations are presented in the papers comprising this chapter. Great population density characterizes many of the underdeveloped countries situated in Asia and some of those located outside of Asia; low density marks most of the others. In nearly all of these countries the potential and/or the actual rate of population growth is high. There is considerable unemployment, disguised and otherwise. The amount of capital and/or cultivable land per worker is low, and capital is formed at a low rate in comparison with income, in part because so many incomes provide little if any more than subsistence. In most of the underdeveloped countries a relatively large fraction of the labor force remains engaged in agriculture. The economies of but few of these countries have undergone considerable modernization, and in most of them persons with technical, professional, or engineering skills form but a small part of the labor force. As a rule, prevailing motivation patterns are not well adapted to the needs of modern economies. While all of these countries are looked upon as underdeveloped, and while the productive capacities of their populations are generally augmentable, the productive *potentials* of these countries apparently vary widely, ranging from very low in those where land and resources are lacking to high in those where land and/or resources are relatively plentiful, or where manufacturing opportunities abound.

The situation of the populations of many present-day underdeveloped countries is worse, Simon Kuznets has found, than were the situations of the populations of the economies of Western and Northern Europe and North America and Oceania 100–200 years ago when the modern industrial revolution was getting under way and spreading. Incomes are appreciably lower in many of the present-day underdeveloped countries, population is more dense in many and growing more rapidly in most. Land and natural resources are not nearly so accessible or available for exploitation as they were in much of Europe, America, and Oceania in the early nineteenth century.

Population factors—in particular, population density, the rate of population growth, and changes in age-composition—play an important role in the determination of the rate of economic development, though, of course, the developmental process is conditioned by many non-demographic factors as well. (a) When a nation's population is dense, it is likely that its land and other resources are in nearly full use, with the result that economic progress tends to be restricted by the increasing scarcity of these agents of production. When, on the contrary, a nation's population is sparse, its numbers may not yet be adequate to permit most effective utilization of its resource equipment. (b) A high rate of population growth entails the use of considerable capital and thereby makes it impossible to augment appreciably the amount of capital in use per head. As children grow up to adulthood they absorb resources and productive efforts that might otherwise be used to form capital. When these children attain adulthood and enter the labor force they require industrial and other capital to equip them. They of course need economic and social overhead capital to sustain them at various stages throughout their lives. It has been estimated, therefore, that a one per cent rate of population growth requires for its support capital formation at a rate approximating 4–5 per cent of national income; it therefore operates to make the rate at which per capita income annually advances something like 0.5–1.0 per cent less than it otherwise would have been. Since net capital formation in underdeveloped countries often approximates only 3–5 per cent of national income, it can contribute very little to the improvement of per capita income. Yet a somewhat similar rate was accompanied by sustained improvement in England in 1688–1760, largely because population was then growing only about one-fourth per cent per year and most of the new capital could be used to provide workers with better equipment. (c) When age-specific fertility and natural increase begin to fall, a population's age composition becomes more favorable to production, since the ratio of persons of working age to total population rises. Changes of this sort may in time augment productive power per head 10–15 per cent or more in underdeveloped countries with age compositions of the sort associated with high age-specific fertility rates.

Inasmuch as persistence of high age-specific fertility rates decelerates both economic development and the progress of per capita income, investment and other programs designed to stimulate economic development and income growth need to slow down rather than to stimulate population growth; hence they need to diminish natality in greater measure than mortality. Presumably, then, development programs should favor types of economic activity, modes and kinds of investment, and patterns of industrial location that are decidedly unfavorable to fertility and hence to natural increase. Otherwise population growth will counterbalance investment and related programs, and in the end, because of the resulting utilization of reserve land and resources, it will be much more difficult than it otherwise would have been to augment per capita income.

It is not possible, by simply correlating rates of growth of population with rates of growth of per capita income, to assess the retardative influence that population growth exercises upon the progress of per capita income. Data are available only for a few countries and for limited time periods. Moreover, although the progress of per capita income depends upon a variety of conditions, little quantitative and other information concerning the separate effects of these conditions is available. Accordingly, even though mere correlation of income and population growth-rates yields insignificant results, it does not follow that the progress of per capita income is influenced only slightly by the rate of population growth. Well-conceived models suggest this influence to be great; and, presumably, it would be found to be great, if the effects of other income determinants could be quantitatively assessed and allowed for.

THE POPULATION OBSTACLE
TO ECONOMIC BETTERMENT *

By Joseph J. Spengler

> "The sire of gods and men, with hard decrees,
> Forbids our plenty to be bought with ease . . ."
> *Virgil,* Georgic I

> "When goods increase, they are increased that
> eat them; . . ."
> *Ecclesiastes,* 5.11

The population factor is only one of the many by which the course of human betterment is affected; but it is one of the most important. Of this we have evidence in man's frequent manifestation of concern lest population grow too much or too little to maximize some variable in which he is interested.

If we would discuss economic betterment meaningfully, we must choose an index suitable to reflect its course. Of the indices available, the most satisfactory appears to be net output per capita per time period, for this index is both a summary measure of many elements after which man aspires and an end result of that process of technological and industrial change which has transformed the economies of at least a quarter of the world's population and raised its levels of living far above the Oriental plane found almost everywhere two centuries ago. We shall make use of this index, therefore, though without implying that it is, of necessity, highly correlated with that inner state known as physiopsychic well-being.

This paper consists of four parts. The first treats of the determinants of economic betterment; the second, of prevailing population trends; and the third, of the nature of the improvement-retarding effects of population growth. In the fourth part, a quantitative estimate of some of these effects is attempted.

I

The determinants of economic betterment, as represented by the movement of per capita real income, may be variously classified. For the purposes of this paper they are categorized on the basis of their sensitivity to changes in the population factor (i.e., to changes in population density, composition,

* Reprinted from Papers and Proceedings of the American Economic Association, Sixty-third Annual Meeting, Chicago, Illinois, December 27–30, 1950, *American Economic Review*, 41 (May 1951), pp. 343–354, by permission of the publisher. (Copyright 1951 by the American Economic Association.)

or total), most sensitive being those included under *A* and least sensitive those listed under *C:*

A.1 Ratio of a nation's labor force to its population.
A.2 Productive assets *in use* per employed worker.
A.3 The effectiveness with which economic activities are organized.
A.4 Genetic composition of the population.

B.1 International exchange relations.
B.2 Ratio of the employed portion of the labor force to the total labor force.
B.3 Extent to which occupational and spatial distribution of employed human and nonhuman agents of production is optimal in character.
B.4 Skill and efficiency of labor force, properties which reflect (i) the state of the industrial arts and (ii) the educational, scientific, and cultural attainments of a population.

C.1 Social structure.
C.2 Culture.

D.1 Residual determinant.

Since the information available does not permit us to show with precision how per capita real income responds to changes in each of these determinants and how they in turn respond to changes in population, we shall merely indicate how population change affects per capita income through the medium of some of the more sensitive of these determinants. We shall ignore A.4 and determinants listed under *C* and *D* and treat only incidentally some listed under *B*.

A.1—the ratio of a nation's labor force to its population—tends to be most favorable when this population has become stationary under Western mortality conditions. For this ratio is conditioned by (*a*) the age composition of the population and (*b*) its state of health. This ratio is most unfavorable to per capita output, therefore, in the underdeveloped countries where the age composition may be something like one-sixth less favorable than in the United States, and where, largely because of poverty due in considerable part to population pressure, the incidence of illness and disease is much higher than in advanced countries. If conditions "*a*" and "*b*" were westernized, per capita income in underdeveloped countries might rise 20 to 30 or more per cent above current levels, other circumstances remaining unchanged.

Determinants A.2 and A.3, while of significance for all countries whose population has passed the income optimum (in which category fall most countries),[1] are of greatest importance for countries which are both overpopulated and characterized by a high population growth potential. Respecting A.2 and A.3 this may be said. (1) Output per worker is highly correlated with the amount of productive assets in use per worker. (2) For this reason, and because the consumption of raw materials is highly correlated with national income, population growth eventually tends to make necessary recourse to natural resources which, because they are inferior or less accessible, cost more to exploit. (3) Population growth is accompanied, within limits, by economies of organization which operate to increase output per worker. (4) An increase in numbers makes for an increase in output per capita so long as (*ceteris paribus*) the increment in output per capita due to the increase in economies or organization consequent upon an increment in population more than offsets the associated decrement (if any) in output per capita due to cost-increases in the extractive industries. (5) The population of a country may be said to be of optimum size when, given the cost of supporting the economically unproductive part of the population,[2] the aggregate population is of the minimum size required to maximize per capita income in a manner compatible with the relevant rate of interest and the assumption that other conditions remain constant.[3]

It follows that the attainment by a country's population of a magnitude in excess of the optimum is an important deterrent to that population's economic betterment. This conclusion is reinforced by the fact that nations whose populations have passed the optimum seldom are again presented with an opportunity to halt their population growth when their numbers have moved into the neighborhood of the optimum. For it is difficult to reduce an actual population in magnitude until it has attained optimum size; and it is rare that circumstances so change as to increase the magnitude of the optimum beyond that already attained by the actual population. The task confronting overpopulated nations, therefore, is not that of striving after an unattainable optimum but that of doing whatever is necessary to increase their per capita income levels even though their numbers are too great. This task includes the prevention of further population growth, however, for reasons to be indicated and because such stimulus as population growth sometimes gives to invention, innovation, and progress, is at a minimum in countries where density of numbers and lowness of per capita income occur jointly.

Let us turn now to determinants B.2-B.4. While one may, under given circumstances, accept the thesis of the stagnationists, it is nonetheless apparent that only under certain institutional conditions does a low or a negative population growth rate make for unemployment. Presumably, an analogous argument may be made in respect of countries where great population density, together with continuing population growth, appears to be producing unemployment. Regional and occupational differences in the rate of natural increase may operate to prevent a country's employed population from becoming optimally distributed in space and among occupations when these differences are not offset by social arrangements designed to secure an optimal distribution. Underutilization of labor of demographic origin appears to be most pronounced in underdeveloped countries where there is considerable agricultural overpopulation. Of importance also is the absorption of capital by population growth. For, as will be shown, such absorption reduces the rate at which the labor force can improve its health, skill, efficiency, and material equipment.

II

It is growth rather than nongrowth of population that is a major obstacle to man's economic betterment in all but a few countries. The stagnationist's explanation of unemployment, insofar as it can be formulated in valid terms, is relevant at present only to about a fifth of the world's population; and this fifth has attained a relatively high income level and is capable of making effective unemployment-preventing adjustments to the nongrowth of its numbers. Most of the remainder of the world's inhabitants are found in countries where population growth is already retarding the improvement of man's living standards. It is of these countries, therefore, that the rest of my paper treats.

That population pressure is a major obstacle to economic betterment in most of the world is readily suggested, though not always demonstrable with precision. Data indicate that per capita income tends to be low where crude population density is relatively great and to be high where it is relatively low. This relationship would be even more marked were the influence of differences in transfer and trading relations taken into account, since these are relatively favorable in most if not all of the densely populated countries where per capita income is relatively high.

That population growth will continue to be a major obstacle to the betterment of man's material lot is apparent. Only about one-fifth of the world's population appears to be approaching a stationary state, and this fifth is composed principally of peoples already enjoying relatively high per capita incomes. Something like another fifth, though describable as proto-stationary, may experience an increase of 50 or more per cent in a half-century. Yet, many of the peoples composing this fifth already have difficulty extracting more than mediocre incomes from their limited equipment of land and resources. The balance of the world's population, close to 60 per cent, is expanding, even though most of its members already receive very low incomes and are badly equipped with land and resources essential to the comfortable support of expanding numbers.[4] Evidently, a major fraction of the population growth in prospect will take place among peoples not well equipped to supply even their present wants.

How much population growth will take place in high-growth-potential countries is not empirically determinable with certainty at present. However, judging by past experience and abstracting from the possibility that a cheap contraceptive could be widely and rapidly diffused, the 1.5 billions concerned and living in Asia,[5] Africa, and Latin America may, in the absence of pronounced obstacles, increase by 100 to 200 or more per cent before they acquire Western fertility patterns and develop a Western age structure; for life expectancy at birth is only about half as high in most of these regions as in the Western World. The order of magnitude of the growth in prospect is suggested by the fact that, should the populations of these regions treble, the population of the world, now close to 2.4 billions, would exceed 5.5

billions a century from now. It is evident, therefore, that, unless a cheap, easily-used contraceptive is developed and widely diffused, population growth is likely to eat up much of those fruits of technical progress which escape the maws of war.

III

Improvement of the economic condition of the some 60 per cent of the world's population whose incomes are very low, often miserably low by Western standards, is possible only on condition that the economies of these peoples are completely transformed. The outstanding characteristic of these economies is their dominance by nonmechanized agriculture, something like three-fourths of their working population being engaged in agriculture pursued in an archaic manner. Accordingly, economic progress presupposes a considerable mechanization and transformation of the agriculture of these countries together with the transference out of agriculture of such "excess" labor as is engaged therein and the creation of a labor force that, in both its agricultural and its nonagricultural branches, has acquired the attitudes, values, and occupational aptitudes essential in rational, mechanized economies.

The development of branches of industry and commerce suited to absorb both the growing nonagricultural labor force and the workers flowing in from agricultural areas involves a number of coinciding steps. (1) There must be brought into being a sufficient supply of persons capable of performing "entrepreneurial" functions. (2) A system of incentives suited to an industrial society must be created. (3) Appropriate facilitating economic, educational, and governmental institutions must be formed. (4) Adequate support must be given to the development of public utilities in appropriate amount and to the establishment of industries which, for one or several reasons, are highly advantageous to economies in the stage of development characteristic of most of the countries under consideration; i.e., industries capable of utilizing available resources and labor, or of satisfying the more urgent wants, or of easing the pressure for foreign exchange, or (because they are complementary to other industries in existence or being established) of reinforcing the industrial development under way.

Industrial evolution along these lines involves two further conditions, the capacity to meet which tends often to be greatly reduced by population growth: (a) the availability of a sufficiency of land and/or natural resources, (b) the formation and/or acquisition of capital at a rate commensurate with the rate of industrial development projected.

Further population growth will accentuate such shortages of land and/or resources as exists in countries where a condition of population pressure already obtains. In North America and Oceania, most of whose population is approaching a stationary state, both resources and land are relatively abundant. In Europe both land and resources are relatively scarce, but much of the population is approaching a stationary state. In Africa, where the population growth potential is high, resources and in some measure land are relatively abundant; but their distribution in space relative to that of population is not such as to afford relief to more than a portion of the inhabitants. Further growth, therefore, will retard the improvement of the economic state of those African populations which lack ready access to lands and resources unexploited or ineffectively exploited at present. In South America, where the population growth potential remains high, both land and ore resources are relatively plentiful; not withstanding, industrial development promises to be greatly restricted by the shortage of coal, water power constituting the principal widespread potential source of energy. Land and energy resources appear to be relatively plentiful in the Soviet Union; still, according to some estimates, iron ore resources are both relatively scarce and not too well located in space. The most acute actual and/or potential shortages, however, are found in Asia, where live over half the world's population and where numbers may well treble in a century. For already Asia's population is short of land, hardly as well equipped with power resources relative to population as are the peoples of Europe, and only about one-fifth as well supplied with iron ore reserves as is the rest of the world. Furthermore, the spatial factor is unfavorable, the bulk of the iron resources of Asia being situated in India, and the bulk of the power resources in China. Presumably, then, only in parts of Africa and South America will further population growth prove economically advantageous. Redistribution of population will serve to correct such localized shortages of numbers as are to be found on other continents.

When a country is short of land and/or raw materials and this shortage is being aggravated by continuing population growth, it may resort to several complementary remedies. First, it may attempt to step up its rate of capital formation, since capital is needed to exploit such natural resources as are at hand, to provide substitutes for critical resources in relatively short supply, to facilitate technical progress, to create good health, and to implant productive skills and attitudes in the labor force. Yet, it is difficult to establish a very high absolute or relative rate of capital formation, when, as is the case in most lands where population pressure and high growth potentials are found, per capita income ranges between $25 and $150 and the relatively wealthy minority devotes most of its income to consumption instead of to capital formation. Second, relief may be sought in foreign lending and foreign trade. However, foreign loans can relieve in but limited measure a shortage of capital imputable to a low rate of domestic capital formation, how much foreign capital an economy can effectively absorb being governed, for technical and economic reasons, by its rate of domestic capital formation. Furthermore, international trade can significantly (but by no means completely) counterbalance a domestic shortage of natural resources only after the domestic economy has been appropriately developed and other relevant conditions have been met. The capacity of a people to find relief for poverty in capital accumulation will be less, in all cases in which the population is of supra-optimum size and land and/or resources are relatively lacking, when a population is growing than when it is stationary.

In sum, population growth operates in four ways to retard the betterment of man's material condition. First, it increases the pressure of numbers upon a nation's land and resource equipment as of any given time. Second, it tends to accentuate this pressure through time by accelerating the rate at which the store of exhaustible and non-replaceable natural resources is used up and the costs of their use are increased. Third, it diminishes the rate at which capital can be accumulated, and this diminution is greatly accentuated when, as is the case in most overpopulated countries, much potential capital is utilized in maintaining for a few years children who eventually die before they reach a productive age.[6] Fourth, given the rate of capital formation, the rate at which the equipment of the labor force can be increased is reduced. Only in the small number of countries where the population is of infra-optimum size will an increase in numbers, through its salutary influence upon economic organization, more than offset the adverse effects enumerated.

IV

Both the problem being posed and the consequences of population growth may be translated into terms of per capita real income. Consider first the problem itself. Per capita income in many lands is only a minor fraction of per capita income in Oceania, North America, and Northwest Europe. Furthermore, judging by the past, we may assume that for some time to come per capita real income will increase 1 to 2 per cent per year in these parts. It follows that, if the material condition of peoples living in very low-income areas is to improve both absolutely and relative to that of high-income populations, these peoples must advance their per capita incomes appreciably more than 2 per cent per year for many years to come. While such an advance may tend to be restrained by the relatively slower rate of growth of the high-income countries,[7] it will be facilitated by the higher rate of technical progress of which the low-income countries are susceptible in virtue of the fact that their economies remain founded upon technically primitive methods of production.

Since an increase in a nation's capital equipment per worker tends to be accompanied by an increase in output per worker, population growth may be looked upon as a deterrent to the increase of per capita income whenever a nation's population is of supra-optimum size. For population growth, together with excessive mortality among those of infra-working age, diverts resources from the formation of capital to the formation of population, whilst the necessity of equipping increments in population makes the magnitude of the increment in per capita equipment lower than it would have been had the population not grown.

Let us first suppose that both the rate of saving and the income-producing power of capital are independent of the rate of population growth. Then a 1 per cent increase in population will be purchased at the cost of something like a 1 per cent increase in per capita income. Given the validity of these assumptions, the 1 per cent per year increase in population roughly characteristic of many densely populated low-income countries operates to prevent an increase of about 1 per cent per year in per capita income. Thus, if per capita income would grow 3 per cent per year in the absence of population growth, it will grow only about 2 per cent per year when the population is increasing 1 per cent per year.[8]

The assumptions just made must be modified, however. First, the income-producing power of capital is not independent of changes in the size of the labor force. On the basis of past experience, when a 1 per cent increase in both the employed labor force and the stock of capital or wealth in use is accompanied by a 2 per cent increase in income, this 2 per cent may be imputed to the forces generating it somewhat as follows: technical progress, 1; labor, 0.7; other productive agents, 0.3. Accordingly, given a 12 per cent saving rate, a 1 per cent increase in the labor force, and technical progress as indicated, about 7/26 of the 2.6 per cent increase in national income would be attributable to the 1 per cent increase in the employed labor force. In general, it is probably safe to say that 25 to 35 per cent of the annual increase in output consequent upon increases of 1 and 1 to 3 per cent, respectively, in labor and capital are attributable to the increment in labor.[9] Secondly, account must be taken of the absorption, by population growth and relevant premature mortality, of resources that would otherwise have been transmuted into wealth or capital. When these two conditions are taken into account, a 1 per cent increase in population is usually found to be purchased at a cost of between somewhat less and somewhat more than a 1 per cent increase in per capita income.[10] It should be noted finally that the productivity of reproducible capital will be higher *ceteris paribus* when the land and natural resources with which this capital can be combined are relatively plentiful. The absence of this condition from many low-income economies makes more difficult their counterbalancing population growth by capital formation.[11]

By way of summary it may be said that population growth is a major obstacle to economic betterment in most parts of the world. It is retarding capital formation, accelerating the rate of depletion of the world's limited store of nonreplaceable resources, augmenting the rise of costs in increasing cost industries, and decelerating the rate of increase of per capita income. Whether a cheap contraceptive, together with a set of motives conducing to its widespread use in the overpopulated parts of the world, can be developed in good time remains to be seen. It is evident, however, in view of the limitedness of the fund of nonreplaceable resources at the disposal of mankind and in view of the dangers to the security of the relatively stationary peoples implicit in the continued growth of peoples living in overpopulated lands, that the former should not give impetus to the multiplication of unfriendly components of the latter.

REFERENCES

1. See my "Measures of Population Maladjustment," *Proceedings* of the Fourteenth International Sociological Conference, Rome, 1950–51. As is shown in this paper, the population optimum tends to be confused with the spatial optimum. There is no evidence to suggest that the population optimum has increased in recent decades; but there is, as the analyses of A. Toynbee and others suggest, evidence to indicate that the magnitude of what constitutes a viable politico-economic system has been increasing for some decades. If this inference be valid, consolidation of the many nonviable small systems into a small number of large viable systems would be accompanied by some alleviation of both consciousness of population pressure and concern lest numbers be growing too slowly. Presumably, as A. Sauvy suggests (in *Population et Richesse*, Paris, 1949, pp. 34–35), consolidation of smaller units tends to alter their individual optima.

2. By unproductive population is meant that part of a population which, though it produces no income, must be or is supported by the productive population at some aggregate, variable cost C. The best example of an unproductive population is that sequesterable part of a population which is continually required to provide a nation's military forces and which, therefore, includes women, children, and both retired and active military personnel. Since the determinants of the magnitude of this "unproductive" population are not describable with precision in a few words, we shall represent it by p' and the cost of supporting it by $C = f(p')$. Then the total population P may be defined as made up of p' and p, with p representing the "productive" population. Let Y represent the national income which, by definition, is produced by p; y, the per capita income retained by p, which equals Y/P when p' and C have zero values and $(Y-C)/p$ when p' and C have positive values; and y', per capita production of income at the margin; namely $\Delta Y/\Delta p$. If p' and C have zero values and therefore p is identical with P, the population of optimum size is the smallest population associated with the condition of that $y = y'$. (The stipulation that the optimum be the smallest population compatible with this condition must be made if the maximization of income through time is the desideratum since, other conditions being given, the smaller the optimum population, the smaller the drain on nonrenewable resources.) If, however, p' and C assume positive values, the income retained per capita by p will no longer by Y/p but $(Y - C)/p$ which is less than Y/p. It will therefore be to the advantage of the productive population p to increase its magnitude; for, although in the original position y and y' were equal, in the new position y', whose value as yet remains at the original level, exceeds y whose value has been reduced from Y/p to $(Y-C)/p$. The optimum size for p is attained when y' and $(Y-C)/p$ again become equal. Whence, given the magnitude of p', the optimum size for P may be defined as p' *plus* the optimum size for p given by the fact that p is required to support p' to the extent of outlay C. Of course, it being given that p' may feasibly be reduced to zero, the preferred optimum is p ($= P$), with $y = y'$. If, however, for reasons of security or otherwise, p' cannot be reduced to zero, it is to the advantage of p that its size be increased so long as such increase augments p's retained income y. While this note has been suggested by A. Sauvy's analysis (see *op. cit.* p. 27), the concept of the cost of supporting the economically unproductive population component, if any, has been substituted for his concept of "general expenses."

3. That the optimum is affected by the relevant rate of interest i may be illustrated as follows, it being assumed that C and p' as defined in the preceding note have zero values. Let W represent productive assets in use; Y, national income; P, population; and y, per capita income Y/P. Now suppose an increase ΔP in population requiring an increase ΔW in W such that the assets/population ratio is unchanged from its initial W/P value. Suppose further that increment ΔP in population is accompanied by Δy_0, an increment

in y due to increased economy of organization and Δy_r, a decrement in y due to increased costs in the extraction of raw materials. So long as W and i may be ignored, whether increment ΔP is economically advantageous turns on whether Δy_0 is greater or less than Δy_r. But W and i may not be ignored. The increment $P\Delta y$ in the income of the initial population P, which accompanies the increment ΔP in population, entails an increment ΔW in the nation's stock of capital for the equipping of the increment ΔP in population. This increment ΔW entails an annual interest cost $i\Delta W$. Accordingly, the initial population P will find advantage in the increment Δy in its per capita income (an increment supposedly associated with increment ΔP in population) only if $(P\Delta y/\Delta W) > i$. Of course, if the initial population P derives from ΔP some noneconomic advantage such as a feeling of greater security, it will deem ΔP advantageous even though $(P\Delta y/\Delta W) < i$. Should p' and C have positive values (see note 2) these may be taken into account.

4. For supporting data see my "Aspects of the Economics of Population Growth," *Southern Economic Journal*, 1948, and my "Economic Factors in the Development of Densely Populated Areas," *Proceedings* of the American Philosophical Society, Philadelphia, February, 1951.

5. In 1947 that 20 per cent of the world's population which lived in noneastern Europe, North America, and Oceania enjoyed a mean expectation of life at birth of 50 to 60 or more years; the 15 per cent living in Eastern Europe and Japan, 40 to 50; the 6.6 per cent in Latin America, 35 to 40; and the 58 per cent in Asia and Africa, close to 30, as a rule. See *World Population Trends*, United Nations, pp. 10–13. Let e represent life expectancy at birth and k the annual number of births. Then, on the assumption that k remains unchanged, the population of a country will approach and finally reach ek, increasing as e increases. If, as has always been the case in the past, fertility fails to fall fast enough to offset increases in e, k will increase for a time, with the result that the final population becomes not ek but $e(k + \Delta k)$. Thus, if e doubles and k increases by one-half before it levels off, the population will treble. For example, by the time Japan's population has completed the growth cycle begun in the mid-nineteenth century, its population will have attained a magnitude three or more times that obtaining in 1850. Having indicated that "at least a threefold multiplication is implicit in the processes by which people hitherto have achieved low birth and death rates," M. C. Balfour, R. F. Evans, F. W. Notestein, and I. B. Taeuber conclude that "in the Far East . . . we have no reason to expect a smaller multiplier." See *Public Health and Demography in the Far East* (Rockefeller Foundation, 1950), pp. 6–7. What is said here is applicable to other parts of Asia and to much of Africa and Latin America.

6. D. Ghosh estimates at something like 22.5 per cent of the Indian national income the cost of maintaining those who die before they reach the age of 15. The corresponding figure for England is put at 6.5 per cent. See *Pressure of Population and Economic Efficiency in India* (New Delhi, 1946), p. 22. In 1934–38, according to C. Clark, capital formation approximated only 6 per cent of India's national income. Analogous conditions are found in many other parts of Asia.

7. Suppose we divide the countries of the world into two categories, the rapidly growing, G, and the slowly growing, S, with their rates of growth represented by R_g and R_s. Then $R_g = f(R_s)$, the specific relation between the two rates turning on whether G and S are primarily substitutes for each other, complements to each other, or independent systems. If, as appears likely, the dominant form of relationship will be a complementary one in the early stages of the development of G, R_s will exercise a restrictive influence upon R_g. This influence will diminish in time, however, as the complementary type of relationship gives place to one that is substitutive or independent. Presumably, an economy that is large (e.g., the Russian or the Chinese) can more easily free its rate of expansion of the conditioning influence of expansion elsewhere than can an economy that is small and relatively short of elements requisite for economic expansion. That the less developed countries are significantly dependent upon the more developed countries is suggested by data presented in F. Hilgerdt, *The Network of World Trade* (Geneva, 1942), especially pp. 37 ff., and Tse Chun Chang, "A Statistical Note on World Demand for Exports," *Review of Economic Statistics*, 1948, pp. 106 ff.

8. Let Y represent national income; W, the wealth or capital used to produce that income; ΔY and ΔW, the annual increment in Y and W, respectively; r, the annual rate of growth of population P; y, the per capita income Y/P; j, the annual rate of increase in per

capita income, $\Delta y/y$; a, the annual rate of capital or wealth formation expressed as a percentage of Y, namely $\Delta W/Y$; and s, the increment in Y consequent upon an increment in W, namely $\Delta Y/\Delta W$. Let us assume for the sake of simplicity, furthermore, that s remains constant for the period under consideration. It follows that

$$j = \frac{1 + as}{1 + r} - 1$$

If population is not growing and r has a zero value, $j = as$. Accordingly, if the value of s were independent of that of r, the value of j would be reduced by approximately r. Thus if a has a value of 0.1, the annual rate of saving approximating 10 per cent of the national income and s has a value of 0.25 (on the assumption that W/Y has a persisting value of about 4), j will have a value of 0.025 so long as population is not growing and r has a zero value. If, however, r has a value of .01, the value of j will approximate 0.015 instead of 0.025. If a has a lower value when r has a value of .01 than when r has a zero value, the value of j will be further reduced. See note 10 below.

This formulation does not take net capital imports into account. If these are represented by A, then as in the above equation becomes $(a + A)s$. There is a practicable upper limit to A/a. In the paper cited in note 4 above it is suggested that the average upper limit to A/a may be in the neighborhood of one-third. If it be true that the poorest half of the world's population produces only one-tenth of the world's income, and if it should save and invest 0.3 of this, it still could use (on the supposition that A/a cannot long exceed one-third) only about one-fifth of the savings which the richest tenth can supply if they save and invest 10 per cent of the 55 per cent of the world's income which they supposedly receive.

9. See J. Tinbergen, "Zür Theorie der langfristigen Wirtschaftsentwicklung," *Weltwirtschaftliches Archiv*, 55 Band, Heft 3, 1942, pp. 511–547. See also E. C. Olson, "Factors Affecting International Differences in Production," *American Economic Review*, May, 1948, pp. 502–522. In the four largest industrial nations in 1870–1913, at the time when about 10–15 per cent of the national income was saved, population was growing about 1 per cent per year, and national income was increasing 2.1–2.5 per cent per year, this increment was distributable somewhat as follows: population, 0.7; capital accumulation, 0.4–0.8; technical improvement, 1.0 Cp. Tinbergen and J. J. Pollak, *The Dynamics of Business Cycles* (Chicago, 1950), p. 128.

10. Let s, as defined in note 8 above, be divided into s_r and s_n where s_r is due to population growth r and s_n is due to other circumstances. Further, let $a = a_n - a_r$ where a_n represents the annual rate of saving or capital formation when $r = O$, and a_r represents the reduction in a_n due to r's having a positive value. Then the annual rate of increase in per capita income

$$j = \frac{1 + a_n s_n + a_n s_r - a_r s_n}{1 + r} - 1$$

When r has a value of zero, the value of j becomes as_n. It follows that j will have a greater value when r has a zero instead of a positive value so long as $(r + a_r s_n) > (a_n s_r)$. The values to be assigned to these variables vary with situation. Suppose we make $a_n = 0.2$, and $a_r = 0.1$. Let the elasticity of productivity for capital be 0.3 and that for population be 0.7. Finally let technical progress increase Y one per cent per year. (Actually the capacity of technical progress to increase income is itself a function of a, but here it is treated as a constant fraction of Y.) If $r = O$, j becomes .025; but if $r = .01$, j approximates .0094. Under the assumed conditions, therefore, r's having a value of .01 instead of zero reduces the annual rate of increase in per capita income by about three-fifths. The value to be assigned to a_r in any particular case depends both upon the magnitude of r and upon the amount of resources absorbed by premature mortality associated with r and destined, in the absence of such mortality, to be saved and invested.

The income optimum population may be defined in terms similar to those used above in this note. Let $s = s_n [1 + f(r)]$ where s and s_n are defined as above and $f(r)$ replaces s_r. Then

$$j = \frac{as_n [1 + f(r)]}{1 + r}$$

When r has a zero value j becomes as_n. When r has a positive value j is higher than when r has a zero value only on condition that $f(r) > r$. Accordingly, population maladjustment may be said to increase whenever, as is usually the case, $r > f(r)$.

11. Colin Clark concludes that the value of s, when only reproducible capital is taken into account, rises as reproducible capital per worker and output per worker per hour increase. With income and reproducible capital per worker represented by y and c, the ratio y/c rises from about 0.22 when real income in I.U. per man-hour approximates 0.10 (the figure for India in 1944 is put at .09) to about 0.28 when hourly real income is 1.0 (as in the United States in 1945). (See *Review of Economic Progress*, II, 1950, No. 1.) Since this increase in y/c, granted the accuracy of the data on which it is based, is not attributable to an increase in nonreproducible capital or labor, it must be attributed to technical progress and similar output-increasing forces. While Clark's data relate more largely to time than to space, they lend support to the view that, insofar as space may be equated to time, the spread of Western methods in space will be accompanied for a while by an increasing rate of technical progress in the underdeveloped countries.

POPULATION AND THE FURTHER SPREAD
OF INDUSTRIAL SOCIETY*

By Kingsley Davis

From a world standpoint the transition to industrialism is still in its infancy. Incomplete even in the West, it has barely started (though its effects have been felt) in the rest of the world. Mankind thus finds itself at the critical point in a socio-economic revolution transcending anything ever known in the past. Those peoples still in the *previous* stage of development—the pastoral and agricultural stage—suffer an extreme disadvantage vis-a-vis the more advanced peoples. Not only are they poorer, but, since the presence of industrialism anywhere affects men everywhere, they have been caught in a worldwide economic and political net that has exploited their weakness, and ironically, affected their opportunities for acquiring industrialism.

To contemporary eyes the spread of industrialism may seem painfully slow, but viewed in archeological perspective it is amazingly rapid. Premonitory signs and conditions aside, the actual transformation came in the last 150 years.[2] Since borrowing is easier than invention, the recently industrialized areas (U.S.A., Australia, Argentina, Japan) have made the transition more rapidly than did northwestern Europe; the pace of industrial change has tended to accelerate.[3] There are reasons to believe, therefore, that the transformation may become worldwide within a century or so.

It is not surprising that the fast rise and spread of such a fundamental transformation has given rise to insecurity and turbulence in human society, particularly in view of the sharp regional inequalities created by a partial industrialization of the world. A new kind of insecurity has been born, an insecurity not so much of bread (though that too still occurs) but of institutions and social expectations. A new scale of conflicts has been reached, global in scope and armed with the newest psychological and material weapons of our latest stage of civilization. This turbulence, however regrettable from a humanitarian standpoint, is functional in the great transformation, for it is by the cataclysmic occurrences that old ways of life can be sloughed off hastily; it is by instability that new modes of stability can arise. The archaic agricultural regions of the world are now the battleground. Because they are weak and poor, because they are industrial vacuums, because they embrace huge areas and large populations, they are important

* Reprinted from *Proceedings of the American Philosophical Society*, 95 (February 1951), pp. 8–19, by permission of the author and the American Philosophical Society. Read April 20, 1950, in the Symposium on Problems of Development of Densely Settled Areas.[1]

pawns in the struggle. They face the greatest potential change and hence the greatest instability.

THE DIMENSIONS OF AGRICULTURALISM. A country can be safely regarded as still in the peasant agricultural stage if more than 50 per cent of its gainfully occupied males are engaged in farming, fishing, hunting, and forestry. This definition excludes the type of nation whose economy rests primarily on products of the land but whose farming is mechanized. The latter cannot have half of its occupied males in agriculture, because mechanized farming requires little labor and yet produces a sufficient surplus to support a substantial labor force in secondary and tertiary industry.[4] Since this kind of country is sometimes called "agricultural," a better designation for the type that interests us would perhaps be "non-mechanized." But regardless of the name the distinction is clear, as our data will show.

World Distribution of Peasant Agriculturalism. Applying the 50-per-cent criterion and using computations and estimates prepared by the Bureau of Applied Social Research for dates around 1940–47,[5] we find that the non-mechanized, or archaic, agricultural countries and colonies embrace 74 per cent of the world's habitable area and 76 per cent of its people. They are distributed by major continents or regions as shown in table 1. Their location is seemingly governed in the main by the complex interrelations of climate, indigenous population density, and accessibility to international trade. It is a striking fact, for example, that archaic agriculturalism is heavily concentrated in tropical areas, modern industrialism in temperate areas. One possible explanation of this fact is that tropical climates are a deterrent,

TABLE 1

PROPORTION OF AREA AND POPULATION LIVING IN
AGRICULTURAL COUNTRIES, BY CONTINENTS

	Area (per cent)	Population (per cent)
World	74	76
Africa	100	100
Asia (excl. U.S.S.R.)	99	93
Central America and Caribbean	94	88
South America	79	77
Europe (excl. U.S.S.R.)	42	30
Oceania	7	16
U.S.A.-Canada	—	—
U.S.S.R.	100	100

though not an impregnable barrier, to industrial development. However, it would appear to be also true that industrial retardation in tropical areas is due in greater degree to their past success as agricultural regions, to their uncongeniality for persons of temperate-zone European culture, and to their inaccessibility. Bearing in mind the factors of climate, indigenous density, and accessibility, we find that the "europeanization of the world" has in fact proceeded along four different lines at different rates:

(A) *Temperate—Accessible—Vacant.*

In temperate areas accessible to trade but with sparse indigenous populations, the Europeans have tended to take possession of the land, to settle, and to grow in numbers by immigration and natural increase. Here industrialization has generally occurred and colonial political status has disappeared. Examples: Australia, New Zealand, Canada-U.S.A., and temperate South America.[6]

(B) *Tropical—Accessible—Vacant.*

In tropical and semi-tropical areas accessible to trade but with sparse native populations, the Europeans have tended to engage in estate agriculture, using imported African slaves or indentured Asiatics to supplement the scarce and unwilling native labor. Such areas have remained in a colonial status more frequently than the areas mentioned above and have failed to industrialize. Examples: West Indies, Malaya, and the Fiji Islands.[7]

(C) *Accessible—Occupied.*

In areas accessible to trade but with dense native populations, the Europeans have not settled in great numbers but have used political and economic dominance to gain their ends. The past success of native agriculture in such regions, nearly all of them tropical, is what enabled them to support dense populations and to ward off European settlement if not European control, and thus eventually to make a strong bid for independence. Examples: India, Ceylon, Java, and China.

(D) *Inaccessible—Vacant.*

In non-accessible and sparsely settled areas European penetration has been light, although colonial control or political annexation has been established and maintained. Since accessibility is a matter of degree, however, depending on the state of the technology, where the resources appear favorable this type of area is now being opened up and is facing potentially rapid development. One reason for inaccessibility has been the past inability of Europeans to cope with certain kinds of tropical conditions. Examples: New Guinea, much of tropical Africa, central South America and parts of the Netherlands Indies.

It follows from these four lines of European penetration that most of the tropical areas of the world, with a few exceptions, have remained in an agricultural stage. It follows also that most of them have until recently remained under outright political control or at least political and economic dominance. As of 1950 the relation between agriculturalism and outright dependence can be shown by the fact that only 1 per cent of the people in industrial areas were dependent, whereas 10 per cent of those in agricultural countries were so classed.[8] Expressing the matter differently, we find that 98 per cent of the population of dependent areas are in agricultural countries and only 2 per cent in industrial ones, whereas the figures are 75 and 25 per cent in the case of independent areas.

Agricultural Density. With reference to population density, both the urban-industrial and the peasant-agricultural areas differ remarkably among themselves. Using a functional definition of density as the number of agricul-

turally employed males per square mile of agricultural land,[9] we find the
highest figure in an industrial country—namely Japan, which has a density of
410. On the other hand, the United States and Canada, also industrial, have an
average of only 10 agriculturally employed males per square mile of agricultural soil. Similarly there is great variation between one agricultural country
and another. In India-Pakistan, for example, the average farmer-farmland
density is approximately 152 per square mile, whereas it is only 61 in Spain. In
spite of this variation among both industrial and nonindustrial countries, the
averages for the two types differ significantly. The industrial countries of the
world have an average agricultural density of only 32 male farmers per square
mile of farm land, whereas the agricultural countries have an average over
three times as large—namely, 113 per square mile. This is what one would
expect, since industrial countries usually practice a mechanized type of
farming and hence need less manpower in relation to the land.[10] Table 2

TABLE 2

AGRICULTURAL DENSITY ACCORDING TO DEGREE
OF AGRICULTURALISM

Per cent of occupied males in agriculture	Agricultural males per square mile of agricultural land
0–29.9	18
30–49.9	55
50–69.9	73
70+	139

shows that the more agricultural a country is, the higher its agricultural
density tends to be. Table 3 shows that, as between the urban-industrial
and peasant-agricultural countries, the difference in density tends to be
consistent in direction within major continents or regions. The only exception is Asia, where only one country—Japan—represents the industrial category. Japan is interesting as showing that labor-intensive agriculture *can* be
combined with modern industrialization. Japan started its industrialization
on an intensive and densely settled agricultural base, whereas no other industrial country started with anything like such a high agricultural density.[11]

If three-fourths of the world's people still live in agricultural countries,
how many of them live in countries of high agricultural density? From one
point of view they nearly all do, for as we have just seen, the agricultural
countries, which are poor, generally have a higher agricultural density than
the industrial countries, which are rich. It comes as a shock, for example, to
find that the rural countries of South America, the "empty" continent, have
an agricultural density almost as great as the rural countries of Europe.
To use the agricultural density in industrial areas as a yardstick, therefore,
leads us to the true conclusion that most agricultural countries have too
many people on the land. It is of some interest, however, to locate some of
those agricultural countries which are above the average (113) in rural

density. The following list gives the figures for selected countries of importance:

Egypt	382	Colombia	217
Indo-China	322	Peru	174
Indonesia	302	Puerto Rico	170
Jamaica	297	Ecuador	166
Ceylon	282	Thailand	153
Korea	279	India*	152
China	260	Union of South Africa	145
Albania	220	Mexico	138

* Including Pakistan.

The problem of acute agricultural density is primarily a problem of Eastern and Southern Asia, although it is also a major problem in the Caribbean and Middle American region. Table 4 shows the truth of this generalization.

TABLE 3

AGRICULTURAL DENSITY BY CONTINENT AND TYPE OF COUNTRY*

	Agriculturally occupied males per square mile of agricultural land[a]		
	All countries	Urban-industrial countries[b]	Peasant-agricultural countries[b]
World	88	32	113
U.S.A.-Canada	10	10	[c]
Oceania	17	14	25
South America	57	16	101
U.S.S.R.	62	[c]	62
Africa	64	[c]	64
Europe (excl. U.S.S.R.)	74	69	79
Caribbean and Central America	128	85[d]	135
Asia (excl. U.S.S.R.)	182	410[e]	178

[a] Agricultural males are those gainfully occupied in farming, hunting, fishing and forestry. Agricultural land is defined as including land under crops, lying fallow, and in orchards.

[b] Urban-industrial countries are those which have 0–49 per cent of their occupied males in agriculture; peasant-agricultural countries are those which have 50 or more per cent of their occupied males so engaged.

[c] No countries in the category. Africa has no industrial countries. If only the white population of South Africa were included, it would be defined as industrial; but most of the population is actually rural black.

[d] The only industrial country in Central and Caribbean America is Cuba.

[e] The only industrial country in Asia is Japan.

* Data on males gainfully occupied in agriculture taken mostly from censuses when available, from the United Nations "Demographic Yearbook" 1948, or from estimates made by the Bureau of Applied Social Research. Data on agricultural areas taken mostly from Food and Agriculture Organization "Yearbook of Food and Agricultural Statistics, 1948, 1 Production" (Washington, 1950), adjusted by the Bureau in some instances, or from estimates made by the Bureau.

Agricultural density throughout the globe shows a relationship to the different lines of "europeanization" mentioned above. The temperate regions accessible to trade but with sparse native populations (type "A"), regions which have been occupied by Europeans and rapidly industrialized, now show some of the lowest rural densities in the world. For instance, Australia and Canada-Newfoundland have only 11 male agriculturalists per square mile of farm land, the United States and Canada only 10. Agricultural settlement in these new countries is remarkably sparse when compared to the world average for industrial countries—32 male agriculturalists per square mile of agricultural land; or when compared to the average for European industrial countries—69.

The tropical and semi-tropical areas accessible to trade and with sparse native populations (type "B"), where Europeans have for long periods engaged in estate agriculture using imported African slave or Asiatic indentured labor and where therefore a now predominantly non-European population has largely replaced the original natives, show high but by no means the highest agricultural densities. The region that most typifies this type of settlement is the Caribbean. The whole Middle-American and Caribbean region has an average of 128 male farmers per square mile of agricultural land, but most of the islands have figures above this. For instance, Jamaica has a figure of 297; Puerto Rico, 170. What is interesting about this region, however, is that industrialization is beginning. Cuba has crossed the threshold of industrialization (by our 50-per-cent criterion), and consequently has a density figure of 81 only. Puerto Rico is on the verge of crossing the line, but shows some signs of moving in the direction of Japan with a high rural density combined with industry.

TABLE IV

AGRICULTURAL COUNTRIES: PROPORTION OF AREA AND POPULATION ABOVE OR BELOW WORLD AGRICULTURAL DENSITY*

Region	Area (per cent)	Population (per cent)	Region	Area (per cent)	Population (per cent)
World			Europe		
Above	40	71	Above	13	15
Below	60	29	Below	87	85
Asia (excl. U.S.S.R.)			Oceania		
Above	86	94	Above	6	11
Below	14	6	Below	94	89
America, Central and the Caribbean			U.S.S.R.		
			Above†	—	—
Above	93	90	Below	100	100
Below	7	10	U.S.A.–Canada		
Africa			Above†	—	—
Above	33	52	Below†	—	—
Below	67	48			
America, South					
Above	25	28			
Below	75	72			

* The average agricultural density for the agricultural countries of the world is 113 gainfully occupied males per square mile of agricultural land.

† No countries in this category.

The highest agricultural densities are found in regions with teeming native populations where Europeans have not settled in great numbers (type "C"). To illustrate, China has something like 260 male farmers per square mile of farm land, Indo-China approximately 322, Ceylon 282, and India 152. Since most of these countries are located on the Asiatic continent and constitute the bulk of the Asian population, they explain Asia's continental average of 178—the highest average for the non-industrial countries of any continent. Few of these countries are as yet anywhere near making the transition across the 50-per-cent-line. Japan alone has accomplished it; only Russia and Malaya approach it.[12]

The lowest agricultural densities, outside of the newly industrialized areas of European immigration, are found in the non-accessible and sparsely settled backward regions (type "D"). Not every country or colony in this category shows a low agricultural density. For instance, Kenya has an estimated 194 male cultivators to every square mile of agricultural land, and Tanganyika has 138.[13] Nevertheless, in most such areas the technology is so poor that not only is manpower the chief implement of work, but a fairly large area is required even for the sustenance of this manpower. The agricultural countries of Oceania, for example, have an average of 25 male agriculturalists per square mile of agricultural land. Africa, with an average of 64, compares favorably with the nonindustrial countries of Europe (average 79) and with the U.S.S.R. (62). As yet these type "D" areas are generally the most retarded of all, having been left that way because of their inaccessibility to markets or their deadliness. Yet because they have generally a small ratio between cultivated land and potentially useful land, and because they often have other unexploited resources, their prognosis for modernization may be more favorable than the other two types of agricultural country which have, as we have seen, crowded populations. If their untapped resources were quickly put to use, they could accomplish the industrial transition almost overnight, without building up a huge population. Heavy capitalization, mechanization of large-scale agriculture, and growth of industry, together with a shortage of labor, a ban on coolie immigration, and social opportunity for all classes (no race barriers) could not only bring in a moderate but important number of European immigrants with European fertility habits but could possibly change the fertility pattern of the natives within two generations. Such areas, when developed, would therefore have a chance of resembling Australia, New Zealand, and Argentina rather than Japan or India. At any rate, since relatively few people live in such areas at present, their current poverty does not pose the great human problems that the more crowded agricultural countries pose.

SOCIAL STRUCTURE OF CROWDED AGRICULTURALISM.—The preceding analysis of agricultural densities in relation to the different modes of europeanization helps us to understand the currently high densities in particular areas. The problem of excess numbers is most acute in those parts of the world that were relatively well settled prior to European contact and were at the same time readily accessible to Europeans. It is also acute, but less so at present, in those areas in which Europeans carved out for themselves large landed estates, bringing in natives from other areas to replace or supplement the sparse indigenous population. In the first case, as observed in countries like China, Egypt, and India, there was, prior to European contact, a sufficient amount of farm technology, soil resources, and trade to support rather thick populations on the basis of traditional agriculture. But this agricultural civilization had its inherent limits. Organized on a village basis, with poor transportation and an oxcart technology, the surplus it produced was relatively small, hard to store and hard to distribute to famine areas. Some of the surplus was used, furthermore, to support relatively small groups at high levels of consumption, such as priests, soldiers, medicine men, and a ruling elite. Under such circumstances, in comparison with the present situation, only a moderate density was reached. Although the thickness of settlement in some fertile alluvial plains was greater than anything human society had known before, it was far less than what can be widely found in modern times.

With the origin of industry in Western Europe and its spread to other areas of European settlement, the only densely peopled agricultural country outside of Europe to become industrialized was Japan. The others—mostly in Asia but also in North Africa—evolved a new mixed type of society based on contact with and political and economic subordination to the industrial peoples. Under this stimulus their agriculture became commercialized, more efficient, less diversified, and more individualistically controlled. The peasants were drawn willy nilly into a money economy, producing for a foreign market over which they had little control; the handicraftsmen were impoverished by the competition of cheap manufactures from foreign factories; the native leaders lost their control or became identified with the foreign masters as kept princes, landlords, and bureaucrats. The profits from this commercialized peasant agriculture were partly syphoned off by the industrial peoples and partly used by the local population to buy foreign manufactures, not to finance local industrial development. The native death rate was reduced through the control of famines, wars, and epidemics, but the birth rate remained static because, owing to the lack of industrial development, the people remained agricultural. The bulk of the native people became to a phenomenal degree a sort of rural proletariat, producing with its labor raw materials for the rest of the world but itself living at a very low level and not controlling the source of its income. The population did not grow as fast as it did in industrializing countries (some of which were industrializing on the basis of their colonies) but fast enough to add considerably to already heavy densities. In fact, the influence of colonial agriculturalism on population growth can be seen by the fact that some wholly new countries—such as Puerto Rico and Jamaica—soon also came to have a dense agricultural settlement, and in the countries of the oldest agriculture, new tracts were opened up for cultivation which soon reached densities the equal of old tracts. In short, the countries not settled by Europeans but having either an already substantial native population or acquiring a population through the slave trade, indenture, and coolie migration had a commercial revolution thrust upon them but did not achieve an industrial revolution. Demographically, they wound up in the situation of having an industrial density with only an agricultural economy. Now their pressing problem is how to acquire the industry when numbers have already grown so large as to bankrupt the agricultural system which alone is their avenue of capital.

Old Versus Mixed Culture. It is fashionable to say that the densely settled peoples of Asia have a variety of traditional cultures different from one another and different from that of the West, and that it is necessary to understand these cultures before one can understand the current predicament of the peoples in question. But while the initial premise is partially true, the conclusion does not fully follow. To a degree all of these overcrowded agricultural countries are alike. They are alike, in the first place, because the pre-industrial conditions of village farming made for a certain basic similarity in the traditional cultures themselves. All of the old cultures emphasized the family, kinship, and the joint household, all had some kind of village polity; all had a handicraft system; all took a religious and magical attitude toward the world; all gave women a position identified with home and children. It was these generalized traits, rather than the differences intriguing to the anthropologist, that determined the economic and demographic response to western contact. In terms of consequences the significant fact about traditional cultures was not so much the differences among themselves but the profound contrast between all of them and modern industrialism. And this leads us to the second cause of similarity among present-day agricultural peoples—namely, the fact that nearly all of them have been subjected to dominance and diffusion by industrial nations. Caste in India, familism in China, Mohammedanism in Egypt, communalism in Java—whatever differences these involved (and it is easy to exaggerate them) have been profoundly altered by western impact. The full force of this impact has been ably described by Furnivall.[14] Although the main nexus between the native and the European has been economic, Furnivall points out that economic behavior is in itself anarchic. It has to be subordinated to other ends by law and custom if there is to be an ordered society, and so, once released by the European from the customary native controls, it could not be stopped, because the native could not under the circumstances absorb the whole European social system.

. . . the West comes to the tropics as a liberator; it liberates the people both from the oppression of arbitrary personal authority, and from the burden of social abuses that the people have tolerated in the name of custom. Soon, however, there succeeds a second stage. So far as the people are released from customary inhibitions, economic forces are subject to no restraint but that of western law. In the West the law is an expression of social will, proceeding from the society itself and reinforcing custom, while adapting old customs to new circumstances. But in the tropics western law is imposed on society from outside, and, because it is not an expression of social will, it is powerless to restrain anti-social economic forces. These forces, liberated from the control of custom by the impact of the West, pursue their natural course, breaking down the social order, disintegrating native organic society into individual atoms, and, by thus depriving man of social protection against natural selfishness, operate more intensively, eliminating social values, and diffusing poverty.[15]

The village organization, with its restraints upon the use of land, quickly disintegrated. It no longer served as an intermediary between the individual and the state. The native leaders who naturally supported local cultural achievement by patronizing the arts, the priesthood, and the medical profession, were replaced by individuals, whether foreign or native, whose advantage lay in purely commercial activity. There was sometimes secondary colonization, as with the Indians in Fiji, Malaya, and Burma, or the Chinese in Malaya and the Netherlands Indies. Thus was created the plural society, with each ethnic group living in its own social world and dealing with the others only in economic terms. The native, often at the bottom of the scale, became increasingly caught in the pecuniary network, increasingly reduced to a standard pattern. The old division of labor was lost in the addiction to monoculture and the disappearance of handicrafts. Poverty came to be unrelieved by the former satisfactions of life. In short, the net effect of European contact upon most agricultural peoples has been social disintegration and a sort of progressive proletarianization of whole societies. The problems arising from such contact have been numerous and almost universal. Whether Dutch, British, French, or American contact reigned, there appeared the phenomena of minute subdivision of land, of landlordism and tenancy, of estates and estate labor, of undernourishment and malnutrition, of moneylenders and indebtedness, of village decay and lawlessness, of chronic underemployment, of monoculture, soil erosion, and low productivity. These common problems, as well as the common conditions of contact which have given rise to them, allow us to talk about the densely settled nonmechanized agricultural countries as a class. Differences between them there are, but they are not so much differences due to the traditional cultures as differences due to the time and extent of European influence.

The weakness of agricultural areas vis-a-vis industrial nations is inevitable. Either they cease to be peasant-agricultural or they continue to be dominated by urban-industrial nations. The superiority of industrial production, mechanized and highly capitalized, lies in the great multiplication it gives to human effort. It follows that almost *any* industrial country has a higher level of living than any agricultural country.[16] New Zealand, often cited as an agricultural country with an extremely high real income, actually has over half of its population in cities of 17,000 or above, and in 1936 only

27 per cent of its workers were employed in primary production. Its basic exports come from the land, but actual cultivation and herding are so highly capitalized that only a small portion of the total manpower is required to produce a surplus big enough to employ the rest in other activities.[17] One factor in New Zealand's ability to reach this envious position may well be its sparse population, a joint product of restriction of immigrants and low fertility, which are in turn a consequence of high standards of living and industrial achievement. The great dividing line between the rich and poor peoples of the earth is therefore not solely or even primarily population density, even when refined measures are used to gauge it, but rather the presence or absence of industrialization. The great agricultural densities in some of the peasant-agricultural countries are mainly important, not as an explanation of the existing poverty, but rather as an obstacle to the industrial transition. It seems easier to industrialize a country such as Argentina or Brazil, where people are few in relation to resources, than to industrialize one like China or Egypt, where the reverse is the case. The great tragedy of colonialism was that it built up huge population densities without changing the economies from an agricultural to an industrial type.

The gap between industrial and agricultural countries can be illustrated in numerous ways, but two alone will suffice. (1) In 1939 the average per capita income for 30 countries that we have defined as agricultural was $76 per annum whereas in 22 industrial countries it was $287, or four times as great.[18] At the extremes, of course, the differences are much greater. (2) In the years around 1947 the average proportion illiterate aged 10 and over was 69 per cent in all countries having 50 per cent or more of gainfully occupied male workers in agriculture, whereas it was only 3.5 per cent in all countries having less than that portion.[19] The great chasm separating the two kinds of society could scarcely be shown more clearly.

POLICY AND REALITY.—If our findings are correct, the only means to higher levels of living in peasant countries is industrialization. The governments themselves realize this. Although an occasional Gandhi may wish to turn back the clock and retrieve the traditional culture, all governments now favor higher economic productivity. Any specific measure to increase the people's welfare must therefore be viewed from the standpoint of how it affects this master means.

Population Control. High on the list of conceivable measures is the control of population, because in many ways the pattern of dense settlement and prospective growth is a handicap to economic change.[20] Yet population control alone, without industrialization, would have little effect on the level of living. The difference in real income as between British Guiana and India, for example, is slight, despite the difference in overall population density. In other words, whatever effect the ratio of population to resources has on real income depends primarily on the state of the technology.

In the past the reduction of fertility has had to wait upon the growth of industry. It therefore appears strange to speak of lowered fertility as an initial aid to industrialization, and the prospect certainly appears unlikely. Yet, although the traditional cultures yielded a high birth rate[21] which has been maintained because they remained agricultural, the fertility pattern should not be regarded as inherently unmodifiable in the early stages of industrialization. As mentioned earlier, the traditional cultures have already been modified in many other respects; perhaps they can be modified with regard to fertility as well. Evidence is admittedly scarce, but the following points deserve consideration.[22]

(1) The technology of contraception may possibly be improved for peasant use. Little medical research has been devoted to contraception. With adequate attention, however, a scientific revolution in contraceptive technique might be accomplished which would ease the task of spreading birth control in backward areas. The popularity of sterilization in Puerto Rico suggests that a long-term contraceptive, if discovered, might prove more satisfactory than existing methods.

(2) Systematic interviewing and public opinion analysis have been insufficiently used for us to know the attitudes of peasant populations concerning limitation of offspring. One modern study in a rural section of India showed the following female answers to the question, "How many living children should a woman have when she is 40?"[23]

Number of Children	Frequency
0	3
1	110
2	353
3	353
4	299
5	102
6 and over	147

A modal preference for two or three living children suggests a desire among Indian peasants for small families.[24] It is also known that differential fertility exists in India as between city and country and as between literate and illiterate castes,[25] and that the fertility of certain highly placed groups is declining.[26] The pattern of lower fertility thus appears to be incipient. Further social research of a scientific character might reveal the latent resources that could be seized upon to undermine the present supports to high fertility.

(3) No all-out governmental campaign backed by every economic inducement, educational device, and technical assistance to diffuse contraception has ever been tried. We know that when birth control clinics have been set up in backward communities, the response has been discouraging.[27] We also know that in certain parts of Asia there has been some exposure to birth control propaganda. The reaction in these cases has apparently been mixed.

Perhaps because the effort was not vigorous, the opposition was not vigorous either. It seems certain, however, that the present mixed culture in agricultural societies will not itself spontaneously evolve a widespread pattern of family limitation in advance of industrial change. The necessary all-out government-sponsored campaign, although it might conceivably have some effect, is not likely to be tried. Both in India and in Puerto Rico the government has taken a somewhat favorable attitude toward limitation of offspring,[28] but this is far from sponsoring an adequate campaign.

In a democracy, even when there is a latent private desire to limit offspring, it is difficult for a government deliberately to set about altering the institutions and attitudes that give high fertility (viz., early and universal marriage, restriction of women to the home, dependence of female esteem upon male offspring, the economic use of children at an early age, and the adoption of a religio-magical approach to reproduction). These social factors are changing gradually,[29] but more as a reaction to incipient industrialization and urbanization than as a response to a deliberate public policy in advance of these developments.

A totalitarian government is less restricted by the predilections of the people, but in the past such governments have not felt that a general reduction in fertility would give more industrial and military power to the state. To eliminate undesired populations they have tended to rely upon increased mortality rather than lowered fertility. It is too early yet to know what will happen in this matter to the new colonies controlled by a totalitarian state, but it may turn out that the dominant power will have no more interest in the local standard of living than did the old seats of empire.[30]

Accelerated Modernization. Whatever the policy toward fertility, other means of facilitating industrialization are required. The probable population growth in agricultural countries makes the speed and character of these measures crucial. The faster the rate of modernization, other things equal, the quicker will be the response of fertility, the earlier the end to population growth, the smaller the ultimate population reached, and the higher the eventual level of living. These effects will be even greater if, in the process of rapid industrialization, those elements of modernization known to depress fertility are emphasized, such as education, urbanization, geographical and class mobility, multi-family dwellings, commercial recreation, and female employment.[31] Since such measures also facilitate industrialization, there is no necessary conflict between them and rapid economic development.

The means required to accelerate industrialization, however, are so disruptive to the existing social order that the people and the vested interests tend to resist them.[32] Furthermore, the requisite economic controls are so complex that most agricultural states do not have the administrative machinery, technical competence, and public knowledge to carry them out with entire success.[33] Weak governments therefore find difficulty in carrying out obviously necessary measures, and outsiders are limited in what they can do for them, by the identification of nationalism with the existing social structure and with economic autarchy.

Unfortunately, the weakness of agriculturalism that led to its previous colonial servitude still persists. At the very moment when rural nations have finally won their independence under one kind of world system, nationalism strong in sentiment but weak in practice is showing signs of proving unworkable under an emerging new kind of world system. Nominal political independence is not today, and has never been, a guarantee of industrial development.

Despite these difficulties, agricultural nations will doubtless industrialize eventually. Short of permanent world catastrophe, the new stage of cultural evolution will complete its diffusion. That it is continuing to spread is shown by the fact that virtually everywhere the literate and urban population is growing faster than the illiterate and rural, public health is improving, and village isolation is breaking down. The question is not whether industrial society will spread to all the world, but how soon and under what circumstances.

Particular conditions will govern modernization in different countries. Some may make a relatively smooth transition without major conflicts; others have such heavy obstacles that a smooth transition seems utopian. In the latter case the efforts made by native governments and by international agencies and friendly nations may prove too gentle to accomplish rapid industrialization, despite the tremendous resources that could be brought to bear. If this proves to be the case, if the status quo is allowed to obstruct and dissipate the effort, then such nations will remain too weak to prevent turmoil. They will either gain strength through internal revolution or be conquered by some new totalitarian colonialism of the right or left.[34] In either case the sweeping away of old barriers may provide a chance for mechanized agriculture and industry to come speedily, although not in the institutional forms familiar to us. Whether or not communist or fascist industrialism will bring the same demographic reactions as occurred under liberal capitalist industrialism cannot be predicted with certainty, but there are reasons to think it will. Even if totalitarianism should view a growth of numbers as advantageous, an increasing population would eventually prove self-defeating. Furthermore, a condition of demographic glut can be written off in a fairly short time by a sudden increase in mortality—an increase that need not necessarily retard industrial development commensurately. Possibly a world struggle several times more deadly than the last will be the cataclysm that will give agricultural nations a demographic breathing spell and a stimulus to such social change as will make future population pressure unlikely. At any rate the present situation in crowded agricultural nations cannot be regarded as anything but a temporary stage in the world transformation from illiterate agriculturalism to literate industrialism. Both the ascription of hopelessness to the situation and the opposite view of the world's resources and human science as capable of providing for a population of any size may reflect our natural desire to eliminate war, strife, and suffering from the process of social change. The actual course of events, however, may not respect this desire.

REFERENCES

1. From the Division of Population Research, Bureau of Applied Social Research, Columbia University (Publication No. A-122 of the Bureau).

2. Levy, Marion J., *The family revolution in China*, 274–278, Cambridge, Harvard Univ. Press, 1949.

3. Heaton, Herbert, *Economic history of Europe*, 417–418, N.Y., Harper, 1936.

4. Argentina is a case in point. Though it depends heavily on agricultural exports, less than a third (approximately 30 per cent) of its occupied males are engaged in agriculture and 48 per cent of its population lives in cities of 20,000 and over. Its agriculture is highly mechanized and rationalized. See Kingsley Davis and Ana Casis, *Urbanization in Latin America*, 17–21, N.Y., Milbank Memorial Fund, 1946 and Carl C. Taylor, *Rural Life in Argentina*, 105–123, 143–148, 274–290. Baton Rouge, L. State Univ. Press, 1948. Another illustration, the case of New Zealand, is discussed later.

5. These computations, together with other research used for the present paper, were done under a grant from the Carnegie Corporation as part of a larger study of population and international relations. The assistance of Dr. Hilda Hertz, research associate in the Bureau's Division of Population Research, is gratefully acknowledged.

6. Hawaii is an interesting case in this respect. At first tropical and relatively vacant it was so moderate in climate, and so accessible, fertile, and commercialized that its imported labor moved up in an expanding economy. As a result, the Islands now fall into the urban industrial group.

7. It is of course realized that a given country or region may have parts which fall into different categories. For instance, the South in the United States had, prior to the Civil War, a substantial plantation development using slave labor.

8. What is a "country" is not always easy to determine, especially as regards dependent areas. In general an area is counted as a separate dependent unit if it is not closely integrated into a wider dependent administrative unit. The ambiguity surrounding "independent" countries has to do mainly with those in the Russian orbit. Thus Rumania might well be regarded today as a dependent country. We have, however, counted as independent all countries where at least the fiction of sovereignty is maintained, although the Ukraine and other integral units of the Soviet Union are not so counted.

The Communist Bloc, including China, Northern Korea, and the Eastern zone of Germany, has 65 per cent of its occupied males in agriculture, the rest of the world only 57 per cent.

9. Not the most refined measure of population pressure on agricultural resources, but one of the best that can be obtained for all countries. Where precise data allow, better measures are possible. See Wilbert E. Moore, *Economic demography of Eastern and Southern Europe*, chap. 2, Geneva, League of Nations, 1945.

As defined by us, "agricultural land" does not include permanent meadows and pastures, forests, or potentially arable land. At times this may lead to distortion—as in cases where ranching or nomadic herding is highly important—but it was thought better to keep a standard definition throughout.

10. Colin Clark found that the output per head of males engaged in primary production varies inversely as the density of such males on farm land. See his *The economics of 1960*, chap. 4, London, Macmillan, 1944.

11. If one assumes that Japan had in 1870 the same ratio of arable land to total area that she had in 1936, the number of people (both sexes, all ages, and all occupations) per square mile of arable land was approximately 1,500 which is higher than that in India today (about 600).

12. Russia, of course, does not conform to type "C," as do most Asiatic countries. In part it is a European country to begin with and in part it has been colonized by European

settlement in areas of sparse native population. According to 1939 estimates, Russia has slightly more than 50 per cent of her gainfully occupied males in agriculture, with an average of 62 of these males per square mile of agricultural land. Doubtless the country has now crossed the line into the industrial category, with the advantage of a density figure slightly below the European average and far below the Asiatic average.

Malaya, including both the Federation and the Crown Colony of Singapore, has according to the 1947 census, 52 per cent of its gainfully occupied males in agriculture, with a density figure of 110. It does not belong in type "C" but rather in type "B."

13. Such areas, like industrial regions, show strikingly the difference between overall or average density and functional density. Tanganyika, for instance, is larger than France and the British Isles combined but has only about 7 million inhabitants. It is, therefore, sparsely settled in relation to its total area and resources, yet its *agricultural density* is quite high—about one person per acre under crops. Taeuber, Irene, *The population of Tanganyika*, 1, 43, Lake Success, United Nations, Population Division, 1949.

14. Furnivall, J. S., *Colonial policy and practice*, chap. 8, Cambridge, Univ. Press, 1948. See also his papers in Talbot, Phillips, (ed.), *South Asia in the world today*, Chicago, Univ. of Chicago Press, 1950.

15. Furnivall, *Colonial policy and practice*, 292–293.

16. The only exceptions are those near the line on one side or the other, e.g., Japan vs. Hungary or Greece.

17. Capitalization is illustrated by the fact that New Zealand has approximately 20 times as many miles of railroad per 1,000 population as India.

18. Computed from *Point Four*, 113–114, Washington, U. S. Department of State, 1950. These averages are not weighted by population. If so weighted, the averages become $55 for agricultural countries and $358 for industrial countries. See also Piquet, Howard S., Point Four and world production, *Ann. Amer. Acad. Polit. and Soc. Sci.* 268: 150–151, 1950.

19. Based on computations and estimates of literacy for the world's countries and colonies made by the Bureau of Applied Social Research. Urbanization does not differ so sharply. The agricultural countries had, in years about 1947, 11 per cent of their population living in cities of 20,000 or more, whereas the industrial countries had 39 per cent living in such places.

20. Ghosh, D., *Pressure of population and economic efficiency in India*, New Delhi, Indian Council of World Affairs, 1946. Davis, K., The economic demography of India and Pakistan, *in* Talbot (ed.), *op. cit.*, 86–107. Perloff, Harvey S., *Puerto Rico's economic future*, part 3, Chicago, Univ. of Chicago Press, 1950.

21. The birth rates, though high, have by no means been as high as was physically possible. Also, some primitive cultures have exhibited a rather low fertility. The Yap Islanders, for instance, have taboos, customs, and practices that severely limit births, and with the higher death rates brought by civilized contacts, their population declined sharply for many decades. See Peabody Museum Expedition to Yap Island, *The Micronesians of Yap and their depopulation*, mimeographed, Cambridge, Peabody Museum, Harvard Univ., 1948. A rather low fertility may have been a functional adaptation to a fairly low death rate in some primitive communities protected by isolation from infectious diseases. Agricultural civilizations, however, do not have this protection and consequently must have a high birth rate.

22. For a fuller discussion of fertility prospects in an agricultural region, see the writer's book, *The population of India and Pakistan*, chap. 22, Princeton, Princeton Univ. Press, 1950.

23. Sekar, C. Chandra, and Mukta Sen, Enquiry into the reproductive patterns of Bengali women, Indian Research Fund Association and All India Institute of Public Health, not yet published. The sample of rural women was obtained in Bengal, about 20 miles from Calcutta.

24. Similar findings have been obtained in Puerto Rico in a study directed by the writer and now being analyzed by Paul K. Hatt, who was in charge of the field work.

25. Davis, Kingsley, Human fertility in India, *Amer. Jour. Sociol.* 52: 243–254, 1946.

26. Sekar, C. Chandra, Some aspects of Parsi demography, *Human Biology* 20: 47–89, 1948.

27. Beebe, Gilbert W., *Contraception and fertility in the southern Appalachians,* Baltimore, Williams & Wilkins, 1942. Also Beebe and Jose S. Belaval, Fertility and contraception in Puerto Rico, *Puerto Rico Jour. Pub. Health and Trop. Med.,* 18: 3–52, 1942.

28. National Planning Committee, Sub-Committee on Population, *Population,* 22, 30–31, 53, 77–78, 81, Bombay, Vora, 1949. Perloff, *op. cit.,* 229–235.

29. In both India and China the age at marriage is apparently rising and women are being increasingly employed away from the home. On China, see Levy, *op. cit.,* 299–302, 309–313, 323–324.

30. For an excellent description of what is here called "totalitarian colonialism," see Yakobson, Sergius, Soviet concepts of Point Four, *Annals Amer. Acad. Pol. and Soc. Sci.* 268: 129–139, 1950. The success of such colonialism in achieving economic development is shown by Warren Wilhelm, Soviet Central Asia: Development of a backward area, *Foreign Policy Repts.,* 25: 218–228, 1950.

31. The social accompaniments of modernization have been well summarized by Levy, *op. cit.,* part 3. See also Moore, Wilbert E., Utilization of human resources through industrialization, *Milbank Mem. Fund Quart.,* 28: 52–67, 1950.

32. Hoskins, Halford L., Point Four with reference to the Middle East, *Annals Amer. Acad. Pol. and Soc. Sci.* 268: 88–94, 1950. Davis, Economic demography of India and Pakistan, *loc. cit.,* 41–42.

33. A fact frequently mentioned in the United Nations *Economic survey of Asia and the Far East* 1948, Lake Success, U.N. Department of Economic Affairs, 1949.

34. For an excellent analysis of sources of instability in India see Thorner, Daniel, Problems of economic development in India, *Annals Amer. Acad. Pol. and Soc. Sci.* 268: 96–103, 1950; also, his, Prospects for economic development in Southern Asia, *Foreign Policy Repts.* 26: 18–28, 1950.

BASIC DATA ON ECONOMIC DEVELOPMENT*

By Joseph J. Spengler

Explanatory note.—Tables 1–4 summarize the main reported and measurable economic and cultural differences between the relatively industrialized and the non-industrialized countries. In table 1 information is given for three categories of countries, classified on the basis of per capita income in 1939; (a) Upper, over $200 (b) Middle, $101–200; (c) Lower, $100 and below. Data are given for only 1,836 of the world's 2,170 millions of population,

* Extracted from "Economic Factors in the Development of Densely Populated Areas," *Proceedings of the American Philosophical Society*, 95 (February 1951), pp. 20–53; reprinted by permission of the American Philosophical Society.

TABLE 1

ECONOMIC AND SOCIAL INDICATORS, BY COUNTRIES GROUPED
ACCORDING TO INDUSTRIALIZATION

Item	Upper	Country group Middle	Lower
1. Per cent of world's population in 1939	17	14	69
2. Population per sq. km. in 1947 (range)	1–285	7–151	2–204
3. Per cent of population aged 15–59 years	[62–64]	[59]	[54–55]
4. Income per capita in 1939 (dollars)	461	154	41
5. Income per capita in 1939 (range in dollars)	201–554	101–200	22–100
6. Index of per worker income in 1925–34	[100]	[34]	[13]
7. Index of per capita income of farm population	100	39	8
8. Per cent of occupied populations in agriculture	[22]	[57]	[75]
9. Index of industrial equipment per worker	[100]	[39]	[11]
10. Energy consumed per capita per day (H.P.H.)	26.6	6.4	1.2
11. Miles of railroad per 1,000 sq. mi. of area	40	29	13
12. Annual freight carried per capita (ton miles)	1517	927	58
13. Line 12 ÷ line 11	37.9	32	4.5
14. Motor vehicles per 1,000 population	111	7	1
15. Telephones per 1,000 population	90	7	2
16. Per cent illiterate (population age 10 and over)	Below 5	20	78
17. Elementary school teachers per 1,000 population	3.98	3.42	1.76
18. State of population growth	Controlled	Controlled or transitional	Uncontrolled
19. Physicians per 1,000 population	1.06	0.78	0.17
20. Expectation of life at birth (years)	63	52	30–40
21. T.B. death rate per 100,000 population	64	143	333
22. Net annual textile consumption per capita (lbs.)	18.63	7.52	4.8
23. All foods: calories per capita per day	3040	2760	2150
24. Animal proteins, oz. per capita per day	1.6	0.9	0.3
25. Fats, oz. per capita per day	4.0	2.3	1.3
26. Typical per cent of calories of animal origin	[20–40]	[10–15]	[under 10]
27. Steel consumption per capita (kilos)	[100–500]	[25–80]	[10–20]

* Figures in brackets are for roughly comparable group of countries, or are estimates.

Sources: Lines 4–5, 7, 10–12, and 14–25 are from U. S. Department of State Publication **3719**, "Point Four," 103–113 (mean values), Washington, 1950. Lines 1–3 are based upon United Nations publications. Lines 6, 8, 9, and 26 are from my *Some Aspects,* loc. cit., 261–265. Line 27 is roughly estimated from United Nations, "European Steel Trends," 120–123, 132–136.

as of 1939. Presumably, however, nearly all of the 336 millions for whom data are lacking in 1939 fell in category (c). On the assumption that this was the case, the world's population was distributed as follows in 1939: (a) 361 millions; (b) 304 millions; and (c) 1,505 millions.

TABLE 2

ECONOMIC INDICATORS, BY COUNTRY

Country	Population (1947) Total (millions)	Density per sq. km.	Income Per worker 1925-34	Income Per capita 1939d	Product per man-hour (highest yr.)	Miles railroad (per sq. mi. of area)	Energy consumed per day (H.P. hrs. per capita)	Energy reserves in tons of bit. coal per sq. km.	Arable land per capita (hectares)	Per cent of labor force in agriculture e
(1)	(2)	(3)	(4)	(5)	(6)	(7)	(8)	(9)	(10)	(11)
United States	144.0	18	$1,381	$554	$1.19	80	37.6	320,665	1.55	22
United Kingdom	49.5	203	1,069	468	.62	222	27.1	565,647	.11	7
Argentina	16.1	6	1,000	218	.44	23	5.0	5,750	1.68	(36)
Union of So. Africa	11.6	10	276	188	.15	30	10.1	172,152	[.46]	26 [75] f
Chile	5.5	7	550	174	—	20	10.7	12,724	0.26	(36)
U.S.S.R.	200.0	9	320	158	.18	14	6.8	62,034	—	67
Cuba	5.1	44	—	98	.20	70	2.6	—	0.39	(41)
Yugoslavia	14.8	58	330	96	.14	72	2.1	45,802	—	79
Poland	23.8	76	352	95	.19	89	5.6	250,981	.54	65
Japan	78.0	204	353	93	.20	102	6.6	109,052	0.07	52
Venezuela	4.4	5	—	92	.21	2	5.1	14,375	—	(51)
Egypt	19.2	20	325	85	—	9	1.7	1,881	0.31—	67
Palestine	1.9	72	360	81	.19	30	1.0	—	—	31
Algiers	8.5	4	300	—	—	—	2.2	267	—	—
Turkey a	24.1	25	200+	(100-125)	.11	—	1.1	[3,720]	.51	82
Morocco b	11.5	20	200+	—	—	—	0.8	1,700	—	—
Costa Rica	0.8	15	—	76	—	22	1.4	—	—	—
Colombia	10.5	9	—	76	.08	5	1.5	10,521	0.26	(74)
Peru	7.9	6	—	72	—	4	1.1	11,569	0.25	(62)
Panama	0.7	10	—	71	—	17	12.3	—	—	(52)
Ceylon	6.9	104	—	63(91)	—	38	1.4	Negligible	0.20	(62)
Mexico	23.4	12	360	61	—	19	2.2	9,221	0.28	(65)
Uruguay	2.3	12	650	56	—	26	3.2	4,701	0.43	—
Iran	17.0	10	—	(85)	—	—	0.8	5,929	—	76
Dom. Republic	2.2	43	—	51	—	8	0.5	—	—	High
Haiti	3.6	127	—	50(36)	—	14	0.4	—	—	High
Nicaragua	1.1	8	—	50	—	4	[0.7]		—	(73)
Guatemala	3.6	33	—	48	—	17	0.6		—	—
Bolivia	3.9	4	—	47	—	5	0.3		—	—
Honduras	1.2	8	—	45	—	17	1.4	26,259	—	—
El Salvador	2.0	60	—	45	—	30	0.6		—	—
Brazil	47.6	6	435	46	.11	6	1.9	8,607	0.33	(67)
Ecuador	3.4	12	—	44	.11	7	1.0	9,694	—	—
Paraguay	1.2	3	—	39	—	4	0.6	12,795	—	—
Afghanistan	12.0	18	—	(50)	—	—	0.2	2,254	—	—
Ethiopia	15.0	17	—	(40)	—	—	0.2	13,022	—	—
Saudi Arabia	6.0	2	—	(40)	—	—	0.1—	365	—	—
India	411.0	101	200	34(43)	.09	26	0.5	21,297	0.31	(67)
Philippines	19.5	66	375	32(88)	—	8	0.6	14,848	0.20	(69)
China	463.0	48	110c	29(23)	.03	3	0.5	246,584	0.24	70-75
Indonesia	76.4	40	200—	22(35)	—	21	0.4	16,231	0.18	(69)
Rest of Asia	—	—	200—	—	—	—	[1.0]	—	—	—
Rest of Africa	—	—	200—	—	—	—	—	—	—	—
Rest of America	—	—	350	—	—	—	—	—	—	—

a Includes Syria and Lebanon. b Includes Tunisia. c Includes Korea. d Figures in parentheses are United Nations estimates for 1946 or 1948. e Figures in parentheses are for agriculture only. f Figure in brackets for colored population.

Sources: See under table 1 for sources of cols. 2–5 and 7–8. Col. 6 is from Clark, "Review of Economic Progress," I, No. 4, 2, 1949. Col. 8 is taken in part from Guyol, op. cit., Col. 9 is from Usher, op. cit., 40–43; it represents major energy reserves converted into terms of tons of bituminous coal. Col. 10 is from FAO, "State of Food and Agriculture, 1948," 51, 72, and "Mission For Greece," 155. Col. 11 is from United Nations, "Economic Survey of Asia and the Far East, 1948," 110, and "Economic Survey of Latin America, 1948," 87, and Hilgerdt, op. cit., 26–27.

In tables 2 and 3 information is reported by country, and particularly for class (c) countries for which data are available. The United States stands at the top of the class (a) and Argentina at the bottom. The Union of South Africa, Chile, and the USSR represent class (b). The remaining countries, beginning with Cuba, are in class (c). It should be noted that population growth is essentially uncontrolled in class (c) countries, whose potential rate of growth is high. It is controlled in class (a) countries, whose potential rate of growth is very low. It is either controlled or rapidly passing under control in class (b) countries.

In table 4 information is given by continent and subcontinent. While no per capita income data are reported by continent, fairly good measures of relative standing in respect of income are provided in lines 9, 10, and 13.

TABLE 3
CULTURAL AND DEVELOPMENTAL INDICATORS, BY COUNTRY

Country	Annual freight carried in ton miles		Motor vehicles (per 1,000 population)	Telephones (per 1,000 population)	Newsprint consumed per capita (kgs.)	Per cent of population age 10 and over illiterate	Daily per capita food supply			Physicians per 1,000 population	T.B. death rates per 100,000 population
	Per capita	Per capita per 1,000 sq. miles					All foods (calories)	Animal proteins (ounces)	Fats (ounces)		
(1)	(2a)	(2b)	(3)	(4)	(5)	(6)	(7)	(8)	(9)	(10)	(11)
United States	2,977	37.2	250	148	31.8	Below 5	3,098	1.8	4.3	1.37	47
United Kingdom	424	19.1	53	59	26.1	Below 5	3,095	1.6	4.3	1.13	62
Argentina	671	29.2	21	27	7.9	17					
Union of							2,777	2.2	3.3	1.05	103
So. Africa	777	25.9	30	15	3.7	60	2,354	1.2	1.8	.41	Low
Chile	324	16.2	20	13	3.7	24	2,322	0.8	1.5	.63	264
U.S.S.R.	1,134	9.6	5	3	—	19	2,827	—	—	.76	160
Cuba	119	1.7	11	11	4.8	35	2,626	0.8	1.7	.63	76
Yugoslavia	43	0.6	1	3	0.8	45	3,013	0.7	2.1	.31	234
Poland	432	4.8	1	8	1.5	27	2,710	0.8	2.2	.32	195
Japan	138	1.3	3	16	5.5	Below 10	2,230	0.4	0.9	.87	207
Venezuela	—	—	10	5	2.0	63	—	—	—	.41	233
Egypt	69	7.7	2	3	0.8	86	2,496	0.4	1.5	.21	52
Palestine	77	2.6	10	12	—	69	—	—	—	1.38	56
Costa Rica	43	2.0	6	5	—	35	2,014	—	—	.25	172
Colombia	12	2.4	4	4	—	44	2,004	0.7	1.5	.29	Low
Peru	45	11.3	3	3	1.1	90	1,835	0.5	1.4	.19	High
Panama	26	1.5	23	11	—	47	—	—	—	.21	119
Ceylon	—	—	5	0.3	—	60	2,059	0.3	1.6	.15	62
Mexico	182	9.6	5	7	2.4	62	1,855	0.7	1.5	.51	56
Uruguay	514	19.8	31	16	7.6	30	2,426	1.0	3.3	.71	101
Dom. Republic	1	0.1	2	2	0.3	71	2,130	—	—	.20	Medium
Haiti	—	—	0.8	0.8	0.1—	90	—	—	—	.09	High
Nicaragua	10	2.5	0.7	1.5	—	57	—	—	—	.28	Medium
Guatemala	13	0.8	1	0.7	—	72	—	—	—	.11	Medium
Bolivia	—	—	0.6	0.9	0.4	92	—	—	—	.15	Medium
Honduras	19	1.1	1	3	0.3	68	2,079	—	—	.11	Low
El Salvador	9	0.3	2	2	—	73	1,944	—	—	.16	High
Brazil	94	15.7	4	5	1.3	62	2,173	1.1	1.8	.31	250
Ecuador	18	2.6	1	3	1.1	80	—	—	—	.24	High
Paraguay	23	5.8	2	3	0.4	65	2,813	—	—	.28	102
India	60	2.3	0.3	0.2	0.1	91	1,976	0.3	1.0	.12	283
Philippines	—	—	3	1.9	0.9	51	1,855	0.7	1.2	.26	298
China	17	5.7	0.2	0.5	0.2	85	2,234	0.2	1.4	.04	400–500
Indonesia	9	0.4	1	0.6	—	92	—	—	—	.02	High

Source: See under table 1 for sources of Columns 2a, 3–4, and 6–11. Column 5 is from the United Nations, "Statistical Yearbook," 1948 (the figures are the higher of the 1935–39 and 1948 averages). Column 2b is obtained by dividing Column 2a by Column 7 from table 2.

TABLE 4
ECONOMIC AND CULTURAL INDICATORS, BY REGION

Sources: Lines 1–3 are based on United Nations publications. Lines 4 and 5 are from United Nations, "Mission for Greece," 155 (orchards and vineyards excluded). Lines 6–7 are from FAO, "State of Food and Agriculture," 1948, 28. Lines 8 and 13 are taken or computed from FAO, "State of Food and Agriculture, 1949," 134, 140. Lines 9 and 12 from United Nations, "European Steel Trends," 132–136 (data for 1937 and 1939, whichever is higher) and 41. Line 10 from Guyol, op. cit., 90 ff. Line 11 from Usher, op. cit., 40–43.

Item	North America	Oceania	Europe excl. U.S.S.R.	U.S.S.R.	Latin America	Africa	Eastern Asia	South Central Asia	Near East	World
1. Population growth, 1920–1947 (per cent)	36.5	33.3	17.7[a]	23.3[b]	62.8	41.5	24.8	37.0	29.8	31.1
2. Population in millions	157	12	384	195	153	191	738	426	74	2,330
3. Population per square km.	8.0	1.4	71.2	9.2	7.4	6.3	45.0	98.0	17	7.6
4. Acres crop land per capita	3.95	4.03	0.88	[2.00]	1.48	—	0.52	0.84	1.01	1.04
5. Acres crop land per head farm population	17.10	11.27	2.64	—	3.95	—	0.74	1.16	1.31	1.90
6. Productive forested area per capita (hectares)	3.0	4.2	0.3	3.2	4.7	2.0	0.3	—	0.2	1.1
7. Accessible productive forested area per capita (hectares)	1.96	2.2	0.3	1.6	2.2	0.95	0.15	—	0.07	0.6
8. % of world tractors ÷ % of world crop land	3.568	1.188	1.261	0.05	0.206	0.056	0.009	—	0.036	1.0
9. Steel consumption per capita (kilos)	371[c]	—	139	110	20	11	12	10	10	63
10. Energy consumed per capita (K.W. hrs.)	10,074	3,543	3,117	1,873	741	686		286		1,676
11. Energy resources (in tons of bituminous coal per sq. km.)	155,503	17,783	147,382	62,034	9,592	25,560	142,562	21,001	2,721	65,503
12. Known and probable iron ore reserves (million tons)[d]	58,000	600	8,000	100,000	12,500	1,400		12,000		192,500
13. Textile consumption per capita (kgs.)	18.3	7.7	6.3	3.7	3.7	1.5		2.3		3.9

[a] Non-eastern Europe only. [b] Eastern Europe and Asiatic U.S.S.R. [c] United States only.
[d] Central America and Mexico are included with North America; Latin America includes only South America; Oceania includes only Australia. World known reserves total 24,050 million tons.

CHAPTER 7

POPULATION GROWTH AND INTERNATIONAL RELATIONS

*I*nternational relations may be variously affected both by the comparative magnitudes of the populations of nations and by their comparative rates of growth. The extent and the composition of international trade may be affected. The volume and the direction of international migration are likely to be influenced, together with the international distribution of capital and technology. The conditions of international political equilibrium will be affected in a marked degree by these demographic factors; and other aspects of international relations may be affected.

International trade arises from the fact that, in the absence of such trade, international differences in prices are much greater than when trade is being carried on. These differences make it more profitable to sell some goods abroad than at home, and more economical to buy some goods abroad than at home. In fact, it is only through trade that certain goods are to be had at all in any given country, since no country is capable of producing every kind of good and service commercially. Differences in the prices of internationally exchangeable products arise principally from international differences in the resource endowment and the state of technological development of countries; for particular goods can be produced relatively cheaply in countries which are relatively well endowed with factors of production that enter significantly into the composition of these particular goods, provided, of course, that technology is sufficiently advanced in the well-endowed countries. The extent to which a country is dependent upon international commerce is governed largely by the comparative shortages which characterize its resource equipment and by the degree to which it has been able to emancipate itself from these shortages through technological progress. In general, the ratio of the value of imports to national income tends to be associated with a country's geographical extent, since the smaller a country the more likely is it to be relatively short of some resources and relatively long on others.

The structure of a country's productive capacity, together with the extent to which it is dependent upon international commerce, depends significantly upon the comparative magnitude of its population. For, as population and hence the labor force increase, labor tends to become relatively abundant in comparison with land and other natural resources and, if all forms of capital are not increasing sufficiently rapidly, in comparison also with some forms of productive equipment. In consequence the wages commanded by at least some kinds of labor tend to be lower in relation to the prices of capital and natural resources, with the result that goods and services into which this labor enters significantly fall in relative price at home and therefore become more attractive to foreign buyers. In general, when labor is relatively plentiful and land and natural resources are relatively scarce (e.g., in the case of Japan or Italy), and this scarcity is not redressed by offsetting technological improvements and capital formation, a country's exports are made up predominantly of goods and services into the production of which comparatively abundant forms of labor enter in relatively large measure. With such a situation, of course, relatively low wages are associated, since wages tend to be lower than they would have been had labor not been so plentiful.

Population growth may further exaggerate this downward pressure upon wages by worsening the terms of trade (i.e., the ratio of export to import prices) in the longer run and by making precarious a nation's capacity to maintain balance between its payments abroad and its receipts from abroad. As a country's labor force increases and its volume of exports rises, these exports tend to fall in price unless demand rises sufficiently in other countries. Meanwhile, imports tend to rise in price, since more and more raw materials and produce are required from abroad to meet domestic needs and the requirements of export industries, even though the raw materials and produce in question are forthcoming only under conditions of rising supply price. The resulting adverse turn in the terms of trade entails a reduction in per capita income in the longer run unless, meanwhile, there has taken place an offsetting increase in output per worker in the export industries; and in this event, income would have been still higher had the growth of the labor force not taken place. Even in the short run an adverse turn in the terms of trade may prove more difficult for a nation to cope with, when a relatively large fraction of its imports are deemed essential, since it is less easy under these circumstances to adjust imports to diminished receipts from abroad than when many imports are non-essential.

It is evident, in view of what has been said, that population growth, by increasing the dependence of some countries upon foreign trade, intensifies competition for both markets in which to sell exports and markets in which to buy raw materials and produce. This intensification of competition may stimulate the tendency of producers, always present in some degree in many countries, to seek tariff, quota, and other forms of protection against this intensified competition. In consequence, commercial relations may undergo strain, and heavily populated countries, which are dependent upon foreign markets for the sale of their manufactured products and for the purchase of produce and raw materials, may find their capacity to cope with internal population pressure weakened. Under some conditions this outcome might result in an increase in the probability of international strife; or it might be made the basis of claims (e.g., those made by Japan and Germany in the late 1930's) that could give rise to international strife; or it could generate tension within a relatively overpopulated country, for which crafty leaders might seek easement in external war.

Within limits international migration and international trade may be looked upon as substitutes for one another. In general, in the absence of legal and other obstacles to movement, migrants tend to move from countries where their economic and/or political prospects are less good to countries where these prospects appear better. Population pressure, by operating to depress or to hold down wages and income, conduces to emigration, since then potential migrants are likely to expect that employment opportunities and wages will be better in countries other than that in which the potential migrants are situated. Emigration, when it takes place under these circumstances, is likely to relieve population pressure in the country of emigration, thereby reducing somewhat the dependence of that country upon international trade. When, however, relief for population pressure is not obtained through emigration, it may be obtained through international trade, since trade will operate to increase the demand for labor and hence the level of real wages and income in the country wherein population pressure exists. It may be said, therefore, that either emigration, or trade, or both are likely to be stimulated by increases in population density.

Capital tends to flow in the same direction as emigrants, for capital is complementary to emigrants, being required to help set them to work in countries of immigration, and being drawn there when the comparative plentitude of resources in the country of immigration makes for a relatively high return on capital invested there. Since the introduction of capital into a country and its use there usually entail the introduction of relatively advanced forms of technology, and since emigrants are bearers of technology, it may be said that emigrants, capital, and technology tend to move together from relatively advanced countries where resources are relatively scarce and population pressure exists to countries where an opposite set of conditions prevails. Such at least was the kind of movement that, in 1800–1930, carried some 60 million emigrants from Europe to the Americas and Oceania, together with billions of capital and the know-how to make use of this capital in the exploitation of these relatively underpeopled areas.

While it is sometimes said that population pressure is an important cause of international war, this statement is incorrect unless very much qualified. It is true that, when population pressure increases in a country because of a continuing growth of numbers or because of the exhaustion of resources (e.g., through dessication), new problems arise and old problems are intensified. A population may react to this new situation in a variety of ways, particularly in modern times when a much greater number of alternatives is likely to be open to a country than formerly. A population will not, therefore, resort to war merely because of an increase in population pressure. It may, however, resort to war if enough other circumstances besides increase in population pressure are conducing to war. Population pressure may not, therefore, be defined as a cause of war; but it may be looked upon as a factor which may become part of a complex of factors that may make for war. That this is the case is borne out by the fact that many wars have been in no way occasioned by population pressure, and that almost invariably when an increase in population pressure has preceded the outbreak of war, it has been but one of many antecedents which together have made for war.

Inasmuch as the comparative political and military power of a state depends in varying degree upon the comparative magnitude of its population, population is one of the determinants of the conditions whereunder the power of a state, or of a group of allied states, is balanced by the power of an opposed state, or group of allied states. Accordingly, whenever the population of one such state, or group of states, begins to outstrip that of the other, the latter must take steps to offset this population growth and thereby restore the balance of power hitherto obtaining. This may be done by adding states to the group that is growing relatively weaker, or by subtracting states from the group that is growing relatively stronger; that is, by pursuing a course of action that is possible so long as there exists no single state that is significantly more powerful than any opposed combination of states which can be brought together. If such compensatory action is not taken, a relatively higher rate of population growth may throw the advantage to one or another of two states or groups initially in balance.

While population is a determinant of political and military power, its influence may be overestimated, for power has many determinants besides mere magnitude of population, as a comparison of the bases of Chinese and American power will readily suggest. One cannot even compare two populations unless one takes into account differences in their age composition, their education, their technical training, and so on. When these conditions have been allowed for, there remain to be taken into account differences in technology, capital equipment, land and resources, situation, and so on. Historically, the relative importance of the population factor as a determinant of power has diminished whenever, as occasionally in ancient times and more particularly in the past century, countries have come to differ significantly in technology, social organization, capital equipment, political structure, etc.

The selections comprising this chapter deal with aspects of the role of the population factor as a determinant of power, and suggest possible ways in which the population factor may affect the nature and course of international relations.

POPULATION AND POWER IN THE FREE WORLD*

By Kingsley Davis

During World War II and the succeeding decade, the struggle between the Communist and the Free countries has become not only more intense but also more equal. The Communist bloc has apparently accomplished the feat of progressively expanding its territory without losing (at least yet) the solidarity of its member states. The Free World on the other hand, lacking the principles of unity that hold together the Communist group, has achieved much less solidarity. Its member states have little to unify them other than their common fear of Communist expansion.

Necessarily, the cleavage between Communist and non-Communist peoples has its roots in the past, as does the relative strength or weakness of each side. One fact to bear in mind is this: the present struggle, recent and in many ways unique has grown out of the much older conflicts and imbalances inherent in the origin and spread of the Industrial Revolution. Communism, which received its initial philosophical formulation in the industrial nations, has paradoxically had its subsequent applications in predominantly agrarian states. It has learned to promise an energetic and simple solution of major problems in the development of backward areas—problems which the pre-Communist world was not able to solve—and to institute drastic reforms by force when it gets control. As yet the Free World, no matter how superior its long-run influence may be, has worked out no solution of comparable directness and clarity, or at least none that it can agree on. It is handicapped thus in its appeal to backward areas.

The historical roots of the present conflict have not, however, arisen simply out of the interplay between industrial and non-industrial people. They have also sprung from a closely related interaction between the West, on the one hand, and the rest of the world on the other. It is significant that the Communist and the non-Communist blocs alike include both Western and Eastern, as well as industrial and agrarian, countries. Indeed, each political philosophy represents a competing way of handling relationships between these four overlapping classes of nations. Any analysis of population and political power in the Free World, therefore, must necessarily take into account the complex ways in which the interdependencies of the Western and non-Western dichotomy cut across those of the industrial and non-

* Paper presented at the Thirtieth Institute of the Norman Wait Harris Memorial Foundation, University of Chicago, November 24–28, 1954; to be published in *Population and World Politics*, edited by Philip M. Hauser. The paper is included in this volume by permission of the author and the Harris Foundation Committee.

industrial hiatus. It is in their different ways of handling these interdependencies that Communism and the Free World seek to win the cold war.

THE CHANGING CHARACTER OF EUROPEAN INFLUENCE.—For roughly 300 years, from around 1600 to 1914, a dominant feature of the world was the fact that two aspects of European influence—the growth and spread of European peoples, and the growth and spread of European culture—were both rising together. Gaining momentum with the industrial revolution and thus reaching their combined pinnacle in the nineteenth and early twentieth centuries, these two processes went along together because they were intimately related. The Europeans were evolving a culture which gave them an increasing capacity to multiply at home and to migrate abroad; and this multiplication and dispersion, in turn, enabled them to make still further advances in their culture. With the entire Western hemisphere and Australia and New Zealand colonized, the territory settled predominantly by European stock and characterized by European culture was approximately ten times in 1850 what it had been in 1600. By 1950 the number of people of European ancestry had risen to approximately eight times what it had been 300 years earlier—that is, to almost a third of the world's population from perhaps 18 per cent at the earlier date.

Since 1914, however, it has become increasingly apparent that the two aspects of European influence need not go together, that they are in fact tending to pursue separate paths. European peoples are no longer settling new areas by mass migration as they once did, and their rate of population growth in the areas already settled is no longer, on the whole, so strikingly ahead of that of the rest of the world. Indeed, the more economically advanced of the European peoples have slowed down in their growth, particularly in northwest Europe. Although certain areas of European culture—notably those of Latin America, Canada, and the Soviet Union—are still growing rapidly, the total picture is one of rough parity with the rest of the world in population growth.

Yet the diffusion of certain aspects of European culture, as distinct from European people, has been accelerated. Peoples who are not European in race, whose cultural roots are far different from those of Europeans, who are in some cases anti-European in sentiment, are absorbing the instrumentalities of urban-industrial civilization at a rapid rate. These instrumentalities embracing technology, economic organization, and political forms, are in fact so universal now that they are no longer considered to be European. They are regarded simply as the well-known means by which any nation, whatever its background, can enhance its national power and its level of living.

This tendency of European cultural diffusion to outlast European demographic expansion was already foreshadowed in the nineteenth century—most strikingly in the economic and military achievements of Japan, but also in the progress of dependent areas, such as India and Malaya, where few Europeans were settled. Since World War I the tendency has been accelerated. Curiously, one factor leading to this result has been the rapid liquidation of colonialism and the rise of nationalism among non-European peoples. Since most of the colonies were controlled by European nations, their demise would appear to signal a decline of European influence, and in a sense this was true; but the fact is that the rise of nationalism among non-European peoples has stepped up the acquisition of technology from the West.

The transformation of colonies into nations occurred on a large scale, for it involved some 600 million persons. It also occurred quickly. By 1950 only about 8 per cent of the world's population lived in officially dependent areas, whereas in 1913 the figure was around 30 per cent. This emergence of new non-European nations was both a consequence and a stimulant of Western contact. The modern idea of a nation-state was itself a Western idea, and both the goals and the propaganda techniques employed in the independence movements were predominantly Western. Once created, the new nations have been forced to find ways of maintaining their independence and their integrity as nations in a highly competitive world. They have been forced, in short, to try to acquire the same essential techniques that have given power to Western nations. Hence they have shown on the one side a strong desire to borrow industrial and economic instrumentalities, and on the other side, an equally strong desire to reject domination by the West and to reject those elements of Western culture which offend their traditional values. Their acquisition of Western ways has not therefore implied a solidarity with Western peoples. Whereas the extension of European culture by the emigration of Europeans overseas added to the political hegemony of the West, the new diffusion of European technology to independent non-European nations has had the opposite effect.

Into this delicately balanced and changing relationship between the West, led by the industrial nations, and the non-West, struggling to establish itself, came the split between Communism and non-Communism. This split appeared within the Western world, but it gained its international scope largely from the fact that the two sides have offered radically different solutions of East-West relationships. The Communists have said, in effect, that nothing short of swift revolution will accomplish the economic and political goals of the newly emerging non-Western nations. They have offered the techniques and leadership for carrying out such revolutions, and have not hesitated to use external force to help along the process. The price, of course, is the loss of democratic freedom as the Free World understands it; but the gain in power is undeniable. Characteristically, the gain in power is not so much that of the individual nation as that of the entire bloc; for the Communists have, as already mentioned, solved at least temporarily the problem of international solidarity within their ranks. They have accomplished this, perhaps more apparently than actually, by using force and propaganda to diffuse their rigid ideology from the top down, by linking the different national dictatorships through Party control, and above all by the overwhelming balance of power held by the Soviet Union itself. The result is evidently a new and more systematic imperialism than was ever achieved before.

The Free World, in contrast, has continued to rely on more informal and voluntary means of maintaining unity among the European and non-European peoples within its orbit. Resting its appeal on the dissolution of colonialism and the creation of a free community of sovereign states, it has attempted to give its underdeveloped members the instrumentalities they need through technical assistance and economic aid, and has offered them protection through voluntary alliances.

An important phase of the struggle between Communism and the Free World is thus the effort of each side to draw in the weaker and more unstable nations. The Communists have found it possible to bring into their camp certain peoples of the East, partly because of their geographical proximity to the Soviet Union and partly because of chaotic internal conditions and opposition to past treatment by Free Western powers.

Though the ultimate outcome of the struggle is not clear, it does appear that the non-Western nations outside the Communist camp are succeeding in acquiring the instrumentalities of the West. Though progress may appear slow, painful, and spotty, it is nevertheless, when we are able to measure it, often more rapid than it was at a similar stage in the now developed countries. Rapid urbanization, the rise of literacy, the spread of mass communication, the decline of mortality, the growth of trade and industry—all indicate a process of fundamental change. This massive transformation cannot be expected in all cases to result quickly in higher levels of living, nor does it guarantee future loyalty to the Free World. It does, however, set the stage for further changes and disturbances and for a possible shift of power in the direction of non-Western countries.

Demographically, the progress of the non-Western Free nations is showing itself in population growth. Between 1935 and 1952 the average annual rate of increase in 18 of these countries was 1.3 per cent, whereas that in 43 countries in the Free Western category was 1.2 per cent. In the future the rate of population increase may shift still more in favor of the non-Western countries.

Indicative of changing circumstances is the growing voice of non-Europeans in international affairs. The desire of white South Africans, for example, to get help from the West in their effort to dominate the African majority and the Indian minority, is doomed to disappointment. The Christian nations, even if they were not restrained by principle (which they certainly are), could not afford to encourage South African racialism. The population of countries holding membership in the United Nations is two-thirds non-European. In the British Commonwealth itself, often taken as a bulwark of Western unity, the non-Europeans constitute 85 per cent of the population; and in the Empire the population is overwhelmingly colored. Even within the areas of European culture, racial diversity bars any unanimity of racial attitudes. The diplomacy of the Free Western powers must inevitably, in the struggle with Communism, be directed toward keeping the allegiance of the non-Western nations.

POPULATION SIZE AND NATIONAL POWER.—In appraising the political power of the Free World, we shall do well to keep the Western and non-Western parts in mind, not because of any implied conflict between them but because of the possibly greater vulnerability to Communism of the non-Western nations.

If we had a perfect measure of power, it would take into account the degree of solidarity among the states joined together in a common struggle; but at best we have only imperfect measures of the strength of individual nations, let alone groups of nations. Probably the best single index of a nation's power is its total income. This in turn is a function of its population size and its productive efficiency. Since these two elements vary independently, a nation may have a high national income primarily because it has a huge number of citizens or primarily because it is highly productive. Thus, of the twenty nations with the highest national income, some rank low in per capita income. India, for example, ranked fifth in total income in 1949, but fifty-fifth in per capita income. Similarly, Italy was ninth in national income but twenty-ninth in per capita income. These are nations whose high position is gained through bigger-than-average population rather than through high productivity.

The reasons why population size is a major determinant of national power seem clear. First, the magnitude of the total population is the principal factor in the size of the labor force, and it is impossible to substitute completely other factors of production for labor. In fact, as an economy develops the price of labor increases because its level of living rises, so that, from a cost standpoint, the share of labor in production remains high. In the United States in 1951, for example, the payments of salaries and wages in manufacturing establishments amounted to 55 per cent of the value added by manufacture. Second, given the adequacy of resources, the larger the population integrated in one economic system, the greater the potential advantages of scale to be gained from mass production and mass distribution. Third, since military personnel is drawn most heavily from restricted age groups, a large population is necessary to furnish a sizeable army and to sustain losses in fighting strength. Fourth, the consolidation of a victory in war often requires a sizeable occupation force, which cannot be supplied if the population is small.

With these considerations in mind, let us look at the total population of 81 countries in 1950 (see Table 1). Seventy of these, constituting the Free World, had a total of 1,450 million inhabitants, as against approximately 800 million in the 11 countries under Communist control. Within the Free World, the 46 Western countries had a combined population of 648 million, while the 24 others—the non-Western Free countries—had a population of 800 million. Approximately 57 per cent of the Free World was therefore non-Western in culture, whereas (even counting all of Russia as "Western") something like 65 per cent of the Communist World was non-Western. It can thus be seen that both camps contain only a minority of Western people, and that the balance of the Communist World in particular is shifting Eastward, as the addition of Vietminh in 1954 indicates.

From the figures just given, it is plain that the average Communist country is larger than the average Free country—72 million inhabitants as against 21 million. This is because two of the world's largest countries, China and Russia, dominate this small bloc of nations. Within the Free World, the non-European countries have bigger populations than the Western ones. In fact, the average population of non-Western Free countries is 33 million, as of 1950, whereas that of the Western Free nations is 14 million. Since, if other things are equal, advantage lies in having a large population concentrated within one political unit rather than divided up into several units, the greater average size of Communist countries represents a demographic advantage over the Free World, and the greater average size of non-Western countries represents a similar advantage over the Western ones. One would think that the West, which invented the modern nation-state and developed mass production and mass communication, would have achieved larger political aggregates; but the truth is that the Asians and other non-Europeans have, at least temporarily and with the help of Western powers, managed to combine more people into single national states than have the Westerners.

TABLE 1

SOME DEMOGRAPHIC FEATURES OF 81 COUNTRIES, BY CULTURE AND
POLITICAL ALLEGIANCE, 1950[1]

	Number of Countries	Population (000's)			(000's Km.^{2})		Persons per Km.^{2}
		Total	Average	Median	Total	Average	
Free							
European	46	647,804	14,083	5,144	51,316	1,116	12.6
Non-European	24	801,902	33,413	16,656	17,319	722	46.3
Total	70	1,449,706	20,710	7,488	68,635	981	21.1
Communist							
European	8	a 279,697	34,962	14,220	23,287	2,911	12.0
Non-European	3	510,185	170,062		11,449	3,816	44.6
Total	11	789,882	71,807	12,340	34,736	3,158	22.7
Grand Total	81	2,239,588	27,649	9,350	103,371	1,276	21.7

a. The population of Communist China in 1950 is assumed to be 500 million. This is larger than the 456 million given by the United Nations "Demographic Yearbook," 1953, for the year 1951, but smaller than the figure of 583 million purportedly found by the Communists in their census of 1953. With reference to the Chinese census, see United States Census Bureau, "The Population of Communist China: 1953, "International Population Reports, Series P-90, No. 6 (March 4, 1955).

[1] Except in the case of the population of China, the figures from which this table is computed are taken from the U.N. "Demographic Yearbook."

Of course, we are making the untrue assumption that the population of each state is effectively integrated as a nation. The extent to which this is or is not the case is a function of the efficiency of political and social organization. For the moment, however, our attention is focused on sheer population, recognizing that in fact it is an important but by no means the sole factor in national power.

The preponderance of non-Western people in both the Communist and Free camps will probably increase, since their rate of population growth has already achieved parity with that of the West. Moreover, we have ignored colonial areas, which are mainly non-European in culture and have rapidly growing populations. Among the Western nations it is generally those that are still relatively underdeveloped that exhibit the fastest numerical increase. The demographic picture in Mexico, for example, resembles that in India more than that in the United States; yet we have grouped Mexico among the Western peoples. It seems, then, that insofar as power results from sheer numbers, the importance of non-Western and less developed areas will increase, and that these will continue to be the main prizes in the cold war between Communism and anti-Communism.

DEMOGRAPHIC FACTORS AFFECTING EFFICIENCY.—There are, however, several demographic factors other than sheer population size which, by their influence on economic and social efficiency affect national power. Among these are the following: (1) the relation of population to resources; (2) the stage of mortality and morbidity; (3) the level of fertility; (4) the age structure; (5) the rate of internal migration; (6) the degree of urbanization.

The greatest differences in these factors occur between industrial and non-industrial countries, not between Communist and non-Communist countries. This fact must be borne in mind as we discuss the international significance of each of these factors.

Population and Resources. When other things are equal, a large population represents a source of power; but when other things are not equal it may at the same time represent a source of weakness. Examining the physical territory of our 81 countries, we find that the 70 free nations occupy an area nearly twice as large as that occupied by the 11 Communist countries—69 million square kilometers as against 35 million. Indochina and some small or relatively unknown countries have been excluded from the calculations, as have all the colonies. Since their combined population is also nearly twice as large, the overall average density comes out about the same. It is 21.1 persons per square kilometer for the free nations; 22.7 for the Communist nations. If the land were equally valuable as between the two groups, there would be no particular advantage on either side. Unfortunately, no certainty exists as to the relative resources of the two areas taken as a whole. There is, however, no reason whatever to think that the resources of the Communist area are greater, square mile for square mile, than those of the Free World. This being the case, the Free World enjoys still a tremendous potential advantage. With a population and a territory twice as large as that of the Communist world, it could, if it stuck together, greatly excel in power. Furthermore, in none of the calculations given above are the dependent territories (colonies, trust territories, etc.) included. These, as of 1950, embraced about 8 per cent of the world's total population and 23 per cent of the world's inhabitable area. Since the dependent areas are wholly controlled by countries of the Free World, they add considerably to the Free World's advantage in potential power.

Within the Free World, as Table 1 shows, the preponderance of territory is to be found in the Western parts. The 46 Western nations in our tabulation have three times the total land area that the 24 non-Western nations have. In population, as we have seen, the opposite is true; for the Free Western nations have less than half the number of people represented by the Free non-Western nations. From these two facts it follows that the average population density in the non-Western nations is much greater than the density in the Western nations—in fact, it is about four times as great.

Curiously, much the same situation is true of the Communist nations. The European nations behind the Iron Curtain (including all of the Soviet Union) have twice the territory but only half the population of the Communist World. The density in the non-Western parts of the Communist realm, like that in similar parts of the Free World, is roughly four times what it is in the Western parts.

The inequality in population density as between Western and non-Western nations would represent no disadvantage for non-Western peoples if (a) the resources per unit of land were correspondingly greater, if (b) the efficiency with which resources are utilized were greater, or if (c) the population size of all countries were below the optimum for the maximum utilization of resources in the given stage of technology. Actually, it appears that none of these conditions is true. The land that lies in the non-Western countries is, if anything, less rich in soil and minerals than that which lies in the Western countries, particularly in the Free World. The efficiency with which resources are utilized in the non-Western lands is known to be much less. Furthermore, in the Free World and probably in the Communist World too, the availability of utilized resources for the local population is limited, because the industrial nations control the exploitation to a marked degree. Finally, some countries, particularly those in Asia, appear to have so many and such rapid growth rates that, given the existing state of the arts, they find it more difficult than it would otherwise be to reach a more advanced stage of exploitation. It appears therefore that the greater population density of non-Western areas represents for them a real disadvantage.

Whether or not a nation has too many people is independent of the absolute size of its population. Some small countries appear to be overpopulated, some big ones not. Moreover, the difficulty of overpopulation is obviously not confined to non-Western countries alone. There are several in the Western category—e.g., Italy, Greece, Mexico, El Salvador—which would probably be more powerful if they had fewer people. Yet it happens that the non-

Western nations as a whole are more afflicted with redundant populations than the Western nations, as the cases of India, Pakistan, Egypt, Lybia, Japan, China, and Indonesia illustrate. The disadvantage for the non-Western countries is indeed great, and it is also fundamental and relatively permanent. It will not disappear overnight.

If a nation finds its population too dense and too rapidly growing for public efficiency, it has two alternatives. It can elect to reduce the rate of population growth, or it can attempt to find ways of continually increasing the national income so as to take care of the increased population. These are obviously not mutually exclusive possibilities. No nation today would pursue the first policy and ignore the second. Virtually all nations, except perhaps a "hermit kingdom" or two, are committed to the goal of economic development. The strange thing, however, is that most nations, even those which plainly have too many people, actually do pursue the second policy and ignore the first, and there are many individuals who refuse to consider the first an alternative at all.

If we ask why nations generally shy away from a policy of checking population growth, the answer is not simple. Doubtless governments fear to offend the sentiments of their people, and officials often share the popular sentiments. But we find that even in countries controlled by dictatorships, where state policy is a matter of hard-boiled power politics, no attempt is made to lessen the rate of population growth, even when such growth is obviously detrimental economically. China is a case in point, as are also Portugal, Poland, Haiti, and El Salvador. To reach a fuller explanation, therefore, one must realize that a policy of limiting population growth jettisons an important source of national power, namely, the military and industrial value of a greater population when other things are improved. Consequently, it is only nations with a strong and liberal sense of the importance of the level of living, an attitude which plays down the primacy of sheer national power, that are likely to adopt a population-limiting policy real enough to be effective. There is thus the possibility that in the highly competitive international world, no nation, however overpopulated it may be or may regard itself as being, is going to carry through such a policy. Perhaps an anti-natalist policy is least likely precisely in those new, insecure, and emotionally nationalistic nations that have arisen out of the ashes of colonialism in the non-Western regions. It is noteworthy that India has authorized such a policy, that Japan seems hospitable to the idea of fostering birth control, and that Egypt is considering possible measures, but as yet no successful implementation of a national anti-natalist policy is on record. It seems more likely that most nations—and this includes liberal Western countries—will adopt exclusively the economic policy of more wealth, more territory and more trade to feed ever more people. This, in its expansionist form, is the familiar *lebensraum* policy made famous by pre-war Japan, Italy, and Germany. It has the advantage of appealing to a very deep and elementary sense of justice (people must have enough room to "live and breathe" in). It also tends to lead to warfare, which, if there are too many people, is an honorable and apparently inadvertent way of reducing their number. In an atomic age, the acquisition of territory by warfare is not as attractive a venture as it used to be, but the idea that economic development can be endlessly spurred on is sufficiently strong to lead most governments to forego measures aimed at checking population growth by limiting fertility.

The Role of Mortality and Morbidity. Most of the demographic disadvantages of non-Western countries, whether Communist or not, arise from the fact that, on the average, they are more underdeveloped than the Western countries. This can be seen, for example, in the mortality figures. Although the data do not permit average mortality rates to be computed for all non-Western countries, we do know that in underdeveloped countries generally, and hence in most non-Western countries, death rates are still relatively high. It is true that the rates have been declining remarkably in recent years, and in some cases spectacularly; but they are still high enough in most non-Western areas to exact a considerable penalty. The chief wastage lies in the death of people before they have a chance to repay, by economic production, the cost of their birth and rearing. Whereas in Australia, according to life tables for the period 1946–48, the percentage of males surviving to age 20 was 95, in Egypt for the period 1936–38 it was 57, and in India for 1941–50 it was 58 (see Table 2). When 20 to 40 per cent of the males are dead before they reach age 20, it is not only their productive life that is lost, but also the effort and expense of bearing them and rearing them to that age. In this respect,

TABLE 2
PERCENTAGE OF MALES SURVIVING TO AGE 20 ACCORDING TO
LIFE TABLES: SELECTED COUNTRIES[1]

	Period Covered	Percentage of Males Surviving
Sweden	1946–50	95.4
United States	1949–51	94.7
Australia	1946–48	94.6
France	1950–51	92.6
Japan	1953	90.7
Argentina	1947	86.2
Portugal	1949–52	82.2
Ceylon	1952	82.1
El Salvador	1949–51	76.2
Mexico	1940	64.0
India	1941–50	58.0
Egypt	1936–38	57.4

[1] Taken from United Nations, "Demographic Yearbook," 1953 and 1954.

while some of the non-Western countries are better off than some Western ones (e.g., Japan or Ceylon as compared to El Salvador), on the whole the advantage still lies with the West.

Where a high death rate is found, so is a high rate of ill health. Accordingly, Western countries, with their low mortality, have on the average a smaller proportion of their labor force or their soldiers incapacitated and enervated by sickness; a lesser proportion of their territory left idle because of health hazards (malaria, sleeping sickness); and a small proportion of their population dependent.

The Level of Fertility. Though there is resistance to admitting the fact, a high birth rate has many disadvantages. It tends to remove women from the labor force, to restrict the activities of those who do enter the labor force, and to increase the vulnerability of women to disease and death. If mortality is very high, then a nation must necessarily bear these costs; but if mortality has been reduced, as it has been in most underdeveloped countries, the persistence of high fertility incurs not only these costs needlessly but also adds others as well. Notably it increases the dependency ratio in the population, puts extra obstacles in the way of adequate education and vocational training, brings too rapid a population growth, and reduces internal migration.

Since the non-Western nations are on the average less developed than the Western, they suffer more from the disadvantages of high birth rates. Indeed, it is probable that in South Asia and the Near East, though not perhaps so much in large parts of Africa, birth rates today are higher than they were in Europe in the Middle Ages.

The Age Structure. The age structure of the industrial nations, due largely to previous rapid declines in fertility, has been heavily weighted in the productive ages. These are also the ages most exposed to the risk of conception and relatively little exposed to the risk of death. Consequently, the actual number of births in relation to the total population is higher than it would otherwise be, and the number of deaths lower. The industrial nations have thus had a maximum birth rate in relation to the actual reproductive effort put forth, and have had a minimum death rate in relation to the medical effort expended. Not only has there been a larger proportion of persons in the active ages and therefore available for the labor force, but there has been a rather safe natural increase incurred at the least cost.

The advantages of the industrial nations in this respect, however, will not last forever. The end-product of the trend is an aging population. Unless means are found to keep the old vigorous as well as alive, the possibility of weakening the economy with costly security schemes or of stultifying progress by allowing authority to gravitate to the old but incompetent, is frighteningly real. It should be noted that the influence of age is different in different kinds of activity. In highly capitalized warfare as well as in any other kind, military efficiency requires the use of the young in large numbers. Old age therefore sets in, for military purposes, at age 35 or 40. In rapidly developing fields of science old age also sets in early. The penalties of an aging population may therefore be greater than the mere non-participation of the aged in the labor force would imply. In the near future it appears that the industrial societies of the West may reap more disadvantages than advantages from their age structure unless both biological and sociological measures are taken to prevent this result.

The Rate of Internal Migration. The movement of people in peasant countries tends to be much less than that of people in industrial countries. Such movement, when it occurs, is often a cause as well as a consequence of economic development. The new activities associated with economic growth are seldom located where the old activities were, and they involve concentrations of workers in particular spots to a much greater degee than was possible with agriculture. Hence economic development requires a massive internal movement of people, often made all the greater by the fact that the new industrial jobs are for the most part regarded as temporary. The fixity of people in underdeveloped countries, particularly in those of non-Western culture, is partly a result of rigid social stratification, close kinship organization, regional cultural and linguistic barriers, and sharply defined age and sex roles. Western culture, even before the Industrial Revolution, was free from some, though not all, of these barriers—a fact which was perhaps one of the conditions giving rise to rapid Western development. Today in most non-Western countries the rate of internal mobility may be rising, but it is still far less than in the average Western country. The barriers appear to be greater in the non-Arabic than in the other parts of Asia, and perhaps least in Negro Africa. In any case, the Western countries seem to enjoy an economic advantage in this respect.

The Degree of Urbanization. The industrialization of agriculture and the growth of manufacturing bring a shift of the population from the countryside to the city, because the city, for many reasons, is the most economical location for most productive and distributive functions which involve land as merely a site and do not require close proximity to raw materials. A country that is not yet heavily urbanized is one that still has to go through the process and bear the costs of urbanization, whereas one that is already urbanized has already met the costs and reaped the advantages. The industrialized countries are approaching what appears to be the saturation point in urbanization —some 70 per cent of the population living in cities of 20,000 or more. Their further economic development can assume the advantages of urban location. Asia outside the U.S.S.R. has only 13 per cent of its people located in such places and Africa even less (9 per cent). In this respect the Western nations, and again the more industrialized ones, appear to have an advantage, at least economically. Whether in the future urbanization will prove an unmixed military blessing is a hard question, but one that should not go unmentioned.

SOME POLITICAL IMPLICATIONS.—Cross-cutting the political division between Communist and Free countries, as we have seen, is a cultural division between the West (more heavily industrial) and the non-West (more heavily agrarian). This cultural division forms one of the main lines of competition and conflict between the Communist and the Free World, because the struggle has increasingly devolved into an effort to win the underdeveloped areas, particularly those of non-Western culture. What has been said here concerns certain of the demographic causes and conditions of this effort. On the one hand, it can be seen that the prize is great, because nearly 60 per cent of the population of the 81 nations with which we have been dealing is contained in the 27 non-Western countries. The potential manpower at stake is therefore enormous, not to mention the natural resources. On the other hand, the explanation of why these countries have not realized the potential power latent in their huge populations and why they are "at stake" in the struggle between Communism and non-Communism, is that they are underdeveloped and plagued with social and economic problems. Prominent among their problems are the demographic factors contributing to inefficiency: redundant populations, high death and sickness rates, extremely high birth rates, immobility, and high agrarian density. These and other problems make them relatively impotent and also extremely "ripe" for change, with Communism and anti-Communism offering alternative solutions.

Although "the West" embraces heterogeneous countries, some rich and some poor, as does also the "non-West," the greater average inefficiency of the latter can be seen in the fact that in 1949 the mean per capita income for the people in 21 non-Western countries was $47, whereas it was $639 in 44 Western countries. Although the methods of calculating these estimates may falsely exaggerate the differences, it is clear that a pronounced inequality is there. The preponderance of the Western nations on the side of efficiency is still so great that it overbalances their disadvantage on the side of sheer population. This can be seen in the fact that in 1949 the total national income of the 44 Western nations was estimated at 379 billion dollars, whereas that of the 21 non-Western nations for which data were available was estimated at 58 billion. In 1952 the two figures were approximately 500 billion to 75 billion. By this measure, then, the locus of power within the Free World, and doubtless in the Communist World as well, definitely resides in the West.

The West's advantage comes from the fact that it invented the Industrial Revolution and then continued to reap advantages from it. But, as industrialization spreads to non-Western peoples, this advantage will not necessarily last. As we have seen, the weight of sheer numbers may increasingly favor the non-Western countries in both the Communist and the Free Worlds. For this advantage, some of them (the already overpopulated countries) may have to pay a penalty—the depressing effect of dense population on the level of living; but if economic advance moves ahead of population growth, the power of these countries can be expected to grow prodigiously. Furthermore, some of the current demographic advantages of the West may turn into liabilities. For instance, the population may become so burdened with the aged that the crude death rate will rise, ill health increase, and the replacement of military losses become more difficult. Under certain conditions, the concentration of people in metropolitan areas may prove a hardship. In addition, certain nondemographic factors may tend in time to lower productivity in the older industrial nations. It may be that a hardening of the sociological arteries, only dimly seen today in such things as the quest for individual security at the expense of national strength, will set in. Assuming that the non-Western nations eventually move through the demographic transition, they will enjoy some, though not necessarily all, of the demographic advantages the West has enjoyed. If they also acquire more of the technological and social instrumentalities of the West, their superior numbers should count for much more than they do now. The struggle between the Communist and the Free camps is not therefore merely a struggle for the non-Western areas as they are at present. It is a struggle for areas with great potentialities for international power.

Since the struggle may at any time break out into major warfare, it is impossible to deal with the demographic future without also reckoning on the possibility of conflict. In this regard, although the future role of atomic and hydrogen weapons is not clear, it stands to reason that such weapons, *if used in a major war*, will prove far more destructive of human life than have the weapons of the past. It has to be remembered that the death rate is unrestricted at its upper limit. While the birth rate can scarcely rise above 65 per thousand per year, the death rate can, with the proper lethal instruments, approach 1000 in a given area. It is therefore unsafe to assume that the world's population, or that of any particular region, will go on doubling every sixty to seventy years until we have untold billions. Indeed, it is strange to believe that the ingenuity and science necessary to make such population growth possible will not also be used in the relatively simple direction of controlling fertility. If men with all their science and technology are so irrational as not to control their fertility, they cannot be expected to be so wise as to use all of their increased capacities only for productive purposes. They may use these capacities for destructive purposes as well.

The demographic effects of nuclear weapons, if they should be used on a large scale, are impossible to forecast under prevailing conditions of rapid advance and secrecy. It can be assumed, however, that since nuclear bombs are expensive to make and to deliver, they would probably be used on those centers where industry and hence population is highly concentrated. Since the more industrialized the nation, the more concentrated is the population, the weapons would probably do more damage to the populations of the industrial nations than to those of the underdeveloped countries. With the greater concentration of capital equipment in industrial nations, destruction on the economic side would also be greater than in underdeveloped areas. The latter areas, even though their total capital is far less, would have a lesser proportion of it destroyed. In short, the population and the production of underdeveloped areas are more spread out, more dependent on the land, less dependent on equipment. Such areas would not only be less subject to attack with nuclear bombs but would also possibly be better able to survive. On the other hand, of course, such regions would be less capable of retaliating with nuclear might.

In sum, nuclear warfare, if it should occur on a world scale, might end up by increasing in a short time both the relative demographic and the relative technological advantages of the underdeveloped and hence the non-Western peoples.

If it be granted that the demographic problems of the underdeveloped countries, especially in the areas of non-Western culture, make these nations more vulnerable to Communism, the question arises as to what population policies the Free World can pursue. It would appear that an appropriate policy would be the control of birth rates in addition to such activities as the lowering of death rates, the provision of technical assistance and economic aid, and the formation of military alliances. Such a combination of policies, if carried through effectively, would strengthen the Free World in its constant fight against encroachment. On the purely demographic side, however, there is little agreement on goals and certainly none on instrumentalities. The philosophy of population in overpopulated Holland bears no resemblance to that in overpopulated India. The official reticence in the United States seems not to be matched in Japan or Egypt. It is therefore too much to expect that a concerted policy will somehow emerge as if by magic in the Free World. The dominant force in this community of nations is still nationalism. Such being the case, the population policies are likely to be those of individual countries, each pursuing its course separately according to its notion of its own interest. Some Free nations, bearing in mind the prospect of frightful mortality, may elect to put their faith in numbers, making a higher level of living a goal subsidiary to the sheer weight of manpower. Others may aim at economic efficiency in part through demographic moderation. If the Free nations go their own individual way and fail to unite on a population policy, it means that they are giving up one possible means of strengthening their cause. The only compensation is that the Iron Curtain countries, in their search for ways of winning and keeping the backward areas, seem equally bent on ignoring the problems of population.

POPULATION PRESSURE AND THE FUTURE OF WESTERN CIVILIZATION IN EUROPE*

By E. W. Hofstee

Those who know something about the demographic situation in western Europe ask whether there is still some sense in speaking about population pressure in relation to the future of Western civilization. Anyone acquainted with the excellent studies published during the past few years by American authors on population problems in Europe will certainly have drawn the conclusion that, generally speaking, western Europe will not show an increase of population of any importance henceforth. Probably the time of decrease is near. In *Europe's Population in the Interwar Years*, Dudley Kirk[1] publishes a map in which is indicated for the different parts of Europe the net reproduction rate according to Kuczynski. It shows that before the last war it had already diminished in the greater part of western Europe to a level of less than 1, which means that, if the situation does not change considerably, the population of western Europe will not be able to maintain its present number. Notestein *et al.*[2] have come to the same conclusions in their study of the future population of Europe and the Soviet Union. They calculate that the population of western Europe has already almost reached its maximum and that it will decrease before long.

Before trying to answer the question mentioned above, it is necessary to determine exactly what population pressure is, what its origins are, and what dangers lie in it.

Population pressure can be defined as the "social tension originating from an absolute or relative disproportion between population and available resources." An absolute disproportion exists when the proportion is such that it endangers the provision for the minimum needs of the population and thereby endangers the lives of a considerable part of the population, as is the case in different parts of Southeastern Asia. We can take it for granted that such a proportion will always cause dissatisfaction, even though it may not lead to collective action. A relative disproportion exists if, without in reality endangering the provision for the minimum needs, the people react upon it with a feeling of dissatisfaction.

It is clear that we have to understand by "population pressure" something else than overpopulation in the strictly economic sense. Overpopulation in the economic sense comes into being when the density of population rises

* Reprinted from *The American Journal of Sociology*, 55 (May 1950), pp. 523–532, by permission of the author and the University of Chicago Press. Paper read at the summer course, "The Future of Western Civilization," given for foreign and Dutch students at the University of Utrecht, Holland, in 1949.

above the optimum density, i.e., above the density at which the proportion between population and resources is such as to bring the population in question the highest possible prosperity. The density of population in a given country can differ considerably from the optimum density without causing social tensions, that is, without causing population pressure. Population pressure exists only when, by the population as a whole or by a considerable part of it, the proportion between population and resources is consciously or unconsciously felt as a mental or material burden. As is pointed out, too, by Kulischer[3] and by Thompson,[4] the population pressure is a phenomenon that cannot be determined by statistical data only; the subjective feeling of the people in question is of paramount importance.

It is necessary to emphasize that population pressure, where it exists, will not always be felt as such, that is, as an unsatisfactory disproportion between resources and population. Only in an uncomplicated agrarian society will this disproportion be felt directly, viz., as a disproportion between the available land and the number of people which must get a living from it. In modern countries, with well-developed industry and trade, the disproportion will be felt as permanent unemployment or as a standard of living considered insufficient by the people. The consequent dissatisfaction in these countries will be distinguished with difficulty from tensions originating from other causes. In general, the mass of the population will hardly be aware that its feeling of dissatisfaction has something to do with this disproportion unless this is pointed out by its leaders. So it is clear that there was a considerable population pressure in Germany between the two world wars, but it was only through the propaganda of the Nazis that the desire for more *Lebensraum* became common among the German people.

This ignorance of the background of existing social tensions does not make them less serious, and especially in modernly developed countries a heavy population pressure can cause situations which are not only an internal danger but a threat to international peace as well.

Population pressure can come into being from many causes. Generally speaking, in a more or less stable society population pressure will not manifest itself easily. Conditions that remain long unchanged will generally be considered as normal by the social group in question and will not cause strong reactions. This holds, too, for the proportion between population and resources and the phenomena related to this. If the population increases little or not at all, if the resources remain about the same, if there are no changes in the economic system or in the technical possibilities, etc., the proportion between population and resources will not be felt as a burden even if it differs considerably from the proportion which would be optimal in the economic sense. Population pressure will come into being when a certain social group or its available resources are changing to such a degree that the proportion between population and resources is no longer adjusted to the felt needs. So, population pressure can be considered as the consequence of a not yet successful readjustment to new conditions. The most important influences which, on the one side, compel a people to a readjustment and, on the other side, determine the possibility of this readjustment—influences on which, therefore, the existence of population pressure depends—are the following: (1) the development of the number and composition of the population, especially the age composition; (2) the natural conditions for the development of resources; (3) the political and economic conditions, which influence the availability of resources; (4) the availability of capital needed for the exploitation of existing resources; (5) the development of organization of economic life; (6) the technological development; (7) the development of the opinion about an acceptable standard of living.

I may recall briefly the development of the situation in western Europe during about the last one hundred and fifty years. In the nineteenth and the first part of the twentieth century we were confronted in Europe with an enormous increase of the population, caused by the diminishing death rate. By different means Europe succeeded in readjusting itself to the consequences. In the first place, it was possible by improvement of the techniques and organization of economic life to exploit the resources existing inside western Europe (e.g., agriculture) much more efficiently than before and to develop new resources. In the second place, Europe succeeded in developing, to a very great extent, resources outside Europe. In tropical and other territories overseas the production of raw materials and food was developed with the help of European capital, techniques, and organization. For a considerable part these products from overseas went to Europe in exchange for exported products of European industry and as a reward for labor done by Europeans. In the third place, millions of Europeans emigrated during the nineteenth century, especially to the United States. Finally, especially since the end of the past century, the decline of the death rate was counterbalanced more and more by a decline of the birth rate, so that the surplus of births, which rose sharply in most countries during the nineteenth century, decreased gradually. But what is the present situation and what can be expected in the future? Answering this question requires an analysis of the factors which influence the coming into being of population pressure. A complete analysis in this paper is impossible, but a general survey follows.

NUMBER AND COMPOSITION OF THE POPULATION. As was pointed out above, at first glance the present demographic situation seems to hold hardly any menace for the future, in view of the decline of population which we may expect before long. But this superficial impression is not right in all respects.

In the first place, it should be emphasized that, especially in countries with a considerable development of industry and trade, the existence of population pressure is not determined in the first instance by the proportion between the total population and the resources but by the number of people who seek employment. This number is to an important degree dependent on the age composition of the population. The calculations of Notestein *et al.*

show us that during the coming years the age composition of the western European population will change to such a degree that, even if after some time the total number of the population should decrease, the number of those who want work—the age group of 15–65 years—will still increase. Taking Europe west of the Iron Curtain as a whole, there must be created in the coming ten to fifteen years some millions of new subsistencies to give employment to all who ask for it.

In the second place, we must take into account that under existing conditions it is only relatively correct to speak about the problem of population pressure in western Europe as a whole. In spite of all good intentions, western Europe is still a complex of independent states which pursue their own economic and social policies and look first to their own interests. But demographic conditions in the different western European countries are not identical, and, if the political situation in Europe does not change, each will have to solve its demographic problems for itself. Some countries will have little difficulty and will perhaps have to do rather with a shortage of people than with a surplus; others will be confronted with very serious problems. The number of people between 15 and 65 years in Belgium, according to Notestein and others, will decrease between 1945 and 1960 by 40,000, while in Holland, which today has about as many inhabitants as Belgium, this class will increase by about 900,000. In reality the difference will perhaps be more, for Notestein underestimated the anticipated increase of the Dutch population.

As long as Europe is not a real economic unit, each country will think only about providing a good living for its own inhabitants and will not trouble to give the surplus population of its neighbor a subsistence, too. Only if there is a shortage of labor for its own economic development will immigration be stimulated. As the practice in Belgium and France shows, for the greater part of the immigrants only the less desired positions, such as those of the miner and the farmhand, are open. If economic unity does not become a complete reality, it is possible that in the near future in some parts of western Europe there will be hardly any population pressure, while in other parts of Europe very dangerous tensions will be brought about, as is already the case in Italy.

In the third place, it should be pointed out that there is danger in the fact that the number of people who will want employment in production will in the near future show irregularities caused by recent fluctuations in the birth rate. This can cause, locally and temporarily, a heavy population pressure, which can lead to a variety of difficulties. Kulischer points out the sharp rise of the number of births in Germany during the Hitler regime, which will cause a rise of the supply of labor before long. Here should be emphasized especially the remarkable phenomenon that in western Europe, already during the war but still more after the war, a sharp rise of the birth rate has come into being. In Holland the number of newborn babies in 1946 and 1947 was about one and a half times as much as in the years before the war. The birth rate is already declining again everywhere, but, nevertheless, in fifteen or twenty years in Holland and several other countries there will be a suddenly increased supply of labor that undoubtedly will cause social tensions. Because of the temporary character of this increased supply, adjustment will be very difficult.

In the fourth place, it is not certain that the suppositions on which the different prognoses of the future population of western Europe are constructed are right. It is difficult to draw conclusions, now, but there are symptoms pointing to the possibility that the population of western Europe may be more numerous in the future than Notestein calculated. I have already mentioned the rise of the birth rate after the war. A second point, which Notestein could not take into account, is the important migration from east to west, caused by the war, by which, especially, the population of Germany was considerably increased.

Finally, apart from the increase of population in the future, which we still have to expect, conditions in several parts of western Europe are already unsatisfactory. Already before the last war clear symptoms of a population pressure could be observed in several countries, for example, in Italy. That the origin of World War II can be attributed to such a high degree to population pressure, as it is by Kulischer, may be doubted; but it is a matter of fact that there was a heavy population pressure in Germany, showing itself, for one thing, in the migration to Holland, which was already so densely populated.

THE DEVELOPMENT OF RESOURCES. Resources are a product of nature and culture. The gifts of nature are resources for mankind only if mankind is mentally and socially able to use them for its needs. Oil really became a resource only after the invention of the internal-combustion engine and after society had developed in such a way that this engine could play an important part in economic life. Nature gives the chances; mankind has to develop them. But the natural conditions are primary. If they do not give the chance to meet the demands originating from an increase of the population or rising needs, then social tension, a population pressure, comes into being. What about these natural conditions for western Europe?

Though there is no country in the modern world which depends only on resources inside its own territory and though every country, by means of exchange, has the resources of all parts of the world at its disposal, the resources inside its own territory are of primary importance; the possibilities of exchange, too, are determined to a high degree by the production of its own resources. So, for western Europe, also, the natural conditions in its own territory are of first importance.

It may be sufficient to discuss the natural conditions for the development of the two most important resources, agriculture and the resources for energy. As for agriculture, the soil is used in western Europe more intensively than anywhere else in the world. By a high development of the techniques of agriculture and by an intensive care for the crops, the output is generally, as compared with that in other parts of the world, extremely high. The average output of wheat per acre in Holland, under normal conditions, is about three times as high as in the United States or Canada. Practically all the land which comes into consideration at all is used for agriculture in western Europe. Even the poorest sandy soils give, by means of an abundant use of fertilizers, substantial crops. As has been pointed out already, it was possible to meet the needs of the increasing population of western Europe, among other things, by raising the agricultural production. Notwithstanding that, Europe during the nineteenth and twentieth centuries became to an ever higher degree dependent for its food supply on other parts of the world. This dependence involves serious difficulties, especially since the war, while the still-increasing population and the increased wants, especially for protective foods, stimulate the demand for food even more than before. Is it possible to enlarge agricultural production in Europe? Extension of the area of cultivated land will hardly be possible, even if we make the greatest efforts, as in Holland through reclamation of the Zuider Zee. Undoubtedly there will still be important discoveries in the field of agriculture, while the technical knowledge of our farmers still can be increased. But it must be doubted very much if such a sharp rise of the output of the land as we have seen during the preceding period will even under the most favorable conditions be possible again. We must not forget that the law of diminishing returns still holds for agriculture! The higher the production, the more difficult it is to raise it still more; precisely because western Europe has already progressed so far, a further improvement will be difficult. There are agriculturists who take an even darker view of the future. They are convinced that because of an excessive use of fertilizers and a lack of organic manure the producing qualities of the soil in western Europe threaten to diminish or are already decreased considerably. They point out the increasing number of plant diseases and plagues which attend this forced and very specialized agrarian production and which can be suppressed only by the use of an ever increasing number of poisons. We will have to wait to see whether these pessimists are right, but it seems certainly unjustified to expect that western Europe will be able to provide its own food supply to a higher degree than in the past.

As for the resources for energy, for the present we have practically to do with only three: coal, oil, and hydroelectric power. As for coal, even if some of the most favorably situated coal mines do become exhausted in time, the reserves are large enough to be able to provide for the needs of western Europe, even if these needs should increase. This does not mean that the supply of coal for western Europe will bring no difficulties in the near future; but probably these difficulties will originate from the supply of labor and be caused by the unattractiveness of mining, a drawback which perhaps can be reduced by a further mechanization.

Not favorable are the conditions as to the possibility of the production of oil in western Europe. The geological structure of Europe is such that, in the greater part, the chances for tracing oil are completely nil, while the rest is to be considered as promising little, even though the painstaking exploration during and after the war gave some results. Yet in western Europe the progress of economic life becomes more and more dependent on oil, and, therefore, it has to rely for its supply of energy on overseas countries more than ever before. Indeed, it is possible to convert coal into liquid fuel, but apart from the difficulties, already mentioned, which will perhaps arise with regard to the supply of coal, there is the fact that synthetic oil is still extremely expensive, so that if western Europe had to solve the problem of oil supply in this way it would be in an unfavorable position as compared to the countries with natural oil wells at their disposal.

As for hydroelectric power, the possibilities in this respect are not yet exhausted, but they are by no means sufficient to provide for the increasing needs of energy of western Europe.

An inspection of the other resources would lead us to similar results, and generally the conclusion may be drawn that natural conditions are not such that western Europe can rely in the future on its own resources to a much higher degree than in the past.

POLITICAL AND ECONOMIC CONDITIONS. Therefore, if Europe is to maintain a fair level of prosperity in the future and if it wants to prevent a heavy population pressure from being felt, then it will have to rely to a high degree on resources outside its own territory; and so it is of paramount importance that these foreign resources be politically and economically accessible to western Europe. In the past these resources were politically accessible because a great number of the countries where they were found were brought into some form of political dependence upon western Europe, or, as far as they were independent (e.g., the states of South America), the governments did not hamper the exploitation of the resources for the benefit of western Europe. Economically the resources were accessible because western Europe exported commodities to these territories and west Europeans worked there, in return for which were received all sorts of products which western Europe itself supplied in insufficient measure. We can take it for granted that the political dependence of a considerable part of the world upon western Europe has gradually come to an end. This fact does not necessarily mean that the resources in the territories in question become inaccessible, for Europe did profit, too, from the resources of the independent countries. But often there exists among these newly independent peoples a strong economic nationalism. They try to transform themselves from suppliers of raw materials into industrial countries and so to exploit their resources only for themselves. They try, also, as soon as possible to take over positions in economic life which were held formerly by Europeans; in brief, they try to make themselves independent of the services, commodities, and capital of western Europe, and by doing that they take away the foundations of the system of exchange, which made it possible to exploit these foreign resources for the benefit of western Europe. Moreover, in many cases political independence leads to unstable conditions (Burma, Philippines, Indonesia), by which the exploitation of resources generally is hampered very much. In several countries that were already independent which of old acted as suppliers of food and raw materials for Europe we see, too, a strong aspiration for economic independence and for loosening of economic ties with Europe. Of this, Argentina is a clear example. On the other side, Canada gives the example of a development in the direction of an independent and all-round economic life which is coupled with the maintenance of close economic relations with the Old World and the opening of its own resources for the providing for the needs of Europe.

It is still difficult to express a definitive opinion, but it seems probable that Europe will have much more trouble in the future in getting the resources which it needs for its development from outside its own territory than was the case in the past.

THE AVAILABILITY OF CAPITAL. Apart from labor for the exploitation of existing resources, capital is needed. In the past century western Europe showed a permanent increase of the available amount of capital, by which it was possible, on the one side, to meet the rising needs caused by the increase of the population, while, on the other side, the new technical possibilities could be realized, and so the level of prosperity could be raised. This more or less regular and gradual growth of capital was twice interrupted seriously during the past decades by a world war. Not only was a large quantity of capital destroyed by the wars directly, but during them and in the first years after them the necessary extension and renovation of capital was stopped, and by this the arrears increased. The destruction of capital due to World War II, directly as well as indirectly, was enormous, and, notwithstanding the great amount of labor which has already gone into rehabilitation, the exploitation of the resources of western Europe is still hampered to a high degree by lack of capital.

To bring the supply of capital in this part of the world to an adequate level again and to maintain for the population an acceptable standard of living, western Europe was compelled to sell a considerable part of its foreign investments. An example is the sale of the Argentine railways by England. But the liquidation of these foreign investments was not at all sufficient to solve the problems, and only by the granting of credits by foreign countries, especially by the United States and lately by the ERP (the Marshall Plan) was it possible to restart gradually the production in Europe and to keep it going. Notwithstanding this help, it will be very difficult to find the capital needed for the exploitation of the available resources, which increases the likelihood of population pressure.

Though the efforts to bring back the capital invested outside Europe as much as possible and to re-establish economic life with this capital must be considered as being right, it is clear that, on the other side, the exploitation of resources outside Europe becomes thereby much more difficult, directly in many cases because, with the withdrawal of capital where it cannot be replaced by other capital, the exploitation of resources is endangered. So the rapid withdrawal of European capital from Argentina without sufficient replacing capital being available certainly contributed to the existing economic difficulties and to the declining exploitation of resources in that country. Where replacing capital is available, as in the case of the sale of Dutch shares in American industries, of course it becomes impossible to use the revenues of this capital to purchase overseas resources.

In another respect, too, the insufficient supply of capital hampers the availability of resources outside Europe. Because of the inadequate supply of raw materials and machinery, the productivity of labor in west European industry is low, and so the costs of production are high. So the sale of products outside Europe becomes difficult, which means generally that the exchange of European commodities against the products of resources outside Europe is hampered.

ORGANIZATION OF ECONOMIC LIFE. In the foregoing, by "exploitation of resources" was meant the whole process of production, transport, working-up, etc., of raw materials until the commodities in their final shape reach the consumer. As already pointed out, the question as to whether some gift of nature becomes an economic resource depends to a high degree on the cultural level reached by a given people; also, the way in which the exploitation is accomplished expresses the whole culture of the people. Of special interest in this connection are the forms of organization of economic life. In the development of new forms of organization adapted to the changing conditions, Europe has achieved exceptional results since the Middle Ages. The organization of modern big industry, the modern organization of transport, modern banking, modern management, which are now spread all over the world and which made possible an exploitation of resources as never before, all originated from Europe. But the danger threatens Europe that by the continued development of the organization of modern economic life it will fall behind, especially as compared with the United States and perhaps with Russia. At the moment the productivity of labor in industry in America is three to four times higher than in western Europe. This is caused not only by the abundance of capital and the richer resources of America but by the better organization of the processes of production in the widest sense. For such commodities as motorcars and aeroplanes America has organized production and sale in such a way that Europe in considerable part has become dependent upon America for them, though the natural conditions, the skill of the laborers, and the technical knowledge are certainly sufficient to equal America in this respect. By this, Europe not only becomes dependent upon American resources but, moreover, often cannot compete with America in foreign markets, whereby the possibility of getting foreign products by means of exchange is reduced.

The most important reason by which in western Europe an organization of economic life in accordance with the possibilities of modern techniques is prevented is the still-existing division into a great number of sovereign states. By this, production and markets are broken up, an adaptation of the available labor to the natural and economic conditions is prevented, and the combination of capital needed for the establishing of industries which could expand over the whole world is hampered. If Europe is to develop in the future, if it is to raise the exploitation of its own resources as high as possible and organize this exploitation as efficiently as possible, and if it is to get access to the resources elsewhere in the world by an export trade as large as possible, then the promotion of the economic and political unity of Europe is the first necessity.

THE TECHNICAL DEVELOPMENT. Technical progress can lead to the result that new resources become available which formerly, for technical reasons, were not and that resources which were already available can be exploited with less labor or with less capital than before. The availability of new resources will always lead to a lessening of population pressure, of course; but the possibility of exploiting resources with fewer laborers than before will be an advantage only if the unemployed workers find a field of activity in the exploitation of new resources. If that does not happen, then the prosperity of those who remain engaged in the exploitation of the resources in question will increase; but a number of workers will be permanently unemployed, and exactly this permanent unemployment is one of the most dangerous symptoms of population pressure in modern society.

Undoubtedly, continued technological development will be an advantage in many respects; thus the modest production of oil which developed in Holland after the liberation would have been impossible if the techniques of exploration and production had not progressed so much during the past decades. Indirectly, technological progress will perhaps benefit western Europe if by this more and better products of industry can be produced and a more extensive exchange with countries producing raw materials and food can be brought about. But if for one reason or another an extension of this exchange is not possible, then it will not be possible to get more foreign resources, and a technological progress becomes a disadvantage rather than an advantage.

The dangers just mentioned are not only theoretical. In Holland the technological progress in agriculture threatens to lead to problems. After the liberation, a strong tendency to mechanization in agriculture, caused, among other things, by a raising of wages, came into being. The consequence of this tendency will be that a considerable number of workers will be turned out of agriculture. The Dutch economists are racking their brains now about how to increase the export of products of industry to such a degree that, not only for the increasing population, but for this surplus of agricultural workers, too, a living will be created, which means, in fact, to get by this export an access to foreign resources on which this people can base a subsistence.

OPINION ON AN ACCEPTABLE STANDARD OF LIVING. As already pointed out, in a modern industrial and commercial country the disproportion between population and resources will demonstrate itself in permanent unemployment or in a standard of living which is considered by the population in question to be insufficient. Permanent unemployment will always be felt as unsatisfactory and will lead to social tensions. The question as to whether a given standard of living is considered insufficient is dependent not only on the absolute level of this standard but also on the opinion that the social group itself has formed about an acceptable standard of living. This opinion is generally influenced very much by the standard of living of other social groups with which the group in question compares itself. With the development of modern trade, the group with which one compares one's self has increased permanently. Formerly, a farmer compared himself only with his own kind in his own region. Today he compares himself, too, with the inhabitants of the cities, and he asks for a higher standard of living. As for western Europe as a whole, the contact between the old world and the new becomes closer continually, and we can observe more and more a tendency to take the American standard of living as a yardstick and to consider, in consequence, our own standard of living to be insufficient. This, too, can be a cause for tensions in the near future, which, because they can be solved only by a change in the proportion between population and resources, will accentuate the problem of the population pressure.

Objectively speaking, the conditions in western Europe are much more favorable than in many other parts of the world. But population pressure is only partly a question of objective conditions; it is also, and especially, a question of the subjective experiencing of these objective conditions. Conditions which in Southeastern Asia would be felt as a blessing from heaven would perhaps cause in western Europe social tensions which would disturb the whole world.

There is a fair chance that western Europe will overcome all these difficulties. But this will be possible only if we direct our full attention to them and are inclined, inside Europe as well as outside, to fulfil the conditions which must be fulfilled if we want to offset the threatening danger. The most important condition is the establishment of a real west European unity. But a united Europe, too, will be able to prevent a heavy population pressure only if the world outside Europe will open itself to products and men from Europe. Europe must be enabled to co-operate in the development of resources over the whole world, and it must have the chance to exchange the products of European industry with raw materials and food from overseas territories. European emigrants must be accepted in those parts of the world where, by an extension of the population, the exploitation of resources could be intensified.

If we do not succeed in solving the problems in this way, western Europe will be a danger spot for the world. Authors like Thompson and Kulischer emphasized the great dangers which population pressure in some parts of the world holds for peace. It does not seem probable that an unfavorable development in western Europe in the next years will be a direct cause of a new war. In western Europe, at the moment, not a single nation possesses the power to make a successful war if it is not sure of the help of the United States of America or the Soviet Union. But an increasing population pressure can lead certainly to internal unrest, which could be the beginning of a dangerous political development threatening the cultural values of the whole of Western civilization.

REFERENCES

1. Dudley Kirk, *Europe's Population in the Inter-war Years* (Geneva: League of Nations, 1946).
2. Frank W. Notestein *et al., The Future Population of Europe and the Soviet Union* (Geneva: League of Nations, 1944).
3. Eugene M. Kulischer, *Europe on the Move* (New York: Columbia University Press, 1948).
4. Warren S. Thompson, *Population and Peace in the Pacific* (Chicago: University of Chicago Press, 1947).

CHAPTER 8

SOCIO-CULTURAL CONTEXT OF POPULATION DYNAMICS

Probably no sociologist would assert that there exists a well-reasoned and highly developed "sociological theory of population" comparable to the theory of population available in economics (as represented, for example, in Peacock's paper included in Chapter 4). For that matter, sociological theory in general is not yet as highly elaborated as economic theory, and sociologists have given sustained attention to population questions for a much shorter time than have economists. However, there is a considerable literature in which sociologists (and others writing from a sociological viewpoint) have shown the relevance of their concepts for the study of population problems. Moreover, in the United States at least, the role of administering collegiate instruction and graduate training in the field of population studies has fallen largely into the hands of the sociologist.

At least two major ways in which writers have sought to justify sociological treatments of population questions are discernible. First, they have attempted to show that analysis in terms of the socio-cultural context discloses forces at work which are lost sight of if population problems are approached strictly from the perspective of biology, geography, or economics. For example, in *Cultural Sciences* (1952), Florian Znaniecki urged demographers to view the population of a territory as a "dynamic complex of changing social groups," and, when dealing with the relevant resource and environmental factors, to give due regard also to the value systems of the persons comprising the population. Second, some studies indicate what particular aspects of the socio-cultural context are demographically relevant, and point out ways in which these aspects may be causally or functionally significant. Unfortunately, such hypotheses, gotten from broad comparative studies, frequently are stated with too little specificity to permit rigorous testing; they may then commend themselves primarily on the grounds of their plausibility. However, there is some indication in the most recent literature that sociologists are beginning to formulate demographic hypotheses of a fairly specific, detailed kind.

The papers included in this chapter illustrate several approaches taken by writers concerned with the sociological aspects of population. Hiller's paper is a prolegomenon to the systematic study of population problems in a cultural context; it consists largely of a demonstration of the inadequacy of theories which neglect this context. In quite a different way, Dedrick's paper emphasizes the cultural relativity of demographic phenomena. His discussion shows how the cultural variability of family and occupational structure renders difficult the task of making precise international demographic comparisons.

Lorimer's work on *Culture and Human Fertility* (the conclusions of which are excerpted here) represents what might be called the "cross-cultural comparative approach." Examining fertility in a number of societies, it seeks to isolate those aspects of social structure and value systems that are functionally related to fertility, and to discover what conditions favor the maintenance of high fertility and what circumstances dispose a population to keep its fertility at a low level. An alternative method of relating cultural to demographic variables is to analyze the impact of cultural change on population processes. If a group with a relatively static culture has achieved an approximate demographic equilibrium, and significant cultural changes are then introduced, one can interpret the situation as a crude experiment. The new cultural pattern is the experimental variable; the observed population changes constitute the experimental effect. Palmer's paper on the impact of European culture on non-European populations generalizes from several instances of this kind. The effects of cultural changes are, of course, not confined to situations where a new cultural pattern is introduced from the outside; but they may, perhaps, be more readily isolated under this condition than in the case where cultural change from period to period is less dramatic.

A growing tendency in sociological work is to direct research to specific hypotheses about social structures and situations, in preference to constructing inclusive syntheses of patterns of socio-cultural variation. Applied to population studies, this trend has involved the formulation and testing of hypotheses that consider the social experiences and predicaments of individuals to be determinants of their demographically relevant behavior. Innumerable such hypotheses can be suggested *ad hoc*. But it appears that more or less haphazard hypothesis-testing is not likely to be fruitful, except, perhaps, in the earliest exploratory stage of research. Such, at least, can be argued from the experience of the Indianapolis study on fertility (briefly reviewed in Westoff's paper). Rather, it seems likely that cogent results are more apt to be obtained in carefully designed studies dealing with a relatively few variables—these variables having been selected for their theoretical relevance to the problem under investigation—and utilizing appropriate observational, experimental, and statistical controls. On some such premise, Westoff marshals the fragmentary evidence indicating the importance of social mobility as a determinant of family size, and suggests that systematic study of this variable may clarify the empirical results of previous studies of fertility.

Sociological writings on population often stress the notion of "multiple causation" and the inacceptability of so-called "deterministic" theories. Not only the multiplicity of causes affecting a particular dependant variable—e.g., a population change— but also the interrelations of changes in different parts of society and culture are signalized in the sociological literature. The paper by Duncan exemplifies the multiplicity of elements present in the situational context of behavior (in this case, migration), each of which may be viewed alternately as an independent or a dependent variable. A general rationale for considering population as both an independent and a dependent variable is given in Ogburn's paper. Each point of view is the necessary complement of the other, because "demographic determinism" is an inadequate sociological theory, and a "socio-cultural determinism" would neglect the demographic factor in the growth of culture and the evolution of society. Where reality has the aspect of a system of mutually interdependent and interacting variables, any single variable may be taken as "independent" only as a provisional simplification for convenience of analysis.

A CULTURE THEORY OF POPULATION TRENDS*

By E. T. Hiller

Attempts to supply a theory of population growth or decline have been based largely on biological and economic premises. The formulas advanced are usually reducible to the dichotomy, physiological organism and food. Births and deaths are obviously biological facts, and their ratio determines the increase or decrease of population. But this commonplace is no indication that a particular rate of population growth is specifically controlled by biological mechanisms. Though food sets limits to possible growth, the theoretical possibility does not explain the actual trends. A review of existing theories leads necessarily to the rejection of assumptions based exclusively on biological and economic interpretations, and compels the substitution of a cultural interpretation of various population phenomena.

The biological determinism implied by Malthus and other early students of the population question has been made more explicit by later writers. An outstanding recent example is found in the mathematical formulas of Pearl and Reed. Assuming that the statistical aggregate of a population is the resultant of the physiologically fixed reproductive capacity and the organism's need of nutrition, these investigators have deduced what they venture to call "universal laws" of population growth. According to their formulas the rate of growth is a function of the size of the population already attained, and the amount of the unutilized subsistence or resources still available at a given date, in the supporting area.[1] An initial slow rate of absolute growth is supposed to be followed by an acceleration, and this by a subsequent retardation.

Corroboration for their so-called laws of human population growth, these authors think, is found in analogies of increase in the number of fruit flies, the rate of growth of yeast, pumpkins, and tadpole tails, and the egg-laying performance of hens. Underlying these analogies is the assumption that the reproductive potentiality in a human population, as in aggregates of insects, is released or limited solely by environmental physical factors such as temperature, light, nutrition, air, and humidity. The mechanisms of growth are inferred to be the same in all cases, whether the increase be that of size or of number of organisms. "Population growth, in respect of its rate," Pearl affirms, "appears to be a fundamental biological phenomenon in which insects and men behave in a similar manner."[2] This approach attempts to reduce humanistic phenomena to "naturalistic" or physical terms.

Such "laws" are invalidated by the methods used in their construction.

* Reprinted from *The Journal of Political Economy*, 38 (October 1930), pp. 523–550, by permission of the author and the University of Chicago Press.

The logistic curves have no explanatory value and, in their universalized form, contain logical inadequacies. The affirmation of a conceptual similarity between such widely different subjects sheds no light on any one of them. Willcox has said,

I see no convincing reason to believe in regular curves of growth susceptible of representation by mathematical equations, through the help of which it is possible to foresee the future growth of populations. . . . My skepticism goes deeper. I do not believe in the existence of any simple law of population growth.[3]

Wolfe concludes,

One fallacy in any such analogy lies in the fact that any phenomenal change that takes place at a decreasing rate in time can be represented by a logarithmic curve. Even for the analogy between growth of an individual organism and growth of an aggregate, it is, to the present writer, impossible to see any rational warrant in a study of the population problem.[4]

Similar vague mechanical or "natural" connections between nutrition and population growth are implied or affirmed by other writers. One of these asserts: "Population pressure is to some extent analogous to pressure of gas or vapour in physics."[5] Sir James Steuart in his *Inquiry into the Principles of Political Economy* (1767) said:

The generative faculty resembles a spring loaded with a weight, which always exerts itself in proportion to the diminution of resistance. When food has remained some time without augmentation or diminution, generation will carry numbers as high as possible; if, then, food comes to be diminished, the spring is overpowered, the force of it becomes less than nothing, inhabitants will diminish. . . .[6]

Roscher states:

A basin entirely filled with water can be made to contain more only in case it is either increased itself, or a means is found to compress its contents. Otherwise as much must flow out on one side as is poured in on the other. And so, everything else remaining stationary, the fruitfulness of marriages must, at least in the long run, be in the inverse ratio of their frequency.[7]

Woodruff supposes that "the saturation point for population closely corresponds to the mean annual rainfall. That is, the more rain there is, the more grass and grain, and therefore more flocks and herds for man to eat."[8] This statement ignores the fact that some areas of great rainfall have sparse populations. Equally untenable are the beliefs that variation in fertility is associated with altitude and Sadler's theory that fecundity stands in direct ratio to the fertility of the soil.[9] More guarded is his theory that the children per family become less as the population becomes more numerous, and Verhulst's argument that

if a population is expanding freely over unoccupied territory, the percentage rate of increase is constant. If it is growing in a limited area, the percentage rate of increase must tend to get less and less as the population grows, so that the percentage rate of increase is some function of the population itself, which falls continuously as the numbers of the population rise.[10]

Though some writers give recognition to the fact of control over the environment, their explanations still rest upon physiological premises. The theories upheld by Achille Loria, Levasseur, Sumner, Keller, and others were of this character. In 1854 G. K. Rickards spoke of "the true law of population as a self-regulating power, capable of adjusting itself to the most opposite phases of society, and, in the absence of disturbing causes, proportioning the supply to the demand, under all the infinitely varying circumstances of human nature."[11] Bastiat believed that population has a tendency to proportion itself to the means of subsistence, and that these means increase with the growth of population. Holmes observes that "increased means of production may, for a while, keep pace with the growing numbers of inhabitants. But in time the growth of population must bring about its own checks."[12] This writer, like Malthus, sees population growth as a calamity, while others, including Darwin, regard it as a source of "progress." Woodruff believes that social progress depends upon food supply, since the pressure of population upon subsistence stimulates invention and control over nature.[13] This theory is a variation of Keller's formula which holds that inventions and numbers are functions of each other.[14] From this point of view, the simple equation, "food and population," offers the solution of the enigma of progress.[15]

While such theories are corroborated by some facts, they are invalidated by others. The inadequacy of population theories which rest on the organism-food, or on any other exclusively "naturalistic" premise is indicated by the fact that in some sections where the per capita quantity of goods and the general physical well-being have increased the birth-rate has declined.[16] This decline, which has been obvious for more than half a century in the most prosperous nations, has recently been accelerated, as shown by Kuczynski's study of Northwest Europe and by the unprecedented low rates in the United States during the last few years.[17]

The organism-food dichotomy is also invalidated by the fact that in the Western nations the families of wealthy people are at present generally smaller than are those of the poor. This differential birth-rate was evident in Roman times, as shown by the designation applied to the working people, *proletarii* ("bearers of children"), and by the rapid extinction of many patrician families. The same demographic phenomenon was noted by Adam Smith and Malthus, and has since been shown to hold in so many countries and cities that the fact has become a commonplace.[18] Alison (1840) and Thomas Doubleday (1841) observed that the birth-rate stood in inverse ratio to the standard of living.[19] Darwin mentioned the fact that 19 per cent of the English nobility were childless, and that this percentage was three times the average for the whole nation. Investigations such as those made by Quetelet in Brussels, Farr and Heron in London,[20] Nitti in Naples,[21] and Bertillon in Paris, Berlin, Vienna, and London,[22] Hindelang in Bavaria, and Schwabe in Berlin,[23] Dunlop in Scotland,[24] and many other students with reference to various times and places[25] have shown the differences in the birth-rate of the

social classes. Gillette observes that a low birth-rate is associated with af-
fluence, high rating of the educational system, and high frequency of notables
in the population.[26] English statisticians have often noted the high birth-rate
peculiar to mining and industrial districts. In Germany, the largest proportion
of births to women of childbearing age was found in the industrial cities of
the Rhine-Westphalian districts, while the lowest rate was found in the commercial cities, where there has been the greater wealth and comfort. Some
attempts have also been made to prove that the number of children tends to
decrease in proportion to the accumulation of property.[27]

The attempt to account for these variable birth-rates has led to a variety of
theories, some of which rest on false methodological premises, since they
suppose the phenomena to be physiological rather than cultural in nature. For
example, Newsholme and Stevenson hesitatingly say: "It is not unlikely that
up to a certain point improvement in prosperity favors fertility, though beyond this it may act to a limited extent in the opposite direction."[28] Pearl,
when faced by inconsiderate facts, is forced to expostulate:

> It is the very harshness and inadequacy of the human environment which is the
> inevitable and indeed necessary concomitant of real poverty, which tends both
> directly and indirectly through psychological reactions to produce a high birth
> rate. And, on the other hand, it seems to me to be equally clear that the probably
> superoptimal environment, biologically speaking, which even moderate wealth is
> able to command, tends both directly and indirectly to low fertility and even a good
> deal of actual sterility.[29]

Doubleday, in a similar dilemma, argued that when the existence of a species
is endangered, "A corresponding effort is invariably made by Nature for its
preservation and continuance by an increase of fertility, and that this especially takes place whenever such danger arises from a diminution of proper
nourishment or food."[30] Spencer advanced the theory that the power of multiplication diminishes as differentiation of function and complexity of the
organism increase.[31] Similar views were expressed by De Candolle, Jacoby,
Delaunay,[32] and more recently by F. Carli.[33] From the data at hand Fourier
deduced the principle that "just in proportion as individuals or a community
become perfected in civilization, in the same proportion the race inclines to
run out."[34] A. K. Chalmers[35] and Corrado Gini[36] likewise stress the physiological factors underlying the declining birth-rates.

Others have shared this belief in a naturalistic population theory with
equal disregard of supporting data. Pell declared variations in animal fertility
to be in inverse ratio to the development of nervous energy.[37] Brownell found
a relation between a low birth-rate and the incidence of nervous diseases.[38]
Dr. Brownlee maintained that increases in population were due to rhythmic
variations in germinal vitality, similar to those resulting in remarkable literary
output, "racial adventure," plagues of field mice or locusts.[39] Bluhm attributed
the lessening fertility of the Germans to racial deterioration,[40] and Jules
Simon accounted for the slow growth of the French people in a similar way.[41]

Dr. Cyrus M. Edson and Dr. Billings hold like views with reference to the lower birth-rate in the United States.[42] Hansen thought he discovered a correlation between the declining birth-rate and the inferiority of the first-born.[43]

However, available data fail to show that the lowering birth-rate is due to changes in fecundity, that is, in physiological capacity of reproduction. The intensive investigations made by the English Birth Rate Commission, and by Ethel Elderton show no evidence of a reduction in fecundity. Dudfield likewise concludes:

There is no direct evidence, statistical or medical, in favor of any suggestion that any decrease has taken place in the potential fecundity or fertility of the human race in general or the English race in particular. . . . There is no data for arriving at any measure of the loss of fertility resulting from late marriages.[44]

Darwin and others believed that the powers of reproduction have increased, rather than diminished.[45] Some investigators have stated that modern civilized races do not differ in fecundity. That the variable rate of increase is not due primarily to biological variations is shown by the fact that the birth-rate of some so-called races varies from place to place, and conforms to that of the population among which they are located.[46]

A physiological explanation of the declining birth-rate is also refuted by facts concerning the marriage rate and the age of marriage. All European countries and all American states, as Brentano points out, have shown a decline in the birth-rate since 1870 irrespective of an advance or decline in the marriage rate.[47] In France the birth-rate has steadily declined since the beginning of the nineteenth century, even when the marriage rate has increased, as it did between 1890 and 1907.[48] During the period when the birth-rate has decreased, the marriage rate has remained fairly constant throughout Europe[49] and has increased in the United States.[50] During the same time the average age of marriage has decreased in France, Prussia, Bavaria, Oldenburg, Finland, Würtemburg, and Saxony.[51] Likewise in the last half-century the age of marriage and also the percentage of single persons in the lower age groups and in the entire group fifteen years of age and over have diminished in the United States.[52] The tendency shown by the upper classes in the last two generations to postpone marriage, although having some effect upon the birth-rate,[53] could not, Heron concluded, be responsible for more than 50 per cent of the decline.[54] Young men of the wage-earning class, according to Rubin, who made an intensive investigation of Danish marriages in the period covering the sixteenth to the nineteenth centuries, marry earlier today than formerly.[55] Neither the marriage rate nor the age of marriage, therefore, can be regarded as the cause of the diminishing birth-rate.[56]

Every purely "naturalistic" explanation advanced to account for the variable rate of population growth illustrates Huxley's definition of a tragedy —a theory refuted by a fact. Any adequate population theory must not only indicate some channel for the regulation of numbers, as these explanations attempt to do, but must also take into consideration the psychological and cultural factors which the purely biological explanations ignore. Many writers on this subject have admitted the influence of prudential considerations in reference to prospective pain, discomfort, or deprivations.

Among these writers, economists have been most concerned with the reaction of individuals to variable quantities of actual or prospective economic goods. Although the problem is held to be one of economic determinism, the mechanism is assumed to involve a psychological, rather than a chemical and physical, connecting medium between environment and numbers. Prudence, rather than physiological wants, is assumed to be the deciding factor. Adam Smith, Montesquieu, and Malthus supplied the model for much of the current discussion relative to this point. Recent opinions have been summarized by Thompson, who concludes that it is not only actual pressure upon sustenance but also "fear of pressure in its manifold forms which keeps population from multiplying more rapidly than it does."[57]

These deductions have been reduced to various formulas. One writer says: "The number of births is in an inverse ratio, not to the density of population, but to the difficulty of providing for a family."[58] Holmes, after expressing the thought that there is no longer reason for fearing the scourges which formerly checked increase, declares: "It is now becoming probable that the automatic checks will not depend so much upon the increase of the death rate, as upon the decrease of the birth rate."[59] East, who apparently accepts the logistic curves of Pearl and Reed without reservation, nevertheless concedes that "there is no good reason for saying that the upper limits of food production will be reached because of population pressure," since (in true ethnocentric style) it is "to be assumed that Americans will have sufficient foresight to adjust the birth rate to the death rate."[60]

The declining birth-rate is believed by the German economist, Julius Wolf, to be the effect of "an increasing rationalism of life."[61] Sidney Webb, noting that the decline in the birth-rate was largest among the well-to-do classes, supposed that these were especially endowed with thrift and foresight.[62] A similar hypostatization is contained in Barton's belief that a state of poverty is generally accompanied by a great want of foresight.[63] Dumont, in particular, stressed the thought that the decrease of population is not an economic question, but an intellectual, political, and aesthetic matter.[64] His theory of social capillarity has found a parallel in the statements of many other writers. For example, the British Commission of Inquiry on the declining birth-rate concluded: "Wherever political and social conditions bring a man or a class into a position in which he hopes to rise or fears to fall, the family will be restricted."[65] Leroy-Beaulieu attempted to show statistically that "a low birth rate goes hand in hand . . . with democratic aspirations."[66]

Psychological explanations of conduct are implicit in the various studies which have been made to determine the correlation between demographic and economic factors. Quételet pointed out the relation between the price of grain and the number of marriages. Yule in 1906 investigated the connection between changes in price levels and the marriage rate.[67] "It is clear," said Guillard, "that the twofold production of corn and of men has proceeded in a parallel proportion."[68] Hector Denis showed that the number of marriages in Belgium followed the rise and fall of prices in coal.[69] Ogle discovered that the marriage rate varied in accordance with export values.[70] Dorothy S. Thomas noted the seasonal variations in the English marriage rate, corresponding to fluctuations in employment.[71] The study made by Ogburn and Thomas with reference to the United States (1870–1920) showed that in states for which statistics were available the marriage rate increased during times of prosperity and diminished during times of depression.[72] R. H. Hooker showed a close correlation between the marriage rate in England and Wales (1861–95) and the amount of foreign trade.[73] Davies found a correlation for the United States between marriage rates and wholesale prices (1887–1906).[74] Giddings says: "The rate of population increase has actually been determined by the economic position of women."[75] Carr-Saunders and others have discussed practices which they suppose to indicate efforts to maintain the "optimum numbers," that is, the population conducive to the highest desirable standard of living in the various stages of civilization.[76] According to Keller, "This means, primarily, that people will not propagate beyond the capacity of the environment or the stage of the arts to support them according to their customary notion of what satisfactory living is."[77]

Although facts and opinions such as the foregoing might seem to supply adequate backing for a psychological theory of population, various contradictions are encountered. Facts are at hand which cannot readily be fitted into the theory. For example, it is impossible, as Sir William Beveridge has shown, to see the selective influence of prices in bringing about a fall of the birth-rate in one province of Holland and no fall at all in the next province.[78] Several studies of the relation between economic conditions and marriage rate show wide variations and inconsistencies from one country and period to another.[79]

The correlation between economic conditions and the birth-rate is even less marked than between these and the marriage rate. There is no uniform relation between the degree of national prosperity and the birth-rate. "Norway and Ireland, both relatively poor countries," as pointed out by Newsholme and Stevenson (1906), "have a high fertility, but Bavaria and France, which are relatively more prosperous, have one a high, and the other a low, birth rate."[80] During periods of extreme social disorganization the birth-rate may be voluntarily restricted, as was done by the Melanesians. They said: "Why should we bring children into the world only to work for the white man?" Before the time of Malthus the Marquis d'Argenson noted: ". . . The population and marriage [are] quite dying out on all sides. . . . They never marry and they do not even think of it. If others prompt them to it, they all make one reply, that it is not worth bringing into the world other unfortunates as miserable as they themselves."[81] On the other hand, the "masses" living in the disorganized conditions of England in the early nineteenth century were said not to have diminished the size of their families. According to one writer, they "were reckless, improvident, intemperate . . . at the same time multiplying as carelessly as rabbits."[82] In Northern and Western Europe during the last six decades, the improvement in the standard of living has been accompanied by a decline in the birth-rate.[83] However, in Japan, according to G. C. Allen, a similar rise in the standard of living has not been accompanied by either a declining or a differential birth-rate.[84]

The variations between the birth-rates of the economic classes are likewise inconstant. In the latter days of Greece and Rome noble families became extinct because of the failure to reproduce,[85] but during the Middle Ages the so-called upper classes are said to have contributed more to succeeding generations than did the lower classes.[86] As a result of his study concerning the fertility of the various social classes in England and Wales from 1850 to 1911, Stevenson concluded that a differential birth-rate is, broadly speaking, a new phenomenon.[87] Other investigators have also shown that the upper classes in many societies of the past, as well as in some oriental societies today, have not contributed a relatively smaller proportion to the number of births.[88] The differential rate is again tending to disappear in the Euro-American culture. In Holland and Germany today the different economic classes are approximately equal in fertility.[89] In Stockholm the professional and upper classes have a higher birth-rate and are reproducing more rapidly than the working classes, according to Dr. Karl Edin.[90]

From the contradictory nature of the various data it is evident that a declining birth-rate does not coincide uniformly with either a high or low, or with a rising or a falling, plane of living. Within the bounds set by the conditions of survival both are culturally determined and there is no uniform or invariable connection between them. "The means of existence," Bastiat said, ". . . do not constitute a fixed quantity; they depend upon the state of manners, of opinion, and of habits."[91] The requisite provision for marriage and a family, according to Rickards,

is regulated, not by a fixed quantity or kind of food, but by usage and opinion [and] is continually enlarged as civilization advances. . . . The English peasant would not increase and multiply upon such means of existence as suffice for the Russian serf or the Hindoo at the present day; neither would he do so if his scale of comforts were suddenly reduced to that of the villeins who preceded him a few centuries ago upon his own soil. . . . Increased self-respect follows upon each step that elevates him in the social scale, and the virtues of prudence, economy, and forethought are its fruits.[92]

The causes of these differences in customs of consumption, another early economist says

are to be found in everything that has affected the past or affects the present, condition of society,—in ancient institutions, in modern improvements, in past and present laws, in battles lost and won, in reformations of religion, in the progress of science, in the manners of the higher classes, in the information of the lower, in everything which man can neither suddenly alter nor create, and which connects his present mode of existence with that of his ancestors and his posterity.[93]

The separable character of the birth-rate and economic questions has been recognized by some writers. Dumont asserted that "if rich nations, like England, have preserved the standard of births at the same level, this is caused by a persistence of family spirit and of tradition."[94] Mill observed:

Where a labouring class who have no property but their daily wages, and no hope of acquiring it, refrain from over-rapid multiplication, the cause, I believe, has always hitherto been, either actual legal restraint, or a custom of some sort, which, without intention on their part, insensibly moulds their conduct, or affords immediate inducements not to marry.[95]

T. A. Coughlan correctly, though with insufficient analysis, has noted that the birth-rate and marriage rate do undoubtedly respond to the ease of securing a living, but that the decline has been so constant as to point "to something outside the economic factors." He thought it to have been due to "a change of moral tone, a matter entirely apart from and independent of prosperity and adversity."[96] If the "moral" is made to comprise general culture, this suggestion is a significant improvement upon most of the theories, explicit or implicit, which burden current literature. It implies that the birth-rate is subject to non-economic factors, and that to this extent it may be less dependent upon individual psychology than upon the group mores in providing behavior ways and motivations for their adoption.

The reaction of the standard of living upon the birth-rate in the Euro-American and other cultures seems logical because it is sanctioned in the given mores, and because the hierarchy of accepted values suggests and encourages the given form of "prudential" behavior. But since the same type of economic situations may be met in other ways, the conclusion must be drawn that (within the limits permitting of survival) there is no inherent and inevitable connection between the birth-rate and economic situations. This is implied in the varied types of responses made to similar economic situations by people of different classes and civilizations and in different periods of history. By custom, individuals of one group resort to the small family system as a means of improving their economic status, while those of another group, which is lacking in such a custom, fail to make the same connection. The supposition that this difference is due to psychological factors implies that the individuals concerned differ in regard to the nature of their mental processes. This is not supported by any demonstrated facts, and furthermore is based on the *pars pro toto* fallacy.

Standardized behavior ways, in the aggregate, are not individual inventions. There are "always cultural influences which cannot be determined or modified at will, superindividual powers which go on working, independent of efforts either to accelerate or to prevent."[97] Therefore the explanation of the behavior relative to the birth-rate in large groups must normally be sought in the institutional facts, rather than in the individual's rationalizations about his own custom-dictated behavior. While there are psychological and biological accompaniments in this, as in all behavior, these do not explain the custom; for they would have functioned equally readily in reference to some other custom. The cultural facts are data which exist in their own right.[98] They do not require naturalistic and psychological postulates as justification and interpretation. Neither do they *sui generis* yield to explanation in physiological or psychological terminology. The "effective desires" of which Rae spoke[99] are complex sociological facts, mediated by culture and by interaction between persons. Consequently, in every civilization births are, according to expectations, contributed by the persons who have acquired the prevailing culture and who have been conditioned by the stimuli arising in society.

These stimuli are themselves highly complex systems of moral, utilitarian, and aesthetic sentiments. They are embodied in literature, commercialized entertainment, folk lore, codes, and innuendoes. In the words of Alfred Marshall, "Society exercises pressure on the individuals by religious, moral, and legal sanctions, sometimes with the object of quickening, and sometimes of retarding, the growth of population."[100] This control is exercised through the esteems bestowed in the group upon marriage, the possession of heirs and of large or small families, and through the integration of these items with other cultural or social factors in the given society.

In many societies marriage is essential to the acquisition of a favorable position in the group.

> The Korean is nobody until he is married. He is a being of no account, a "hobble-dehoy." The wedding-day is the entrance on respectability and manhood and marks a leap upwards on the social ladder. . . . His name takes the equivalent of "Mr." after it; honorifics must be used in addressing him—in short, from being "nobody," he becomes "somebody."[101]

Similarly, to the Hindu, who holds celibacy in disesteem, "marriage is the most important and most engrossing event in his life; it is the subject of endless conversation and of the most prolonged preparations."[102] At some Spartan festivals bachelors were dragged around the altars and beaten by the women, as a sign of disgrace.[103] Epaminondas, when asked what one unmarried and childless could do for his country, replied,"Die for it."[104] Most European countries at some time within the modern centuries have imposed disabilities upon bachelors and bestowed recognition or rewards upon the married.[105] On the other hand, asceticism, such as that practiced by the early Christians and other religionists, indicates the disesteem which was sometimes attached to marriage.[106] Constantine gave special privileges to celibates.[107]

Not only the married state but also the numbers of children are regarded differently in various cultures. In early patriarchal society, according to C. E. Stangeland, the social rank of a man was determined by the number of his children.[108] This was also true of the Persians, according to Herodotus.[109] In some tribes of American Indians, Heriot relates, the chiefs were elected because of their numerous offspring.[110] Children have also been desired to carry on the family name or to serve as agents for attaining or perpetuating family ambitions and honor.[111]

When numbers are esteemed, the pressure of the group is exerted upon the individual for the purpose of encouraging increase. Religious sanctions may be invoked with this intention. "Multiply and replenish the earth" is the command of many religions. Pythagoras declared that men should marry in order to leave new adorers of God.[112] "The greater the number of souls that are added to the numbers of the elect," it has been believed, "so much the richer is nature's hymn of praise."[113] Another doctrine holds that children are sent directly as blessings from God. Luther's statement, "The more children, the more good luck,"[114] and the belief that "for every mouth there are two hands"[115] are further expressions of this attitude.

Again, the rearing of children may be regarded as a patriotic duty, owed to the state by every citizen. In ancient Greece children were considered desirable for strengthening the ties between the individual and the state. The laws of Sparta gave special privileges to citizens having three or more children. The *Bevölkerungspolitik* which prevailed throughout Europe from the time of Colbert till the middle of the eighteenth century was based upon the belief that populousness was necessary for the happiness of the people and especially for the security and greatness of the state.[116] Similar statements were expressed more recently by Roosevelt, Harding, and Mussolini. Roosevelt's assertion is representative: "Even more important than ability to work, even more important than ability to fight at need is it to remember that the chief of blessings for any nation is that it shall leave its seed to inherit the land."[117] "To be a worthy citizen, you must have four children, at least," declared Mr. Roosevelt. "If you have three, you will receive land in the Campania," promised Julius Caesar, in keeping with the traditional policies of state.[118]

On the other hand, small families are encouraged by some cultures. The Thracians are said to have mourned when a child was born and to have rejoiced at its death.[119] Various preliterate groups made regulations prescribing the maximum number of children that might be reared in each family. This number varied considerably. For example, in Radeck, as one writer relates, no woman was allowed to bring up more than three children unless she were the wife of a chief.[120] The Abipones of South America do not rear more than two children per family. But the small family system, as a culture trait, is not restricted to preliterate groups. It is a growing characteristic of some Euro-American areas, where it is re-enforced and aided by other dominant elements of this culture, such as individualism, conspicuous consumption, mass education, high mobility, and the organization of the family on the basis of the simple marriage group.[121] One might readily grant that the prudential factor is also increasing and that this is stimulated by urbanization and child-labor legislation.[122] But a reduction of the family in response to these changes is given in the culture itself, and is not known to be an independent invention by individuals.[123] Indeed these situations might be met in other ways or might evoke responses not designed to decrease the burden of rearing children.

The present-day notions favoring the small family have also been linked with the cult of "the lady," which, with various adaptations, has come down from the days of chivalry. According to this cult, emphasis has been placed upon the wife as a symbol of social status, and this status has been thought to be enhanced by the scarcity of children. Conventional tastes of the dominant class have favored the delicate and fragile type, in contrast to the more robust build of the peasantry and other subordinates. Even the athletic girl, when favored in customs, has been required to preserve these traditional labels of femininity. In this cult the "lady" is esteemed, not for her maternal or her economic and intellectual functions, but for her adventitious character.[124]

The current attitudes are a popularization of those prevailing in the eighteenth century, when Defoe commented that it was considered "below a lady of quality to trouble herselfe in the nursery, as 'tis below the gentleman of quality to trouble himself with a library."[125] These attitudes are further illustrated by the statement of a recent French writer: "A family of five or six children was once an ordinary thing; now it is regarded as a veritable affliction. The unhappy parents are blamed; the fact is regretted and they are laughed at; this is worst of all; this is the reason why the upper classes are failing."[126] A similar viewpoint, divorced from economic considerations or needs, was expressed by Mill, who said: "No advance in public morality can be looked for until numerous families come to be regarded with the same contempt as drunkenness and other corporeal excesses. The moral obligation not to have too many children could, if the case called for it, be changed into a legal obligation."[127] "We were learning . . . ," said William Godwin, "to look askance and with suspicious eye upon a human being, particularly upon a little child."[128]

The preference for the small family which has long existed among the upper classes has gradually spread to wider areas, and to other strata and other culture groups, the progression being retarded by distance and by differences in the general culture and the customs with reference to the family. Already the working classes, it has been observed, have smaller families, on the average, than they did a half-century ago.[129] The French peasants soon adopted the preference noted among the upper classes for small families, thereby keeping their numbers almost stationary. Though resistance against subdividing landholdings be granted to have been an objective,[130] this does not place the given economic datum outside the total culture complex. This conclusion is implied in the fact that other groups meet the same situation in other ways.

Like other cultural facts, the family system migrates or fails to migrate into new areas, depending upon factors comparable to those aiding or hindering other culture diffusion. Dumont noted that when the rural regions begin to copy the customs of the city, the birth-rate records the effect.[131] Newsholme and Stevenson found that both the urban and the rural counties of England reduced their birth-rates between 1881 and 1903, but that the greater reduction took place in the rural areas, thus approximating the birth-rate of the urban centers. There was, they thought, no essential reason why the urban birth-rate should be lower than that of the rural areas. "The fact that in Germany and elsewhere the reduction of the birth rate is chiefly shown in great cities," they say, "is an indication not that urbanization favors a low birth rate, but that the operative causes of a low birth rate have not yet affected the rural population of that country to a great extent."[132] That is, the folk ways regarding the size of the family have not yet been extended to the rural areas.[133]

Similar tendencies for the diffusion of the "small family system" from one culture area to another have been noted. It has been frequently shown that immigrants tend to approach in fertility the index of the native populations where they take up their abode.[134] Sweeney has noted that the less prolific races tend to become more prolific in new countries, as, for example, the French in Canada and the British in Australia.[135] In America, however, where "having a family is not an American 'ideal' . . . this is affecting everyone down to the poorest immigrant. . . ."[136]

As in the case of births, so with reference to deaths, a system of beliefs and practices designed to control the biological event is built up. The physiological and psychological theories of population growth make provision for the elimination by death, chiefly as the result of pressure upon subsistence. But it is evident that customs are also a factor in this regulation of numbers. There is no proof that the majority of the practices of taking life or of trying to prolong it were intended to carry out a population policy. Whether there shall be fœticide or infanticide, paracide, human sacrifice, blood feuds, or war is largely a matter of the mores. Theoretically, the sentiments and ideas involved may include economic considerations, but usually the utilitarian factors are interwoven with various elements in the culture complex.

It is safe to assume that infanticide was often prompted by the desire to preserve the food supply. However, many customs pertaining to infanticide were obviously non-economic in origin, and were connected with other cultural items. Various kinds of abnormality, such as albinism, malformation or unusual dentation, irregularities in delivery or in the number of children at a birth, or other incidents which, according to primitive beliefs, implied spirit intervention, or which might result in misfortune, were considered adequate reasons for depriving children of life.[137] "The Kamachadales used to destroy children who were born in very stormy weather; in Madagascar infants born in March or April or in the last week of a month, or on a Wednesday or Friday were exposed, drowned, or buried alive."[138] The Chinese in one village, according to a traveler's account, destroyed one-half of their female infants.[139]

The widespread custom of abandoning or killing the sick or aged, although probably resting at times upon economic considerations or perchance having other prudential advantages, were often prompted by magical beliefs. Other forms of homicide, such as blood feuds, suicides, human sacrifices, and witch-executions, all of which materially retarded numbers, were not, so far as is known, designed for this purpose.[140] They belong to other complexes. Likewise wars, which are frequently asserted to be the direct results of population pressure, are patently parts of cultural systems and yield to explanations as do other social institutions.[141] The approved patterns may prescribe wars for spreading a given culture,[142] universalizing a religious creed, for gaining spoils, attaining glory, or disciplining the young men. Elimination of numbers by customary practices, as well as the restriction of the birth-rate, therefore, fails to establish a sufficient physiological or psychological premise for the explanation of trends in population growth.

Aside from the customs relating to generation and to removals by homicide, there are other cultural items which affect the growth of population. Fluctuations in methods of food production or conservation and in medical practices also bring about variations in survival rates, other factors remaining constant. The cycles of population growth are thus complex affairs, which comprise unequal rates of change in several phases of the group culture. In recent centuries this growth was accelerated because the methods of food production and preservation increased simultaneously with improvements in medical science and with the persistence of the former birth-rate customs. Since the upward trend of factors reducing the death-rate has continued, the present declining rate of population increase must be ascribed to changes in the customs regarding births. These customs, like other social and humanistic facts generally, are subject to modification by innovation, diffusion, growth, and decline, and like other cultural data can be investigated without postulating naturalistic "laws."

In fine, a *general* population theory must rest upon culture premises. Such a theory will not imply a single or uniform factor as the cause for the varying rates of growth. It will search for distinctive types of causal factors in different social groups, and will assume that varied combinations of material and non-material culture elements may account for observed statistical trends. Such trends measure, but do not disclose nor explain, the processes which are actually involved. These are normally mediated through social factors which are subject to change. Therefore any attempt to predict long-time population cycles will probably go as far astray as did the forecasts of Malthus.

REFERENCES

1. Raymond Pearl, *The Biology of Death* (Philadelphia, 1922), pp. 247–48.
2. Raymond Pearl, "Some Eugenic Aspects of the Problem of Population," *Eugenics in Race and State—Papers of the Second International Congress of Eugenics* (Baltimore, 1923), II, 213.
3. W. F. Willcox, "Population and the World War," *Journal of the American Statistical Association*, XVIII, No. 142 (1923), 710–11.
4. A. B. Wolfe, "Is There a Biological Law of Human Population?" *Quarterly Journal of Economics*, XLI (1926–27), 585.

5. J. Swinburne, *Population and the Social Problem* (New York, 1924), p. 58.

6. Quoted by Frédéric Bastiat, *Harmonies of Political Economy* (Edinburgh, 1880), p. 402.

7. William Roscher, *Principles of Economics* (New York, 1878), II, 276–77.

8. C. E. Woodruff, *Expansion of Races* (New York, 1909), p. 21.

9. Michael T. Sadler, *The Law of Population* (London, 1830).

10. A summary of Verhulst's three memoirs (1838, 1845, 1847) on this subject is given by G. U. Yule, "The Growth of Population and the Factors Which Control It," *Journal of the Royal Statistical Society*, LXXXVIII (1925), 4.

11. George K. Rickards, *Population and Capital* (London, 1854), Preface, p. xii.

12. Samuel J. Holmes, *Trend of the Race* (New York, 1921), p. 122.

13. Charles E. Woodruff, *op. cit.*

14. William G. Sumner and A. G. Keller, *The Science of Society* (New Haven, 1927), I, 72.

15. R. Mukerjee, *Regional Sociology* (New York, 1926), pp. 109–10.

16. A. M. Carr-Saunders, *The Population Problem* (Oxford, 1922), pp. 285–86; F. S. Nitti, *Population and the Social System* (London, 1894), pp. 92–109; A. Niceforo, "Development of the Population in Italy," *Proceedings of the World Population Conference, 1927* (London, 1927), pp. 65–70; J. Bourdon, "Is the Increase in the Population a Real Danger for the Food Supply of the World?" *ibid.*, p. 111; George K. Rickards, *op. cit.*, pp. 62–67, 118–25; Sir William Beveridge, "Mr. Keynes' Evidence for Overpopulation," *Economica*, IV (1924), 17 ff.; James Caird, "General View of British Agriculture," *Journal of the Royal Agricultural Society of London*, XIV, Part II, 277–332; Andrew Carnegie, *The Gospel of Wealth* (New York, 1901), pp. 48–52; Helen Bosanquet, *The Standard of Life* (London, 1900), pp. 340–71.

17. R. R. Kuczynski, *The Balance of Births and Deaths* (New York, 1928), p. 140; British Commission of Inquiry into the Declining Birth Rate, *The Declining Birth Rate* (New York, 1920), pp. 1–37; W. S. Thompson, "Population," *American Journal of Sociology*, XXXIV (July, 1928), 3–15, and XXXIV (May, 1929), 959–75; Arthur Newsholme and T. H. C. Stevenson, "The Decline of Human Fertility in the United Kingdom and Other Countries as Shown by the Corrected Birth Rate," *Journal of the Royal Statistical Society*, LXIX (1906), 34–87; W. S. Thompson, "Population Facts for the United States and Their Interpretation," *Journal of the American Statistical Association*, XVIII (March, 1923), 575–87; William Rossiter, "An Adventure of Population Growth," *ibid.*, 561–74; P. K. Whelpton, "Population in the United States (1925–75)," *American Journal of Sociology*, XXXIV (September, 1928), 253–70; E. Sydenstricker, "Population Statistics of Foreign Countries," *Journal of the American Statistical Association*, XX (March, 1925), 80–89; L. I. Dublin and Alfred J. Lotka, "On the True Rate of Natural Increase," *Journal of the American Statistical Association*, XX (September, 1925), 305–39; G. U. Yule, *The Fall of the Birth Rate* (Cambridge, 1920); Edward L. Thorndike, "The Decrease in the Size of American Families," *Popular Science Monthly*, LXII (1903), 64–70; Ray E. Baber and E. A. Ross, *Changes in the Size of American Families in One Generation* (Madison, 1924).

18. Cf. Stewart Johnson, "The Relation between Large Families, Poverty, Irregularity of Earnings and Crowding," *Journal of the Royal Statistical Society*, LXXV (1912), 539–50; T. H. C. Stevenson, "The Fertility of Various Social Classes in England and Wales, from the Middle of the Nineteenth Century to 1911," *ibid.*, LXXXIII (1920), 401–32; *Report of the British Commission of Inquiry on the Declining Birth Rate* (1920), pp. 8–12; E. M. Elderton, "Report on the English Birth Rate," *Eugenic Laboratory Memoirs* (London, 1914), Nos. 19, 20, Part I; W. F. Willcox, "Differential Fecundity," *Journal of Heredity*, V (1914), 141–48; Lucien March, "The Fertility of Marriage According to Profession and Social Position," *Problems in Eugenics—Papers of the First International Eugenics Congress* (London, 1912–13), I, 20–22.

19. "By a singular anomaly, the rapidity of increase is in the inverse ratio of the means which are afforded of maintaining a family in comfort and independence. It is greatest when these means are the least and least where they are the greatest."—Archibald Alison, *The Principles of Population* (Edinburgh, 1840), I, 112. See also Thomas Doubleday, *The True Law of Population* (London, 1841), *passim*.

20. David Heron, "On The Relation of Fertility in Man to Social Status," *Drapers Company Research Memoirs*, No. 1 (London, 1906).

21. F. S. Nitti, *Population and the Social System* (1894), pp. 156–58; "Agricultural Contacts in South Italy," *Economic Review*, III (July, 1893), 376–77.

22. J. Bertillon, *La Dépopulation de la France; ses consequences ses causes, mesures à prendre pour la combattre* (Paris, 1911).

23. *Report of the British Commission of Inquiry on the Declining Birth Rate* (1920), p. 31.

24. James C. Dunlop, "The Fertility of Marriage in Scotland: A Census Study," *Journal Royal Statistical Society*, LXXVII (1914), 260–88, 313–16; LXXVIII (1915), 35–40.

25. W. S. Thompson, "The Size of Families from Which College Students Come," *Journal of the American Statistical Association*, XX (1925), 481–95; Hornell Hart, *Differential Fecundity in Iowa* (Iowa City, 1922), p. 39; "Occupational Differential Fecundity," *Scientific Monthly*, XIX (1924), 527–32; "Familial Differential Fecundity," *Journal of the American Statistical Association*, XX (March, 1925), 25–30; P. K. Whelpton, "Differentials in True Natural Increase," *ibid.*, XXIV (September, 1929), 233–49; A. M. Carr-Saunders, "Differential Fertility," *Proceedings of the World Population Conference* (London, 1927), pp. 130–43; Lucien March, "Differential Increase in the Population in France and in the World," *ibid.*, pp. 143–49; Corrado Gini, *ibid.*, pp. 157–69; A. Grotjahn, "Differential Birth Rate in Germany," *ibid.*, pp. 149–57; H. W. Methorst, "Results of Differential Birth Rate in the Netherlands," *ibid.*, pp. 169–205; Karl Pearson, "On the Correlation of Fertility with Social Value," *Francis Galton Eugenics Laboratory Memoirs*, XVIII (London, 1910), 72.

26. J. M. Gillette, "Community Concepts," *Journal of Social Forces*, September, 1926, p. 677.

27. *Report of the British Commission of Inquiry on the Declining Birth Rate* (1920), pp. 41–42; Leonard Darwin, "Eugenics in Relation to Economics and Statistics," *Journal of the Royal Statistical Association*, LXXXII (1919), 5.

28. Arthur Newsholme and T. H. C. Stevenson, "Human Fertility as Shown by the Corrected Birth Rate," *ibid.*, LXIX, 63.

29. Raymond Pearl, "The Differential Birth Rate," in *Problems of Overpopulation*, edited by Margaret Sanger (New York, 1926), p. 23.

30. Thomas Doubleday, *op. cit.*, pp. 5, 6.

31. Herbert Spencer, "A Theory of Population Deduced from the General Law of Animal Fertility," *Westminster Review*, LVII (April, 1852), 468–502; *The Principles of Biology* (New York, 1875), II, 446–508.

32. F. S. Nitti, *op. cit.*, pp. 75–76.

33. F. Carli, *L'Equilibrio delle nazióni* (Bologna, 1920), pp. 177 ff., quoted by P. Sorokin, *Contemporary Sociological Theories* (New York, 1928), p. 551, footnote 69.

34. Quoted by Nathan Allen, *Population: Its Law of Increase* (Lowell, Mass., 1870), p. 23.

35. A. K. Chalmers, "Testimony before the British Commission of Inquiry on the Declining Birth Rate," in *Report* (1920), pp. 24–25, 336–39.

36. C. Gini, "Considerations on the Optimum Density of a Population," *Proceedings of the World Population Conference* (London, 1927), pp. 118–28; "Decline in the Birth Rate and the Fecundability of Women," *Eugenics Review*, XVII (1925–26), 73–77; 258–74.

37. Charles E. Pell, *The Law of Births and Deaths* (London, 1921), p. 190.

38. J. L. Brownell, "The Significance of a Decreasing Birth Rate," *Annals of the American Academy of Political and Social Science*, V (1894–95), 65.

39. See the following statements by John Brownlee: "Testimony before the British Commission of Inquiry on the Declining Birth Rate," in *Report* (1920), pp. 149 ff.; discussion on T. H. C. Stevenson's paper, "The Laws Governing Population," before the Royal Statistical Society, December 16, 1924, *Journal of the Royal Statistical Society*, LXXXVIII (1925), 82, 83; "Germinal Vitality," *Proceedings of the Royal Philosophical Society*, Glasgow, April 29, 1908.

40. Agnes Bluhm, "Zur Frage nach der generativen Tüchtigkeit der deutschen Frauen und der rassenhygienischen Bedeutung der ärztlichen Geburtshilfe," *Archiv für Rassen- und Gesellschafts-Biologie*, IX (July–August, 1912), 454–74.

41. M. Jules Simon, "L'Ouvrier de huit ans," reviewed in *Journal of the Royal Statistical Society*, XXX (1867), Part II, 343–45.

42. Cyrus M. Edson, "American Life and Physical Deterioration," *North American Review*, CLVII (1893), 440–51; John S. Billings, "The Diminishing Birth Rate in the United States," *Forum*, XV (June, 1893), 467–77.

43. Sören Hansen, "Über die Minderwertigkeit der erstgeborenen Kinder," *Archiv für Rassen- und Gesellschafts-Biologie*, X (Copenhagen, 1913), 701–22.

44. Reginald Dudfield, "Some Unconsidered Facts Affecting the Birth Rate," *Journal of the Royal Statistical Society*, LXXI, 15.

45. A. M. Carr-Saunders, *op. cit.*, pp. 100–110.

46. C. E. Pell, *op. cit.*, p. 19.

47. L. Brentano, "The Doctrine of Malthus," *Economic Journal*, XX (September, 1910), 371–93.

48. S. J. Holmes, *The Trend of the Race* (New York, 1921), p. 148.

49. Arthur Newsholme, *The Elements of Vital Statistics* (New York, 1923), p. 67.
Changes in the marriage rate, Thompson believes, are but temporary and local.— W. S. Thompson, *Population: A Study in Malthusianism* (New York, 1915), p. 96.

50. Department of the Census, *Marriage and Divorce, 1927* (Washington: U.S. Government Printing Office, 1929), p. 5.
A recent study shows an increase of the marriage rate for the younger age groups.— R. S. Lynd and Helen M. Lynd, *Middletown* (New York, 1929), pp. 110–111.

51. S. J. Holmes, *op. cit.*, p. 149.

52. United States Department of Commerce, Bureau of the Census, Fourteenth Census, Vol. II, *Population* (1920), p. 387; William B. Bailey, "Some Recent Changes in the Composition of the Population of the United States," *Journal of the American Statistical Association*, XIII (1912–13), 390–91; E. R. Groves and William F. Ogburn, *American Marriage and Family Relationships* (New York, 1928), pp. 151–293.

53. According to Dunlop, the calculated influence of one year of marriage is to raise the average by 0.29 of a child; in other words, by three children in ten years.—J. C. Dunlop, *op. cit.*; cf. C. E. Pell, *op. cit.*, p. 21.

54. D. Heron, "On the Relation of Fertility to Social Status," *Draper's Company Research Memoirs*, No. 1 (1906), pp. 18–20.

55. Marcus Rubin, "Population and the Birth Rate," *Journal of the Royal Statistical Society*, LXIII (1900), 600–609.

56. *Report of the British Commission of Inquiry on the Declining Birth Rate* (1920), p. 37; cf. George C. Whipple, *Vital Statistics* (New York, 1923), 2d ed., pp. 249, 250; Arthur Newsholme, *op. cit.*, pp. 68–70.

57. W. S. Thompson, *op. cit.*, p. 14.

58. J. E. Wappaues, *Allgemeine Bevölkerungsstatistik* (Leipzig, 1859–61), I, 173.

59. Samuel J. Holmes, *op. cit.*, p. 112.

60. E. M. East, "The Agricultural Limits of Our Population," *Scientific Monthly*, XII, 551.

61. Julius Wolf, "Die letzten Ursachen des Geburtenrückgangs unserer Tage," *Archiv für Sozialwissenschaft und Sozialpolitik*, XXXVII (1913), 919–29; *Der Geburtenrückgang und die Rationalisierung des Sexuallebens in unserer Zeit* (Jena, 1912); cf. Lucien March, *op. cit.*, p. 255.

62. Sidney Webb, "Physical Degeneracy or Race Suicide," *Popular Science Monthly*, LXIX (December, 1906), 512–29; *The Decline in the Birth Rate* (London, 1907), *Fabian Tract Number 131*.

63. John Barton, *An Inquiry into the Causes of the Progressive Depreciation of Agricultural Labor in Modern Times* (London, 1820).

64. Arsène Dumont, *Dépopulation et civilisation: Etude démographique* (Paris, 1890).

65. *Report of the British Commission on the Declining Birth Rate* (1920), p. 41.

66. P. Leroy-Beaulieu, "The Influence of Civilization upon the Movement of Population," *Journal of the Royal Statistical Society*, LIV (1891), 378.

67. G. U. Yule, "On the Changes in the Marriage and Birth Rates in England and Wales during the Past Half Century," *Journal of the Royal Statistical Society*, LXIX (1906), 88–132.

68. F. S. Nitti, *op. cit.*, p. 95.

69. H. Denis, *Recherches sur la matrimonialité en Belgique* (1883), I, *passim*.

70. W. Ogle, "On Marriage Rates and Marriage Ages," *Journal of the Royal Statistical Society*, LIII (June, 1890), 253–80.

71. Dorothy S. Thomas, "Changes in Marriage Seasons," *Economica*, IV (1924), 97–106.

72. W. F. Ogburn and D. S. Thomas, "The Influence of the Business Cycle on Cer-

tain Social Conditions," *Journal of the American Statistical Association,* XVIII (September, 1922), 324–40.

73. R. H. Hooker, "On the Correlation of the Marriage Rate with Foreign Trade," *Journal of the Royal Statistical Society,* LXIV (1901), 485–92.

74. George R. Davies, "Social Aspects of the Business Cycle," *Quarterly Journal of the University of North Dakota,* Vol. XII, No. 2 (January, 1922).

75. F. S. Giddings, *Democracy and Empire* (New York, 1900), p. 173.

76. A. M. Carr-Saunders, *op. cit.;* Edward Cannan, "The Malthusian Anti-socialist Argument," *Economic Review,* II (1892), 71–87; *Wealth* (London, 1924), pp. 52–71.

77. William G. Sumner and A. G. Keller, *op. cit.,* I, 72.

78. Sir William Beveridge, "The Fall of Fertility among European Races," *Economica,* V (1925), 10–27.

79. For a brief summary of these studies see P. Sorokin, *Contemporary Sociological Theories* (New York, 1928), p. 553.

80. W. H. R. Rivers, *Essays on the Depopulation of Melanesia* (Cambridge, 1922), p. 104.

81. F. S. Nitti, *op. cit.,* p. 97.

82. H. Ellis, *Problems of Race-Regeneration* (New York, 1911), pp. 10–11; cf. M. O. Buer, *Health, Wealth and Population in the Early Days of the Industrial Revolution* (London, 1926), p. 25.

Concerning increase of slaves, as compared with free negroes in the United States, see George Tucker, *Progress of the United States in Population and Wealth in Fifty Years* (New York, 1843), p. 118.

83. G. M. Mulhall, *Dictionary of Statistics* (London, 1892); *History of Prices since the Year 1850* (London, 1895); W. S. Thompson, "Standards of Living as They Affect the Growth of Competing Population Groups," *Scientific Monthly,* XVII (July, 1917), 57–65.

84. G. C. Allen, "The Population Problem in Japan," *Economica,* XVII (1926), 180–82; *Modern Japan* (New York, 1928), pp. 180, 191, 197, 198.

85. J. R. Seeley, *Lectures and Essays* (London, 1870), pp. 51–52; C. E. Stangeland, *Pre-Malthusian Doctrines of Population* (New York, 1904), pp. 29, 33; W. C. D. Whetham and C. D. Whetham, *The Family and the Nation* (New York, 1911), p. 149; Nathan Allen, *Lessons on Population Suggested by Grecian and Roman History* (Boston, 1871).

86. A. M. Carr-Saunders, *op. cit.,* p. 457.

87. This difference was found to be small for marriages contracted before 1861, and its increase was at the maximum for those marriages contracted from 1891 to 1896.— T. H. C. Stevenson, "The Fertility of Various Social Classes in England and Wales from the Middle of the Nineteenth Century to 1911," *Journal of the Royal Statistical Society,* LXXXIII (1920), 401–32.

88. P. Sorokin, *op. cit.,* p. 550.

89. A. Grotjahn, "Differential Birth Rate in Germany," *Proceedings of the World Population Conference, 1927* (London, 1927), pp. 153–54; A. M. Carr-Saunders, Discussion before World Population Conference, in *Proceedings* (1927), p. 203.

90. Karl Arvid Edin, "Fertility in Marriage and Infant Mortality in the Different Social Classes in Stockholm from 1919 to 1922," *Proceedings of the World Population Conference, 1927* (London, 1927), pp. 205–7.

91. Frédéric Bastiat, *Harmonies of Political Economy* (Edinburgh, 2d ed.), p. 422.

92. George M. Rickards, *op. cit.,* pp. 44–48.

93. T. Perronet Thomson, *True Theory of Rent* (London, 1830), p. 16.

94. Quoted by F. S. Nitti, *op. cit.,* p. 77.

95. J. S. Mill, *Principles of Political Economy* (New York, 1909), p. 338.

96. T. A. Coughlan, discussion of Arthur Newsholme and T. H. C. Stevenson's paper, "Human Fertility as Shown by the Corrected Birth Rate," *Journal of the Royal Statistical Society,* LXIX (1906), 135.

97. H. W. Methorst, "Results of Differential Birth Rate in the Netherlands," *Proceedings of the World Population Conference* (London, 1927), p. 177.

98. Cf. Charles H. Judd, *Psychology of Social Institutions* (New York, 1926); A. L. Kroeber, "The Possibility of a Social Psychology," *American Journal of Sociology,* XXIII (1917), 635–50; "The Superorganic," *American Anthropologist,* N.S., XIX (1917), 163–

213; W. D. Wallis, "The Independence of Social Psychology," *Journal of Abnormal and Social Psychology*, XX (1925-26), 147–50; Robert H. Lowie, "Psychology and Sociology," *American Journal of Sociology*, XXI (1915–16), 216–29; *Culture and Ethnology* (New York, 1917).

99. John Rae, *The Sociological Theory of Capital* (New York, 1925), pp. 354 ff.; "Letters of Rae (1796–1872) to Mill on the Malthusian Doctrine of Population," edited by C. W. Mixter, *Economic Journal*, XII (1902), 112–20.

100. Alfred Marshall, *Principles of Economics* (New York, 1905), p. 173.

101. W. G. Sumner and A. G. Keller, *op. cit.*, III, 1534.

102. O. Chrisman, *The Historical Child* (New York, 1920), p. 87.

103. George Ensor, *An Inquiry Concerning the Population of Nations* (London, 1818), p. 3.

104. *Ibid.*, p. 9.

105. C. E. Stangeland, *op. cit.*, pp. 122–37; George Ensor, *op. cit.*, pp. 9, 12–15.

106. Monier Williams, *Buddhism and Its Connection with Brahmanism and Hinduism* (New York, 1889), p. 152; Henry C. Lea, *Celibacy* (Boston, 1884).

107. Harold Wright, *Population* (New York, 1923), p. 17.

108. *Op. cit.*, p. 40.

109. George Ensor, *op. cit.*, p. 5.

110. George Heriot, *Travels through the Canadas* (London, 1807), p. 551.

111. "In the days when a man owed his existence in the first instance to himself, and only in a very secondary manner to the State, it was very important, not only that his sons should be able to speak with the enemy in the gate, but that they should be resolute to leave no wrong unavenged."—Karl Pearson, *National Life and Character* (London, 1900), p. 245.

112. George Ensor, *op. cit.*, p. 8.

113. Henry Pratt Fairchild, "Optimum Population," in *Problems of Overpopulation*, edited by Margaret Sanger (New York, 1926), pp. 31–32.

114. Martin Luther, *Tischreden* (Weimar, 1914), III, 458, No. 3613.

115. Henry George, *Progress and Poverty* (New York, 1879), p. 126; Piercy Ravenstone, *A Few Doubts as to the Correctness of Some Opinions Generally Entertained on the Subjects of Population and Political Economy* (London, 1821), pp. 177 ff.

116. C. E. Stangeland, *op. cit.*, pp. 118–37.

117. C. V. Drysdale, *The Small Family System* (New York, 1917), p. 100, quoting Mr. Roosevelt's lecture at the Sorbonne, April, 1910, as given by the *London Daily Chronicle* of April 25, 1910.

118. Elsie Clews Parsons, *Social Rule* (New York, 1916), pp. 36–37.

119. George Ensor, *op. cit.*, p. 10.

120. See Carr-Saunders, *op. cit.*, pp. 197–242 for examples.

121. W. S. Thompson, "Race Suicide in the United States," *American Journal of Physical Anthropology*, III, No. 1 (1920), 97–146; Lucien March, "The War and the Birth Rate in France," *Eugenics, Genetics and the Family—Papers of the Second International Congress of Eugenics*, I (Baltimore, 1923), pp. 243–65; Nathan Allen, *Population* (Lowell, Mass., 1870), pp. 22–24; T. Veblen, *The Theory of the Leisure Class* (New York, 1911), pp. 15, 17, 38, 68, 169.

122. David Heron, *op. cit.*, p. 19.

123. Cf. Arsène Dumont, *Dépopulation et civilisation* (Paris, 1890), pp. 279–92; 321–36.

124. For a discussion of many other ways in which the position and function of women have been organized in different civilizations, see Robert Briffault, *The Mothers* (New York, 1927), 3 vols.

125. Quoted by Mary Burt Messer, *The Family in the Making* (New York, 1928), p. 304.

126. J. Rochard, *Traité d'hygiène sociale*, p. 322, quoted by F. S. Nitti, *op. cit.*, p. 115.

127. J. S. Mill, *op. cit.*, I, 362–63.

128. William Godwin, *Enquiry Concerning Population* (London, 1820), p. 110.

129. H. Ellis, *The Problem of Race Regeneration* (New York, 1911), p. 57.

130. J. S. Mill, *op. cit.*, I, 157; 281 ff.; C. V. Drysdale, *op. cit.*, p. 105.

131. Arsène Dumont, *op. cit.*, p. 339.

132. Arthur Newsholme and T. H. C. Stevenson, "Human Fertility as Shown by the Corrected Birth Rate," *Journal of the Royal Statistical Society,* LXIX (1906), 63.

133. Although the birth-rate of Stockholm, according to Edin's statistics, is but one-half that of the surrounding rural districts, the fertility of the city population is greatest among the couples born in Stockholm.—Karl Avid Edin, *op. cit.,* pp. 206, 207.

134. Joseph A. Hill, "Comparative Fecundity of Women of Native and Foreign Parentage in the United States," *Journal of the American Statistical Association,* XIII (1912–13), 583–604; W. S. Thompson, "Race Suicide in the United States," *American Journal of Physical Anthropology,* III, No. 1 (1920), 97–140; Frederick S. Crum, "The Decadence of the Native American Stock," *Journal of the American Statistical Association,* XIV (1914–15), 215–23; R. P. Kuczynski, "The Fecundity of the Native and Foreign-born Population in Massachusetts," *Quarterly Journal of Economics,* XVI (1901–2), 136; 141–86.

135. J. S. Sweeney, *op. cit.,* p. 71.

136. *Report of the British Commission of Inquiry on the Declining Birth Rate* (1920), p. 426.

137. Dudley Kidd, *Savage Childhood* (London, 1906), pp. 46–47. Some villages in India have been known to be almost entirely lacking in grown-up girls. This, according to Colonel McCullough, was due to the superstition which condemned to death those born in a particular position.—*Selections from the Records of the Government of India, Foreign Department,* No. LXXVIII, cited by T. C. Hodson, "Female Infanticide in India," *Man,* XIV (1916), 92.

138. Edward A. Westermark, *Origin and Development of Moral Ideas* (London, 1912–17), I, 394–95.

139. Cf. John Weyland, *The Principles of Population and Production* (London, 1816), 132–33.

140. It has been estimated that nine million victims, mostly women, lost their lives during the Christian era, as a result of witchcraft delusions.—M. M. Knight *et al., Taboo and Genetics* (New York, 1920), p. 198.

From twenty to fifty thousand persons were thought to have been slain each year as sacrificial offerings by the Aztecs.—O. Chrisman, *Historical Child* (New York, 1920), p. 28.

141. Cf. Archibald Alison, *The Principles of Population* (Edinburgh, 1850), I, 273 ff.

142. Ezra Bowen, "Paleo-Malthusianism," *Scientific Monthly,* XXIX (1929), 538–45.

CULTURAL DIFFERENCES AND CENSUS CONCEPTS*

By Calvert L. Dedrick

One of the questions most frequently asked about the 1950 Census of the Americas is, "Will all the countries use the same population schedule, or questions?" When this is answered with a categorical "No," the next question usually is, "How, then, are you going to get international comparability of the censuses of the twenty-two American nations?"

For many people, including some statisticians, the essential element in attaining comparable results in a statistical inquiry is to ask exactly the same questions in exactly the same way of all the respondents and then tabulate the answers in accordance with a uniform mechanical pattern. Differences between the various sub-groups of the population universe are then measurable with a high degree of accuracy. How often this accepted statistical procedure fails to yield the desired results when used in measuring the relatively homogeneous population of the United States, we do not know. We do know that it is *not* a satisfactory technique when applied to widely divergent culture patterns such as those of the Western Hemisphere.

The Committee on the 1950 Census of the Americas has never concerned itself very much with census *questions*. Its emphasis has been on census *topics*, or items, for which as nearly comparable data as possible are desired for all countries. The Population Commission of the United Nations has also placed its stress on census topics or items rather than questions. Indeed, the close working relations between the Committee (often referred to as COTA) and the Population Commission and staff of UN have resulted, for all practical purposes, in a single international list for population census purposes. The definitions of these topics are in most instances very general, capable of adaptation to various culture patterns, and related to social and economic problems as widespread as mankind—those related to sex, age, marital status, place of birth, citizenship, language, literacy, occupation, etc.

With agreement reached on the most necessary general topics to be covered by population censuses, *i.e.*, a minimum international list, a great step toward international comparability of censuses has been taken. But, this is only a first step, and to rest here with the hope that each country will be able to take a census conforming to these international standards is sheer wishful thinking. Quite naturally we think first of the administrative and physical difficulties; for example, the lack of census offices with trained personnel, the inadequate financial support of statistics, the lack of maps, com-

* Reprinted from *The Milbank Memorial Fund Quarterly*, 27 (July 1949), pp. 283–288, by permission of the author and the Milbank Memorial Fund.

munication and transportation facilities, etc. These are serious indeed in many countries of the Western Hemisphere, but they are problems to which many different available skills and interests can be applied and are being applied in preparation for 1950.

The conversion of an international minimum list of census topics into a practical census schedule, with instructions, procedures, and tables for each country presents problems which have not been solved and on which research is now just beginning. I consider this one of the most important fields for research by demographers and statisticians at the present time. Until we know how to draft census schedule questions and instructions suitable for each cultural group, *i.e.*, meaningful in the language, concepts, values, and experiences of different peoples, we cannot hope to have comparable international population statistics, or even know when they are not comparable.

The cultural pattern of the Western Hemisphere can be divided into two major areas: the two countries north of the Rio Grande which are basically Northwestern European and dominantly English; and the twenty countries south of the Rio Grande which are basically Southwestern European, and dominantly Spanish.

Through centuries of intimate contact the French and English elements of Canada have come to have an essentially common culture, and it probably is not significantly different from that in the United States for census purposes. This does not mean that, in this English-speaking area, there are no areas which should be studied for the application of special census techniques.

Latin America presents a greater number of cultural problems to the statistician, both because of the diversity of cultures within the area, and because of the difficulties of securing exact conceptual equivalents among the official languages—Spanish, Portuguese, French, and English. As to language, Guatemala, with a population of about 3,000,000, has six Indian dialects in addition to the official language, Spanish. Other countries with significant population groups which do not speak the national language, and in many instances differ culturally from the main population of the country are Mexico, El Salvador, Panama, Ecuador, Peru, Bolivia, Paraguay, Brazil, and Venezuela. In each of these countries, and to a lesser extent in some others, it will be necessary to frame the population census instructions in such a way that the agreed-to topics will have the desired meaning to the respondents in their own language.

Recently our Committee prepared a questionnaire on the basic census topics. We used Latin American technicians who are studing in the United States to translate the original English version to Spanish. To do so required the invention of new terminology in Spanish and Portuguese, terminology which, when tested on other Spanish-speaking trainees, was not readily understood. For example, a topic on the international list for data collection by all countries is the number of "households." In neither Spanish nor Portuguese could a term be found which had the exact equivalent of the concept "household." The invented term is "census family" (in Spanish, "familia censal.") Now there are statistics on "families" and "census families" both included in some of the plans. On the other hand the Spanish word "vivienda" is superior in concept for census purposes to our closest equivalent "dwelling unit."

When that which is approved by law or the Church differs materially from the customs of the people there are other types of statistical classification difficulties. For example, what is called "common law" marriage in the United States is very widespread in certain Latin American countries. The statistics of a number of countries, however, do not recognize it at all. Thus thousands of women who, for statistical as well as legal purposes, are "single" are mothers and grandmothers. Under these cultural circumstances the adoption of the United Nations definition of marriage as including all forms of marital unions which are socially acceptable is difficult, if not impossible for the census technicians. Since only a civil ceremony has full legal standing in Mexico, but many people prefer a religious ceremony, their marital classification reports separately (1) civil marriage only, (2) religious marriage only, (3) both civil and religious marriage, (4) living together, not married, (5) widowed, (6) divorced, and (7) single. Some countries hesitate to recognize the "living together, not married" as a standard census category. The effect of this on certain types of fertility analysis is obvious.

Cultural differences in the organization of education and the attitude of the population toward education will materially affect international comparability of census data on this subject. There are wide differences between different Latin American countries and even within some countries as to the number of years and level of schooling in "primary," "secondary," and "college." Nor can these differences be avoided by using the number of years of schooling as a census classification because of the wide variation in what constitutes a school year. The statistics on education from the 1950 Census of the Americas will require very careful handling for international comparability.

Probably no aspect of a census of population is more useful in measuring the economic potential of a people than data on the "economically active population," i.e., the "gainful workers," or the "labor force." Relatively few countries of Latin America have attempted seriously to develop more than simple occupation data in their past censuses. How successful will be the application of modern census concepts and techniques in this field is not known. It seems reasonable to assume that the larger cities of Latin America such as Rio de Janeiro, Buenos Aires, Santiago, Mexico City, Havana, etc., are similar enough to corresponding cities in the United States and Europe to permit the use of the same census procedures. Here either the gainful worker or the labor force approach would find the industrialized economy which they are best designed to measure.

A rural Indian village in the Andes, on the other hand, presents a different problem of economic activity. It would be almost ridiculous for an enumerator to ask an illiterate family which persons were usually gainfully employed, or even which ones worked. Every child almost as soon as he can walk becomes a "worker." His education consists of doing things with his mother, father, sisters, and brothers. He has no "job," or even a concept of one; he is part of the family, and the family works together for their own support. The concepts of being an employer or employee, of having a job, of being employed or unemployed are most applicable to highly industrialized countries. Some of these probably disappear entirely in a primitive, self-sufficient agricultural economy. We are not sure just what approach to such a culture will yield the best data for national and international purposes.

One of the important topics on the international minimum list concerns agricultural population. For many purposes it is desirable to have a measure of the number of persons "dependent on agriculture," however that term may be defined. Again the problem of cultural differences complicates our techniques. In many parts of Latin America there is an almost complete admixture of home industry with agriculture. This occurs not only among the native Indian population but throughout the entire lower-income group of the population except in the larger cities. Cloth weaving, shoe-making, wood carving, carpentry, preparation of food for sale, and many other activities utilize the time of all workers in the family when they are not directly needed for farming. At certain times everyone works in agriculture; in other seasons, scarcely anyone. The practice of diversified home industries and sales or exchanges in the village market place of non-agricultural as well as agricultural goods by the same family makes the classification of such families very difficult.

The above examples of the difficulties of the census taker faced with different cultural situations are but a few of many which must be solved in the 1950 Census of the Americas. Especially when we talk about securing internationally comparable data for countries with widely diverse cultures and levels of industrial development, we are apt to be overoptimistic. Much research in which the statistician joins forces with the sociologist and the anthropologist must be completed before we shall know just how true comparability—as distinguished from apparent or "census label" comparability—can be attained.

Some research of this type is now under way in Latin America. Several countries are planning to take trial censuses, using the topics of international lists and the best definitions now available in their language and adapted to their culture pattern. Technicians from the United States are assisting in these trial censuses. We hope that the regional census training institutes which are planned for the next year will bring technicians from all the countries together to analyze the experience gained from the trial censuses under different conditions. But, only after the 1950 censuses are all taken and analyzed shall we be in a position to say whether census techniques have been able adequately to measure radically different cultural areas.

CULTURE AND HUMAN FERTILITY: CONCLUSIONS*

By Frank Lorimer

The hypotheses developed in this study suggest the operation of five major conditions as tending to induce high fertility.

1. Perpetual groups of a corporate character, with membership wholly or mainly determined by descent, and with established lines of authority usually imply emphasis on inter-group economic and cultural competition within a society, and are frequently associated with a tribal organization oriented toward military power in competition with other societies for the control of natural resources. Such groups tend to motivate and support high fertility.

2. Sacred values and religious sanctions in some cultures, though not in all cultures, motivate the procreation of large families as an ideal, or motivate early marriage as a means for assuring the perpetuation of family lines, or inhibit interference with reproductive processes.

3. Cohesive groups, such as extended families, provide strong support for their members in fulfilling expected roles and they tend to enforce conformity to norms approved by their leaders and generally by their members. They do not necessarily stimulate high fertility, if·dissociated from emphasis on competitive relations or sacred values that require high fertility. But in the context of most agrarian cultures under premodern conditions, they have generally tended to promote high fertility. In other situations their influence might, at least in theory, be directed toward restriction of fertility—though the pattern in Tikopia provides the only non-ambiguous concrete illustration of such an emphasis. However, the highly structured societies of Japan and the Parsi community in India have permitted spontaneous action by individual families in the control of fertility. It may even be that, in spite of the absence of official encouragement or even the presence of official opposition to these trends, the highly disciplined personal character of the members of these societies has been an important factor in the efficacy of their spontaneous responses.

4. The lack of efficient, convenient, or culturally acceptable means of controlling human fertility has tended to prevent effective restriction, especially in societies with a strong cultural preference for early marriages, except in response to very strong motivation.

Motivation for limitation of families in premodern Europe was sufficiently strong to cause widespread postponement of marriage but not sufficiently to

* Reprinted from *Culture and Human Fertility*, by Frank Lorimer and others (Paris: United Nations Educational, Scientific and Cultural Organization, 1954), pp. 247–251, by permission of the author and publisher. (Copyright UNESCO 1954. Columbia University Press, Sales Agent in the United States.)

cause any widespread resort to available antinatal practices. The early phase of the modern movement toward family limitation in European society was due to the rise of more intense motivation for the control of fertility or a shift in cultural attitudes toward available means, or both. But in its later phases this movement has been powerfully influenced by the development of more efficacious and convenient and more culturally acceptable techniques of regulating procreation.

The future prospects of present agrarian societies with respect to the control of fertility may be affected by the wider range of measures now available and the possibilities of new developments in this field.

5. Apathetic acceptance of circumstances—especially in situations where traditional values have been weakened through processes of social disorganization, but which are relatively free from acute social conflict or a prevalence of sterility-inducing diseases—tends to promote a high level of fertility through relaxation of restraints on man's biological propensity for procreation.[1]

Conditions which, it has been suggested, may induce reduction of fertility come under two main categories.

1. Acute social disorganization may release modes of behaviour that are inherently incompatible with any stable patterns of social life, and may be associated with the spread of sterility-inducing diseases. These conditions may lead to declines of fertility that have no necessary limit short of the extinction of the society in which they prevail, or a transition toward more orderly social life and improvements in health.

2. Social and cultural adjustments to actual conditions of living tend to induce widespread restriction of fertility when such restriction is recognized, or assumed, to be favourable to the achievement of accepted goals.

The first conditions in each of the two preceding lists can be considered in the same context. The free play of tribal societies and the maintenance in full force of their traditional forms of authority and of the control and transmission of property is nearly at an end. In most parts of the world such societies where they still exist are subject to outside interference and restrictions; their social structures are either in process of dissolution or are undergoing important modifications.

Societies with traditional cultures may or may not develop the necessary adaptability to meet changed conditions without disruptive disorganization. The factors which determine whether or not this happens are very complex. The subject is one that merits and is receiving major scientific attention; it far exceeds the scope of this limited study. We will note only a few aspects, directly related to our topic.

Any transition to new modes of stable social life—involving stable conditions of economic enterprise or employment, stable patterns of family life, and improved conditions of health—will, quite inevitably, involve rapid increases of population over a very considerable period. Any concern about limitation of families as a means of improving the adjustment of population to resources is so foreign to traditional modes of thinking in most tribal societies that any suggestion along this line is likely to be immediately repudiated. It is likely, in fact, to be interpreted as a device to distract attention from claims for more ample resources against other native populations or colonists. Fortunately, tribal societies by their nature rarely make intensive use of resources, so that there is generally a relatively low ratio of population to natural resources in their situations. A period of rapid growth of population must be expected as a result of such transition—as, for example, a doubling of the native population in Africa south of the Sahara during the next forty to fifty years—except where this is checked by chaotic social conditions or disease. Eventually, as social progress is advanced, the trend toward rapid increase may be checked by a rationalistic restriction of fertility; but we noted that even in the coastal region and university circles of the Gold Coast any such tendency is, as yet, barely incipient.

Conditions that seem to be important in arresting tendencies toward acute social disorganization, or correcting such a tendency already in force, include stable economic enterprises and employment, improved health, and the emergence of new emphasis on the values of marriage and parenthood in the nuclear, monogamous family. The latter trend involves a shift from attitudes toward wives and children as possessions to be 'claimed' and exploited to attitudes of greater respect for wives and children as *persons* to be cherished and enjoyed, and to greater sense of responsibility for the nurture and education of children. This trend will, in part, emerge as a response to new opportunities for the education of children. Such conditions, which appear essential for the promotion of stable social relations, may also be required as an essential basis for an eventual orderly and rational control of fertility.

Sacred values lie outside the scope of the social scientists, except as regards the study of their objective relations, including conditions affecting their development and their role in human affairs. Such values are constantly in process of development, re-interpretation, and new application in any living society. For example, ancient religious dogmas are interpreted in application to industrial relations to which they originally had no explicit reference. Moreover, their implications, as viewed by those who cherish them most deeply, involve issues of precise interpretation and emphasis not fully appreciated by others. Only those who cherish these values sincerely are capable of developing them, in the context of changing conditions, in such ways that religious values can function as vital forces in the culture of any society.

Cohesive groups with firm lines of authority have, in the past, rarely exerted a positive influence in the direction of any restriction of fertility, as noted above. The moderate, but significant, control of fertility in premodern Europe, mainly through postponement of marriage, and the more drastic control of fertility through its restriction within marriage in modern European society have been brought about by the spontaneous responses of nuclear families to their actual conditions of living, in societies with a rather loose structuring of personal relations. Even in modern Japan the trends toward postponement of marriage and toward restriction of fertility within marriage have been spontaneous individual responses rather than socially directed movements—at least prior to the last few years. But this is not an inevitable relation, inherent in the nature of cohesive groups.

It is by no means impossible that socially directed movements, sometimes with government sponsorship, led by intellectual, social, and religious leaders, teachers, physicians, and councils, such as the panchayats in India, may play a far larger role in this sphere of human interests in Asia than has been the case in Europe. It is important to note in this connection that the cultural conditions that have tended to sustain high fertility in most Asiatic societies have not explicitly required unlimited fertility. They have required early marriage, but this seems subject to modification. And, with improved conditions of child health, the deep cultural need for a surviving son can be assured with smaller families than were required in the past.

Any significant trend toward lowering of fertility must, however, in the last analysis be a 'democratic process'—in the sense that it can only be achieved by a widespread popular response in matters of sexual behaviour and family interests to actual conditions of life, as perceived and interpreted by the many individuals who form a nation. It will, therefore, be affected by two sets of background conditions:

First, ways in which objective conditions of living impinge on the affairs of individuals and primary families in towns and villages—opportunities for raising real levels of living through diligence, prevention of the economic exploitation of children, possibilities of improved positions for children through their attendance at schools, opportunities for gainful employment by women, possibilities of improvement in health through greater emphasis on sanitation, nutrition, and improved methods of child care, etc.

Secondly, factors affecting the ability of individuals to understand objective relations, and to draw correct inferences about the relation of behaviour to welfare—through the acquisition of words and concepts useful in analysing these relations, and increased understanding of mechanics, agronomy, contracts, politics, physiology, etc.

Any public policy directed toward lowering fertility, to be effective, must not only provide efficient and acceptable means of controlling fertility, but must also be concerned with the development of 'background conditions' favourable to such control.

In view of the infinite complexity of the factors tending to induce a demographic transition in the context of an economic and social transition, problems of policy and administration influencing these changes can only be adequately resolved by political leaders and scholars who comprehend these problems, both in detail and in broad perspectives. In any case, recognition of the responsibility of the people of any nation and of their accepted leaders for guiding its affairs is a basic principle of international relations. Even from strictly demographic considerations, as suggested in the following paragraph, there is added reason for insistence on strict adherence to this principle.

Cultural inertia, such as that likely to result from the breakdown of social institutions and the disorganization of personal relations, tends to leave elemental impulses toward procreation relatively unrestrained and thus to hamper any rational adjustment of reproductive patterns to objective conditions. In the opinion of the present writer, it is the most powerful obstacle in the modern world to the rational ordering of personal behaviour influencing population trends. This may be a gross exaggeration of the importance of this condition, but there can be no doubt that it is one of the major factors in perpetuating levels of fertility that now hamper real economic advance in many countries. The Charybdis of social disorganization and irresponsible procreation can be avoided in escaping the Scylla of obsolete custom only if the processes of economic, social, and demographic transition are guided by accepted and well-equipped leaders.

This leads to a final conclusion. It is important that there be in every society a core of competent scientists equipped to analyse and interpret social and demographic trends, and to discover the larger implications of actual and possible changes. The degree to which a society is able to determine its own destiny depends in part on the extent to which it participates in advancing the general fund of the world's knowledge about human affairs and on its capacity to interpret accurately the conditions affecting its own life.

REFERENCES

1. The influence of new access to unlimited resources available for exploitation with traditional techniques—as in colonial America—should logically be listed as a sixth major condition. It is omitted from this brief summary in view of its lack of relevance to the modern scene.

THE CHANGING FOCUS OF DIFFERENTIAL FERTILITY RESEARCH: THE SOCIAL MOBILITY HYPOTHESIS *

By Charles F. Westoff

Intensive research in the field of differential fertility according to socio-economic levels began, in the United States, in the late 1920's and early 1930's. Despite the fact that fertility and various types of socio-economic data were available from earlier censuses, it was not until nearly 1930 that data from the 1910 census were first exploited.[1] Since that time a rash of studies has appeared, many of these concentrated in the early '30's, which have employed various approaches to the subject of differential fertility. The development of these studies has proceeded along three different but related lines.

The first of these may be called the descriptive empirical studies. The main purpose of these was to establish the nature of the relationships and to confirm their stability.[2] From these analyses the inverse relation of fertility to social class became the familiar expectation to students of the subject. The purpose of the frequent repetition of these descriptive studies, apart from the application of more refined techniques of measurement, has been to measure time trends in the differentials, the central question being whether class differences in fertility were contracting or becoming greater. From this "second wave" of statistical studies,[3] it became evident that the usual inverse relationship had been superseded by a type of relationship which assumed the form of an oblique "J" curve, with the inverse relationship of marital fertility only continuing up through the business class, the high school graduate group, or the upper-middle income or rental groups, while the topmost groups manifested either similar or higher fertility rates. These exceptions to the inverse association have been interpreted as evidence of a general contraction of class differences in fertility. This interpretation was given substance by the theory of the differential rate of diffusion of birth control information and practice which presumably began in the upper classes and only gradually seeped down to the middle and lower classes. A recently published study by Kiser, using the fertility ratio data of the 1947 and 1949 Current Population Surveys, indicated still further contractions since 1940 which are the result of differential *increases* in fertility as opposed to the earlier contractions due to differential *declines* in fertility.[4]

* Reprinted from *The Milbank Memorial Fund Quarterly,* 31 (January 1953), pp. 24–38, by permission of the author and the Milbank Memorial Fund. Paper presented at the annual meeting of the Population Association of America held in Princeton, April 19–20, 1952.

These descriptive studies have been indispensable in defining the subject but, nevertheless, are only preliminary to the equally important task of ascertaining the causal complexes involved. The use of birth control techniques is *per se* an unimpeachable *immediate* cause of differential fertility and family limitation in general, but is in turn a cultural product. The mere possession of its knowledge is no guarantee of its utilization. The social scientist, therefore, is obligated to go further and to ascertain within which subcultural or class environments and under what social circumstances this knowledge is applied. In other words, what are the differences in subcultural value-systems which encourage or discourage the use of birth control devices and which influence motivations governing the size of the planned family?

Most of the theories which were advanced to explain the relationships discovered in these early studies were largely of the so-called "ex post facto" variety and at best, under the circumstances and in the absence of supporting deductive research, can be considered as only more or less plausible inferences. In other words, although many insightful sociological hypotheses have been stimulated and derived from these descriptive studies, the data were collected and analyzed without substantive, analytical hypotheses in advance.

The second line of interest in differential fertility may be classified as the "evaluative" approach. Eugenicists, demographers, biologists, and sociologists alike contributed many articles to various journals in which differential fertility was usually deplored and feared.[5] Gloomy predictions for the genetic future were forecast. Extrapolating the class differences in fertility, they predicted that in some few hundred years the so-called "best" elements in American society would die out because of under-reproduction. In assessing these qualitative implications, the only redeeming feature seen by some observers was contained in the theory that differential fertility facilitated vertical mobility and thus contributed to the maintenance of an open-class system and democratic values in general.[6] In some instances, at least, this was considered as only slight consolation since the process of vertical mobility itself was believed to lead to a waste of society's "best" biological stock. On the whole, it was a rather pessimistic picture of the future.

The third area of interest in the differential fertility of socio-economic groups—research into its causes—represents the most recent development.[7] The Indianapolis Study, a study of the social and psychological factors affecting fertility and a landmark in this research field, is the first major study to test empirically substantive hypotheses which raise the question "why." The Study Committee in 1939 selected and formulated twenty-three hypotheses involving the relation of many sociological variables to fertility planning and fertility. The completed analyses of seventeen of these have already been published; the remaining ones are in the final stages of preparation. Up to date, one of the major results of the Indianapolis Study has been to highlight the analytical importance of socio-economic status. This importance is manifested, with only few exceptions, in the fact that given relationships between specific variables, for example, general planning, feeling of economic security, feeling of personal adequacy, religious interest, and others, and fertility planning and planned fertility are either considerably weakened or disappear completely when socio-economic status is held constant. For example, Freedman and Whelpton report that:

To a large extent—but not entirely—the relationship between general planning and fertility planning is a function of the socio-economic status of the couple. (8)

Kiser and Whelpton in their report on economic security conclude that:

Among the couples studied, success in fertility planning is directly associated with economic security but this relation virtually disappears when socio-economic status is held constant. (9)

In this particular instance, however, the direct relation of economic security to the *fertility* of planned families does persist to some extent with socio-economic status controlled. Freedman and Whelpton, in another analysis, indicate that:

A slight negative relationship exists between the effective practice of contraception and degree of religious interest as determined in this study. However, this relationship is mainly a function of socio-economic status. It is not maintained with any consistency within categories based on the Index of Socio-Economic Status. (10)

and

A large part, if not all, of the relationship between (religious) denomination and effective planning is a function of the distinctive socio-economic status of the different denominations. (11)

In a recent article in this series relating to feeling of personal adequacy, the authors state:

The data indicate that when socio-economic status is held constant, much of the original association of fertility planning with personal adequacy disappears, although the positive direction of the relationship is, for the most part, still maintained. (12)

and

No systematic relation of fertility to the index of personal adequacy of either the wife or the husband is found when the factor of socio-economic status is held constant. (13)

This is only a partial list. Other factors, such as Traditionalism also experienced a considerable, if not entire, loss of association with fertility planning and/or fertility when socio-economic status was controlled.[14] In most of these side-analyses where socio-economic status was held constant, statistical treatment necessitated retaining only three class levels instead of the original five. In view of the resultant loss of homogeneity in these groups, it is even more surprising that socio-economic status exerted as strong an influence as it did.

The Index of Socio-Economic Status employed throughout this Study represented the summation of scores assigned to couples on the basis of eight factors: average annual earnings of the husband since marriage, shelter rent at the time of interview, net worth, husband's longest occupation since marriage, purchase price of car, education of husband, education of wife, and rating on Chapin's living room scale.[15] In essence, these factors can be reduced to three basic phenomena: financial position, occupation, and education. Ideally, in view of the evident importance of this Index as revealed in the quotations above, it would be very desirable to perform the same type of factor analysis using these three major components as controls rather than the summary index by itself. This might possibly establish some indication of the relative importance of one or the other component in "outweighing" the previously observed strong relationships between economic security, general planning, personal adequacy, etc., and fertility planning and size of family. Although it is of course true that all of these sociological and psychological variables are themselves related to socio-economic status, the relationships are by no means so high as to preclude automatically independent influences on fertility and fertility planning.

The fact that these relationships are considerably reduced when socio-economic status is held constant at least leaves open the definite possibility that social mobility may be the dynamic variable that empirical research has for so long ignored. One hypothesis (the analysis of which has not yet been published) which was formulated in the Indianapolis Study—relating to the difference between actual level of living and standard of living desired—represents a pioneer attempt to explore a part of the subjective aspect of social mobility in its relation to fertility planning and fertility. Unfortunately, the basic interview questions designed to test this hypothesis which asked the couples, for example, the amount of income they would need to live satisfactorily, the kind of car they would like to own, the amount of rent they would have to pay for a house in which they would like to live, and so forth, were of a nature that encouraged, among low-income groups, wide relative differences between actual and desired standards of living and did not distinguish couples who were actively oriented toward closing these gaps from couples to whom these expressed desires were only idealistic aspirations never seriously entertained.

Two other analyses of the Indianapolis Study data, currently in process, are attempting to relate data on occupational, income, and educational mobility to fertility planning and size of family. Unfortunately, only tentative and completely unreliable inferences can be drawn about the aspirational dimension of mobility from these data. Riemer's preliminary findings indicate that upward occupational mobility is associated with greater relative success in fertility planning but her analysis of the fertility of planned families suggests that a higher rate of deliberate childlessness, rather than a lower average number of children, is associated with upward mobility. This latter relationship is by no means, according to Riemer, conclusively demonstrated.

It is impossible, within the limits of this paper, to discuss in any detail the various social and psychological implications of social mobility.[16] Very briefly, however, the ideal-type of the couple either in the actual process of vertical mobility or effectively geared toward its anticipation probably has the following characteristics: a maintained rationality of behavior; intense competitive effort; careerism with its accompanying manipulation of personalities; psychological insecurity of status with its attendant anxieties; and an increasing exhaustion of nervous and physical energies; in short, a pervasive success-orientation and all that is implied by it. In reality, of course, not all of these elements will be found necessarily to be either operating together or of equal intensity.

It would seem very probable that social mobility is present in varying degrees in and between all strata of American society, although sociologists have maintained that mobility and its accompanying personality structure are most characteristic of the middle class. As a matter of fact, one sociologist has defined the middle class as "that class whose members have welded their attitudes and values into a life-long striving toward an improvement of personal socio-economic position within the class-structure."[17] Although this emphasis on the so-called middle class is probably quite justified, it by no means obviates the necessity for studying the mobility patterns in the other classes.

All of these characteristics of social mobility would appear to have definite implications for fertility planning and size of family. Arsene Dumont, for example, recognized this relationship some 60 years ago in his theory of social capillarity which claimed that "just as a column of liquid has to be thin in order to rise under the force of capillarity, so a family must be small in order to rise in the social scale."[18] The theoretical relationship is clear enough; what is suggested here is the need for quantitative research into the extent of the precise empirical relationship of these variables.

On the assumption then, that having children is considered inimical to social and economic ambitions, the following hypothesis emerges: social mobility, both in its subjective and objective dimensions, is directly related to fertility planning and inversely related to the size of the planned family—both relationships persisting within otherwise homogeneous socio-economic groups. Furthermore, it is quite possible that the direct relationships manifested between socio-economic status and feeling of economic security, feeling of personal adequacy, general planning, and the like, would not retain their original intensity if social mobility were introduced as the test factor. In other words, it is just as plausible to hypothesize that these social-psychological variables in addition to fertility planning and planned fertility, are as much dependent upon the presence or absence and type of social mobility as they are on the more static phenomena of a given occupation, financial status, and educational level. At the very least, it would seem necessary to take into account the *process* of achieving a certain status as well as the end result.

The theoretical extension of these assumptions for *differential* fertility would be that social class differences in fertility planning and differential fertility itself are related to the differential frequency of socio-economic ambitions and social mobility within and between class levels—the middle classes exhibiting the clearest manifestation of this type of "atmosphere" and having the lowest fertility.

One of the most difficult methodological obstacles to designing a study to test these hypotheses is the problem of quantifying and measuring social mobility. In its most simple outline, there is a three-point continuum: upward mobility, immobility or stability, and downward mobility. In addition to direction, there is the question of intensity or degree of movement. Many of the existing statistical studies of mobility (they are mostly studies of occupational mobility) have measured movement between occupational categories as defined by the Bureau of Census classifications. This certainly leaves much to be desired since it leaves untouched what probably amounts to the most frequent type of mobility, namely, movement within the same broad occupational class from one position to another.

Advancement from the proprietorship of a newsstand to the presidency of a bank, for example (although undoubtedly not too frequent an occurrence), would not be perceived if the "Managers, Officials, and Proprietors" classification were the smallest breakdown, as it so frequently is in these studies. Countless other illustrations could be offered of many routine occupational movements which are necessarily overlooked in the use of these broad classifications. These census groupings were clearly *not* designed as indices of personal occupational mobility and their use for this purpose, particularly at the level of individual mobility, is quite meaningless. Another pattern of these studies has been to consider mobility in terms of the comparison of father's and son's occupations, which has definite limitations from the point of view of fertility studies. It would also seem that an ideal study of the relation of mobility to family limitation should include the more strictly economic as well as occupational mobility and the changes in position that might connote prestige as well as actual occupational changes within a given career line. Some of these factors might possibly be reconstructed in terms of their influence on motivations governing size of family or could certainly very profitably be included in future studies of couples in their reproductive age periods.

An extremely important dimension of the sociology of vertical mobility is the so-called subjective aspect, that is, the effect upon individual motivation of the anticipation of socio-economic advancement. With respect to factors influencing decisions on size of family this aspect of mobility is probably the most important. This so-called subjective aspect of mobility cannot be deduced in its entirety from *actual* mobility since there is the type that aspires but is not mobile and, conversely, within the general type that is upwardly mobile, the amount and intensity of ambition and effort required is a relative and non-inferable variable. Also, individuals who feel that their existing status is of uncertain tenure and who react in an "economizing" fashion to the fear of loss of status must also be included in this subjective concept of mobility. It is suggested here that aspirations for advancement and increasing success are important factors in the making of decisions regarding the size of family planned as well as the extent and effectiveness of contraceptive practice, while, conversely, the actual degree of subsequent mobility is at least partially due to the conditions resulting from these decisions. In addition to all of these facets of the subject, there is another, this emphasized by Dumont, namely, that small families may be motivated by the desire of parents to provide better opportunities for the advancement of their children rather than by their own mobility ambitions.

There are two recent empirical studies of European populations which have yielded some information about the relationship of social mobility to size of family. One of these studies, by Marcel Bresard and Alain Girard,[19] is based on data collected from a national sample of about 3,000 males in France. The research concentrated primarily on job changes and comparisons of grandfathers', fathers', and sons' occupations and educational levels, in other words, the objective rather than the subjective aspects of mobility. The data collected on size of family were restricted to information about only the actual number of children in the different families that is, no information was obtained on the extent of fertility planning or anything to do with birth control practices. It would not have been feasible in this particular study to obtain such information. Ideally, however, we are more interested in the extent to which social mobility operates in affecting the size of the *planned* family as well as fertility and fertility planning *per se*. Nevertheless, the statistical analysis did reveal that the proportion of small families was highest in instances of upward mobility, lowest in downward mobility, and generally intermediate in stable families. In summarizing this part of the study, Bresard concludes that ". . . it is in the group of small families that we note the largest proportion of persons who have risen socially."[20]

The other major study, by Jerzy Berent[21] based on close to 2,000 marriages taken from a nation-wide sample of 10,000 cases which were collected by the Social Survey in England and Wales in 1949, also analyzed the relationship between fertility and both intergenerational and personal social mobility. Similar to the studies of the French population, Berent's analysis did not include either data on socio-economic ambitions or contraceptive practice. The findings of this study are in general agreement with other studies of the subject. When the family size of persons in the same class of origin is considered, those who have moved "up" have the smallest families, on the average, and those who have moved "down" have the largest families, with static families having an average size intermediate between the two. On the other hand, when persons of the same present social status are compared, the pattern is reversed. Berent resolves this apparent contradiction by the theoretical isolation of two phenomena: "the acquisition of the fertility characteristics of the class into which the sons have moved and the maintenance by them of the family building habits of the class in which they were born."[22] The author's analysis of personal mobility, that is, change in occupational status since marriage (all marriages in this study were of at least twenty years duration) reveals, with some irregularities, the expected pattern of upward mobility associated with low fertility and downward mobility characterized by high fertility.

A recent study[23] by E. Digby Baltzell of the size of families listed in WHO's WHO IN AMERICA and in the SOCIAL REGISTER also suggests, rather than conclusively demonstrates, a confirmation of the mobility hypothesis. His analysis of a relatively homogeneous social class in Philadelphia indicates consistently that those parents who have *achieved* their class position have smaller families, on the average, than those whose class positions were *ascribed*.

The most neglected area of study in this field has been research into the relation of fertility and fertility planning to mobility *aspirations* or socio-economic *ambitions* which, as has been suggested, would appear to be potentially a very rewarding line of investigation. Although the various methodological problems which would be encountered in such a study are very complex, an increasing amount of psychological research on levels of aspiration is being undertaken which demographers may be able to incorporate in future fertility research. Certainly both the theoretical significance of mobility aspirations and the extremely sketchy empirical studies of actual mobility would seem to dictate the desirability of future research oriented in this direction.

In summary, the changing focus of the study of class differences in fertility is from descriptive to causal research. The latter type of research has repeatedly indicated the greater relative importance of socio-economic status over a number of discrete sociological variables in relation to fertility planning and planned fertility. It is proposed here that both aspirations for upward mobility and social mobility itself may be the crucial variables as yet not explored to any extent in empirical research.

REFERENCES

1. Sydenstricker, Edgar and Notestein, Frank W.: Differential Fertility According to Social Class. *Journal of the American Statistical Association* XXV, No. 169, March, 1930, pp. 9–32.
2. Pearl, Raymond: Differential Fertility. *The Quarterly Review of Biology* II, No. 1, March, 1927, pp. 102–118; Sallume, Xarifa and Notestein, Frank W.: Trends in the Size of Families Completed Prior to 1910 in Various Social Classes. *American Journal of Sociology* XXXVIII, No. 3, November, 1932, pp. 398–406; Kiser, Clyde V.: Fertility of Social Classes in Various Types of Communities of the East North Central States in 1900. *Journal of the American Statistical Association* LXVII, No. 180, December, 1932, pp. 371–382; Pearl, Raymond: Some Data on Fertility and Economic Status. *Human Biology* IV, No. 4, December, 1932, pp. 525–553; Kiser, Clyde V.: Trends in the Fertility of Social Classes from 1900–1910. *Human Biology* V, No. 2, May, 1933, pp. 256–273; Notestein, Frank W.: The Differential Rate of Increase Among the Social Classes of the American Population. *Social Forces* XII, No. 1, October, 1933, pp. 17–33. For a systematic listing

of many additional references to this early period, *see* Moore, Eldon (ed.): *A Bibliography of Differential Fertility in English, French, and German.* Edited on behalf of Commission II of the International Union for the Scientific Investigation of Population Problems, Edinburgh, 1933; Finch, F. H. and Nemzek, G. L.: Differential Fertility. *Journal of Social Psychology* VI, 1935, pp. 458–473 (contains an extensive bibliography); Notestein, Frank W.: Class Differences in Fertility. The *Annals* of the American Academy of Political and Social Science, November, 1936, pp. 1–11.

3. Edin, Karl and Hutchinson, Edward P.: *Studies of Differential Fertility in Sweden.* London, P. S. King and Son, Orchard House, Westminster, 1935; Kiser, Clyde V.: Trends in Annual Birth Rates Among Married Women in Selected Areas According to Nativity, Age, and Social Class. The Milbank Memorial Fund *Quarterly* xv, No. 1, January, 1937, pp. 1–27; Notestein, Frank W.: Differential Fertility in the East North Central States. The Milbank Memorial Fund *Quarterly* xvi, No. 2, April, 1938, pp. 186–191; Innes, John W.: *Class Fertility Trends in England and Wales.* Princeton University Press, 1938; Kiser, Clyde V.: *Group Differences in Urban Fertility.* Baltimore, The Williams and Wilkins Company, 1942; U.S. Bureau of the Census: *Differential Fertility 1940 and 1910* (Women by Number of Children Ever Born) Washington, Government Printing Office, 1945.

4. Kiser, Clyde V.: Fertility Trends and Differentials in the United States. *Journal of the American Statistical Association* 47, No. 257, March, 1952, pp. 25–48. See p. 45.

5. For example, *see:* Elderton, E. M.; Barrington, A.; Jones, H. G.; Lamott, D. G.; Laski, Harold J. and Pearson, Karl: On the Correlation of Fertility with Social Value. *Eugenics Laboratory Memoirs* xviii, London, Dulau and Co., Ltd., 1913, pp. 1–72; Tompkins, Herbert W.: The Suicide of the Middle Classes. *National Review*, 92, 1928, pp. 601–606; Hankins, Frank H.: Is the Differential Fertility of the Social Classes Selective? *Social Forces* xii, No. 1, October, 1933, pp. 33–39; Dublin, Louis I.: Discussion of the Differential Fertility of Social Classes. *Social Forces* xii, October, 1933, pp. 43–45; Osborn, Frederick: Characteristics and Differential Fertility of American Population Groups. *Social Forces* xii, October, 1933, pp. 8–16; Lorimer, Frank and Osborn, Frederick: DYNAMICS OF POPULATION. New York, The Macmillan Co., 1934; Woods, Frederick A.: Thoroughbreds Have More Children. *Journal of Heredity* xxvii, No. 11, November, 1936, pp. 415–426; Dorn, Harold F.: Genetic and Social Significance of Differential Fertility: 1. Present Knowledge Concerning the Effects of Differential Fertility. The Milbank Memorial Fund *Quarterly* xxv, No. 4, October, 1947, pp. 359–366.

6. Sorokin, Pitirim A.: *Social Mobility.* New York and London, Harper and Bros., 1927, p. 359.

7. Some of the non-statistical discussions of the causes of differential fertility and the declining birthrate in general are contained in: von Ungern-Sternberg, Roderich: The Causes of the Decline in the Birthrate within the European Sphere of Civilization. *Eugenics Research Association.* Monograph Series No. iv, Cold Spring Harbor, Long Island, New York, August, 1931; Notestein, Frank W. and Kiser, Clyde V.: Factors Affecting Variations in Human Fertility. *Social Forces* xiv, No. 1, October, 1935, pp. 32–41; Cottrell, Leonard S.: Research in Causes of Variations in Fertility: Social Psychological Aspects. *American Sociological Review* ii, No. 5, October, 1937, pp. 678–85; Heberle, Rudolph: Social Factors in Birth Control. *American Sociological Review* vi, No. 6, December 1941, pp. 794–805; Thompson, Warren S.: *Populations Problems.* New York and London. McGraw-Hill Book Co., 1942 (*see* Chap. 13: Factors in the Decline of the Birth Rate, pp. 201–215); Landis, Paul H.: *Population Problems.* New York, American Book Co., 1943 (*see* especially Chap. 8: Factors Producing the Differential Birth Rate, pp. 127–144); For an insightful discussion of the effects of the social philosophies of "individualistic competition," "progress" and "economic insecurity" from the Victorian era to the time of monopolistic capitalism in Great Britain on declining fertility, *see* Chaps. 6–9 in Titmuss, Richard and Kathleen: *Parents Revolt. A Study of the Declining Birth-Rate in Acquisitive Societies.* London, Secker and Warburg, 1947. For a recent summary of this literature in addition to some of the leading empirical studies *cf.* United Nations, Population Commission: Economic and Social Factors Affecting Fertility. Chap. II in *Findings on the Relationships between Population Trends and Economic and Social Factors.* New York, 1951.

8. Freedman, Ronald and Whelpton, P. K.: Social and Psychological Factors Affecting Fertility. xii. The Relationship of General Planning to Fertility Planning and Fertility Rates. The Milbank Memorial Fund *Quarterly* xxix, No. 2 April, 1951, p. 230

(Reprint p. 570). "General planning" as the term is employed in the analysis refers to the planning of personal economic affairs.

9. Kiser, Clyde V. and Whelpton, P. K.: Social and Psychological Factors Affecting Fertility. xi The Interrelation of Fertility, Fertility Planning, and Feeling of Economic Security. The Milbank Memorial Fund *Quarterly* xxix, No. 1, January 1951, p. 112 (Reprint p. 238).

10. Freedman, Ronald and Whelpton, P. K.: Social and Psychological Factors Affecting Fertility. x. Fertility Planning and Fertility Rates by Religious Interest and Denomination. The Milbank Memorial Fund *Quarterly*, xxviii, No. 3, July, 1950, p. 333 (Reprint p. 456).

11. Ibid.

12. Westoff, Charles F. and Kiser, Clyde V.: Social and Psychological Factors Affecting Fertility. xvii. The Interrelationship of Fertility Planning, Fertility and Feeling of Personal Inadequacy. The Milbank Memorial Fund *Quarterly* xxx, No. 3, July, 1952, pp. 270–271. (Reprint pp. 772–773.)

13. Ibid., p. 285. (Reprint p. 787.)

14. Freedman, Ronald and Whelpton, P. K.: Social and Psychological Factors Affecting Fertility. xv. Fertility Planning and Fertility Rates by Adherence to Traditions. The Milbank Memorial Fund *Quarterly* xxx, No. 1, January, 1952, p. 73. (Reprint p. 687.) The slight direct relation of the fertility of planned families to traditionalism does persist, however, within socio-economic status categories.

15. For the details of the method by which this Index was constructed, *see* Kiser, Clyde V. and Whelpton, P. K.: Social and Psychological Factors Affecting Fertility. ix. Fertility Planning and Fertility Rates by Socio-Economic Status. The Milbank Memorial Fund *Quarterly* xxvii, No. 2, April, 1949, p. 244 (Reprint p. 415).

16. For a systematic conceptualization of differences in psychological responses to different rates of mobility and for the development of a number of theoretical models of mobility-types, *cf.* Bensman, Joseph: Communities of Meanings and Differential Mobility in Large Scale Organizations. (Unpublished manuscript.)

17. Green, Arnold W.: The Middle-Class Male Child and Neurosis. *American Sociological Review* xi, No. 1, February, 1946, pp. 34–35 (footnote 9).

18. Dumont, Arsene: *Dépopulation et Civilization*. Paris, 1890. Also *see* Dumont's *Natalité et Démocratie*. Paris, 1898.

19. Bresard, Marcel: Mobilité sociale et dimension da la famille. *Population*, No. 3, July–September, 1950, pp. 533–566; Girard, Alain: Mobilité sociale et dimension de la famille. Deuxieme Partie: Enquête dans les lycees et les facultés. *Population*. No. 1, January–March, 1951, pp. 103–124.

20. Bresard, Marcel: *Op. cit.*, p. 563. ". . . c'est dans le groups des familles restreintes que l'on compte la plus forte proportion de personnes s'etant socialment elevées."

21. Berent, Jerzy: Fertility and Social Mobility. *Population Studies* v, No. 3, March, 1952, pp. 244–260. This study represents the first report of an inquiry undertaken by the Population Investigation Committee and the Nuffield Research Unit of the London School of Economics into various aspects of the relationship between social stratification and fertility.

22. Ibid., p. 248.

23. Baltzell, E. Digby: The Elite and the Upper Class in Metropolitan America: A Study of Stratification in Philadelphia. Ph.D. Dissertation, Columbia University, 1952.

CULTURE CONTACTS AND POPULATION GROWTH*

By Edward Nelson Palmer

Numbers affect profoundly collective human behavior. The old saw, "Two is company and three is a crowd," and the important sociological duality, primary and secondary groups, both imply that intimacy is a function of small numbers; that fragmentary, anonymous social contacts derive from groups of larger size; in short, that social interaction among individuals varies in aggregates of different sizes. Jingoists, politicians, and demographers have commented upon population numbers as they relate to war. The intense specialization in production and the standardization in tools and equipment, two of the characteristic features of modern Western societies, rest on large population concentrations. The homogeneous, *Gemeinschaft* character of preliterate societies has its genesis in small numbers.

E. B. Reuter and C. W. Hart summarized trenchantly the relationship between numbers and social organization:

Numbers and density, in turn, are important in the determination of social life and culture development. Numbers make for protection and safety from marauding groups and give the peace and security necessary to possession and accumulation. Numbers make possible a division of labor with its increased productiveness and a modicum of leisure. All inventions and discovery upon which culture advance depends are the work of superior men who are relatively rare in any society. The larger the population the greater the likelihood of the appearance of extraordinary men, hence the greater the likelihood of invention, discovery, and the ability of control. Density increases the frequency of contacts and the amount of communication. Various facts basic to culture advance come directly from the size and density of population. . . .[1]

It follows that serious research into culture contacts must consider population numbers as they influence and are influenced by the meeting of peoples of diverse cultures. The present paper is addressed to the latter aspect of the problem. Specifically, it will treat the interrelation between culture contacts and population growth and investigate the hypothesis that population growth of surviving subordinated peoples is an inevitable accompaniment of the acculturative process following upon European-native contacts. In other words, the paper purposes to examine the proposition that the so-called native or colonial populations, if they are not destroyed in the course of European cultural expansion, increase ultimately to sizes greater than existed prior to the coming of the Europeans.

The hypothesis can be stated succinctly in two parts: The population size of isolated peoples is in balance with culture and sustenance; and European

*Reprinted from *The American Journal of Sociology*, 53 (January 1948), pp. 258-262, by permission of the author and the University of Chicago Press.

cultural invasion disrupts the dynamic balance of numbers in non-European societies and creates an imbalance which ultimately involves larger numbers.

THE BALANCE OF NUMBERS.—The number of organisms occupying a given habitat at a particular time is fundamentally a function of the available sustenance. This principle grows out of a fact, noted by Malthus, and later by Darwin, that the insurgence of life—the drive to live—is hedged in by a finite food supply. The biotic community is a web of interrelated plant and animal life in a territorial locus, wherein every animal form, having adjusted to the plant community base, is hunter and prey, eater and eaten. In such a natural order, numbers tend to balance with sustenance; insurgent life tends to increase to the limit of the means of subsistence.

Man's place in the biotic community is remarkably variable. The preliterate peoples whose cultures are most rudimentary adjust to the biotic community in almost the same way as do the fauna of the region. They live in a natural sort of economy balanced with the rest of life. In the more complex cultures the people, on the other hand, disturb the balance of nature. They do not adjust to natural life. They adjust the latter to human needs and goals— grow what wheat they want and nurture the cattle they desire. Man's dominance in the biotic community enables him to regulate the entrance and departure of other forms of life into and from the biotic community at his will.

The size of human populations, while ultimately dependent upon available sustenance, is more immediately a function of culture, since culture influences strongly the food supply. Thus, the number of human beings in an area is a consequence of (1) culture and (2) means of subsistence.[2] The aspects of culture involved are of two categories: the state of the arts, that is, the artifacts and techniques used to exploit the natural resources of the area or to import resources to the area; and beliefs supporting customary controls of natural increase—either by birth control or by practices, such as infanticide, which heighten the death rate.

One of the most intriguing theories dealing with the balance of human numbers is the optimum theory of population advanced by A. M. Carr-Saunders, the English populationist.[3] The theory, in part an application of the economic law of diminishing returns, sets forth two propositions:

1. That there is for any given area a size of population which produces maximum economic welfare, i.e., maximum real income per head. Carr-Saunders states: "There will be taking into account, on the one hand the known arts of production and on the other hand the habits and so on of any people at any one time in a given area a certain density of population which will be the most desirable from the point of view of return per head of population. There will, in fact, under any given circumstances always be an optimum number; if the population fails to reach that number or if it exceeds it, the return per head will not be so large as it would be if it attained that number."[4]

2. That isolated preliterate populations tend to approach their optima.

Carr-Saunders asserts that native peoples maintain nearly optimal size through the customary restriction of fertility. The customs operating in this manner include infanticide, abortion, and prolonged abstention from sexual intercourse between married persons. He marshals considerable evidence[5]— some of it admittedly untrustworthy but much of it apparently reliable—to enable him to state: "No matter in what quarter of the world we look wherever there are native races, one or more of these three customs is practiced except where native customs have been destroyed by European influence."[6] In order to explain the prevalence of these customs, Carr-Saunders relies on the social Darwinian doctrine of natural selection. He holds that since optimum size of population is a desideratum in the struggle for survival and since customs which diminish fertility aid in the attainment of this goal, the peoples who practice them are selected for survival. Hence, he comes to the conclusion: "Among existing primitive races, therefore, the checks which are set upon multiplication probably result in an approximation of the density of population to the optimum number."[7]

The validity of the optimum theory is not germane to the present paper except as it indicates that the population sizes of preliterate peoples are relatively small and stable and that these sizes are equilibrated to cultural as well as to physical factors.

THE EFFECTS OF CULTURAL INVASION ON NON-EUROPEAN PEOPLES.—1. *Small Preliterate Societies.* Imbalance in the living patterns of preliterate peoples issues from their contacts with European cultures. The means of subsistence are increased with the introduction of advanced technology. Folkways, mores, traditions, beliefs, and institutions are modified. Old attitudes and values fade out, and new ones emerge. When the coming of the Europeans produces this cultural disintegration, the immediate effect appears to be, generally, a diminution in the numbers of natives.[8] Population decline seems to have occurred, for example, among the American Indians and the South Pacific Islanders.[9]

Cook reports on the most striking illustrations of population reduction among the American Indians in *The Conflict between the California Indian and White Civilization.* In the century following 1770 the California Indian population, exclusive of the Modoc, Paiute, and Colorado River tribes, shrank from 135,000 to 30,000[10]—a decline of more than three-fourths (77.8 per cent). In the South Pacific the Fijian population fell from an estimated 200,000 in 1859 to 120,000 in 1901—a decrease of 40 per cent.[11] The Tasmanians and the Marquesans were entirely destroyed. The importation of European diseases, notably tuberculosis, malaria, syphilis, and pulmonary disorders, previously unknown to the natives, is probably the major cause of the depopulation.[12] Psychological factors, variously described as loss of morale, lassitude, and the lack of zest for living, also contribute to diminishing numbers.

However, if the natives survive, the decline in numbers eventually halts, and population growth sets in when the acculturative process becomes fairly well established. The major factors that operate to produce the increase appear to be (a) a sharp curtailment of positive checks to population growth and

(b) an introduction of more effective techniques for exploiting natural resources. A notable decline in the death rate comes about from the first set of factors, and a significant rise in the number of persons which the area can support stems from the latter. Because of the lowered death rate there is an increase in the number of women in the child-bearing ages and a consequent rise in the birth rate. The net result is a rapid rate of natural increase which, in Malthusian terms, impels the population to press with increasing force on the means of subsistence.

The positive checks which are weakened with the spread and establishment of European cultures include, among others: (a) disease (morbidity declines as a result of scientific medicine); (b) war (colonial rule suppresses intertribal warfare); (c) fertility-limiting customs (infanticide, abortion, and other life-destroying practices are curtailed); (d) hunger (the food supply becomes more dependable by way of augmented technology).

The total Indian population of North, South, and Central America experienced rapidly declining numbers following European conquest and increased later. Julian H. Steward, commenting on this point writes:

The first European contact had devastating effect on the numbers of Indians, bringing a sharp decline everywhere and rapid extinction in some areas. During the first two centuries after the Conquest, the number was at least halved. . . . Once adjustment was achieved many Indians showed a remarkable increase . . . and some multiplied beyond all expectation. The Navajo, for example, increased in a century from 8,000 to more than 50,000. Mexico, Guatemala, Honduras, and the Andean countries have almost certainly more than regained their aboriginal number. In fact, if mestizos are included, they have doubled it.[13]

Steward estimates that there were 13,170,000 American Indians in 1500 as compared with 15,262,000 in 1940.[14] His estimate lends credence to Carr-Saunders' assertion ". . . it seems certain that there are now more American Indians of pure blood in the world than in 1492; therefore, they have more than reversed the heavy losses which they sustained."[15]

The Indians of the United States do not seem to have recovered, as yet, their estimated original numbers of 770,000 although they have demonstrated an erratically upward trend, at least since 1870. The census figures, somewhat unreliable because of differential emphases on the enumeration of Indians from census to census,[16] show that their 1940 population (333,969) is thirteen times larger than that of 1870 (25,731).[17]

The native population of the island of Fiji has undergone a similar shift. The 40 per cent loss in numbers during the latter half of the nineteenth century has already been mentioned. However, the population rose by nearly two-thirds (65.1 per cent) between 1901 and 1936—from 120,124 to 198,379,[18] an increase due, in part, to the transplanted Indian population of the colony.

2. *Large Literate Societies.* The contact of European peoples and cultures with non-European literate societies seems similarly to bring about population growth. In these instances, however, the numbers tend to increase immediately and without prior diminution. According to Carr-Saunders, this

is the history of Japan, India, China (with some exceptions), Ceylon, Java, Egypt, Formosa, Algeria, and the Philippines.[19]

Among these peoples, Western contacts simply accelerated the development of already existing conditions productive of population growth. The culture patterns, especially religious practices, withstood the shock of contact and were not destroyed. Fertility-limiting customs were not widespread among these peoples at the onset of Westernization. On the contrary, the birth rate was relatively high and the unrestricted family system prevailed. The effect of the European influence was to add to natural increase by encouraging a continuance of high levels of reproduction and by reducing the rates of mortality. Increased sustenance, the establishment of order and security, the development of transportation and communication were among the consequences of European contacts which served to induce population growth. As sanitation and scientific medicine are more widely disseminated, the death rate will tend further to diminish and the population will continue to enlarge.

Java and Madura, in the Netherlands Indies, are illustrative of the direction of change in native populations. The initial contact between Europeans and the Netherlands Indies occurred when the Portuguese established a trading center in the Moluccas early in the sixteenth century. The Dutch began their conquest of the area in the first decade of the following century. The earliest available estimate of the native population of Java and Madura is for 1815, but the population curve has risen rapidly and steadily since that time. Java and Madura's estimated fifty million natives in 1943 are eleven times more numerous than they were in 1815. Robson[20] cites the following figures for Java and Madura:

Year	Population
1815 (rough estimate)	4,500,000
1880	19,540,813
1890	23,609,312
1900	28,386,121
1905	29,924,558
1920	34,433,476
1930	40,890,244
1943 (estimate)	50,000,000

Algeria affords another example of an increasing native population following European expansion. Pearl, after noting that "by 1850 the essential work of conquest had been accomplished," cites census figures of the indigenous native population from 1856 to 1921.[21] The Algerian increase is steady, although not so rapid as that of Java. During the sixty-five-year period the aboriginal Algerians more than doubled their numbers.

CONCLUSIONS AND IMPLICATIONS.—The conclusions from this brief analysis of culture contacts and ensuing population change validate the hypothesis that population growth of native peoples is an inevitable resultant of European cultural incursion. The conclusion is, of course, qualified by the assumption that the native peoples are not destroyed by the initial and early contacts. The expansion of Europe carries in its wake a disruption of the balance of numbers in non-European societies. The populations, especially of preliterate peoples, tend to be transformed from relatively stationary, near-optimal numbers to aggregates which increasingly follow the Malthusian law of the increasing pressure of numbers on the food supply. The disequilibrium thus created is apparently neither guided nor restrained by the motives, expectations, and plans of either the cultural invader or the culturally invaded. It seems rather to stem from impersonal forces which weaken population checks and stimulate population growth.

Implicit in these conclusions for those social planners who seek to alleviate starvation and misery is the necessity for bringing into existence a rational means of limiting population growth. This will be required for many non-European peoples until there is more widespread utilization of efficient techniques for enlarging and distributing the world supply of sustenance.

INDIGENOUS NATIVE POPULATION OF ALGERIA[21]

Census	Total Observed Indigenous Native Population
1856	2,307,349
1861	2,723,851
1866	2,652,072
1872	2,125,052
1876	1,462,936
1881	2,842,497
1886	3,287,217
1891	3,577,063
1896	3,781,098
1901	4,098,355
1906	4,477,788
1911	4,740,526
1921	4,924,938

REFERENCES

1. Reuter and Hart, *Introduction to Sociology* (New York: McGraw-Hill Book Co., Inc., 1933), p. 91.

2. A. B. Hollingshead, "Human Ecology," in R. E. Park (ed.), *An Outline of the Principles of Sociology* (New York: Barnes & Noble, Inc., 1939), p. 78.

3. *The Population Problem: A Study in Human Evolution* (Oxford: Clarendon Press, 1922); *Population* (London: Oxford University Press, H. Milford, 1925); *World Population: Past Growth and Present Trends* (London: Oxford University Press, 1936).

4. Carr-Saunders, *The Population Problem: A Study in Human Evolution*, p. 200.

5. *Ibid.*, chaps. IV–IX, esp. Appen. I.

6. *Ibid.*, p. 16.

7. *Ibid.*, p. 36. The optimum theory of population has been vigorously criticized by many population authorities (see, for example, Gunnar Myrdal, *Population: A Problem for Democracy* [Cambridge, Mass.: Harvard University Press, 1940]).

8. Carr-Saunders, *World Population*, pp. 295–96.

9. *Ibid.*, pp. 295–306. The population figures for most non-European peoples are exceedingly inadequate; see, e.g., Robert R. Kuczynski, *Colonial Population* (London: Ox-

ford University Press, 1937), who summarized the situation in this way: "For some countries, such as Ethiopia, Liberia, Iran, and Peru, all population figures are wild guesses, and the same is true, for example, of most Spanish colonies where all data for a reasoned guess are lacking. The same conditions prevail in particular areas of many territories, for example, the 'unpatrolled' regions of New Guinea. . . . The proportion of the colonial population which actually has been enumerated varies greatly for the various parts of the world. In Africa it is only a very small fraction. Moreover, in many colonies where the population has been enumerated the last census was taken in 1921. The most recent figures published there again either are reasoned guesses or estimates."

10. S. F. Cook, *The Conflict between the California Indian and White Civilization* (Berkeley: University of California Press, 1943), Part III.

11. R. W. Robson (ed.), *The Pacific Islands Handbook, 1944* (New York: Macmillan Co., 1945), p. 181.

12. Carr-Saunders, *World Population*, p. 297.

13. J. H. Steward, "The Changing American Indian," in Ralph Linton (ed.), *The Science of Man in the World Crisis* (New York: Columbia University Press, 1945), pp. 291–92.

14. Steward, *op. cit.*, p. 292.

15. Carr-Saunders, *World Population*, p. 300.

16. See *Fifteenth Census of the United States: Population*, II, 27.

17. *Ibid.*, p. 32, and *Sixteenth Census of the United States: Population*, II, 20.

18. Robson, *op. cit.*, p. 181.

19. Carr-Saunders, *World Population*, pp. 260–94.

20. Robson, *op. cit.*

21. Raymond Pearl, *The Biology of Population Growth* (New York: Alfred A. Knopf, 1925), Appen. p. 225, Table 12.

THE THEORY AND CONSEQUENCES OF MOBILITY OF FARM POPULATION*

By Otis Durant Duncan

The purpose of this paper is to discuss the topic of mobility of farm population under the following principal headings: Causes of Mobility, Types of Movements, The Volume of Movements, Recent Westward Movements, and The Consequences of Movements. The discussion applies to the farm population primarily and secondarily to the nonfarm population.

Necessarily, in this case mobility is to be understood as having reference to spatial, territorial, or geographic movements of agricultural people, although throughout the discourse will be the implicit assumption that there are also shifts in the social positions of people which are of at least as great importance as place changes. It should be recognized also that changes occur in the social milieu which sometimes produce effects that are similar in most respects to those which accompany migration. This may be called social mobility or, perhaps more appropriately, adjustment to cultural change. Such changes as this involves are resultants of cultural, political, economic, or other influences, which may force man to alter his mode of living without necessarily changing his habitat or his residence. Suburbanization, industrialization, or any other fundamental transformation made in the use of land and other natural or socio-economic agents in a given locality may be taken as examples of the case in point. This is also an assumed fact for the purposes of this study. While it is proposed to confine the comments about to be made to the subject of territorial mobility, it would be impossible to deduce anything of value from them unless the factors and processes involved in social mobility are kept continually in the forefront.

The data from which the inferences and generalizations to be presented are drawn are entirely documentary in character, and no special investigation has been made as a background for this particular presentation. The task undertaken here is one of synthesizing and organizing materials available from scattered sources into an integrated discussion. For that reason, the representativeness, the reliability, and the validity of the data used have been

* Reprint of Experiment Station Circular No. 88 (May 1940), Oklahoma Agricultural Experiment Station, Stillwater, Oklahoma; reprinted by permission of the author and the Director of the Experiment Station. The main body of this paper was read before the Agricultural Economics and Rural Sociology section of the Association of Southern Agricultural Workers meeting in Birmingham, Alabama, February 7-9, 1940. While the text of the paper has been somewhat enlarged and amplified by the addition of new materials since it was presented in the original form, the main theses developed remain unaltered.

accepted upon faith in the competence and maturity of the agencies and persons who have supplied the statistics used. For the most part these materials have been gathered and organized by responsible official public bodies, and may be regarded as authentic and dependable.

The purpose of the discussion is fourfold: First, to show, on the basis of the most recent data available, the conditions which give impetus to human migration.[1] Second, to show the kinds of migratory movements which take place among the farm population and in other social groups as movements into and out of these groups affect the farm population directly. Third, to call attention to the volume of migration and the frequency of the movements of specific groups of the farm population. Fourth, to attempt to point out some of the consequences which accompany migration.

While the factual materials offered and the interpretations given them are somewhat limited geographically to the South and especially to the Cotton Belt, there is no intention that their uses and applications are to be confined to this region. No doubt the inferences drawn may be, and often are, as pertinent to one agricultural section of the United States as to another.

CAUSES OF MOBILITY.—One of the first questions which confronts the student of mobility is: Why do people move from one place to another? There are many reasons which collectively may be called the search for opportunity. If a farmer moves from one side of the road to the other, it is because he hopes to be able to do something, to have an advantage, to enjoy a privilege, or to experience something which he thinks will be more difficult of realization if he remains where he is than if he seeks a new location. This is, however, an oversimplification of the matter, for social causation is extremely complex and often is remote and indirect. Each move undertaken by a farmer is an effort to make an adjustment to a crisis in the situation he faces. Although the dilemma before a particular farmer may seem trivial or farcical to others, it usually appears grim and even staggering to him who is confronted by it. There are, therefore, numerous causes or even classes of causes for moving. They may be reduced partially to categories somewhat as follows:

I. Economic and Technological Causes.
   1. Changes in production techniques.
   2. Changes in farm organization and practices.
   3. Market and price situations.
   4. Specialization in production.
   5. Relative differences in wage levels.

II. Social Causes.
   1. Institutional development.
   2. Public land and production policies.
   3. Development of transportation and communication.
   4. Growth of population.
   5. Advancement and spread of knowledge.

    6. Class conflict and competition.
    7. Social decay and disorganization.
    8. Changes in family maintenance requirements.

III. Personal Causes.
    1. The insatiability of wants.
    2. Enlargement of intellectual horizons.
    3. Health.
    4. Sense of isolation or nearness.
    5. Attitudes toward neighbors.
    6. Temperamental characteristics.

IV. Natural Causes.
    1. Climate and weather.
    2. Flora and fauna.
    3. Pests and plagues.
    4. Catastrophes, floods, earthquakes, avalanches, etc.
    5. Continual hazards, malaria, hookworm, etc.
    6. Seasonal variations.
    7. Depletion of soil.

V. Miscellaneous Causes.
    1. Labor disturbances.
    2. Real estate promotion.
    3. Discovery or exhaustion of resources.

VI. Combinations of two or more of the above causes.

A limited amount of information on reasons for long distance migration is available. The data apply to Oklahomans who went to California during 1939. (See Table 1.) These figures indicate in a rough way the nature of the causes for leaving Oklahoma. Perhaps they do not mean much as to why the migrants went to California; that is a matter which will have to be left to conjecture. However, there can be little doubt that the factors named were potent influences that would contribute immediately to unrest in Oklahoma.

TABLE 1

REASONS FOR MIGRATION GIVEN BY OKLAHOMA FARM
MIGRANTS TO CALIFORNIA DURING 1939

Reason for Migration	Number	Percent
Total	1873	100.00
Drouth	831	44.37
Lack of work	807	43.09
Health	109	5.82
Replaced by machine	35	1.87
Flood	13	.69
Other reasons	78	4.16

(Source of Data: California Farm Security Administration)

Probably drouth, lack of work, flood, and replacement of men by machines may be only different ways of expressing the same condition to a large extent. However, it is undoubtedly a fact that something had happened which broke the individual loose from his mooring and gave him a strong feeling of insecurity and uncertainty in the community of his origin. In other words, it should be obvious that dislodgement, of which the Oklahoma data are cited as examples, is likely to be a fruitful cause for movement.

The foregoing groups of causes of movement of population are stated in rather general and inclusive terms. They are by no means peculiar to farmers, nor are they exhaustive. In fact, not a small part of farmer mobility is attributable to the mobility patterns of non-farmers. If sixty per cent of the farm tenants of a given state are occupying their farms for the first time this year, it is partly because non-farmers have moved to the farm and farmers have moved to non-farm centers of population. It should be said that no scientific approach to the problem of mobility can single out any one cause and say this is *the* cause of a particular move. What has been attempted here is to break down the general cause given, search for opportunity, into some of its more obvious and more elemental components, realizing at the same time that this does not constitute even a beginning of an inquiry into the problem of causation.

TYPES OF MOVEMENTS.—Are there any regularities or uniformities as to the movements of farmers, or of people relative to farms? Roughly, some are thought to exist. As far as is known, types of farm population movements may be identified as (1) local farm to farm shifts which are confined to a rather small area, perhaps a local neighborhood, for periods of from one to many years, in which the farm occupied changes often but without resulting in a change of church, neighborhood, school, or trade center; (2) short moves which involve changes of school and church but not necessarily of trade center; (3) moves that transgress minor political boundaries and require changes in all socio-economic institutions which are pertinent to locality; (4) interstate, or inter-regional movements; (5) movements from farms to cities or towns and vice versa, as well as non-agricultural movements within the open-country movements, and (6) international movements. All of these types of movements are occurring continually, at least in the United States, and when taken together they comprise an enormous turnover of population, both on farms and elsewhere.

The short distance, local movements, so far as we have data on them, do not seem to obey any law of direction. Sometimes they appear to proceed spirally; and, at other times, observation shows that they occur in a zigzag path. Apparently these types of shifts bespeak a rather strong attachment to locality. It may be acquaintances, relatives, type of farming, climatic conditions, or any of a great many different attractive forces that tend to hold a family near a favorite place. Some of the relatively short distance movements may proceed by stages and ultimately acquire a directional path.

As for the longer distance moves, it is certain that they proceed principally from east toward west and secondarily from south to north except for Florida and California in which cases the southward flow of population is heavier than the northward.[2] However, it should be understood that each movement of population is likely to be accompanied by a counter movement in the opposite direction which exhibits characteristics that are similar to those of the main movement except that it is of smaller volume. Therefore, when we speak of the direction a movement takes, what is referred to is in reality the net movement. Moreover, there are within the track of all these major movements a great many eddies and whirlpools which result in much geographic confusion, if Webb and Brown's analysis is correct.

It is unlikely that these westward and northward movements of population can be perpetual. In the past, the westward flow has meant a ruralization of the population, while that which has been northward has been largely an urbanization process. Undoubtedly, with immigration from the Old World practically a thing of the past, an eastward flow of people will begin, since the large cities can maintain themselves at a stationary level neither by their own natural increase nor by the absorption of foreigners, unless the mechanization of productive processes should be so complete as to reduce labor requirements in the East to unheard of low levels. In fact, there are indications that this eastward movement has been under way for some time already. At the present time the balance of the farm-city population movement is in favor of the city; and, but for a stubbornly high rate of natural increase on the farms, it might soon start losing population rapidly.

As soon as movements become long enough in distance to transcend locality boundaries, they begin to assume regularities and uniformities. That is because such movements tend to exercise selective influences upon the persons who move. For example, when interstate movements occur the migrants usually settle in states adjoining the state of origin in larger proportions than in more remote states and seem to be projected more towards the north and west than in other directions.[3] Movements from farms to cities must proceed largely from the south toward the north and east, since the areas of heaviest density of farm population lie to the west and south and also because the larger cities which are mostly in the north and east attract population from the farms in greater proportions than the smaller cities of the agricultural regions.

Our data on the exodus of American population to foreign countries are too inadequate to justify any conclusions whatever as to the direction which those movements follow. However, the bulk of all foreign peoples coming into this country have entered from the east and have been gradually dispersed toward the rural areas of the west, except for Mexicans and the relatively few orientals that have come to our shores. Such have been the historical movements of population in this country.

If we confine ourselves to the Cotton Belt, it is possible to identify at least four phases of population movements. First, there was a Colonial phase during which there was a primary flow from the Mother Country to the Carolinas, Georgia, and other coastal areas in the 17th and the first half of the 18th centuries. Secondarily, the movement proceeded to Tennessee, Alabama, Mississippi, and North Louisiana in the 18th century. The tertiary movement was toward Arkansas and Texas in the first half and Oklahoma in the second half of the 19th century. A study of these settlements reveals that they have been largely stage movements and that they have occurred roughly in the order given. Each of these areas was first an area of absorption and later of dispersion. As long as there was a new region to the west there was an easy outlet for excess population. The fourth and present phase began more or less gradually at a time when all of these areas reached the saturation point and were forced simultaneously to seek outlets for their overflow populations.

Relief from population pressure in the fourth phase has been sought in the South in several ways. First, population has moved to cities in the North and to Florida and California. Second, cities have been built rapidly within southern regions themselves. It may be observed that the most rapid relative growth of cities in the United States since 1910 has been mostly south of the Mason and Dixon Line and west of a line extending from Duluth and Superior to Galveston. There are some exceptions to this rule, of course, but it holds in the main.[4] Third, a desperate effort has been made to bring industrial capital to the South in the futile hope that it would absorb the surplus labor off the farm. Fourth, in an attempt to increase its capacity for supporting its population, the South has sought ways and means of increasing the productivity of its land, such as soil conservation, flood control, drainage, the application of fertilizer, the substitution of the hen and the dairy cow for the mule and the cotton basket, and, in many parts, new types of farm organization and new techniques of production. Fifth, there has been a tremendous increase in the utilization of human energy in public and social services such as building and maintaining schools, highways, health services, agricultural extension and adult education, and in many other ways. All of these things, directly or indirectly, are bound up in the problem of farm population mobility; they either require that shifts be made in the farm population, or else they follow shifts which are initiated through the operation of other forces. In any event they are outlets through which a large share of the movements of farm people are being channelized and stimulated at the present time.

VOLUME OF MOVEMENTS.—The volume of farm population mobility is difficult to measure or even to estimate accurately because the Census data are not only quite indefinite for such uses but are also collected over long intervals of time and without regard to intercensal movements. However, the Federal Bureau of Agricultural Economics estimates that from 1920 to 1938, inclusive, 31,174,000 persons left the farms of this country for cities, towns, and villages and that 22,957,000 persons arrived on farms from cities, towns, and villages, thus creating a net loss to the farm population of 8,217,000 persons for that period.[5] In spite of this enormous volume of farm population movement, the total number of persons on farms on January 1, 1939, was not significantly lower than in 1910, which was the peak year for all time so far as records show. Nobody knows how great the farm to farm movement during the whole of the past two decades has been. However, observation and scattered data which are available lead one to believe that movements between farms in most sections of the country, and of the Cotton Belt in particular, are surprisingly frequent.

At this point it is necessary to say that farm to farm shifts of population as well as farm to city movements are closely associated with farm tenure status, and probably vary inversely, within limits, according to the age of farmers and their tenure positions. It should be noted parenthetically that tenure status is inseparably linked with the age of farm operators in most areas of the country, except possibly in sections where ghosts of the old plantation are still extant. Whether the alleged "agricultural ladder" is a reality or a figment of someone's imagination, it is inescapable that age is a correlative of socio-economic status and also of mobility of all types. Perhaps this statement may sound somewhat complicated, but the writer is confident it can be demonstrated by existing data which must be omitted here for lack of space.[6]

Another angle on the problem of farm population mobility is the proportion of farm operators who have occupied the farms on which they reside for a specified period of time. One-tenth of the farm owners in the United States had lived on the farms they occupied in 1935 one year or less. (See Table 2.)

TABLE 2

DISTRIBUTION OF FULL OWNERS ACCORDING TO LENGTH OF
RESIDENCE ON FARM OCCUPIED IN 1935

Length of Residence in Years	PERCENT OF FULL OWNER-OPERATORS			
	United States	Cotton Belt	Oklahoma	South Carolina
Total	100.0	100.0	100.0	100.0
Under 1	6.0	7.4	10.0	7.1
1	4.0	3.9	4.7	3.6
2	4.3	4.3	5.1	3.6
3	3.9	3.9	4.2	3.6
4	5.0	5.5	5.5	5.4
5– 9	16.9	17.6	17.4	15.4
10–14	15.0	14.7	13.5	14.6
15 and over	44.9	42.7	39.6	46.7

(Source: U.S. Census of Agriculture, 1935)

In the Cotton Belt, 11.3 per cent of farm owners had been on the farms they occupied in 1935 one year or less. The corresponding figures for Oklahoma and South Carolina were 14.7 per cent and 10.7 per cent, respectively. On the upper extreme, 44.9 per cent of the farm owners of the nation as a whole and 42.7 per cent of those of the Cotton Belt had lived on the farms they occupied in 1935 for 15 years or longer. The corresponding proportions for Oklahoma and South Carolina were 39.6 per cent and 46.7 per cent, respectively.

The situation of tenants is much different from that of owners in respect to stability or mobility. For the United States as a whole, 47.3 per cent of the tenant farmers had occupied the farms on which they were located in 1935 for one year or less, and for the Cotton Belt the proportion was 52.6 per cent.[7] The corresponding proportions for Oklahoma and South Carolina were 54.9 per cent and 46.4 per cent, respectively. On the other hand only 28.6 per cent of the tenants in the entire country and 24.2 per cent of those in the Cotton Belt had occupied the farms they were on in 1935 for five years or longer. In Oklahoma, the corresponding figure was 21.9 per cent. (See Table 3.)

TABLE 3

DISTRIBUTION OF TENANTS ACCORDING TO LENGTH OF
RESIDENCE ON FARM OCCUPIED IN 1935

PERCENT OF TENANT OPERATORS

Length of Residence in Years	United States	Cotton Belt	Oklahoma	South Carolina
Total	100.0	100.0	100.0	100.0
Under 1	34.2	40.2	42.9	35.4
1	13.1	12.4	12.0	11.0
2	9.9	9.3	9.4	9.2
3	7.0	6.6	7.0	6.9
4	7.2	7.3	6.8	8.4
5 and over	28.6	24.2	21.9	29.1

(Source: U.S. Census of Agriculture, 1935)

From the foregoing comparisons, it is possible to arrive at several significant deductions. First, mobility in the South during recent years probably has not been as much greater than that of the country as a whole as might have been expected. However, it should be recalled that the national situation is as it is largely because of the tremendous weight of the South in the nation's total farm population. Second, the mobility pattern of the South is probably not due as much to the prevalent types of agricultural organization as such as to the degree of socio-economic maturation to which the region has attained. Third, there are as great contrasts in mobility within the Cotton Belt itself as there is between this region and the nation as a whole. Fourth, the mobility of farm population, even within the South itself, seems to be somewhat greater in areas where there are alternative uses for manual labor outside agriculture. A particular instance is the case of the oil fields and mines in Oklahoma.[8] The processes of selection and elimination of workers in industries of the types referred to work fiercely and relentlessly, which forces much shifting of population from non-agricultural pursuits to farms.

Fifth, the factor of mechanization, which is now making rapid headway in the South, is forcing many moves to be made which otherwise might not occur. Sixth, the Census definition of a farm undoubtedly creates fictitious mobility of farm population in sections where urbanization and suburbanization of farms are proceeding rapidly. Much of this high mobility is at the outskirts of growing cities where farms are being cut up into "acreages." All of these speculations come to mind as one surveys the data on farm mobility in its quantitative aspects.

One point on which there is definite agreement among students of population, at least in the United States, is that a high degree of mobility is a distinctive trait of the American population, both city and farm.[9] It is also true that the populations of some areas are more mobile than those in others. In Oklahoma, for example, we have an area where mobility has been a prominent characteristic of the people wherever they may be located, in respect to both those who reside in the State and those who were born there. In 1930, almost 52 per cent of the resident native white population of Oklahoma was born in other states, and about 29 per cent of the persons who were born in Oklahoma were living elsewhere. For the country as a whole, 23 per cent of the native white population was residing outside the state of birth. At the same time approximately 12 per cent of the native white population residing in South Carolina lived elsewhere. As we go west into the Mountain and Pacific states, we find the proportions much higher in both cases than in either Oklahoma or South Carolina. In the Cotton Belt proper, Arkansas was found to be the area of the heaviest dispersion and Oklahoma of the heaviest absorption.[10] Sometimes, the more mature a state becomes the greater is the exodus of its population and the smaller is its population intake relatively. However, this can scarcely be regarded as a general rule, urbanization being one of the principal disturbing factors. No doubt, there are other important influences, such as climatic cycles, mechanization of productive processes, specialization in agricultural enterprises, and the degree of exploitation of natural resources, to mention only a few of the more obvious forces which affect mobility.

One of the important questions that may arise at this point is: What kinds of people move most? Unfortunately, the information which may be offered in answering this question is limited and fragmentary. However, if one may use Oklahoma again as an example, it is possible to throw some light upon the problem. The Census of 1930 showed that 41.4 per cent of the American-born urban population of Oklahoma was born in the State, while the corresponding figures were 49.7 per cent for the rural non-farm and 56.5 per cent for the rural farm population. From these simple facts it is readily apparent that interstate migration is a more important phenomenon for the urban than for the farm population, and few people who are informed on population movements would claim for a moment that mobility as a serious problem is peculiar to the farm population.

Again, of the total native population of Oklahoma in 1930, 51 per cent of the males and 49 per cent of the females were born in other states. However, at the same time there were 106 males to 100 females in the entire population of the State, while among those who were born elsewhere there were 112 males to 100 females as compared with 102 males to 100 females for the Oklahoma-born portion of the population. Thus it can be seen that in an area of absorption like Oklahoma has been, mobility tends to be associated significantly with a high proportion of masculinity of the population. Unfortunately, this comparison cannot be carried far enough to show differences for farm and nonfarm populations. However, it is known that agricultural areas attract heavier proportions of males than of females, while cities, for the most part, attract relatively more females than males. This tends to leave on the farms highly distorted sex ratios in the population in which there are more than one and one-half times as many marriageable men as women left on farms in the United States, and almost twice as many in Oklahoma. The effects of these conditions upon important social relationships, such as the family institution, potential population increases, labor supply, economic productivity of the population, and demand for housing and many other consumers' goods, may be surmised readily.

RECENT WESTWARD MOVEMENTS.—The westward movement of population has been referred to at some length in a foregoing section of the paper. Perhaps it may be desirable to amplify what has been said so as to indicate something of its effects. Oklahoma has been sending out population for some time. In 1930, there were 63,608 Oklahoma-born persons living in California and 125,647 residing in Texas. This was approximately half of all the people born in the State who were living elsewhere at that time. Not a great deal is known of the characteristics of those people, and we must turn to specific studies to find out much about them. On June 30, 1935, there were 2,633 families whose origin was Oklahoma who were registered in transient camps of the country, and 916 of these, or 34.8 per cent, were located in California. In return, Oklahoma had received 607 transient families, only 30 of which came from California.[11]

More recently, the Works Progress Administration in cooperation with the Farm Security Administration studied 6,655 migrant households receiving emergency grants in California during 1938.[12] A study of the results of this California movement may prove to be highly enlightening. The migrants composing this group originated chiefly in four states, Oklahoma, Texas, Arkansas, and Missouri. Of the total 6,655 households studied, 2,771, or 41.7 per cent, were from Oklahoma, which state was the chief contributor. Particular attention will be given briefly to the movement to California from Oklahoma.

In the migration that is now proceeding from Oklahoma to California it is possible to gain at least an approximate idea of the volume of mobility among various classes of the population. From the figures in Table 4 it is obvious that the greater part of the emigration from Oklahoma to California was from population groups which had been long established. Other evidence which will be cited later leads to the supposition that a very large proportion of these migrants were young adults, many of whom, doubtless had spent practically their entire lives before emigrating in Oklahoma.

TABLE 4

NUMBER OF YEARS OF RESIDENCE IN OKLAHOMA PRIOR TO MIGRATION TO CALIFORNIA

Years of Residence in Oklahoma	Percent of Migrants
Total	100.0
1– 2	3.7
3– 4	5.7
5– 9	13.3
10–14	13.0
15–19	11.0
20 and over	53.3

(Source of Data: California Farm Security Administration)

On the other hand, the time interval between departure from Oklahoma and arrival in California is of some significance at this point. (See Table 5.) An inspection of the data in Table 5 will reveal that slightly over 75 per cent of the migrants from Oklahoma to California spent less than one year on the road before arriving there and a little more than 25 per cent of them had spent three months or less while enroute. This suggests two things at least. First, these migrants probably worked as they traveled in order to make a living along the way, which if correct would mean that they were in rather straitened circumstances financially and that they might have settled anywhere else if they had been able to find a foothold. Second, it seems that the bulk of them were bona fide migrants and not a mass of vagabonds or habitual wanderers.

TABLE 5

DISTRIBUTION OF OKLAHOMA MIGRANTS TO CALIFORNIA ACCORDING TO TIME ELAPSING BETWEEN DEPARTURE FROM OKLAHOMA AND ARRIVAL IN CALIFORNIA

Months since migrant left Oklahoma	Number of migrants	Percent of migrants
Total	1696	100.00
Less than 1 month	128	7.55
1 to 3 months	304	17.92
4 to 6 months	344	20.28
7 to 11 months	502	29.60
12 to 35 months	357	21.05
36 months and over	61	3.60

(Source of Data: California Farm Security Administration)

The speculations suggested in the preceding paragraph seem to be borne out by further data which have been provided. In Table 6, the agricultural migrants are distributed according to tenure status. These figures show that not only has dislodgement been a factor in migration but also that those who were dislodged were principally from the poorer classes of farmers.

TABLE 6

DISTRIBUTION OF OKLAHOMA MIGRANTS TO CALIFORNIA BY TYPE OF
AGRICULTURAL OCCUPATION OR TENURE STATUS

Type of agricultural occupation	Number of agricultural workers	Percent of agricultural workers
Total	1280	100.00
Owner	35	2.73
Tenant	285	22.27
Sharecropper	186	14.53
Laborer	774	60.47

(Source of Data: California Farm Security Administration)

Obviously, even when unstandardized data are used, the incidence of migration among the farm population falls more heavily upon the classes which are likely to be detached from their homes and communities. This may be verified by taking notice of the inordinately heavy numbers of laborers, sharecroppers, and tenants in contrast with the very small number of farm owners who migrated.

TABLE 7

NUMBER OF MONTHS OF EMPLOYMENT DURING 1937 OF HEADS OF
OKLAHOMA HOUSEHOLDS MIGRATING TO CALIFORNIA

Number of months employed during 1937	Agricultural Workers		Non-Agricultural Workers	
	Number employed	Percent employed	Number employed	Percent employed
Total	1,468	100.0	1,539	100.0
None	114	7.77	38	2.47
Less than 1 month	8	.54	6	.39
1	43	3.93	24	1.56
2	82	5.59	57	3.70
3	127	8.65	105	6.82
4	140	9.54	152	9.88
5	128	8.72	147	9.55
6	279	18.99	333	21.64
7	114	7.77	143	9.29
8	126	8.58	155	10.08
9	76	5.18	91	5.91
10	80	5.45	102	6.63
11	28	1.91	41	2.66
12	123	8.38	145	9.42

(Source of Data: California Farm Security Administration)

A similar interpretation may be drawn from the employment data given in Table 7. Having a job tends to check population movements, except, of course, those types of work in which travel is itself a primary feature of the work. In agricultural and in most industrial labor the work is fairly stationary by its very nature. Farm work exhibits this characteristic to an even greater extent than do many forms of non-agricultural labor, as may be surmised from the data.

From the figures we have here, it may be observed that approximately 64 per cent of the agricultural workers and 56 per cent of the non-agricultural workers had been employed for six months or less when they were interviewed. Also, about 21 per cent of the agricultural and 25 per cent of the non-agricultural workers had been employed for nine months or more when they were registered in California. Among the agricultural workers it seems that about the same proportion, around 8 per cent, had been unemployed altogether as had worked continuously for twelve months prior to registration in California. But only about one-third as large a proportion of non-agricultural as of agricultural workers had been without jobs for the whole year, while a larger proportion of the non-agricultural than of the agricultural workers had been employed for the full year preceding registration for emergency loans at the hands of the Farm Security Administration.

One popular idea to which these California figures seem to deal a severe blow is the prevalent notion that the emigres from Arkansas, Missouri, Oklahoma, and Texas went principally from the "dust bowl" counties. In Oklahoma, according to the sources cited, the bulk of the exodus was from the populous counties of the central parts of the State. Those who went from Kansas were mostly from the border fringes of the State, along the northern, eastern, and southern boundaries, with very few from the western parts. The families which had gone to California from Missouri and Arkansas were largely from the Ozark region, while it was from the black prairies and the central plains that most of the movement from Texas began. Although there are evidences that the droughts of recent years have had some part in the movement of population from the Southwest, it is the opinion of the writer that there are other factors which are of far greater and much more fundamental importance than lack of moisture for a season or two.

These studies blast numerous other popular assumptions about migrant households. In the first place, the distribution of the households according to size was almost identical with that for the general population. The majority of the children in the migrant households were under 10 years of age, only one-fifth being 15 years of age or over. The heads of the migrant families were practically all men, 96 per cent, in their best working years, more than 75 per cent of them being between 20 and 44 years of age and only 7 per cent being 55 years of age or over. The median age of all heads of households was 33.5 years. The most usual household was composed of three persons, two adults and a child under five years of age. The usual occupation prior to movement for the majority of the heads of households was farm labor. Of those who gave their usual occupation as farmer, 67.8 per cent were farm laborers, 17.7 per cent were tenants, 10.8 per cent were sharecroppers, and 3.7 per cent were owners. Of the non-agricultural workers, 33.7 per cent were unskilled manual laborers, 27.8 per cent were semi-skilled laborers, 19.7 per cent were skilled laborers, 10.6 per cent were servants, and all others accounted for 8.2 per cent. These transients were not, as is often supposed, a nomadic class of people. The majority had long been residents of the states of their origin. Almost half of them had spent over 20 years in the states of their prior residence, and only 17 per cent had lived less than five years in the states of their last residence. The median amount of work reported by these family heads for 1937 was six months, although 66 per cent of them had worked six months or longer, and less than 24 per cent had worked nine months or more.[13]

The data suggest again that there are many factors operative to cause emigration. While droughts have doubtlessly played an important part in the matter, they have not been sole causes of population disturbances. Low wages while employed, with resultant inadequate incomes, and unemployment have been potent causes of distress. Mechanization of agricultural production, labor-saving processes in industrial production, restriction of crop production under the AAA, low prices for the staple products grown on farms, low agricultural purchasing power for dollars received, seasonal unemployment in industry, interference in labor conditions both by private and public agencies, and even the fact that charitable and benevolent institutions both public and private have aided and abetted transiency, as well as many other factors, have provided a tremendously impelling motive force upon population movements. That is not to say that these phenomena alone are sufficient to explain population movements. Undoubtedly, there are personal factors, psycho-social traits, temperamental characteristics, and other personal variables, as well as many natural conditions, which are important determinants of mobility. Consequences of Movements.—What are the effects of mobility? Effects, like causes, are of difficult determination. However, there are certain accompaniments of mobility which do not seem to be present in as great a frequency where there is a low incidence of mobility as where it is high. From what was shown above, mobility is selective of certain bio-social traits of the population, particularly with reference to age. This is true also in regard to sex. Young adults move more often than other people. The consensus on this is that the farm to city movement is primarily a phenomenon of adolescence and early adulthood, the age limits of the period of heaviest migration extending from around age 17 up to 25. However, no age group is entirely free from migration. This is because the migrant must be old enough for his services to be economically valuable so that he can provide for himself. Also the mover must be young enough to be easily adaptable to new modes of living. This has led many writers to assert that migration often drains off the more vigorous and virile elements of a population. Unmarried persons are more mobile than those who are married, partly because of the greater expense of moving families than of single individuals. Marriage increases the number of bonds between the individual and his own group and also increases the burden of moving and the economic responsibility of the mover.

Not all movements are equally selective with regard to a given trait. Farm to city movements are disproportionately selective of females. Movements to new agricultural areas are disproportionately selective of males. It is believed, though not definitely known, that the back-to-the-farm movement which was characteristic of the depression period was made up more heavily of men and of families than of unmarried women because urban unemployment was several times as great among men as among women, and because agriculture even at its worst gave refuge to men more often than to women.

From the standpoint of socio-economic status, Zimmerman developed the thesis that the city attracts the extremes of population while the country retains the means. He and his students have suggested that the same thing probably happens with respect to physical traits, social status, and intelligence. If this be true, the net result is that the city does not gain a great advantage nor does the country suffer a severe disadvantage through the rural exodus.[14] E. C. Young claims that the hired man, the farmer's son, the share tenant, the cash tenant, and finally the farm owner leave the farm in the order named.[15] If race may be considered a social as well as a physical characteristic of population, one of the important socio-economic features of rural-urban migration has been the movement of Negroes from the agricultural South to the cities of the North. In this Negro migration, contrary to the usual principle, there has been a disproportionately higher proportion of males than of females. Limited data collected by Galpin indicate that the landward movement of urban population is made up predominantly of persons who have had prior farm experience and who are largely from 30 to 50 years of age.[16] Perhaps there are many other correlatives of rural-urban population movements which are of importance, but so little is known of them that one dare not speculate beyond what has been said here.

In the foregoing data there are evidences of a rather fierce selection. First, the incidence of mobility falls heaviest upon the smaller families. Perhaps this is partly because these families can move more cheaply and more easily than larger families. Second, there appears to be a selection of young and incompleted families. This accounts partly for the rather small size of the families. It also suggests that the more virile elements of the population constitute the largest proportions of the moving classes. Third, from the descriptions given it is apparent that those whose socio-economic positions at home were most precarious and insecure were moving out in the largest proportions. Moreover, the reports indicate that the exodus has been heaviest among those classes which are least able to bear the costs of moving and that the economic conditions which necessitate moving bear down most relentlessly upon the low-wage-earning groups.

In the discussion of farm-city movements of population, it has been pointed out either implicitly or explicitly that the net results are: (1) a masculinization of the country and an effeminization of the city; (2) a relative deficit of children and old people in the cities and a deficit of young adults and persons "in prime of life" in the country; (3) a strain upon the farm family induced by a distorted proportion of unmarried men stranded on the farms; (4) a relatively high proportion of prospective producers in the city population and an unduly high proportion of potential consumers in the farm population. Then it may be mentioned further, without offering supporting proofs, although such proofs are readily available, that there are other social results which have not been implied up to now. They are presented as self-evident facts: (1) that there is a continual drain of agricultural wealth to the city in the form of the costs of education and rearing of the migrants who leave the farms at the thresholds of their most productive years; (2) that there has been a cultural depletion of the rural communities in the form of loss of local leadership; (3) that per capita economic productivity of the cities has been increased at the expense of the farms because of the disturbing effects of migration upon the age composition of the farm population; (4) that the national birth rate has been depressed because of childless marriages and postponed marriages in the cities and because of limited opportunities for marriage to males in the country; and (5) that rural culture is being rapidly refashioned after patterns resembling that of the cities. This is not to say that these things are either good or bad, but they are forces which must be dealt with in any attempt at dealing with the social problems which confront us as a people at this time.

CONCLUSION.—In conclusion, it may be said that the problems of mobility inhere in the fact that it tends to be destructive of existing social bonds and established relationships. We have a predisposition to view with alarm that which breaks down socially sanctioned patterns of life which have been built up by a slow and difficult process of trial, error, and accommodation. A high degree of mobility brings together conflicting points of view and dislodges vested interests. It breeds conflict, a feeling of dissatisfaction with things as they used to be. It brings together antagonistic racial, nationality, political, linguistic, religious, economic, and psychological elements of population, and generates contempt, skepticism, and cynicism with respect to "the sacred verities." On the other hand, it stands to reason that a society in which the members are tied down and immobile may disintegrate easily. It is in societies which are the most stable that military dictatorships, feudal overlordship, and autocratic social systems have arisen and flourished. There is no surer index of subjugation and servility of the masses of human beings than absolute fixity of place and social condition. Change of social condition in one way or another is inevitable with change of location. Moreover, mobility may be compared to metabolism. It is a method of removing worn out social structures and making way for new structures to grow and multiply. Migration is and has been one of our chief carriers of new thought, new culture, and new forms of collective existence.

While there are thought to be no new continents to be discovered, it remains that new frontiers must be discovered if a large portion of the present population of this country is not to die without issue. Perhaps migration holds the solution for our present debacle, but who knows?

REFERENCES

1. Dorothy Swaine Thomas defines internal migration as change of residence from one community, or other clearly defined geographical unit, to another within the national boundaries. See *Migration Differentials*, SSRC, Bul. 43, New York, 1938, p. 4. Her definition presupposes that persons actually give up one residence and go to another, and excludes vagabonds, "trailer nomads" and other casual wanderers. This is essentially what is to be understood by migration in this paper. However, transient laborers are not wholly excluded as they have been by Dr. Thomas because to all appearances those who have been included were persons actually seeking to establish themselves in a new residence, having given up an old one. The fact that such people often have difficulty in finding a new place to live should not necessarily stigmatize them as vagabonds.

2. See John N. Webb and Malcolm Brown, *Migrant Families*, WPA Research Monograph XVIII, pp. 40–44. Also Cf. T. Lynn Smith, *The Sociology of Rural Life*, Harpers, New York, 1940, pp. 42–44, 183–197.

3. See T. Lynn Smith, *idem;* Webb and Brown, *idem;* Charles J. Galpin and T. B. Manny, *Interstate Migrations Among the Native White Population as Indicated by Differences Between State of Birth and State of Residence*, Washington, 1934.

4. For confirmation of this point, witness the phenomenal growth of such cities as Miami, Charlotte, Winston-Salem, Durham, Atlanta, Birmingham, Memphis, Shreveport, Dallas, Houston, Fort Worth, San Antonio, Tulsa, Oklahoma City, Denver, El Paso, and Los Angeles, as compared with most of the northern and eastern cities with few exceptions.

5. See United States Bureau of Agricultural Economics, *Farm Population Estimates,* January 1, 1939, Washington (Released June 22, 1939).

6. For example, employment, wealth accumulation, marriage, social participation and many other aspects of socio-economic status are conditioned significantly by the age factor, and these characteristics of a population are related functionally to mobility. It is axiomatic that a migrant must be old enough to go from place to place easily and to provide for himself; yet he must be young enough to adjust himself easily to new situations. Otherwise, the dead expense of migration itself operates as a check to movement.

7. If the South be taken out of the picture entirely, it will be found that, in the remainder of the United States, 9.4 percent of the farm owners and 36.8 percent of the farm tenants have resided for a period of one year or less on the farms they occupied in 1935.

8. Although workers engaged in the extraction of minerals are often loath to take up farming, the experience of Oklahoma and other mineral areas in the Southwest has been that, when the mineral deposits were exhausted, the workers left unemployed were disposed of in one of three ways: Some of them went on to new areas, following the industry; others crowded into nearby towns and either found casual work or depended upon the relief agency; still other released workers became squatters and survived as best they could by very small scale subsistence farming, or part time farming, by getting supplementary aid from the relief agency, or by salvaging what they could from the abandoned mineral properties and leases.

9. See C. E. Lively and Conrad Taeuber, *Rural Migration in the United States*, WPA Research Monograph XIX, Washington, D. C., 1939, p. xi.

10. See Galpin and Manny, *Op. cit.*, pp. 6–7.

11. See Webb and Brown, *Op. cit.*, p. 140.

12. See *Study of 6,655 Migrant Families in California*, 1938, Report No. 765–08–3–4; also News Release R9–5–FRS, April 20, 1939, Farm Security Administration, San Fran-

cisco. Also, the writer received a personal communication from Mr. Frederick R. Soule describing additional details of this report for Oklahoma.

13. This summary is condensed from the sources cited above.

14. See C. C. Zimmerman and O. D. Duncan, "The Migration to Towns and Cities," *Jour. Farm. Econ.* X, 4, October, 1928, pp. 506–515. Noel P. Gist and Carroll D. Clark contend that this is an over simplification of the problem. See their paper, "Intelligence as a Selective Factor in Rural-Urban Migration," *Amer. Jour. Sociol.* XLIV 1, July 1938, pp. 36–58.

15. E. C. Young, The Movement of Farm Population, Cornell, AES Bul. 426, Ithaca, 1924, p. 88.

16. Sorokin, Zimmerman and Galpin, *A Systematic Source Book in Rural Sociology,* University of Minnesota Press, Minneapolis, 1932, Vol. III, pp. 625–627. Also, T. Lynn Smith, *op. cit.*, p. 183.

ON THE SOCIAL ASPECTS OF POPULATION CHANGES*

By William Fielding Ogburn

The expansion of activity in the study of population has been so great and so rapid that it is appropriate to make some observations as to scope. Such observations may be of value for future researches in this field.

Scope. The field may be viewed as of two kinds. One is concerned with the collection and measurement of data on population in different areas and in different times. These measurements include components such as deaths, births and migrations by age, sex and other characteristics of people, such as the diseases which cause death, and marital conditions. Most of these characteristics are anatomical or physiological. The inquiries in this field constitute the traditional work of demographers and actuaries.

The second field of activity in population studies is concerned not with measuring population, but with the relation of population variations with variations in social institutions and human behaviour, such as business and political activities. Civilization consists of parts such as religion, family, community, government and economic organizations. These vary from place to place and from one time to another. Changes in population may be related to these variations.

Research in this second field has not been confined to demographers. Investigations have been made by sociologists, economists and political scientists.

This paper is not concerned with the major field of demographers, that is, with the measurement of population and its components. The achievements in this field indicate as high degree of science as is to be found anywhere in the social sciences. Indeed this branch of social science with its accumulation of reliable knowledge shows evidence of considerable maturity.

But demographers are reaching out beyond and writing on the various social aspects of population variation. This field of interrelations of population with social institutions and human behaviour in general, is not only important, but methods of research and the orientation are somewhat different from the usual demographic procedures. For these reasons then this paper will deal with research in this field of the interrelationships with population change.

The Social Aspects of Population Changes. The significance of population phenomena lies in the meaning for human activity. Population numbers mean markets, military forces, land values. Deaths mean ill health and disabilities.

* Reprinted from *The British Journal of Sociology,* 4 (March 1953), pp. 25–30, by permission of the author and the London School of Economics and Political Science.

Population statistics without these social and human implications would be dry and uninteresting data. It is natural therefore that students of population should want to study the social implications of their population data.

Indeed the most well known writing in the earlier history of population study dealt with social implications. The contribution of Malthus was on the relationship of population growth to income and human welfare. The contribution of Galton dealt with the relationship of the biological and racial quality of population to the progress of civilization. But as time went on more effort and more time were required by statisticians to gather and marshal their data not for use by themselves as the etymology of the word might imply, but for use in statecraft, and policy making by others.

Such contributions deal with the social *effects* of population change. But the social implications of population change deal with the social *causes* also.

The Social Causes of Population Changes. Students of population who range beyond the collection and measurement of population data have perhaps dealt more with the causes of population change than with effects, thus there have been a large number of studies of the causes of the decrease in births. So also the literature is extensive on the causes of death. These causes of death have naturally been sought in medical science. But the social conditions which foster different types of disease have also been carefully investigated and related to urban life, to poverty, to bad housing, and to life in factories. Then, too, in the case of migration a good deal of work has been done in relating the causes of migration to crop failures, to the search for new lands, to the cyclical changes of business, to religious persecution and to policies of victors in wars. The causes of population change have been the result of studies of its relationship to changes in the family, in agriculture, in trade, in business, in religion and in transportation.

Qualifications for Interrelationship Study. It is not an accident that Malthus was a careful student of political economy. Galton could not have founded eugenics without a knowledge of biology. The causes of the decrease in births have been made by social scientists with little skill in demography. Historians and economists have made the best studies of the causes of migration. Medical knowledge and biological orientation are helpful in investigating the causes of death. Sociologists have been particularly successful in relating the conditions of urban and rural life to births, deaths and migration.

Studies, then, in the interrelationship of population changes to the different parts of civilization require a wide range of knowledge and a variety of skills in economics, medicine, sociology, biology, as well as in demography. No one person can have all this orientation. Such intercorrelations will be done by many different persons operating in the various social sciences.

Since all such intercorrelations involve population as the dependent or independent variable the common factor in them all is knowledge of the facts of population and the techniques of their manipulation. Demographers are then in a key position for such research. True, they may not know the other social sciences. But, of course, it is not necessary to know them all. For any particular study it is necessary only to know the part concerned. Thus, if one is correlating death rates with business cycles, an extensive knowledge of the whole field of economics is not needed; nor indeed of business cycle theory. A considerable knowledge of the measurement of business cycles and of their components is required. It is not too difficult to learn by an outsider.

If the correlation of population phenomena with the business cycle is done by economists, they must learn a good deal about the sources, meaning and accuracy of the different demographic series, perhaps in different countries and for many years back. Thus for death rates for different diseases for different countries in prior decades there is need for familiarity with subjects quite outside economics.

In addition to these specialized skills and knowledge, there is a pattern of analysis that may be helpful. It can be demonstrated by a consideration of the social effects of population variation.

The Social Effects of Population Changes. There is a definite process by which the effects of a population change are worked out on society and its institutions. The restriction of immigration to the United States of America in the 1920's resulted in various social changes many of which were quite complex. These changes were related to wage rates, the introduction of machines, the migration of negroes from the southern States into the northern, civil rights for negroes, housing problems, relations with Mexico, etc. These social effects are not miscellaneous or disorderly. The process by which they follow constitute a pattern. This pattern may be divided into four parts each of which will be presented in succeeding paragraphs. The first one is the direct process.

The Direct Process. The effect of a population change is often simple and direct. Thus as towns increase in population there is an increase in governmental functions. Large cities which are more densely populated furnish more social services to their citizens than small towns; in police, traffic regulation, play space for children, recreation facilities, etc. The discovery of such a direct effect is often important in itself and may answer our curiosity or our need.

(It may be observed that a correlation of social characteristics with size of community does not always mean a causal correlation. For instance, that foreign born immigrants were found in larger numbers in big cities than small ones in the United States, does not mean that an increase in population of cities causes a larger proportion of foreign-born persons to live there. Their presence may be due to other variables such as wage rates, or shipping or railway routes and terminals, rather than to population increase. The meaning of correlations with population aggregates of different sizes is difficult to determine because of the large number of variables.)

But the increase in governmental functions of cities is a result of a direct process of the influence of population increase, even though there be other factors than an increase in population density.

The Succession Process. The influence of a change in population does not end with its direct and more or less immediate effect. Thus a decrease in births has the direct effect of increasing the proportion of elders in a population. But the influence of the decrease in births does not stop there, for the increase in the proportion of elders adds to the burden of support of the family and relatives of the elders. This influence on the family and kinship function may be called a derivative effect of the decrease in births. But the effect does not end with its first derivative. There are families without children or nearby kin and so the care of elders falls upon others, notably the government. The development of state pensions for the old may then be called a second derivative of the influence of a decrease in the birth rate. When the payments for pensions to employees of the government and of private business become large the burden is felt by the taxpayer and by business, so there follows a movement to extend the age of employment for elders, a third derivative. These derivative influences string out like the beads on a chain.

In observing the successive derivative influences of a population change, it is not to be understood that the influence of population change is the only one operating to produce the change.

The succession process is like a game of billiards. The force of the cue on the cue ball is passed on the ball struck by the cue ball. This second ball may also hit a third ball.

The Convergence Process. In discussing derivative influences the reader was warned not to consider the influence of a factor as the sole cause of a change. I have never seen a zero-order correlation coefficient of 1 between social phenomena. Often the influences of several varying factors converge to produce a change. Thus the increased proportion of old in the population of the United States is not due solely to the decrease in the proportion of the very young because of the influence of a falling birth rate. Another influence in the 1920's in the United States was the restriction of the number of immigrants coming across the Atlantic, who were generally young adults or persons in the early middle ages. A third converging influence operating to increase the proportion of elders was successful research in medicine, particularly in the earlier detection of cancer and in care and treatment of difficulties of the circulatory system, especially in the late middle ages. Thus there are at least three converging influences that increased the proportion of the aged. Similarly, the increase in the percentage of the elders is not the sole influence operating to increase or create pensions for old age. Other factors whose influence converge to produce pensions are the decline of kinship responsibilities due to dispersion of the family by improved transport to other places of work and of residence, the growth of the idea of the welfare state, and the efficiency movement in industry.

Thus the increase in the proportion of the aged is one of at least four converging influences that led to old age pensions. And since the decreasing birth rate is one of three influences causing an increased percentage of the old in the population, then a decrease in the birth rate is one in six factors causing old age pensions. As derivative influences extend in succession the share of one factor in causing remoter derivative influences diminishes. Like the billiard ball whose force gets less and less, so the share of one factor becomes less and less. It should be noted that not all converging factors are equal in influence. The birth rate may be more important than decreasing migration in causing a larger proportion of aged in the population.

The Radiation Process. The reverse of the convergence process is the radiation process. A population change may influence not just one phenomenon, but its influence may radiate outward in many different directions, like the spokes from the hub of a wheel. Thus a fall in the birth rate will be a factor in women working away from home, in divorce, in the personality of children, in early marriage, and in the support for education.

The Combination of Processes. When population changes are occurring in several aspects of population, as for instance in birth rates, in death rates, in migration, in population increase, these four processes just described become combined. The successive derivatives radiate influences outward in various directions and are impinged upon by various converging forces coming from different directions. The simile of links in a chain does not indicate the pattern as well as does the picture of a network. The process is not hopelessly complex, for the derivative influences eventually fall away to nothing; and not all parts of the network are activated at one time; finally some direct influences are very slight. Often measurement of these influences may not be needed, or they may not be worth the trouble to measure. Where measurement is needed, the usual techniques, such as partial and multiple correlation may be used.

The Future. It seems probable that the social aspects of population change will become increasingly the subject of scientific investigation. Whether these investigations are made by demographers or by other social scientists may be only of jurisdictional importance. If demographers move over in large numbers to this field of studying the interrelationship of population change with other social phenomena, the foregoing analysis will indicate something of the complexities to be met.

Sometimes experts in population study have perhaps not approached the problem of these interrelationships with the seriousness with which they do their usual demographic work, as when they see an increase in the sale of wheel chairs as an economic effect of the increase in the aged. More often they rely upon ominous suggestion, for instance, as to the dire consequences of the falling birth rate or of the menacing growth of population in India. Malthus took it more seriously; though he would have profited by a greater awareness of convergence, as for instance of the technological factor as well as the population factor on the plane of living.

There are some problems of interrelationship between population and social phenomena of considerable importance for public policy and of significance for a science of society. In closing, I mention two, as illustrations.

One concerns the relation of population to war. Is population pressure related to the augmentation of the warlike attitude? Much has been said on the subject, though the analysis calls for an adequate conception and measure of population pressure. Changes in density and changes in the plane of living, measured in various ways, need to be considered as well as a comparison by countries of densities and planes of living. Migration has been shown to be correlated more highly with the "pull" than the "push". Could a similar relationship exist between population and warlike moves? Are rates of growth of population related to attitude of aggression in both urban and rural countries irrespective of density? Such questions as these suggest the intricacies and magnitudes of an adequate inquiry.

Another important problem of the interrelation of population and other social phenomena concerns the relation of density of population to social organization. Small communities with low densities would seem to offer less possibility of a multiplicity of social organizations. On the other hand, large cities with high density seem to imply many governmental services of the type of the welfare state. Then there is the fascinating question of the social characteristics of cities of different sizes, that is, the influence of population aggregations on collective behaviour as shown in institutions and customs. The problem of optimum populations then breaks down into optima. There are also indices of adjustment and maladjustment to populations of varying density, as seen in morbidity rates, death rates, prevalence of psychoses and neuroses, extent of juvenile delinquency, frequencies of problem children in schools, etc.

Great variations in population probably affect all social institutions one way or another to some degree.

CHAPTER 9

POPULATION POLICY

A population policy embraces the objectives sought by a state in respect of the magnitude or the composition of its population, together with the means recommended for the realization of these objectives. The term may also be applied when the objectives are sought and the means are employed by a less inclusive social or political group, such as a church. It is usually confined, however, to the pursuit of objectives by the state.

When a policy relates only to a population's magnitude, it may be restrictive or expansionist in character. It is definable as restrictive when the objective sought is retardation of population growth. Historically, this type of policy has not often been pursued. It was endorsed by Plato and Aristotle (see Chapter 1), who believed that a city-state's population might become too large. It was advocated by Malthus, who believed that numbers usually tended to increase too rapidly for man's welfare. It was approved by many nineteenth century writers who believed, with Malthus, that population normally tends to increase too fast. It was subsequently endorsed by writers who believed that populations tend to grow beyond a size that is optimum for them under circumstances most likely to obtain (see Chapter 4). Today a restrictive policy has widespread support in some countries in which, by most any criterion, too many people already are seeking a livelihood (e.g., Japan, India).

Advocates of a restrictive policy agree that in the absence of such a policy numbers would become too great and per capita income or welfare would not be so high as it would be were numbers fewer. Advocates of a restrictive policy may differ, however, respecting the means to employ. Some favor deferment of marriage and non-marriage; others favor recourse to so-called "natural" methods of birth control (e. g., restriction of sexual relations to the so-called "safe period"); some may even endorse medically supervised abortion; but most favor use of effective modern contraceptive methods. Advocates of restrictive policies sometimes differ somewhat respecting how individuals may be induced to pursue restrictive policies, though they usually agree that the necessary goals, motivations, etc., must be built into a nation's culture and subcultures.

An expansionist population policy is one advocating an increase in a nation's population, or in its rate of population growth. This objective has been based upon various assumptions. Off and on, particularly with democratization of war and the development of mass armies after the late eighteenth century, the military advantages of numbers have been stressed. During periods (e. g., when mercantilist policies were widely approved; when, as under communism and fascism, the ends of the "state" rather than the welfare of the individual were stressed) when the individual was looked upon as essentially the instrument of the state, the economic advantages supposedly derived by the state from populousness were emphasized, in large part because labor was looked upon as by far the most important factor of production and hence the most important source of gold, wealth, etc. In recent times, with the decline in net reproduction to a level barely adequate to replace the existing population, it has sometimes come to be supposed that a population is not likely to replace itself in the absence of state assistance for mothers, parents, and children. Here, of course, emphasis is placed upon the maintenance of existing numbers rather than upon their augmentation.

Exponents of what has been called an expansionist policy favor recourse to divers means that confer advantages of sorts upon parents or upon children. Preferential treatment with respect to employment opportunities and military service may be accorded the head or other members of the family; wages or salary may be based in part upon family size; marriage and birth bonuses, tax advantages, and child subsidies may be provided; and other forms of assistance in money or in kind may be made available. Propaganda and the award of honors may also be utilized by the state. Access to means of family limitation may be denied or highly restricted. While exponents of expansionist policies tend to look with favor upon immigration, they seldom advocate unrestricted immigration; and if they did, they could hardly win support for such a policy, since it would adversely affect various groups and since it would have none of the popular appeal that income-equalizing, birth-stimulating policies are likely to have.

Modern expansionist policies seldom if ever give much weight to the fact that, in the longer run, population growth is likely to depend upon the rate of income growth more than upon any other circumstance. For if they did, they would stress capital formation, technological improvements, freedom of trade, and other policies highly favorable to the growth of national income.

Qualitative population policies have commanded some attention since the late nineteenth century, having earlier enjoyed the support of Plato and Aristotle and several later Roman policy-makers. These policies have been defended either on the ground that they would make for improvement of the genetical structure of the population, or because they would favor the relative increase of families and groups that were the creators and/or the bearers of the kinds of values deemed of relatively the greatest significance for the future of a society. Qualitative population policies have not had widespread support and have rarely been implemented, in part because information concerning genetical selection is considered too incomplete, and in part because explicit recognition of individual differences, together with the provision of subsidies, etc., for their maintenance, runs counter to egalitarian and democratic dogma.

The selections comprising this chapter review many aspects of population policy, indicate some of the policies that are in effect, and disclose the foundations on which some policies rest. Meadows describes how a socialized policy comes into being. Spengler indicates how theory may contribute to the formulation of suitable population policies. Whelpton suggests what is a suitable policy for the United States, a country of which population pressure in the orthodox sense is not yet characteristic, while Notestein treats of the policy problems faced in areas, of which there are many, in which population pressure already is great. Johnson deals with policy aspects of mobility, a subject of great importance to students of population. Peterson's paper outlines some of the population policy in effect in the Netherlands, a densely populated country with relatively high incomes, and touches upon considerations underlying this policy. In the last paper are presented policy and other findings made by the British Royal Commission on Population in respect of economic aspects of Britain's population situation.

TOWARD A SOCIALIZED POPULATION POLICY*

By Paul Meadows

The study of population is, as a sociological discipline, only about a half century old.[1] The temporary eclipse of Malthus[2] during the nineteenth century tended to obscure relevant sociological aspects of population study. Population was usually considered a branch of economics or of actuarial science. The political and economic questions arising from the volume of immigration during the period before the first World War opened the way to a rather careful study of the vital rates of Western peoples. The facts about the birth and death rates gave rise to much speculation about future population growth. These calculations began to have a practical bearing on social and economic problems and programs. In the last two decades the field of population study has for social scientists become a very extensive one.

The academic problems of population may be distinguished from the social problems of population. Academically, population may be the subject of scientific curiosity: the accumulation of data on trends, quality, composition, distribution, and migration.[3] Again, for the scientist there may be a good deal of interest in the explanation of population data. What are the causes of changes of one sort or another in a given population? On the other hand, population may be the subject matter of social policy. Certain attitudes may develop toward changes; the latter may be defined as having a particular significance for the nation as a whole. What can be done? How may certain goals regarded as desirable be achieved? The present paper is limited to these latter questions. The procedure will be to describe the general theory of population change and the framework of population policy.

CHANGING CONCEPTIONS OF POPULATION.—It is impossible to say that human society has followed any single policy toward human numbers; indeed there has never even been any single policy. Roughly, three types of concern with numbers may be noted: one which definitely desires population increase, for one reason or another; another which seeks to check the growth of population because of certain social or economic considerations; and finally a third which regards the question of human numbers as a phase of, if not actually an instrument of, general social policy. These three public policies stand in decided contrast to the prevalent *laissez faire* optimism of the nineteenth century which held that private interests would, if left free for expression, naturally and inevitably contribute to the common good.[4] This was hardly a policy at all; rather it represented a wish that a policy would not be necessary.

*Reprinted from *Psychiatry*, 11 (May 1948), pp. 193–202, by permission of the author and publisher. (Copyright 1948 by the William Alanson White Psychiatric Foundation.)

Safety in Numbers. Historically, the most common attitude toward population has been one of fervently desiring increase. Rooted in primitive phallicism with its worship of sex, the appetite for numbers has taken many forms.[5] The political-dynastic argument for large and growing populations hinges on the importance of a sizeable manpower. It has not been an unused argument in recent decades, and it has been important in the unsatisfied hunger for colonies and other systems of control over lands and people. How much of it entered into the motivations for World War II is difficult to say, but it was present in the common cries of *Lebensraum* and "population pressure."

The industrial-dynastic argument likewise assumes the necessity of a large labor force to carry on production as well as of a large consuming public to buy the products of business and industry. Many hands to work and many mouths to feed are indispensable to an expansive industrialism. Less obvious, perhaps, but none the less strong is the religious-dynastic argument which, though clothed in the language of mysticism and sacred scriptures, also assumes the desirability of large numbers of children of the faith: "Be fruitful and multiply." The zeal with which orthodox church representatives fight efforts to control population via birth control testifies in some measure at least to the strength of this motivation. Like so-called primitive people, these various groups of dynasts feel that numbers are in themselves some guarantee of safety as well as of other values which these groups prize.[6]

Sanity in Numbers. Although he was not the first person to speculate on the problems of population, Thomas Robert Malthus was the first to succeed in systematizing the general theory of population up to his time in his *Essay on the Principle of Population* (1798).[7] One is not very likely to appreciate the position taken by Malthus in his famous *Essay* if he does not understand the conditions which caused many persons at that time to regard it as an extraordinarily effective plea for sanity in numbers.

To what extent can man deliberately "improve" his society? Malthus' *Essay* was intended to refute the myth, popularized by the French Revolution and the French encyclopedists, that progress is possible through the medium of social legislation. Malthus had seized on an admission in a book by William Godwin, *Political Justice,* which was very popular among advocates of the French cause: "There is a principle by which population is perpetually kept down to the level of the means of subsistence." Malthus proceeded to inquire into the bearing of this proposition on human perfectibility.[8] This principle he formulated as the incompatibility of two equally strong human desires, the desire for food and for sex. Seeing no prospective diminution of either,[9] he found that the best that can be hoped for is the pessimistic realization of limited possibilities in the supply of food; this gloomy future is further depressed by surplus human numbers. There is no help in institutions, because they are superficial; nor in the control of human numbers, because the sex drive is strong; nor yet again in the human arts, because land is subject to diminishing returns.

The popularity of such a thesis can with great credibility be traced to the political circumstance that "it appeared at a time when the upper classes, terrified by the French Revolution, found in it a much needed justification for the existing order as against the radical proposals of Godwin and Condorcet. . . . Malthus' principle, posited as a natural law, involved a condemnation of all such attempts and a defense of the institution of private property which he argued was the basis of the check of prudence."[10] Malthus appealed to the apprehensive proponents of the *status quo* with the philosophy that increase in numbers with no changes in planes of living, along with a lack of supporting resources, spells only the impossibility of permanent improvement in the living conditions of the English people, especially of the new industrial working classes. The only thing he could advise was self-restraint, the voluntary check on numbers, for as a humanitarian he could hardly urge the other alternative—involuntary checks on human numbers by war, disease, and so forth.

Malthus' principle of curbing numbers as a means of social amelioration appealed to a great many people during the nineteenth century. Although critical of many phases of his theory, the socialists also saw a relation between numbers and economic status; however, they argued that the pressure of numbers on nature would be relieved by a more adequate distribution of wealth and income. Those who, following Malthus, advocated reducing the birth rate through the control of conception were known in the nineteenth century as "Neo-Malthusians." Through the work of Francis Place, Robert Dale Owen, Dr. Charles Knowlton, Dr. George Drysdale, Charles Bradlaugh, Annie Besant, Marie Stopes, and Margaret Sanger, this movement has grown enormously since its inception during the first quarter of the nineteenth century. Variously known as the Malthusian League, the Birth Control League, the Voluntary Parenthood League, the Planned Parenthood Federation, the movement has become institutionalized in clinics, contraceptive industries, and formalized social hygiene. The spread of birth-control information and technics has undoubtedly had a great influence on the decline of the birth rate in most industrial countries since the third quarter of the nineteenth century.[11]

Human Numbers and General Social Welfare. In point of fact, during the century which followed the final edition of Malthus' *Essay*—a century in which his preaching ultimately began to be practiced—the interest in limitation of offspring was a family affair, not the result of public discussion of birth-control measures.[12] The new *mores* came actually in utter opposition to declared State policy.[13] It is not at all clear, indeed, that the State can—should it so desire—modify trends in population reproduction.[14] None the less, modification of the birth trends, which have declined more rapidly than even the Neo-Malthusians probably imagined they would, has been very actively sought in the last three decades by the State, chiefly by European governments.[15] This promotional work, however successful it may have been (there has been some controversy over this point), was prompted by the apparent threat of depopulation and by the realization of the incompleteness and inadequacy of the Neo-Malthusian remedies. Indeed, the greater the success of Neo-Malthusianism, the greater the concern of modern governments. In a sense, then, there has been a return to the pre-Malthusian point of view. Quantity is again important.[16] However, there has not been a wholesale or wholehearted return to a "numbers" policy, for the purpose has been not merely to control fertility but (at least in some cases) to provide for human welfare on a broader scale.[17]

THE FRAMEWORK OF POPULATION POLICY.—Contemporary population policy, therefore, is not characterized by singleness of purpose or by uniformity of methods. Unfortunately, we have not yet arrived at a completely socialized conception of population, but the methods and the information for such conception are at hand. Certain facts about modern population trends have begun to cause alarm. It is not a case of undue fright, for rational norms of population growth and change have come to be formulated. Socialized goals and means appear to be available, subject only to certain limitations which policy in the field of population must always face. These items constitute the next objects of attention in this paper.

Some Areas of Immediate Concern. Three types of population problems may be distinguished.[18] The demographic problems center on questions of vital rates, age composition, and quality. The socio-economic problems consider the relationships between the trends in the demography of a nation and the trends in the society and economy. The bio-ecological problems focus on the spatial distribution of a people. If, as Alva Myrdal has said, "a population policy can be nothing less than the social policy at large,"[19] it should be readily apparent that in considering population one runs the whole gamut of modern social problems. Since such a scope is impossible within the brief confines of this paper, it is necessary to limit the present discussion to selected phases of these three groups of interest.

Not all aspects of population should be considered as problems. A case in point is the decline of the death rate. The huge increase in human numbers during the nineteenth century was not due to any change in reproductive behavior but was solely a result of the fact that more people survived and that they survived for a longer period of time. This lengthened life expectation has been especially characteristic of the industrial countries.[20] Life expectancy has radically altered under the conditions of modern industrialism. Four centuries ago in Europe, life expectancy stood at less than 25 years—a century ago at 35 years. In 1900 the life expectancy in countries of the industrial West was about 50 years; in 1940, almost 64. In other words, it has almost trebled in four centuries. However, as Thompson has shown,[21] this lengthening life expectancy—and conversely the decline in death rates—cannot continue indefinitely. For as a nation ages, it becomes subject to the risks of aging.[22] Against these risks little has been accomplished, especially in

found our public domain placed almost as freely at their disposal as that of our native citizens: For example, foreigners as well as natives could obtain a farm by homesteading. Nor were national policies favorable to growth limited to immigration; the Comstock law was interpreted to include contraceptive materials and appliances, while various State laws proscribed abortion. To the extent that attempts to enforce these laws were successful, the birth rate and population growth from natural increase were higher than they otherwise would have been.

CHANGING OUTLOOKS. Since the World War, however, our policy toward immigration has changed radically. The discovery that the Americanization of pre-war immigrants had not gone on as rapidly as popularly supposed, plus the realization that millions of persons wanted to leave war-torn Europe, contributed to the passing of the quota laws in the 1920's. Early in the 1930's the unemployment problem led to even more rigorous control through the "public charge" regulation, which denied admission to newcomers unless their support was guaranteed by their own wealth or by responsible persons already here. As a result, the immigration stream is now a mere trickle instead of a rushing torrent and, judging from the present temper of the nation, will remain so for some years to come. Not until conditions change greatly will we again allow large numbers of foreigners to cross our borders annually.

At the same time, an extremely significant change from the standpoint of population growth has occurred in the public attitude toward contraception. This is not to say that contraceptive methods have only recently been used in the United States. On the contrary, most students of population believe that birth rates in rural areas were half again as high as in urban areas as far back as 1820 chiefly because some type of contraception was practiced by a larger proportion of urban families than rural families. Similarly, these scientists believe that our birth rate was cut in half from 1800 to 1890 primarily because birth control in some form became more widely practiced. Until recently, however, there was little relation between the attitude of individuals toward spacing their own children and their attitude toward birth control clinics and the intelligent public discussion of contraceptive problems. Compare, for example, the persecution of Margaret Sanger and her associates in their first clinic during 1916 with the general tolerance toward clinics at the present time in most states. And try to imagine Mr. Pringle's article "What do the Women of America Think about Birth Control?" being published by the *Ladies' Home Journal* in 1900 instead of 1938!

Looking ahead, it seems likely that information regarding some means of spacing births will continue to spread through the population, gradually reaching the groups not yet informed. It may be expected to bring about a decrease in the birth rate among the lower socio-economic groups in urban centers and among rural people in general, especially those less affected at present by city influences. In contrast, little change in birth rates may occur among the groups which have gone farther in cultural assimilation of contraception and in the stabilization of fertility. To be explicit, the rapid decline in birth rates among southern whites and Negroes during recent years may be expected to continue, especially in the open country, while the fertility of the native white population of New England may remain at the level it has held since 1910.

A further decrease in the death rate can offset part of the decrease in the birth rate, of course, but only a small part. Medical and public health authorities realize it will be extremely difficult to increase the expectation of life of our white people from 63.3 years, the present figure, to 70 years by the end of the century. Such a gain will be wiped out by a 10 per cent decline in the birth rate, which can easily come about—witness the decline of over 20 per cent from 1920 to 1930.

In the absence of effective changes in population policy, therefore, a continued slowing up of population growth may be expected. My colleague, Dr. Warren S. Thompson of the Scripps Foundation, and I have computed the future course of population growth with various trends of immigration, fertility, and mortality. According to our medium assumptions for future trends —no immigration, an increase in expectation of life of white persons to 70 years in 1980, and a decline in the average number of children in a completed native white family from 2.2 in 1930–34 to 1.9 in 1980—the population will increase from the present 131,000,000 to a maximum of nearly 154,000,000 in 1985 or thereabout, after which it will begin to decline. If the average number of children per native white woman declines from 2.2 to 1.5 (our low fertility assumption), a maximum population of not quite 140,000,000 will be reached about 20 years from now, and by the end of the century our numbers will be little, if any, greater than in 1920. Even if present birth rates should be maintained, which seems extremely unlikely in view of past trends, the population peak would be reached during the next century. It is clear, therefore, that unless there is a marked change in population policy, and unless the new policy is effective, our population will slowly reach an upper limit during the next 20 to 60 years and then begin to decline.

OPTIMUM POPULATION. The official attitude in most European countries is that a larger population is needed. Faced with the probability of a maximum number of people a few years hence, should we, too, adopt measures designed to achieve greater size? Let us consider first the relation between the size of our population, our resources and our level of living. More specifically, is a larger or smaller ratio of people to resources more desirable from the standpoint of the welfare of our population?

If this nation could choose between having a stationary population of 131,000,000 (our present size) or 150,000,000 or 100,000,000, it can be shown quite conclusively that the smaller number would be best from an economic standpoint. The supporting argument involves some economic theory with which I will not bore you. Simply stated, the essential point is that the larger the population the larger the amount of farm land, mineral deposits, and other natural resources which must be used, or the more intensively a given amount must be worked to provide the basic necessities of life. Since our farm lands and mineral deposits vary in quality and accessibility, working a larger quantity of them will necessitate working poorer grades. Both this expansion and an intensification of methods tend to reduce the average production per worker, which in turn tends to lower wages in these industries or raise the prices of their products. Either will lower the living levels of the population.

From the standpoint of the efficiency of workers in manufacturing and trade, it matters little whether our population amounts to 100,000,000 or 150,-000,000. In either case the number of people to provide for is so great that innumerable factories and stores are needed. The essential difference under the two conditions is in the number of factories and stores, not in their human efficiency.

In transportation and communication an important part of the cost of service rendered is the construction of the highway, railroad, or telephone line. Once these are built, the number of people and tons of freight transported and the number of messages sent can increase greatly with little increase in the annual cost for upkeep or replacement. A population considerably larger than that of today, therefore, should be beneficial to output per worker in these industries, and hence to the general standard of living.

Summing up, a population of 100,000,000 as compared with 150,000,000 in the United States should have a higher output per worker in agriculture, forestry, and mining, about the same output in manufacturing and trade, and a lower output in communication and transportation. Considering the fact that in 1930 agriculture and mining employed about three times as many workers as transportation and communication and supported a still larger proportion of persons, the net advantage lies clearly on the side of a smaller population than the present, rather than a larger population. The United States is *now* overpopulated from the standpoint of per capita economic welfare, but fortunately not as seriously overpopulated as most nations.

You will notice I have not referred to the 12,000,000 persons now unemployed as evidence that our present ratio of population to resources is too high. My belief is that the present high unemployment is connected very remotely, if at all, with our overpopulation. There seems to be plenty of evidence that the main reason why so many people lack jobs is the failure of our economic system to function smoothly, which in turn results from our failure to develop an adequate mechanism for controlling it.

GROWTH VS. DECLINE. To talk about the advantages and disadvantages of a population of 100,000,000 compared with one of 150,000,000 is one thing; to talk about those of a growing compared with a decreasing population is another. Although a lower ratio of population to resources favors a more comfortable level of living than does the present ratio, it may be that this is more than offset by disadvantages associated in some degree with a slowing up of population growth and in a greater degree with a decrease in numbers.

No one denies that a rapid growth in population and a substantial improvement in living conditions have gone on together for a century or more in most western nations. It is not so clear, however, that the people in the nations with the most rapid increase have had the largest gains in living levels; on the contrary, in some of the slower growing nations the change has been equally favorable. Nor does the fact that living conditions improved during a period when population was growing prove that the latter was an important cause. In the light of the evidence available, it is much more reasonable to conclude that both have resulted from a common set of causal factors, among which scientific discoveries and inventions are of extreme importance.

Nevertheless, certain advantages of a growing population have been advanced by various persons and merit attention in considering the aims of a population policy. For one thing it is said that rapid growth helps to minimize the harm done by overexpansion of facilities in various lines. If factory capacity is increased too rapidly, if real estate developments take place on too large a scale, it will be possible to market the factory products and rent or sell the homes or offices in a shorter period if the population increases rapidly than if it increases slowly. But the other side of the picture should not be overlooked—if these developments go on in some period at too slow a pace, the seriousness of the situation is increased by a rapid population growth. It seems to me, however, that the proper solution for problems of this type is not the stimulation of population growth, but more intelligent planning on the part of private and public agencies.

Another advantage claimed for an increasing population is its higher proportion of young people in the working ages. Youth is supposed to represent progress, the development and adoption of new manufacturing processes and business methods which increase human efficiency. A rapidly expanding population is believed to offer them more opportunity to forge ahead, achieve positions of control, and put their ideas into practice. In a stationary population, in contrast, elders constitute a larger proportion of workers; they are likely to fill relatively more of the dominant places, and being more cautious and conservative, to retard the rate of change. The force of this argument depends in part on the extent to which change is progress, and in part on whether or not soundness of judgment increases with age and offsets any loss in the willingness to experiment and take chances. Opinions will differ on these matters, though perhaps the preponderance will be in favor of youth.

As far as the ratio of workers to dependents is concerned, there may be little choice between a rapidly growing population and one which is stationary. The former will have many children to raise but few old people to support; the latter will use more of its budget for elders and less for children, but may live equally well.

ECONOMICS OF EXPANSION AND STABILIZATION. In recent months much has been said about another advantage of a growing population. The logic runs somewhat as follows: Prosperity—that is, high per capita income—depends on full employment in the producers goods industries, which depends on a large flow of capital into long-time investments, which in turn depends on the development of new industries or on an increase in population. It may be true that in the past per capita income has varied from year to year with the amount of long-time investment and the increase in people, but let us examine the broader implications of this theory. By and large, the productive effort of a nation can be utilized to provide goods and services for current consumption or to develop facilities for greater production in the future. The more rapidly a population is increasing, the larger the share of its productive effort which should be directed toward expanding capacity for the future, and the smaller the share left to produce for present day needs. A stationary population thus has the advantage over a growing population that it can put more emphasis on producing for itself and less on producing for the future, which should mean more consumption goods per capita and higher living standards. The important thing in either case is that the working force be fully employed. This need not be left to depend on population growth; it should be susceptible of direct influence if the emphasis laid on improving our social and economic knowledge and practice is more nearly commensurate with that heretofore placed on the so-called physical sciences.

I hope what I have been saying has not given you the impression that I believe our standard of living will fall in the future with the population growth which I anticipate will occur. On the contrary, I believe our standard of living will rise. My argument has been that our people will live better not *because* they become somewhat more numerous, but *in spite of it*. The improvement will be caused primarily by an increase in our technical knowledge in such fields as production, business management, and government and in our ability to put this knowledge into practice. I have tried to make it clear that an increase of population helps to give a high level of living only when a nation is underpopulated judging from the ratio of people to resources, or when it is somewhat overpopulated but does not know how to regulate its economic life. The United States is now somewhat overpopulated, but in my opinion it need not remain indefinitely in its present ignorance about economic controls. Since our economic education may proceed slowly, however, it may be well to adopt a population policy which will retard somewhat the slowing up of growth. This will prolong the period during which increasing numbers may help our economic system and provide time for the development of more direct controls.

Most of my talk so far has been devoted to the quantitative goals of a population policy because it seems to me that even an intelligent group like this is heavily influenced by the general but uncritical acceptance of a large and increasing population as the ideal. I cannot hope that many of you who are "big population" people have changed your minds already, but I do hope your future thinking will lead you to change.

WHAT TO DO. As far as the qualitative goal of a population policy is concerned, it seems to me there is general agreement that we want a better population, and that improvement should be sought as rapidly as is feasible.

Accepting as the goals of population policy the prevention of too rapid slowing up of growth and the improvement of the quality of the population, we face the knotty problem of determining the specific measures which should be adopted. Manifestly we could add large numbers of people in a short time by again opening our doors to foreign immigration. While our moral or spiritual duty may be to do this, a majority of even the "big population" advocates do not appear to favor such action. Apparently it is generally agreed that under present conditions, the only people who should be admitted in large numbers are those who are sufficiently rich to live without working. Only they will swell the number of consumers without increasing the competition for jobs or becoming dependent on workers or relief agencies. In addition, there is the remembrance of the problems of assimilation and Americanization which arose after a period of rapid immigration in the past. As far as our immigration policy is concerned, it may well be that only minor changes, such as admitting refugee children, should be sought for some years to come.

If relaxing the immigration restrictions is ruled out as the way to check the slowing up of population growth, attention must be turned to measures affecting the birth rate. The first suggestion from some quarters would be the prevention of abortion, the banning of dissemination of information regarding contraception, and of the manufacture and distribution of the materials or appliances used for this purpose. By controlling the severity of the preventive measures it should be possible to check the decline of the birth rate and even bring about a significant rise, thus achieving the ends desired from a quantitative standpoint. Qualitatively, however, such measures would do much more harm than good, for it would be most difficult to affect the more able, intelligent and farsighted portion of the population. Such persons would be able to continue to limit the size of their families in the future much as they have in the past, hence the additional children would come chiefly from the other groups. Clearly the qualitative need is for measures in the opposite direction. Instead of curtailing contraception there should be a rapid increase in facilities for giving sound contraceptive advice to those groups which have not yet been able to obtain it. In addition, the materials and supplies should be provided free when necessary, so that poverty alone could no longer prevent the spacing of children. Manifestly such a task is too costly to be undertaken by private or philanthropic agencies; it must be a function of Government.

There is no question but that a system of publicly supported birth control clinics adequate to help in improving the quality of our population would also tend to speed up the cessation of growth and the beginning of a decrease in numbers. To prevent this from going on too rapidly, I believe we need measures akin to those being tested in Sweden, a democracy faced with similar problems. There the endeavor is to lessen the cost of children to the parents rather than to pay money to people for having large families, as in Germany. Although this may sound like two ways of saying the same thing, there is a fundamental psychological difference in the procedures. Money paid directly to parents can be used in a wide variety of ways, many of which may not be desirable from the standpoint of the children, the parents, nor society in general. In contrast, such things as rent subsidies for families with two or more children, free medical care for mothers during pregnancy and for children until working age, and public creches or kindergartens to relieve mothers of part of the care and confinement of raising children would appeal equally well (if not better) to couples wanting children for their own sake and not for their money value. Since there is plenty of evidence that the cost of raising children and the load they place on the mother's time and energy play an important rôle in limiting the size of families, it is reasonable to expect that family assistance of the type outlined could go far toward checking the decline in the birth rate. Conducted on an adequate scale, it could even bring about some increase, even if birth control information were made generally available.

It may be argued that it will cost too much to maintain the clinics, housing projects, health subsidies, creches, etc., suggested above. That they would be expensive is admitted. But that such a program would be a worthwhile national investment is, I think, susceptible of proof. Certainly we can afford to lay out large sums in ways which will gradually improve the quality of our population and forestall too rapid a shift from population growth to population decline.

PROBLEMS OF POLICY IN RELATION TO AREAS OF HEAVY POPULATION PRESSURE*

By Frank W. Notestein

In the next half century the size and distribution of the world's population will change rapidly. These changes will bring new demographic problems, and shift both the locus and form of old ones. Areas of Europe and Europe overseas in which technological civilization is most fully developed face slowing growth and perhaps gradual population decline. The phase of rapid growth which formerly characterized their populations is shifting to less fully developed areas such as Eastern Europe, the Soviet Union, and Japan. There, declines in fertility are well established but have not yet overtaken those in mortality which modernization has induced; hence growth is rapid.

In the remainder of the world, actual population change ranges from apparent decline in parts of Central Africa to very rapid increases in many areas of the Near and Far East and of Latin America. However, virtually all of these populations have high birth and death rates. In any of them the application of established techniques for the reduction of mortality would bring about a very rapid population growth. Irrespective of their past actual growth, such populations have the potentiality for rapid future growth. Populations with high growth potentials include most of those of Latin America, and, except for Japan, virtually all of those in which non-European cultures are dominant—in short, virtually all of the populations in the technologically undeveloped regions of the world.

Many of the world's undeveloped regions could absorb substantial growth readily enough. Throughout large parts of South America, Africa, and the Middle East, developments that would foster rapid population increase would also elicit the economic product to support that increase for a considerable period. In such areas population growth will present no considerable barriers to economic and political development for some time to come.

This paper deals with the much more serious problems of the regions that are already densely settled and still have high growth potentials, hence regions in which population growth may present serious obstacles to future economic and political development. They include Egypt, India, China, Korea, Formosa, Java, much of the Caribbean, and to a lesser extent the Philippine Islands and a number of other areas. However, the analysis treats the problems of this type of area in principle only. Illustrative materials are drawn from India, the Netherlands Indies, and the Philippines without any

* Reprinted from *The Milbank Memorial Fund Quarterly*, 22 (October 1944), pp. 424–444, by permission of the author and the Milbank Memorial Fund.

intention of suggesting that their situations are unique in principle. The essentials of the argument are equally applicable to the situation of Puerto Rico, Korea, Ceylon, and many other areas. We shall consider (1) the demographic situation, (2) the possibilities for checking growth, (3) solutions to the problem of pressure, and finally (4) problems of policy.

THE DEMOGRAPHIC SITUATION. Under conditions of stable government and economic development many colonial and semi-colonial areas have become densely settled for predominantly agricultural economies. In these areas human reproduction is grossly inefficient, for both birth and death rates remain high. Fertility is close to the biological maximum, and the presence or absence of growth depends principally on the course of mortality. Economic innovations that increase the production of the region serve to reduce mortality somewhat, thereby stimulating a growth that tends to consume the added product. Living levels have therefore risen little. Governments in a number of regions face the necessity of constantly expanding production merely to support growing numbers of people at the same subsistence level.

Populations living close to the margin of subsistence are highly vulnerable to the shocks of even minor economic dislocations. Such shocks hold a constant threat of catastrophe. The low nutritional status of people increases susceptibility to disease, and minimum cereal diets permit no substantial contraction when food production falls below normal. Although the improvement in transportation effected by colonial governments has done something to check famine, in general the development of the regions as sources of highly specialized and valuable raw materials has introduced new risks to the populations arising from their dependence on world markets. The potentialities for increased productivity inherent in modern agricultural techniques have been utilized to some extent but have not effected any substantial modification of the demographic situation. Fertility remains high; hence the growth potentialities of the population remain unimpaired.

The dangers of overpopulation in densely settled agricultural economies with high growth potentials may be illustrated by the situations in India, the Netherlands Indies, and the Philippines. In details their demographic positions and prospects differ widely from each other, and from those of other areas of the same type. However, each has the fundamental characteristics of the type, which is the potentiality for future population growth of a magnitude that sooner or later threatens to become a serious obstacle to political and economic development.

India is the giant of the colonial areas by all measures of its importance. Its population is only a little smaller than that of all Europe west of Russia. It increased by 50.7 million between 1931 and 1941 to reach a total of 389 million at the latter date. By now the population almost certainly exceeds 400 million. The record of its past growth is typically Malthusian. The decade 1871–1881 was one of famine and negligible growth; that following was one of prosperity and had a recorded increase of 11 per cent. The great famines of 1899 and 1900 cut the increase of the decade 1891–1901 to less than 2 per cent. In the recovery from 1901–1911 growth rose to 6.5 per cent. Between 1911 and 1921 a negligible increase of 1.2 per cent resulted from the death of at least 16 million people in the influenza pandemic and other high mortalities of the war years. Then for the first time since 1871 there were two successive decades of substantial growth. Between 1921 and 1931 the increase was 10.6 per cent and between 1931 and 1941 it was over 14 per cent. There is reason to believe that this rapid growth was due in part to a public health program that was increasingly effective after 1925.

Both the presence of growth in the favorable years and its absence in the unfavorable ones must be considered normal in India. As may be seen from the data in Table 1, if growth were continued at the rate of the favorable years 1921 to 1941 it would require only 57 years for the population to double itself. Such doubling would doubtless be possible if there were a rapid economic development. In the absence of such change it is quite unlikely. There are already 95 persons per square kilometer of territory that contains much arid and semi-arid land. Moreover, 67 per cent of the population is dependent on agriculture, less than 9 per cent of it lives in cities of 10,000 or more, and 91 per cent of the population ten years or more is illiterate (about 88 per cent in 1941). We may conclude that in the absence of sweeping economic development recurrent catastrophes are virtually inevitable.

The underlying demographic situation is reflected in the vital rates presented in Table 1. In the years 1930–1931, which seem typical of relatively favorable conditions, the birth rate was probably between 43 and 49 per 1,000 and the death rate was between 30 and 36.[1] The mortality experience of favorable years suggests an expectation of life at birth of slightly over 30 years, a figure that times of catastrophe sharply reduce. In spite of such terrific mortality the natural increase exceeds one per cent per year. Given the perpetuation of past trends, one may expect increases of the order of 50 million per decade until they are checked by new and larger catastrophes.

The Netherlands Indies have a notable record for economic development and "beneficent rule" in an area containing at once some of the world's most densely as well as most thinly settled regions. Much of the area of the Outer Islands is virtually uninhabited. On the other hand, no more perfect laboratory for the study of the Malthusian theory can be found than Java and Madura. There internecine wars, insecurity of person and property, primitive productive techniques, and the uncontrolled spread of disease kept the population in check until the eighteenth century. Then the colonial administration of the Dutch began to maintain peace and order, improve agricultural techniques, and introduce elementary sanitation and hygiene. The native population grew from about 5 million in 1816 to 13 million in 1860, 30 million in 1905, and 41 million in 1930. In the seventy years from 1860 to 1930 the native population apparently multiplied more than three times. By 1930 there were more than 800 persons per square mile (316 per sq. km.) and in three provinces density exceeded 1,000 persons per square mile. Such densities are frequently found in industrial economies, but in agricultural economies like that of Java they are found elsewhere only in the Ganges and Nile valleys and in some parts of China. At the rate of growth of the decade 1920–1930 it would require less than 40 years for the populations to double (Table 1).

TABLE I
SELECTED DEMOGRAPHIC INDEXES FOR INDIA, THE NETHERLANDS INDIES, AND THE PHILIPPINE ISLANDS.[1]

Index	India Date	India Amount	The Netherlands Indies Date	Total Amount	Java and Madura	The Philippine Islands Date	Amount
Population (000 omitted)	1941	389,001	1930	60,727	41,718	1939	16,000
Density Population per Km.²	1941	95.4	1930	31.9	316.1	1939	53.8
Growth Average Annual Per Cent Growth	1921–1941	1.21	1920–1930	2.08	1.76	1918–1939	2.20
Years Required to Double Population at this Rate		57		33	39		32
Vital Rates (Est.) Births per 1,000	1930–1931	43–49	1929–1930	43–51	41–51	1930–1931	42–52
Deaths per 1,000	1930–1931	30–36	1929–1930	27–37	25–35	1930–1931	21–31
Natural Increase per 1,000	1930–1931	10–16	1929–1930	5–20	11–21	1930–1931	17–27
Illiteracy Per Cent Population Age 10+ Illiterate	1931	91	1930	92	93	1939	51
Urbanization Per Cent Population in Cities of 10,000+	1931	8.75	1930	6.98	8.27	1939	10.6?
Dependency on Agriculture Per Cent Population Dependent on Agriculture	1931	67	1930	73	70	1939	76

[1] From the Office of Population Research, Princeton University. The values entered are those that seem most reasonable in view of all available evidence. They are not necessarily those given in official reports.

Unless there are drastic changes, sooner or later there must come a point at which continued increase forces down living levels, so that mortality will begin to rise. The colonial administration has pushed that point back and back by the development of agriculture and, to a lesser extent, of industry. Until recent years, the needs of the growing population have been met by the expansion of cultivated areas onto virgin soil, the increased productivity of the lands already under cultivation, the construction of improved irrigation works, and the development of better varieties of native and commercial crops. However, the limits of such development had been virtually reached by 1930. In 1938 the natives of Java and Madura had .20 acres of irrigated rice land per capita and .27 acres of nonirrigated land, or a total of less than half an acre of agricultural land per capita. The 19 million acres in native agriculture and fisheries constituted 60 per cent of the area of the islands. This native agriculture was highly vulnerable to changes in the world demand for its products. In 1937, 36 per cent of the total value of exports was the product of native enterprise. Natives produced 49 per cent of the export value of rubber, 67 per cent of that of coffee, and 95 per cent of that of coconut products. The general situation is that of a relatively efficient and highly specialized agricultural development which has scarcely more than kept pace with the population growth and now faces the limit of its expansion with the growth potential of the population unchecked.

The depression made necessary the immediate facing of a problem that had to be met in the near future at any event. Government statisticians point out that a continued increase of 1.5 per cent per year would yield a population of 116 million by the year 2000, an obviously impossible figure. The only solution that appeared to the government as having a reasonable chance of success was the planned colonization of the less densely settled Outer Provinces. Colonists transferred under this program increased from 13 thousand in 1936 to 45 thousand in 1939. Before the war the government had set an ambitious goal of 100 thousand colonists a year to be reached in eight years, the colonists to be carefully selected young married people in order to yield a maximum population reduction in the home islands. It was estimated that with an average annual emigration of 80 thousand couples with one child, the population of Java and Madura would increase from 42 million in 1930 to only 74 million in 2000—a density of a little over 1,400 persons per square mile. However, apparently scant attention was given to the need for innovations calculated to reduce fertility and check population growth at its source. The experience of the Netherlands Indies exemplifies the fact that good administration, of itself, offers no escape from the dilemma of all-consuming growth.

The Philippine Islands illustrate the problems of a less congested area where considerable improvement in health and education has been effected with unusual rapidity. Fortunately, the pressure here is less than in either Java or India, the average density being only slightly more than half that of India and one-sixth that of Java and Madura. This relative sparsity does not arise from factors fundamentally different from those of the other two areas, but simply from the fact that the Philippines have been under the control of a progressive nation for a shorter length of time. Thanks to efforts since 1900 in the fields of public health and education illiteracy stands at 51 per cent and death rates are now relatively low, probably between 21 and 31—the lowest among Asiatic colonial populations. However, 76 per cent of the people are dependent on agriculture, and only 11 per cent live in communities of 10,000 or more inhabitants. Birth rates remain those characteristic of colonial peoples, being probably between 42 and 52 per 1,000. Natural increase in peacetime probably ranged between 17 and 27. Between 1918 and 1939 the population apparently increased by an average annual rate of 2.2 per cent. Maintenance of this increase would double the population in about 32 years. The problem of the Philippines is less pressing than that of Java or India because the carrying capacity of the Islands is less fully utilized. However, at recent rates of growth it will not require many decades for congestion to become severe.

The fundamental causes of rising population pressures are substantially the same in all densely settled colonial areas. Prior to the advent of modern government, more efficient economic production, and elementary sanitation, death rates were very high and populations were more or less in balance at the densities possible with inadequate economic techniques. All such societies, if they are to survive, must have high fertility, and universally their social structures are those that elicit high birth rates.[2] Family form and function, religious doctrine, and community custom are all focused toward the maintenance of high fertility. High evaluations are placed on the perpetuation of the family, clan, or other group, but low evaluations on the individual and his welfare. These values are deeply imbedded and rigidly enforced by social sanctions. Even under the impact of a rapidly shifting environment, they change only gradually.

At the first advent of the European, native populations were often decimated, and occasionally wiped out, by exposure to diseases to which they had no immunity. However, after the initial stages, mortality began to decline.[3] The areas have been developed by the technologically advanced countries primarily as sources of agricultural and mineral raw materials, often of a specialized kind, and as markets for manufactured goods. Such development has required the introduction of strong government, improved transportation, simple sanitation, and a modicum of epidemic control, together in many instances with sufficiently ameliorated living conditions to ensure a supply of tolerably efficient labor—the whole often stimulated and supported by genuinely humanitarian ideals. All such innovations reduce mortality.

Fertility, on the other hand, has declined not at all or very little. In fact, the only societies in which low birth rates have appeared are those dominated by the values developed in modern urban life.[4] Such societies set great store by the individual, his health, welfare, initiative, and advancement. They develop a rational and materialistic outlook on life, view man as the master of his own destiny, and come to hold the deliberate control of fertility to be as reasonable and desirable as that of mortality. The transition from the earlier set of values to the new individualistic ones is gradual. Therefore, universally the decline in the birth rate lags behind that of the death rate until both reach rather low levels. The interim affords a period of rapid population growth. Europe is only now coming to the end of its period of expansion.

The uses to which technologically backward regions have been put, and the nature of the policies of dominant nations toward them, have been such as to impede the transition to low fertility. Agricultural life has been promoted; native industries have faced the competition of established industries of technologically advanced countries. Industrialization and urbanization have developed very gradually. Moreover, in general and especially under the more enlightened colonial regimes, there has been considerable protection of native customs, religions, and social organization, all of which foster the maintenance of high fertility. In short, the technologically advanced nations have disseminated and imposed that part of their culture which reduces mortality, while withholding, or at least failing to foster the transfer of, that part of their culture out of which the rational control of fertility and the small-family pattern develop. The population grows a good deal as it did in the West, but unlike the situation in the West, the growth stage has not been accompanied by the social changes that eventually lead to an end of expansion.

The significance of rapid growth for future political and economic development in the areas under consideration depends on a variety of factors, such as the stage of economic development, the resources on which new industries may be based, the outlets for settlement, the sheer size of the populations, and the future policies of the dominant powers toward them.

Given a perpetuation of the past policies of developing the regions primarily as sources of raw materials, it is altogether probable that population will increase more rapidly than the means of subsistence in some areas. In such cases hunger, pestilence, and war will remain the major controls of growth in any future that matters. The areas will undergo recurrent catastrophes that will shock the conscience of the world. They will be increasingly expensive and troublesome to administer, and unsatisfactory to do business with. Of themselves they will be too impotent to threaten the peace, but probably they will be discontented, disloyal, and ready, if somewhat inefficient, materials for each new political conflagration. India is a likely candidate for this group.

Other regions, those whose readily available resources are now less fully developed, may emerge with sufficient political unity and industrial strength to give their growing numbers power. Failing to find a solution to their problems within their own borders, they may easily become threats to world peace by their endeavors to expand. Sections of the Near East and China are perhaps the most likely candidates in this group.

Neither of these situations is satisfactory from the point of view of the humanitarian ideals, economic interests, and the peaceful security of the United States. Its interests are almost as directly involved as are those of the major colonial powers and, in an ultimate sense, they are more directly involved in the problems of areas not under its control than in those of the smaller areas that it governs. Since past policies have failed to prevent the development of critical situations, it is necessary to consider possible alternatives to their re-establishment.

THE POSSIBILITIES FOR CHECKING GROWTH. The obvious solution to the demographic problem of the regions under consideration might seem to lie in measures designed to check growth. There are only three factors to manipulate: birth, death, and migration. Losses can be increased by raising mortality and stimulating emigration, or gains can be reduced by checking fertility. However, since none of these factors is independent of the others, the problems are far from simple.

Death rates could be permitted to rise; indeed it will be difficult to prevent their rise. Policies designed to yield such a trend are occasionally suggested as a temporary expedient to obtain release from pressure, pending a decline in fertility. However, as will appear below, the suggestion is based on a misconception of the factors governing growth. A period of increasing mortality would in fact impede the developments essential to induce a decline in fertility. Rising mortality in the areas under consideration means in reality rising population pressure, and not a solution to that pressure.

Moreover, it is essential to remember that death rates remain high, and that such improvements as have taken place are largely the result of innovations essential to the economic development of the regions on whose specialized products much of the economic welfare of the West depends. A deterioration of existing conditions would disrupt the economies of the regions. Increasing economic intercourse between West and East cannot be profitably maintained in the face of recurrent catastrophes or lower levels of physical health than already exist.

Any policy that permits an increase of mortality would not solve the problems of population pressure and would adversely affect the economic interest of the American citizen, as well as grossly offend his humanitarian attitudes. It could be rationally advocated only as a means of weakening the power of peoples that might at a later date gain sufficient strength to threaten the security of the Western world.

Emigration obviously increases the losses of the sending population. However, it does not necessarily reduce the size of the total population. If fertility is so high that the population is pressing on the means of subsistence, and mortality is the principal check to growth, emigration will temporarily relieve that pressure, but will then lower mortality and increase growth to cancel the effect of the outward movement. Other factors remaining equal, in this situation emigration would not permanently alter the problems of the sending areas, but would vastly increase the total size of the sending stock in the world. Thus the calculations of officials in the Netherlands Indies are somewhat naive. They presuppose the maintenance of a rate of increase of 1.5 per cent per year until the year 2000 for Java-Madura, then subtract quotas of migrants. In the absence of rather profound changes in the economy, there is no reason to suppose that the growth could be maintained at that level, or that the population of Java-Madura would be any less with the scheduled migration than without it.

Whether emigration can reduce population depends largely on the magnitude of the migration in relation to the parental stock, on the duration of the movement, and on intervening social developments. These factors are principally a function of the size of the population under consideration. Emigration as the sole solution to the problems of Egypt, India, China, Java-Madura, and other areas would increase the number of Egyptians, Indians, Chinese, and so on without substantially altering the problems or conditions of life in their countries, at the same time probably tending to create similar conditions in the areas of destination.

On the other hand, heavy and lasting emigration from small to large regions, as, for example, from Puerto Rico to the United States (or the past migration from Ireland), would assist the development of social changes out of which low fertility develops, thereby facilitating a permanent solution. The solution depends on the availability of receiving areas. Analogous migrations probably could help solve the problems of many small congested islands in the Pacific.

In general, however, emigration will not check growth in the most important areas of population pressure at the present stage of their demographic evolution. It would be unfortunate to waste the open spaces of the world in a fashion that could only intensify future problems of adjustment.

It is frequently suggested that efforts should be made to reduce birth rates before further declines in the death rate are permitted. To this end there are some advocates of the view that a widespread dissemination of contraceptive knowledge and materials should replace efforts now being made in the field of public health. The proposal arises from a misunderstanding of the factors controlling fertility, and of the role of birth control. Both indirect evidence and that of pertinent experiments have shown that:

1. Populations whose social institutions and personal aspirations are those developed in high mortality cultures are little interested in contraception and will not make effective use of the methods normally at their disposal. Of course, in nearly all cultures some individuals practice contraception and resort to a variety of other controls of fertility. However, they do not do so in sufficient numbers and with sufficient effectiveness to bring about any very substantial reduction of the fertility of the group.

2. Conversely, populations whose institutions and personal aspirations are those of modern individualistic cultures will control their fertility in substantial degree with or without the assistance of modern contraceptive techniques. Nearly all peoples have at their disposal the knowledge of contraceptive practices that are in fact used with great effectiveness in some populations.

The dissemination of contraceptive knowledge as the *sole* solution to the problems of population pressure is of little importance. In an appropriate social-economic setting, birth control propaganda, contraceptive and other, and birth control clinics undoubtedly can and do serve important educational purposes, and can be very useful in hastening the reduction of fertility. Contraception is an important means, among others, by which people can control their fertility. Whether they control it depends on the social setting; hence new patterns of behavior are to be established principally by the alteration of that setting.

From the foregoing analysis it must be concluded that, in the regions under consideration, population growth can be promptly checked only by rising mortality. However, that check would afford no solution to the problems of population pressure, and would react unfavorably on the immediate economic interests of our own population and on that of other dominant powers.

SOLUTIONS TO PROBLEMS OF POPULATION PRESSURE. There is no quick demographic solution to the problems of population pressure in the areas under consideration. However, there are solutions, at least in principle. Population pressure in the short run is no more a matter of too many people than it is of too little product. Pressures may therefore be relieved by a rapid expansion of product. It is not the problem of doubling, or perhaps even tripling, the product of backward regions that staggers the imagination; it is the need for an indefinite continuation of such an expansion in order to keep up with an unending growth. The demographic problem is not that of putting an immediate end to growth, but of checking growth before the populations become unmanageably large—for example, before the present numbers are doubled. The immediate and pressing demographic problem, therefore, is the early reduction of the potentialities for future growth.

Paradoxically, a reduction of the growth potentialities can be achieved only on terms of increased population growth in the near future. Both mortality and fertility have a long way to fall before a balance is achieved. Fertility declines will come gradually and only after the people acquire new interests and aspirations. These new interests are likely to develop only in a period of rising levels of living, urbanization, widespread education, and growing contacts with foreign cultures. All such developments would initially reduce mortality more rapidly than fertility and therefore temporarily enhance growth. In its analogous period of transition from high to low vital rates, European population increased from two to fourfold. There is little reason to suppose, if the situation is allowed to drift along past lines, that today's backward people could accomplish their vital transition with less growth.

The crux of the problem is the greatest possible reduction of the lag between the downward trends of mortality and fertility. If relief from population pressure is the goal, it is dangerous to continue frittering away the productive power of modern techniques in a social setting calculated to maintain high fertility. There is urgent need to apply in synchronized fashion every device for the creation of a social setting favorable to reduced fertility. This in fact would require a complete and integrated program of modernization.[5]

Something of the scope of changes required to bring as rapid a decline of fertility as possible is suggested by the following outline.

1. Economic—The Substitution Within Feasible Limits of the Rounded for the Colonial Economy

a. The development of industries to support large urban populations. Such a development takes people out of their former context, breaks the cake of custom, and permits the growth of new individualistic aspirations. Moreover, it is essential to draw a surplus and ineffective agricultural population into effective production. The development of light industries, such as textiles, in which women can be employed away from the home, is especially important as a means of giving women new independence and a milieu for the dissemination of new ideas.

b. The rationalization and extension of agriculture. Such rationalization would include the improvement of techniques, the reform of land tenures and credit systems, the development of new areas, and such diversification of production as the requirements of high productivity permit. It would not include the extension of subsistence farming as a substitute for commercial agriculture.

c. The promotion of international trade. Trade is one of the most important means of diffusing new ideas and attitudes.

2. Educational

The rapid extension of popular education through all available mediums designed, unlike the education in some colonial systems, to create new wants for physical and material well-being, and the skills appropriate to modern techniques in industry and agriculture.

3. Birth Control

It is important that specific and widespread propaganda be directed to developing an interest in the health and welfare of children rather than in large families for their own sake. Such education would also involve propaganda in favor of controlled fertility as an integral part of a public health program. As a matter of economic necessity, the efforts would have to be confined largely to the educational level.

4. Public Health

The matter cannot be rigidly proved, but the writer is profoundly convinced that only a society in which the individual (child or adult) has a reasonable chance for survival in healthy life will develop that interest in the dignity and material well-being of the individual essential to the reduction of fertility. He therefore firmly believes in directly fostering public health *as part of the program required to reduce growth potential.*

5. Political

It is important to develop a native leadership that will acquire new values rapidly and serve as a medium for their diffusion. To this end native political leaders, civil servants, and native middle classes are needed.

6. Social

It is important that caste and other barriers to the advancement of the individual be broken down as rapidly as possible.

7. Migration

If a train of events of the sort suggested above were under way, migration could be of invaluable assistance in facilitating the transition to low fertility. Under such circumstances emigration becomes more than a substitute for reduced fertility. By relieving the pressure of population during the transitional stage of rapid growth, it fosters the rising levels of living essential to the maintenance of that transition. Much of Europe's migration to the United States has been of this character. If the curtailment of the growth potential is the object, the world's areas available for settlement should be reserved for migrants from regions in which the downward trend of fertility is already established. The empty regions are none too plentiful and should be used to some lasting effect.

Temporary migration, seasonal or other, should in all circumstances be encouraged as part of any program for the reduction of fertility. It is one of the most effective means of spreading new ideas, new skills, and new interests in the home population.

CONSIDERATIONS FOR AMERICAN POLICY. The foregoing analysis has indicated that a continuation of past policies toward the technologically undeveloped regions of dense settlement would almost certainly yield an intensification of population pressures with their resultant train of human poverty and suffering, perhaps to the extent of creating situations that are permanently insoluble. It has been pointed out that such a situation would adversely affect the immediate economic interests of this country and of other Western powers that are heavily dependent on the specialized products of these regions, and that the resulting catastrophes would grossly offend the humanitarian sensibilities of our people and the world.

The analysis has further shown that the escape from this situation of rising population pressure, if escape there be, lies in a highly complex and integrated program of modernization. Such a program would yield populations that would be larger and stronger than those that would arise from the perpetuation of past policies. By launching a program of modernization the now dominant powers would in effect be creating a future world in which their own peoples would become progressively smaller minorities, and possess a progressively smaller proportion of the world's wealth and power. The determination of national policy toward the undeveloped regions must be made in the light of that fact.

It is the writer's belief that the perpetuation of past policies toward undeveloped regions involves greater risks to the peaceful security of the American people than a policy consciously designed to create larger and more powerful populations in these areas.

A program of repression must be universally successful to prevent disturbances of the world peace. Such universally successful repression is hardly to be expected in a world in which the spread of education and modern technology has gone too far to be stopped. Almost inevitably some major population would acquire the political unity and industrial skill to give its people power while its growth potential remained high. In a world where dominant nations jealously withhold economic assistance, the emerging nation would receive new and punishing lessons on the impossibility of achieving a demographic balance within its own borders. Such people could be expected to learn these lessons, and to threaten the peace by their efforts to obtain a solution through expansion.

On the other hand, a program of modernization would amount to giving a practical demonstration for some decades of the possibility of achieving an internal solution to the most serious problems of population pressure on the basis of industrial production, increasingly efficient agriculture, and world trade. The fact that the demographic problems were on the way toward solution would, of course, be no guarantee of peaceful inclinations, as the present experience with Japan amply proves. Many other factors are involved in the formation of an aggressive spirit. However, it would mean that one stimulus to aggression would be removed, and that there would be large vested interests in the perpetuation of peace.

Although the writer prefers to accept the risks of modernization, he doubts in fact that the choice of policy will, or should, be exclusively based on the balancing of distant risks. Other considerations seem more compelling and sounder bases for the formulation of policy in the light of values held by the American people. The immediate economic interests of the American people lie in the direction of a program of modernization of backward areas. Such a program would permit the continuation and expansion of mutually profitable economic intercourse, and there are powerful pressure groups to call that fact to the public attention. Of even greater importance is the fact that such a program of modernization coincides with the humanitarian ideals deeply imbedded in our culture.

The above consideration suggests that:

1. The interests of the United States, and of other major powers, are deeply involved in the problem of population pressure in technologically backward areas.
2. A goal of American policy, and of that of other leading powers, with respect to such areas should be to foster a reduction of the potentialities for population growth.

If this goal is accepted, it is essential to realize that:

1. There is no simple nor quick solution. The goal can be achieved, if at all, only by an integrated program of modernization, designed to establish a social milieu in which fertility will come under control.
2. Any such program requires the review of all social, economic, and political innovations from the point of view of their impact on fertility. Such a review can be made only with much more information about the details of social organization of each area than is now at hand.
3. The requisite changes cannot be made without the assistance of the dominant powers. Neither can they be imposed by them. They can only be developed cooperatively with leaders in the areas concerned.
4. Since the interests of all nations are affected by the population growth of such areas, there should be appropriate international machinery for the consideration of broad policy with respect to such areas, for the formulation of policy with respect to international migration and settlement, and for the rendering of technical assistance.
   Such an agency, or at least some agency, should also be concerned with fostering the development of information by which the demographic situations of these areas could be accurately appraised.
5. Having regard to the fact that any program of the sort suggested will be exceedingly difficult to carry out, it would be wise to concentrate the most intensive efforts on regions in which there are reasonable prospects for success. India is probably the last region on such a list. There, a deterioration of the existing situation will be avoided only with great difficulty, and a major catastrophe is easily within the bounds of possibility.
6. The United States is in the unpleasant position of having an interest in the demographic development of large areas outside its political control, while having

conspicuously failed to solve the much simpler problems of smaller areas that it has governed. If it is to urge its interest in the colonial policies of other nations, it should undertake an energetic attack on the problems of its own colonial areas, notably those of Puerto Rico.

REFERENCES

1. Though official figures are available, many births and deaths are not registered, so that published rates are clearly too low.

2. There is no evidence that innate biological differences in the ability to reproduce, if they exist, have been of substantial importance in creating the differences in reproduction. Differences in social attitudes toward controls of fertility have been the dominant factors.

3. Statistical records throughout the areas under consideration are highly inadequate and inaccurate, so that careful assessment of the trends over long periods is impossible.

4. There have been instances of fertility rates inadequate for the maintenance of a stationary population, but only under conditions of mortality rates that were high by modern standards. A fertility that would be sufficient only to maintain a stationary population in ancient Rome, where the expectation of life at birth probably did not exceed 30 years, would maintain rapid growth in a population with an expectation of life at birth of 60 years.

5. The question may be raised whether the transition to low fertility can be made by the peoples of today's undeveloped regions even under the most favorable conditions. Will people living in different climates, having different racial origins and widely different cultural backgrounds, modify their reproductive behavior in response to changing environments in the same way that persons of European origins have done? The weight of available evidence suggests that they will. That evidence cannot be marshalled in the present paper, but two or three points may be noted.

There is clear evidence that fertility is not primarily a matter of race or climate. Examples of fertility of the European type exist among all important races and in all important climates. Neither is low fertility a characteristic of European culture as such. The low fertility of today came only as the modern technological, urbanized society developed. Moreover, in cultures as diverse as those of the Soviet Union, Eastern Europe, Western Europe, New England and the Southern United States, and Australia, there has been a notable similarity in the way trends toward lower fertility have developed in relation to improving health, increasing urbanization, and rising educational and economic status. Careful study of these patterns suggests that well-rounded modernization is susceptible of transfer to people of widely different cultural backgrounds, and elicits similar modifications of reproductive behavior.

The conclusion is supported by the experience of Japan. There is clear evidence that its demographic behavior closely parallels that of Western Europe as to its time trends and its geographic and social-economic patterns. The lower fertility of large cities than of rural areas in India is further evidence of the same sort. However, the apparent failure of the differentials to increase in recent years, and their virtual absence in Egypt, should serve as a warning. Western patterns of reproduction cannot be expected to develop from the imposition on other cultures of one or two gross externals of Western life. More adequate knowledge of the precise determinants of reproductive behavior, especially in the many Oriental cultures, would undoubtedly permit greater efficiency in inducing a fertility decline, and this knowledge is among that most urgently needed in the field of demography. Pending its acquisition, we must assume that the reduction of fertility among today's backward peoples will come only in response to a combination of the major elements which preceded that response in the modern nations of the West.

MOBILITY AS A FIELD OF ECONOMIC RESEARCH*

By D. Gale Johnson

The history of all industrial nations has had several things in common. One of the more important common characteristics has been the declining significance of agriculture in the national economy. In the United States the rapid advances in agricultural technology, the high birth rates in farm areas, and the slow growth of demand have necessitated a large transfer of labor from agricultural to urban employment.

The magnitude of the farm-to-urban migration, and the large reverse movement, may well surprise many. Between 1920 and 1946 some 45 million people moved from farms to nonfarm areas. About 28 million did exactly the opposite—returned from cities and villages to the farms. Yet the net movement of 17 millions must be considered to have been large. Large as the net of farm movement was, not until World War II was any substantial reduction achieved in farm population.[1]

Consequently at the beginning of World War II there were in agriculture far more people than could earn satisfactory incomes. This was true of even the best agricultural areas. Even after the large reduction in farm population during the war, at least half—perhaps more—of American agriculture is still subject to serious excess supplies of labor.

The excess supply of labor in agriculture is significant from two points of view. One is the effect which the excess employment in agriculture has upon the total national product or income, or, put another way, the efficiency with which the nation's resources, particularly labor, are used. A second point of reference is the impact of a too large supply of labor upon the level of per capita farm incomes.

Not all of the inefficiency existing in agriculture, nor all of the low incomes, are due to a larger population in agriculture than can obtain a level of earnings equivalent to that received by labor of comparable skills elsewhere. Yet so many of the forces leading to inefficiency and low incomes are related to excess supply of labor that one must accept the overwhelming importance of migration and mobility in seeking a solution to the resource and income problems in agriculture.

The social and political significance of the problems related to migration and mobility are alone sufficient to warrant extensive research investigations. But research in mobility is important from another standpoint. Mobility, as an empirical aspect of human behavior, has had the interest of social scientists

* Reprinted from *The Southern Economic Journal*, 15 (October 1948), pp. 152–161, by permission of the author and publisher. (Copyright 1948 by the Southern Economic Association.)

in several different disciplines. Consequently, for this reason and because of the nature of the problem, mobility and migration offer considerable opportunities for joint and cooperative research by individuals specializing in the study of different aspects of social behavior. For the most part, the following approach bears the imprint of the training of the writer as an economist.

I

Viewed pragmatically, analysis of the nature, extent, results, and motivating factors of private migration as it has occurred in the past is important for two reasons: (1) Why has private and unguided migration failed to equate labor returns in agriculture and the rest of the economy? (2) What conditions are conducive to achieving the optimum rate of migration and mobility? These two points are important because of their implications to the formulation and promulgation of agricultural policy. In addition, systematic analysis of migration and mobility can add significantly to our body of knowledge and generalizations concerning social behavior. In a dynamic and changing world, there is probably no adjustment of greater significance than is involved in migration.

Our insight into the basic characteristics of migration has been extended only modestly since Ravenstein's epic study, "The Laws of Migration," published in 1885.[2] From an analysis of English census data, Ravenstein set forth seven "laws of migration." He found that migrants move only short distances and that females are more migratory than males. He showed that migration proceeds through a process of absorption—individuals near an attracting center move to that center, others move into the area left, and so on. Migration thus occurs in stages, though specific individuals may make only one move. Ravenstein also found that each main current of migration is accompanied by a countercurrent.[3]

Additional empirical generalizations have been developed with reference to American experience. The more important may be briefly noted. Youth and young adults are more migratory than older people. Small family units are more likely to migrate than large. Males move longer distances than females. Regional or area differentials in the net rate of rural-urban migration seem to be related to the economic status of the areas in a manner fulfilling analytical expectations. In addition, regional or area differentials are affected by the proximity of the area to large cities—the attracting centers.

Perhaps the most significant of the generalizations explaining migration has been that net off-farm migration is closely related to the availability of job opportunities in nonfarm sectors of the economy. People leave farming communities when unemployment is of modest proportions; when unemployment is high the migration is small.[4]

It should, however, be possible to go beyond empirical generalizations of this sort, important as they are, to a theoretical schema that will be capable of explaining the important aspects of behavior involved in migration and mobility. Such a theoretical formulation should include, first of all, a reasonable explanation of the important motivating factors. Though there undoubtedly are a number of more or less personal factors—such as illness, physical disability, desire to be near family members, and poor relations between landlord and tenant, for example—it seems reasonable to presume that the most significant motive underlying rural migration is the desire for improved economic conditions.

The theoretical formulation should also provide a set of generalizations regarding the conditions conducive to (or retarding) migration sufficiently powerful to explain the great variations in the extent that migration has reduced the degree of excess labor supply. Emphasis would undoubtedly be placed upon the effects of urbanization, level of education, racial and ethnic differences, past incomes, savings, and the cost of movement.

Broadly speaking, it may be said that over the past 30 years private migration has failed to eliminate the excess of labor in agriculture. Migration has been inadequate to equalize economic opportunity, either within agriculture or between agriculture and the rest of the economy. Yet the disparities in opportunity would have been greater at any particular time if less migration had occurred.

II

The effects of mobility and migration, either in response to positive policy or in the absence of any policy, can be evaluated only in terms of certain goals or objectives. There are two broad goals toward which a mobility policy should be oriented. The two goals are: (1) Labor in agriculture should receive real economic returns equivalent to the returns in other sectors of the economy for work of comparable skill, training, and difficulty. (2) Farm families should receive sufficient income to provide a socially accepted minimum scale of living.

The mere enunciation of the two goals does not make them relevant guides for the evaluation of the results of migration and mobility. From the economic point of view it can be argued that the two goals are important and significant. But it should be possible to go beyond the theoretical formulation of economics to determine suitable objectives. Research undertakings should emphasize the possibilities and necessities of applying systematic methods of study of acceptable social goals. The materials which must be scrutinized are probably different from those usually studied by most of us. It seems evident, however, that a study of past and current legislation, the statements and positions of various interest groups, the attitudes of the press and political parties, and the objectives and purposes of social action dealing with related problems can indicate what goals and objectives are likely to be acceptable.

The two goals noted above have rather distinct implications. The first— equivalence of real economic returns—is a necessary condition for efficient utilization of resources. However, this goal accepts the resources as they are—

with their given level of productivity. The second goal implies that steps will be taken to insure a minimum level of investment in every individual. Poverty breeds poverty by restricting the development of productivity—skills, attitudes, mental capabilities—in youth. Labor productivity is produced in the same sense as any other type of productivity. If the second goal is achieved, all individuals will be assured of a certain level of investment and, given their innate capacities, a certain level of productivity to serve as a basis for earning power.

However, research must go beyond the statement of goals in so general a context. The goals must be given an empirical formulation to permit their application to concrete situations. The empirical formulation of the concepts is required for later aspects of research on migration and mobility as well as for testing the effectiveness of actual policies.

Two general problems must be solved in applying the first goal. One is the determination of labor returns in agriculture. Because the farmer supplies most of the labor, capital, and land, the determination of labor returns is a difficult task. The other is the evaluation in real terms of the monetary incomes in agriculture and in other segments of the economy. It may, of course, be necessary to broaden the concept of equivalent real income to take into account other attributes of work and life in agricultural and urban areas. Such considerations as the quality of public services, uncertainty, difficulty of work, and similar phenomena may have to be given weight.

The goal of a minimum scale of living presents the same problems of comparison as are presented in calculating equivalent returns. In addition there is the problem of determining the actual content of an accepted minimum. Though there does not seem to be any "scientific" solution to the question, various specialists—nutritionists, educators, social service workers, economists —can make clear to policy making groups the implications and effects of various minimum levels. Furthermore, while there may be considerable disagreement about some parts of the budget, other elements such as education, health service, and perhaps food may be subjects of considerable unanimity.

III

An adequate analysis of the required movement of labor out of agriculture if the goals are to be met should consider regions or areas of considerable homogeneity. However, as an indication of the magnitude of the required change of employment, some crude estimates are made for the nation as a whole. It should be noted that the method used is inferior to others that might be employed.[5]

Stated simply, the achievements of the migration goals in the short run require that labor must leave agriculture until the real returns in agriculture are the same as for comparable labor elsewhere. In estimating the amount of migration and change of occupation required to bring about an equivalence of returns, certain empirical formulations are required. One is the determination of differences in the purchasing power of income in different occupations and places of residence. This problem is not considered in detail here. On the basis of extremely crude manipulations, it may be said that the purchasing power of income on farms is (roughly) a fourth to a third greater than the income received by factory workers in small and large cities.[6]

Another problem of an empirical nature is the determination and segregation of the various components of agricultural income.[7] A third is the consideration of the effect of a change in the agricultural labor force on the output of agricultural products and thus gross farm income. The degree of inefficiency in agriculture and the failure to use capital in appropriate amounts leads the writer to the conclusion that, after a short period of adjustment, employment in agriculture could fall by at least a quarter—perhaps a third—before output declined. In fact, given one to two decades for readjustment, output might be larger with a smaller than with a larger labor force.[8]

If it is remembered that the purchasing power of income on farms is perhaps a third larger than income received by factory workers, the following income comparisons are of significance (on a per worker basis):

	1939	1944	1946
1. Net agricultural income	$ 510	$1,560	$1,885
2. Net total farm income[9]	670	1,960	2,310
3. Labor income from agriculture[10]	380	985	1,270
4. Annual income of hired farm workers[11]	380	1,005	1,181
5. Labor income—commercial farms[12]	540	1,375	1,795
6. Labor income—all farm workers—all sources	540	1,335	1,695
7. Income of employed factory workers	1,200	2,325	2,240

It is obvious that in 1939 farm incomes, regardless of how calculated, were considerably below the incomes of factory workers. The highest of the figures —net total farm income—is only $670 or considerably less than the income of factory workers. The most comparable estimate of farm labor income is that of labor income on commercial farms (roughly the largest 50 per cent) of $540. This is at least a third lower than the factory worker income, after adjustments are made for differences in living costs.

By 1944 there was a considerable improvement in the relative status of agricultural workers. The real labor income of workers on commercial farms was probably only slightly below that of factory workers. If an adjustment were made for nonfarm labor income, income equivalence might have been achieved. However, the workers on 3,000,000 farms received considerably less than the $1,660 received by workers on commercial farms. This is indicated by the average labor income on all farms of $940. Though there is undoubtedly some over-estimate of the actual labor performed on the smaller half of the farms, the data indicate extremely low income.

How many people must leave agriculture to equalize income earning opportunities? In part the answer depends upon how well the economy as a whole is operating. The higher the level of employment and incomes the greater the number of people that could remain in agriculture.[13] In 1940 there were approximately 10,600,000 man-years of work performed in agriculture. Our estimates indicate that 2.5 to 3.5 million fewer workers than were employed in 1940 would permit attaining the goal of equivalent incomes.

If 1939 cost, price, income, and employment conditions represented long-run expectations there might well be 4,000,000 farm units employing 7,000,000 farm workers and providing a place of residence for 20,000,000 farm people. This estimate, crude as it is, was arrived at in the following manner: (a) There were about 950,000 farms that provided labor returns equivalent to the earnings of factory workers. These farms provided employment for 2,750,000 workers. (b) There were about 1,250,000 farms that may be classified as nominal farms. They are so designated because the total value of product was less than $750 and no power source was owned by the operator. These farms include largely part-time, residence, retirement and gentlemen's farms. It is assumed that no change should be made in the number or size of these farms as most of the operators do not depend upon farming for their livelihood. These farms provided employment for 1,300,000 workers.[14] (c) There were an additional 125,000 farms reporting little or no labor. Presumably these farms represent land left fallow or idle, farms operated on a share arrangement, or part-time and residence. (d) The remaining 3,825,000 farms provided employment for 6,650,000 workers. These farms must be considered to be of inadequate size. The largest percentage of the farms provided a labor income per worker of less than $500 in 1939. (e) On the basis of land and buildings required per worker to obtain an adequate labor income in 1939, the 3,825,000 farms should be replaced by no more than 1,500,000 farms with 3,000,000 to 3,500,000 workers.[15]

If 1941 cost, price, employment, and income relationships represented long-run expectations there would be more—but not many more—job opportunities in agriculture than under 1939 conditions. While labor income on commercial farms increased from $540 to $790, factory workers' income increased from $1205 to $1495. The absolute increase in industrial workers' income was the greater, but farm workers gained relatively. Another factor in improving the position of nonfarm workers was the reduction of unemployment from 16 to 6 per cent. As a result, the increased urban opportunities almost offset the gains made by agriculture. At most, it would seem that farm employment might be about 250,000 higher than under 1939 conditions.

If 1944 cost, price, income, and employment conditions represented long-run expectations, one might anticipate that a total farm labor force of 8,000,-000 might be adequately employed. Most of the movement out of agriculture would occur in the South. The total farm population might be slightly more than 23,000,000 compared to more than 30,000,000 in 1940 and 27,000,000 in 1946.

When the migration and mobility goal is achieved, there will remain a continuing need for a relatively large net out-migration from agriculture. An annual movement of 250,000 to 300,000 people including about 80,000 to

100,000 adult workers will be required merely to offset the excess of births over deaths. This off-farm movement should be compared with actual experience in recent years if one is to understand its importance.[16]

In addition, if the past is an adequate guide for the future, more workers will be displaced by technological advance. How important this will be depends largely upon the rate of growth of national income and the rate of technological advance in agriculture. It would not seem unreasonable, however, to assume that the annual rate might be as high as 50,000 workers (150,000 people) for at least two decades. If this were true, the net off-farm migration might have to be in the neighborhood of 400,000 or more per year to maintain an equilibrium position once it had been reached.

IV

Mobility of the human agent out of agriculture can take two principal forms: (1) a change of residence to an urban area and (2) a change of occupation involving part-time or full-time nonfarm employment by one or more members of the family, who retain residence on the farm. Most of the mobility that has occurred in the past has been of the first type—actual migration. There are many interested individuals who would like to encourage the second. For the present, however, we shall be concerned only with actual migration of people out of agriculture.

The impact of migration and rural depopulation on the social and economic structure of rural communities represents an interesting area of analysis and research. By and large, relatively little is known of these effects. The nature of the problem can perhaps be best posed by raising the extreme question: When does the population density of an area become so limited that on both social and economic grounds the area should be completely depopulated? It may well be that a minimum density is required to support the functioning of basic institutions and services, such as schools, churches, roads, medical care, markets, and police protection.

In the less extreme cases, some attention should be devoted to the ways and means rural communities may utilize to adapt themselves to a reduced population. Many ways of doing things become obsolete. Changes are required. An important consideration is the effect on the cost of schools, public services such as roads, public utilities, and churches. In most instances rural depopulation is likely to be cost increasing.

Yet such a conclusion is not a valid argument against migration. In fact, one might anticipate that the effect of reduced population density, up to a certain point, would increase incomes much more rapidly than the aforementioned cost. Consequently the ability to pay the increased costs of services may increase more rapidly than the costs. Past experience has certainly indicated that within wide ranges the density of farm population is inversely related to the quality of rural education and other services.

Equally as important as the increased cost of services is the necessary readjustment of the modes of operation of such institutions as the church, school, and local government.

The reduction of farm population density will have significant repercussions upon the local trading centers and commercial institutions serving the area. Migration of farm people will probably be accompanied by a reduction in village and town population—or the so-called rural nonfarm population. Not only will fewer people be required in villages and towns, but the nature and character of services will change as rural population declines.

V

Though the most important end of a mobility policy is that of achieving equivalent returns for comparable resources, two important conditions should be accepted as guides in the selection of means and the operation of the policy. One condition is that the mobility policy should try to minimize the social disorganization of the rural community as it is depopulated. The other is that the mobility policy should aid in creating the most favorable economic development of the resources of the areas involved.

At the present there seems to be little to say concerning the necessary measures to minimize social disorganization. This is an area requiring analysis and research. In this case the trite thing may be the correct one, namely, that education which creates an awareness of the basic problem confronting the poorer agricultural areas and shows the necessity of migration may do much to permit the community to plan for and adjust to the new situation.

Nor does there seem to be much that can be said, given our present knowledge, about measures required to develop the total resources of a rural community, area, or region. The desirability of increased investment and industrialization in the overpopulated areas seems evident, if the long-run expectation is that such investments will prove profitable. If subsidies are necessary to encourage original investment, such subsidies should not be ruled out.

The desirability of developing new opportunities for employment near the excess labor supply lies in the relationship between distance and the rate of migration. If the cost of movement, the degree of the break in family or community ties, and the relative change in environment can be minimized, migration will occur more rapidly and probably result in fewer disappointments and less personal and social disorganization.

What major features should a mobility policy have? One cannot be sure at present, yet there are a few evident things that would need to be done:

1. The productivity of many persons on farms must be improved through more and better education, improved nutrition, increased medical and dental facilities, and superior sanitation.

2. The education afforded rural people must be such as to permit individuals more readily to adapt themselves to an urban environment. This probably

means less rather than more vocational education. Emphasis should be placed upon an understanding of economic, social, and political processes.

3. A system of grants and loans must be established to aid people who wish to migrate. If you are poor enough, you may not have the funds necessary to pay transportation costs or the necessary reserve to withstand the risk of unemployment.

4. A labor outlook program must be provided to give migrants a more adequate basis for choosing a particular destination and type of employment and a federal employment service that can obtain jobs in advance of migrating.

5. The maintenance of a high level of employment is not only a desirable goal in itself, but is a basic precondition for the successful operation of a mobility policy.

Given our existing political framework and general moral and social values, migration will have to be undertaken by the individual involved on a voluntary basis. The final decisions will be made by those who migrate. The function of a mobility policy must be largely to create incentives that make movement desirable, to provide financial assistance under certain conditions, to give individuals the necessary data for making a rational choice, and, where possible, actually to obtain jobs for individuals before movement occurs.

VI

Our analysis of mobility and migration of the human resource in agriculture has considered at least five significant aspects. These may be described briefly as follows:

1. The extent, nature, motivating factors, and results of personally undertaken migration of people out of, within, and into agriculture. The emphasis should be upon the development of generalizations that explain the behavior involved in mobility and migration and the analysis of the effects and consequences of migration.

2. The socially accepted goals of a mobility policy. These goals should not be separated from the consideration of the general goals of the desired social-economic-political organization of our entire society.

3. The necessary amount and direction of migration and mobility required to achieve the migration goals. Consideration should be given to state or regional situations and the possibilities of migration from one agricultural area to another.

4. The effects of rural depopulation on the general social, economic, and political structure and institutions of rural communities.

5. A mobility policy that will facilitate the movement of people out of agriculture, minimize the social disorganization of rural communities, and make possible the most favorable economic development of the resources involved.

In this paper no attempt has been made to treat any one of these significant facets of migration in a definitive fashion. The purpose has been to indicate some of the significant issues that must be considered in research undertakings dealing with mobility and migration. Consideration of each of these aspects will give a broader focus to research than has generally been true of most research conducted in this field. As a result such research should serve as a more adequate base for policy formulation.

Migration and mobility is a field of study that cuts across the boundary lines of several social science disciplines. The economist is interested in migration as a means of improving resource allocation and the regional distribution of income. The sociologist is largely concerned with the impact of mobility and migration upon the community. The psychologist is likely to approach it in terms of the effect of migration upon personality development. The political scientist sees migration in terms of its effect upon the balance of power, particularly in its regional and occupational effects.

It is obvious that the nature of science makes it possible for each social scientist to concentrate upon that particular analytical element of social or individual behavior that can be conceptually isolated. But when policy formulation is at issue, social behavior as a concrete entity—and not separate analytical elements—is involved. Migration has such pervasive effects upon the whole fabric of human behavior that it is necessary to combine the insights of several social science disciplines if reasonable policy recommendations are to emerge.

REFERENCES

1. In 1920 farm population was 31.6 millions: in 1940, 30.3 millions, and in 1946, 26.8 millions. For data on farm population and migration, see *Farm Population Estimates, United States and Major Geographic Divisions, 1910–46*, issued by the Bureau of Agricultural Economics, June 1946.

2. E. G. Ravenstein, "The Laws of Migration," *Journal of the Royal Statistical Society*, June 1885.

3. Three articles on labor mobility in England by H. Makower, J. Marschak, and H. W. Robinson represent the most definitive work on migration from an economic viewpoint. These articles are published in *Oxford Economic Papers*, No 1. (Oct. 1938), pp. 83–123; No. 2 (May 1939), pp. 70–97, and No. 4 (Sept., 1940), pp. 39–62.

4. Cf. T. W. Schultz, *Agriculture in an Unstable Economy*, chap. IV.

5. A more refined technique would involve the derivation of production functions, the demand and supply functions for agricultural products, the demand and supply functions for labor and other resources, and certain general functions determining the level of economic activity. Cf. Trygve Haavelmo, "Quantitative Research in Agricultural Economics: The Interdependence Between Agriculture and the National Economy," *Journal of Farm Economics*, XXIX (1947), pp. 910–24.

6. Nathan Koffsky of the Bureau of Agricultural Economics had made certain preliminary studies in this field. He had compared the cost of living in farm and urban areas by pricing a farm budget at farm and urban prices and a budget of a city family at farm and urban prices. His results, which have not been published, were presented at the 1946 Income Conference of the National Bureau of Economic Research held in New York in November 1946.

Koffsky found that the farm budget cost 30 per cent more when valued at urban prices than when valued at prices paid by farm people. The urban budget cost 14 per cent more in the urban area. However, it may be argued that these cost of living differences are too small. Koffsky assumes that housing costs are the same in urban and farm areas. Assuming that comparable housing costs 30 per cent more in urban areas than on farms, Koffsky's cost of living differentials would be about 35 and 22 per cent.

7. This step is necessary to evaluate the income earned by comparable labor in the available nonagricultural occupations.

8. A fourth factor which warrants investigation is the effect of a large off-farm migration upon absolute and relative wages in those occupations best suited for the migrants. For Negroes and other individuals having very modest skills, the extent of migration might be sufficiently important to result in significant reductions in relative incomes for many off-farm migrants.

9. Includes income to farm people from off-farm labor and capital employed outside of agriculture owned by people living on farms.

10. Labor income of all farm workers, including farm operators, unpaid family labor, and wage labor. For method of making estimate see forthcoming article by writer, "Allocation of Agricultural Income," which is to appear in the *Journal of Farm Economics*.

11. The estimate of the annual income of hired farm workers is derived by dividing the total farm wage bill by the number of hired farm workers. For estimates of the wage bill, see "Net Farm Income and Parity Report: 1943," issued by the Bureau of Agricultural Economics, and *The Farm Income Situation*, June–July 1947.

12. Commercial farms include all farms that had a total value of products sold, traded, or used in excess of $600 in 1939.

13. Throughout in these estimates the assumption is made that farm migrants suffer the same amount of unemployment that prevails in the economy as a whole. Studies of census data for 1939 seem to substantiate the assumption that recent migrants to an area are as likely to be employed as natives.

14. Ronald W. Jones of the Bureau of Agricultural Economics has stated that the census data for 1939 indicate that many, if not most, of these farms do not have any outside source of income and are operated by men less than 65 years old. This information would indicate that the estimates of required migration are too small.

15. The basic assumption used in estimating the required net migration was that income per worker increases in a consistent fashion when the amount of capital and land per worker is increased. Cf. D. Gale Johnson, *Forward Prices for Agriculture*, pp. 91–108.

16. In 1938 net off-farm migration was 420,000; in 1939 it was 491,000.

FAMILY SUBSIDIES IN THE NETHERLANDS *

By William Petersen

That Holland is a demographic anomaly in Northwest Europe has long been recognized by social scientists. Its natality has been consistently the highest in this culture area, and its mortality (except for the war years) has generally been at one of the lowest rates in the world. The consequent increase in the population is startling, especially when compared with that of Northwest Europe as a whole, as in Table 1.

TABLE 1

POPULATION INCREASE IN THE NETHERLANDS AND THE REST OF
NORTHWEST EUROPE, 1850–1950

	Netherlands		Rest of Northwest Europe[a]	
	Mean		Mean	
	Population (thousands)	Percentage Increase	Population (thousands)	Percentage Increase
1846–1850	3,058		107,611	
1896–1900	5,026	64	149,251	39
1946–1950	9,784	95	189,993[b]	27

Compiled from R. R. Kuczynski, "The Measurement of Population Growth: Methods and Results" (London: Sidgwick & Jackson, 1935), supplemented by United Nations "Demographic Yearbooks" and "Monthly Bulletins of Statistics."

[a] Eire, United Kingdom, Norway, Sweden, Denmark, Germany,[b] Belgium, Luxemburg, France, Switzerland.

[b] For 1947–50, population figures were available for West Germany only; these were adjusted on the assumption that the ratio to the population of all of Germany remained the same as in 1946. However improbable this may be, the difference will not affect the total sufficiently to invalidate the comparison.

In the general upswing of the birth rate during and after the war, Holland's reached a maximum of 30.2 in 1946, almost half again as large as that of any other country in Northwest Europe. When the cohorts born in the middle 1940's begin to enter the labor market, this will increase by 50,000 to 75,000 persons per year—a disturbingly large figure for a country of this size.

Holland's economy, in contrast to its population, has deteriorated sharply from its prewar position. The Netherlands East Indies, which used to account for fully one-sixth of Holland's national income, is now independent Indonesia. Every element of the Dutch economy, from rollingstock to manpower, was depleted by the German occupation; and the difficulty of the postwar reconstruction has been aggravated by the general maladjustments of the

* Reprinted from *Marriage and Family Living*, 17 (August 1955), pp. 260–266, by permission of the author and publisher. (Copyright 1955 by the National Council on Family Relations.)

European economy. The contrast between the rapidly growing population and the war-damaged economy stripped of Indonesia has created an almost tangible population pressure. At all levels of social intercourse, the public is acutely aware of this. The government is attempting to alleviate it by sponsoring expensive industrialization and emigration programs, which to date have been only partly successful.[1]

It is against this background that Holland's new family endowment policy is being administered. Under such circumstances, whether family subsidies affect the birth rate is a decidedly relevant question; and this is the principal subject of this paper. Secondly, Holland affords an example of the interaction between Socialist and Catholic family policies, and of the consequent tendency of family subsidies, once they have been instituted, to grow in size and importance.

Advocates of a family endowment policy have been motivated by one or more of four general considerations:

1. Catholic philosophy: The natural unit of society is not the individual but the family, and wages should therefore be paid at least in part according to family needs, rather than individual worth.

2. Egalitarianism: Since in general there is a negative correlation between income and family size, family subsidies help effect a more equitable distribution of income.

3. Social welfare: The children of large families are often those who most need assistance.

4. Population: To the extent that the secular decline in the birth rate has been caused by economic factors, it can be checked by family subsidies.

These four principles are ranked in order of decreasing importance, from a fundamental norm to a contingent expedient of unproved value. In general, therefore, the strongest advocates of family subsidies have been Catholics, especially those most in accord with the doctrines of Leo XIII and in countries (particularly France) with especially low natality. Fascist countries (and, since the middle 1930's, the Soviet Union) have also uniformly adopted some mode of family endowment, particularly because of the assumed value to the nation of a rapidly growing population. Socialists and liberals, on the other hand, have been less consistent. In Anglo-Saxon countries, they have sometimes been among the most vigorous proponents of a family wage (for example, Eleanor Rathbone in Britain, Paul Douglas in the United States); but the historic role of continental Socialist parties and their affiliated trade unions has been forthright opposition, petering down in recent years to acquiescence.

Socialists are caught between two contradictory tenets, the underlying ideology of "To each according to his needs" and the trade union slogan of "Equal pay for equal work." In general, family subsidies are paid at the expense of the wages of unmarried workers—either directly, when the total wage fund remains equal, or indirectly, through the inflationary pressure created by an increase in income with no corresponding increase in production. This conflict of interest tends to weaken union solidarity, especially since employers' contributions to family subsidies have often been gained in place of other union demands. Moreover, unless administrative safeguards are established, various abuses are possible: undue interference in the worker's family life, discrimination against married workers, and others. Thus, in the decade following the First World War, when family endowment programs got under way in most countries, Socialists and trade unionists opposed them. In Limoges, CGT members went so far as to refuse to accept benefits after the system had been established; in Berlin, members of the metalworkers' union threatened to leave the organization unless the system was effectively opposed. However, it became increasingly difficult, particularly during the depression, to align this stand with fundamental Socialist principles; for one could hardly find a more direct translation of "To each according to his needs" into social action than a law regulating workers' pay according to the number of minor children they had to support. Fundamental opposition to family subsidies, therefore, tended to give way to differences over administration and other details.

In Holland,[2] the family-subsidy principle began as a wholly Catholic concept. The Minister of Labor during the depression following the First World War, P. J. M. Aalberse, was a Catholic economist of progressive views. At his initiative, the government established the Supreme Council of Labor (*Hoge Raad van Arbeid*) to give it information and advice on economic and social questions, and this Council stimulated a rapid extension of Holland's social legislation.[3] Articles by Aalberse in the *Catholic Social Weekly* advocating family subsidies were supported by such larger works as *The Regulation of Pay Rates According to Catholic Sociology* by Professor J. D. J. Aengenent. Such organizations as the Union of Parents and Heads of Families and the Roman Catholic League for Large Families helped circulate these views more widely. The first application of these concepts was also under Catholic auspices: the successive groups of government employees to get family subsidies—post office employees, teachers, railroad employees, government mine-workers, etc.—received them as a result of the Catholic bloc's persistent fight for the principle in Parliament; and the first private employers to sign union contracts under which they paid bonuses for children were Catholic textile mill owners in the South.

Dutch Socialists were strongly opposed to this trend, for the reasons noted above. Moreover, this division was to be expected in terms of rational self-interest, for Catholics tended to have the largest families and the secularist urban intellectuals and skilled laborers who led the Socialist Party the smallest ones. Socialists attacked the family subsidy as a premium for breeding. De Walle, a Socialist pamphleteer, termed the Union of Parents and Heads of Families a "Union of Reactionaries." In 1921, the secularist trade union federation (NVV) called a special "Anti-Family-Subsidy Congress." In spite of the vigorous language in which it was voiced, however, this opposition was evanescent, for principled criticism of family subsidies was compromised, as has been noted, by the certain contradiction with Socialist ideology. Practical criticisms, on the other hand, had the paradoxical result of extending and strengthening the system. The mineworkers' union objected, for example, on the ground that mine-owners, who paid part of the subsidy, tended to give preference to single men; and this made it harder for married men to find employment. More generally, Socialists regarded all needy families as entitled to special benefits, not merely those of certain government employees or certain workers. While the intent of these arguments was to advocate other modes of social welfare or of income redistribution (particularly differential income taxes), they were easily diverted to support the Catholic effort to extend and rationalize the family endowment system. From 1925 on, all persons employed by the state were paid in part according to the number of children they had; and the proportion of all workers covered by trade union contracts who received family subsidies increased from 12 per cent in 1920 to 27 per cent in 1938.[4]

TABLE 2

AVERAGE SUBSIDIES, IN DUTCH CENTS PER WORKING DAY, PAID IN THE
NETHERLANDS FOR EACH CHILD OF EACH BIRTH ORDER, 1945–54

Birth Order	1945	1947	1952	1954[a]
1	0	40	44	48
2	0	40	46.5	54
3	13	40	47	54
4	20	42.5	51.5	75
5	24	44	54	75
6	27	45	56	85
7	29	46	57	85
8	30	46	58	85
9	31	47	58.5	85
10	32	47	59	85

[a] Proposed in a bill before the Second Chamber.

Sources: F. J. H. M. van der Ven. "Terug naar Rommel," Economie, XVI: 5 (February, 1952), 197–203; "Keesings Historisch Archief," November 22–28, 1953.

In 1937, C. P. M. Romme, one of the Catholic Party's principal leaders and then Minister of Social Affairs, introduced a bill extending family subsidies to all workers, and the Socialists supported it except for differences on administrative details. Principled opposition came only from the Liberals, who denounced giving government support to this "morality of the unreasoning animal," and from some of the Orthodox Calvinists, who oppose insurance of any kind as an affront to God.[5] It went into effect on January 1, 1941, but the differences between the Catholic and the Socialist principles underlying it did not affect its development until after the war. By Romme's interpretation, the purpose of his bill was to aid families with more than the average number of children; thus, subsidies began with the third child and increased progressively for children of each higher order of birth.[6] For the Socialists, on the other hand, the purpose of the bill was less to help large families than all families, and at the end of 1946, the law was amended in this sense.

Neither the Catholic principle of progression nor the Socialist one of virtually equal subsidies for all children has any necessary relation to the total amount paid out in subsidies, but the effect of the successive compromises between these two positions has been to raise this total substantially, for each new amendment has been made with the highest current figure as the base. Table 2 shows the amounts paid under the law at three postwar dates, and those proposed under a current bill.

Other revisions of the law in line with the Socialists' arguments in 1937, such as its extension to cover illegitimate children and the small self-employed class,[7] have also been additions rather than substitutions. Thus, the cost of the program, which Romme estimated at ƒ15 million, had grown to more than ƒ225 million by 1950, or by considerably more than can be accounted for by the postwar population growth and inflation.

In this context, the key question concerning family subsidies is their effect on fertility, and this is not one that can be answered definitely. Most of the discussion in other countries, including such an excellent work as David Glass's book on population policy,[8] is not directly relevant, because of the important differences between Holland and the rest of Western Europe in this respect. Once parents have come to view their role largely in rational terms, it is generally impossible either to revive traditionalist attitudes towards child-rearing or to pay them enough to make up for their financial loss.[9] Thus, in such countries as France and Germany, where family subsidies were introduced after a sharp decline in average family size had taken place in order to *raise* fertility to its previous level, their effect was probably small. In Holland, however, the family-subsidy law was less remedial than preventive: its purpose was to help *preserve* the traditional system of family norms still prevailing. As an incentive, subsidies are generally regarded as ineffective, but as a counter to economic deterrents, they may strongly reinforce other, nonrational incentives.

Under such circumstances, the size of the subsidy need not be great for it to be effective. According to a sample survey made by the Central Bureau of Statistics in 1950, the average subsidy paid to industrial workers amounted to 13 per cent of their weekly wage for an average of 2.4 minor children.[10] Since the amount of subsidy paid is the same for all classes, it is proportionately much higher for low-income families, or those with the highest fertility. Thus, a person with a monthly income of ƒ640 receives a subsidy equal to 6 per cent of this for three children, while someone with an income of ƒ160 gets 24 per cent; for seven children, the equivalent proportions are 17 and 67 per cent.[11] Moreover, the average cost of bringing up a child *decreases* with the number of children,[12] while the amount of the subsidy *increases* with the birth order of the child.[13]

Moreover, the family subsidy is only the most direct of the many rational advantages of parenthood. To some degree, any social welfare program tends to shift the financial burden of raising a family from the parents to the community, and in Holland this tendency has been reinforced by scaling various advantages or disadvantages according to family size. Even to list all these would require a special study, but several examples will suffice to give some notion of their range. In 1946, men with five or more children, including reserve officers, were exempted from military service. In June 1950, the government provided interest-free loans to persons repatriated from Indonesia, ranging from f1,200 for a married couple with no children to f3,000 for one with eight children. In April 1952, the cost of schooling was reduced to three-quarters of the usual rate for the third child, and to half of the rate for the fourth and subsequent children. Taxes are steeply graduated: in the various income brackets, bachelors pay more than the highest married person's rate, which falls sharply with the size of the family.[14] The principle is observed also in private industry: in February 1952, when the mammoth Philips plant reduced the working week to 40 hours, pay was cut to that for 42 hours for single men, while for married breadwinners it remained at the 48-hour rate. More important than any of these examples, or of the similar more or less incidental cases that could be added, are the facts that all increases in pay are now made through general contracts arranged jointly by the employers, trade unions, and government, and that these contracts are usually based in part on the concept of a "just wage." As one example, a general increase in February 1950 can be cited:

> Married workers, of either sex, below 23 years of age, with two or more children; and breadwinners, of either sex, below 23 years of age, belonging to a family of at least four persons, and whose normal earnings constitute at least two-thirds of the total income of the family, including any government subsidies and pensions, are entitled to a 5 per cent increase in salary (provided it has not already been increased to 105 per cent of the salary as of January 1, 1950, in accordance with prior regulations or increases).[15]

Whether the cumulative effect of these measures is to keep Dutch fertility high cannot be shown one way or another—first, because the determinants of fertility are very imperfectly understood; secondly, because in any case it would probably be impossible to isolate the effect of these measures. Actually, however, no one doubts their effect, but advocates of the family-subsidy program now tend to stress either that its avowed purpose is not to raise the fertility rate or that the supposed causal relation cannot be proved.[16]

A recent pamphlet issued by the Catholic Social-Ecclesiastical Institute, for example, distinguished sharply between family and population policy. Zeegers and Godefroy write: "Catholic family policy is based on principles of natural right and, especially, of social justice, which apply always and everywhere. The aims of population policy differ according to time and place."[17] While the differentiation may be valid, its relevance is slight. Among some Catholic publicists, there is a conscious desire to have the larger natural increase among Catholics continue until they become a majority in the Netherlands,[18] and the authors' wholly unobjectionable demonstration that this is unlikely to happen within the next seventy to eighty years could indicate only over how long a range some policies are set. In any case, even if the *purpose* of family subsidies is indeed only to further social justice, their *effect* on the birth rate may be to stimulate fertility. "Since the family subsidy," the authors argue, "covers only a portion of the outlay that must be made for the child's food, clothing, recreation, and education, an increase in the size of the family must always lower its relative standard of living. Thus, family subsidies can never act as an incentive to procreation."[19] This would be true only of economic men; the acts of real persons are influenced but not necessarily determined by monetary factors. Moreover, this very discrepancy between the costs of bringing up a child and the extra income acquired for this has been the principal argument in the continuous, and largely successful, effort to increase subsidies.

Before the war, when population pressure was not a problem, the relation between subsidies and fertility was freely admitted. The Catholic sociologist Kohlbrugge, for example, advocated a graduated tax system (thus, not even family subsidies but their milder negative equivalent) on the ground that it would "encourage" a high fertility rate.[20] Bomans declared that Socialists "fight with all their strength against the system of family subsidies, which they scornfully term a '*fokpremie*' [premium for breeding]; this is understandable, for they see in it, and rightly, a brake to neo-Malthusian practices."[21] Sometimes current proponents of the family-subsidy system, even while they deny that it tends to increase fertility, accuse those who disagree with their program of trying to "depress" the birth rate because of their principled opposition to the large family.[22] Similarly, the extension of subsidies to mothers of illegitimate children has been opposed on the ground that this would increase extramarital fertility.

In summary: Dutch Socialists now accept family subsidies as a legitimate element of social security, and the repeated Catholic-Labor compromises have resulted, paradoxically, first in the extension of the system to all wage-earners and then in a continual increase in the amount of the subsidy. Superficially, the Catholics have won, but their victory may have unanticipated consequences highly deleterious to their fundamental aims. The principal bond uniting the human family is neither romantic love nor moral and legal sanctions, but the joint parental task of caring for the children. Communal assistance to children in need strengthens the family, but when the state begins to take over the father's economic function, the family is thereby weakened.

In the 1920's the Dutch feminist Mrs. Mansholt-Andreae advocated what she termed a "motherhood wage" (*moederloon*)—that is, a direct remuneration by the state to mothers for the social work done in giving birth to children and bringing them up to be healthy and responsible citizens, to be made independently of the husband's wage or of his employment or unemployment.[23] By most of the arguments used to support family subsidies, this was a better system: it made little sense in social welfare terms, for example, to deprive a family of the subsidy when a man lost his job. In Mrs. Mansholt's eyes, the "motherhood wage" had the added advantage of increasing the wife's economic independence, so that the force impelling a woman to remain with her husband for financial reasons would be less strong. Dutch policy is tending in this direction. The persistent pressure to reduce the gap between the cost of raising a child and the amount of the subsidy will continue to effect increases. Zeegers and Godefroy attempt to estimate the cost of extending the system from wage-earners to the whole of the population,[25] and if this goal is reached, the present link between the husband's wage and the mother's income will necessarily be weakened, if not broken. As Kingsley Davis has put it, the logical outcome of such pecuniary measures is a change in reproductive institutions:

Undoubtedly, as many people fear, some families at the bottom of the social scale (and perhaps others) would find this a delightfully easy method of earning a livelihood. Now see what would happen. The Government would meet this situation by commanding that persons who live by producing children must prove their fitness. It would thereby produce, gradually and probably unwittingly, a new profession—the profession of child-rearing. It would take only one step more to introduce required training for the professional child-rearers, thus elevating both the standards and the social status of this occupational group. With training there would come specialization. The different subsidiary functions in the creation of new citizens would be taken over by specialized groups within the profession. Some women would merely *bear* children, others would care for them physically, others would educate them. Thus, by a gradual evolution unforeseen at the start, the use of monetary rewards for having children would lead to a system in which the father's role is assumed by the state, the mother's role by professional women paid by the state for their services. A new kind of reproductive organization compatible with modern society would have been substituted for the family.[25]

REFERENCES

1. Cf. William Petersen, *Some Factors Influencing Postwar Emigration from the Netherlands* (Research Group for European Migration Problems; The Hague: Martinus Nijhoff, 1952).

2. Most of the facts concerning this early development, but not their interpretation, are from an unpublished manuscript by H. H. Heringa, "Sociale organisate en reorganisatie," Amsterdam, 1950. See also Hugh H. R. Vihart, *Family Allowances in Practice* (London: King, 1926), especially pp. 36–41.

3. Among its 44 members, representing employers, labor and the government, the balance of power was held by twelve social scientists representing "the public." Measures adopted during this period included a workmen's compensation act (1921), supplemented by special accident-insurance laws for seamen and farm laborers; old-age pensions (1919); increased doles to the unemployed—as well as an extension of the 40-hour week to 48 hours.

4. L. P. van der Does, *De economische beteekenis der sociale verzekering* (Deventer: Kluwer, 1946), p. 104.

5. W. F. de Gaay Fortman and A. C. M. van der Ven, *Handleiding voor de toepassing der kinderbijslagwet* (Alphenaan-den-Rijn: Sansom, 1941), pp. 22–32. P. Zandt, the leader of a splinter preserving Calvinist principles in fossil form, announced in Parliament that he could support the bill only if he could be sure it was not insurance; while

the Socialist Van der Waerden was opposed to subsidies on principle but would support an insurance bill. It was a measure of Romme's parliamentary adeptness that he was able to satisfy both. The bill passed the Second Chamber by 66 votes to 22 and, after a delay occasioned by the fall of the government, passed the First Chamber by 27 to 7. It was signed by the Queen and became law on December 23, 1939, but during the five months before the German invasion there was no time to put it into effect. However, "after the German army was replaced by a [German] civilian administration, it developed that these authorities desired to have the law put into effect quickly." There were slight differences between Romme's bill and a "decree of the Führer," and the authors discuss whether the Dutch or the German text was the final authority (*ibid.*, pp. 34–37).

6. Romme is in this respect a mild Malthusian. Malthus was in general opposed to laws that shifted the burden of support from parents to the community, but he was for allowances to families with six or more children, for these would give needed assistance to the parents without encouraging improvident marriages. Cf. Joseph J. Spengler, "Malthus' Total Population Theory: A Restatement and Reappraisal," *Canadian Journal of Economics and Political Science*, XI: 83–110, 234–264, 1945.

7. But see also Centrum voor Staatkundige Vorming, *Proeve van een ontwerp van wet op het verlenen van kinderbijslag aan zelfstandigen* (The Hague: Katholieke Volkspartij, 1948).

8. D. V. Glass, *Population Policies and Movements in Europe* (Oxford: Clarendon Press, 1940).

9. In the United States around 1930, middle-class "parents spent between $9,180 and $10,485 in rearing a child through the age of eighteen. Dividing this figure (say, $10,000) by 18, and multiplying by the number of children in the country, we can calculate the total annual amount a nation would need to spend to cover cash expenditures made on children. For the United States it would be around $23,990,079,540, or more than six times the total government expenditures in 1930. . . . At least this amount would be required if genuine economic rewards for having children were given" (Kingsley Davis, "Reproductive Institutions and the Pressure for Population," *Sociological Review*, XXIX, 289–306, July, 1937).

10. Centraal Bureau voor de Statistiek, *Statistiek der lonen*, IV:2 (July–September, 1951), 35–84.

11. D. J. M. Knibbeler, "Heeft de kinderbijslag in Nederland invloed op de gezinsgroote?" *Mens en Maatschappij*, XXVIII: 3 (May 15, 1953), 153–174.

12. According to a survey of employees and government clerks made in 1951, the average weekly outlay per child amounted to ƒ9.60 when there were 1.4 children, ƒ8.97 with 1.8 children, ƒ7.49 with 3.4 children, and ƒ6.9 with 5.4 children (Centraal Bureau voor de Statistiek, *Nationaal Budgetonderzoek*, "Enkele utikomsten over het eerste kwartaal 1951," p. 14).

13. In order to prevent the fostering of very large families, Douglas suggested that, on the contrary, subsidies should cease after the fourth child, or should be provided in a diminishing scale (Paul H. Douglas, *Wages and the Family* [Chicago: University of Chicago Press, 1925], p. 256).

14. Cf. B. J. M. van Spaendonck, "Verhoging van de kindertoeslag als noodzakelijke maatregel voor de vermindering van de spanning tussen lonen en prijzen," *Economie*, XII: 3/4 (December, 1947–January, 1948), 117–137.

15. *Keesings Historisch Archief, VII*, 8619. The added italicization emphasizes the range of criteria by which wage rates are now usually set; note that neither skill nor productivity is mentioned.

16. For example, Knibbeler, "Heeft de kinderbijslag in Nederland invloed op de gezinsgrootte?" *op. cit.*

17. G. H. L. Zeegers and J. Godefroy, *Demografie en Gezinspolitiek* (Katholiek Sociaal Kerkelijk Instituut; The Hague: Pax, 1953), p. 30.

18. So important a man as Romme, then parliamentary leader of the Catholic People's Party and editor of one of the largest Catholic dailies, wrote that "full Catholic emancipation" can be achieved only when "our people will have become Catholic in the vast majority" (*De Volkskrant*, October 25, 1951). It is not necessary to postulate, as Zeegers and Godefroy do, that non-Catholics have projected their irrational fears as Catholic aims.

19. Zeegers and Godefroy, *op. cit.* p. 69.

20. J. H. F. Kohlbrugge, *Practische sociologie,* VI: *Sociale nooden,* II: *Sexueele en geestelijke problemen* (Groningen: Wolters, 1929), 73–74.

21. J. B. Bomans, *Het gezinsloon en de groote gezinnen* (Haarlem: Spaarnestad, 1919), p. 23.

22. E. J. Hoogenstraaten, "Gezinspolitiek," *Katholiek Staatkundig Maandschrift,* V:7 (September, 1951), 246–252.

23. Cf. Vibart, *op. cit.,* pp. 150–154.

24. Zeegers and Godefroy, *op. cit.,* pp. 54–60.

25. Davis, "Reproductive Institutions," *op. cit.*

THE ECONOMIC CONSEQUENCES OF THE PRESENT TREND OF POPULATION: SUMMARY OF CONCLUSIONS*

By the Economics Committee, Royal Commission on Population

I. *Introductory*

1. If in future British fertility rates remain below replacement level, as they have been for many years past, the population of Great Britain, unless sustained by immigration, will presently cease to increase and begin to decline. The subject-matter of this report is the economic consequences that may be expected to follow from such a demographic trend.

2. That important changes in the general economic situation will be brought about by future population trends may be regarded as certain. We discuss the nature of these changes, and have been particularly concerned to draw out their implications for Government policy in various fields.

3. The economic consequences of the prospective future trend of population also have a bearing on the desirability of intervention by the State to promote a recovery in the birth-rate. To this aspect Section V of the report is particularly related, but it is kept in mind throughout.

II. *External Consequences*

4. The outstanding feature of the economic development of Great Britain during the Victorian age was the rapid expansion of overseas trade, coupled with large-scale overseas investment in opening up the productive resources of new Continents and with large-scale emigration. This process provided for Great Britain the key to the riddle of how to obtain the additional food which a growing population needed.

5. During the inter-war period there was a tendency for supply to exceed demand in world markets for agricultural products, owing mainly to progress in agricultural technique, but in part also to the slowing down of population growth in Western Europe. This change was on the whole advantageous to Great Britain.

6. At the same time, however, industrialisation was proceeding in agricultural areas all over the world; and as a result it has become increasingly difficult for Great Britain to maintain an adequate export trade.

7. It is possible that in future the Eastern countries where populations are large and growing rapidly and where industrialisation is proceeding fast,

* Excerpted from *Papers of the Royal Commission on Population*, Vol. III, *Report of the Economics Committee* (London: H. M. Stationery Office, 1950), Chapter VI. Although published in 1950, the report was completed in December, 1945. Reprinted by permission of the Controller of Her Majesty's Stationery Office. (Crown Copyright 1950.)

may become importers of primary products on a considerable scale. The repercussions of such a development on Britain's capacity to obtain supplies overseas might be grave.

8. This is one (though not the only) reason for fearing that the British balance of payments problem, which is acutely difficult at present, may remain a source of anxiety even in the more remote future owing to long-term economic developments. If so, we shall have cause to be glad that our numbers will soon cease to grow, for an increase of the population by 10 per cent would call for an increase, according to our estimate, of about one quarter of the pre-war volume of British export trade.

9. If, however, pre-war conditions of abundance in the supplies of primary products available for export to world markets return and are maintained in the long run, it should be possible for Britain to find some way of overcoming her balance of payments difficulties. Whether this is likely to occur is a speculative question on which different views may be entertained; but it would be imprudent to assume that the problem will be of short duration.

10. In any event, it will be out of the question for Great Britain to resume for a long period to come her pre-1914 role as a large-scale international lender.

11. During the inter-war period, migration to the United States and other new world countries was greatly reduced. The outlets for the overpopulated countries of Southern and Northern Europe were virtually closed, and at the same time the disposition to emigrate was greatly weakened in the less prolific parts of Europe and especially Great Britain.

12. So long as Britain has a birth-rate below replacement level, the maintenance of a large flow of emigration is neither practicable nor desirable. On the other hand, the arguments for allowing a substantial immigration would acquire increased force if the population were tending to decline.

III. *Internal Consequences*

13. The output of new houses hitherto has been mainly directed to meeting the increment in the demand for housing accommodation. If this demand should become stationary, after the shortage resulting from the war has been made good, there would no longer be any need to build new houses, except for replacement.

14. The unit in the demand for housing accommodation is the family. The fall in the annual number of births which took place after the early years of the present century had, of course, no immediate effect on the number of people arriving at the ages at which families are founded, and the number of families grew rapidly throughout the inter-war period. This increase is now slowing down markedly and may be expected to disappear altogether in a comparatively short period.

15. It seems probable therefore that after the wartime arrears of house-

building have been overtaken the demand for additional houses will fall off rapidly. This will give an opportunity to raise housing standards by replacing inferior dwellings, but it will probably also become necessary to transfer part of the labour previously engaged in building houses to other work.

16. The altered trend of population is likely to exert similar repercussions, subject to a similar time-lag, on other forms of building and constructional activity; and the same broad morals apply, viz. that it will be wise to seize the opportunity to modernise and improve our capital equipment, but that there are limits to the extent to which it would be reasonable to carry such a policy.

17. Within a measurable period, therefore, the aggregate output of capital goods is likely to decline, and we shall then be faced with the task of effecting a transition from an economy adapted to a high level of investment activity to one adapted to a lower level of investment and a correspondingly higher level of consumption.

18. The common assumption that the aggregate of urban land values will continue to grow in future at much the same rate as hitherto may cease to hold good under conditions of stationary or declining numbers.

19. The difficulties of the budgetary problem are likely to be increased by the present trend of our vital statistics. First, the buoyancy of the revenue will be reduced, as the population of working age ceases to grow. The existence of a huge national debt lends importance to this consideration.

20. Secondly, the charges falling on the budget for the relief of old age will rise materially, owing to the rapid increase in the number of persons of pensionable age. The automatic increase so arising may be expected eventually to exceed £200 millions. Increases of expenditure may also arise from measures designed to promote a recovery in the birth-rate.

21. Thus the altered population trend is likely to exert adverse long-run repercussions on both public revenue and public expenditure. In these circumstances the maintenance of low interest rates will be of prime importance, so as to keep the debt charge as low as possible.

22. These difficulties will limit the use that can be made in future of taxation as an instrument of economic stability and social progress, and cannot, therefore, be regarded lightly. But they do not express any probable inadequacy of productive resources to meet consumers' needs, and fundamentally therefore they represent a less disquieting problem than that of the adverse balance of international payments.

IV. *Employment*

23. Stationary or declining numbers tend to make the maintenance of full employment more difficult. It will be increasingly unsafe in future to rely solely on the automatic adjustment of an unregulated economic system to ensure that our labour-power and productive resources are fully used.

24. Four objectives of policy will be especially important:

(1) increased mobility of labour;
(2) appropriate location of industry;
(3) stability of investment, and the adjustment of saving to any long-term changes in investment;
(4) a steady and sufficient export trade.

25. Many of the consequences of the altered population trend which carry with them an increased danger of unemployment carry with them also increased opportunities for a higher standard of life. The degree in which these opportunities are realised will depend largely on the degree in which the danger of unemployment is overcome.

V. The Standard of Life and the National Welfare

26. For two reasons a stationary population is likely to find it easier than one which is growing rapidly to increase its standard of life. First, the resources which a growing population would have to devote to maintaining capital equipment per head become available for raising standards.

27. Second, the amount of land per head ceases to decline when the population ceases to grow, with the consequence that the difficulty of obtaining a supply of natural products (which may become serious for Britain in her changed international position) will be at least mitigated.

28. On the other hand, the cessation of growth has the disadvantages (1) that the average age of the population will increase; (2) that there may be some loss of the economies of large-scale production; (3) that the difficulties of maintaining employment will be increased.

29. If, however, employment policy is only moderately successful, we think that for Great Britain today the balance of economic advantage is strongly in favour of stationary as compared with increasing numbers.

30. Unless fertility rises, the population will not merely cease to grow but must in time decline. There can be no question as to the necessity of restoring our fertility rates sooner or later to replacement level, since the alternative is national extinction. There is, however, a question whether it is important that the recovery should be effected quickly enough to avert any material decline.

31. The consequences of a decline of numbers are broadly similar in kind to those of a cessation of growth, but may differ greatly in degree. There will be advantages from the fact that accumulated capital per head of population will increase; but these advantages are likely to be speculative, transient, and double-edged. A smaller population would be advantageous on balance of payment grounds, but it is difficult to forecast whether this advantage would be slight or important. There would also be a gain on the score of amenity.

32. The offsetting disadvantages of the cessation of the growth of population—in particular, the extra difficulty of maintaining full employment—would acquire some added practical importance if numbers were to decline materially. The burden that might result from an increase in the proportion

of dependents to the working population would, however, be less formidable than is often supposed.

33. Thus while a smaller population would, as such, be on the whole advantageous, the *process* of decline would be difficult. Whether there would be a net gain would depend mainly on the long-term development of our balance of payments position.

34. To the issues of population policy, however, three other considerations are relevant. First, a sub-replacement birth-rate will encourage immigration and so reduce the proportion of home-bred stock in the population. Second, intervention to raise the birth-rate is not likely to have quick results. Third, measures to aid parents and to improve the care of children will strike at one of the main causes of poverty and malnutrition.

35. We conclude accordingly that in Great Britain at the present day the case for reasonable and well-considered measures to mitigate the burden of parenthood is fully made out on economic and social grounds.

‍

The bibliography that follows is intended to aid the student to supplement the reading he has done in this volume. Titles of articles reprinted in the present volume have not been included. The bibliography has been limited almost entirely to the titles of articles appearing in English-language journals in recent years. For titles in other languages the student may consult such sources of bibliography as *Population Index, Population,* and the *Economic Journal.*

The following abbreviations are used in referring to journals cited frequently:

Annals: *Annals of the American Academy of Political and Social Science*
AER: *American Economic Review*
AJS: *American Journal of Sociology*
ASR: *American Sociological Review*
CJEPS: *Canadian Journal of Economics and Political Science*
EQ: *Eugenics Quarterly*
GJ: *Geographical Journal*
GR: *Geographical Review*
HBR: *Harvard Business Review*
IJE: *Indian Journal of Economics*
ILR: *International Labour Review*
JPE: *Journal of Political Economy*
JRSS: *Journal of the Royal Statistical Society*
LE: *Land Economics*
MMFQ: *Milbank Memorial Fund Quarterly*
MS: *Manchester School*
PAPS: *Proceedings of the American Philosophical Society*
PS: *Population Studies*
QJE: *Quarterly Journal of Economics*
SF: *Social Forces*
SM: *Scientific Monthly*
SR: *Social Research*

I. *Development of Population Theory*

Aldridge, Alfred, "Franklin as Demographer," *Journal of Economic History,* 9 (May 1949) 25–44.

Carr-Saunders, Sir Alexander, *et al.,* "A Discussion on the Reports of Royal Commission on Population," *JRSS,* 94 (Part 1, 1951) 38–49.

Cook, R. C., "A New Science Emerges," *Population Bulletin,* 10 (July 1954) 57–66.

Davis, Kingsley, "Malthus and the Theory of Population," in *The Language of Social Research,* edited by Paul F. Lazarsfeld and Morris Rosenberg (Glencoe: Free Press, 1955) 540–553.

Glass, D. V., "Gregory King's Estimate of the Population of England and Wales, 1695," PS, 3 (March 1950) 338–374.

Glass, D. V., "The Population Controversy in Eighteenth Century England, Part I. The Background," PS, 6 (July 1952) 69–91.

Grebenik, E., "Two Reports on Population," Economica, 17 (February 1950) 91–107.

Meek, Ronald L., "Malthus—Yesterday and Today," Science and Society, 18 (Winter 1954) 21–51.

Notestein, Frank W., "The Report of the Royal Commission on Population: A Review," PS, 3 (December 1949) 232–240.

Petersen, W., "John Maynard Keynes' Theories of Population and the Concept of 'Optimum,' " PS, 8 (March 1955) 228–246.

Sauvy, A., "Some Lesser Known French Demographers of the Eighteenth Century: De la Morandière, de Caveirac, Cerfvol and Pinto," PS, 5 (July 1951) 3–22.

Smith, Kenneth, "Some Observations on Modern Malthusianism," PS, 6 (July 1952) 92–105.

Spengler, J. J., "French Population Theory Since 1800," JPE, 44 (October and December 1936) 577–611, 743–766.

Spengler, J. J., "Malthus's Total Population Theory: A Restatement and Reappraisal," CJEPS, 11 (February and May 1945), 83–110, 234–264.

Spengler, J. J., "Marshall on the Population Question," PS, 8 (March 1955) 264–287, 9 (July 1955) 56–66.

Spengler, J. J., "Messance: Founder of French Demography," Human Biology, 12 (February 1940) 77–94.

Spengler, J. J., "Pareto on Population," QJE, 58 (August 1941) 571–601, 59 (November 1944) 107–133.

Spengler, J. J., "Population Doctrines in the United States," JPE, 41 (August and October 1933) 433–467, 639–672.

Spengler, J. J., "Population Prediction in Nineteenth Century America," ASR, 1 (December 1936) 905–921.

Spengler, J. J., "Population Theory in the Ante-Bellum South," Journal of Southern History, 2 (August 1936) 360–389.

Taeuber, I. B., "The Development of Population Predictions in Europe and the Americas," Estadística, 2 (September 1944) 323–346.

Thompson, Warren S., "Population Studies," AJS, 50 (May 1945) 436–442.

Unsigned, "Population Studies in the United States," Population Index, 12 (October 1946) 254–269.

Wolfe, A. B., "The Population Problem Since the World War: A Survey of Literature and Research," JPE, 36 (October and December 1928) 529–539, 662–685, 37 (February 1929) 87–120.

II. The Role of Theory in Population Studies

Bladen, V. W., "The Population Problem," CJEPS, 5 (November 1939) 528–547.

Bladen, V. W., "On Population," CJEPS, 8 (May 1942) 273–288.

Boulding, K., "The Malthusian Model as a General System," Social and Economic Studies, 4 (September 1955) 195–205.

Haavelmo, T., A Study in the Theory of Economic Evolution (Amsterdam: North Holland Publishing Co., 1954).

James, Preston, "Toward a Further Understanding of the Regional Concept," Annals of the Association of American Geographers, 42 (September 1952) 195–222.

Leibenstein, H., A Theory of Economic-Demographic Development (Princeton: Princeton University Press, 1954).

Lotka, Alfred J., "Population Analysis as a Chapter in the Mathematical Theory of

Evolution," in *Essays on Growth and Form Presented to D'Arcy Wentworth Thompson*, edited by W. E. Le Gros Clark and P. B. Medawar (Oxford: The Clarendon Press, 1945) 355–385.

Lotka, Alfred J., "Contact Points of Population Study with Related Branches of Science," *PAPS*, 80 (February 1939) 601–626.

Park, T., "Analytical Population Studies in Relation to General Ecology," *The American Midland Naturalist*, 21 (January 1939) 235–255.

Park, T., "Ecological Experimentation with Animal Populations," *SM*, 81 (December 1955) 271–275.

Spengler, J. J., "Population Theory" chap. 3, in *A Survey of Contemporary Economics*, edited by B. F. Haley (Homewood: Richard D. Irwin, Inc., 1952).

Trewartha, Glenn T., "A Case for Population Geography," *Annals of the Association of American Geographers*, 43 (June 1953) 71–97.

III. *Theory of Population Growth*

Blacker, C. P., "Stages in Population Growth," *Eugenics Review*, 39 (October 1947) 88–102.

Brown, S. P., "Analysis of a Hypothetical Stationary Population by Family Units— A Note on Some Experimental Calculations," *PS*, 4 (March 1951) 380–394.

Davis, Kingsley, "The World Demographic Transition," *Annals*, 237 (January 1945) 1–11.

Dublin, Louis I. and Lotka, Alfred J., "On the True Rate of Natural Increase," *Journal of the American Statistical Association*, 20 (September 1925) 305–339.

Goodman, Leo A., "Population Growth of the Sexes," *Biometrics*, 9 (June 1953) 212–225.

Hatt, P. K., Farr, Nellie L., and Weinstein, E., "Types of Population Balance," *ASR*, 20 (February 1955) 14–21.

Karpinos, Bernard D., "A Stationary Population," *Human Biology*, 7 (December 1935) 514–538.

Karpinos, Bernard D., "The Length of Time Required for the Stabilization of a Population," *AJS*, 41 (January 1936) 504–513.

Krishnaswami, G. V., "Some Aspects of the Tendency of Population," *IJE*, 30 (July 1949) 69–75.

Kuczynski, R. R., "Economic Causes of Population Movement," *Index*, 11 (November 1936) 223–233.

Leslie, P. H., "On the Distribution in Time of the Births in Successive Generations," *JRSS*, 111 (Part I, 1948) 44–53.

Leslie, P. H., "On the Use of Matrices in Certain Population Mathematics," *Biometrika*, 33 (November 1945) 183–212.

Notestein, Frank, "Economic Problems of Population Change," *Proceedings of the Eighth International Conference of Agricultural Economists* (London: Oxford University Press, 1953) 13–31.

Notestein, F. W., "Population—The Long View," in *Food for the World*, edited by Theodore W. Schultz (Chicago: University of Chicago Press, 1945).

Noyes, C. R., "The Weather Chart of Population," *Yale Review*, 12 (1922–23) 813–825.

van Nort, L. and Karon, B. P., "Demographic Transition Re-Examined," *ASR*, 20 (October 1955) 523–527.

Vianelli, S., "A General Dynamic Demographic Scheme and its Application to Italy and the United States," *Econometrica*, 4 (July 1936) 269–283.

Wolfe, A. B., "Is There a Biological Law of Human Population Growth?" *QJE*, 4 (August 1927) 557–594.

Wolfe, A. B., "The Rationalization of Production and Reproduction," in *Carver Essays* (Cambridge: Harvard University Press, 1935) 226–243.

IV. *Population, Resources, Technology, and Levels of Living*

Barlowe, R., "Population Pressure and Food Production Potentialities," *LE*, 25 (August 1949) 227–239.

Baykov, A., "Note on the Trend of Population and the Labour Problems of the USSR," *JRSS*, 106 (Part IV, 1943) 349–359.

Bennett, M. K., "Population and Food Supply: The Current Scare," *SM*, 68 (January 1949) 17–26.

Bennett, Merrill K., *Population, Food, and Economic Progress,* The Rice Institute Pamphlet, Vol. 39, No. 2, July, 1952 (Houston: The Rice Institute, 1952).

Berry, W. J., "The Capacity of the United States to Support Population," *GJ*, 102 (August 1943) 56–62.

Bertram, F. C. L., "Population Trends and the World's Resources," *GJ*, 107 (May–June 1946) 191–210.

Boone, A., "Land Resources and the Growth of World Population," in *Research Council of Israel*, Special Publication No. 2, (Jerusalem, 1953) 464–477.

Brewster, J. M., "Farm Technological Advance and Total Population Growth," *Journal of Farm Economics*, 27 (August 1945) 509–525.

Bowen, Howard, "Capital in Relation to Optimum Population," *SF*, 15 (March 1937) 346–350.

Chatfield, Charlotte, "Changes in World Consumption of Calories and Proteins over the Last Decade," *MMFQ*, 27 (April 1950) 103–113.

Clark, Colin, "Population Growth and Living Standards," *ILR*, 68 (August 1953) 99–117.

Clark, Colin, "World Supply and Requirements of Farm Products," *JRSS*, 117 (Part 3, 1954) 263–296.

Cressey, George B., "Land for 2.4 Billion Neighbors," *Economic Geography*, 29 (January 1953) 1–9.

Dalton, H., "The Theory of Population," *Economica*, 8 (March 1928) 28–50.

Davis, Joseph S., "The Population Upsurge and the American Economy, 1945–80," *JPE*, 61 (October 1953) 369–388.

Dunsdorfs, E., "The Optimum Theory of Population," *Weltwirtschaftliches Archiv*, 71 (No. 2, 1953) 221–233.

El-Shafie, Mahmoud Ahmed, "Population Pressure on Land and the Problem of Capital Accumulation in Egypt," *Journal of Farm Economics*, 34 (December 1952) 979–981.

Gottlieb, M., "Optimum Population, Foreign Trade and World Economy," *PS*, 3 (September 1949) 151–169.

Grove, A. T., "Soil Erosion and Population Problems in Southeast Nigeria," *GJ*, 117 (September 1951) 291–306.

Hainsworth, R. G., "How Many People Can The Earth Feed?" *Foreign Agriculture*, (February 1953) 23–29.

Healey, Derek T., and Nilson, Sten S., "Population Growth and Living Standards, Replies to Mr. Clark's Article," *ILR*, 69 (January 1954) 68–76.

Henderson, A., "The Cost of Children," *PS*, 3 (September 1949) 130–150, 4 (December 1950) 267–298.

Hoffman, E. S., "Food Supplies and National Incomes," *Quarterly Review of Agricultural Economics*, (April 1951) 51–55.

Huntington, E., "Agricultural Productivity and Pressure of Population," *Annals*, 198 (July 1938) 73–92.

Leighly, John, "Population and Settlement: Some Recent Swedish Studies," *GR*, 42 (January 1952) 134–137.

Lestapis, S. de., "Population, Living Standards and Sense of Responsibility," *ILR*, 70 (November 1954) 442–445.

Lorimer, Frank, and Roback, Herbert, "Economics of the Family Relative to Number of Children," *MMFQ*, 18 (April 1940) 114–136.

McDougall, Frank L., "Food and Population," *Carnegie Endowment for International Peace, International Conciliation*, No. 486, (December 1952) 537–584.

McFall, R. J., "Is Food the Limiting Factor in Population Growth?" *Yale Review*, 15 (1925–26) 297–316.

Nevett, Albert, "Population Growth and Living Standards," *ILR*, 70 (November 1954) 445–449.

Nilson, Sten S., "The Threatening Overpopulation of the World," *The Norseman* (London), 10 (September–October 1952) 289–301.

O'Dell, Andrew C., "Population and Natural Resources," *Scottish Geographical Journal*, 68 (September 1952) 49–56.

Ozaki, Iwao, "Theoretical Approach to Measurement of Over-rate of Population Growth—Econometric Analysis of The Rate of Economic Growth," *Archives of the Population Association of Japan*, (No. 2, 1953) 25–33.

Richter, J. H., "Population and Food Supply," *SR*, 20 (Autumn 1953) 253–266.

Saunders, Harold W., "A General Theory of Population Pressure," *Journal of Business, University of Iowa*, 24 (May 1944) 11–15.

Spengler, J. J., "Aspects of the Economics of Population Growth," *Southern Economic Journal*, 14 (October 1947 and January 1948) 124–147, 233–265.

Spengler, J. J., "Limitational Factors in Population Theory: A Note," *Kyklos*, 7 (Part 3, 1954) 227–244.

Spengler, J. J., "The World's Hunger—Malthus, 1948," *Proceedings of the Academy of Political Science*, 33 (January 1949) 53–72.

Taylor, E. G. R., "An Under-Nourished World," *GJ*, 118 (September 1952) 348–350.

Thompson, W. S., and Whelpton, P. K., "Levels of Living and Population Pressure," *Annals*, 198 (July 1938) 93–100.

Villard, H. H., "Some Notes on Population and Living Levels," *Review of Economics and Statistics*, 37 (May 1955) 187–95.

Weaver, Warren, "People, Energy, and Food," *SM*, 78 (June 1954) 359–364.

V. *Population and Level of Economic Activity*

Adler, H. A., "Absolute or Relative Rate of Decline in Population Growth," *QJE*, 59 (August 1945) 626–634.

Colm, G., "Comments on W. I. King: Are We Suffering From Economic Maturity?," *JPE*, 48 (February 1940) 114–118.

Davis, Joseph S., "Our Changed Population Outlook and its Significance," *AER*, 42 (June 1952) 304–325.

Dickinson, H. D., "A Note On Dynamic Economics," *Review of Economic Studies*, 22 (No. 3, 1954–55) 169–179.

Drucker, Peter F., "Population Trends and Management Policy," *HBR*, 29 (May 1951) 73–78.

Fellner, W., "The Technological Argument of the Stagnation Thesis," *QJE*, 55 (August 1941) 638–651.

Franzsen, D. G., "The Secular Stagnation Thesis and the Problem of Economic Stability," *South African Journal of Economics*, 10 (December 1942) 282–294.

Gillies, F. D., "Population and Public Capital," *Economic News* (Queensland, Bureau of Industry), 22 (November 1953) 1–6.

Glass, Ruth and Davidson, F. G., "Household Structure and Housing Need," *PS*, 4 (March 1951) 395–420.

Goldenberg, L., "Savings in a State with a Stationary Population," *QJE*, 61 (November 1946) 40–65.

Hansen, A. H., "Extensive Expansion and Population Growth," *JPE*, 48 (August 1940) 583–585.

Hansen, A. H., "Population Problems," *AER, Supplement*, 30 (March 1940) 383–398.

Harrod, R. F., "Modern Population Trends," *MS*, 10 (April 1939) 1–20.

Hauser, P. M., and Jaffe, A. J., "The Extent of the Housing Shortage," *Law and Contemporary Problems*, 12 (Winter 1947) 3–15.

Jewkes, J., "The Population Scare," *MS*, 10 (October 1939) 101–121.

King, W. I., "Are We Suffering From Economic Maturity?," *JPE*, 47 (October 1939) 609–622.

Lange, O., "Is The American Economy Contracting?," *AER*, 29 (September 1939) 503–513.

Lederer, E., "Is the Economic Frontier Closed?," *SR*, 6 (May 1939) 153–162.

Long, Edwin J., and Dorner, Peter, "Excess Farm Population and the Loss of Agricultural Capital," *LE*, 30 (November 1954) 363–368.

Neisser, Hans, "The Economics of a Stationary Population," *SR*, 11 (November 1944) 470–490.

Pedersen, J., "Interest Rates, Employment, and Changes in Population," *Kyklos*, 2 (No. 1, 1948) 1–16.

Petersen, William, "John Maynard Keynes' Theories of Population and the Concept of 'Optimum'," *PS*, 8 (March 1955) 228–246.

Reed, H. L., "Economists on Industrial Stagnation," *JPE*, 48 (April 1940) 244–250.

Rosen, M. M., "Population Growth, Investment, and Economic Recovery," *AER*, 32 (March 1942) 122–125.

Schiff, E., "Family Size and Residential Construction," *AER*, 36 (March 1946) 97–112.

Slichter, S. H., "The Conditions of Expansion," *AER*, 32 (March 1942) 1–21.

Spengler, J. J., "Population Growth, Consumer Demand, and Business Profits," *HBR*, 12 (1933–34) 204–221.

Spengler, J. J., "Population Threatens Prosperity," *HBR*, 34 (January–February 1956) 85–94.

Spengler, J. J., "Population Trends and the Future Demand for Teachers," *SF*, 19 (May 1941) 465–476.

Spengler, J. J., "Prospective Population and Income Growth and Fiscal Policy," *National Tax Journal*, 3 (March 1950) 36–63.

Spengler, J. J., "Population Movements and Investment," *Journal of Finance*, 6 (December 1951) 343–360 and 7 (March 1952) 10–27.

Spengler, J. J., "Population Movements and Economic Equilibrium in the United States," *JPE*, 48 (April 1940) 153–182.

Staudinger, H., "Stationary Population–Stagnant Economy?," *SR*, 6 (May 1939) 141–153.

Stolper, W. F., "The Demand for Houses: The Population Factor," *QJE*, 45, Part II (November 1941) 79–107.

Stone, R., "Misery and Bliss: A Comparison of the Effect of Certain Forms of Saving Behaviour on the Standard of Living of a Growing Community," *Economica Internazionale*, 8 (February 1955) 72–96.

Sweezy, A. R., "Population Growth and Investment Opportunity," *QJE*, 55 (November 1940) 64–79.

Tsiang, S. C., "The Effect of Population Growth on the General Level of Employment and Activity," *Economica*, 9 (November 1942) 325–332.

VI.   *Population Growth and Economic Development*

Anonymous, "Population and Social Problems," *ILR*, 39 (March 1939) 291–318.

Belshaw, Horace, "Some Social Aspects of Economic Development in Underdeveloped Countries in Asia," *New Zealand Institute of International Affairs*, Paper No. II, 1954, processed.

Belshaw, Horace, "Population Growth and Levels of Consumption in New Zealand," *Economic Record*, 31 (May 1955) 1–17.

Bromberger, E., "The Growth of Population in Palestine," *PS*, 2 (June 1948) 71–91.

Chambers, J. D., "Enclosure and Labour Supply in the Industrial Revolution," *Economic History Review*, 5 (No. 3, 1953) 319–343.

Chandrasekhar, S., "Population Growth, Socio-Economic Development and Living Standards," *ILR*, 69 (June 1954) 527–546.

Chiang Hsieh, "Underemployment in Asia, I. Nature and Extent," *ILR*, 65 (June 1952) 703–725.

Davis, J. S., "Adam Smith and the Human Stomach," *QJE*, 68 (May 1954) 275–286.

Davis, J. S., "The Population Upsurge and the American Economy, 1945–80," *JPE*, 61 (October 1953) 369–388.

Eldridge, Hope, "Population Growth and Economic Development," *LE*, 28 (February 1952) 1–9.

Hoselitz, Bert F., "The Role of Cities in the Economic Growth of Underdeveloped Countries," *JPE*, 61 (June 1953) 195–208.

Husain, A. F. A., "Industrialization and the Problem of Population," *IJE*, 30 (July 1949) 55–59.

Merton, R. K., "Science, Population and Society," *SM*, 44 (February 1937) 165–171.

Myrdal, Alva, "Population Trends in Densely Populated Areas," *PAPS*, 95 (February 13, 1951) 1–7.

Ogburn, W. F., "A Design for Some Experiments in the Limitation of Population Growth in India," *Economic Development and Cultural Change*, 1 (February 1953) 376–389.

Pan, Chia-Lin, "The Population of Libya," *PS*, 3 (June 1949) 100–125.

Roberts, G. W., "Some Observations on the Population of British Guiana," *PS*, 2 (September 1948) 185–218.

Shaul, J. R. H., and Myburgh, C. A. L., "A Sample Survey of the African Population of Southern Rhodesia," *PS*, 2 (December 1948) 339–353.

Singer, H. W., "The Mechanics of Economic Development. A Quantitative Model Approach," *Indian Economic Review*, 1 (August 1952) 1–18.

Spengler, J. J., "Economic Factors in the Development of Densely Populated Areas," *PAPS*, 95 (February 1951) 20–53.

Whelpton, P. K., and Badenhorst, L. T., "Population Statistics in Relation to the Development of Underdeveloped Areas," *Journal of Social Research*, 3 (No. 1, 1952) 5–13.

VII.   *Population Growth and International Relations*

A. J. B., "Population Trends and Power," *International Affairs*, 21 (January 1945) 79–86.

Chandrasekhar, S., "Population Problems and International Tensions," *International Social Science Bulletin*, 1 (Nos. 1–2, 1949) 54–63.

Corbett, Davis, "Immigration and Canadian Politics," *International Journal*, 6 (Summer 1951) 207–216.

Davis, Kingsley, "The Demographic Foundations of National Power," in Morroe Berger, *et al.*, editors, *Freedom and Control in Modern Society* (New York: Van Nostrand, 1954).

Forsythe, W. D., "Population Growth—Some Comparisons," *Economic Record*, 17 (December 1941) 248–252.

Friedman, W., "Migration and World Politics," *International Journal* 4 (Summer 1952) 196–203.

Hankins, F. H., "Pressure of Population as a Cause of War," *Annals*, 198 (July 1938) 101–108.

Irwin, J. O., "World Population," *MS*, 8 (No. 1, 1937) 63–68.

Kuczynski, R. R., "World Population Problems," *International Affairs*, 20 (October 1944) 449–457.

Lasker, B., "Displacement of Population in Eastern Asia," *Annals*, 234 (July 1944) 13–21.

Lebon, J. H. G., "Population Distribution and the Agricultural Regions of Iraq," *GR*, 43 (April 1953) 223–228.

Lorimer, F., "Population Trends in the Orient," *Foreign Affairs*, 23 (July 1945) 668–674.

Notestein, F. W., "Population and Power in Postwar Europe," *Foreign Affairs*, 22 (April 1944) 389–403.

Ostrolenk, B., "The Economics of an Imprisoned World. A Brief For The Removal of Immigration Restrictions," *Annals*, 203 (May 1939) 194–201.

Pearl, Raymond, "War and Overpopulation," *Current History*, 43 (March 1936) 589–594.

Sandwell, B. K., "Population Pressures and the Problems of World Peace," *Proceedings of the Royal Society of Canada*, 44, series III (June 1950) 155–167.

Shirras, G. F., "The Population Problem in India," *Economic Journal*, 43 (March 1933) 56–73.

Staudinger, Hans, "Problems of Population," Chapter IV in *War in Our Time*, edited by Hans Speier and Alfred Kähler (New York: W. W. Norton and Co., Inc., 1939).

Wright, Quincy, "Population Trends and International Relations," in *Compass of the World*, edited by Hans W. Weigert and Vilhjalmur Stefansson (New York: Macmillan, 1944), 408–428.

Young, Kimball, "Population and Power: Some Comments on Demographic Changes," *SF*, 25 (October 1946) 1–9.

VIII.   *Socio-Cultural Context of Population Dynamics*

Awad, Mohamed, "The Assimilation of Nomads in Egypt," *GR*, 44 (April 1954) 240–252.

Cattell, Raymond B., "A Quantitative Analysis of the Changes in the Culture Pattern of Great Britain, 1837–1937, by p-Technique," *Acta Psychologica*, 9 (1953), 99–121.

Cattell, Raymond B., and Adelson, Marvin, "The Dimensions of Social Change in the U.S.A. as Determined by p-Technique," *SF*, 30 (December 1951) 190–201.

Gibbons, W. J., "The Catholic Value System in Relation to Human Fertility," in *Studies in Population*, edited by George F. Mair (Princeton: Princeton University Press, 1949), 108–134.

Glass, D. V., editor, *Cultural Assimilation of Immigrants*, Supplement, *PS* (March 1950.

Heberle, Rudolf, "Social Factors in Birth Control," *ASR*, 6 (December 1941), 794–805.

Kirk, Dudley, "Dynamics of Human Populations," *EQ*, 2 (March 1955) 18–25.

Ogburn, W. F., "Inventions, Population and History," in *Studies in the History of*

Culture, American Council of Learned Societies (Menasha, Wis.: Banta Publishing Co., 1942).

Parsons, Talcott, "Population and Social Structure," in *Japan's Prospect,* edited by Douglas G. Haring (Cambridge: Harvard University Press, 1946).

Russell, J. C., "Demographic Values in the Middle Ages," in *Studies in Population,* edited by George F. Mair (Princeton: Princeton University Press, 1949), 103–107.

Taeuber, Irene B., "Culture, Technology and Population Change," *Bulletin of the Atomic Scientists,* 7 (August 1951) 206–208.

Taeuber, Irene B., "The Reproductive Mores of the Asian Peasant," in *Studies in Population,* edited by George F. Mair (Princeton: Princeton University Press, 1949), 95–102.

Thompson, C. H., editor, "The Relative Status of the Negro Population of the United States," *Journal of Negro Education,* Yearbook Number, 22 (Summer 1953).

IX.   *Population Policy*

Beveridge, W., "The Population Problem," *Political Quarterly,* 17 (April-June 1946) 133–136.

Booker, H. S., "Income Tax and Family Allowances in Britain," *PS,* 3 (December 1949) 241–247.

Cartter, Allan M., "Income-tax Allowances and the Family in Great Britain," *PS,* 6 (March 1953) 218–232.

Chambers, Rosalind, "Family Allowances in Great Britain, Canada, Australia, and New Zealand," *EQ,* 1 (March 1954) 21–27.

Doublet, J., "Family Allowances in France," *PS,* 2 (September 1948) 219–239.

Douglas, J. W. B., and Rowntree, Griselda, "Supplementary Maternal and Child Health Services. Part I. Postnatal Care. Part II. Nurseries," *PS,* 3 (September 1949) 205–226.

Eldridge, Hope T., *Population Policies: A Survey of Recent Developments* (Washington: International Union for the Scientific Study of Population, 1954).

Elton, G. R., "An Early Tudor Poor Law," *Economic History Review,* 6 (August 1953) 55–67.

Fairchild, H. P., "Postwar Population Problems," *SF,* 23 (October 1944) 1–6.

Gille, H., "Family Welfare Measures in Denmark," *PS,* 6 (November 1952) 172–210.

Gille, H., "Recent Developments in Swedish Population Policy," *PS,* 2 (June and September 1948) 3–70, 129–184.

Gille, H., "Scandinavian Family Allowances: Demographic Aspects," *EQ,* 1 (September 1954) 182–190.

Hammons, Helen G., "International Family Legislation," *Eugenical News,* 37 (December 1952) 65–85.

Kiser, Clyde V., "Implications of Population Trends for Postwar Policy," *MMFQ,* 23 (April 1944) 111–130.

Kotok, E. I., "International Policy on Renewable Natural Resources," *AER,* Proceedings, 35 (May 1945) 110–119.

Lorimer, Frank, "European Governmental Action Regarding Population," *Annals,* 262 (March 1949) 56–61.

McCleary, G. F., "Pre-War European Population Policies," *MMFQ,* 19 (April 1941) 105–120.

Mukerjee, Radhakamal, "On the Criterion of Optimum Population," *AJS,* 40 (November 1935) 344–348.

Mukerjee, Radhakamal, "Population Theory and Politics," *ASR,* 6 (December 1941) 784–793.

Ross, Rhona, "Population Policy in Great Britain," *South African Journal of Economics,* 17 (September 1949) 320–328.

Rowntree, Griselda, "Supplementary Child Health Services, Part III, Infant Welfare Centers," *PS,* 3 (March 1950) 375–385.

Sovani, N. V., "Population Planning in India," *IJE,* 27 (January 1947) 299–316.

Spengler, J. J., "Some Economic Aspects of the Subsidization by the State of the Formation of 'Human Capital'," *Kyklos,* 4 (No. 4, 1950) 316–343.

Spengler, J. J., "Measures of Population Maladjustment," in *Proceedings of the XIVth International Congress of Sociology,* (Rome 1951) III, 336–364.

Spengler, J. J., "Welfare Economics and the Problem of Over-population," *Scientia,* 89 (April and July 1954) 128–138, 166–175.

Susswein, E., "Family Allowances in Belgium," *PS,* 2 (December 1948) 278–291.

Timlin, Mabel F., "Economic Theory and Immigration Policy," *CJEPS,* 16 (August 1950) 375–382.

Usher, Thomas H., "An Appraisal of the Canadian Family Allowance System," *Review of Social Economy,* 9 (September 1951) 124–136.

Watson, Cicely, "A Survey of Recent Belgian Population Policy," *PS,* 8 (November 1954) 152–187.

Watson, Cicely, "Birth Control and Abortion in France Since 1939," *PS,* 5 (March 1952) 261–286.

Watson, Cicely, "Housing Policy and Population Problems in France," *PS,* 7 (July 1953) 14–45.

Watson, Cicely, "Population Policy in France: Family Allowances and Other Benefits," *PS,* 7 (March 1954) 263–286, and 8 (July 1954) 46–73.

Watson, Cicely, "Recent Developments in French Immigration Policy," *PS,* 6 (July 1952) 3–38.

Wolfe, A. B., "On the Criterion of Optimum Population," *AJS,* 39 (March 1934) 585–599.

Clarence L. Barber is Associate Professor in the Department of Economics and Sociology, University of Manitoba. His writings include papers on tariff policy and the trade cycle. He is co-author of *The Canadian Electrical Manufacturing Industry: An Economic Analysis* (1955).

K. E. Boulding is Professor of Economics at the University of Michigan. While his books and papers have dealt principally with theoretical-economic subjects, he has written on general system theory and on the Malthusian model as a general system. His books include *A Reconstruction of Economics* (1950).

Melvin D. Brockie is Associate Professor of Economics at the California Institute of Technology. His research interests lie principally in the field of business cycles.

Donald Olen Cowgill, Professor of Sociology at the University of Wichita, has published research on population mobility and human ecology.

Kingsley Davis, Professor of Sociology, University of California, is author of *The Population of India and Pakistan* (1951), *Human Society* (1950), and numerous shorter sociological and demographic studies; he edited the symposium, *World Population in Transition* (1945).

Calvert L. Dedrick is Coordinator of International Statistics, U.S. Bureau of the Census; he is co-author of *The Madison Community* (1934) and *The Enumerative Check Census* (Vol. IV of the 1937 Census of Unemployment).

Otis Durant Duncan, Professor of Sociology, Oklahoma Agricultural and Mechanical College, is co-author and editor of *Social Research on Health* (1946), and has published numerous studies in population and rural sociology.

The *Economics Committee, British Royal Commission on Population,* was composed of H. D. Henderson, E. C. Ramsbottom, Alexander Gray, J. R. Hicks, W. B. Reddaway, and Mrs. Joan Robinson. Its function was to formulate the economic factors relevant to the inquiry conducted by the Royal Commission on Population and to advise the Commission on the economic aspects of the inquiry. The report of this committee is Vol. III of the *Papers of the Royal Commission on Population* (1950).

Manuel Gottlieb is Associate Professor of Economics at the University of Kansas City. His writings include, besides papers on optimum population, studies in the history of economic thought, taxation, economic potential, and the theory of economic systems.

Alvin H. Hansen is Professor of Economics at Harvard University and a former president of the American Economic Association. He has published many books dealing with the trade cycle, employment theory, fiscal policy, interest-rate determination, etc. Both in these books and in many papers he has treated the impact of population change upon the behavior of the economy.

Philip M. Hauser is Professor of Sociology and Director, Population Research and Training Center, University of Chicago; he was formerly Acting Director and Deputy Director of the U.S. Bureau of the Census. He is author of *Workers on*

Relief in the United States, March 1935 (1938) and co-editor of *Government Statistics for Business Use* (1946 and 1955), and has published many demographic studies, particularly in the field of labor force analysis.

E. T. Hiller, Professor Emeritus of Sociology, University of Illinois, has made extensive contributions to sociological theory, including such volumes as *The Strike* (1928), *Principles of Sociology* (1933), and *Social Relations and Structures* (1947).

E. W. Hofstee is Professor of Rural Sociology, Agricultural University of Wageningen, The Netherlands. He is interested in regional sociology and regional demography, in internal and international migration, and in population forecasting. Among his recent publications are *Some remarks on selective migration* (1952) and *Economische ontwikkeling en bevolkingsverspreidung* (1949).

D. Gale Johnson is Professor of Economics at the University of Chicago. His major research interests lie in the field of agricultural economics. Among these interests is population mobility. Among his studies, some of which deal with mobility, are *Forward Prices for Agriculture* (1947) and *Agricultural Price Policy and International Trade* (1954).

Frank Lorimer is Professor of Sociology, The American University, and Administrative Director, International Union for the Scientific Study of Population. He is author or senior author of *Dynamics of Population* (1934), *Foundations of American Population Policy* (1940), *The Population of the Soviet Union* (1946), and numerous other demographic studies.

August Lösch (died May 30, 1945) was a member of the Institute for World Economy at Kiel. His most notable study is the pioneer work, *The Economics of Location* (1954), a translation from the second revised German original. Among his writings on population the most important are *Bevölkerungswellen und Wechsellagen* (1936) and *Was ist vom Geburtenrückgang zu halten?* (1932).

Alfred J. Lotka (1880–1949), acknowledged as the "father of mathematical demography," retired as Assistant Statistician of the Metropolitan Life Insurance Company in 1947. His many contributions to population analysis were summarized in *Théorie analytique des associations biologiques* (1934 and 1939) and *Elements of Physical Biology* (1925). He was also co-author of *Length of Life* (1936 and 1949) and *The Money Value of a Man* (1930 and 1946), and a prolific contributor to demography and mathematical statistics.

Paul Meadows, Professor of Sociology, University of Nebraska, is author of *The Culture of Industrial Man* (1950) and other sociological studies.

Frank W. Notestein is Professor of Demography and Director, Office of Population Research, Princeton University; he is co-editor of the quarterly journal, *Population Index* and co-author of *Controlled Fertility* (1940) and *The Future Population of Europe and the Soviet Union* (1944).

William Fielding Ogburn is Professor of Sociology, Florida State University, and Professor Emeritus of Sociology, University of Chicago; among his principal demographic studies are *American Marriage and Family Relationships* (1928) and *Social Characteristics of Cities* (1937); he is well known for his work on social effects of technology, including *Social Change* (1922), *The Social Effects of Aviation* (1946), and *Technology and the Changing Family* (1955).

Edward Nelson Palmer, Professor of Sociology, Hampton Institute, is a specialist in the field of race and culture contacts.

Alan T. Peacock is a member of the faculty of the London School of Economics and Political Science with special interests in public finance, insurance, and national income accounting. He is Assistant Editor of *Economica*. Among his publications are (with H. C. Edey) *National Income and Social Accounting* (1954) and *The Economics of National Insurance* (1952).

William Petersen, Assistant Professor of Sociology, University of California, is author of *Planned Migration: The Social Determinants of the Dutch-Canadian Movement* (1955) and other demographic studies.

The *Population Division, United Nations*, is responsible for the annual compilation of international population statistics, *Demographic Yearbook*; its staff has also prepared a number of methodological and monographic studies in population.

Harold W. Saunders, Professor of Sociology, State University of Iowa, has written on the theory of population pressure and done research on the interrelations of demographic and economic phenomena.

Joseph J. Spengler is Professor of Economics at Duke University. He has published books and papers dealing with differential fertility, migration, the economic aspects of population change, and the history of population theory.

Rupert B. Vance, Professor of Sociology, University of North Carolina, is known for his research in regional sociology as well as his contributions to demography; among his publications are *Human Geography of the South* (1932), *Research Memorandum on Population Redistribution in the United States* (1938), and *All These People* (1945).

Charles F. Westoff, Research Associate, Office of Population Research, Princeton University, has published several studies on differential fertility, among them his contributions to the collaborative study of *Social and Psychological Factors Affecting Fertility*.

P. K. Whelpton is Director of the Scripps Foundation for Research in Population Problems; among his numerous demographic studies are *Needed Population Research* (1938) and *Cohort Fertility: Native White Women in the United States* (1954); he is also co-author and co-editor of the series of studies on *Social and Psychological Factors Affecting Fertility*.

A. B. Wolfe is Professor Emeritus of Economics at Ohio State University and a former president of the American Economic Association. He has published many important papers and three books on population questions and on economic and social theory. His publications include *Conservatism, Radicalism, and Scientific Method* (1923) and "Neurophysiological Economics," *Journal of Political Economy*, LVIII, 1950, pp. 95–110.

BOOKS PUBLISHED BY
The Free Press

3,56